Sport

and the Law

To the Memory of
My Parents

and

For all who believe
in
The Corinthian Ideal
of
Fair Play and the Rule of Law
In Sport, and Society, too

Sport
and the Law

Third Edition

Edward Grayson MA (OXON)

Barrister of the Middle Temple and of the South Eastern Circuit;
Visiting Professor of Sport and the Law in the Anglia Law School,
Anglia Polytechnic University;
Founding President, British Association for Sport and Law;
Fellow of the Royal Society of Medicine

Foreword by

Jimmy Hill OBE

President, Corinthian-Casuals Football Club;
Former Chairman, Professional Footballers' Association

Butterworths
London Edinburgh Dublin
2000

United Kingdom	Butterworths, a Division of Reed Elsevier (UK) Ltd, Halsbury House, 35 Chancery Lane, LONDON WC2A 1EL and 4 Hill Street, EDINBURGH EH2 3JZ
Australia	Butterworths, a Division of Reed International Books Australia Pty Ltd, CHATSWOOD, New South Wales
Canada	Butterworths Canada Ltd, MARKHAM, Ontario
Hong Kong	Butterworths Asia (Hong Kong), HONG KONG
India	Butterworths India, NEW DELHI
Ireland	Butterworth (Ireland) Ltd, DUBLIN
Malaysia	Malayan Law Journal Sdn Bhd, KUALA LUMPUR
New Zealand	Butterworths of New Zealand Ltd, WELLINGTON
Singapore	Butterworths Asia, SINGAPORE
South Africa	Butterworths Publishers (Pty) Ltd, DURBAN
USA	Lexis Law Publishing, CHARLOTTESVILLE, Virginia

© Reed Elsevier (UK) Ltd 1999

A CIP Catalogue record for this book is available from the British Library.

First edition   1988
Second edition   1994

ISBN 0 406 90505 3

Printed by Hobbs the Printers Ltd, Totton, Hampshire

Visit us at our website: http://www.butterworths.co.uk

Foreword

by Jimmy Hill OBE

President, Corinthian-Casuals Football Club
former Chairman, Professional Footballers' Association

Fair play in sport and justice in the law are beliefs which Edward Grayson and I have shared for many, many years. "Two sides of the same coin," is how he describes that involvement, and as it has turned out, our lives have affected the destiny of many of those involved in sport in the strangest of ways.

Whilst Edward was frustratingly recovering from a broken leg, occurring as it did in the trials for a place in the Oxford soccer XI, his passion for sport was channelled into correspondence with the incomparable G.O. Smith, and his *Corinthians and Cricketers* publication. It was inevitable perhaps that his inquiring and clinical mind would find a satisfactory haven as it did, within the uncertain areas of professional practice at the Bar.

Some years later, our equal devotion to all sports, in particular Association Football, led me into a professional career, first with Brentford and then Fulham football clubs. During that time I was elected to chairmanship of the Players' Union, almost immediately changing its name to the Professional Footballers' Association. In 1961, the maximum wage was abolished, as well as the iniquitous 'retain and transfer' system. When the Football League reneged on the second principle in that deal, it took the George Eastham case (funded by the PFA), and Mr Justice Wilberforce to restore the second fundamental right.

Meantime, I was coaching Oxford and later London University football teams, endeavouring to maintain the high profile created by Pegasus's success in the FA *Amateur* Cup competition not long since, on two occasions, in front of 100,000 people at Wembley. Leaving Fulham happily restored to the Premier (then 1st) Division, I moved to Coventry City, Charlton Athletic and Fulham as a director, for which my lasting reward has been to be made President of the Corinthian Casuals, thus completing the circle.

During that time, the game we all learned to love from early schooldays, stimulated by caring masters, has become part of a world-wide, professional entertainment industry. Not surprisingly, such dynamic progress provided a multitude of problems, not the least to preserve fairly and accurately the difference between right and wrong, on and off the field. Edward stepped into that lonely arena in a formidable way, alongside other principals, notably Sir Stanley Rous.

Perhaps the first problem they tackled was the current injustice, whereby cricketers were able nearing or on retirement to promote a benefit match from which they pocketed the proceeds – without tax deduction. In contrast, footballers' benefits were taxed fully. In the 1958/59 season, after five years' service with Fulham, I was granted a benefit match, which was organised independently from the Fulham club, in order to circumvent the law. Over £1000 was raised from which I was paid a cheque for £750 (the maximum under Football League regulations). A year or two later, I was taxed between £2-300 on that sum. At the same time, Denis Compton, of Middlesex and Arsenal, and Willie Watson of Huddersfield and Yorkshire, were totally absolved from tax on their publicly subscribed benefit match payments.

Had I met Edward at that time, I surely would have challenged such a quirk of the current practice. In truth, I was unaware that he had been working with my predecessor at the Players' Union, Jimmy Guthrie, and a committee member, George Swindin, Arsenal's goalkeeper, to rectify this injustice. I am wiser now. Together they raised the restraint of trade flag for the first time in football's history in the Aldershot County Court on behalf of Ralph Banks. He had been transferred for £500 from Bolton Wanderers to the local club, after being mesmerised by Stanley Matthews in the memorable 1953 Coronation Cup Final. It resulted in his release on a free transfer to Weymouth, eight whole years before Mr Justice Wilberforce's ruling re Eastham. The Bosman case later squared the legal circle, but I'm afraid destroyed the practical balance to the detriment of the professional game.

All this is encapsulated in these pages, together with the unsuccessful attempt to establish the joint Oxbridge/Pegasus inspiration of the university spectroscopy professor, Tommy (later Sir Harold) Thompson, and future FA Chairman, as a valuable educational and sporting charity, with all the social and fiscal advantages flowing from it. Twenty-five years later, in 1980, the House of Lords judicial committee, in another landmark ruling, made it clear that this would have been consistent with correct legal principles.

As a former Oxford University coach, then chairman of Fulham, I was able to persuade the board to provide a new home for the Oxford v Cambridge fixture, which had been played, without interruption, annually since 1874, at Craven Cottage. Under Al Fayed's chairmanship, that hospitable concession has continued.

On leaving Fulham FC, I was invited to become President of the Corinthian-Casuals about the same time as Edward was invited by Maurice Watkins, the solicitor director of Manchester United, and Dr Ray Farrell from the Law School at Manchester Metropolitan University, to become Founding President of the British Association for Sport and Law.

During a High Court trial about a football injury last autumn, Edward and I found ourselves on opposite sides of the courtroom. I, an expert witness and President of the Corinthian-Casuals, was cross-examined with more than a twinkle in those eyes which had seen so much in his extraordinary life, by my fellow life member of the Casuals, who was none other than Professor Edward Grayson. In our mutual exchanges, and without compromising our professional integrity I trust, we found some measure of agreement on the scarcity of modern players fully competent with both feet. Football should also be a challenge for a head with two functions, as the game itself, and indeed nearly all sport embraces two dimensions, and two cultures – grass roots joy, and showbiz entertainment.

The laws in sport and society should be applied uniformly at all levels, and to all those who embrace games and life, a philosophy which gallops through the pages of Edward's book, and his race – some marathon – through life. I share his view that without the Rule of Laws in society, there could only be anarchy. Without the Rule of Laws in sport, chaos. The law of the land does not stop at the touchline, boardroom, nor council chamber as the following fascinating pages confirm.

'…aversion to law and courts of law is naturally strong in the human mind'

Lord Hewart, The Lord Chief Justice of England
Introduction to Uncommon Law
by AP Herbert (1935)

'To many lawyers it will seem that it is all to the good that legal principles and procedure should be discussed in public in any guise.'

Lord Atkin
Introduction to Uncommomn Law
by AP Herbert (1935)

Preface

Sir Alex Ferguson and Michael Watson, among many others, may not be aware how they have proved from different points of the Sport and Law compass, during the autumn of 1999, why the Rule of Law in Society outside of sport fills a void created by sport's own self-regulatory Rule of Law within it. In doing so they point to the factual and evidential basis for all who care or wish to know how this exists today for every different sporting discipline.

Sir Alex's publicly subscribed testimonial benefit match, between a Manchester United and an International All-Stars Celebratory XI, was freed from the burden of income tax by a celebrated House of Lords judicial ruling of more than seventy years antiquity, unchallenged and unaltered down the years. It concerned a greatly admired professional Kent County Cricket club batsman, James Seymour. A Court of Appeal's reversal of a wise and experienced taxation judge, Mr Justice Rowlatt, was in turn overruled in a House of Lords judgment which caused Viscount Dunedin to explain

"honestly, had it not been for the fact that honourable judges, whose opinions I respect, have come to another conclusion, I would have thought the contention [ie in the Court of Appeal] was quite preposterous".

Appendix 1 to this text explains how its now seventy two years old ruling (*Seymour v Reed* [1927] AC 554 at Pages 560–562) was extended to football forty years ago in 1959 (*Rigby v IRC*, unreported except in the *Peterborough Citizen and Observer*, 16 June, 24 July).

Michael Watson obtained a High Court judgment on Friday 24 September 1999 against the British Boxing Board of Control after his world title championship fight with Chris Eubank in 1991, because of its negligent failure to provide appropriate medical assistance at the ringside; and that in consequence, a largely remediable condition became irremediable. For reasons unknown at present, leave has been granted for an appeal hearing after this publication. This was not the first, and it will certainly not be the last time, when the law is required to fill a gap which a recreational governing body has failed to control correctly. Yet when the judgment was publicly reported in the general media sources, it was hailed as a landmark verdict for the first time, to establish liability for negligence and damages against a sporting governing body.

This was incorrect for two reasons. Six years earlier in 1993, Wendy Morrell, a disabled wheelchair athlete, obtained judgment against the then British Les Autres Sports Association ("BLASA") when she was seriously injured by a discus thrown against a net (*not* a safety) curtain while preparing for the 1992 Barcelona Paralympics (*Morrell v Owen*: Times : 14 December 1993). Furthermore, sixty years before that occasion, in 1933, a colourful Irish singing heavyweight boxer, Jack Doyle, was disqualified for hitting below the belt against Jack Petersen in a fight for the heavyweight championship of Great Britain. Doyle was disqualified; Petersen declared the winner, and Doyle's contracted purse of £3,000 was forfeited. A claim against the White City Stadium for return of the sum was dismissed by Mr Justice Mackinnon, but judgment was entered for that amount *against the British Board of Control* which was a co-defendant to the action. The Law Report of the successful appeal, *Doyle v White City Stadium Limited* [1935] 1 KB 110 raises four important issues for the worlds of sport, the law and society generally.

1.   The title to the action, as cited above, incorrectly omits the name of the successful appellant, the Board of Control.
2.   The successful appeal was not required to overcome the little known current hurdle introduced by the present government in a Blue Paper entitled *MONITORING JUSTICE* (Cm 4155) 15 December 1998 (following a Practice Note of 17 November 1998, published in [1999] 1 All ER 186), which will be referred to frequently within these pages, when it claims with a curious blend of ignorance compounded by arrogance (with my own emphasis here)

> "In a well-functioning justice system, the emphasis should be on *assuming that the court of first instance has reached the right decision*; so that there should not be an automatic right of appeal".

Every modern practitioner will recognise the flawed premise inherent in this claim: a flaw which is emphasised and confirmed by the number of landmark sports-related appellate decisions which might never have changed the face of British sport and society if this ludicrous governmental decree had existed before its introduction without debate during Christmas and New Year vacation of 1998–99. It suffices here to list only two of those which appear in the last column of the 251 years outline list of cases 1748–1999 which can be seen in the last column attached to the Introduction at pages 24–62 below.

(1) *Nagle v Fielden* [1966] 2 QB 633 freed women racehorse owners from the Jockey Club's embargo as trainers, too, except by a fiction through their head lad, only when the Court of Appeal overruled two earlier judges and

(2) the House of Lords landmark ruling in *IRC v Macmullan* 1981 AC 1 which linked the F.A. Youth Trust Deed with a 65 years-old earlier Aldenham School charitable bequest also required reversal of earlier judicial opinions. If the new development collides with the wrong adjudicator, Magna Carta's magic formula, "To no one will we sell, to no one will we deny or delay right or justice" would never get to first base; and Sport and the Law is only a tiny cameo of a much greater cosmos which we will now suffer from it.

(3) Juridically the appeal decision in *Doyles* 1933/1935 cases is important. It validates the Board's rule against Doyle's then infant status as an 18 years old boxer, even though its effect was to cause financial loss by forfeiture of his purse. Of equal significance are the words stated by one of Lord Denning's perhaps forgotten today but nonetheless contemporaneously highly regarded predecessors, Lord Hanworth, MR at Page 126, which are repeated later in this text:

> "It is as much in the interests of the plaintiff himself as of any other contestant that there should be rules of clean fighting, and that he should be protected against adversary misconduct in hitting below the belt or doing anything of the sort".

As I explain hereafter (2nd edn, p 150:) many standard textbook citations are silent on this extract. Doyle's celebrated counsel, Serjeant Sullivan in his memoirs, *The Last Serjeant*, is equally remiss, although they dwell extensively on one of his better known and non-sporting clients, Sir Roger Casement, who was hanged for treason during the First World War. In all earlier editions I have suggested, and repeat here, that Lord Hanworth's words threading the true spirit of sport with the law and the law with sport should also be 'hanged' as a warning against sporting treason, in every schoolroom, dressing room, changing room, board room and club room throughout the land.

In turn they also recall the claim by Lord Hailsham of St Marylebone, thrice Lord Chancellor, who earlier created in 1962 the role of a Government Minister for Sport when a senior member of Mr MacMillan's Cabinet. After nearly thirty years he explained in his memoirs *A Sparrow's Flight* (1990)

"In a sense there is no such thing as sport. There is only a heterogeneous list of pastimes, with different governing bodies, different ethics and constantly varying needs";

Two years later in 1994 he was corroborated from an unexpected legal source under a Treasury HM Customs and Excise notice VAT 701/45/94. It lists 113 UK 'heterogenous list of pastimes with different governing bodies, different ethics and constantly varying needs' which qualify for exemption as non-profit-making activities for VAT purposes.

List of UK sports activities for VAT purposes, which qualify for exemption as non-profit-making activities for VAT purposes, which inevitably require different and differing legal and medical services. [HM Customs and Excise VAT 701/45/94]

Aikido	Fives	Petanque
American football	Flying	Polo
Angling	Gaelic football	Pony trekking
Archery	Gliding	Pool
Arm wrestling	Golf	Quoits
Association football	Gymnastics	Racketball
Athletics	Handball	Rackets
Badminton	Hang/para gliding	Racquetball
Ballooning	Highland games	Rambling
Baseball	Hockey	Real Tennis
Basketball	Horse racing	Roller hockey
Baton twirling	Hovering	Rosser skating
Biathlon	Hurling	Rounders
Bicycle polo	Ice hockey	Rowing
Billiards	Ice skating	Rugby League
Bobsleigh	Ju jitsu	Rugby Union
Boccia	Judo	Sailing/yachting
Bowls	Kabaddi	Sand/land yachting
Boxing	Karate	Shinty
Camogie	Kendo	Shooting
Canoeing	Korfball	Skateboarding
Caving	Lacrosse	Skiing
Chinese martial arts	Lawn tennis	Skipping
Cricket	Life saving	Snooker
Croquet	Luge	Snowboarding
Crossbow	Modern pentathlon	Softball
Curling	Motor cycling	Sumo wrestling
Cycling	Motor sports	Squash
Dragon boat racing	Mountaineering	Street hockey
Equestrian	Movement and dance	sub-aqua
Exercise and Fitness	Netball	Surf life saving
Fencing	Orienteering	Surfing
Field sports	Parachuting	Swimming

Table Tennis	Trampolining	Volleyball
Taekwondo	Triathlon	Water skiing
Tang soo do	Tug of war	Weightlifting
Tenpin bowling	Unihoc	Wrestling
		Yoga

The list was an arbitrarily Treasury inspired document, which did not include chess and pigeon racing, each of whose respective regulatory governing bodies is still protesting at its omission. Two years earlier on 5 December 1992 in Cliff Morgan's never to be forgotten BBC *Sport on Four* radio programme, axed contentiously in the face of strong public protests by an unappreciative BBC directorate, the celebrated *Daily Mail* columnist and award winning Sportswriter of the year, Ian Wooldridge, illuminated all of this after ejection of the four United Kingdom national soccer teams, from the 1994 World Soccer cup competition, when he posed and answered a question,

> "Does Sport still exist?
>> Well it does; but you have to go out into the suburbs and shires to find it. Village cricket, soccer on Hackney Marshes, Old Boys rugger teams getting legless afterwards, point-to-pointing, county golf, darts leagues in Dorset.
>> What we have been watching in the frenetic World Cup soccer action this week was hardly about sport at all. It was all about [a] high performance branch of the entertainment industry."

He thereby crystallised the present public persona of whatever sport may mean; not a game of two halves, but a game of two conflicting and contrasting concepts: showbiz v grass roots, and exercise for health and education within the Rule of Law on and off the playing field.
Those two conflicting and contrasting concepts or cultures reflect C.P. Snow's two cultures, Art and Science, and D'Israeli's *Two Nations*, poverty and prosperity. They are evidenced by the daily blurring in the public and media minds and eyes which refuse to recognise and identify, for example,

Manchester United Football Club plc
proudly presents at its
Old Trafford Theatre of Dreams,
International All Stars Football Entertainment,
including David Beckham (with Victoria
Adams and Baby Brooklyn in the Stands)
under the management of
Sir Alex Ferguson

alongside

Clayton Playing fields at Oldham:
Foster's Field in Dorset:
New Milton Recreation Ground in Hampshire:
Town Moor, Newcastle-upon-Tyne:
Charterhouse-v-Westminster 1863 to date:
Oxford-v-Cambridge 1893 to date:
Corinthian-Casuals 1882/3 at Tolworth, Surrey since 1989 to date:

Yet none of those 113 different activities can exist within the above equation. No common cultural or legal thread connects any of them apart from their self regulation and subjection to the overriding Rule of Law in both Sport and Society.

Nevertheless, they all require such differing and different levels of legal services, that they thereby demolish the arcane, arid, and artificial arguments about whether there is a Law of Sport or Sports law. As a tabloid headline or sound bite, the shorthand version serves a convenient, practical and populist purpose. As a juridical concept it does not and never will exist, evidenced by the 52 different volumes of *Halsbury's Laws of England* 4th Hailsham Edition, many of which have a sliver of sports-related issues without any further basis for finding a connecting thread between the 113 non-profit-making VAT activities.

Furthermore, anyone who would wish to challenge Lord Hailsham's entitlement to adjudicate in this area would be unaware of his impeccable pedigree, apart from his creation of the ministerial role in Government. His landmark House of Lords judgment in the F.A. Charitable Youth Trust case of *IRC v Macmullan* [1981] AC 1 overturned the Inland Revenue; Walton, J.; and a Court of Appeal majority to bring U.K. charity law in relation to sport into line with Australia 33 years earlier. That was when the Sydney University Rugby Club decision in *Kearins v Kearins* (1957) SR 286 (NSW) followed Eve, J.'s First World War establishment of the Aldenham School athletics bequests in *Re Marriette* [1915] 2 Ch 284 to qualify for valid charitable status with their true meaning of health and education within the Rule of Law.

Curiously, Kearins was never referred to by any Counsel or any of the judges at any stage of the eight years saga developing *MacMullan* and its ultimate landmark ruling from Walton, J, via the Court of Appeal to the House of Lords. It nevertheless followed *Marriette* specifically. His father, Viscount Hailsham, was MCC President during the 1932–33 Leg Theory imbroglio, inspired by the immortal Jardine-Larwood combination, which nearly split the then Dominion ties with Australia; and his grandfather, the first Quintin Hogg, pioneered with Lord Kinnaird the first Scotland v England soccer internationals in the early 1870's, played for Old Etonians in the F.A. Cup Final of 1875–76, and is the subject of the *only London statue* with a football, facing his own landmark education foundation Regent Street Polytechnic (now University of Westminster), outside the BBC in Portland Place. He is portrayed alongside a boy holding a ball, consistent with his goalkeeping position for that Old Etonians FA Cup Final XI, in 1875–76 and in the earliest unofficial Scotland-v-England international matches.

Lord Hailsham's senior, in constitutional precedence after the Royal Family, was always the Archbishop of Canterbury. The present incumbent, Dr. George Carey, without proclaiming his allegiance as Arsenal Football Club's most celebrated supporter, during a House of Lords debate on *Society's Moral and Spiritual Well-being* on the eve of the European Football competition in July 1996, explained

> "We take it for granted that you cannot play a game of football without rules. Rules do not get in the way of the game; they make it possible".

Tottenham Hotspur's renowned manager, Bill Nicholson, OBE, who steered it to the 20th century's first F.A. Cup and Football League Double in 1961 captained by the unforgettable Danny Blanchflower, would always refine this concept with the admonition to me:

> "Laws, Laws of the Game, not rules";

and he was right. The Laws of any Game, subject to the overriding *national laws* of the land, create their own legal structure for every different organisation to bring order out of chaos, namely

1. Playing laws:
   (a) rules of play
   (b) sanctions and penalties for playing field offences (e.g. sending off, dismissals from play);
   (c) disciplinary sanctions and penalties (e.g. suspensions and/or fines)
2. *Consequences for breaches*
   Fines and/or suspensions.

Nevertheless those overriding *national laws* of the land are wheeled on stage by Parliament and the Courts inevitably when the frequent gaps in sports' own self regulation demand action for justice for participatory and spectator victims of personal injury and administrative abuse which are incapable of provision or ignored or omitted within sport itself. Parliament has been concerned with protecting the peace of the realm and private property rights from "times immemorial" in the Middle Ages, down to later

20th century control of mob violence and stadium safety. The Courts have cranked into action from 18th and 19th century gaming disputes to their now inevitable cascade of 20th Century current controls over criminal and civil playing field misconduct, and abuses of administrative powers, which are delineated chronologically for the first time ever in the Introduction's list selected — but not claimed to be exclusively comprehensive of recorded representative cases over the 251 years since 1748 hereafter.

Each of these circumstances which brings the *national legal system* on to the fields of play and sport and recreation affairs has never created, whether jointly or severally, and never can create its own jurisprudence. They have all been absorbed when required, within those 52 volumes of *Halsbury's Laws of England*, spanning the publicised *Bosman* European Court of Justice verdict to the more significant and valuable grass roots levels of school and club sport.

That span embraces twelve interlocking reasons which have precipitated this third Butterworths edition within a decade of *Sport and the Law* (and a fourth when including its earliest version from the *Sunday Telegraph* more than 20 years ago in 1978). These are:

1. Update with original and new research material
2. True meaning of sport
3. Two cultures: showbiz-v-grass roots
4. No modern phenomenon
5. Rule of Law benefits sport and recreation
6. Government overlapping complexities
7. Uncontrolled sales of playing fields and school sport generally
8. Reaction to new challenges
9. Local developments
10. Judicial limitations and error
11. Denials of Justice by bars on appeal
12. Readers' conclusions on true meaning of sport.

The purpose and original *structures* of 15 Chapters and 15 Appendices, from those two earlier editions in 1988 and 1994, have been retained here

> 'To create a level of awareness among all readers of the extent to which...the law can and should come to the help of sport; and indeed, how sport with its high public profile and image can come to the help of the law. For sport without rules and their control creates chaos. Society without laws and their enforcement means anarchy'.

That readership embraces everyone within a Sport for All policy from the cradle to the grave, and particularly the unbalanced framework between the relatively miniscule number of showbiz celebrity professionals and the 30,920,000 United Kingdom grass roots participants associated with 421 national sports governing bodies identified by the United KingdomSports Council in March 1999. All of them are equally in need of legal services as are their higher profile competitors, and summarily this can be seen through the analysis prepared for this edition under the stimulating and encouraging guidance of Sport England's (formerly the Sports Council's) Chief Executive, Derek Casey.

Sports Participation in England:

Table 1: Participation by children

Total Population in England aged 5 to 15	Participation in one sport outside of school at least 10 times in in previous year	Number of children participating
6,964,000	87%	6,059,000

Source: Young People and Sport in England, 1994 (English Sports Council) and mid year population forecasts. 1997 (Office for National Statistics)

Table 2: Participation by adults

Total Population in England 16+	Participation in at least one activity in the previous 4 weeks	Number of adults participating
39,214,000	63.4%	24,862,000

Source: General Household Survey 1996 (Office for National Statistics) and mid year population forecasts. 1997 (Office for National Statistics)

Table 3: Total participation

Total Population in England 5+	Number participating	Regular participation (i.e. 10 times in the previous year or one in previous 4 weeks)
46,178,000	30,920,000	67%

Governing Bodies:
Table 4: Recognised governing bodies:

Remit	Number of NGBs
UK	43
GB	76
England	136
Wales	94
Scotland	98
Northern Ireland	94
Total Number of NGBs	**421***
Number of sports covered	96

Source: English Sports Council (1999)

*Total is less than the sum of the NGBs in each country as an individual NGB can cover more than one country

In his Foreword to the 1978 *Sunday Telegraph* edition, the then Chairman of the Sports Council and former British Lions and England captain and scrum-half, Dick Jeeps CBE wrote:

"Sport and the law may seem a world apart to casual sportsmen and women playing their weekend game of tennis, squash or golf. But there are, in fact, many key areas of overlap which directly affect both participants and administrators.

As sport becomes more and more a part of everyday life for millions of people and the staging of major, international events takes governing bodies into the realms of big business and financial management, there must be a greater understanding among all concerned of the requirements and constraints of the law.

In an increasingly complex world, sport can no longer exist in a vacuum, sustained by its own rules and administrative regulations. Sport belongs to the real world and its rapid development in recent years has made ignorance of the law among decision makers unacceptable."

Those twelve interlocking reasons cover the latest perceptions which have surfaced since the last edition in 1994, to highlight the basic conflict between showbiz -v- grass roots alongside the overriding true meaning of sport and recreation as a vehicle for health and education within the Rule of Law, on, as well as off the field of play. They have been adjusted to absorb developments with the inevitable passage of time since their respective initial formations in the two earlier Butterworth editions in 1988 and 1994.

They also have had the benefit of hindsight by reflecting upon twenty years of changing perspectives after the *Sunday Telegraph's* 76 pages booklet in 1978. What emerges through successive editions of Butterworths *Sport and the Law* in 1988 and 1994, is a subject which merits adaptation of the football philosophy from the renowned and deep thinking Tottenham Hotspur manager during the early 1950's in the mould of Herbert Chapman, Bill Shankley, Sir Matt Busby and Sir Alex Ferguson: Arthur Rowe. He steered the team containing Sir Alf Ramsey and Bill Nicholson to successive Second and First Division Football League Championships, and supervised his professional players' coaching of Pegasus, the joint Oxbridge twice winning F.A. *Amateur* Cup Club in the Corinthian tradition before 100,000 crowds at Wembley Stadium. "Football is a simple game; the players make it difficult", was his theme.

Correspondingly, the law applied to sport and recreation is simple when recognised to be appropriate. Only evidence, clients, and particularly lawyers at all levels in both practice and academe make it difficult as these pages will show. The concept and nature of sport's often unrecognised, unidentified and thereby unknown complexities are themselves elusive, as appears throughout this text, to compound the difficulty.

A sample example can be fund in the relatively old but nonetheless oft-cited leading case, which supports the juridical proposition that there is no obligation to guard against unusual dangers at sports venues. When dismissing a six year old's appeal against rejection of a claim for an eye injury suffered at an ice-rink, *Murray v Harringay Arena* [1951] 2 KB 529, Singleton, LJ, at pp 531–2 said, with words never cited in conventional sources:

> "The evidence given on the hearing was meagre. There was no evidence from anyone connected with the management; no evidence to show the number of persons who normally attended matches; and no evidence to show whether there had been any other accidents there. In a sense this appears to be unsatisfactory, and yet it would seem that there are ways in which the Plaintiffs might have obtained information on these matters".

Furthermore how many of those concerned as administrators, lawyers and media commentators are aware that the true nature of sport at its grass roots and all activities listed on pages xii-xiii above is health and education within the Rule of Law? Furthermore, any who may doubt or challenge this opinion should reflect upon the source behind the landmark schoolcoaching and insurance High Court decision in *Van Oppen v Bedford School Trustees* [1989] 3 All ER 389. It was based upon the now 20 years old MOSA Report recommending compulsory insurance for schools rugby, because of the overwhelming evidence of consistent injuries at school rugby levels. Yet how many within sport and recreation and indeed society at any level know what MOSA stands for? *Medical Officers Schools Association*. Finally, how many concerned with any area of whatever, however, or whenever sport is claimed to be understood, know or care that in the early 1990's, a British Sports Council's Sheffield University commissioned survey concluded in the '*Summary of the injuries and exercise main report — national study of the epidemiology of exercise related injury illness*':

> Six million new sports injuries require treatment each year. Accident and Emergency departments are well equipped to deal with the more serious injuries, but family doctors may be less familiar with the management of sports injuries. To help reduce costs and improve effectiveness, the way in which sports injuries are managed should be reviewed. NHS Sports Injury Clinics may be needed to fill the gaps.

Six years later, a leading article in the *British Journal of Sports Medicine* from Robin Knill-Jones (June 1997 at pp. 95–6) recorded that:

> Sports related injuries form a significant part of the workload of the National Health Service. Patients with acute injuries account for between 3.9% and 7.1% of total attendances at casualty departments, and a higher proportion of these attendances — 28% by children. An unknown proportion of these injuries go on to become chronic or recurrent problems which later involve orthopaedic clinics or general practitioners. Clearly, there is an unmet need for expert advice and treatment, for which, for whatever reason, NHS resources are unavailable.

Thus, it may be argued that sports medicine (and its ethical criteria based upon World Medical Association Guidelines as I have explained in *Ethics, Injuries and the Law in Sports Medicine*), with its uniquely complex and rarely recognised general and specialist multi-disciplinary requirements, which are rarely understood within both sport and society and medicine generally, stands apart from other medical and paramedical areas. This also reflects the clear division between *sport as a branch of the entertainment industry* and *sport in its health and education role*, with or without a competitive regulatory framework.

Lord Hailsham, with his family background and professional practical barrister experiences, and comprehensive grasp of the subject, understood all this in an area now more than ever before swamped superficially today by celebrity cult image conscious and commercial considerations and explained in *The Door Wherein I Went*, published in 1980. This appeared twenty years after the Central Council of Physical Recreation (CCPR) published in 1960 its now forgotten landmark *Wolfenden Report* on *Sport in the Community* with its 57 paragraphs of conclusions and recommendations.

It had appointed a Committee under the chairmanship of Sir John Wolfenden during 1957 to report on the future of sporting administration "in promoting the general welfare of the community". Significantly and symbolically a year later in 1958 Parliament passed the Recreational Charities Act to widen the scope of charitable status in a context built in to its title (although the Act was not construed effectively within a sporting context until nearly a quarter of a century later in the North Berwick Sports Centre House of Lords decision of *Guild v IRC* [1992] 2 All ER 10).

As Minister for Science and Technology and Lord President of the Council in Mr MacMillan's Government, Lord Hailsham recalled during 1980

'It occurred during a Cabinet Meeting [in 1962] in which government responsibility for Sport was being discussed. It was being said that, properly speaking, responsibility for sport was being shared between quite a number of departments and authorities, education, local government, universities, the services, and all the voluntary bodies dealing with athletics, from the Olympic and Commonwealth Games and League and Cup football at the top, to badminton, fives and even chess at the most refined and esoteric end of the spectrum. I pointed out that recreation generally presented a complex of problems out of which modern government was not wholly free to opt, and which government funds were, in fact, and were likely to continue to be, committed in one way or another in coaching, in the provision of playing fields, in matters of safety at racecourses and football grounds. I waxed eloquent on this subject, talking of the fares for Olympic competitors and many other topics. I suggested that there was need, not for a Ministry but for a focal point under a Minister, for a coherent body of doctrine, perhaps even a philosophy of government encouragement. Paradoxically, I thought there was in fact a kind of analogy in the way in which I had tried to administer government science, making use of independent expertise, but not seeking to impose regulation or central administration. My eloquence had its effect on the Prime Minister and, before I knew where I was, I was left to organise the first government unit of this kind under Sir John Lang, who had been Secretary of the Admiralty when I was First Lord. As in most of the other things I have done in public life, except the Party chairmanship, I always strive to work through other people with the minimum of fuss, as I find that this is the best way to get things done. This particular activity was a minor matter, and I thought comparatively little of it at the time since it occurred at a period when other things were occupying my mind [as a Cabinet Minister].'

Nearly 30 years after what he had regarded in the context of the time to be "a minor matter" he reflected further in *A Sparrow's Flight* published in 1990

'Sport, I believe....is an essential part of education. Years later, in my judicial capacity as Lord Chancellor, I was part-author of a judgment which authenticated the legal status of a fund for Association Football as a charitable trust [*IRC v McMullan* [1980] 1 AC 1]. Organised sport is undoubtedly part of our national culture. In mountain-climbing, cricket and most kinds of football, in hunting, fishing and game shooting, the British were the pioneers in the field of sport as it burgeoned in the nineteenth century.'

Organised sport today, while the curtain comes down on the 20th Century, is now part of the world's culture dominated by the International Federations, FIFA, IOC, IAAF, IRB, ICC, FINA as the most prominent: and while the three previous editions of *Sport and the Law* have unfolded in 1978, 1988 and 1994 they have reflected on patterns in which sport mirrors the social climate of its time.

Thus Stephen Pile, writing in *The Sunday Telegraph Review*, as its media correspondent, on 8 November 1992 on the occasion of the launch of UK Gold, which he described as 'the all-repeats satellite channel', recalled

'I have now watched the first episode of every major soap, drama and comedy series in the past 20 years. And they make a fascinating study of social history. Here, in half-hour chunks, we can see the brutalisation of British life over two decades.

The shift from *Terry and June* (all sweetness and light in the 1970s, laughing affectionately at British incompetence) to *Eastenders* and *The Bill*, where everyone is snarling with anger and frustration all the time, is disturbing to watch when laid end-to-end.'

That brutalisation was not confined to Britain. Television has globalised it, not only in the world of sport. In the previous year of 1991 the balanced and comprehensively experienced team of London *Evening Standard* sports writers prepared and published a remarkable and illuminating anthology which confirmed the shift in emphasis from the days of my schoolboy's innocence, reflected in my hero-worshipping correspondence published as *Corinthians and Cricketers* initially in 1955, to the self-evident sordidness of today's amoral public sporting climate under the title *Sporting Spite: Rebels and Rebellion in World Sport*. The admirable Introduction by the paper's then assistant editor and head of sport, Michael Herd, contained this passage at page 11:

'Isn't it time [1991] to reflect on what has happened to sport? I suggest we have allowed ourselves to confuse the pursuit of sporting excellence with the scramble for money or political prestige. And as a result too many of us today condone what seems to be an irresistible compulsion for participants to behave badly. Let there be no doubt, though, that whatever external pressures exist, at the end of the day each participant is able to act according to his own moral values.

As fists and four-letter words fly, is sport a mirror of our society in which, with arrogance and disdain, rules are bent so that Authority is tested? Do we all see what we can get away with on the field of play and off it? Perhaps E.M. Forster was correct when he wrote that it is international sport that has helped to kick the world downhill?

All things considered, this is the appropriate time [1991] for sport's ruling bodies to declare enough is enough. How much violence will be tolerated before rugby and other sports act to replace anarchy with authority? At the very moment that baseness seems to have become a daily feature of our sporting lives, is there a way back to a golden age, to the Corinthian era? Some will say that sport should not look over its shoulder while the rest of the world makes what is declared as progress. But surely we want to return to the good old days?'

The answer which I suggested in Butterworths 2nd 1994 edition, to what might appear to be a rhetorical, at most a wistful question is simple: of course we do, with the overriding criteria, namely a return to the Rule of Law within sport itself, as the only 'way back to a golden age, to the Corinthian era'.

In the intervening years very few, if any responsible commentators on the global or domestic public sporting scene would suggest that any improvement has occurred since that assessment in 1991. At the beginning of 1999 Simon Barnes wrote in the London *Times* [20 January]

'A sporting dispute is not like a dispute between unions and management. A sporting dispute is something that involves and invades everyone who cares for sport. It feels – perhaps irrationally – like a personal attack. It does, after all, affect ourselves and our pleasures.

People have said that agents, or sponsors, or television will kill sport. Or journalists. But it is sport that is killing sport; sportsmen are killing sport, and so – and especially – are sporting administrators".

Two days later in the *Financial Times* for Friday 22 January 1999 Patrick Heverson explained how the Rugby Football Union was at war on no less than three separate fronts; the rest of the Five Nations from which competition it was initially rejected; the International Rugby Board, and finally "in a long feud with the top English clubs, which want to wrest control of club competitions and their revenues from it". In his final paragraph he concluded,

"If the game can then rid itself of the incompetent administrators who have landed it in such a mess, rugby union in Britain has a future as professional sport. Its long-suffering supporters, whose patience is wearing thin, deserve no less".

Barely two-and-a-half weeks further forward on Saturday 6 February 1999 *The Daily Telegraph* editorial Sports Team produced a Special Report headed '*Time for real action*', with an introductory *Comment* from its Sports Editor; David Welch, supported by detailed analysis from each of his specialist contributors:

> "Sport is in a mess. Internationally and in this country, too. From 10C bribery and world-wide drug scandals, to suggestions of race-fixing, football bungs, disputes between Five Nations rugby boards, the twaddle over Hoddle and the dithering of MCC over women members: the problems in sport demand urgent attention.
>
> Its traditions are being sullied and betrayed on an almost daily basis by a succession of tawdry, chaotic or corrupt revelations involving most of our major sporting bodies.
>
> Sport is being brought into disrepute, and a way has to be found of making those in nominal charge accountable for their failure to protect the image of the sports concerned.
>
> Not everyone, of course, will appreciate our raising such issues (in a special report on our centre pages today). Indeed, many may find it disturbing that they are being highlighted by those who make a living out of sport – but how else are we to avoid the sins of the fathers being visited on the sons (or ourselves reincarnated [N.B. for later readers, a "twaddle over Hoddle" allusion]) when we are running the risk of handing over sport to future generations in a state of such confusion and corruption".

For sons, of course, add daughters; and the final conclusion,

> "The Government must assume responsibility by creating a passionate, universally respected, Commissioner of Sport. It is no laughing matter for the Commons. Sport deserves and requires, this degree of recognition and will not survive in an acceptable form without it".

Sadly the intervening months have witnessed the most unsporting contributions to the welfare of the sporting spirit of fair play within the Rule of Law at two high profile Prime Ministerial levels. When the England Football Coach and Manager Hoddle was at his most vulnerable after ill-thought out comments about disabled people, Mr Blair joined the crescendo which led to his resignation; and correspondence disclosed in *The Daily Telegraph* during August from his junior Minister in the Department of Culture Media and Sport, Tony Banks, to Sir John Smith, Chairman of Manchester United Plc, confirmed that he was aware of pressure on Manchester United to destroy the tradition and spirit of the Football Association *Challenge* Cup Competition by withdrawl from participation to defend its retention of the trophy for a universally acknowledged debateable public interest and benefit, for which FIFA's secretary and President later rejected any suggestion of their pressure or influence.

Since the above earlier forebodings at the commencement of 1999 it is hardly surprising that in the last week of October 1999 on Monday 25, David Hands, *The Times* Rugby Correspondent wrote

'FOR the first time in the history of rugby union's World Cup, not one of the four home countries has reached the semi-final stage, completing a gloomy year for British team sports.

After the failure of England's cricketers in their World Cup in the summer and the struggles of the footballers to qualify for Euro 2000, England's rugby players crashed 44–21 in Paris yesterday to South Africa, the holders.

The failure of Scotland in Edinburgh, against the tournament favourites New Zealand, completed a sad week for domestic rugby. Despite a brave rally by the Scots, who lost 30–18 in a constant down-pour, the All Blacks go through to a semi-final against France at Twickenham next Sunday. South Africa will play Australia, victors over Wales in Cardiff, on Saturday, also at Twickenham.

Only France could fly the flag for the northern hemisphere, beating Argentina 47–26 to reach the semi-finals for the third time'.

For those who would seek a reason for these contrasting failures in the northern hemisphere, an examination of Dr Mary Malecka's comparison in Appendix 2 between the attitudes of the successive recent governments of Britain and France, with its Sports Minister in the Cabinet, to school and youth sport and culture, may not be unrewarding as an initial inquiry. Furthermore, after Australia's ultimate defeat of France in the Final, the *Times* further crystallised the victors' overriding national attitude following a concurrent address from one of Australia's leading medical practitioners, Professor Peter Fricker, to the BASM (British Association of Sports Medicine) Congress. He explained his country's graded progressions, beginning at the ages on entry into secondary eduction within structured monitored levels, to echo Gwyn Jones in the *Times* for Tuesday, 9th November 1999, p 57:

'Australia's success in the World Cup along with that at cricket, netball and rugby league is all important to a nation that uses sport to express its identity. They have an ambition and willingness to act with massive investment on a scale unparalleled in Britain'.

These contrasting international attitudes to Britain's national cricket, soccer and rugby playing failures, during the dying months of 1999 and the century, are reflected in the diversions from assessing their causes by such irrelevant posturings with proposed Parliamentary legislation to ban fox hunting by the non-sporting Blair barrister dominated government, while neglecting comparable contemporaneous legislative opportunities to protect school and recreational playing fields within the Rule of Law in the manner proposed specifically in Part (2) of the Second Appendix on School Sport to this text.

Additionally and realistically the Australian Government has proclaimed its intention to criminalise drug-related athletic offenders during the 2000 Olympic games, notwithstanding the IOC's artificial attempt to claim territorial jurisdiction for their duration. In the same sports-related legal areas Dave Moorcroft, the Chief Executive of UK Athletics, has highlighted the sinister significance in the IAAF's intention to refer all doping cases to arbitration with the arguably challengeable and unlawful decision for the loser to pay all the costs, notwithstanding exoneration from any culpability after a UKA inquiry. As Moorcroft explained, reported in the *Guardian* 27th November 1999:

> 'It's probably an effective way of protecting their system. Even if people are innocent they will figure they cannot afford to run the risk of not winning'.

This development is consistent, of course, with the unreality inherent in the IAAF's retention if its title as the International *Amateur* Athletics Association, notwithstanding its creation of trust funds and direct payments for its participants.

Looking back to the *Daily Telegraph* Saturday, 6th February 1999 Special Report beginning 'Sport is in a mess', I had not realised until now the supreme irony in its timing after thirty years. On Friday 7th February 1969 I had moved from being concerned in the mid and later 1950s with problems of taxation of players' benefits, restraint of trade and Pegasus' potential charitable status, explained throughout these pages. A *Police Review* proposal for prosecuting fouling footballers causing serious injury in order to solve the spiralling criminality of foul play produced a reaction in the *News of the World* two days later on Sunday 9th February 1969. A headline over Frank Butler's column read:

'STAR'S BEHIND BARS
IT'S JUST CRAZY'

followed by a text which began:

> 'I've read some crazy sporting gimmicks, but the silliest suggestion comes from a barrister who wants the police to have power to arrest footballers who commit dirty fouls'.

It ended:

> 'The day the police take over from the referees will be the day the sport dies.'

Many will recognise from the pages which follow how sport within its true meaning of health and education within the Rule of Law has died at many different levels. When this is understood and rectified by returning the Rule of Law within sport itself and when required, by invoking it from outside, the new millennium can cleanse this great slice of society's current culture from the sickening mess it has created for itself and all of us throughout the dying 20th Century.

Edward Grayson

9-12 Bell Yard,
London, WC2A 2LF

Acknowledgements

Teamwork for publishers is equivalent to all team groups, on and off the field; and some players in such dimensions are more equal than others. Furthermore, during the last twenty-odd years which have followed since *Sport and the Law* surfaced in 1978 from within the *Sunday Telegraph* not everyone who has added to its development within that period would expect recognition here. For this third Butterworths edition in ten years, however, I would be guilty of gross ingratitude if I were not to record the debt I owe in what has been at times a battle against prejudice, hostility, naivity, and ignorance compounded as happens so often by arrogance. To combat these elements I have been blessed with allies who could always see the cause to be fought, whereby this is an appropriate occasion for acknowledgement in two dimensions.

A happy coincidence has timed Jimmy Hill's Presidency of Corinthian-Casuals Football Club after his crusading Chairmanship of the Professional Footballers' Association, and so many other successful soccer sources, to turn history's wheel full circle and link his generous Foreword with how this book began from his own Corinthian inheritance and his predecessor Jimmy Guthrie's earlier Players' Union Chairmanship.

My co-founders of the British Association for Sport and the Law, Maurice Watkins as Manchester United's solicitor director in line with the great Harold Hardman's Olympic Games soccer gold medallist traditions, and Dr Ray Farrell from the School of Law at Manchester Metropolitan University, have balanced practical commercial expertise and learning for me with solid academic foundations. They have reaffirmed my own native southern impressions that what Manchester thinks to-day Britain and particularly London thinks to-morrow, evidenced here by the rapid rush of other practitioners and writers to enter into this hitherto barren territory before our foundation on the 35th anniversary on 6th February 1993 of the Munich Airport disaster which decimated Sir Matt Busby's Babes; and the Anglia Sports Law Research Centre at Anglia Polytechnic University's own Law School has further encouraged our creation as pioneers in their own chosen unique and valuable field.

Derek Casey at Sport England (formerly the Sports Council), and Nigel Hook at the Central Council of Physical Recreation, have long guided me constitutionally through what the late Lord (Dennis) Howell in his Forewords to each of the two earlier 1988 and 1994 Butterworth editions described as a 'legal minefield'; Gerry Boon and Richard Baldwin with their specialist accountancy expertise at Deloitte & Touche have steered me away from some of the delayed action fiscal dangers lurking there; Brian Glanville has always been ready to balance his unrivalled perspective as football's leading international chronicler with his Charterhouse and Chelsea-Casuals grass roots; and M'Learned Friend and neighbour at 1 Brick Court, Temple, Edward Garnier, QC, MP, has generously allowed me to draw upon his specialised politico-legal experiences and opinions when sporting issues have spilled over into them.

Finally, each of the specialist contributors to the Appendices has generously responded to bring a particularly vivid insight to their respective experiences and supplement the main text of this comprehensive 'complex of problems', identified by Lord Hailsham when he persuaded the Prime Minister Harold Macmillan nearly forty years ago now in 1962 to create a government minister with responsibility for whatever can be regarded as sport.

In a wider context, the BBC World Service and the whole of its world-wide sports unit expertise, alongside the libraries of Middle and Inner Temple, the Football Association and the Scottish Football Association, the Royal Courts of Justice, the Royal Society of Medicine, and the *Daily* and *Sunday Telegraph*, *The Times*, *The Yorkshire Post*, and Malcolm Henson at Staffordshire University, and Stephen Green, Curator and Librarian at Lord's Cricket Ground, have all responded readily to enquiries to fill gaps in the jig-saw puzzle which this subject will always create as its global explosion daily demands new solutions to its expanding problems.

Nearer home, Mrs Christine Martins gallantly converted countless drafts alongside more formal solicitors' instructions in Chambers where my successive Heads, Edmund Lawson, QC, and D Anthony Evans, QC, with their staff have responded when required in the spirit which my publishers have now endured for three successive editions.

Butterworths have now edited all three with enthusiasm, patience, restraint, understanding and wise guidance which is every author's ideal; and timing and a happy coincidence have combined to draw stumps with the law existing on the birthday anniversary of G O Smith, Corinthian and Cricketer, England's greatest centre-forward, and one-time headmaster, Ludgrove School, whose letters to me at school, and published in *Corinthians and Cricketers*, were the acorns from which this particular oak-tree has grown: 25 November 1999.

Contents

PART I

Overview

CHAPTER 1

PART II

Personal Relationships

PART III

International Sport

CHAPTER 9

CHAPTER 10

Single European Market and UK Sport   373

PART IV

Administration

CHAPTER 11

Fair Play and Reason in Court   385

CHAPTER 12

Administrative Advice   419

Table of statutes

Table of statutory instruments

Table of cases

B

F

G

H

PAGE

Introduction

1. LEGAL SIMPLICITY

Arthur Rowe's philosophy: 'Football is a simple game: the players make it difficult' was adapted almost imperceptibly after the Second World War in the early 1950's to 'the law applied to sport is simple: others make it difficult'. The harmonisation of professional footballers' and professional cricketers' tax-free benefits payments demonstrated it. This was required to destroy the imbalance which then existed between Denis Compton of Arsenal and England paying tax on his footballer's *Company-Club employment linked* discretionary benefit payment under the then Football League Regulations, and Denis Compton of Middlesex and England receiving his *publicly subscribed* cricket bounty tax-free *outside* the terms of his cricketer's employment contract.

A simple re-arrangement, with the approval of the then Association Football Players' and Trainers' Union (now the Professional Footballers' Association PFA), was effected, to delete the *discretionary contractual element* for payment of a benefit within the professional footballer's *employment contract* during the 1950's. Thereby it came into line with a professional cricketer's, and reliance upon public funding and goodwill outside the *contract of employment* and Football League Regulations encasing it. The concept was based upon the House of Lords cricketer's ruling in *Seymour v Reed* [1927] AC 554, which had held the publicly subscribed professional cricketer's benefit to be tax-free. The simple solution achieved the desired result and harmonised the tax free basis for the two separate benefits. It is explained in more detail in the contemporaneous contributions during 1953 which are reproduced in the first Appendix to this text. It thereby circumvented the adverse results of two misconceived professional footballers' cases respectively in 1927 and 1941 [*Davis v Harrison* [1927] TLR 623: and *Dale v Duff, etc* [1941] KB 730] which misguidedly and vainly attempted to apply the *Seymour v Reed* tax-free situation and circumstances to a contractual regulated relationship.

2.   SPORT COMPLEXITY

The converse to such legal simplicity is illustrated by three well-known examples from the Court of Appeal (Civil Division) of judicial and procedural practitioners' errors, in the days before the present Government's unjust and illiberal practice to ban any appeal without leave of a trial judge or the Court of Appeal. For in a remarkably unpublicised and little known administrative action slipped in to the procedural litigation framework under cover of the Christmas-New Year Court Vacation in December 1998 with the title, '*Modernising Justice*' CM 4155, unknown to the general public, and accepted without demur or challenge by all branches and at all levels of a supine legal profession, Paragraph 4.17 at Page 44 proclaimed with breathtaking arrogance compounded by ignorance [with my emphasis]

'In a well-functioning justice system the emphasis should be on *assuming the court of first instance has reached the right decision*: so there should not be an automatic right to appeal.'

In the first of those three well known frequently cited examples, *six days of factual analysis and legal argument* in the Court of Appeal, reversed an experienced judge after a trial inquiry into injuries suffered at a White City Horse Show. It established as a precedent a key element in the duty of care required for sports-related personal injury negligence cases (i.e. to take into account all the relevant circumstances) in now an oft cited ruling. The Appeal Court held that the wrong inferences *of fact had been drawn from the evidence* of 12 different witnesses seen and heard by the trial judge, including the injured Plaintiff cameraman and Defendant horse rider (*Wooldridge v Sumner* [1962] 3 WLR 616). Twenty years later in 1982 another Court of Appeal ordered a re-trial of J.P.R. Williams' libel action against *The Daily Telegraph* (which was ultimately settled) because on that occasion the trial judge wrongly left to the jury

'both the interpretation of the [International Rugby Football Board] regulations (which he should not have done) and the decision of what evidence to believe and inferences to be drawn from the oral and documentary evidence',

(*Williams v Reason and Daily Telegraph* [1988] 1 All ER 262); finally, a decade later in 1993 H.H. the Aga Khan's legal practitioner advisers persisted perversely in vain in the face of sustained adverse authorities to challenge, by the *judicial review procedural remedies*, in lieu of available clear-cut contract claims, as explained clearly in the Court of Appeal Judgments, a Jockey Club's disqualification of the 1989 Epsom Oaks victory of his filly Ailysa, with the ultimate consequential withdrawal of his horses from English racing training stables to Ireland and France. (*R v Disciplinary Committee of the Jockey Club, Ex parte Aga Khan* ([1998] 2 AER 853 at 876).

3. THE TWELVE INTERLOCKING REASONS WHICH HAVE PRECIPITATED THIS 3RD EDITION

1. Update with original and new research material
2. True meaning of sport
3. Two cultures: showbiz -v- grass roots
4. No modern phenomenon
5. Rule of Law benefits sport and recreation
6. Government overlapping complexities
7. Uncontrolled sales of playing fields and school sport generally
8. Reaction to new challenges
9. Local developments
10. Judicial limitations and error
11. Denials of Justice by bars on appeal
12. Readers' conclusions on true meaning of sport.

Accordingly, those twelve interlocking reasons follow on from each other in an irresistibly logical sequence, to explain how and why this third edition emerges. The relevant applicable *legal principles* remained unchanged down the years and since the last edition in 1994. Only their application to the daily developing differing emerging problems, issues and then admissible evidence which command, domestic, national and international reportage, demands attention. They are summarised in their twelve separate categories listed here above.

(1) To *update* with original and new research material the earlier Overview and details from those two earlier editions for existing loyal readers; the ever increasingly interested enquirers, students and general public concerned about the subject, and especially for the newly qualified and/or younger generations of practitioners and all others linked to the subject who would be unaware of its historical background and progressive development explained thereafter.

(2) To explain whatever *meaning* can be ascribed for sport, as assessed at the outset here in the Preface[1] for all three required identifiable

---

1   I.e. an earlier Hailsham context.

levels; namely, internationally, nationally and domestically, within each particular self regulatory recreational activity; and how all are subject to the overriding Rule of Law within any civilised constitutional government community. Thus, the now celebrated 1995 European Court of Justice judgment in favour of the Belgian *professional* footballer, *Jean-Marc Bosman*, transcended every *economically structured* recreational governing body foundation throughout whatever may be identified as the sporting world, within the European Community (EC), including FIFA (the world governing football body), UEFA (its European limitation), and every commercially based domestic football association. It surfaced within the framework of the *economically* structured Treaty of Rome, without having any *direct* effect upon the overwhelming majority of 30,920,000 adults and children aged 5 to 15 of recreational participants, comprising 67% of the population, and their 421 organisations of recognised United Kingdom Sporting Governing Bodies, explained in detail from Sport England (formerly the Sports Council) sources, as at March 1999, cited in the Preface above. Nevertheless it epitomises two all-too-forgotten or deliberately and too frequently ignored concepts.

(i)   Without the Rule of Law in Society anarchy reigns; without the Rule of Law in Sport, chaos exists.

(ii)   The law of the land does not stop at the touchline, boundary, board or committee room.

(3) To emphasise how the fall-out from the explosion of international sport and recreation, dominated to-day by the international governing body federations, IOC (Olympics), FIFA (football), IAAF (athletics), IRB (rugby), ICC (cricket), FINA (swimming), to name just a few of the most popular and easily identifiable, has thereby created differing and complex concurrent cultural gaps comparable to D'Israeli's *Two Nations* and C.P. Snow's Two Cultures of *Art and Science:*

(i)   the division between sport and recreation at the public, entertainment media- orientated and commercial levels on the one hand, and the fun-seeking, healthy, recreational grassroots (but nevertheless competitive) and educational dimension on the other; and

(ii)   the even more insidious gap between those with respect for the Rule of Law in Sport (reflective of the Rule of Law in society generally) and those demonstrating an unconcealed contempt for such doctrinal idealism generally, beyond sport, evidenced by the daily mounting casualties in breach of road traffic regulations with their comparable breaches of the laws of sport. In each discipline, medical evidence provides damning proof of callous social and sporting misconduct. These cultural divisions and distinctions exist universally without any national boundary differences and often any awareness of how

(a) the modern global explosion of sport and recreation began in mid-Victorian nineteenth century Britain as a grass roots vehicle for fun and healthy exercise and pleasure;

(b) before it was taken round the world as a chunk of the commercial entertainment and leisure industries alongside its retention of a two dimensional healthy educational example of its origins.

(4) To disabuse all those within and without the legal profession who believe application of the Rule of Law in society to sport and to recreation is a *modern phenomenon*; and to explain how the weapons in the legal armoury from Parliament and the Courts have been waiting in the wings and used when required since the Middle Ages, to come on stage to protect victims of unlawful and illegal practices off as well as on the field of play, for centuries before their current explosive invocation in our own times. This is evidenced clearly from the chronological tabulated lists of 251 years of cases spanning 1748 to 1999 and events summarised in this Introduction at pages 24ff hereafter, with their kaleidoscopic range of known identifiable legal areas, covering contracts, crime and charity to negligence, tax, tribunals, trade restraints, with dashes of defamation in between.

(5) To explain contrary to many misconceptions, within and without the varying worlds of recreational activities at all levels, public and private, how the general national *Rule of Law* outside sport and recreation is essential for protecting individual and the public interests within each particular discipline when sport and recreation are incapable of providing appropriate sanctions within their own self-regulatory structures. The world's two most popular pastimes, horse racing and football, vividly illustrate the point.

(i) Jenny Pitman is modern steeple chase horse racing's most celebrated woman trainer. In her autobiography *Jenny Pitman* she generously acknowledges her debt to Florence Nagle. This indomitable lady took on the then chauvinistic Jockey Club who had created an unwritten rule that women trainers could and would not be granted a licence to train racehorses in their own name but required the fiction through their head lad. After two procedural rejections of her claim by the Queen's Bench Master in Chambers, and on appeal to Mr. Justice John Stephenson, she arrived ultimately in the Court of Appeal presided over by the liberal Lord Denning. They raised the starting gate to continue her claim. Before she reached a judgment winning post, the Jockey Club capitulated, (see *Nagle v Fielden* [1966] 2 QB 633). Nearly twenty years later in 1983, Corbiere won the Grand National trained by Jenny Pitman. Because Mrs. Nagle's claim in 1966 was without a binding precedent, present commentators and future historians may justifiably enquire whether she would have achieved her goal under the present Court of Appeal practice which requires leave to appeal from a trial judge's decision or the Court of Appeal itself; introduced after Production of the *Modernising Justice* publication cited [here P1 above] without Parliamentary or public debate by statutory instrument, to take effect during the Christmas - New Year holiday over 1998-1999, under the regime of Lord Denning's less liberal minded successors, with a Government campaign misleadingly described as *'Access to Justice'* yet concealing in reality a Denial of Justice.

(ii)   The European Court of Justice *Bosman* ruling, which has emancipated *professional* footballers generally from the restrictive practices within that old style feudal world, was the logical corollary to an English campaign led by successive Chairmen of the former Association Professional Players' and Trainers' Union, now the Professional Footballers' Association (PFA), James Guthrie and James Hill. In the years after the Second World War Jimmy Guthrie, who had captained Portsmouth's F.A. Cup winning team in the last Final played before that war, campaigned under the banners of *Soccer Slaves* and *The Last Bonded Men in Britain*. Jimmy Hill, who had supported and ultimately succeeded him, and progressed from a distinguished playing to managerial and communicating careers until he became President of the most prestigious club in the world of international sport, Corinthian-Casuals, and synonymous with its fair play ethic, built progressively under his own flag of *Striking for Soccer* on Guthrie's pioneer work in their successive preludes to the well-known and oft-cited case *Eastham v Newcastle United, Football Association and Football League* [1964] Ch 413. This ensured freedom of contract for United Kingdom professional footballers linked ultimately to *Bosman*. It allowed Sir Matt Busby and later Sir Alex Ferguson, initially under the stewardship of the only *professional solicitor* to have won full England and Olympic Games international and F.A. Cup winning honours as an *amateur* player, Harold Hardman, as club chairman in the early 1950's, to bring glory for Manchester United and British football generally, with its inspiration for future generations, by blending overseas and local United Kingdom talents.

(iii)   More recently at the other end of professional football's financial spectrum, the relatively unfashionable A.F.C. Bournemouth, which once gave the Manchester United Busby Babes an F.A. Cup 6th Round fright in 1957, was rescued from extinction during the mid-1990's by the legal commercial initiatives of a local solicitor, Trevor Watkins. He achieved it while commuting from his coastal home to his London solicitor's office until his own transfer between practising solicitors firms coincided with the Club chairmanship and leadership of a consortium in Bournemouth to link it all with a community more renowned traditionally for less strenuous recreational pursuits. An exodus of 34,000 citizens to a Wembley Stadium competition final appearance from the edge of Club bankruptcy following his inspiration was a classic example of the law in sport filling a gap beyond the capacity of conventional football administration.

(6) To emphasise for greater public and professional awareness how the subject's complexities in the United Kingdom command the attention of 14 overlapping Whitehall and Westminster *government* departments in the land of its origin *in addition to the* Department of Culture, Media and Sport ostensibly concerned with sport and recreation, in the manner summarised in previous editions and updated at p 129 in Chapter 2. They in turn are inter-connected with those 421 United Kingdom recognised Sporting Governing Bodies, and 30,920,000 participating adults alongside participating children between the ages of 5 to 15, throughout the United Kingdom, already identified authentically in the Preface.

(7) To direct attention concurrently with this complex inter-departmental network of sport and recreationally related Government activity, to the hitherto neglected opportunity to initiate primary Parliamentary legislation for solving the apparently intractable problem of the national concern for uncontrolled *sales of schools and other playing fields*. This is an area where the Law in Parliament is available for the benefit and welfare of the health and education dimensions to this particular national issue, inherent in sport and recreation, if any member of either of the two Houses of Parliament would ever have the vision, wit, will or even interest to initiate activity for it. This interaction between health, education and the law was climaxed when the Medical Officers' Schools Association (MOSA) Report of 1979 resulted in the Rugby Football Union's response to activate it. Compulsory insurance was recommended, but activated ultimately too late for circumstances which emerged in *Van Oppen v Bedford School Trustees* [1989] 1 All ER 273; affirmed [1989] 3 All ER 389, CA.

(8) To emphasise how application of the law in relation to sport and recreation can respond positively to *new challenges* when the evidence, facts and circumstances permit. Thus, the socio-political campaign to Kick Racism out of Football in particular, and sport generally, was absorbed with the racially aggravated legislative provisions enacted with all-party support in the Crime and Disorder Act 1998. Accordingly, while these pages were in preparation a Swansea City football fan, who raced on to the Vetch Field playing area during a Third Division Football League match, and abusively

called a visiting Brighton and Hove Albion player 'a black nigger', was convicted by a Swansea Crown Court jury and gaoled for 12 months. He was prosecuted and convicted and gaoled for 12 months under the statute for putting the player in fear while being racially motivated (*R. v Neil Roberts* (BBC Radio Wales: 16 July 1999).

(9) That example in turn leads to an often overlooked or even ignored unawareness of how the Law is regularly applied to and or the benefit of sport and recreation in *local developments* and circumstances which are never recorded or reported at national or professional sources and journals. A classic example, capable of countless repetitions, was the broken leg injury suffered in a Leamington, Warwickshire, local league football match between Whittle Wanderers and Khala Football Club during the early 1980's. Initially it was of little interest beyond the parties, players and local interest involved, even when Judge Wootton in the Warwick County Court in March 1984 awarded £4,900 to the victim of a foul tackle. Because the offender Gurdever Basi and/or his advisers and/or insurers appealed against the judgment in favour of the victim James Condon, the event has become a legal Court of Appeal landmark, not without criticism of it; on liability for football personal injury as *Condon v Basi* [1985] 1 WLR 866.

(10) The debate about that *judgment's* authenticity, notwithstanding its reliance and citation in subsequent cases again, leads on to what appeared in Appendix 9 to the 1994 edition and is repeated here. This is that on every one of the near dozen occasions, except for the last in 1993 [*Customs and Excise Commissioners v Professional Footballers' (Association) Enterprise Ltd* [1993] STC 86], whenever the House of Lords over a sixty years period since its first foray with the professional cricketers tax-free benefits case of *Seymour v Reed* [1927] AC 554 has entered into this penalty area, it has reversed a lower court; and thereby reflected at least a disagreement with often judicial and other practitioners' errors. Thus, Viscount Dunedin at pages 560-561 [1927] AC explained, as cited partially in the Preface supra

'When I think of this little nest egg....being treated, the whole sum, as income, honestly, had it not been for the fact that honourable Judges, whose opinions I respect, have come to another conclusion, I would have thought that contention preposterous'.

(11) Similarly in many landmark sports-related decisions, such as *Nagle v Fielden*, already explained in relation to Jenny Pitman and Corbiere, the Court of *Appeal* also has reversed a lower court decision; and we shall see throughout this text, how, if the present draconian denial of automatic right of appeal in civil trials had existed before 1999, the

development of Sport and the Law and justice for the successful parties might never have been achieved, to re-emphasise the reality of an alleged Access to Justice present British Government policy cloaking deceptively a *Denial of Justice*.

(12) Finally, and by no means the least of these twelve reasons which precipitate this third Butterworths' edition, is to let the reader judge for himself and herself the true *meaning* of sport. Whether in reality it is a branch of an over hyped, over indulged, overpriced, and often corrupt commercial chunk of the vast internationally orientated entertainment leisure industry with its unregulated agents or an irregular drug testing territory; or what the medical and teaching professions which have to pick up the fall-out from its industrial illegalities recognise as health and education within a regulated conducted framework: the Rule of Law, in both sport and society.

4. HOW THE INTERLOCKING REASONS INTEGRATE

These twelve interlocking reasons for this 3rd Edition will appear threaded throughout the narrative which follows. They will also remain constant as the dynamic nature of the subject- matter drives forward to create new boundaries of awareness which are already in the pipeline while these pages are being prepared during the last year of the century, and will spill over into the millennium and beyond. Parliament has processed at last legislation for further control over football and crowd hooliganism overseas as well as at home, with its Football (Offences and Disorder) Act 1999, based in principle upon the draft Safety of Sports Persons Act which I included in an Appendix to each of the three earlier editions in 1978, 1988 and 1994. The House of Lords judicial committee is due, at the time of writing in the autumn of 1999, yet to adjudicate with finality upon Diane Modahl's long-standing claim for damages against the British Athletic Federation (BAF) for alleged flawed drug testing procedures and Lindford Christie and Lawrence Delaglio were also subjected to administrative enquiries under this area. Not surprisingly and perhaps significantly, the London *Independent* newspaper in a leading article [Saturday 7 August] at the end of a week when sports-related drug reports dominated national and international headlines concluded

'The criminal justice system - police and courts - are the way to take drugs out of sports. Self-regulation has failed.'

Indeed, the Australian Government has already served notice of its intention to act on this basis against drug-related offenders during the

2000 Olympic Games. London's High Court has adjudicated while these pages were in preparation on a crucial commercial dispute between the F.A. Premier Football League and the Office of Fair Trading about control of television for the national game. Bruce Grobbelaar obtained £85,000 libel damages against the *Sun* newspaper after two Criminal Court jury disagreements. A judgment upheld in London's High Court of boxer Michael Watson's claim against the British Boxing Board of Control's alleged failure to organise effective emergency medical measures for urgent transport and treatment after he was knocked out and suffered serious brain damage at Tottenham Hotspur's football stadium in a world title contest with Chris Eubank during 1991 is now perhaps surprisingly benefiting from leave to appeal, contrary to the refusal of Huddersfield Town's similar application against Gordon Watson, also in 1999.

The numerically more important area for competitive school sport, and its future and dangers still debated at adolescent levels between the ages of 14 and 16, are subject to a Qualitative Curriculum Authority (QCA) quango, created under Section 21, the Education Act 1997, with a core remit to promote quality and coherence in education and training. The Human Rights Act 1998, due to enter United Kingdom Law in the year 2000, promises new uncharted territories which may yet add further weapons in the legal armoury for deployment, beyond the dreams of all who have seen how the Law can be invoked to regulate sport and recreation issues, when they are clearly incapable of self-regulation from within whatever may be regarded as sport itself. Jenny Pitman, Jimmy Guthrie and Jimmy Hill, *Eastham, Bosman*, Trevor Watkins, the explosive drug cocktails, and more recently Neil Roberts in Swansea Crown Court, have already illustrated what can be seen as the head of potentially bubbling sporting legal volcanoes which are yet to spill over on to whatever can be regarded or interpreted as part of the recreational scene, both nationally and internationally; and in the widest socio-politico legal dimension, the *British Association of Sports Medicine Journal* special edition on Women in Sport, at the time of preparation of these pages, contains a sombre warning for all concerned with the health of sport and future generations; the greatest potential danger stems not so much from drugs as the insidious risks from child and sexual abuse available to sports coaches working in the closest possible physical relationship with vulnerable younger participants.

In turn that all raises a more urgent and immediate assessment of what the subject-matter of Sport and the Law means and covers. The distinguished cricket writer and philosopher, C.L.R. James, observed in his classic *Beyond a Boundary* 'What do they know of cricket who only cricket know?' Concurrently, it is equally appropriate to enquire 'What do they know of Sport and the Law who only Sport and the Law know?'.

Within whatever can be an accepted and understood meaning of Sport and Recreation, many are reluctant to accept how the Laws of Sport can be subject to prosecution or compensation claims implemented in the courts and jury and judicial surveillance [*not* in England and Wales, as distinct from Scotland under the technical procedurally described and titled judicial *review*], and also if oppressive irregular administrative domestic tribunal sanctions penalties are imposed. This was illustrated by the oft forgotten reversal by Mr. Justice Cantley two decades ago now during 1979 of the Football Association's 10 years ban on its former England team manager, Don Revie, after he had walked out of that role for alternative employment in United Arab Emirates (see *Revie v The FA* [Times: 19 December 1979]. More recent examples come from the principality of Wales. Its Football Association and R.F.U. each bit the dust when High Court injunctions were required respectively during the 1990 decade to protect victims of oppressively unlawful administrative sanctions against Newport and other soccer clubs [1995], and an Ebbw Vale rugby player, Mark Jones [1997]. The media and even some members of the profession in the case of Jones appeared to believe as a messianic revelation or as a new dimension how a sporting governing body had been brought within the jurisdiction of the law courts. Everyone concerned with such belief appeared to have been unaware of the countless precedents over the last 45 years which began with the British Amateurs Weightlifters Association (BAWLA) over forty years earlier in *Baker v. Jones* [1954] 2 AER 553.

BAWLA still exists as one of the 136 recognised governing bodies in England to-day, out of the total number of 421 in the United Kingdom identified by the English Sports Council (now Sport England) in 1999. Very few of the 30,920,000 participatory adults and children aged 5 to 15 and/or members of the 421 United Kingdom recognised Sporting Governing Bodies would have recourse to the sources available to the moguls of the F.A. Premier League except for legal aid: but their personal proprietary rights are equally entitled to protection within the Rule of Law.

That Rule of Law is constant throughout society. Thus, a Yorkshire schoolboy Maxwell Casson's £3,000 Bradford County Court interim award during May 1999 against negligent Army football players was qualitatively equal in principle and in accordance with legal precedent to the £900,000 final award adjudicated around the same time in the High Court for the privately funded F.A. Premier League professional Gordon Watson of Bradford City. He had succeeded against Kevin Gray and Huddersfield Town in an arguably challengeable judgment on negligence liability, for which leave to appeal was refused under the newly introduced controlled mechanism for civil justice appeals from debateable judicial decisions based upon the fallacious assumption that 'the court of first instance has reached the right decision' under the present Government's Denial of Justice misleadingly cloaked under its title of *Modernising Justice* [Cmnd 4155: December 1998, para.4.17 at page 44] with an equally misleading populist described policy of *Access to Justice*.

Finally, there is a deeper and wider meaning behind the message inherent in the Primate's claim during the debate on *Society's Moral and Spiritual Well-Being* on the eve of Euro '96,

'Rules do not get in the way of the game, they make it possible'.

Significantly, the only contributor in the debate in addition to Britain's longest serving Sports Minister, the late Lord Howell, who took up this theme, was Lord Borrie, who had created the Institute of Judicial Administration at Birmingham University and is a Bencher of the Honourable Society of Middle Temple. He began by saying,

'Society's moral well-being is or should be, an important objective for people of all religions, and, indeed, for those who have none. The most reverend Primate, the Archbishop of Canterbury, has no doubt very rightly put the emphasis on the responsibility of schools,'

but in the wider context which embraces the Law in relation to sport and recreation Lord Barrie continued, with my own emphasis,

'However, this afternoon I should like to stress not just the responsibility of schools and other educational institutions, and, of course, parents, in all such matters, vital though that is, but also the responsibility of influential leaders in our society. Most obviously, I refer to our politicians and other business and commercial leaders. I suppose that *there is also a responsibility*, though it may be less easy to persuade them, *on all the people whose* utterances and *behaviour have an impact on citizens of all ages, especially the young.*

I include among those people editors, *sporting heroes* and pop stars. *They can be role models. They may not choose to be* influential but, *whether or not they choose to be so, their impact through the publicity given to their activities and behaviour both on and off the sports field* and on and off the stage, *involves, to my mind, a responsibility to behave in a moral and ethical way.*'

Nearly ten years earlier, another lawyer, the then retiring Lord Chancellor, Lord Hailsham of St. Marylebone, in 1987, twenty-five years after he had conceived the idea in 1962 of a Government Minister with special responsibility for sport, in his Carlton Lecture *Morality, Law and Politics,* discussed 'Values' with the following explanation:

'It has been our fortune, good or bad, to live in an age of conflict, violence and confusion, one in which old certainties have faded into agnosticism, when new fanaticisms, new bigotries have arisen and new sources of political power or disruption have first challenged and sometimes overthrown established authority. Partly this has been due to the speed of travel, and partly, possibly as a result of the conflicts which this produces, by a decline in religious belief in the West, overawed as it is by the triumphs of its own science and technology. But, although science and technology are capable of demolishing, up to a point, certain types of superstition, they are not by themselves capable of creating a new system of values, and, if the old systems of value are to be re-established, the need for them will have at the least to be restated in the light of prevailing confusion and doubt. At the heart of the problem lies the uncertain frontier between morality, politics and law, the framework of an ordered and civilised life.'

No greater example of the

'uncertain frontier between morality, politics and, the framework of an ordered and civilised life',

exists than the current problems inherent in domestic and international sport at all levels. A few weeks after Dr. Carey's House of Lords debate in 1996 the Independent Schools Association felt obliged to issue a 'Code of Honour for School Sport' after two famous independent schools, Marlborough and Radley discontinued their cricket fixtures because of alleged sledging during play. During early 1999 a Schools Sports Forum condemned the misconduct by public professional football players of misleading younger generations with the claim by the Headmaster of Queen Elizabeth's Grammar School, Blackburn 'A fish rots from the top'; and shortly before Maxwell Casson obtained his £3,000 *interim* damages award for negligent physical play by the Army, during a Work Experience activity, another schoolboy was convicted of smashing a schoolboy opponent's jaw in an inter-school rugby match. Upon conviction the offender's father complained: ' Why should my son go to jail? It was only a game'. [*R v Calton* : *Yorkshire Post*: 29 September 1998].

In a similar context the Everton Football Club expressed disbelief when their transferred Scottish International player Duncan Ferguson, from Rangers, was imprisoned after conviction for head-butting a professional opponent during a Scottish Premier League game. Later this trend was confirmed when David Sole, the former Scottish rugby international captain, was reported as having written to a Scottish court supporting a fellow player, Jason Fayers (*Times*, 14 February, 1997) who had been fined £1000 and ordered to pay £500 compensation for breaking an opponent's jaw during a game. Earlier, he had been subjected by the Scottish Rugby Union to a four-year worldwide ban against participating in rugby in any format or role, concurrent with his court sentence; and it will be recalled how the England cricket captain, Michael Atherton was subjected to criticism for alleged apparent ball tampering.

Internationally, the President of the International Olympic Committee, Juan Antonio Samaranch, raised the temper of and, fuelled the flames in this medico-pharmacological-ethical climate when commenting in an interview with a Spanish daily newspaper and recorded in the London *Daily Telegraph* (26 July, 1998) and the BBC World Service that 'substances that do not damage a sportsman's health should not be banned'.

The reverberations from this bombshell were heard worldwide. A week later the Head of the International Olympic Medical Commission, Prince Alexandre de Merode, was recorded in the *Independent* (18 August, 1998) to have been 'appalled' after Samaranch was reported to have said he saw no harm in athletes taking certain drugs as long as they were not a threat to health.

'I don't understand,'

he said

> 'people who want to reduce the list of banned drugs are those who want doping to continue. President Samaranch has always been against doping and he has always supported the a]ction taken by the medical commission. I know where these ideas have come from - doctors who have forgotten their professional ethics.'

More recently England's rugby captain, Lawrence Delaglio was sanctioned by the Rugby Football Union for curiously contentious statements to *News of the World* reporters about drug issues and at the time of writing towards the end of 1999, disparities between the British Athletic Federation (BAF) and the International Amateur Athletic Federation (IAAF) in their approach to alleged offenders using the substance nandrolone create a diet of daily reading which now appears to be never-ending.

Ironically, the *News of the World* thirty years ago on 9 February 1969 had protested at suggestions I had published in the *Police Review*, two days earlier, that offending players against the *national law* should be prosecuted or sued if sufficient sanctions within sport and recreation itself did not exist or are not applied effectively to regulate fair play. They had been inspired or rather incited by what many to-day may not know or have forgotten about the manner in which the great Brazilian star, Pele, during the 1966 World Cup competition won by England was brutally and viciously assaulted and ultimately excluded from it by foul play committed without any retribution or sanction by known and named offenders in his book *My Life and the Beautiful Game*. Brian Glanville's narrative and 1966 World Cup film *Goal* has it all recorded for posterity. Two years later in 1968 the then Minister with responsibility for Sport, Mr. Denis Howell, MP. received a Report he had commissioned from a Birmingham Research Group directed by Dr. J.A. Harrington on *Soccer Hooliganism*. In its summary of '*Main Findings and Recommendations*'

'The evidence for a close relationship between player misbehaviour and misbehaviour in the crowd was examined. Our conclusion [as at 1968] is that it is not possible to divorce one from the other as they are not independent entities.'

Thirty odd years later at the time of writing, professional footballers' field misconduct on 2 May 1999 in a Celtic-Rangers match was attributed [*Independent*: 10 August 1999] specifically to consequential criminal crowd activities, when a Scottish Premier League Commission of Inquiry ruled that the Celtic Club

'..had refused to heed police advice to emphasise to their players beforehand that their behaviour during the match would have a direct impact on that of the crowd'

Plus ca change: Plus la meme chose.

The subsequent years since Lord Hailsham's and Dr Carey's respective attentions to moral issues have seen an ebb and flow of local, national and international examples of an apparent never ending exploding social phenomena. It erupted again during the 1998 World Cup Competition in France, and stirred the British Parliament a year later to enact the Private Member's and Government supported Football (Offences and Disorder) Act aimed at overseas as well as domestic offenders, in principle following the draft Safety of Sports Persons Act which I had prepared for each of the previous editions of this book for the Sunday Telegraph (1978) and Butterworths 1988 and 1994.

Towards the end of 1968 football's first known playing field fatality after its last seventy years earlier prosecution in similar circumstances in 1898 [*R. -v- Moore*] (14 TLR 229), reached the courts at Essex Assizes. Transferred to Maidstone in Kent for a guilty plea to manslaughter [*R. -v- Southby*] (Times: 21 November), it was followed shortly after towards the end of 1969 by the first traceable personal injury assault judgment for a foul football tackle during a minor local league Sussex match which later led to a £4,500 damages award recorded subsequently in the *New Law Journal*: 1970: *Lewis v Brookshaw*. [Vol.120. 413]. Its trial details never surfaced beyond the local Sussex sources, consistent with *R v Neil Roberts's* Swansea Crown Court conviction for a racially aggravated offence on 16 July 1999, at p 8, above.

In that year of 1969 the then Chancellor of the Exchequer, the then Roy Jenkins, MP now Earl Jenkins of Hillhead; Chancellor Oxford University, in a well publicised speech to the Abingdon Labour Party (*Times*, 21 July p3) proclaimed the self-styled permissive society to be the 'civilised society', with permanent undesirable consequences many may consider are evidenced throughout these pages and well beyond them. Twenty-five years further forward America's *Sports Illustrated's* 40th Anniversary issue [1954-1994] claimed with justification

> 'Sometime in the second half of the century, sports became an axis on which the world turns. ....There have been comparable times in history when sports have been at the centre of a culture and seemed to dominate the landscape. Whether in Greek society or in what used to be called the Golden Ages of Sports. But everything is magnified by television.'

Television therefore inevitably enters the legal arena with legal commercial battles which now appear to be never ending. The 1992 law suit between BBC and BSKYB [1992] Ch.141 has been followed more recently by the BSKYB-Manchester United Monopolies and Merger Commission Report, and the Commercial Court judgment between the Office of Fair Trading and the F.A. Premier League mirrored wider issues reflecting the commercial stakes in public media entertainment. Yet while Access to Justice or Denial of Justice will always have echoes of Mr. Justice Maule's celebrated aphorism 'The Law Courts like the Ritz Hotel are open to all', the substantive and clear-cut Law in relation to sport and recreation is no different qualitatively and substantively in its application to those who are 'magnified by television', and to any one of the 30,920,000 participants identified in the Summary of Sports Participation in England' prepared for this edition by Sport England, formerly the Sports Council.

5. BEFORE TELEVISION BEGAN

With, or without television, structured sport and recreation will always be a cameo illuminating any civilised community's legal system's target area: society's preservation and stability linked to the national interest, individual freedom and property protection.

So long as participatory sport and recreation sporting Governing Body organisations associated with the 113 VAT exempt activities based upon voluntary services retain a *non*-profit making and thereby amateur identity (crystallised in the United Kingdom by H.M. Customs & Excise Treasury Regulations cited in the Preface hereof above), their needs for special Parliamentary legislation and personal litigation will often be less necessary than the requirements of conflicting tensions, fuelled by personal pique or more publicised commercial disputes. The battles for Nationwide Football League or the F.A. Premier League [1992] supremacy and Packer against cricket's establishment in *Greig v Insole* [1978], between full *profit* making taxable and Vatable general activities, need hardly be recalled here, to illustrate the point. They returned more recently on an even more recognisable public stage with the Monopolies and Merger Commission's and British Government's rejections of BSKYB's interest in Manchester United, and the marathon court case between the Office of Fair Trading and the Premier League for the right to control Pay-per-View television [*Times* 18 August 1999].

Consequently, when comparable compensatory and other industrial and road traffic circumstances are adapted to the *financial* as distinct from the non-profit sector of sport and recreation, exemplified by the stadium disasters below, the floodgates of Parliamentary legislation and personal litigation inevitably open; and progressively developing patterns can be traced from 18th and 19th century precedents which lead up to what at one time was a novelty: is still regarded with tinges of the hostility in many sporting and even wider circles, to what now is accepted, often with grudging reluctance, as a norm and necessary reality.

Parliament's role after the middle ages in sport and recreation was quiescent and untroubled with any need to intervene in national recreational affairs beyond its traditional protection of archery; public order; and rural proprietary rights and pastimes, until the social thrust of D'Israeli's government created the Public Health Act, 1875. This in turn progressed to beneficial education statutes and their build-up to the Physical Training and Recreation Act 1937 in anticipation of Hitler's war in 1939. A century later the crowd disasters at Bolton (1946), Ibrox (1971), Bradford (1975), Hillsborough (1989), and World Cup overseas hooligans (1998), spawned litigation and legislation which are threaded in the texts which follow and are still continuing while these pages are in preparation and will continue during and after publication. Indeed as a prelude to the future, the twentieth century began with its 110, 820 crowd at the Tottenham Hotspur v Sheffield United FA Cup Final in 1901 at the relatively safe natural Crystal Palace bowl in South London followed a year later by the first Ibrox, Glasgow, disaster with 26 dead and 500 injured when Scotland played England.

Not all sports related recreational court cases hit the formal law reports, or national and even local newspaper and other media headlines; and the patterns which appear below in this Introduction can be traced from conventional sources or others which emerge from anecdotal and personal recollections. Yet looking back with hindsight to those pioneering original 1978, 1988 and 1994 earlier editions of *Sport and the Law*, with further citations and developments since then, what is now discernible are identifiable trends. These are consistent with the parallel growth and emergence of sport and recreation as a crucial slice of cultural and social life, with the Law through Parliament and the courts with their consequences, travelling, if not in tandem, then not far behind self-regulatory and structured developments. Recourse to the courts as a last resort reflects this when internal controls of an appropriate recreational authority cannot provide a solution to a disputed problem. Thus the

Blackburn Rovers grandstand collapse with personal liability proved against its committee in *Brown v Lewis* [1896] 12 TLR 445 was followed swiftly in 1897 by corporate incorporation to become Blackburn Rovers Limited; and the Football Association in London and Scottish Football Association in Glasgow reacted similarly in 1903 after that first Ibrox disaster in 1902, to establish the Football Association Limited and Scottish Football Association Limited. To-day at the time of writing in late 1999 the localCounty Football Associations within the Football Association's jurisdiction are re-structuring their constitutions within the framework of companies limited by guarantee, and thereby avoid the legal consequences of personal liability experienced at Blackburn in 1896.

Gaming disputes with their essential commercialism, incapable of amicable settlements, have sustained a continuity down the years. Ultimately, examples of a more variable mosaic joined them to create a kaleidoscopic picture reflective of the 113 non-profit making sources listed in the VAT catalogue cited in the Preface. Even prior to formulation of cricket's first Laws of the Game in 1774, *before* foundation in 1787 of MCC (who own their copyright to-day), *Jeffreys v Walter* in 1748 arrived in Volume I Wilson's King's Bench Reports 220. It was an unresolved and ultimately out-of-court settlement about whether or not cricket was included in the category of 'other game or games whatsoever' under Section 1 of the Gaming Act, 1710 [9 Ann. c.14]. In 1825, judgment for yet another club cricket wager was upheld on appeal from Hertford Assizes in *Walpole v Saunders* in volume 1, Dow and Ryl Reports 130. Eight years later a £20 wager between the Warwick and Birmingham Cricket Clubs was contested at Warwick Assizes and reported as *Hodson v Terrill* [1833] 1 Crompton and Meeson [797]. On this occasion cricket qualified for inclusion within the Act, but in the judgment of Baron Vaughan, 'The question here turns, not on the legality of the game, but on the amount of the stake rendering it illegal' (at p 805). These earliest examples of cricket's current global commercial tensions, and enquiries, are an echo from the past to diminish any novelty about modern practices: and I am indebted to two retired solicitor cricketing enthusiasts, John Scott and the late E.B.V. Christian for their erudite initiatives in their respective publications *Caught in Court*, and *At the Sign of the Wicket* for these important sources.

Eleven years further forward in 1844 illegality hit the Epsom Derby. The first past the post was described, in Roger Mortimer's *History of the Derby Stakes* (1973) 'as Mr. A. Wood's Running Rein. He was, in fact, a four year-old-called Maccebaeus'. When objections included the second horse's owner's claim for the winning stakes, 'the Jockey Club wisely stood back and awaited a settlement by law'. *Wood v Peel* was listed and began at Westminster before Baron Alderson (*Daily Telegraph,* 1 July 1844). The case collapsed when the Plaintiff would or could not meet the trial judge's demands: ' Produce the horse? Produce the horse?'. Orlando was awarded the race on Running Rein's disqualification. Its owner Col. John Peel, brother of the Prime Minister, received the stakes; and Roger Mortimer's citation from the Judge,

> 'if gentlemen condescended to race with blackguards, they must condescend to be cheated',

has echoed down the years, with the Hon. George Lambton's celebrated disclosures in *Men and Horses I Have Known* of doping his own horses to force the Jockey Club into sanctioning its offence against the Rules of Racing at the turn of the century in the early 1900s.

1844 was a watershed. Racing's integrity had been controlled in the courts after the Derby in June; and the first Grand National Archery meeting was held a few weeks later during August in York, for what *'The Oxford Companion to Sports and Games'* 'can claim the oldest ancestry of any sport actively pursued to-day'. Its governing body, the Grand National Archery Society was founded in 1861, significantly and almost symbolically, two years before the world's most popular team game's modern formation with The Football Association's creation in 1863. Not everyone to-day knows how initiatives from schools, clubs and university sources inspired its formation to harmonise and fuse their own disparate rules to establish the Association and Laws of the Game which have survived to-day. Thereafter, development of recreational and commercial sporting self-regulation can be traced within concurrent and contemporaneous court controls in circumstances beyond the capacity of any regulatory sporting authority. Ten years earlier cricket had pointed the way ahead with an example at Norfolk Spring Assizes and the Queen's Bench Court, on appeal in London, *outside the MCC's jurisdiction*, about a spectator turned-cricketer-ejected from the playing area between the Lynn and Lytcham Cricket Clubsfor non-removal of a coat! (*Holmes v Bagge* (1853) 1 Ellis & Blackburn [782 QBD]). Throughout the decades since then different tensions have surfaced with well publicised struggles for control of county and local cricket and football clubs, and more recently International Federations and Organisations.

Three years after the F.A.'s foundation 1863 Blackheath and Richmond in 1866 broke away to prepare formation of the Rugby Football Union in 1871, the year in which the oldest *Challenge Cup* competition followed Harrow School's Cock-house concept and survived as a Challenge Competition until the the present British Government's pressure on Manchester United to devalue and withdraw from it in 1999. 1866 witnessed a collapsed grandstand with fortunately no fatalities at the celebrated Cheltenham Steeplechase Festival in April which arrived in the High Court four years later as a test case for the first reported traceable sports-related Personal Injuries claim (*Francis v Cockrell* [1870] 5 QB 501): The first reported traceable trial of a boxing fatality from sparring with gloves, a few weeks before Cheltenham, resulted in an acquittal at the Central Criminal Court, Old Bailey (*R v Young* [1866] 10 Cox CC 371.

Moving onwards two decades later, the amateur administrative Football Association in 1885 legitimated professionalism. Almost symbolically a year later, with commercial considerations authenticated, Burslem Port Vale and Stoke City professional Clubs were locked in combat over the contractual services of one of England's future international goalkeepers William Rowley in Burslem County Court with damages and injunctive issues at the heart of Arnold Bennett's *Five Towns* [*Wilkinson and Oliver v Rowley* (sub nom *Burslem Port Vale v Stoke City*): *The Staffordshire Sentinel*: 9 Nov. 1886]. 'The case created unusual excitement. The Court room being inconveniently crowded so long as it lasted'. The editorial subheading billed it as 'the most important case of the century'.

Henceforth the chart of sport's involvement with the law unfolds with a gradual evolving inevitability alongside self-regulation of sport itself, and courts and more recently Parliament filling gaps which sporting sources could not fill within themselves. It also demolishes any claim that their interaction for the benefit of each other is a modern phenomenon emerging on our own late twentieth century stage.

Looking backwards down the years in a climate of end-of-century reflections towards the millennium, a pattern of how the law has become entwined with sport and recreation can be seen from a survey of recent Parliamentary and court activities, charted at three different periods.

PART 1	1748 - 1853	Early years
PART 2.	1866 - 1918	Developing patterns until the end of the First World War
PART 3.	1919 - 1939	Between two Wars
PART 4.	1939 - 1959	Creating Sport and the Law
PART 5	1959 - 1999	Forty years on

PART 1 summarises those earliest traceable citations.

PART 2 at page 25 below until the end of World War 1 traces what should be regarded as merely 20 representative and in no way comprehensive cases in 52 years. Their diverse legal categories listed in their end column reaffirm Lord Hailsham's concept of a heterogenous collection of different activities. Parliament during this period was not required to come on stage, but portents for the future could be seen at the turn of the century. In 1901 the F.A. Cup Final at the old Crystal Palace arena in Sydenham, South London with its bowl shaped structure carved out of natural sources with vantage viewpoints and no need for grandstands of the kind which collapsed a year later at Ibrox, Glasgow, drew a crowd of 110, 820 spectators to the first appearance at that stage of the competition of a professional

London club, Tottenham Hotspur, against a leading representative from the North, Sheffield United. It was also the first occasion when a South of England Club appeared in the final stage of the competition after the last fling of the grass roots pioneering amateur Old Etonians had succumbed to Blackburn Olympic at Kennington Oval in 1883 nearly twenty years earlier after extra time.

A year later, at Ibrox Stadium, Glasgow, a collapsed grandstand during Scotland's international game against England caused 26 fatalities and 145 injuries among the crowd which had attracted an attendance of reportedly 80,000 spectators. On this occasion there was no government or other inquiry, but in lieu thereof a curiously selective prosecution was mounted for cuplable homicide against the timber merchant whose alleged defective timber bearings and joists caused the collapse (*R v McDougall*: Glasgow Herald 8 July 1902). After conflicting evidence, it ended in an aquittal, when with sound Scottish prescience the *Glasgow Herald* at the *end* of the trial *commented* (and as cited more comprehensively in Chapter 5 at p 203-4)

'The uneasy feeling remains that what occurred at Ibrox may occur again, and that at present there is no adequate means of preventing it. Obviously a stand such as that set up by the Rangers Club might be perfectly safe when occupied by a placid, orderly crowd, and yet become a source of terrible danger when filled by a mass of people labouring under the excitement invariably aroused by a football match. As for the future, does the Ibrox disaster, with its sequel in the trial brought to a close yesterday, not point to the necessity for some very drastic regulations for the construction of the huge arenas required for the patrons of football? Surely modern skill and science should be equal to the production of something quite as stable as the ancient Roman circus.' 10 July 1902.

As already noted a year later the Football Association in London and Scottish Football Association in Glasgow understandably converted its unincorporated status into corporate liability. The tone and scene were therefore set at the beginning of the century for Sport and the Law and particularly Football and the Law, which were to intensify through the years to the present worldwide manic obsession with what began and will always remain as a school and grass roots recreational game.

PART 3 at p 28 and below accentuated the process with 24 cases, again to be regarded representatively in 20 years; and again with no need for Parliamentary intervention, apart from the 1937 Physical Recreation and Training Act in preparation for the inevitability of a Second World War. Within this period, however, there are further portents for the future with Arsenal Football Club directors challenging in the Courts the Football Association's disciplinary jurisdictional authority; the Jockey Club's jurisdiction over horse doping similarly disputed; the famous Brooklands motor car racing circuit reflecting a future pattern for injured spectators; and protection of amateur golf's status, sporting educational charities, and revenue matters for professional sports practitioners, all required court intervention which could not be resolved within sport itself. The Chart of Cases is self-explanatory, again re-affirming Lord Hailsham's insight,

> 'only a heterogenous list of pastimes, with different governing bodies different ethics and constantly varying needs'

PART 4 at page 32 covers the first twenty years period from the outbreak of the Second World War in 1939 until the time in 1959, when the campaign to harmonise professional footballers' and cricketers' tax-free benefits, explained at the outset here in the Preface, was consolidated with a Peterborough United experiment, now enshrined in the *Special Commissioners of Income Tax decision in Rigby v IRC* (Peterborough Citizen Advertiser 16 June, 24 July). This designed cut-off point in 1959 after twenty of the sixty years of Sport and the Law from 1939-1999 in Parts 4 and 5 and explained at page 20 here above is appropriate for two reasons.

For it was during this period between 1939 and 1959 when this book and Sport and the Law were born as a coherent identifiable concept of legal consciousness, and is one of two reasons for selection of the cut-off date of 1959. The other results from the never ending stream of litigation and legislation which appears in *Part 5. 1959 - 1999*.

First, because the remaining forty years from 1959 and until now are still continuing while these pages are being written and in production; and the varied pattern of those twenty years between 1939 and 1959 reflects sufficiently the mirror image which the Law will always show for developments in society generally, and sport and recreation particularly, as an accurate cameo of it at any particular time.

Second, *Rigby v IRC* (1959), (unreported except in the *Peterborough Citizen and Advertiser*, 16 June, 24 July) is the practical and lasting outcome, unchallenged since then in Parliament and the Courts, which has stood the test of time after I had stumbled on the easily soluble anomaly, as explained in the Preface generally and with more detail in Appendix 1: *How It All Began* (1953), between professional footballers' and cricketers' benefit tax arrangements, while preparing my homage to their true health and education values within the Rule of Law in Sport during the 1950's through *Corinthian and Cricketers*

That homage did not escape criticism in a generous and acceptable approbation for the second 1994 edition in the *Scots Law Times*. The reviewer from the world of academe had only minor reservations, of which one was that preservation of Corinthian values was 'naive and inappropriate in a modern treatise devoted to the legal environment of sport'. That premise indicated an unawareness or refusal to recognise and/or acknowledge of the great divide between industrial and thereby commercial and potentially corrupting influences upon the grass roots, school, club and vast village green majorities when contrasted numerically with the relatively minuscule number of influential professional players on a global stage.

One of the many vindications for preserving Corinthian values appeared during early 1999 when a School Sports Forum emphasised the opinion among teachers that

'increasing numbers of youngsters were disregarding both the laws and spirit of the game';

and a principal headmaster contributor, Dr David Hempsall at Queen Elizabeth's Grammar School, Blackburn, Lancs, explained paradoxically

'We are in an Orwellian world of double-speak when honest men become mealy-mouthed'

and then concluded,

'While he did not believe that Britain could return to Corinthian values of fair play, soccer should be played in a fair and honest spirit'.

The unintentional inconsistency within that last statement is self-evident, and the final rebuttal to the *Scots Law Times*, albeit 'minor' reservation was the welcome invitation upon my appointment as a Visiting Professor of Sport and the Law at the Anglia Polytechnic University to deliver an inaugural lecture under the auspices of its Sports Law Research Centre, to be reproduced in due course with the title '*Sport and the Law: A Return to Corinthian Values*'. Those Corinthian Values will appear throughout this text. For without those Corinthian Values of Fair Play, self-discipline, and health and education within the Rule of Law, where would sport and recreation be to-day?

IN THE COURTS AND PARLIAMENT: A CHRONOLOGICAL OUTLINE
1748-1999: 251 years

Part 1: Early Years: 1748-1853
Part 2: Developing patterns until First World War: 1866-1918
Part 3: Between Two Wars: 1919-1939
Part 4: Creating Sport and the Law: 1939-1959
Part 5: Forty Years On: 1959-1999

Monitoring Justice
Cm 115 December 1998: '…assuming court of first instance has reached the right decision'. Decisions of courts 'of first instance' that have been reversed are marked in bold.

PART 1: Early Years:1748-1853

Date	Event	Legal Issue	Decision	Sport	Citation	Legal Area
1748	Cricket wager	Gaming Act 1710	Out of court settlement	Club cricket	*Jeffreys v Walters* [1748] 1 Wils 220	Gaming
1825	Cricket wager	Monetary claim	£2.15s awarded	Club cricket	*Walpole v Saunders* [1825] 1 D & R 130	Gaming
1833	Cricket wager	Gaming Act 1710	Repayment of illegal stake	Club cricket	*Hodson v Terrill* [1833] 1 C & M 797	Gaming
1844	Epsom Derby	Claim for winning stakes	Awarded	Horse racing	*Wood v Peel* (1844) Daily Telegraph 1 July	Gaming
1853	Cricket ground dispute	Civil assault	Damages £20	Club cricket	*Holmes v Bagge* (1853) 1 E & B	Civil assault

PART 2: Developing Patterns until First World War 1866 - 1918

Date	Event	Legal Issue	Decision	Sport	Citation	Legal Area
1866	Collapsed grandstand Cheltenham	Breach of warranty/negligence	Liability proved	Horse racing	Francis v Cockrell [1870] 5 QB 501	Environment
1866	Boxing fatality when sparring with gloves see 1866 Cheltenham	Manslaughter	Acquittal	Boxing	R v Young [1866] 10 Cox CC 370	Crime
[1870		above]				
1878	Hunt members trespassing on land	Criminal assault conviction	Liability proved	Field Sports	Paul v Summerhays [1878] 4 QBD 9	Environment
1878	Football field fatality	Manslaughter	Acquittal	Football	R v Bradshaw [1878] 14 Cox CC 83	Crime
[NB		affirmed R v Venna [1976] QB 421]				
1878	Boxing Prize fight	Illegal practice	Conviction	Boxing	R v Orton (1878) 39 LT 293	Crime
1882	Boxing aiding/ abetting consent	Prosecution and consent plea	Conviction	Boxing	R v Coney [1882] 8 QBD 534	Crime
1885	*F.A. legalise professionalism*	*Amateur and Professionalism co-exist*	*Payments lawful*	Football	*Official History Football Association*	Employment

Date	*Event*	*Legal Issue*	*Decision*	*Sport*	*Citation*	*Legal Area*
1886	Professional football injunction	Breach of contract	Injunction damages	Football	Burslem Port Vale v Stoke City Staffordshire Sentinel (1886) 9 November	Employment Contract
1890-91	Cheating at Baccarat	Slander	Procedure rejected	Card playing Baccarat	Gordon-Cumming v Green [1891] 7 TLR 408	Defamation
1891	Cricket ground obstruction	Boundary dispute	Injunction damages	Cricket	Ratcliffe v Jowers [1891] 8 TLR 6	Environment
1895	Yacht racing prize	Charity	Rejected	Yachting	Re Nottage [1895] 2 Ch 649	Charity Environment
1896	Collapsed grandstand Blackburn Rovers	Negligence of Committee	Proved	Football	Brown v Lewis (1896) 12 TLR 455	Environment
1897	**Yacht racing contract**	**Construction rules**	**Proved**	**Yachting**	**Clarke v Dunraven [1897] AC 59**	**Contract Competition rules**
1898	Football Field fatality	Foul charge	Guilty	Football	R v Moore [1898] 14 TLR 229	Crime
1901	Boxing fatality	Manslaughter	Acquittal	Boxing	R v Roberts (1901) Daily Telegraph 29 June	Crime
1902	Ibrox grandstand collapse	Culpable homicide	Acquittal	Football	R v McDougall (1902) Glasgow Herald	Negligence

Date	Event	Legal Issue	Decision	Sport	Citation	Legal Area
1910	Workman's compensation professional	Workman status	Proved	Football	*Walker v Crystal Palace* [1910] 1 KB 87	Employment
1911	Boxing title fight:	Breach of Peace	Bound Over	Boxing	*R v Driscoll and Moran*	Boxing
1912	Football restraints of trade	Conspiracy Contract	Not Proved	Football	*Kingaby v Aston Villa* [Times 12 May]	Employment Contract
1913	Infants Contract	Beneficiaries	Proved	Billiards	*Roberts v Gray* [1913] 1 KB 520	Infants Contract
1915	Educational Charity	Charity or excluded	Proved	Athletics	*Re Marriette* [1915] 2 Ch 284	Educational Charity

[NB   affirmed House of Lords [1980] 1 All ER 844]

<u>TOTAL CASES:21</u>

PART 3: Between Two Wars 1919 - 1939

Date	Event	Legal Issue	Decision	Sport	Citation	Legal Area
1920 - 1927	Professional Cricketers Benefit Fund	Gift or employment emolument	Gift: not taxable	Professional Cricket	*Seymour v Reed* [1927] AC 554	Cricket Benefit Tax free
1922	Public Highway Golf ball injury	Public nuisance	Damages award	Golf	*Castle v St. Augustine Links* (1922) 38 TLR 615	Environment
[1924	Government Wembly Stadium 1923 F.A. Cup Final Report on Crowd Safety: No action]					
1925	Gift for Army promotion of sport (fishing, cricket, football, polo)	Charity or Sport	Valid educational bequest	Multi-sport	*In re Gray Todd v Taylor* [1925] 1 Ch 362	Charity
[1925	National Playing Fields Association created]					
1927	Pre-play Golf injury	Negligence	Damages award	Golf	*Cleghorn v Oldham* (1927) 43 TLR 465	Environment
1927	Professional Jockey owner's gift present	Gift or employment emolument	Taxable	Racing	*Wing v O'Connell* [1927] IR 84	Jockey Tax
1927	Professional Footballer's Benefit payable under contract	Gift or employment emolument	Taxable	Professional Football	*Davis v Harrison* (1927) 11 TC 707	Professional Football Tax
1927	Professional Football Director's Administration	Libel	Not proved	Professional Football Administration	*Norris v Football Association* (1927) *Times, Daily Telegraph*	Defamation Domestic Tribunal

Date	*Event*	*Legal Issue*	*Decision*	*Sport*	*Citation*	*Legal Area*
1927	Professional Football Director's Administration	Company Law injunction to block F.A. directive	Action withdrawn	Professional Football Administration	*Peachey v Arsenal Football Company/Club*	Company Law Domestic Tribunal
1929	**Jockey Club Rules of Racing Test Case**	**Contract or Wager**	**Contract upheld**	**Racing Adm- inistration**	***Ellesmere v Wallace* [1929] 2 Ch 1**	**Gaming Contract**
1929	Bequest to Sussex County Cricket Club Nursery Fund	Charity or sport	Wrongly argued for young professionals invalid	Junior Cricket	*Re: Patten: Westminster Bank v Carlyon* [1929] 2 Ch 276	Charity
1931	Bequest for sports games or pastimes benefiting the district	Charity or sport	Sport invalid [see *Re: Gray* above] [1925]	General Multi- sport	*In re: King: Henderson v Cranmer* [1931] WN 232	Charity
1931	**Amateur Golf libel**	**Impugning Amateur status/ reputation**	**Re-trial settled**	**Amateur Golf**	***Tolley v Fry* [1931] AC 333**	**Defamation**
1932	Polo Pony Spectator injury	Negligence	No liability	Polo	*Piddington v Hastings* (Times) (1932) 12 March	Environment
1932	Pony Turf Club Administration Tribunal	Natural justice libel damages	No liability	Pony Club Administration	*Cookson v Harwood* [1932] 2 KB 478	Administration

Date	Event	Legal Issue	Decision	Sport	Citation	Legal Area
1932	**Jockey Club Drugs Administrative Tribunal**	**Libel**	**No liability**	**Racing**	*Chapman v Ellesmere* **[1932] 2 KB 431**	**Administration**
1932	School playtime personal injury	Negligence	No liability	Playground	*Langham v Governors Wellingborough School* [1932] 101 LJKB 513	Negligence
1933	**Brooklands motor sport personal injury**	**Negligence**	**No liability**	**Motor racing**	*Hall v Brooklands* **[1933] 1 KB 205**	**Negligence**
[1935	*Central Council of Physical Recreation founded: Phyllis Colston]*					
1935	Professional Football Company Club Takeover	Company Law Practice	No liability	Professional Football	*Berry & Stewart v Tottenham Hotspur* [1935] 1 Ch 718	Company Law
1935	**Infant boxer disallowed fee**	**Rule considered**	**Purse forfeited**	**Professional boxing**	*Doyle v White City Stadium* **[1935] 1 KB 110**	**Contract**
1936	School gymnasium personal injury	Negligence	Liability proved	School gymnastics	*Gibbs v Barking Corporation* [1936] All ER 115	Negligence
[1937	*Physical Training and Recreation Act]*					
1938	Physical training athlete adults injured on slippery dance floor used for sport	Negligence	Liability proved	Physical Training	*Gillmore v London County Council* (1938) 4 All ER 331	Negligence

Date	Event	Legal Issue	Decision	Sport	Citation	Legal Area
1939	Swimming bath springboard injury	Negligence Expert evidence	No liability	Swimming	*Clark v Bethnal Green BC* (1939) 55 TLR 519	Negligence
1939	School cricket master's supervision	Negligence	Liability proved	School Cricket	*Barfoot v East Sussex CC*	Negligence

[No Legal Aid available until 1949 Act, implemented 1950]

TOTAL CASES: 22 [20 years]

PART 4: Creating Sport and the Law 1939 - 1959

Date	Event	Legal Issue	Decision	Sport	Citation	Legal Area
1941	Professional Footballers' Benefit payable under contract	Gift or employment emolument	Taxable	Professional Football	*Corbett v Duff & Others* [1941] 1 KB 730	Professional Football Tax
1944	Hotel accommodation refused to world renowned West Indies Test cricketer	Pre-Race Relations Act common law discrimination	Innkeeper liable	Cricket	*Constantine v Imperial London Hotels Ltd* [1944] 2 All ER 171	Innkeepers/Race discrimination pre-Race Relations
1945	Educational game bequest	Chess tournament charity for education	Educationally charitable	Chess	*In re Dupree's Deed Trusts* [1945] Ch 14	Educational Charity
[1946	*Bolton Wanderers crowd disaster: 33 dead. Molwyn Hughes K.C. Report]*					
1947	School injury during game of touch	Negligent supervision	Liability		*Ralph v LCC* (1947) 63 TLR 546	School negligence
1949	1945 Moscow Dynamo Samford Bridge crowd damage	Riot Damages Act 1886 compensation	Receiver Metropolitan Police liable	Professional Football	*Munday v Metropolitan Police Receiver* [1949] 1 All ER 337	Riot Damages Compensation Crowd Safety/Environment

[1949/1950 Legal Aid Legislation initially High Court only]

Date	Event	Legal Issue	Decision	Sport	Citation	Legal Area
1950	Speedway track noise disturbed private residents	Nuisance to private residents -v- public speedway	Injunction granted	Speedway	*Att-Gen v Hastings Cptn* (1950) Sol Jo 225	Environment
1951	**1947 cricket ball injury out of ground**	**Negligence or nuisance**	**Claim rejected**	**Cricket**	***Bolton v Stone* [1951] AC 850**	**Environment**
1951	1948 infant's ice-hockey puck arena injury	Negligence or consent	Not proved	Ice Hockey	*Murray v Harringay Arena* [1951] 2 KB 529	Environment
1951	1949 Jersey Road Race organisation and car crash claim	Negligence	Not proved	Motor car racing	*O'Dowd v Fraser-Nash* [1951] WN 173	Crowd Safety Event organisation
1953	1938 Police Athletic Federation charitable claim	Charitable or taxable	Taxable	Police Athletics	*IRC v City of Glasgow Police Athletic Federation* [1953] AC 380	Charity/ Revenue
1953	Pollution claim for fishery protection	Nuisance and injunction	Injunction granted	Angling Fishing	*Pride of Derby Angling Assn. v British Gelanse & Others* [1953] 1 All ER 179	Environment
1954	1951-1954 dispute over unincorporated association funds	Powers of Court	Courts controls association Declaration	Weight-lifting	*Baker v Jones* [1954] 2 All ER 553	Domestic tribunals subject to Court control

Date	Event	Legal Issue	Decision	Sport	Citation	Legal Area
1955	Property possession claim under restraint of trade contract	Football retain and transfer system/Rent Acts	Suspended Order for possession	Professional Football	*Aldershot F.C. v Banks* (Aldershot News: 4, 25 November)	Landlord tenant Restraint of trade
1955	**Professional Cricketer's Benefit payable under contract**	**Gift or employment emolument**	**Taxable**	**Professional Cricket**	***Moorhouse v Dooland 1955 Ch 284***	**Professional Cricket Tax**
1957	Sydney University Rugby Club bequest	Educational Charity claim	Charitable	Amateur Rugby	*Kearins v Kearins* (1957) SR (NSW) 286	Educational sporting Charity Trust
1957	Club officers vicariously liability for wrongful expulsion by secretary	Unincorporated Association Liability	Libel	Club Membership	*Birne v National Sporting Club Ltd & Ors* (Times) 12 April	Unincorporated
1958	Tennis Club as business under Landlord & Tenant Act 1954	Unincorporated Members Club	Protection under Act	Amateur tennis	*Addiscombe Garden Estates Ltd v Crabbe* [1953] 1 QB 513	Landlord & Tenant
1959	Footballer' Tax-free benefits	Non-contract benefit match proceeds	Not taxable	Professional Football	*Rigby v IRC Peterborough Citizen Advertiser* 16 June, 24 July)	Tax-free Professional Footballers' Benefits
1959	Professional Footballers' benefit payable under contract	Gift or employment emolument	Taxable	Professional Football	*Rigby v IRC Peterborough Citizen Advertiser* 16 June, 24 July	Tax free Professional Footballers' Benefits

PART 5: Forty Years ON 1959-1999

Date	Event	Legal Issue	Decision	Sport	Citation	Legal Area
1960	Disciplinary Tribunal Hearing	Validity challenged through inaccurate notice of hearing	Invalid decision	Professional Rugby League	*Keighley RFC and AnoR v Cunningham* (1960) *Times* 25 May	Natural justice
1961	**Football insurance**	**Penalty or Inadequate damages**	**Damages reasonable**	**Professional football**	***Alder v Moore* [1961] All ER 1**	**Insurance**
1961	Infants' escaping football's fatal injury to motor cyclist	Negligent lack of land control	Liability proved	Infant football	*Hilder v Associated Portland Cement Manufacturers* [1961] 1 WLR 1434	Personal Injury Negligence
1962	**Sunderland Football under counter payments inquiry**	**Irregular Tribunal structure**	**Invalid conclusions expunged**	**Professional Football**	***(1) Elliott & Ors; (2) Ditchburn & Ors. v Football Association Times: 1962 (1) 12 April, (2) 22 June***	**Natural justice**
1962	**White City Horse Show**	**Negligence Judicial evidence**	**No liability on evidence**	**Equestrian**	***Wooldridge v Sumner* [1963] 2 QB 43**	**Personal Injury Negligence Judicial evidence**

Date	Event	Legal Issue	Decision	Sport	Citation	Legal Area
1963	Eastham contract	Restraint of Trade	Declaration Restraint	Professional Football	*Eastham v Newcastle United & Ors.* [1963] 3 WLR 574	Restraint of Trade
1964	**Amateur Rugby signing on professional fee once and for all time**	**Taxability**	**Compensation for loss of amateur status not taxable**	**Pro-Am Rugby**	*Jarrold v Boustead* [1964] 3 ALL ER 76	**Tax free Rugby Union payment**
1965	Oppressive irregular governing body conduct	Irregular Tribunal practice	Tribunal reversal	Professional Football	*St. Johnstone Football Club Ltd v Scottish Football Association Ltd* [1965] LT 171	Natural justice
1966	**Women's Racehorse Trainers' Rights in own name**	**Restraint of Trade Discrimination**	**Reversal strike out procedural judgment**	Horse racing	*Nagle v Feilden* [1966] 2 QB 633	**Procedural framework for Restraint of Trade Sex Discrimination**
1967	**Amateur Rugby future service signing on fee payment**	**Taxability**	**Emolument Taxable**	**Pro-Am Rugby**	*Riley v Coglan* [1967] 1 WLR 1300	**Taxable Rugby Union payment**
1967	Amateur Golf	Remoteness of injury risk from golf ball	No liability	Amateur Golf	*Brewer v Delo* [1967] 1 Lloyds Rep.488	Personal Injury negligence

Date	Event	Legal Issue	Decision	Sport	Citation	Legal Area
1967	Golf domestic family discord	Matrimonial misconduct - golf obsession	Divorce Decree	Amateur Golf	*Lane v Lane* (1967) *Daily Telegraph*, 4 June	Family Law
1968	Corporation Golf	Liability for balls on highway	Foreseeable negligence	Golf	*Lamond v Glasgow Corporation* (1968) SLT 291	Personal injury negligence
1968	Professional Golfer's road traffic injury	Injury quantum	Damages award	Professional Golf	*Mulvain v Joseph* (1968) Sol Jo 927, 22 November	Golfer's personal injury road traffic
1968	Water-ski collision after no warning	Defence of consent to injury	No liability	Water-ski Sport	*Rootes v Shelton* [1968] ALR 33 (Aus)	Consent to negligence
1968	Football field fatality from niggling blow	Homicide	Guilty Manslaughter plea	Amateur Football	*R v Southby* (1968) *Times*: Nov 21 [*Police Review* 1969 7 Feb, Vol. 77: p.110]	Crime
1969	Football field broken leg	Assault trespass to the person	Proved	Amateur Football	*Lewis v Brookshaw* (1970) 120 NLJ 413	Civil assault damages
1970	Domestic Tribunal representation	Right of representation	Discretionary except for difficult points of law	Professional Football	*Enderby Town v Football Association Ltd* [1970] 3 WLR 1021	Natural justice
[1971	Ibrox Glasgow Disaster 68 dead, 145 injured]	See Dougan v Rangers (1974) below]				

Date	Event	Legal Issue	Decision	Sport	Citation	Legal Area
1971	Australian Rules Football assault	Intention or consent	Liable Damages	Australian Rules Football	MacNamara v Duncan (1971) 26 All ER 584	Civil Assault
1971	**Spectator injured at motor cycle scramble**	**Principle for inexplicable accident**	**No liability**	**Motor cycle Rally**	**Wilkes v Cheltenham Home Guard Motor Cycle and Light Car Club (1971) 2 All ER 369**	**Environment Personal Injury Negligence**
1972	Spectator killed at Jalopy Car Racing	Liability excluded Occupiers Liability Act 1957	No liability	Jalopy Car Racing	White v Blackmore [1972] 2 QB 651	Environment Personal Injury Negligence
1972	**Anti-Apartheid Wimbledon Tennis disruption**	**Public Order**	**Conviction**	**Tennis**	**Brutus v Corens [1973] AC 854**	**Crime**
1974	Ibrox Rangers test case	Negligent Safety Crowd Control	Liability	Professional Football	Dougan v Rangers Football Club (1974) (Daily Telegraph 24 October p 19)	Personal injury Environment
[1975	*Safety of Sports Ground Act, 1975; after Ibrox Glasgow 1971 Disaster]*					
[1975	*Sex Discrimination Act]*					
1975	Assault endorsing R v Bradshaw (1878) [supra] Football fatality	Football Criminality	Affirmation R v Bradshaw (1878) [supra]	All football	R v Venna [1975] 3 All ER 788 [at p 793f-g]	Crime

Date	Event	Legal Issue	Decision	Sport	Citation	Legal Area
1976	Boxing injury right to sue	Strike out claim	Rejected	Boxing	*Pallante v Stadiums Property Ltd (No.1)* [1976] VR 331	Boxing
1976	**Football hooligans in Public Place**	**Public Order**	**Conviction**	**Professional Football**	***Cawley v Frost* [1976] 1 WLR 1207**	**Crime**
1977	Rugby assault	Criminal foul play	Conviction	Amateur Rugby Union	*R v Billinghurst* (1977) Crim LR 553	Crime
1977	**Cricket balls escape**	**Negligence Nuisance**	**Damages award**	**Club Cricket**	***Miller v Jackson* (1977) 3 All ER 338**	**Environment Negligence Nuisance Procedural Remedies**
1978	Boxing Promoters Licence	Basis for rejection	Rejected	Professional Boxing	*McInnes v Onslow Fane* [1978] 1 WLR 1520	Natural justice
1978	Medical Ill-treatment soccer injury	Medical Negligence	Proved	Amateur Soccer	*Price v Milawski* (1978) 82 DLR (3d) 130	Medical Negligence
1978	Rangers F.C. Supporters Club copyright breach	Injunction for breach	Granted	Professional Football	*Performing Right Society Ltd v Aristidou* (1978) Times 6 July	Intellectual Property
1978	**School girl banned from football with boys**	**Sex Discrimination**	**Banned**	**School Football**	***Bennett v Football Association* CAT No 591 of 1978**	**Sex Discrimination**

Date	*Event*	*Legal Issue*	*Decision*	*Sport*	*Citation*	*Legal Area*
1978	Company voting irregularities	Company Law Resolutions	Damages	Football Company	Hobbs & Others v Bristol City Football Club Ltd and Others (1978) Times, July	Company Law
1978	Public Order Injunction	Public Order		Football Crowd Control	Bristol City v Milkins (1978) Daily Telegraph 31 January	Crime Injunction
1979	England Football Manager Tribunal	Likelihood of bias. Natural Justice		Professional International Football	Revie v Football Association (1979) Times, 14 December	Natural Justice
1980	**Sport Education Charity**	**Charitable or not**	**Charitable**	**Youth Football**	**IRC v McMullen [1981] AC 1**	**Education Sport Charity**
1980	Football Ground Stand Tax Claim	Expenditure as 'plant' or not	Not allowable tax expenditure	Professional Football	Brown v Burnley Football and Athletic Co Ltd [1980] 3 All ER 244	Tax
1980	**Football Transfer Contract**	**Implied term**	**Breach of reasonable opportunity to score goals**	**Professional Football**	**Bournemouth and Boscombe Athletic Football Club Co. Ltd v Manchester United Football Club Ltd (1980) Times, 21 May**	**Contract Implied term**

Date	Event	Legal Issue	Decision	Sport	Citation	Legal Area
1980	Snooker Sex Women Ban	Sex Discrimination Private Member-ship	Non-exclusive breach of legislation	Snooker	*Bateson v Belfast YMCA* (1980) NI 135	Sex Discrimination
1980	Women's wrestling	Sex Discrimination under Local Government Act 1963 Pre 1975 Act	Pre 1976 Act Non-discriminatory	Women's Wrestling	*GLC v Farrer* [1980] 1 CR 266	Sex Discrimination
1981	Consent to Assault	Legality of consent outside lawful sport	Unlawful		*A-G's Ref (No 6 of 1980)* [1981] QB 715	Crime
1981	Family shooting rights	VAT dispute	Non-VAT assessable	Pheasant Shoot	*Customs & Excise Commissioners v Lord Fisher* [1981] 2 All ER 147	VAT supply

Date 1981	Event	Legal Issue	Decision	Sport	Citation	Legal Area
1981	Separated Bowls Club Structures for VAT purposes	Separate VAT Assessments	Assessments discharged	Bowls	*Hayhoe (AG) (Watchet Blowing Club and Watchet Indoor Bowling Club) v Customs & Excise Commissioner* LON/80/341, 13 January 1981	VAT Assessment
1981	Basketball eligibility	Amateurs seeking selection	Not eligible	Amateur Basketball	*R v British Basketball Association ex p Mickan and Cheesman* [1981] 17 CAT 0111	Court control over sport
1981	Tawain's exclusion from IAAF	Construction IAAF Rules	Exclusion overruled	International Athletics	*Reel v Holder* [1981] 3 All ER 321	(International (Contract (Interpretation of (Rules
1981	Tawain's exclusion from International Badminton Association	Construction IBA Rules	Exclusion overruled	International Badminton	*Shen Fu Chang v Stellan Bohlin* reported in [1981] 3 All ER 324g-h	
1981	**Power boat noise**	**Damages or Injunction**	**Modified Injunction**	**Power Boat Racing**	***Kennaway v Thompson* [1981] QB 88**	**Nuisance Environment**

Date	Event	Legal Issue	Decision	Sport	Citation	Legal Area
1981	**School supervision unfit infant**	**Special category supervision**	**Failure to protect: Liability proved**	**School physical education**	***Moore v Hampshire County Council* (1981) 80 LGR 481**	**Personal Injury Negligence School Sport**
1981	Canadian Ice Hockey Medical Complaint	Vicarious Liability	Club liable Medical Neglect	Professional Ice-Hockey	*Robitaille v Vancouver Hockey Club Ltd* [1981] DLR (3rd) 288	Medical Negligence and Vicarious Liability
1982	Golf Injury without warning	Negligence	Liable failure to warn	Golf	*Bidwell v Parks* (Lewes Crown Court: unreported)	Personal Injury Negligence
1982	Motor Cycle Sidecar Injury	Negligence	Liability Competitor Organisers	Motor Cycle Racing	*Harrison v Vincent* [1982] RTR 8	Environment Personal Injury Negligence
1982	Womens Professional Golf Administration	Contract	Injunction Settlement	Women's Professional	*Edwards v WPGA; APP Publicity Promotions Ltd v C.M. Walker & Others* (1982) *Times, Daily Telegraph*	Contract
1982	Agency Contract	Contract Breach and Interpretation	Damages Award	Professional Football	*Keegan v Public Eye Enterprises Ltd* (1982) *Times,* 28 October *Yorkshire Post,* 21 October (1982)	Contract

Date	Event	Legal Issue	Decision	Sport	Citation	Legal Area
1983	Challenge to Tribunal's Powers	Contract or Judicial Review	Contract only	Greyhound Racing	*Law v National Greyhound Racing Club Ltd* [1983] 1 WLR 1302	Contract Correct Procedure
1983	Challenge to Tribunal's Powers	Penal Points barred F.A. Cup Final appearance	Denied Relief	Professional Football	*Foster v Football Association* (1983)	Natural Justice
1983	**Challenge to Referees Powers**	**Referee's Sanctions Finality**	**Court of Appeal majority upheld**	**Professional Football**	***Machin v Football Association* [1983]**	**Natural Justice**
1983	**Recoverable VAT**	**UEFA Competition Rules for Reciprocal Hospitality**	**Competition obligation not business entertainment**	**European Professional Football**	***Celtic Football Athletic Club v CE Commissioners CS Scotland* May 1983 [1983] STC 420**	**VAT and Sports Competition**
1983	Local Football League Headbut Injuries	Civil Assault Trespass to Person: Damages	Proved	Amateur Club Football	*Hewish v Smailes* (Epsom County Court Archives per HH. Judge John A. Baker DL)	Trespass to the person (Civil Assault)

Date	Event	Legal Issue	Decision	Sport	Citation	Legal Area
1984	School Vicarious Liability for schoolmaster's imbalance tackle on pupil causing injury tackle	Negligence from disproportionate	Liability proved	School Rugby	*Affuto Nartoy v Clarke v ILEA* (1984) *Times*, 9 February	Personal injury School rugby negligence
1984	Conflict between bona fide medical treatment and athletic regulations	Right to be heard overlooked	Life ban overruled by Consent Order	Judo	*Angus v British Judo Association* (1984) *Times*, 15 June	Natural Justice
[1985	Safety of Sports Grounds Act - after Ibrox 1971 disaster]					
[1985	Bradford City Valley Parade Fire Disaster - Popplewell Report]					
[1985	Heysel Stadium, Brussels riot]					
1985	Women football assault	Assault broken jaw	Conviction	Womens Football	*Baker v Bridger* (1985) *Daily Express* May	Crime
1985	Football foul play	Negligence	Damages	Local League Football	*Condon v Basi* [1985] 2 All ER 453	Personal Injury Negligence
1985	Injunction to prevent South African Rugby Tour	Private individual right to challenge tour decision	Injunction granted	New Zealand Rugby	*Finnigan & Another v New Zealand RFU* [1985] 2 NZLR 159	Third party Right to Sue

Date	Event	Legal Issue	Decision	Sport	Citation	Legal Area
1985	Threatened forfeiture of amateur rugby status because of professional Rugby League connections	Anticipated restraint of trade interference contract and potential libel	Threat withdrawn	Rugby cross-over codes	*Ray French v Rugby Union and Lancashire Schools Rugby Union Committee*	Conflict of amateur Rugby Union and professional Rugby League jurisdictions
1985	P.E. teacher discriminated for appointment	Sex Discrimination	Confirmed	Physical Education	*Miller v Strathclyde Regional Council* (Case No.S/2582/85)	Compensation Award
1985	Hunting trespass to land	Master of Hounds position	Liability proved	Staghounds hunting	*League Against Cruel Sports v Scott* [1985] 3 WLR 400	Trespass Environment
1985	Life ban by Brighton & Hove Albion Club after	Public Order	Convictions and Club Life Bans	Football Spectators	*R v Clark & Ors Daily Telegraph*, (1985) 10 April	Crime Public Order
1986	Rugby Foul Play Assault	Crime	Conviction	Rugby	*R v Bishop* (1986) *Times*, 12 October	Criminal
1986	Rugby Foul Play ear-bite	Crime	Conviction	Rugby	*R v Johnson* [1986] 8 CR App R(S) 343	Criminal
1986	Attempted excavation 10th Duke of Beaufort's grave	Common Law Conspiracy	Conviction	Hunting	*R v Curtin & Another* (1986) *Times*, 12 June	Criminal

Date	Event	Legal Issue	Decision	Sport	Citation	Legal Area Jurisdiction
1986	Anti-Apartheid exclusion Commonwealth Games	Exclusion from Selection	Upheld	Swimming	Cowley v Heatley (1986) Times, 24 July	Competition
1986	European Court Reference	Competition Law: At 85 EU	Referral to European Court		Cutsforth v Mansfield Inns Ltd [1986] 1 WLR 558	Competition
[1987	Fire Safety and Safety of Places of Sport Act 1987 - after Bradford City Valley Parade Fire Disaster]					
1987	Golf 'widow'	Divorce	Decree granted	Golf	Lane v Lane (1987) Daily Telegraph, 4 June	Family
1987	Bradford City Fire Disaster Litigation Test actions	Personal Injury Negligence	Damages Awards	Professional Football	Fletcher v Fletcher:Britton v Bradford City, West Yorkshire Metropolitan (1987) Times, 24 February	Environment Personal Injury Negligence
1987	Packer Revolution	Interfere with Contract Restraint of Trade	Declarations Injunctions	Professional Cricket	Grieg v Insole [1987] 1 WLR 302	Contract Restraint of Trade
1987	Extradition after Heysel Riot	Extradition	Granted	European Football	Government of Belgium v Poslethwaite [1987] 3 WLR 365	Extradition

Date	Event	Legal Issue	Decision	Sport	Citation	Legal Area
1987	Football Coach European Work Permits	Treaty of Rome	National qualification requirement breached	European Football	Heylens v Union Nationale des Entraineurs [1987] ECR 4097	Treaty of Rome
1987	Tennis Coach hut tax claim	Plant or Shelter	Treaty Shelter No tax relief	Tennis	Thomas v Reynolds and Broomhead [1987] 59 TC 502	Tax
1987	Rugby Club tax liability	Tax liability	Club liable	Amateur Rugby	Worthing RFC Trustees v IRC [1987] STC 273	Tax
1988	Special police costs	Law Enforcement	Club liable	Professional Football	Harris v Sheffield United Football Club [1988] QB 77	Police Act 1964
1988	Sex Discrimination	Non exemption from snooker room	Club liable	Snooker	Priestley v Stork Margarine Social and Recreational Club (24 June)	Sex Discrimination
1988	Criminal Assaults	Levels of assault	Convictions	Football	R v Birkin (1988) Enfield Gazette, 7 April	Crime
				Football	R v Kamara (1988) Times, 15 April	
				Rugby	R v Lloyd (1988) Times, 13 September	
				Canadian Hockey	R v Cicarelli (Ontario 1988)	

Date	Event	Legal Issue	Decision	Sport	Citation	Legal Area
1989	Illegal Professional football tackle	Personal Injury Negligence	Settled out of Court	Professional Football	*Thomas v Maguire and Queen's Park Rangers* [1989] *Daily Mirror*, 17 February	Personal Injury Negligence
1989	School Rugby Injury and Insurance	Personal Injury Negligence and Insurance	School Rugby	*Van Oppen v Bedford Charity Trustees* [1989] 1 All ER 273		Personal Injury Negligence Insurance
1990	Slipping on wet floor in 5-a-side games	Unincorporated Association potential liability	Association exonerated but officer personally liable	5-a-side football	*Jones v Northampton Borough Council* (1990) *Times*, 21 May	Unincorporated Association and individual members
1990	Collision between Australian Jockeys	Duty of care by one jockey to another	Liability	Australian horse racing	*Johnston v Frazer* (1990) 21 NSWLR 89	Personal Injury Negligence
1990	Smashed jaw in Australian professional Rugby League game	Vicarious liability for injury	Proved	Australian Professional Rugby League Football	*Rogers v Bugden* (1990) and (1993) ATR 81 - 246	Vicarious liability for servants personal injury offence

Date	Event	Legal Issue	Decision	Sport	Citation	Legal Area
1990	Serious foul play injuries in *semi-professional* association football	Liability and Quantum	Line assault from recklessness of tackle £6,000 general and £4,000 special damages	Semi-Professional association	*May v Strong* (1990) Halsbury's Laws Monthly Review	Personal Injury Trespass on the person
1991	Schoolboy swimming injury	Supervision liability apportioned	Liability of school authority and association	School swimming	*Gannon v Rotherham MBC & Others* [Halsbury's Laws Monthly Review 91]	Persoal Injury Negligence
1991	Football Administration	Procedure	Judicial Review negligence	Football	*R v Football Assoc of Wales ex parte Flint Town United Football Club Ltd* [1991] COD 4	Administrative Law
1991	Interest free loan Arsenal Football Club & David O'Leary invested Jersey	Employment source Schedule E or Bank deposit Schedule D	Income from settlement arrangement from employment source chargeable Schedule E	Professional Football Finance	*O'Leary v McKinlay* (1991) Tax Journal 7 March	Tax Off-shore scheme

Date	*Event*	*Legal Issue*	*Decision*	*Sport*	*Citation*	*Legal Area*
1991	**'Golden Hello' payment to encourage football transfer and reduce wage bill**	Emolument of employment or 'Golden Handshake'	Employment payment taxable	**Professional Football**	**Shilton v Welmhurst [1991] 3 All ER 148**	**Tax Inland Revenue**
1991	Conflict of Interest between manager and promoter for professional boxer's contract	Restraint of trade	Unenforceable in restraint of trade	Professional Boxing	*Watson v Prager* [1991] 3 All ER 487	Restraint of Trade Contract
1992	Hillsborough Disaster and proximity for damages claim	Legal interest limitation for damages claim	Only those present in stadium and not those watching on television qualified to claim disaster damages	Professional Association Football	*Alcock v Chief Constable South Yorkshire Police* [1992] 1 AC 310	Personal Injury Negligence Environment
1992	Hillsborough Disaster Injury before death and Evidence	Evidence before Death Injury facts	No interference on facts findings of no injury	Professional Association Football	*Hicks v Chief Constable South Yorkshire Police* [1992] 2 All ER 65	

Date	Event	Legal Issue	Decision	Sport	Citation	Legal Area
1992	Football Ground Hooligans	Occupiers Liability Act 1957 and Negligence	Prior knowledge of potential violence creates negligence	Professional Association Football	*Cunningham v Reading Football Club Ltd* [1992] PIQR 141	Personal Injury Negligence Environment
1992	Professional football Injury	Criminal Assault and debateable evidence	Majority Verdict Aquittal	Professional Association Football	*R v Blissett* 1991 *Times*, 5 December	Crime
1992	Football Company Directors' undertakings for local Council inquiry evidence	Public Policy Agreement	Enforceability Confirmed	Professional Association Football	*Fulham Football Club v Cabra Estates Plc* (1992) *Times*, 11 Sept.	Company Law Evidence Environment
1992	**Recreational Charities Act 1958 bequest to include 'similar purpose in connection with sport' linked to North Berwick Sports Centre**	**Construction of the Act in context of earlier cases**	**Validly Charitable**	**Recreational Charity**	*Guild v IRC* [1992] 2 AC 310	**Recreational Charity**

Date	Event	Legal Issue	Decision	Sport	Citation	Legal Area
1992	Trophy presentations for consideration (dinner tickets)	VAT Assessment	VAT not payable	Professional Football	*Customs & Excise v Professional Footballers' Association (Enterprises) Ltd (1992) Times*, 11 March	VAT
1992	BBC FIFA 1990 World Cup excerpts	Copyright, Designs and Patents Act 1988 fair dealing s 30 (2)	Limited use reporting not breach	International Professional Football	*BBC v BSB* [1992] Ch 141	Intellectual Property
1993	**Playing Fields Charities**	**Power of Sale under Charities Act 1960**	**Remitted to Chancery Division for further evidence**		***Oldham Metropolitan Borough Council v Attorney-General* [1993] 2 All ER 432**	**Playing Fields Charity Law**
1993	Fishing rights infringed	Negligence and nuisance escape of rainbow trout interfering with high quality brown/trout	£10,500 damages for loss of amenity inconvenience and lost employment		*Broderick Brown (for Savernake Fly Fishing Club v Gate & Ainslie Ltd (1993) Times*, 30 March	Negligence Nuisance Environment

Date	Event	Legal Issue	Decision	Sport	Citation	Legal Area
1993	Karate injury	Application to relevant facts of *Condon v Basi* [supra: [1985] 1 WLR 866]	Damages award £30,557 'The Court has to find the facts, apply the law, and that is the end of it'	Martial Arts [Karate]	*Champion v Brown* [24 February (1993)]	Personal Injury Negligence
1993	Disabled participant injured in practice preparation paralympics	Level of duty of care in disabled context	Higher duty than required for *able* bodied athlete	Disabled archery	*Morell v Owen* (1993) *Times*, 14 December	Personal Injury Negligence
1993	Alleged unfair and illegal ball tampering	Defamation	Settled out of Court	Professional Cricket	*Nawaz v Lamb* (1993) *Times*, November	Defamation
1993	Company Law Control	Construction of contracts	Company Control unchanged	Professional Commercial Football	*Venables v Sugar* (May 1993) *Edennote Plc v Tottenham Hotspur Plc, Alan Sugar Armstrong Ltd* (1993) 14 June	Company Law
1993	Sado-masochistic injuries	Consent alleged	Rejected *R v Bradshaw* (supra) [1878: 14 Cox CC applied]	Perverse social-criminal practices	*R v Brown* [1994] AC 212	Crime

Date	Event	Legal Issue	Decision	Sport	Citation	Legal Area
1993	Judicial Review Machinery English Courts procedure rejected by preference to breach of contract remedies			Professional Football	*R v Football Association ex parte Football League Ltd* [1993] 2 All ER 833	
				Horse Racing Administrator	*R v Disciplinary Committee of the Jockey Club* [1] ex p *Aga Khan* [1993] 2 All ER 853 [2] ex p *Massingberd-Munday* [1993] 2 All ER 207) [3] ex p *Ram Racecourses Ltd* [1993] 2 All ER 225)	Administrative Law
1994	Alleged Cheating in amateur golf	Libel	Not proved	Amateur Golf	*Buckingham v Rush and Dave* [1994] *Independent*, 28 April	Defamation
1994	Cricket balls hit out of ground into adjoining property	Nuisance Injunction	Not proved (came to the nuisance)	Club cricket	*Lacey v Parker & Boyle (for Jordans Cricket Club)* (1994) 144 NLJ 785	Nuisance Environment

Date	Event	Legal Issue	Decision	Sport	Citation	Legal Area
1994	Football Association of Wales interfered with member clubs geographical activities	Restraint of trade and procedure	Declaration of Restraint	Professional Football	*Newport Association Football Club Ltd v Law and Football Association of Wales Ltd*	Administrative Procedure
1994	Compensation £500 order for serious intended harm cancelled on High Court reference	Appropriate sentence	Custody	Amateur Rugby	*R v Piff* (1994) *Guardian*, 2 February	Crime
1994	Professional Football Injury	Personal Injury Negligence	Not proved	Professional Football	*Elliott v Saunders and Liverpool Football Club* (1994) 10 June	Personal Injury Negligence
1994	Professional Football Injury	Personal Injury Negligence	Settled out of Court	Professional Football	*O'Neil v Fashanu and Wimbledon* (1994) *Times*, 14 October	Personal Injury Negligence
1995	Stag Hunting Ban	Local Authority's Powers	Excessive overruled	Stag Hunting	*R v Somerset CC ex parte Ewings* [1995] 3 All ER 20	Abuse of Power
1995	Amateur Rugby League	Assault	Conviction with sentence reduction	Amateur Rugby League	*R v Goodwin* (1995) 6 Cr App R(S) 885	Crime

Date	Event	Legal Issue	Decision	Sport	Citation	Legal Area
1995	Professional Football Assault on Spectator	Assault	Conviction (culpably and recklessly kicking into crowd)	Professional Football	*R v Kirk* (1995) *Daily Telegraph*, 17 October	Crime
1995	Professional Football Assault on Spectator	Assault	Conviction Community Service	Professional Football	*R v Cantona* (1995) *Times*, 25 March	Crime
1995	Professional Football Assault on Player	Assault	Conviction Custody	Professional Football	*R v Ferguson* (1992) *Times*, 12 October	Crime
1995	British Olympic Games donations	Tax	Tax-free	Olympic Games	*British Olympic Assoc v Winter (Inspector of Taxes)* [1995] STC 85	Tax
1995	Bosman European Court of Justice Freedom of Contract	Article 48 Treaty of Rome	Transfers outlawed	European Football	*Union Royale Belge des Sociétés de Football Association ASBL v Bosman* (1995) *Times*, December	European Law
1995	Racing Jockey's Licence Application	Legal Relationship	Contract created by Licence Application	Horse Racing	*Wright v The Jockey Club* (1995) *Times*, 16 June	Contract

Date	Event	Legal Issue	Decision	Sport	Citation	Legal Area
1996	Professional Football	Scotland Judicial Review	Scottish Football Association ultra vires	Professional Association Football	*Ferguson v Scottish Football Association* (1996) 1 February	Procedure Administration
1996	Gymnastic coaching	Contributory Negligence	Apportionment of responsibility from contributory negligence	Gymnastics	*Fowles v Bedfordshire County Council* [1996] ELR 51	Personal injury Negligence
1996	Olympic symbols confusion	Passing off	Actionable	Olympic Games	*New Zealand Olympic and Commonwealth Games Association Inc. v Telecom New Zealand Ltd* [1996] FSR 757	Intellectual Property
1996	Professional Football Arbitration and alleged illegal approach to manager	Arbitration Act 1996 stay of proceedings	Stay refused	Professional Association Football	*Notts Incorporated FC Ltd v The Football League Ltd and Southend United FC* (1996) 28 November	Football Administration and Arbitration
1996	Professional Football competitor eligibility dispute	Rule/Regulation construction and restraint of trade	Promotion eligibility claim rejected	Professional Association Football	*Stevenage Borough Football Club Ltd v Football League* (1996) *Times*, 1 August	Football Administration Restraint of Trade

Date	Event	Legal Issue	Decision	Sport	Citation	Legal Area
1996	Amateur Rugby Referee Liability	Inadequate control of game	Negligence Proved	Colts' Rugby Union	*Smoldon v Nolan and Whitworth* (1996) *Times*, 18 December	Personal Injury Negligence
1996	Crowd Control Police Officer injured by player colliding in play	Foreseeable risk of injury	Minimal risk precludes precautions necessary	Professional Association Football	*Gillon v Chief Constable of Strathclyde Police and Another* (1996) *Times*, 22 November	Personal Injury Negligence
1996	Lyme Bay canoeing tragedy	Safety Failure	Corporate and personal criminal liability	Canoeing	*R v Kite and OLL Ltd* (1996) 2 Cr App R(S) 295 CA	Crime
1997	Mountain climbing death	Standard of care due from mountain guide to climber	Liability Proved	Mountaineering	*Hedley v Cuthbertson* (1997) 20 June	Personal Injury Negligence
1997	Welsh Rugby Union Tribunal Procedural Defects	Natural Justice	Injunction	Professional Rugby Union	*Jones v Welsh Rugby Union* (1997) *Times*, 28 February	Natural Justice

Date	Event	Legal Issue	Decision	Sport	Citation	Legal Area
1997	Athletics drugs ban challenge under Treaty of Rome	Attempted application of Bosman European Court ruling to Sport per se	Rejected	Athletics	*Edwards v BAF and IAAF* [1997] Times Law Rep 348	Treaty of Rome
1997	Taxation of Golf Club Steward and Stewardess	Joint Contract of Employment with divisions of duties	Different tax liabilities established	Golf	*McManus v Griffiths (Inspector of Taxes)* [1997] STC 1089	Revenue Taxation
1997	Commercial Golf Manufacturing	Breach of Trade Mark and passing-off	Anton Pillar Orders	Golf	*Cobra Golf Ltd v Rata* [1997] 2 All ER 150	Intellectual Property
1997	Tennis Drug Testing Procedures	Right to sue	Statement of Claim struck out	Tennis	*Wilander v Novacek v Tobin and Jude* [1997] 1 Lloyd's Rep 195	Restraint of Trade
1997	Trade Mark usage	Construction of 'use'	FA's 'Three Lions' logo not trade mark use	Football	*Trebor Bassett v FA* [1997] FSR	Intellectual Property

Date	Event	Legal Issue	Decision	Sport	Citation	Legal Area
1998	British Field Sports campaigning activities and VAT	Link between members subscriptions and campaign	Not liable for VAT	Field Sports	Customs and Excise Commissioners v British Field Sports Society [1998] 2 All ER 1003	VAT
1998	Deflected golf ball	Insufficient injury risk	Liability	Golf	Pearson v Lighting (1998) Times 30 June	Personal injury Negligence
1998	**Schoolgirl's classroom injury**	**Duty and degree of care**	**Not liable**	**School Sport**	**Mullins v Richardson and Another [1998] 1 All ER 320**	**Personal Injury Negligence**
1999	Professional Football Quantum	Loss of earnings in Premier League	£900,000	Football	Watson v Gray and Huddersfield Town [1999] May	Personal Injury Negligence Quantum
1999	Schoolboy footballer Negligence claim	Liability and Quantum	£3,000	Football	Casson v MOD (1999) May	Personal Injury Negligence Quantum
1999	Libel	Defamation	£85,000 damages	Football	Grobelaar v The Sun	Defamation
1999	Natural Justice Drugs Inquiry	Debateable Evidence of offence	Insufficient Evidence	Athletics	Walker v BAF	Natural Justice

Date	Event	Legal Issue	Decision	Sport	Citation	Legal Area
1999	Football Conspiracy to cause floodlight black-out nuisance	Conspiracy	Conviction	Professional Football	*R v Ong Lim Firth* (1999) 26 August *Daily Telegraph*	Crime
1999	Rugby Union Tribunal Inquiry	Disrepute charge after newspaper Interview	Fine and Costs	Professional Rugby Union	*RFU v Delaglio* (1999) 26 August *Daily Telegraph*	Administrative Law
1999	Watson v British Board Boxing Control	Medical negligence	Liability	Professional boxing	*Watson v British Board of Boxing Control* (1999) *Times* 26 September	Medical negligence

PART I

Overview

CHAPTER 1

Genesis

1 PREAMBLE

Preservation of Corinthian values of fair play, self-discipline, health and education within the Rule of Law on and off the fields of play led to *Sport and the Law's* inevitable birth during the early 1950s with an authentic legal-sporting pedigree. It was bred by *Corinthians and Cricketers* out of the then Association Football Players' and Trainers' Union (now the Professional Footballers' Association: PFA) and the joint Oxbridge soccer club, Pegasus.

The name Corinthians was taken over a century ago as a classical foundation for the world's most famous amateur football club of all time: the Corinthian Football Club. Its title has survived the amalgamation with their amateur brother-in-arms, the Casuals FC on the eve of the Second World War in 1939. Brazil's leading football club, Sporting Club Corinthians Paulista, has adopted the name; and letters received by me during a wartime schoolboy friendship and correspondence with two of its most celebrated members, who also distinguished themselves as cricketers, C B Fry and G O Smith, led to the book entitled *Corinthians and Cricketers*. It was first published during the middle 1950s. To commemorate the centenary of both clubs during the 1982–83 soccer season an updated version was published: *Corinthian-Casuals and Cricketers*.

A generous review of the second 1994 edition of Sport and the Law in the *Scots Law Times* which contained a 'minor' reservation about Corinthian values naïveté 'in the legal environment of sport', incited a response for explaining the Corinthian values noted above. This resulted in a further version published in 1996 under the extended title of *Corinthians and Cricketers: and Towards a New Sporting Era'*. Additional Forewords were added to C B Fry's from Hubert Doggart and

Gary Lineker at the specific request of my enterprising publisher Dave Twydell of Yore Publications.

With hindsight, that hero-worshipping correspondence between my enthusiastic enquiring teenage schoolboy and particularly England's greatest centre-forward of 40–50 years earlier, G O Smith, was clearly encouraged by his later career as headmaster of Ludgrove School, in Berkshire, unknown to me at the time. There England's future King William III and his football fan brother Harry were educated before progressing to Eton and its FA Cup-winning heritage of the 1880s. Furthermore, our dialogue had one significant omission in today's context. Whilst it covered conventional topics such as tactics, techniques, training and personalities from W G Grace, C B Fry and Ranji to Steve Bloomer, and even contemplated future post-war problems such as a two-division County Cricket Championship, it never had the slightest thought for the modern issues of violence, drugs, commercial exploitation and political violation. Even during the Second World War (Hitler's war), progressive ideas on sport breathed an air of innocence: an innocence which survived well beyond the end of that conflict while schoolmasterly trained leaders such as Sir Stanley Rous at football, Harry Altham for cricket and John MacGregor Kendall-Carpenter in rugby sustained an awareness of being able to differentiate between right and wrong until the jungle laws of commercial and international administrative sporting corruption misplaced then at the public level for the norm of today, with their poisonous examples for future generations.

An echo of that innocence appeared recently happily in a beautifully produced and written biography of G O Smith's great Derby County and England international inside-forward contemporary who was the Michael Owen of his day: *Steve Bloomer: The Story of Football's First Superstar*, by Peter Seddon. He cites Bloomer's personal recollections of G O Smith's last international appearance before he retired to join his England-full-back colleague, W J Oakley, as joint-headmasters of Ludgrove upon the premature death of its founder Arthur Dunn. In his memory the competition explained in Chapter 8 *Sponsored Gentlemen and Players* was donated in 1902 by yet another England international, the banker R C Gosling. Since then it has been played for continually to remain the oldest surviving *national* football competition after the FA *Challenge* Cup Competition, the Arthur Dunn Memorial Cup.

'Talking of G O Smith reminds me of the game against Scotland at the Crystal Palace in 1901. We were keen to win because, although we had taken the championship again in 1899 we lost it to Scotland in 1900 when I scored the goal in a 4–1 defeat at Glasgow. Probably no match gave me more personal joy than the 1901 game, even though England could only draw. It was 30 March and that afternoon was the Boat Race, which deeply excited "G O" being an Oxford University man. Just as he was leading us on the field, a telegram boy handed him the familiar envelope and "G O" put his hand up to us and said: "Just a minute lads." He opened it and with is face wreathed in smiles turned to us and remarked: "Come on boys, Oxford has won; let's show Scotland how to row a winning oar at football."

'Well, we tried out best to fill his cup of joy by winning, but Scotland were just as keen and in the end we had to cry quits. It ended two goals each and was the only international in which I ever felt tired and weary at the finish. The ground was ankle deep in mud and slush and the going was really terrible but many well-known followers of the game declare I scored the greatest goal of my career that day...and I believe they are correct, too. I received the ball just in my own half and dribbled right through, finishing with a shot which it was such an effort to make that I flopped down practically exhausted... it was the equaliser and it gave us the championship that year. That was the last game G O Smith played for England and I should say that he was worshipped by every professional player in those days. He was the finest type of amateur, one who would always shake hands with us professionals in a manner which said plainly that he was pleased to meet them. In those far off days professional footballers were looked upon with something bordering on contempt and many amateurs would not mix with us. But "G O" was a true sportsman and brilliant centre-forward and he was beloved for it.'

This symbolic memoir from the sporting feudal days, when many of the professional Players were gentlemen, like Bloomer himself, and not a few of the amateur Gentlemen, like G O Smith, were talented players, too, contrasts sharply with a perceptive cameo of to-day's sporting culture caught brilliantly in a monograph, published by John Williams, the well-known Senior Researcher at the Sir Norman Chester Centre for Football Research at the University of Leicester. In *IS IT all over? Can football survive the Premier League* he explains in the final chapter *Some Final Comments* at Pages 64–65

'Football now seeps into almost every aspect of popular culture and sometimes seems to constitute a new civic realm. When the England football team manager expresses an opinion on almost any subject, we tend to expect a response from the Prime Minister or from one of his Cabinet. Clearly, football is also very much part of the political agenda.

In football's darker days no politician was willing to stand up and proclaim him/herself a football fan. Today, virtually every notable public figure wants their football allegiance properly advertised. If they have none, one will soon be invented by a helpful spin doctor.'

A few weeks later when the current holder of the Junior Minister's portfolio, Kate Hoey, was reported in *The Daily Telegraph* for Friday 17 September to be announcing a formal strategy in January 2000 to 'revive and reinvigorate' competitive sport in schools', the *Private Eye* journal on the same day referred in the context of John Williams' assessment, from his research background under its *Quote of the Week* columns to Hoey's views having

'now been exposed by those fine investigative organs, respectively the fanzine and unofficial webside of Arsenal FC.

Hoey tells interviewers she is a dedicated Arsenal supporter, yet in October 1994 Arsenal's Gunners magazine had this to say about the MP for Vauxhall: 'Kate was born in Northern Ireland and fell in love with football as she stood on her stool cheering George Best from the terraces of Windsor Park. Living in London she had ample opportunity to watch Arsenal, but retained her childhood support for Manchester United.

So many members of the new Labour Islington support Arsenal that Manchester United manager Sir Alex Ferguson had a moan last month about 'Arsenal supporters in the government'. Surely the lovely Kate cannot have switched allegiance merely for the sake of political correctness?'

2   CORINTHIANS

Corinthian-Casuals, Cricketers and Pegasus

By the time when those modern 'Letters *from* Corinthians' to me, never *to* St Paul, were being prepared during the late 1940s and early 1950s for general readership, the heirs to the traditional sources were found under two separate footballing flags: Corinthian-Casuals and the newly formed Oxbridge foundation, Pegasus. After the Second World War had ended in 1945 an Oxford don, Dr H W Thompson (later and more widely known before he died in 1983 as Sir Harold Thompson FRS, CBE, Professor of Spectroscopy and Chairman of the Football Association), inspired amalgamation of the two Oxbridge soccer clubs, Oxford University Centaurs and Cambridge University Falcons. Christened Pegasus by his wife, Penelope, an Oxford classic scholar, its meteoric decade of romantic sporting glory upheld *two* profound Corinthian traditions. One was the inclusion of Test Match cricketers within its playing membership who were selected on meritorious grounds: P B H May, D J Insole, F C M Alexander, D B Carr, G H G Doggart, and A C Smith (the first four of whom were Test Match captains). The other was the forging of close links with outstanding *professional* football guides, philosophers and friends: Arthur Rowe, Vic Buckingham, Billy Nicholson from Tottenham Hotspur, George Ainsley from a pre-1939 Leeds United, Joe Mercer of many clubs and England, in addition to many others, including particularly Jimmy Hill, OBE. After his playing and PFA pioneering days were followed by creating Coventry

City's modern structure, he arranged before his departure from management at Fulham, and becoming the current present President of Corinthian-Casuals, for the annual Oxford v Cambridge Varsity match to be anchored at Craven Cottage, alongside the Thames, for Boat Race Day. It is an appropriate turn of history's wheel to recall Steve Bloomer's tale of G O Smith's telegram before England played Scotland in 1901 on the same occasion.

When Pegasus flew to its two Wembley successes in the (now defunct) FA *Amateur* Cup Final ties of 1951 and 1953, 100,000 crowds attended (on each occasion) just before Sir Roger Bannister's four minute mile in 1954 around Pegasus' Oxford Iffley Road playing arena. The story of the *FA Amateur* Cup Final triumphs is told in the final chapter of each *Corinthians* titled publication; and 45 years on modern readers who are conditioned by crowd controls following the Bolton, Bradford, Heysel and Hillsborough crowd disasters, may find the size of those Wembley Stadium crowds to be astonishing. Three years after the second triumph, in 1956, some of the club's founder members, including D J Insole from Cambridge University (later the nominee defendant in the *Greig v Insole* [1978] 1 WLR 302 Packer litigation, now its University representative on the FA Council) appeared before an 80,000 crowd at the same place on the same occasion in Corinthian-Casuals colours, against Bishop Auckland.

Pegasus' Oxbridge captain throughout his all too short career, Denis Saunders, one of Billy Nicholson's coaching pupils, progressed via the Corinthian traditions as a housemaster of Malvern College in Worcestershire, to Principal of England's future professional footballers at the original FA-General Motors-sponsored FA National School of Excellence at the Lilleshall National Sports Centre in Shropshire. It now houses the Lilleshall Sports Injury and Human Performance Centre. Such amateur and professional links have thus been perpetuated also at grass-roots levels.

Those triumphs were chronicled by me only after a badly broken leg during Oxford University's soccer trials. Followed by inadequate treatment, it allowed time for diversions of energies from active sport and examination studies to frame an historical setting to share those Corinthian and cricketing letters with a wider readership. Research prior to publication, but after call to the Bar by Middle Temple and commencement of legal practice in Lincoln's Inn, produced two sporting legal puzzles connected directly with the Corinthian-cricketing and Pegasus texts which appeared to demand solutions. Each concerned the attitudes of the Inland Revenue authorities at the time in the early 1950's towards two separate sporting taxation 'penalty' areas.

With hindsight they were for me the earliest professional threads which started to bind the law with sport, and drew me gradually and inevitably to varying levels of friendships and publications which have led ultimately to the writing of this book. Jurisprudentially they are the true beginnings of what has unfolded and emerged as this dynamic, developing area of sport and the law.

Its real origins, however, can be traced to that personal injury and the inadequacies of its treatment. Time lost from studies in hospital for recuperation and during convalescence produced an emerging awareness then which has now been crystalised in the three chapters: '*Participation Problems*' Chapter 6, p 243; '*Sports medicine and the law*', chapter 7, p 293; and '*Administrative advice*', Chapter 12, p 419.

For players, it illuminated the often misapplied latin tag, *volenti non fit injuria*. My own ill-timed tackle, stemming from blunted reflexes after the pre-term vacation, missed the ball; the foot hit the bone-hard Iffley Road playing surface resulting in a broken fibula. It created no legal liability of the kind which now follows. This is all too rarely recognised and it is also recognised at the public level, notwithstanding the concurrent criminal and civil liability inherent in the misleading descriptions, 'professional foul', 'cynical foul' and 'over-competitiveness'. If a foul is committed with such *professional* efficiency it qualifies inevitably for legal liability. If it claims to be professional, it hardly reflects credit on the profession it purports to serve.

Grossly wrong hospital advice and inadequate treatment were given to me when I was told to walk on the leg while the plaster was being set. This pointed to disaster, until parental intervention and insistence obtained the release from such gross medical negligence. Removal from Oxford to London and specialist orthopaedic surgery saved the limb. The initial medical neglect created a clear legal liability. Parental wisdom on behalf of a then legal infant (below the age of 21 at that time, now 18) declined to enforce it.

That experience demonstrates for players, administrators and sporting medicare personnel the importance of adequate insurance. For me it also proved at an early age, and with startling clarity, how the law is not available to all. This event had occurred before Parliament's limited legal aid legislation in 1950 (and its further controversial cutbacks in 1993 and again to-day, with the present illiberal Government's proclaimed Access to Justice concealing of a Denial of Justice); but it demonstrates how inadequate financial resources preclude access to professional services to mount a claim. The hollow ring to Magna Carta's proclamation, 'To no one will we sell, to no one will we deny or delay, right or justice' became self-evident. Maule J's aphorism still applies: 'The Law Courts like the Ritz Hotel are open to all.'

3   SPORT AND THE LAW IS BORN

Also open to all, for anyone genuinely concerned with the beneficial progress of sport generally and association football in particular, during the 1950s were the pages of the then monthly *FA Bulletin*. The former schoolmaster and international soccer referee Sir Stanley Rous, CBE as secretary [now a Chief Executive] of the Football Association encouraged investigation of the solution to a legal paradox upon which I had stumbled coincidentally and fortuitously during research preparations for *Corinthians and Cricketers*. It concerned Denis Compton of Arsenal, Middlesex, England's Test Match XIs; and wartime and victory soccer international XIs.

He was every games player's sporting hero of that period as the beau ideal of footballing and cricketing professionalism, with the Corinthian style of enthusiasm laced with skill and fair play. When he died on St George's Day, April 23, 1997, his memorial and obituary tributes affirmed his application of Corinthian values. As a county cricketer, his benefit payments from an admiring public were tax-free because of the well-known House of Lords ruling in *Seymour v Reed* [1927] AC 554 which had overturned a Court of Appeal reversal of an experienced taxation judge, Rowlatt J (and thus restored the judgment). As a *professional* footballer, however, his benefit was subject to tax as part of his employment income. This too, was based on earlier litigation and also on the nature of his footballer's contract and the Football League and FA regulations which were incorporated into it.

Suffice it to say here that the paradox produced two articles which are reproduced here in Appendix 1 as they appeared in their contemporaneous 1953 publications. They tackled the problem head-on, while the I was also wrestling with an appropriate formula to present the correspondence with G O Smith, a great Corinthian sportsman of Queen Victoria's England, the country's centre-forward and captain (also an outstanding University batsman). The first was encouraged by Sir Stanley Rous, CBE, then FA Secretary and Chairman of the Central Council of Physical Recreation, ultimately President of FIFA to contribute on the subject for the then *FA Bulletin*. It appeared in April 1953 under the title *Taxation of Player's Benefits*. Later in the same year the more professional publication, *Rating and Income Tax*, allowed extensions of the same arguments with more formal and traditional citations and sources.

The basic theme throughout each article was that the House of Lords' decision in *Seymour v Reed* [1927] AC 554 freed from income tax liabilities the *public funding sources, extraneous to a contract of employment*, of a benefit cricket match granted to the Kent County Cricket Club's opening batsman, James Seymour, for the traditional Canterbury Cricket Week match against Hampshire in 1920. At that time the *professional* footballer's comparable contract of employment contained discretionary and/or *contractual claims* for benefit payments. The then legal advisers to contemporary football players had perversely attempted to apply the *Seymour v Reed non-contractual* circumstances to their own contrasting situation on two separate occasions before I became aware of the position while preparing *Corinthians and Cricketers* (see *Davis v Harrison* [1927] 43 TLR 623: and *Corbett v Duff*; *Dale v Duff*; *Feebury v Abbott* [1941] 1 KB 730).

It was clear to me that so long as the professional footballers' *contract of employment* contained references to a benefit claim, there was no chance of the revenue authorities or the Courts equating the two professional sporting categories in respect of relief for the two kinds of benefits. Indeed, at about the same time, the situation was re-emphasised and reaffirmed by the London Court of Appeal in the contemporary circumstances concerning a claim for tax relief by an Australian Test Match cricketer who received public funded collections, also under his contract of employment, while playing Lancashire League cricket (see *Moorhouse v Dooland* [1955] 1 All ER 93). The only possible solution for professional football was to follow cricket's precedent and take the benefit out of the contract of employment. It was achieved in the following way.

Denis Compton's goalkeeper colleague in the 1950 FA Cup final against Liverpool, George Swindin, was a committee member of the then Association Football Players' and Trainers' Union of which the chairman was the former Portsmouth FC captain, James Guthrie. When Swindin moved to Peterborough United as player-manager during the early 1950s, prior to returning subsequently to Arsenal as manager, Peterborough United at that time was a progressive club outside the Football League to which it was later elected in 1960. The Midland Counties Football League in which it played contained no comparable Regulations equivalent or comparable to the Football League players' contracts for testimonial or benefit payments. A special Peterborough United Benefit Fund Committee extraneous to the club was created. The club's ground was hired to the Benefit Fund Committee to exclude the club from all arrangements. Two benefit matches in 1956 were arranged for the benefit of players, including the club captain Norman Rigby; and three years later the *Seymour v Reed* principle was applied by the Special Commissioners of Inland Revenue, to discharge the local income tax inspector's assessment, *Rigby v IRC* (1959) (unreported except in the *Peterborough Citizen and Advertiser*: 16 June, 24 July).

After Peterborough United were elected to the Football League in 1960 the Football League regulations were amended to delete the contractual element in the professional footballers' benefits to equate them with the professional cricketers. Any future Denis Comptons would no longer experience the sporting legal anomaly which existed needlessly between 1927 and 1956, primarily because of the absence of any apparent awareness on the part of the professional footballers' then legal or tax advisers during the intervening years of the simple solution: simple deletion of the *contractual or discretionary* entitlement, based upon the small print of the Football League Regulations to which the standard contract of employment was subject. As Arthur Rowe would have said: It was a simple problem. Only the lawyers, with their failure to recognise the difference between the 1927 and 1941 cases cited at p 1 above from *Seymour v Reed* in the House of Lords during 1927 had made it difficult.

A year before, and in three subsequent cases after Norman Rigby's Peterborough triumph, that *simple principle of difference* between 'profits of his *employment*' as *income* and payment from sources outside it in sports-recreation related issues, were seen clearly *on the available evidence in all cases*. In 1958 a professional huntsman's regular *customary* Christmas payments from hunt-members were held to be taxable (*Wright v Boyce* [1958] 2 All ER 789). In 1964 bona fide rugby union *amateur* players' payments, on entering the then alien new world of *professional* Rugby League, were held to be not taxable on the basis of once and for all capital compensation payments for loss of office (*Jarrold v Boustead* [1964] 3 All ER 76). This contrasts with how the House of Lords treated the 'golden handshake' signing on fee, paid to Peter Shilton on *his* transfer from Nottingham Forest *to* Southampton in order to reduce its wages bill, to be taxable (*Shilton v Wilmhurst* [1991] 3 All ER 148); and twenty years after Rigby in 1959 had followed the *Seymour v Reed* [1927] cricket road for tax-free benefit payments, Bobby Moore's legal accountancy team had no difficulty in persuading Brightman, in London's High Court that the Football Association's bonus gift payments to himself and his fellow 1966 World Cup warrior victors was not taxable *Moore v Griffiths* [1972] 3 All ER 399. In none of these cases was *Rigby's* Special Commissioners of Income Tax decision cited. It was never appealed and has clearly stood the test of time because it was based clearly on the carefully prepared *evidenciary* arrangements consistent with the *legal principles* established in the House of Lords. It has never appeared in any standard Income Tax or any other book associated with its facts and issues, although sophisticated fund-raising activities associated with it are frequently reported and recognised to be subsequent to careful scrutiny.

These tax publications led to meetings, and ultimately friendship, with the then Chairman of the Association Football Players' and Trainers' Union, Jimmy Guthrie. In 1939 he had captained the last pre-war FA Cup winning team, Portsmouth, to an unexpected 4–1 victory over a youthful Wolverhampton Wanderers team, known to the football world as Buckley's (not Busby's) Babes, because of the youth policy of the then team manager, Major Frank Buckley. Guthrie's persistence in discovering and attempting to solve serious sporting issues included not only the paradox produced by different taxation attitudes towards professional football and cricket benefits with the aid of Peterborough United, then outside both the Football League and also Compton's area of competitive employment with Arsenal and its player-manager, George Swindon. He had been Denis Compton's Arsenal goalkeeping colleague, and, by that crucial time had become a fellow Union committee member. Guthrie was also responsible for launching the first real attack on the restraint of trade vice in the retain and transfer system of the professional footballer's contract of employment in Aldershot County Court proceedings during 1955. For he now placed his Union behind defending a claim in Aldershot County Court for possession of club premises against one of its players, Ralph Banks, and it was a prelude to the better known *Eastham* case and Mr Justice Wilberforce's landmark judgment eight years later in 1963 (*Eastham v Newcastle United* [1964] Ch 413).

Banks had been transferred to Aldershot for £500 from Bolton Wanderers after he had played left-back against Stanley Matthews in the 1953 Coronation Cup Final which led to Matthews' coveted FA Cup winners' medal in the dramatic finish which witnessed his team's, Blackpool's, 4–3 victory. At Aldershot he disputed a wages offer, and in lieu thereof hoped to accept a more favourable offer from Weymouth who were unable to afford Aldershot's wish to recoup their own earlier £500 transfer fee paid to Bolton Wanderers. Although his contract of employment for 12 months from 30 June 1954 to 30 June 1955 had terminated at the date of the court action in October 1955, his Football Association registration permitted Aldershot's retention of his services under the FA Rules under what was then known as the retain and transfer system, analogous to a perpetually renewable lease. The county court Judge, H H Judge Percy Rawlins, who had just been transferred to the Aldershot County Court circuit from his west country circuit base, refused leave procedurally for Banks to join the FA with Aldershot as a defendant to a counter-claim and plead that the club's possession claim was based upon an unenforceable contract in restraint of trade and thereby tainted with illegality. He ordered the FA to attend through counsel and a representative to assist him on the contractual arrangements.

A possession order was made with effect from five months from the date of judgment on 28 October 1955; but evidence was provided by a future FA deputy secretary, Douglas Hawes, in answer to a question by the judge that Banks was under a 'penalty'; ie the retain and transfer system was equivalent to a perpetually renewable lease built into the football governing body rules to which the professional players' contracts were tied.

In his judgment H H Judge Percy Rawlins said,

'It may very well be, although I am not going to decide it, that as the defendant alleges the rules of the Football Association place an intolerable burden upon some professional footballers. But it may well be that as the Football Association says, the rules were necessary for the protection of footballers because the Football Association exists to some extent to protect footballers and to prevent their exploitation.'

(*Aldershot Football Club v Banks*, Aldershot News, 4 November 1955.)

An appeal to the Court of Appeal was under consideration when as Guthrie in his own version *Soccer Rebel* [1976] page 74 explained: 'Aldershot, perhaps under guidance or orders, gave Banks a free transfer'; to the club he wished to join, Weymouth. Guthrie's book, for which the unforgettable Danny Blanchflower, captain of Northern Ireland and Tottenham Hotspur's 1961 FA Cup and Football League Double-winning team, ended a Foreword, with a tribute to

'the debt that professional footballers past, present and future, owe him'

told the full story at pages 74–75 in the chapter entitled/headed appropriately '*Trade Union Membership*' in the following way:

'Aldershot right full-back Ralph Banks had refused terms and been put on the list, and that meant no wages. Only a season before Frank Brennan the Newcastle centre-half, a man who had played in two FA Cup finals for his club had his wages docked by more than a half. When refusing to accept the measly wage he was listed. I went to see Frank and told him we would fight the case under 'restraint of trade'. We had a great case, for Frank had been a wonderful servant to the Tyneside club, but alas Newcastle got off the hook when, in disgust with his treatment, Brennan quit the business.

I was determined to take Aldershot to court. I remembered *Sir Walter Monckton's remark when he first saw a Football League form. 'The worst contract I've ever seen.' With full union support Banks issued a writ [1] alleging that the action of Aldershot was in restraint of trade. We booked Counsel, the Club entered an appearance and we lined up our big guns and ammunition. But they licked us again. Aldershot, perhaps under guidance or orders, gave Banks a free transfer and there was no case for them to answer. However, we did get some reward. Our Counsel, Edward Grayson, in a letter to me said that we were in a position to put the strongest pressure on clubs for the purpose of establishing freedom of contract 'If a player refuses, legitimately, to accept the terms offered to him' Counsel's opinion continued 'one of two things can happen'.

a.   He will run the risk of quitting football in the manner of Frank Brennan in 1954.

b.   He can do what one may assume was appreciated by both sides in the Banks' circumstances—indicate to the club his intention to proceed with restraint of trade proceedings for an injunction.

The opinion continued—'If a player leaves football nothing can be done. If on the other hand he indicates the likelihood of restraint of trade proceedings one of two things can happen.

---

*   *Monckton*: celebrated cricketer, lawyer, Minister of Labour in Churchill's post second World War Government, and Leading Counsel for the successful Kent cricketer's appellant *James Seymour* in the House of Lords tax triumph of 1927.

1   It was a counter-claim in possession proceedings

a.   The majority of clubs would do as Aldershot.
b.   At least one of the wealthier clubs such as those who operate in the North-East would dig its heels in, call the bluff and the fight which was anticipated in the Chancery Division would be joined between whatever club would so act and the player who would legitimately refuse terms.'

Our Counsel not only anticipated the hearings of 1963 but also almost named the club concerned, Newcastle United, in his well organised brief. When George Eastham began his action, about which more anon, I showed him the Counsel's opinion, outlined above. In concluding Counsel said:

'On reflection, the conditions of the football world, or industry, are such that I am of the opinion that with his Committee, Guthrie should now be preparing the way for informing players of their rights and possibilities of invoking the Court's assistance at the time when terms are offered to all players in three months' time. As I visualise the case there can never be another example of knuckling under in the unfortunate manner experienced by Frank Brennan'.'

These were the first occasions when the restraint of trade issue was ever raised in the English courts for professional sport. Over forty years earlier a challenge to the system was made on behalf of a professional footballer, Harry Kingaby, who was dissatisfied with his position at the Aston Villa Club, *Kingaby v Aston Villa* (1912) *Times*, 28 March. Restraint of trade, however, was neither pleaded nor argued.

At that period before 1914 the restrictive elements which today are understood to create a restraint of trade situation between master and servant were already recognised in the legal world (see *Leather Cloth Co v Larsont* (1869) LR 9 Eq 345; *Mitchel v Reynolds* (1711) 1 PWms 181; 18 Sm LC (13 Edn) 462). Unfortunately that was not how it appeared to those who advised the plaintiff, Kingaby. No claim was formulated which challenged the restrictive practice *per se*. A claim was pleaded extraordinarily for damages for

(1)   loss of employment; and
(2)   maliciously charging an excessive transfer fee.

The trial judge, Mr Justice A T Lawrence (who later became the first Lord Trevethin as Lord Chief Justice in 1921 in contentious political circumstances under Lloyd George's premiership), non-suited the plaintiff and withdrew the case from the jury. He ruled there was no cause of action and confirmed the transfer fee and system under attack without adequate advocacy arguments based on appropriate available legal principles and evidence to be legally permissible under the terms of contract of employment (*Kingaby v Aston Villa* (1912) *Times*, 28 March).

Eight years after *Aldershot v Banks*, in *Eastham's case*, ([1964] Ch 413 at 445) when the restraint of trade issue was fully pleaded and established, the trial judge, Wilberforce J explained (with my emphasis) on the pleading issue

'Kingaby brought an action arising out of the fact that the club had placed an excessive transfer fee upon him. This seems to be the only reported case affecting the rules of the Football League. The case is shortly reported in 'The Times, 28 March, 1912, but *I have seen the pleadings,* from which it appears that the action was for damages for breach of contract, damages for conspiracy, damages for maliciously procuring breaches of contract and an injunction. A T Lawrence J refused to allow the case to go to the jury because, as reported, he said *no tort against the plaintiff* had been committed and *there was no evidence of malice.* I find the case of no assistance.'

It is certainly arguable today in 1999 that *if* the restraint of trade had been properly pleaded and argued in 1912 the claim based on the then traditional and established authorities would have succeeded. Yet the perversity or lack of clear thought which created, as much as it does today, an unawareness in sporting legal areas of the true legal issues, was illuminated after the restraint of trade and other principles were reaffirmed in the celebrated Packer litigation thirteen years after the *Eastham* landmark verdict in *Greig v Insole* [1978] 1 WLR 302.

The former secretary to the MCC and the co-defendant with the Test and County Cricket Board (TCCB) in the Packer litigation, the International Cricket Council (ICC), Jack Bailey wrote in *Conflicts in Cricket* (1989),

'As the world knows, ICC and TCCB lost a case which, by the time all the witnesses had been called and the closing speeches had been made by both sides, and Mr Justice Slade had given his comprehensive and enlightening judgment, had lasted thirty-two days. The cricket authorities had lost on every point of law involved, although they had emerged with some credit from a moral standpoint. Had it all been worth it? Or rather, had we anything to show for the damages and costs awarded against us, amounting to some £250,000 (later shared equally between ICC and TCCB) apart from a vast amount of publicity for cricket all over the world?

Well, for one thing, it had been a lesson. It had taught the cricket authorities that good intentions, if not paving the road to hell, certainly are not enough when it comes to the law of the land.

We also learnt the law regarding inducement to breach of legal contract and what was reasonable in the cricket world, both to protect established cricket and to prevent unlawful restraint of trade'.

It is understandable that the cricketing establishment via the ICC and TCCB could not have been aware of the trial run to establish restraint of trade in the Aldershot County Court by Ralph Banks with the backing of Guthrie and his Union. It is beyond belief that thirteen years after *Eastham's* landmark decision the then legal advisers to cricket's establishment had not apparently recognised, alerted its clients to, or even understood the restraint of trade application to professional sport.

Against that background, the chain of events which has led to Jean-Marc-Bosman's now well publicised European Court of Justice ruling on 15 December 1995 under Article 48 of the Treaty of Rome (which is now Article 39 of the Treaty of Amsterdam) concerning restrictions on the free movement of workers, was a judgment waiting to happen, when activated by the appropriate evidence. It emerged in a parallel pattern to the Banks and Eastham judgments under the English Court's jurisdiction, when unacceptable and restrictive contract provisions led to the player's refusal to sign. Bosman was employed by the Belgian FA club Standard Liège. Potential negotiations for transferred employment to the French club US Dunkerque were ultimately blocked by Liège's refusal to obtain a required transfer certificate from the Belgian FA. A damages claim for breach of contract and also challenges to the Belgian FA were referred to the European Court of Justice. Its ultimate effective result was to declare transfer fees to be unlawful after expiry of players' contract periods. Because of the Treaty's *economic* basis, all *professional/commercial* sports-related activities with a European dimension are capable of being affected as distinct from 'grass roots recreative participants'. The detailed consequences are still being worked out with an awareness of the shift in controlling power from clubs' exclusivity to players as free agents with their advisers' guidance. This was illuminated by the highest professional football personal injuries award of £900,000 to Gordon Watson of Bradford City in early 1999, after he had obtained liability judgment against Kevin Gray and Huddersfield Town in the Leeds High Court during late 1998 in an arguably debateable judgment for which leave to appeal to the Court of Appeal was refused. On expiration of his contract at the end of season 1998–99 he rejected a re-engagement offer with the freedom to negotiate his own future under the Bosman ruling: a far cry from *Kingaby, Banks* and *Eastham*, before the Wilberforce J landmark judgment in 1963 for George Eastham.

Watson's quantum judgment in the High Court at Newcastle was obtained concurrently in early 1999 while the 16 year-old schoolboy Maxwell Casson in the Bradford County Court was moving towards a £3,000 interim judgment payment for a similar incurred injury caused by ungallant and foul soldierly play. Watson's result followed an arguably debatable and challengeable earlier liability judgment in Leeds High Court during October 1998, blocked from appealing by the Government's Denial of Justice requirements for leave to appeal against all civil liability decisions. When his contract expired in July 1999 his refusal to re-sign with the club which had supported his litigation, Bradford City, reportedly did not please the chairman Geoffrey Richmond. The club had paid £1m to Southampton for the transfer of his services two years earlier. Accordingly, the balance between short-term contracts with low wages or long term contracts with the opportunity of a transfer fee during its period will be a developing balancing requirement among the higher earning participating parties. It will hardly be an immediate problem for the bulk of grass roots school and park players in the 43,000 registered clubs who are outside the professional ranks, irrespective of the unknown unregistered numbers of clubs and players who play on Hackney Marshes and village greens throughout the land.

At this watershed in the forty years from Banks in 1955 to Bosman in 1995, two features merit attention. First, would the current turmoil have been avoided if the Belgian authorities had possessed the subtle depths of the Football Association's experiences in 1955 to influence Banks' desired free transfer from Aldershot to Weymouth, avoid an Appeal Court hearing by facilitating simply a free transfer and thereby afford Bosman a comparable freedom? Second, would it all have been revealed and decided half-a-century earlier if the Kingaby case had not been the failure recalled by Wilberforce J in his Eastham judgment during 1964 cited at page 77 above? For what is little known generally is how its preparations were fudged by a graphic self-satisfied recollection of the *Kingaby* case in 1912, to be found embedded in *'The Story of The Football League: 1888–1938'*, published by it in 1938 on its Jubilee. Compiled by its officers, C E Sutcliffe, J A Brierley, F Howarth, page 121 recalls,

'......illustrated by a piece of inside history. Mr Shearman, who was afterwards briefed for the defence, had actually given his opinion on a case submitted to him by the Players' Union that the system was contrary to law'.

We now know how this opinion was confirmed fifty odd years later by Wilberforce J after its trial run before H H Judge Percy Rawlins at Aldershot for Ralph Banks in 1955. Remarkably, however, we are told what today would create a professional conflict of interest and potential breach of professional etiquette,

'At a conference [for the Football League in support of Aston Villa] at which Mr Bernard Campion, his joint counsel was present, Mr Shearman explained his difficulty, whereupon he was bluntly told that he clearly had not grasped the scheme, and, as he himself phrased it, did not understand the law applying to it. At the conclusion of the action he was congratulated upon the successful result of the defence, but he generously attributed to the efforts and astuteness of Mr Sutcliffe.'

Montague Shearman was one of the few lawyers who blended athletic skills with sporting learning, evidenced by his monumental *'Athletics and*

Football' in the *Badminton Library* 1887. He followed Oxford University rugby and athletics Blues with active Athletics Association administration and ultimately a High Court judicial appointment. On this occasion his judgment was notoriously offside, and if any congratulations were due, they were applicable to his defence team's good fortune to have been opposed by a former England and Old Etonian FA Cup final winning goalkeeper, J P F Rawlington, KC, MP, who clearly fudged his evidence and causes of action on behalf of his Plaintiff-Client, Kingaby. He thereby missed the golden opportunity to do justice to the professional game which he had served better when playing as a distinguished amateur player.

4   DEVELOPING SPORT AND THE LAW

Concurrent with these economic, employment, industrial and important taxation legal sporting issues was the wider and much farther reaching factor which commanded the Inland Revenue's attention: the Pegasus windfalls from the FA Amateur Cup travels for which the two 100,000 crowds at Wembley Stadium in 1951 and 1953 produced sufficient income to create a prima facie liability to tax. This was consistent with established precedents of over sixty years' unchallenged authority that a sport club's profits from public funding beyond its private subscriptions were assessable to income tax (*Carlisle & Silloth Golf Club v Smith* [1913] 3 KB 75). Pegasus however, with its Oxbridge structure, was no ordinary club. It contained all the elements of classical physical education concepts which are built into the ideal of a healthy mind in a healthy body: *mens sana in corpore sano*.

That was the basis of a judgment delivered by Mr Justice Eve in the High Court during the First World War in the year when W G Grace and Victor Trumper both died, 1915 (*Re Mariette* [1915] 2 Ch 284) and reproduced verbatim *in toto* in Appendix 12 at p 595. He upheld as being validly charitable separate bequests for establishing a fives court and an athletics prize at Aldenham School, near Elstree in Hertfordshire. For reasons which can be attributed only to unawareness among British sporting administrators between the two World Wars (1919–39), it does not appear to have been applied as it could have been in court until 1957 when the New South Wales Equity Court in Australia (more recently concerned during 1986 with well publicised British Government security issues in the Peter Wright *Spycatcher* trial) applied the principles enunciated by Eve J for Aldenham School to a bequest in favour of Sydney University Rugby Football Club (*Kearins v Kearins* (1957) SR 286 (NSW)). In this year, too, the Central Council of Physical Recreation appointed a Committee under Sir John Wolfenden, which produced in 1960 its far-reaching Report on *Sport and the Community*. This in turn led ultimately in 1972 to creation of the Sports Council [now Sport England].)

In the immediate post-Second World War period after 1945 for nearly three years dining beneath the portrait of Eve J in the hall of Exeter College, Oxford, concentrated my attention on his decision in *Re Mariette* [1915] 2 Ch 284). Gradually I became aware during periodic researches of the absence of its citation or reliance upon it throughout the forty year period until its resurrection in Australia by a bequest in a will dated *12 December 1954* and the judgment of McLelland J to benefit Sydney University Rugby Football Club, during 1957 (*Kearins v Kearins* (1957) SR 286 (NSW)). Spurred on by this unexpected antipodean bonus from the other football game, Pegasus, through its creative and driving force the then Dr (later Sir Harold) Thompson , was advised jointly, by me and the late Hubert Monroe, QC, subsequently the Presiding Tax Commissioner, to tackle the Inland Revenue charitable status offices at Bootle in an attempt to protect the club's profits obtained after its *Amateur* Cup Final triumphs as a joint Oxbridge club team in 1951 and 1953 before those 100,000 crowds on each occasion. Because of the lack of funds recorded above, it had to act contrary to its cup-tie character when games were won after early errors, and on this occasion concede defeat after the joint advice was rejected by the Inland Revenue authorities.

A decade later Sir Stanley Rous's successor as FA Secretary, Denis Follows (later Sir Denis Follows, chairman of the British Olympic Association and Treasurer of the Central Council of Physical Recreation), who was aware of the then Council's charitable status, commissioned from me a contribution on *Football and the Law* to an *FA Manual of Administration* in the early 1970s. The opportunity was taken to explain the concept of physical education as a legal charity, and how

> '*educational* foundations could claim to qualify. At one time thoughts existed
> for Pegasus FC'.

On 30 October 1972, the Charity Commissioners registered an FA Youth Trust Deed; and after the eight-year battle to obtain a reversal of its rejection by the Inland Revenue, the Chancery trial judge and a Court of Appeal Majority, the House of Lords *unanimously* in a 'whitewash' ruling endorsed the judgment of Eve J as 'stimulating and instructive' (*IRC v McMullan* [1980] 1 All ER 884 at 892; letters b–c). Under the present Government Denial of Justice, leave would have been required from the trial Judge, Walton J before arguing further with the Court of Appeal, as distinct from the automatic right which existed at that time. Furthermore, bearing in mind the almost bizarre exchange between Counsel and the Appeal Judge recalled at page 82 below, and that a majority upheld the flawed judgment at first instance; it is debateable whether under the present Denial of Justice practice this crucial issue for the welfare of the health and education of the whole community would ever have arrived in the House of Lords for its landmark ruling:

Appeal Judge [Stamp LJ]

'Are you really saying that physical education is education like Latin or Greek?'

Counsel [Andrew Morritt QC]

'Yes, my Lord.''

Curiously, and for reasons which are not clear, *Kearins* was not cited at any level of the FA Youth Trust Deed court disputes. Yet its judgment too, was vindicated. Nearly thirty years later, as we shall see in Chapter 6, *Participation problems*, Australian authorities were relied upon by London's Court of Appeal to apply the principles of common law negligence to an award of £4,000 damages for a badly broken leg from a deliberate foul tackle in an amateur soccer match, and uphold the decision of a county court judge (*Condon v Basi* [1985] 2 All ER 453). More recently in Australia a decision of the High Court, upholding its appellate and New South Wales courts in *Rogers v Whittaker* [1992] 109 ALR 625 [1992] 4 MedL.R.79 (HC of Aust) with the robustness characteristic of its sporting culture has rejected the English Court's traditional deference to medical opinions epitomized in *Bolam* and *Bolitho* as distinct from the grounds of testifying medical expert witness, and asserted the decision of the court itself as a matter of law, in adjudicating whether a medical defendant's conduct has conformed to the standard of reasonable care demanded by the law, and not by the standard of the medical profession or some part of it. This is explained further in Chapter 7, *Sports Medicine and the Law*.

That contrast over a nearly thirty-year span from Australian sources for British courts between university rugby charity (1957) and soccer playing violence (1985) exemplifies the sinister shadows which were taking shape throughout the sporting world, on as well as off the fields of play. This was while the more subtle sporting legal knots with taxation elements were being untied after I had become entangled with them through Pegasus and professional players under Guthrie's guidance during the 1950s.

In 1969, the late J L Manning, an outstanding campaigning journalist, and son of an equally distinguished sporting journalist, Lionel Manning, recognised the appalling gaps in British crowd safety requirements after a relatively minor accident when a crush barrier collapsed in 1969 during a soccer match at Watford's homely ground in Hertfordshire, before the club's admirable progress throughout the later 1970s and 1980s. An invitation by Manning to me to examine the correct legal position for his *Daily Mail* column resulted in the discovery that two British Government Reports which had recommended licensing systems after a crowd overflow at the first-ever Wembley Stadium FA Cup Final in 1923 (Cmnd 2088 (1924)), and thirty-three fatalities in 1946 during a Bolton Wanderers FA Cup-Tie (Cmnd 6846 (1947)) had produced the traditional Whitehall inactivity. This contrasted with legislation later enacted after the Ibrox, Glasgow (1971), Bradford (1985) and Hillsborough (1989) football crowd fatalities, following investigative judicial inquiries by Lord Wheatley (Ibrox), Mr Justice Popplewell (Bradford) and Lord Justice Taylor (Hillsborough).

South America in 1964 and 1968 had recorded, respectively, 301 people killed and 500 injured after one match at Lima, Peru, and 71 people killed and about 200 injured at Buenos Aires in Argentina. Accordingly, when the Ibrox, Glasgow, disaster in 1971 caused 66 deaths and over 140 injuries, Manning did not have to shout very loudly, in the London *Evening Standard* to which he had moved, to steer Parliament into a third Government Report (from Lord Wheatley: Cmnd 4952 (1972)). This followed those two earlier Government Reports upon which no action had been taken: the Wembley Stadium FA Cup Final Report in 1923 and the Bolton Wanderers versus Stoke City 6th round FA Cup-tie Report in 1946. At last the Safety of Sports Grounds Act 1975 followed the Wheatley Report. Thereafter disasters at Bradford City; Heysel, Belgium, (1985) and Hillsborough, Sheffield (1989) were followed by comparable judicial Inquiries and Reports. Popplewell (Final 1986) (Cmd 9700)), Taylor (Final 1990) Cmd 962, and inevitable consequential legislation and litigation threaded throughout this text and particularly in Chapter 5, *Public Protection*.

Furthermore, since each of these Reports and the last edition of this text in 1994 were published, a valuable compendium from Butterworth-Heinemann entitled *Sport & Safety Management* edited by Steve Frosdick and Lynne Walley in 1997 contained *two* startling graphic tables of football stadia disasters which are reproduced here, with permission. They testify to at least forty-four *UK*-related accidents involving deaths and multiple injuries up until 1989, the Hillsborough landmark year, and at least twenty-six football disasters outside the UK in what the editors explained 'might be described as developing countries'.

For the victims of Bolton, Ibrox, Bradford, Hillsborough and others, compensation has been effected primarily by the Courts. Would it still be argued that the law should keep out of sport?

Disasters and incidents involving United Kingdom stadia or supporters

Venue	*Year Fatalities/injuries*	*Disaster/ incident type*
Valley Parade (Bradford)#	1888 1 dead, 3 injured	railings collapse
Blackburn	1896 5 injured	stand collapse
Ibrox (Glasgow)	1902 26 dead, 550 injured	collapsed temporary stand

Venue	Year Fatalities/injuries	Disaster/incident type
Brentford	1907 multiple injuries	fence collapse
Leicester	1907 multiple injuries	barrier collapse
Hillsborough (Sheffield)	1914 70–80 injured	wall collapse
Charlton	1923 24 injured	crowd crush
Wembley	1923 1000+ injured	crowd crush
Burnley	1924 1 dead	crowd crush
Manchester (City)	1926 unknown injuries	crowd crush
Huddersfield	1932 100 injured	crowd crush
Huddersfield	1937 4 injured	crowd crush
Watford	1937 unknown injuries	crowd crush
Fulham	1938 unknown injuries	crowd crush
Rochdale Athletic Ground#	1939 1 dead, 17 injured	roof collapse
Burnden Park (Bolton)	1946 33 dead, 400 injured	crowd crush
Shawfield (Clyde)	1957 1 dead, 50 injured	barrier collapse
Ibrox (Glasgow)	1961 2 dead, 50 injured	crowd crush on Stairway 13
Oldham	1962 15 injured	barrier collapse
Arsenal	1963 100 injured	crushing
Port Vale	1964 1 dead, 2 injured	fall/crushing
Roker Park (Sunderland)	1964 80+ injured	crowd crush
Anfield (Liverpool)	1967 32 injured	crowd crush
Leeds	1967 32 injured	crowd crush
Ibrox (Glasgow)	1967 8 injured	crowd crush on Stairway 13
Ibrox (Glasgow)	1971 66 dead, 145 injured	crowd crush on Stairway 13
Carlisle	1971 5 injured	barrier collapse
Oxford	1971 25 injured	wall collapse
Stoke	1971 46 injured	crowd crush
Wolverhampton	1972 80 injured	barrier collapse
Arsenal	1972 42 injured	crowd crush
Lincoln	1975 4 injured	wall collapse
Leyton Orient	1978 30 injured	barrier/wall collapse
Middlesbrough	1980 2 dead	gate collapse
Hillsborough (Sheffield)	1981 38 injured	crowd crush
Walsall	1984 20 injured	wall collapse
Bradford	1985 54 dead	fire
Birmingham	1985 1 dead, 20 injured	disorder/wall collapse
Heysel (Brussels)	1985 38 dead, 400+ injured	disorder/wall collapse

Venue	*Year Fatalities/injuries*	*Disaster/ incident type*
Easter Road (Edinburgh)	1987 150 injured	crowd crush
Hillsborough (Sheffield)	1989 95 dead, 400+ injured	crowd crush
Middlesbrough	1989 19 injured	crowd crush

Incident at rugby league ground.

Disasters in football grounds outside the UK

Venue	*Year Fatalities/injuries*	*Disaster/ incident type*
Ibague (Colombia)	1961 11 dead, 15 injured	stand collapse
Santiago (Chile)	1961 5 dead, 300 injured	crowd crush
Lima (Peru)	1964 318 dead, 1000+ injured	riot
Istanbul (Turkey)	1964 70 injured	fire
Kayseri (Turkey)	1967 34 dead	riot
Buenos Aires (Argentina)	1968 74 dead, 150 injured	disorder/ stampede
Cairo (Egypt)	1974 49 dead, 50 injured	crowd crush
Port-au-Prince (Haiti)	1978 6 dead	disorder/police shooting
Piraeus (Greece)	1981 21 dead, 54 injured	crush/stampede
San Luis (Brazil)	1982 3 dead, 25 injured	riot/police shooting
Cali (Colombia)	1982 24 dead, 250 injured	crushing/ stampede
Algiers (Algeria)	1982 10 dead, 500 injured	roof collapse
Moscow Spartak (Soviet Union)	1982 69+ dead, 100+ injured	crowd crush
Heysel (Belgium)	1985 38 dead, 400+ injured	disorder/wall collapse
Mexico City (Mexico)	1985 10 dead, 100+ injured	crowd crush
Tripoli (Libya)	1987 20 dead	unknown
Katmandu (Nepal)	1988 100+ dead, 500 injured	hailstorm/ stampede
Lagos (Nigeria)	1989 5 dead	crowd crush
Mogadishu (Somalia)	1989 7 dead, 18 injured	riot
Orkney (South Africa)	1991 42 dead, 50 injured	riot/stampede
Nairobi (Kenya)	1991 1 dead, 24 injured	stampede
Rio de Janeiro (Brazil)	1992 50 injured	fence collapse
Bastia (Corsica)	1992 17 dead	temporary stand collapse

Venue	Year	Fatalities/injuries	Disaster/ incident type
Free Town (Sierra Leone)	1995	40 injured	gate collapse
Lusaka (Zambia)	1996	9 dead, 52 injured	crowd crush
Guatemala	1996	80 dead, 150 injured	crowd crush

Of equal chilling significance to these figures are two separate paragraphs to be found in Lord Justice Taylor's Final Hillsborough Report in the context of John Williams' citation at Page 2A above from his publication: *IS IT all over? Can football survive the Premier League?*

'In football's darker days no politician was willing to stand up and proclaim him/herself a football fan'.

Paragraph 19 at Page 4 begins

'It is a depressing and chastening fact that mine is the ninth official report covering crowd safety and control at football grounds',

beginning with the 1924 Shortt Report in the 1923 FA Cup Final (at which committee the later Bolton Wanderers Meolwyn Hughes Report comments 'the Football Association had not deigned to appear'),
Paragraph 24 on the same page states

'Amazingly, complacency was still to be found even after Hillsborough. It was chilling to hear the same refrain from directors at several clubs I visited:-

'Hillsborough was horrible — but of course, it couldn't have happened here'.

Couldn't it? The Hillsborough ground was regarded by many as one of the best in the country'.

What Lord Justice Taylor's report does not contain, because he was doubtless never told by anyone who prepared or conducted the Inquiry before him, are references to the three collapsed grandstands which made it clear that accidents of the kind listed above were bound to happen, and tragically, may yet happen again.

Date	Occasion	Source	Result/Comment
1866	not a football ground, but first recorded Law Reports citation:	*Francis -v- Cockrell* 1870 5 QB 501	Promoter vicariously liable for negligently constructed grandstand at Cheltenham racecourse

Date	Occasion	Source	Result/Comment
1896	Blackburn Rovers -v- Everton stand collapse at Ewood Park: 5 injured	*Brown -v- Lewis* (QB Div (Cave and Wills JJ) (1896) 12 TLR 455 5 June	Club committee personally liable for defective contractor per HH Judge Coventry Blackburn County Court *Northern Daily Telegraph* 21 April 1896 —"His Honour in giving judgment said that committees of football clubs undertook a heavy responsibility in inviting the people to attend matches on their grounds. They made themselves responsible for the life and limbs of the people who went to the matches and used the stands. They knew that if the stands were not safe possibly hundreds of people might lose their lives or be maimed for life. It stood to commonsense that any football club which invited thousands of people to attend its matches incurred this responsibility. The law, which was generally— though not always— the impersonation of common sense, said that anybody who undertook such a heavy responsibility should see that these stands were as safe as it was possible to have them. In order to absolve themselves from liability, football clubs should show that they had done all they possibly could to secure the safety of the people. In this case he did not think this had been done. THESE IMMENSE "GATES" had grown up, within his memory practically, and he thought that the football clubs in this district scarcely knew the responsibility they were incurring. To call in a joiner who had had no practical experience in regard to the construction of stands, and who probably did not know the right place to which to direct his attention in

Date	Occasion	Source	Result/Comment
			examining them was not, in his opinion, taking every precaution to ensure their safety. He must therefore find a verdict for the plaintiff for £25.—"
1902	Ibrox, Glasgow 26 Dead: 550 injured Scotland -v- England	*R -v- McDougall* Culpable Homicide: Acquittal Glasgow Herald 10 July 1902	Glasgow Herald: 10 July 1902 "The verdict of "Not Guilty" in the Ibrox case is probably what most people who have followed the course of the trial were prepared for. Whatever the amount of the responsibility resting upon the contractor for the ill-fated structure, it became increasingly obvious as the case for the Crown was unfolded that that responsibility did not lie exclusively with any single individual. A jury of ordinary intelligence and of fair mind were little likely therefore to make a scapegoat of the defender, more especially in view of the extraordinary conflict of evidence as to the true cause of the disaster. It is in this conflict of evidence, and not merely in the fate of the contractor, Mr McDougall, that the real interest of the case lies. The witnesses were mutually destructive to a degree that is not often seen in such trials and the public are left in a state of complete bewilderment as to what chiefly conduced to the accident, and in doubt as to the means that should be adopted of preventing similar occurrences in future. Unfortunately, the close of the case does not admit of the questions raised being dismissed from the public mind. The uneasy feeling remains that what occurred at Ibrox may occur again, and that at present there is no adequate means of preventing it. Obviously a stand such as that set up by the Rangers Club might be perfectly safe when occupied by a placid, orderly

Date	Occasion	Source	Result/Comment
			crowd, and yet become a source of terrible danger when filled by a mass of people labouring under the excitement invariably aroused by a football match. As for the future, does the Ibrox disaster, with its sequel in the trial brought to a close yesterday, not point to the necessity for some very drastic regulations for the construction of the huge arenas required for the patrons of football? Surely modern skill and science should be equal to the production of something quite as stable as the ancient Roman circus."

The prescience of HH Judge Coventry at Blackburn County Court in 1896 and the *Glasgow Herald* six years later in 1902 need no emphasis or repetition. Lord Justice Taylor was also never informed of the explosive public interest which not only hovered over the Moscow Dynamo post Second War tour in 1945 at Cardiff, Glasgow and Stamford Bridge London. It was available and recorded for his advisers in *Munday v Metropolitan Police District Receiver* [1949] 1 All ER 337 with its proof of elements of riot proved under the Riot (Damages) Act 1889 1886 s 2(1). A year after the Dynamo tour, the Moelwyn Hughes Report (Cmd 6846) into the 33 dead and 400 injured ended 25th May 1946 (two and a half months after the Burnden Park, Bolton, disaster of 9 March 1946), with the conclusion

'I earnestly hope, that if the proposals I have made in this report, or similar suggestions (for regulatory control) commend themselves to you, Parliament will not be slow in granting, you the necessary powers',

to the Home Secretary on Mr Attlee's so-called progressive Government. 29 years later after all those further dead between 1946 and 1975 listed above, a Parliament was sufficiently stirred to pass the Safety of Sports Grounds Act 1975.

In the near thirty intervening years from Moelwyn Hughes in 1946 to 1975, among players, during soccer's World Cup Competition in 1966, the foul play chickens came home to roost, bred by the self-styled permissive society which the Chancellor of the Exchequer in 1969, the then Roy Jenkins MP, later claimed unwisely during a well-publicised speech to Abingdon Labour Party to be the 'civilised society' ((1969) *The Times*, 21 July p 3.

Six years later as Home Secretary he was directly concerned with the 1975 Act. The Brazilian international player, Pelé, was seen on television and video recordings throughout the world to have been criminally and brutally assaulted out of the competition by Bulgarian and Portuguese opponents who have been later identified and recorded below in Pelé's own words at Chapter 9, p 364, International Interaction, without any effective retribution. The experienced Senior Sports Correspondent, David Miller, recalled in his survey of that series, The Boys of '66, how I had pinpointed the illegality in the *FA Year-Book 1967–68*. In 1969 a conviction at Maidstone Assizes for manslaughter after a local Essex footballer had fatally punched another caused me to contribute a different form of article: 'Crimes of Soccer Violence', and *R v Southby* published in the *Police Review* for 7 February 1969, Vol 77, p 110.

5   SPORT AND THE LAW ARRIVES

A year later, the first recorded substantial damage award of £4,500 for foul play on the soccer field resulted in a further publication by me for the *New Law Journal* (1970 Vol 120, p 413 *Lewis v Brookshaw*). Concurrent with these violent physical developments on the field, behind the scenes, protracted and contentious negotiations, unknown to me, were taking place for the transfer of the CCPR's assets to the newly-to-be-formed government-funded Sport's Council while preserving the CCPR's identity under an on-going contractual relationship which exists to the present day. Nevertheless, physical violence persisted, and after the Scottish international rugby referee, Norman Sanson, was obliged in 1977 to send off two players for fighting in the Wales-Ireland international at Cardiff without much sympathy from the international rugby fraternity, a commission from the *Sunday Telegraph* to assess and recommend remedies for the violence engulfing all body-contact sports resulted in a series published there entitled '*Sport and the Law*'. The legal emphasis thus had shifted a long way from a quarter-of-a-century earlier during the early 1950s, and the taxation imbalance between professional footballers' and cricketers' benefits, restraint of trade, and the concept of Pegasus, as a sporting educational charity. To present the law in sport against a more comprehensive perspective, the series was converted and extended a year later in 1978 into a more general survey under the same title in booklet form. It was the genesis for the present text.

On that occasion two Forewords were contributed. The former Lord Chancellor, Lord Havers (writing in his capacity as a then former Solicitor-General, before becoming Attorney-General), recorded:

'If the rule book is torn up or vicious fouls go unpunished then the sporting element is destroyed and fun for both the player and the spectator is lost'.

The then Chairman of the Sports Council, and a former Rugby Union President and captain of England, Dick Jeeps CBE, wrote:

'Sport belongs to the real world and its rapid development in recent years has made ignorance of the law among decision makers unacceptable'.

If only to preserve that fun element, in addition to alerting decision makers at all levels to the legal consequences of their actions, a partnership between sport and the law is essential. The events during the past 20 odd years since 1978 have done nothing to diminish that need.

Shortly after the *Sunday Telegraph* publication appeared, a senior FA councillor told me 'You lawyers keep out of sport: we can take care of it all'. Ten years later on the eve of publication of the first Butterworths 1988 edition, the then new Chief Executive of the Football Association, Ted Croker, complained publicly at the Annual Conference of the Central Council of Physical Recreation in Birmingham after a paper on *Sport and the Law* had been read by Charles Woodhouse of Farrer and Co and my successor as Founding President of the British Association of Sport and Law, that he did not approve of lawyers coming into Sport: and that it was the fault of Edward Grayson who had invented Sport and the Law.

In response to an invitation to answer for myself I was obliged to point out he had hardly been confirmed by the urgent calls made upon the courts and Parliament to try to put out the social fires which his own game's abject administration failed to control. The extent of this intervention is rarely outside public exposure and continues almost daily during preparation of this text. Indeed for example, Leicester Crown Court throughout mid-summer and near autumn of 1993 was occupied for two months with the Public Order Act 1986 application to the Leicester City versus Newcastle United crowd disturbance at the end of the 1991–92 soccer season. Within my personal and professional knowledge it did not command national attention, but it was of great concern to the local community, sporting and otherwise (*Leicester Mercury* 28 August 1993). The database of intelligence and video evidence monitors the extent to which these experiences to a lesser or greater degree continue to exist for local areas throughout the country and indeed throughout the world in its global sporting village, in circumstances which are never recorded or reported at national or professional sources and journals as explained in the Introduction. Indeed, the national media know we have become too immune to such experiences to bother to record them generally beyond high profile celebrity or seriously grave circumstances.

The misconception behind that quoted FA councillor's line of thought, or lack of it, reflects a wider confusion explained already in the Preface by the former Lord Chancellor and creator in 1962 of the role of Government Minister with responsibility for Sport, Lord Hailsham of St Marylebone, in his Carlton Lecture 'Morality, Law and Politics', delivered shortly after his departure from office in June 1987. Discussing 'Values', he explained:

> 'It has been our fortune, good or bad, to live in an age of conflict, violence and confusion, one in which old certainties have faded into agnosticism, when new fanaticisms, new bigotries have arisen and new sources of political power or disruption have first challenged and sometimes overthrown established authority. At the heart of the problem lies the uncertain frontier between morality, politics and law, the framework of an ordered and civilised life'.

In *Britain: 1991*, an official handbook prepared by the Central Office of Information, for the Foreign and Commonwealth Office explained at the beginning of Section 26 entitled 'Sport and Recreation'

> 'The British invented and codified the rules of many of the sports and games which are now played all over the world.'

When these rules are breached, as Lord Hailsham's successor, Lord Havers, observed, 'If the rule book is torn up... the sporting element is destroyed'. In a sporting context they can be identified and categorised at four separate levels:

(1) playing laws;
    for players and participants to play
(2) playing penal laws;
    for referees, umpires to control and discipline play
(3) administrative laws;
    for fair and sensible organisation and control
(4) national laws;
    for overriding control for justice and fair play at all the above three levels.

Because a Welsh international rugby union player in the autumn of 1985 punched a defenceless opponent during the course of a club rugby match without being seen by the referee:

(1) there was a clear breach of rugby playing laws;
(2) this was not disciplined by the referee in control, and;
(3) the incident was ignored by club administrators (*R v Bishop* (1986) *Times*, 12 October).

Accordingly, as a last resort the *national law* was invoked. The ultimate plea of guilty to a common assault resulted in an immediate custodial sentence reduced to a conditional discharge on appeal. Since then the tariff of criminal violence on playing fields at rugby and soccer has progressively increased to the present penalty of 18 months custody. Damage awards have oscillated between the £4,000 tariff for a broken leg in amateur football in 1970 (*Lewis v Brookshaw* 120 NLJ 413) to a reported £900,000 awarded to Gordon Watson in 1999 for an injury suffered in an FA Premier League game after a judgment for which leave to appeal was refused to challenge a liability decision which contained no identifiable precedent authorities: and the anticipated damages claim by the other Watson, Michael, after he obtained judgment against the British Boxing Board of Control as explained in the opening pages is likely to exceed that amount, subject to an appeal hearing for which leave has been granted notwithstanding the current British Government's fallacious assumption '*that the court of first instance has reached the right decision*'.

Such developments reflect a pattern throughout the 1970s, 1980s and now into the 1990s in which sport mirrors the general social climate of its time. In its widest reflection the law in relation to sport and recreation has developed from its legislative control for peace of the realm and protection of property, in mediaeval days, to the litigation pattern which has unfolded down the years, and is evidenced by the representative host of cases covering the 251 years from 1748 to 1999 listed at the end of the Introduction. Those progressive developments numerically, as the area of sporting and recreational activity has been recorded throughout the century, is illustrated by the tables of disasters listed at pages 83–86 above and the table of *Hooligan-free football ground records in England and Wales (1919–1939)* prepared by Harry Grayson and contained in Appendix 5: and it was not required to identify that earlier Hooligan free crowd of 110,820 at the 1901 FA Cup Final [between Tottenham Hotspur and Sheffield United] with which the 20th century opened.

That pattern crystallised in the circumstances with which this chapter began when I puzzled over the anomalous difference between professional footballers' and cricketers' benefit payments, and also the abortive attempt to establish Pegasus as a valid charitable trust, while preparing for publication that schoolboy's hero-worshipping correspondence with G.O. Smith, as *Corinthians and Cricketers*. Many of G.O. Smith's England and Corinthian contemporaries were practising lawyers while playing alongside him. W.R. Moon the goalkeeper, whose firm still bears his name; the brothers, Walters, at full-back: A.M., a solicitor, P.M., a Chancery barrister and later Bencher of Lincoln's Inn, join 'Morning and Afternoon' as they were known; and Charles Wreford-Brown, who had captained G.O. Smith at Charterhouse, Oxford, Corinthia and on one occasion for England, who progressed to high office in the Football Association. Yet apart from Wreford-Brown's many years of service as *honorary* legal adviser to the National Playing Fields Association, none of them had any public participation in sports-related matters, and indeed, the scope for it did not exist in their days.

Another practising solicitor of a later generation who played and practised in Lancashire was a Corinthian in spirit, Harold Hardman. He gained an Olympic Gold medal in the United Kingdom Olympic Games winning XI in 1908, after playing for Everton in winning and losing FA Cup Finals. Later as chairman of Manchester United in the early 1950's he steered Matt Busby and his club into European competition in the face of intransigent parochial Football League opposition. It was appropriate, therefore, that his practising solicitor successor on the Board of Directors, Maurice Watkins with Dr Ray Farrell, from the School of Law at the Manchester Metropolitan University Law School, should have invited me to become Founding President on the 35th anniversary of the Munich airport disaster on 6 February 1993 and witness the creation of the British Association for Sport and Law at Old Trafford, Manchester under the aegis of the Sports Law Unit at the Law Department of the Manchester Metropolitan University.

If Sport and the Law could not be regarded before that occasion as having arrived at a mature age since its birth in the *FA Bulletin* for April 1953, it can certainly do so now.

CHAPTER 2

Progressive Perspective

INTRODUCTION

When Maurice Watkins, the practising solicitor now of Manchester United
Football Club Plc in the tradition of Olympic gold medallist, Harold Hardman,
and Dr Ray Farrell from The School of Law at the Manchester Metropolitan
University Law School, invited me to become The Founding President of
the British Association for Sport and Law on Saturday 6 February 1993,
with education as its first objective, it symbolised recognition of Sport and
the Law as a subject, which transcends and embraces Lord Hailsham's

> "heterogeneous list of pastimes, with different governing bodies, different
> ethics and constantly varying needs",

corroborated by the 113 non-profit making exempt VAT list of UK sports
activities.

Nevertheless, it is vital to be constantly mindful of the range of issues
connected with Sport, Law, and Sport and the Law: and this chapter aims
to discuss those wider issues that surround the genesis of Sport and the
Law: a discussion that is required because it is difficult to understand all
the elements which continue to affect sport in a modern day environment
without recognising their depth and complexity, as distinct from selecting
the appropriate and often clear-cut legal remedy applicable to them. This
would exist either by requiring an Act of Parliament attempting prevention
of repeated crowd disasters, of selecting the appropriate legal remedy and
relief, such as restraint of trade and injunction, as distinct from the
inappropriate choices in the *Kingaby v Aston Villa* example (see p 77 supra).

My *Sport and the Law* contributions to the *All England Law Reports
Annual Review* from 1987 onwards point the way in which the subject will
inevitably develop in the years ahead. Criminal, civil and fiscal litigation
surfaces regularly alongside Parliamentary attention in its legislative and
debating capacities. Yet at one particular point, the relationship of the law

and sport in the constitutional legal context remains static, and indeed, perversely confusing, in the United Kingdom at least; namely at government levels in Whitehall and Westminster.

At the end of the first page and top of the second page in the Chapter 1, *Genesis* for the first Butterworths edition of *Sport and the Law*, it was necessary to explain:

> 'an expanding and exploding world of sport at the end of the twentieth century as part of a wider recreational and leisure scene. This is the absence of any 'coherent body of doctrine, perhaps even a philosophy of government encouragement'; to cite the words first used to describe how ... in the early 1960s, 'a need, not for a Ministry, but for a focal point under a Minister', exists to identify 'government responsibility for sport': per Lord Hailsham of St Marylebone writing *The Door Wherein I Went*. He 'was left to organise the first government unit of this kind' in 1962 when Minister for Science and Technology in the Government of Mr Harold Macmillan (later Lord Stockton) ... that need has outgrown the constitutional legal status of a junior government Minister at the level of Parliamentary Under-Secretary in the Department of the Environment, with only 20 per cent of his time available for sport and recreation matters. The remaining 80 per cent is allocated to
> 'Gypsies and Gypsy site provision'
> 'mineral planning ... with onshore exploration work'
> 'planning matters, planning appeals'
> 'new towns, those which are still new town corporations'
> 'royal parks and palaces'
> 'ancient monuments and historic buildings, and the area called heritage'
> 'European Regional Development Fund money which comes into the Department of the Environment, and indeed for some matters on derelict land'
>
> (evidence, 11 December 1985: Mr Richard Tracy MP, to House of Commons Environment Committee: HC 198-iii at page 105, col 1, para 321).'

Although progress has now been made in relation to the most fundamental aspect of how Westminster and Whitehall view what Britain's longest serving Sports Minister, Lord (Denis) Howell of Aston, recognised in a debate (Hansard House of Lords 9 June 1993 Col 1025)

> 'about sport and recreation ... that it is a social service'

was followed by the claim (col 1027):

> 'what we need is a strong statement from the Government on the philosophy and purpose that they envisage for physical education within the school curriculum. We do not have such a philosophy and we suffer as a result,'

the constitutional Government status of a British Minister with responsibility for Sport and Recreation still remains in 1999 at Parliamentary Under Secretary level, although before the 1997 change of Government, Ian Sproate MP was elevated Denis Howell's last level of Minister of State and thereby with access to cabinet papers.

When I enquired from Lord Howell whether it is correct to view this as a serious situation he produced the response, irrespective of Home Office for Public Order and other specialist government departments such as the Ministry of Agriculture, Fisheries and Food (MAFF) for angling and water sports, that (at least in relation to playing fields):

'Sport and recreation now covers three government departments. I do not think they talk to each other!'

And as he explained in a subsequent *Observer* contribution:

'we do not have a Minister for Sport these days we have Ministers for Sporting occasions.'

for which the current fourteen different Government departments (apart from the one which houses the junior minister with responsibility for sport in the department of Culture Media and Sports and concerned with British sport), more than confirm this claim at the time of that 9 June 1993 House of Lords debate.

Since that occasion the present junior minister, Kate Hoey, as recorded here on page 67 above, was reported to be announcing 'a formal strategy in January 2000 for competitive sports in schools' and the Office for National Statistics (ONS) publication *Britain 2000* has 'A "Sports Cabinet" was established in 1998 to identify strategic priorities for sport ... the Government intends to publish early in 2000 a new national sports strategy.'

Clearly, one of the causes for this confusion until today is the absence of a concise and convenient definition for sport, which does not detract from Lord Hailsham's concept that it cannot be categorised comprehensively.

In 1980 I tried it and failed when reviewing for the Sports Council publication *Sport and Leisure*, then *Sport and Recreation*, a valuable enquiry by Professor McIntosh entitled *Fair Play: Ethics in Sport and Recreation*. What emerged, however, is that if definition is impossible, description is everything. For while sport to many who view it through traditional eyes and minds is a healthy vehicle for fair play, others have corrupted it through the triple diseases of drugs, violence and commerce, which destroy its healthy honest foundation. Thus, in the process of that review, I structured the following pyramid as a guideline to the facets which constitute sport without claiming then or now that they are necessarily complete. They illustrate some of the different perceptions for sport which are recognisable and identifiable. The base elements of this pyramid are shaped and conditioned by the upper echelons.

Violence
Internationalism
Politics and Power
Commercialism
Entertainment
HealthyCompetition
Free-For-AllFun

The impetus for such structuring came from the Foreword a year earlier in 1979 to McIntosh's book by Sir Roger Bannister, the pioneer who broke the four-minute mile barrier as an undergraduate amateur, and progressed to Master of Pembroke College, Oxford. He wrote of not only;

> 'Sport, which occupies the professional time of a few and the spare time of many, is a fit study for ethics'.

but also

> 'Internationally it is becoming increasingly complex to organise and regulate and has become fraught with commercial and political pressures or even, as in the Munich Olympics, terrorism'.

Subsequent Olympic and Commonwealth Games have confirmed this judgment from the later 1970s with every passing year, and the pyramid justifies sectional attention, with violence at its apex.

Parallel with the pyramid proposal is the categorisation created by Sir Denis Follows' own umbrella sporting association, the Central Council of Physical Recreation (CCPR). Its own sub-divisions are structured in the following way:

Games and Sports	: the traditional concept
Major Spectator Sports	: the public interest
Movement and Dance	: art or sport, or both, eg Torvill and Dean
Outdoor Pursuits	: rural sports out of town
Water Recreation	: rivers, lakes and all round island coasts
Interested Organisations	: the multitudinous residue, with Sports Council government-funded grants

In turn these approach in a modern context the 'fundamental distinctions between rural and urban and between aristocratic and plebeian' identified by Joseph Strutt in 1801 in his classic *Sports and Pastimes of the British People* and developed in Chapter 3, *Under starter's orders*, at p 135.

The pyramid structure with the passage of more than ten years since it was first conceived is still based on realities consistent with current experiences. Indeed, the intervening years have confirmed it. For the reader unfamiliar with Sir Denis Follows' concept of the indefineability of sport it will be appropriate to approach it within the present context at three separate stages, namely:

(1) the different layers of levels of the *sport* pyramid beginning at the top;
(2) the different layers of levels of *law* which are appropriate to sport;
(3) the crucial role of law in the playing and *administrative structures* of all sports.

The different layers or levels of the sport pyramid are consistent with Sir Roger Bannister's awareness that sport 'is becoming increasingly complex to organise and regulate'. The different levels or layers of law which are appropriate and applicable to sport were also identified and expanded in Chapter 1, *Genesis* through an offender's experiences, namely:

(i)   basic playing laws, eg rules prohibiting unfair or foul play;
(ii)   playing penal laws, eg immediate field sanctions, ie dismissals, sinbins;
(iii) administrative laws, eg disciplinary tribunals, ie suspensions, life-bans;
(iv)   national laws, eg civil or criminal.

The crucial quality or true meaning of law generally at all levels or layers was further assessed from across the Atlantic by one of America's leading examples of a practising jurist, Professor Roscoe Pound, one-time Dean of Harvard Law School among many other distinguished offices. Writing in a series of Cambridge University lectures in *Interpretations of Legal History* he explained (at page 153):

> '... the science of law ... must be more than an organising and systematizing of a body of legal precepts. There are three things to consider, which may not be looked at wholly apart from each other and yet must not be confused by ambiguous use of the term 'law'. Putting them in the chronological order of their development, these are, the administration of justice, the legal order and law'.

Applied to the sporting scene, Roscoe Pound's three elements can be recognised clearly when identified with easily recognised illustrations in line with the more restrictive assessment set out above.

(1) *the administration of justice*:
  (i)   balanced refereeing and umpiring for play
  (ii) balanced disciplining administration in committee rooms and
        council chambers
(2) *legal order*: playing and administrative laws for all games and play
(3) *law*: as defined further by Pound below with concepts generally and
     sportingly applicable

'Law is the body of knowledge and experience with the aid of which this
part of social engineering (ie the administration of justice and the legal order)
is carried on. It is more than a body of rules. It has rules and principles and
conceptions and standards for conduct and for decision but it has also
doctrines and modes of professional thought and professional rules of art
by which the precepts for conduct and decision are applied and given effect'.

Against those sporting and legal categories the Sport pyramid can be
assessed.

LEVEL OF THE SPORTS PYRAMID

1   Violence

To ignore or deny this category rejects the evidence proved by the Munich
massacre in 1972, the Heysel Stadium stampede in 1985, and the track record
of British football followers which created their unenviable reputations
during the years preceding this last disaster, and indeed, since then, too.
Violence is an unfortunate apex of the pyramid. It is debatable whether it
should exist at this level at the top of the pile. Nevertheless it affects all
aspects of sport throughout the world.
Indeed with a prophetic vision, George Orwell had written *The Sporting
Spirit* after the Second World War in 1945,

'Serious sport has nothing to do with fair play. It is bound up with hatred,
jealousy, boastfulness, and disregard of all rules and sadistic pleasure in
witnessing violence; in other words it is war minus the shooting'.

The shooting between El Salvador and Honduras at the time of the
qualifying rounds for the World Soccer Competition in Mexico during 1970
coincided with the games between the two countries at that stage of the
tournament; but although the occasion is cited often as an example of sport
resulting in war, there is also a contrasting argument that a third match
play-off took place amicably during the fighting period and in fact

contributed to a reconciliation. Orwell's awareness of sport's 'disregard of all rules' was written before the higher levels of the pyramid merged to dominate sport's public persona.

2 Internationalism

Modern international sport began formally on 3 October 1872 with the Football Association's resolution:

> 'In order to further the interests of the Association in Scotland, it was decided during the current season that a team should be sent to Glasgow to represent England'.

Thus began the earliest regular international sporting fixture in the world. Five years later in the winter of 1876–77 the first cricket tour from England, took place in Australia, followed by the first return visit in 1880, and creation of the mythical 'Ashes' at Kennington Oval in 1882. In 1886 the Four Home British Rugby Unions combined to form the International Rugby Board. In 1896, Baron de Coubertin recreated the Olympic Games from his enthusiasm and inspiration fired by his admiration for the athleticism of the English public school and collegiate university system which he had explored extensively. The foundation of FIFA, the Fédération Internationale de Football Association, followed in Paris during 1904.

A year later in 1905, the non-Government funded British Olympic Games was formed in anticipation of joining the 1908 Olympic Games to be held in Rome. When Rome withdrew as the host city, an Anglo-French trade exhibition at London's White City (then not sacrificed as a sporting centre on the high altar of property development) led to the United Kingdom's replacement for the first time. In the following year, 1909, the three leading cricket countries, England (represented by MCC), Australia and South Africa, formed the *Imperial* Cricket Conference. South Africa's membership lapsed when it withdrew nationally from the Commonwealth in 1961. After the restructured and retitled *International* Cricket Conference replaced it in 1965, applications by the South African governing cricket authority for joining as a new member failed regularly until its re-admission after the formal abolition of apartheid in the early 1990s, because of political opposition to its country's national apartheid policies, notwithstanding justifiable claims to have satisfied the International Cricket Conference's own *sporting cricketing standards* of non-discrimination. With this entwining of sport with politics, a new dimension emphasised what has been recognised by realists as a direct consequence of the First World War.

3   Politics and power

The First World War not only tore up the European map; it enmeshed the USA in the fight for it. The old British empire, now the Commonwealth, joined the mother country automatically in the name of the King Emperor, George V, on its own entry into battle with the Kaiser's Germany. By the time it ended in 1918, with united Imperial heroism and sacrifices in all war zones, the new international horizons heralded profound constitutional, national and political changes. The Versailles Treaty in 1919 contained the seeds for European nationalism which spawned Mussolini's fascism in Italy, Hitler's Nazism in Germany and their blatant exploitations of sporting events for political purposes.

With hindsight it is now possible to identify how three separate strands of events during the 1920s were unwinding to bind sport with national politics inextricably during the run up to the Second World War in 1939, and its near irrevocable cementation after it in the Empire, Europe and international sporting contests.

Firstly, the old British Empire's priceless contribution to defeating the Kaiser inspired a nascent nationalism which culminated in self-government following from three Imperial Conferences, the Statute of Westminster in 1931, the former Dominions' individual roles alongside the mother country at the time of Edward VIII's abdication in 1936 and entry into the Second World War against Hitler's Germany. Within this progression the 1932–33 MCC cricket tour of Australia, under the aggressively thoughtful leadership of the amateur playing professional solicitor captain, Douglas Jardine, exploded into a political crisis which locked the former Dominion Office (now the Foreign and Commonwealth Office) in Whitehall with leading Australian national and cricketing politicians at all levels. It transcended the immediately successful object of winning the Ashes by four Test Matches to one and curtailing the record-breaking batting talents of the then 24-year-old Donald Bradman, whose batting technique many modern readers may not know was based upon a dedicated physical and mental self-discipline to create a legend which in turn transcends the narrow worlds of sport.

Secondly, during the two following years, Mussolini concerned himself personally with substantial bonuses, (including exemption from military service), which were offered to Italy's international football team, for its 1–1 draw with England in Rome during 1933 and the return fixture at Arsenal's North London stadium in 1934. England won 4–2 in what has become known in football circles as the Battle of Highbury. England's captain Hapgood, has recorded it as 'the dirtiest game I ever played in', and Sir Stanley Matthews looked back upon it as 'the roughest in which I have ever taken part'.

Thirdly in December 1935, the Trades Union Congress tried to ban the visit by Germany's national team to North London's other national football centre at Tottenham Hotspur's White Hart Lane ground. It was not the fixture which produced the objections but the possibility of processions and demonstrations in an area bordering upon deeply populated Jewish communities who had been alerted to Hitler's horrendous practices. The German Ambassador called at the Foreign office to discuss a cancellation and the Home Secretary, then Sir John (later Viscount) Simon, and later a wartime Lord Chancellor, wrote in *The Times* with an innocence touching upon naivety;

> 'Wednesday's match has no political significance whatever ... It is a game of football, which nobody need attend unless he wishes, and I hope that all who take an interest in it from any side will do their utmost to discourage the idea that a sporting fixture in this country has any political implications.' [Nearly 60 years later in 1994, the fixture booked to be played on Hitler's birthday, 30 April, was cancelled realistically for recognised political reasons.]

Whatever was the attitude 'in this country' during 1935, Germany was preparing its own showcase for politico-sporting posturing with the Berlin Olympics barely six months later in 1936. Two years later in 1938 England's footballers, still captained by Hapgood, were advised by Britain's Ambassador, Sir Neville Henderson, to give the Nazi salute in Berlin's Olympic Stadium four months ahead of the Munich 'piece of paper' of appeasement. The England team saluted with shame, but there was nothing shameful about their salutary victory 6–3. The 103,000 German crowd was stunned.

This sustained politicisation of sport continued even after the Second World War had ended in 1945. The Moscow Dynamo football tour of the United Kingdom was welcomed by football followers with the warmth shared universally by sporting aficionados. The excitement engendered by its novelty in a country starved of international competitive sport during the war-time period of 1939–45 was evidenced by the later litigation for compensation against the Receiver of Metropolitan Police when fans overflowed from Chelsea's Stamford Bridge into neighbouring garden properties (see *Munday v Metropolitan Police Receiver* [1949] AER 333). It chilled as a prelude to the Cold War with the realisation explained by Mr Colm Brogan in *Our New Masters* (1947) that the team was 'here to demonstrate the superiority of Stalinite football over bourgeois football, and the superiority of Russia over Britain'. The visitors' sustained persistence in playing a makeshift postwar Arsenal XI in the fog at Tottenham Hotspur's White Hart Lane ground, with the referee on one touchline and the two linesmen on the other, symbolised the enigmatic attitudes which shrouded East-West Relationships thereafter. It was a sporting prelude or warm-up for The Cold War. Thirty-three years later Sir Stanley Rous wrote in his memoirs *Football World* (1978):

> 'Russia is now the country that looks on sport as a means of furthering its political aims'.

In more than fifty years since that Moscow Dynamo tour, Olympic and Commonwealth Games and international sport generally have been bedevilled by political poisoning of the sporting atmosphere. With the honourable and memorable exception of the late Sir Denis Follows' resistance to the non-sporting Mrs Thatcher's opposition to the Moscow Olympics, sport had supinely accepted this in a manner which more courageous enlightened and intelligent administrative leadership could have avoided through recourse to the law which has consistently protected victims of sport in oppression within and without it as these pages will demonstrate. Taiwan proved this when its national badminton and athletics governing bodies applied successfully to the English courts for acceptance within their respective international governing bodies which had rejected them until the law was invoked successfully. As we shall see in Chapter 9, '*International interaction*', the means required a legal interpretation of the rule-book: the purpose and consequence were political (*Shen Fu Chang v Stellan Mohlin* (1977) (badminton) unreported except at [1981] 3 All ER 324 g-h; and *Reel v Holder* [1981] 3 All ER 321, CA (athletics)). So successful were the Taiwanaise in achieving justice under the Rule of Law from the legendary Lord Denning and his fellow judges that the International Amateur Athletic Federation (IAAF) moved its offices from the English Courts' jurisdiction in London to Monaco. For reasons explained more fully in Chapter 9, the House of Lords in *Wheeler v Leicester City Council* overruled two other appeal court judges and the first instance judge to uphold Browne-Wilkinson LJ's dissenting judgment and to adjudicate as offside the Leicester City Council's ban on the Leicester Rugby Club's use of council playing premises. This happened because its players, selected for the honour of wearing England's white shirt, exercised their freedom of choice to tour South Africa.

If a sufficiently determined administrative will, of the kind demonstrated by Sir Denis Follows against a Prime Minister alien to and never comprehending any aspect of sport existed, the political spoilsports, who trespass upon sport's traditional administrative apathy and ineptitude could be defeated. For deliberately and intentionally interfering with contractual relations as well as providing compensation for breach of contract, the law of tort can be structured to protect international as well as domestic sport from the political interference which has progressively been permitted to erode the true spirit of sporting comradeship for too long. One reason, of course, has been the hostage given by *public* sport to commercial interests, and the inevitable financial risks inherent in litigation costs with the balance of resources often but not always tilted in favour of governing bodies against victims of their oppression. The shading from political to commercial layers in the pyramid became a natural one when Parliamentary activity in the sporting sphere accelerated at an unprecedented rate, for amending legislation which resulted in the Fire Safety and Safety of Places of Sport Act 1987, alongside preparations for and the hearing in Leeds Crown Court of the compensation claims for the Bradford City fire disaster, and the subsequent crowd control legislation following Lord Justice Taylor's Report and the Hillsborough disaster, with civil and criminal litigation unfolding from it to this day and beyond the Millennium, into the year 2000.

4 Commercialism

Commerce and sport are so wedded in the public mind that it is often forgotten how vast areas of sport from school to club levels are dependent upon voluntary service and private funding, without the vast sums now pumped annually into sport and monitored by expensive reports and enquiries. In November 1983, the CCPR itself published *The Howell Report* from a committee of enquiry into sports sponsorship. Ironically it contained a specific recommendation for Government reference to the Office of Fair Trading to examine whether any monopoly situations exist between certain marketing and sporting associations. The current litigation during 1999 between the Office of Fair Trading and the FA Premier League proved how far down the road this has progressed. In April 1999 the 254 paged Monopolies and Merger Commission Report recommended 'that the acquisition of Manchester United by BSkyB should be prohibited', endorsed by the Government Secretary of State for Trade and Industry: and the financial columns of media sources compete for space and coverage with bona fide sport elements and particularly to the exclusion of those concerned with health and education within the Rule of Law.

If commercial sources are to be harnessed most effectively and beneficially they require skilled professional structuring. Sponsorship is in the beginning and at the end a business deal which must be geared to clear contractual foundations as we shall see in Chapter 13, *Sponsored gentlemen and players*; and the whole of sports funding in the later 1990s should be framed with an eye to the tax, VAT, and charitable situations at both national and local levels to be explained in Chapter 14, *No fine on fun*.

That particular title is taken from the polemical attack by the late Sir Alan Herbert on a greatly resented Entertainment Tax; and this leads logically to the next layer or level of the pyramid.

5   Entertainment

Sir Denis Follows in his potentially posthumous Loughborough College lecture in 1983 explained how:

> 'Sport at top level has become much more part and parcel of the entertainment world and particularly so during the past thirty years. We have reached the stage where sport at top level has become almost completely show business with everything one associates with show biz — the cult of the individual, high salaries, the desire to present the game as a spectacle — with more money, less sportsmanship, more emphasis on winning — and all this has largely come about through television'.

His conclusion contained this express warning:

> 'I have no fear for the future of sport at grass root level. But I do profess a fear for sport at top level.
>   In my lifetime I have more or less seen an entertainment industry born and die. I refer to the cinema. Is there any God given gift that protects League Football and County Cricket from such a fate?'

In the sixteen years which have passed since those thoughts, the fluctuating mobility of different sponsors entering and departing from these two national and other sporting institutions, such as longstanding provincial tennis tournaments, point to the authenticity within Sir Denis' apprehensions about *sport at top level*, and an issue yet to be resolved in 1999. His lack of fear for the grass roots stemmed from his knowledge that it is there that the true meaning of sport exists forever, with healthy competition and free-for-all fun.

Yet even here, too, the years since Follows spoke in 1983 had witnessed changing attitudes to health and education in sport, creating such dangers and apprehensions as the monopolistic control of public entertainment sport by television, commerce and sponsorship which previously did not exist. The almost daily battles for television and other entertainment rights occupy business and front page headlines in all sections of the media as much as the actual sport and recreation reports on the back pages, with no difference in the levels of legal expertise require to conclude them. Furthermore, earlier this year in *Ethics injuries and the law in sports medicine* Butterworth Heinemann 1999 based upon the *World Medical*

Association's Declaration of Principles of Health care for Sports Medicine, I pointed out at pages 38–39 how

'The demands and stresses of competitive professional sport are particularly vulnerable in this category. With a supreme irony, unnoticed by many commentators at the time of the 1996–97 FA cup final, manager Bryan Robson selected, or allowed to be selected, a semi-fit player for the Middlesbrough team, Ravanelli, a quarter of a century after he was himself selected for the England 1970 World Cup tour in Mexico after suffering a dislocated shoulder while playing for Manchester United. This reflected a memorable comment during an interview on the BBC World Service during 1997 given by FIFA Secretary General, Sepp Blatter 2–3 May, 1997 when questioned by Steve Tongue:

"It is always the best players that have to perform. It is too much to demand for every game. The clubs pay a lot for players. They have to make players like horses. They perform but they are not in a circus. They are in a game and they need time off for recuperation. Otherwise there are physical limits and there are mental limits to play a game."

Added to the demands of the club are the contractual pressures of sponsors and agents. No veterinary surgeon would allow horses to perform to the extent demanded of two-legged athletes: indeed, if such demands on animals were ever made, the RSPCA would become involved. It has often protested in the past, for example at the Grand National dangers, for protection of the horses, with a consequential benefit to the riders; and illustrative of the different approaches for four-legged from two-legged animals were the contrasting attitudes explained publicly during the high sporting summer of 1998. The Epsom Derby winner's trainer, Luca Cumani, was recorded in the *Sunday Times* (19 July) by John Karter, to say of his colt, High Rise:

We bypassed the Irish Derby to run at Ascot for the King George VI and Queen Elizabeth Stakes because I have the Prix de l'Arc de Triomphe at the back of my mind and we wanted to save the horse for the autumn.

A week later Britain's women's heptathlon champion Denise Lewis wrote in the *Daily Mail* (24 July) under the headline 'Stop pushing our track stars to the point of collapse':

Athletes' bodies are not machines. All the exertion takes its toll and it is hardly surprising a lot of us end up injured. Our bodies need 12 months without the pressure of a major championship to recharge.

At present, there is no Society for the Prevention of Cruelty to Human Athletes'.

although the spiralling increase in injuries to star public performers is now commanding media attention as an inevitable consequence of commercially driven competition and sponsored seductive financial prizes.

6   Healthy competition

Every sporting competitor should know the difference between healthy and sickening activities. Unfortunately, the corruption of language among media, professional sport commentators and observers has transferred the euphemism for unfair conduct and play from the professional foul, now recognised as a criminally and civilly actionable assault, to a 'good' or 'keen' competitor. Description once more, rather than definition, is appropriate for accurate understanding. One commentary which stands the ultimate test of time was coined by the doyen of modern all-round sporting chroniclers, Bernard Darwin, who trained as a barrister, practised as a golfer, journalist and writer and had many other sporting attributes. Under the title *British Sport and Games*, published by the British Council in a *British Life and Thought* series at the outset of the Second World War during 1940 and revised when it ended in 1945, he wrote over fifty years ago with words requiring no modifications today:

'As long as there is competition in any walk of life, so there will be some sharp practice, but at least it is today generally and severely frowned upon where once it was almost admired'.

He continued interrogatively,

'What exactly are the ideals which make us call the man who lives up to them 'a good sportsman'? One of them and that the chief, because almost everything else is comprised in it, is 'to set the game above the prize', to enjoy the contest or the adventure first of all for its own sake. It is one that in its sternest and narrowest sense is scarcely possible to live up to. Everybody must want to win; that desire is part of the joy of the contest, whether it be with the beasts of the chase or with a human adversary, and those who have such desire are far better otherwise occupied. There is a certain maxim, or rather aspiration, too often quoted, which in its literal meaning is almost absurd — 'May the best side win!'. It is one which must, if we are honest, be accompanied by another unspoken wish, namely, that ours may prove the best side. Otherwise it is an anaemic thing. Of course we want our own side to win. We should be poor creatures if we did not and poor players. The point is, I take it, that we must not want it too much and in the wrong way. First of all we must not want to win by an excessive sharpness. Games must have rules and rules must be kept, but there will always come moments when it is well not to insist too much upon breaches of them, but rather to put the blind eye to the telescope. As to when those moments arise, there will always be differences of opinion. This much at least can be said, that the rules of games are not made for those who mean to break but for those who mean to observe them. You cannot legislate for cheating.'

Nearly sixty years on the last sentence requires qualification. The need to legislate for cheating marks the difference between recognising regrettably that unfair and unhealthy competitors do exist, and carrying on unconsciously as if they do not. The minority who step out of line have to be lassoed, coralled and above all else sanctioned until they learn the norm of good behaviour or forever be outlawed and banished, to all the silent majority within a setting of Healthy Competition their free-for-all fun. Furthermore, this can create a problem if the lawyer assigned to, or entering into sporting or sports related territory, is unfamiliar with dismissal of the culture of the climate within which he operates. Thus, in the Introduction to the second edition of Sport and the Law at Pge xxvii it was necessary to explain the flaw inherent in a claim before the 1994 World Cup Competition during 1994 by one of the Football Association's leading legal advisers, who allowed himself to be described in a Law Society's Gazette interview as a 'commercial litigator who spends nearly a third of his time handling contentious work for the FA'. He had explained:

'A rule change to prevent the types of soccer injury suffered by Spurs centre back Gary Mabbutt and Torquay defender John Uzzell would be "extraordinarily difficult to draft"'.

The solution was clarified by Philip Don, England's World Cup referee, to Michael Parkinson in the *Daily Telegraph* during the opening days of the 1994–95 season,

'The laws weren't changed. All that FIFA did was to remind referees of what their responsibilities are'.

Correspondingly, during an international conference in Monaco during 1991 it was necessary to remind the meeting of the flaws inherent in opinions expressed publicly by a self-satisfied practitioner operating in the drugs scenario. He would have been unwise to persist in a dismissive attitude to what he had described as 'the continuing paper chain of custody' as he did on that occasion. The turmoil which has erupted since then in the esoteric and pharmacological worlds of drug testing recognises, today, at least the essentiality for strict continuity of admissible evidence in the experience of all civilised court procedures, in their appropraie civil, criminal and tribunal jurisdictions.

7 Free-for-all fun

In 1986 a publication prepared by the National Coaching Foundation and the Association for Children's Play and Recreation-Playboard was entitled *Play the Game*. An introductory section entitled 'A New Perspective on winning and losing' explained under these sections

> 'What is needed is a new view of competition which emphasises the personal
> challenges and rewards:
> of trying to do better than last time
> of persistence
> of setting one's goals and finding the discipline to pursue them
> of cooperation of playing for the team
> of sheer athletic joy.'

Under the fun concept it explained

> 'Keeping the fun in sport can be extremely hard. Rather than measure the
> value of sport in terms of whether a child can win or not, score or not, defeat
> or be defeated, emphasis should be on the development of a sense of personal
> worth and achievement ...
>   When competition is kept in perspective, there is room for fun in the
> pursuit of victory — or more accurately, the pursuit of victory is fun.'

A decade later in 1996 The National Coaching Foundation recycled the same concept in its exclusive publication '*Making Sport Fun*'. Its catalogue description crystallises the ideal inherent in the Archbishop of Canterbury's caveat cited in the Preface at Page above 'We take it for granted that you cannot play a game of football without rules. Rules do not get in the way of the game. They make it possible':

> 'Sport can be very rewarding; a lifetime's interest can depend on a child's
> first impression and it is your task to create positive experiences to help
> children explore a lifetime of pleasure'.

These concepts may be elusive in the world of commercial entertainment sport. From different sides of the Atlantic and from different points in time they can be summarised in well known stanzas familiar to some, perhaps not so well known to others. From America, Grantland Rice wrote,

> 'For when the One Great Scorer comes
> To write against your name,
> He marks — not that you won or lost —
> But how you played the game.'

In similar style, Sir Henry Newbolt evoked from Clifton College, Bristol

'There's a breathless hush in the Close to-night —

Ten to make and the match to win —
A bumping pitch and a blinding light,
An hour to play and the last man in.
And it's not for the sake of a ribboned coat,
Or the selfish hope of a season's fame,
But his Captain's hand on his shoulder smote —
'Play up, play up, and play the game?'

Out-dated? Old hat? Or, in the end, nearer to the true meaning of sport than the higher echelons in that pyramid:
Entertainment

Commercialism
Politics and Power
Internationalism
V i o l e n c e

or the modern celebrity cult-concept, sponsored sport? Each reader must judge for himself, or herself. For as we shall see in Chapter 8, the women are rapidly 'catching up the men', and indeed getting ahead of them when allowed to.

THE LEVELS OF LAW APPLICABLE TO SPORT

Against the background of the above perspective of the levels and layers of sporting operations, how does the law fit in or function? To some the answer may be clear-cut; but a moment's reflection should establish that it cannot be as simple as superficial minds would suggest. For sport in its widest, broadest meaning acknowledges the laws' existence at one or more of four separate levels, already explained:

(i)   basic *playing* laws, eg rules prohibiting unfair or foul play;
(ii) playing *penal* laws, eg immediate field sanctions, ie dismissals sin-bins;
(iii) *administrative* laws, eg disciplinary tribunals, ie suspensions, life-bans;
(iv) *national* laws, eg civil or criminal.

Thus a World Cup or Test Match offence against the laws of a particular game, such as the assaults by Portuguese and Bulgarian footballers on Pelé in England during the World Cup Competition of 1966, and the threats to bowl in an intimidatory fashion as explained in Chapter 9, *International interaction,* could or would (subject to any advantage discretion by a referee or prosecuting or litigating source),

(a)   breach a playing law;
(b)   activate a penal playing law;
(c)   initiate an administrative law;
(d)   operate a civil or criminal law.

Thus, *R v Bishop* (1986) illustrates (a), (c) and (d). Because the *referee* did not see the admitted criminal common assault on the rugby field, the offence was initially charged and prosecuted as an assault occasioning actual bodily harm. This was not pursued in the Crown Court where a plea of common assault was the basis of a one month's custodial sentence reduced on appeal to a suspended sentence and thus (b) *could not function*. Furthermore, at one stage the administrative law operated by the Welsh Rugby Union resulting in a season's ban was under consideration for a High Court application during late 1986 and early 1987 resulting in no further action being taken.

For lawyers, however, this alignment may justifiably be considered too restrictive. Yet even if sport is approached from a wider legal spectrum, the practical and ultimate result would be the same. Hence, the application of every restricted legal category, (a) to (d) inclusive above, to the sporting scene within Pound's wider concept at page 100 supra as 'part of social engineering'. Furthermore, beyond sport, this covers the whole legal spectrum from divorce and child abuse in family life to drunken and drugged drivers and homicide as the apex of anti-social misconduct.

Pound's concluding comment is a natural prelude to the next stage, namely, the crucial role which law has played in the playing and administrative structure of sport. He wrote:

'Like the engineer's formulas, they [ie the law's 'doctrines and modes of professional thought and professional rules of art'] represent experience, scientific formulations of experience, and logical development of the formulations; but also inventive skill in conceiving new devices and formulating their requirements by means of a developed technique'.

Another great American practitioner and jurist, Oliver Wendell Holmes, coined the concept in the opening pages of his great work on *The Common Law*: as long ago as 1881. 'The life of the law is not logic, it is experience'. Experience, expediency and experiment through law produced the structure and the framework for modern sport, as we shall now see. Sadly, however, the manner in which it is both played and administered in our time merits the connfirmation of a celebrated source nearer home, with Kipling's immortal couplet [*The Islanders* (1902)]:

'They ye returned to your trinkets; then ye contented your souls. With the flannelled fools at the wicket or the muddied oafs at the goals'.

CRUCIAL ROLE OF LAW IN THE PLAYING AND ADMINISTRATIVE STRUCTURES OF ALL SPORT

Not without significance *The Oxford Companion to Sports and Games* — explains 'Archery can claim the oldest ancestry of any sport actively pursued today'.

Its practice and usage in the interests of national security meant that effective and authentic legislation protected its survival while outlawing other sports and pastimes. Latimer preaching before Henry VIII declared,

'The art of shooting hath been in times past much esteemed in this realme:
it is a gift of God, that he was given us to excell all other nations withal —
It hath been Goddes instruments whereby he hath gyven victories agaynste
our enemyes'.

Edward III forbade the playing of idle games, including football, because they interfered with archery practice, and an Act of 1541 was similarly motivated. It made illegal not only a great variety of customary pastimes, but also ordained that every man under sixty years of age, 'not lame, decrepit or maimed', should possess and use a bow and train up his children and servants in the art.

Modern competitive archery runs true to form with so many other modern sports, and a fall-out from the social progress of emerging leisure pursuits during the mid and later nineteenth century. The first Grand National Archery Meeting was held at York in 1844, and in 1861 the Grand National Archery Society was founded to assume responsibility for this meeting and in due course became the official governing body for archery in the United Kingdom.

Comparable with archery in antiquity, and in one historic instance for national security, is bowls. Contemporaneous evidence confirms Sir Francis Drake's memorable reply to news of the Spanish Armada's sighting off Plymouth Hoe on 19 July 1588, 'There is plenty of time to win this game and thrash the Spaniards, too'; as he did.

Nearly three centuries passed, however, before a Glasgow solicitor during 1848–49, W W Mitchell, was charged to prepare a code which has become standard for what is now a universally popular game within the capacity of all generations and both sexes.

The most popular of all sports with a parallel for antiquity alongside any other, horse racing, was structured with the foundation of the Jockey Club in 1750 to regulate control of the potential corruption from gaming and commercial exploitation. As we shall see, with its disciplinary and drug controls it had almost a century's start on other governing bodies in keeping offenders against its Rules of Racing either in line or warning them off the Turf on Newmarket Heath. Cricket's first dedication of the Laws of the Game are attributable in 1774 to the club which played at the Artillery Ground now used by the Honourable Artillery Company. MCC's foundation in 1787 ultimately took over and has retained trusteeship and copyright of the Laws; although in 1968 it surrendered autonomy for government funding purposes of the domestic English game to the Cricket Council and under it, to the Test and County Cricket Board (TCCB), now the England and Wales Cricket Board (EWCB).

These club and professional sources available to the leisured society of the times created inevitably a class basis for developing British sport. This mould began to crack only when the rapacious fiscal legislation after 1945 allowed commercial predators and business sponsorship to replace the earlier pioneering patronage. The first organised athletics meeting originated at Exeter College, Oxford in 1850, as if to anticipate the vintage period of the 1950s when its ancient walls contained Roger Bannister, to break the four-minute mile barrier; Denis Saunders, captain of the two Pegasus Oxbridge FA *Amateur* Cup-winning teams before two 100,000 Wembley crowds; and John McGregor or Kendall-Carpenter, England's future rugby captain and Rugby Union President, and innovator of the Rugby World Cup Competition before his premature death.

From Cambridge University in 1862 came the final thread to link the differing school rules for playing football in anticipation of the FA's foundation in 1863; and the Gentlemen and Players division epitomised the public fabric of nearly all popular pastimes in their formative years. Dr Arnold's mid-nineteenth century concept of *mens sana in corpore sano* guided those who created the urban, industrial and overseas clubs formed for amateur joys. The public demand and spectator appeal converted them into professional industries by legislative changes of the emerging public bodies such as the FA, Rugby League and the County Cricket Championship. Even Baron de Coubertin's vision of an athletic dream which grew into the modern Olympic Games from 1896 was inspired from these privileged and elitist sources.

Underlying and running throughout this unfolding pattern and progression was the constitutional legal core described so aptly by the judge who was required to sentence the last women to be hanged before Ruth Ellis, Edith Thompson. Montague (later Mr Justice) Shearman was an outstanding Oxford University athlete who later became President of the Amateur Athletic Association until he died in 1930. Author of a classic sporting textbook in the Badminton Library, *Athletics and Football*, he wrote as a young practising barrister a century ago (during 1887) in a chapter entitled 'Athletic Government' which is equally applicable to all sports:

'One of the most remarkable features about modern English Athletic life is the capacity of the athlete for self-government. As soon as any game or sport becomes popular in any district, or throughout the country, clubs are formed; the clubs conglomerate into district associations; and the latter finally become gathered into a national governing body. All these bodies, from the smallest club to the largest association, are the outcome of voluntary effort; they are worked, as a rule, in a sensible and businesslike manner, and the officers, in almost every case, are unpaid. Football, cricket, cycling, athletics, paper-chasing, have all their governing bodies; and at a week's notice the best team in any sport can be picked from the whole country, or the popular opinion as to any change or innovation in the sport ascertained. All this discipline and organisation is so well known nowadays as to excite little notice; but when fairly considered, it is really marvellous and most creditable to the capacity and sound sense of the English sportsman'.

Victorian modesty must have prevented him from also saying what I will say to fill the gap. It was also due in no small way to the pioneering lawyers and also the sense of justice and fair play among the lay administrators, many from the teaching profession, who combined to create the administrative structures and playing laws during the later 19th and earlier 20th centuries which have been adapted universally throughout the world.

Shearman himself played a major role in the development of amateur athletics in the years long before modern accountancy ingenuity has converted them at the public level into trust fund athletics. Cricket's first knight, Sir Francis Lacey, was MCC's non-practising barrister secretary who received his accolade in 1926. That was the year in which Harry Altham from Winchester College produced the first edition of his classic *History of Cricket* before creating the MCC coaching scheme, and later attaining Presidency of that Club and also of his beloved Hampshire County Cricket Club. In that year, too, a Watford Grammar schoolmaster began his public refereeing career before gaining the highest honours within soccer as Sir Stanley Rous. Ultimately he re-wrote the Laws of the Game and invented the ingenious diagonal system of refereeing control to worldwide acclaim. More recently, Upjohn J's judgment in *Football League Ltd v Littlewoods Pools Ltd* ([1959] 2 All ER 546) explains the skill in creating the copyright contained in the League's fixture compilation from the solicitor son, Harold Sutcliffe, of a former Football League President and Solicitor, Charles E Sutcliffe, in its formative years of the last century. These examples can be multiplied in every British sport at national and local levels.

The two World Wars inevitably operated as a catalyst upon the development of British sport which reflected their impact on society generally. They also mark the general unawareness of understanding within sport of how the law was available to benefit it before and during the inter-war years period. As we will see in detail later in Chapter 6, *Participation problems*, and considered already in chapter 1, *Genesis* the advisers to the Plaintiff (Kingaby), in the crucial litigation before 1914 did not apparently recognise or understand the difference in applying the law of restraint of trade in contract, from conspiracy in tort to the professional footballers' retain and transfer contracts which were analogous to a perpetually renewable lease at the employer's discretion — *Kingaby v Aston Villa FC* (supra). The landmark sporting education charity decision in favour of athletics and a fives court at Aldenham School (*Re Mariette* [1915] 2 Ch 284) was propounded by Eve J in line with his former College's contribution to amateur sport, Exeter College, Oxford from its creation of modern competitive athletics in 1850 to the Pegasus triumphs a century later. Outside Australia where the 12 December 1954 bequest to Sydney University Australian Rugby Union Football Club was validated in the New South Wales Equity Court in *Kearins v Kearins* SR (NSW 286) it was also not always followed, recognised or understood by the sporting world until the Charity Commissioners registered the FA Youth Trust Deed in 1972. Thereafter eight years of contested litigation passed before its endorsement and approval by the House of Lords in *IRC v McMullen* ([1981] AC 1). Finally, as we shall see in Chapter 11, *Fair play and reason in court*, even the great and courageous Sir Patrick Hastings, advocate supreme with Norman Birkett, in the inter-war years, and after too, could not find a way to overturn an oppressive FA disciplinary tribunal verdict on the Arsenal Football club chairman, Sir Henry Norris, in the manner which today is utilised by *declaratory judgments* on grounds of denying natural justice as distinct from the at present inapplicable judicial review machinery. Libel was the only relief pursued and more often lost than won, as he experienced on that occasion (*Norris v FA* (1929)) and later in the better known judgments concerning the Pony Turf Club and the Jockey Club, also arising out of the libel claims; respectively *Cookson v Harwood* (1931) [1932] 2 KB 478 and *Chapman v Ellesmere* [1932] 2 KB 431.

Natural justice was not unknown to the courts at that time (see *Maclean v The Workers Union* [1929] 1 Ch 602 at 605); but its applicability to sporting and even more general situations was not recognised as it has become today. Indeed, it was in yet another sporting libel action after the Second World War, again attempting unsuccessfully to attack a sporting disciplinary tribunal (the Jockey Club again: *Russell v Duke of Norfolk* [1949] 1 All ER 109) that Lord Denning MR (at pp 119–220), in what Professor Lowell has called 'a forceful but scarcely cited obiter',

> 'was quietly laying the groundwork for the acceptance of a number of the basic principles behind'

the breaches of natural justice created by the Brighton Watch Committee, and established by the House of Lords' judgment fifteen years later in its police corruption case of *Ridge v Baldwin* [1964] AC 40. This we shall see in Chapter 11, *Fair play and reason in court*.

Concurrently with sport's tentative court appearances after the First World War, two other parallel developments emerged, consistent with a national awareness of the advantages of physical education. As a precedent for R A Butler's Education Act of 1944, before the Second World War ended in 1945, the Education Act 1918 was passed during August, three months prior to the 11 November Armistice Day. Conceived throughout under the guidance of the Minister and eminent educationalist, historian and statesman, H A L Fisher, and consolidated three years later by the Education Act 1921, the legislation extended earlier legislation for public education to include physical and social recreational education at varying levels.

In 1925 the privately-funded National Playing Fields Association was created under the patronage of the then H R H Duke of York, later H M King George VI, a year before he played at Wimbledon; and a letter to Yachting Monthly inspired the first Round Britain Fastnet Rock race.

By the mid-1930s, at a time of developing military nationalism in Europe and mass unemployment, an uneasy awareness was felt of a gap in the nation's physical culture, created by an imbalance when compared with Nazi Germany and Fascist Italy, and a lack of coordination for physical and mental health. Against this background the creative vision and genius of a thirty-year-old physical education teacher, Phyllis Colson, conceived the idea of a nationally coordinated 'umbrella' body of sporting organisations. Thus was born in 1935 the Central Council of Recreative Physical Training (later and now the Central Council of Physical Recreation — the CCPR). A starting gift from private sources covered its initial expenses of £300.

Backed by the then Board of Education (now the Department for Education and Employment), under the patronage of the King (George V) and Queen (Mary), with the Prince of Wales (Edward VIII) as its Vice-Patron, and Lord Astor, its President, its launch was auspicious. And the initial council members included Stanley Rous. The new Jubilee Trust created after 25 years' reign of the present Queen's grandfather contributed £1,000 in February 1936, and a few months later the NPFA added an equal sum and free accommodation.

The Board of Education's parallel involvement became apparent with first a circular in January 1936 encouraging inter alia *Physical Education for Persons no longer attending school*; a Memorandum a year later in January 1937 on *Physical Training and Recreation*, explaining the Government's proposals for the development and extension of the facilities available, and a final enactment, in the first few weeks of Mr Neville Chamberlain's Conservative Party premiership, of the Physical Training and Recreation Act on 13 July 1937. This was the first statute dedicated exclusively and specifically to activities identified in its title (although Public Health legislation since 1875 under Disraeli's Conservative Government had entered into this area fragmentarily). This innovative enactment authorised the then Board of Education to grant aid to voluntary recreation organisations and two years later on the eve of the Second World

War the Social and Physical Training Grant Regulations of 1939 extended it to

'(a) the provision and maintenance of facilities for social and physical training in England or Wales, including payment of leaders, instructors and wardens, and the hiring and equipment of premises;
(b) training of leaders, etc; and
(c) incidental expenses of organisation and administration.'

The war years catalyst carried into battle on the home and service fronts the mixture of voluntary and national service which is the leitmotiv for the mixed economy of today and the keystone for the future funding of leisure and recreation in the community. Sporting rivalries between branches of the armed services and combined services fixtures had been threaded into traditional sporting calendars for decades. In 1938 they were joined by ENSA, the Entertainments National Service Association. In 1939, CEMA, the Council for the Encouragement of Music and Arts, was formed with a mixture of Government and private sources, including the American Pilgrim Trust. When the Pilgrim Trust pulled out in 1942 CEMA's funding became exclusively grant-aided from the then Ministry of Education, alongside the 1937 statutory public funds for Physical and Recreation Training.

Thus the scene was set for the logical pattern which unfolded after the Second World War. In June 1945, a month following the European War's end, CEMA's conversion was approved 'to encourage knowledge, understanding and practice of the arts ... With the name of the Arts Council of Great Britain'. Unfortunately, a decision was made to transfer it from the Education Ministry to the Treasury. From there it was transferred back to the Education portfolio until it became the Office of Arts and Libraries in the 1980s and to-day is linked with Sport and Lotteries within the Department of National Heritage.

The initial grant in 1946–47 was £350,000. The funding of £101m by 1985 was argued by Arts lobbyists to be insufficient; and arguments were fuelled by the uncertain constitutional status in the 1980s of the Minister responsible for its administration with the belief created by the dual roles of *appearing* to be a spending Minister for the Arts and a budgeting Minister linked to Treasury constraints/control until in April 1992, alongside a hotch-potch of other cultural areas, including sport, it was shunted into the Department of National Heritage and in 1997 as a Department of Culture, Media and Sport.

With a Minister covering *all three categories* at the Cabinet table and only Parliamentary Under-Secretaries in both the House of Commons and House of Lords committed collectively to sport with wider heritage areas than those described before the House of Commons Environment Committee as cited at page 96, above (and as appears at the end of this chapter) by the then Sports Minister and his limited areas of activities.

Furthermore, this new Department of Culture Media and Sport and its Minister and civil servants have no *direct* control or jurisdiction over school sport (Department for Education and Employment), planning supervision over playing fields (Department of Environment), sports medicine (Department of Health and Social Security) — the key areas for the future of sport. Thus, the sporting scenario became even more complex than the Arts background, primarily because of any comprehension in Whitehall and Westminster of its true meaning of health and education within the Rule of Law.

The original CCRPT became the CCPR in 1944. In 1957 it appointed a committee under the chairmanship of Sir John Wolfenden to report on the future of sporting administration 'in promoting the general welfare of the community'. In 1958 Parliament passed the Recreational Charities Act to widen the scope of charitable status in a context built-in to its title.

Before the Wolfenden Committee reported in 1960, the Conservative Party's 1959 General Election Manifesto contained a commitment to *The Use of Leisure* specifying:

> 'Measures will be taken to encourage Youth Leadership and the provision of attractive youth clubs, more playing fields, and better facilities for sport'.

The Labour Party's official election booklet, *Leisure for Living*, declared the Party's policy to form a Sports Council within the then Ministry of Education, with an income of £5m to spend.

In 1960 the CCPR's Wolfenden Report ended with 57 paragraphs of Conclusions and Recommendations. They included £5m 'as the amount to be distributed in any one year' by a Sports Development council. Two years later in 1962, a full quarter-of-a-century after the first direct government entry on the playing field and physical recreation and training areas under the 1937 legislation, Lord Hailsham of St Marylebone (*before* his three periods as Lord Chancellor in the 1970s and 1980s) was Minister for Science and Technology in Mr Macmillan's Cabinet. He explained in *The Door Wherein I Went* (at page 207) how he recognised the time had arrived for another leap forward in this crucial area of national activity:

> 'It occurred during a Cabinet Meeting in which government responsibility for Sport was being discussed. It was being said that, properly speaking, responsibility for sport was being shared between quite a number of departments and authorities, education, local government, universities, the services, and all the voluntary bodies dealing with athletics, from the Olympic and Commonwealth Games and League and Cup football at the top, to badminton, fives and even chess at the most refined and esoteric end of the spectrum. I pointed out that recreation generally presented a complex of problems out of which modern government was not wholly free to opt, and which government funds were, in fact, and were likely to continue to be,

committed in one way or another in coaching, in the provision of playing-fields, in matters of safety at racecourses and football grounds. I waxed eloquent on this subject, talking of the fares for Olympic competitors and many other topics. I suggested that there was need, not for a Ministry but for a focal point under a Minister, for a coherent body of doctrine, perhaps even a philosophy of government encouragement,"

and concluded

'This particular activity was a minor matter, and I thought comparatively little of it at the time since it occurred at a period when other things were occupying my mind [as a Cabinet Minister]'.

Belief that 'This particular activity was a minor matter' was, in the context of traditional Whitehall and Westminster thinking, then, as well as now, understandable.

The first ever Wembley FA Cup Final stadium crowd overflow was in 1923 where an estimated crowd of 125,000 gathered at a stadium equipped for 93,000. A government enquiry was established as there were 1,000 casualties but thankfully no fatalities. Its report (Cmd 2088) in 1924 recommended a stadium licensing system and fire precautions. Nothing happened not surprisingly, because the later 1946 Moelwyn Hughes Bolton Report explained as cited above the FA 'had not deigned to appear before the Committee'. After 33 were crushed to death in a crowd overflow in 1946 during the Bolton Wanderers versus Stoke City FA Cup-tie a further government report made similar recommendations (Cmd 6846). Again nothing happened, notwithstanding the 'fast track' Report produced on 25 May 1946 within two and a half months after the 11 March 1946 tragedy.

During the later 1960s an experienced and perceptive journalist, the late J L Manning, son of an equally respected Fleet Street practitioner Lionel Manning, warned vigorously in the Daily Mail that no legal liability protected crowd safety positively. Nothing happened apart from ridicule. Then came Ibrox in 1971, with 66 deaths; another report in 1972 (Cmnd 4952), and at last something did happen: a Highway Code-styled Green Guide in 1973 without legal effect but with common-sense recommendations for stadia safety and the Safety of Sports Grounds Act 1975 with limited provisions confined to First and Second Division Football League Clubs, Wembley Stadium and Murrayfield, Edinburgh, followed by progressive developments after the Fire Safety and Safety of Place of Sport Act 1987 after the Bradford City fire disaster of 1985.

Contemporaneously with the above inactivity on the safety scene, Lord Hailsham's concept took shape administratively. After the 1964 General Election and a change of Government, the Sports Ministry portfolio was handed to a former Football League referee, subsequently the Rt Hon Lord Howell of Aston. He was appointed initially as a junior under-secretary at the Department of Education and Science (with responsibility for sport). After his reappointment two years later in 1966 following his Party's further General Election success, and before the arrival in 1970 of Mr Heath's Government, he was promoted to the role of Minister of State at the Ministry of Housing and Local Government, taking that responsibility for sport with him to a different department.

A four-year period as Opposition Spokesman for Local Government and Sport preceded his return to office in February 1974 for a further five-year period until 1979. On that occasion as Minister of State at the Department of the Environment, he had responsibilities to sport and recreation as well as the countryside, environmental policy, water resources and the Property Services Agency.

Denis Howell thereby held the sports ministry portfolio for a cumulative period of eleven years, a longer span than that experienced by any other occupant of this nationally important but constitutionally junior government role. Indeed, those eleven years are only six short of the collective tenure of all other seventeen holders of the office in the twenty years period since the start of Mrs Thatcher's first Government in 1979. Significantly, his generous and friendly public advice given in the *Independent* newspaper (20 June 1987) after the General Election of 1987 to the seventh and youngest appointee, Colin Moynihan MP, a former Olympic Games rowing cox, included the following warning note:

'The problems ahead are formidable and deepening. He will need to find resources as yet untapped if he is to steer the nation through seas quite unlike the calm waters in which he is used to coxing his boat ... On the international political stage, cricket and rugby will demand more of his time than the 20 per cent allocated by his predecessor to the whole of his portfolio'.

Domestically Denis Howell was responsible during his first ministerial period for implementing the Wolfenden Report's recommendations in 1960 to create a Sports Council by establishing an advisory Sports Council in 1965, of which he became chairman. This occurred prior to the grant of a Royal Charter in 1971 (when his immediate successor, then Eldon Griffiths MP, occupied the ministerial chair) to what became the executive Sports Council.

1972 witnessed not only the transition of Phyllis Colson's 1935 CCPR creation as a collective focal point for the governance of British sport to the Sport's Council for England. Sports Councils for Scotland, Wales and Northern Ireland were structured concurrently with Royal Charters and linked to their respective government offices for funding. Each of the other three home countries retains its equivalent to the CCPR separate from its national Sports Council.

The hard core legal basis for that transition was a contract signed in 1972 under the title of Heads of Agreement by the representatives of the Sports Councils and the CCPR. It was reaffirmed in January 1985 by a document headed Memorandum Agreement produced in evidence to and published in an appendix (No 5, pages 117–118) by a House of Commons Environment Committee Report on the Sports Council and its associated public bodies in early 1986 (HC 241). The contract guaranteed the funding by the Sports Council of the CCPR, which was restructured. The Sports Council inherited from the original CCPR its valuable assets, including its properties, journal, the priceless experience of its professional staffs, and the charitable trusts for administering the National Recreational Centres on land and water.

The Sports Council's prime objectives, as summarised in the House of Commons Committee's Report (para 15, page x):

'as set out in its Royal Charter, are to encourage mass participation in sport and to promote excellence in sporting achievement. Clearly these aims are interlocked. The greater the number of people participating in sport the more chance there is of excellence emerging. The higher the achievements of the top performers, the greater the number of those who will be inspired to emulate them'.

In 1972 the CCPR was restructured, with HRH the Duke of Edinburgh continuing in office as an active President. A new Central Committee elected Denis Howell as its Chairman in 1973, where he stayed until his reappointment as Minister in 1974. Its present role and objectives were summarised in a written Memorandum of evidence to the House of Commons Committee by its then General Secretary, Peter Lawson, thus:

(1) to constitute a standing forum of national governing and representative bodies;
(2) to support the work of the specialist sports bodies and to bring them together with other interested organisations; and
(3) to act as a consultative body to the Sports Council.

This last function was illustrated vividly on two occasions in the years immediately before the House of Commons Committee's Report. Both linked the Sports Council directly, yet were ignored by the Committee's Report. One was contained in the Sports Council's written evidence, the other forms the CCPR's oral testimony.

The written Memorandum of evidence from the Sports Council (pages 81–82) generously acknowledged and adopted the CCPR's proposal in its Paragraph 33:

'that a non-profit distributing body having the purpose of developing and controlling a sport or recreation activity for the public benefit should enjoy tax exemption'.

This issue is considered further at Chapter 14, *No fine on fun*.

In 1981 the CCPR established its own Committee of Enquiry into Sports Sponsorship under the chairmanship of Denis Howell. Its members included the Sports Council's then Director General, John Wheatley, and the subsequent Sports Minister, Colin Moynihan MP. Its report, published as The Howell Report in November 1983 contained 73 Conclusions and Recommendations. These compared consistently with the 77 conclusions and recommendations from a House of Commons Education, Science and Arts Committee Report published a year earlier in October 1982 on the Public and Private Funding of the Arts, (1982 HC 49–1, Ch XIII; pp cxxic–cxxix). They each contrast sharply with the mere nine conclusions and recommendations of the House of Commons Environment Committee on the Sports Council and its associated public bodies (1986 HC 241, Ch 3 pp xxix–xxx).

The then Government's Response published in July 1986 to the House of Commons Committee's Sports Council Report (HC 504) recognised in the context of

'the efficient structure of sport ... some overlapping functions between the Sports Council and the Central Council for [sic] Physical Recreation (CCPR) and with the other main sporting agencies, such as the British Olympic Association and the Sports Aid Foundation. As the Committee found, the structure of sport is a crowded one, having developed over the last century and relying now, for the most part, on long-held traditions and customs'.

Reliance was also placed heavily on public as well as private funds in the manner experienced by the Arts. Before 1971, as the CCPR Memorandum to the House of Commons Committee explained (page 34, Question 1):

'the majority of public funds allocated for sports purposes were dispersed by the Department of Education and Science, largely through the CCPR'.

Its continued funding is sustained by the 1972 Heads of Agreement, alongside sponsorship and subscription sources from its constituent governing body members, approximately 300. The Heads of Agreement were negotiated at arm's length at the time of the 1972 reorganisation of the CCPR and have been the subject of almost continuous contention since then.

The Government's Response also welcomed the House of Commons Committee's endorsement:

'of DOE funding for sport, of the role of the Sports Council and of the division of responsibilities between the Government and its sponsored body'.

ie the Sport's Council. The extent of that funding can be seen in the contrasts between the time of the Royal Charter in 1971 and the date of that Government Response, in July 1986.

In 1971 the initial allocation of Government funds to the Sports Council was £3m. By 1985 it had grown to £30m. Underpinning it at that date in 1985 was a sponsorship source attributed to well over £100m a year. Furthermore, during early 1986 the campaign by Birmingham City Council for the 1992 Olympic Games was underwritten by a Government guarantee for any financial shortfall and in due course the bid by Manchester received comparable support. This publicly funded intervention was separate and apart from a continuing complaint of payment of corporation tax and VAT by non-profit-making organisations such as the British Olympic Association. Only pressure from the Central Council of Physical Recreation and a Kent County Playing Fields senior member who had been associated with the European Commission, Ernest Virgo, and advice from Andrew Park QC, resulted in exposing HM Customs and Excise breaches of EC Directives leading to the Treasury's intention ultimately to exempt from VAT certain non-profit-making organisations and local authorities concerned with sport and physical recreation (see also Chapter 14, *No fine on fun*).

The emergence of central government in sporting recreation fields reached its climax with Prime Ministerial, Home Office and judicial intervention in 1985 after the football crowd tragedies of that year. In 1976, the emerging professional and differing bodies of Recreation Management resulted in a Department of the Environment Committee which took eight years to gestate all relevant facts. The Department published its Final Report in early 1984. A few months earlier in 1983, a discussion paper on behalf of all government agencies concerned with sporting recreation and leisure activities under the title of the Chairman's Policy Group published its *Leisure Policy for the Future*, under the chairmanship of the Sports Council's Chairman, Mr Dick Jeeps CBE.

Each of these publicly funded publications purported to identify the areas of government involvement with leisure services. The corroborative evidence which identifies the complexity of government involvement is graphically illustrated at the end of this chapter. During the early 1990s a new Government department with the title of Department of National

Heritage was created after the General Election of 1992, (followed by the re-titled Department of Culture Media and Sport in 1997). Within the period of hardly more than two years which have passed before the date of publication of this edition no less than five different Government Ministers have been allocated the portfolio for the Minister with Responsibility for Sport as the citations at the end of this chapter demonstrate. Even within the heterogeneous conglomerate of the Department of Culture, Media and Sport, the Sport and Recreation division (SARD) is merely part of a Sport Tourism and Millennium Group, alongside fourteen other Government Departments concerned with Sport.

Against this background it can be seen how sport and recreation and leisure have travelled in space and substance since the Minister for Science and Education in 1962, Viscount Hailsham, thought 'that recreation generally presented a complex of problems out of which government was not wholly free to opt'. The range of that complexity will emerge from the pages which follow, both in the private and public sector in addition to what must have become apparent on even a superficial reading of the text so far.

Chapter 5, *Public protection*, demonstrates the urgency with which Parliament has reacted in 1985 and 1986 and the later 1980s and early 1990s to the consequences of successive parliamentary failures since 1924 to activate methods for crowd safety, apart from the relatively ineffectual interludes with the then Green Guide of 1973 and the halfhearted Safety of Sports Grounds Act 1975. By limiting its implementation to First and Second Division Football League grounds and national stadiums, it demonstrated a total unawareness of and disregard for the system of promotion and relegation that has operated throughout the Football League since the Second Division was added in 1890 to the First Division created in 1888.

The promotion of Bradford City in May 1985 from the Third Division to the Second Division meant that forty-eight hours after its disastrous fire, its ground would have come under starter's orders for the safety provisions of the 1975 enactment. Knowledge of fluctuating sporting fortunes commonly known to the general public for promotion and relegation issues may possibly have escaped the attention of Whitehall and Westminster. The legislation, however, was Home Office responsibility. The Minister with responsibility for Sport had no concern constitutionally or legislatively with its innovation or implementation. If the 1975 Act had provided for *all* Football League Clubs to be designated and licensed, the Bradford City tragedy might have been more likely to be avoided (ie subject to correct procedures being followed), and a more heightened awareness of safety requirements might have prevented the Hillsborough disaster of 1989 or mitigated the quantity of fatalities and injuries.

Thus, nearly forty years after Lord Hailsham conceived the idea of a 'focal point under a Minister, for a coherent body of doctrine, perhaps even a philosophy of government encouragement,' the question must now be asked: 'Is a further leap forward now required by the mere pressure of events?' It must be asked, whatever may be the personal thoughts of the mandarins at Whitehall and Westminster who would never know the difference between a Gentleman and Player or distinguish a Corinthian from a Harlequin, or comprehend how sport has progressed within the changing perspective of the last four decades. They appear to be unaware of the enlightened five overseas Governments which have taken on board Lord Hailsham's vision and elevated their Ministers for Sport to the Cabinet table, three of whom are women:

Canada:	Sheila Cobbs, Minister for Canada Heritage
France:	Marie-Georges Buffet, Minister for Youth and Sport
Jamaica:	Portia Simpson-Miller Ministry of Labour, Social Security and Sport
New Zealand:	Hon Murray McCully Minister for Sport Fitness and Leisure,
South Africa:	Steve Tshwete Minister for Sport and Recreation.

The manner in which the constitutional role and status of the erroneously named Sports Minister in the United Kingdom has fluctuated since it was created is seen from the list and departmental duties of the incumbents, to date, below, at the end of this chapter. It is updated from its position in the previous 1994 edition. The list of Government Departments has been transposed from the Appendices.

Indeed, no greater indictment of the current chaos which pervades Whitehall and Westminster's lack of a comprehensive and intelligent approach to sport and recreation has appeared than the facts known throughout the sporting world which surfaced for the enlightenment of the general public in the report prepared under section 6 of the National Audit Act 1983 for presentation to the House of Commons in accordance with section 9, and dated 23 December 1993 (although not published until 14 January 1994; HMSO 131), from the Comptroller and Auditor General, Sir John Bourn, while the second edition was in its last stage of preparation. The report, entitled *The Sports Council: Initiatives to improve Financial Management and Control and Value for Money*, states in paragraph 1.7, under the heading 'Restructuring of the Sports Council',

'In November 1991 the Government issued a document, Sport and Active Recreation, which set out their policies and priorities for sport. These included the restructuring of the council into a Sports Council for England and a United Kingdom Sports Commission. During the course of the National Audit Office's examination the Government announced that it no longer intended to proceed with the planned restructuring. Instead, fresh arrangements were to be considered to ensure a United Kingdom dimension for sport. Following on from this, the activities and general structure of the Council will also be reviewed.'

Seven months later on 8 July 1994 the then Under-Secretary of State for the Department of National Heritage, Iain Sproat MP, announced the establishment in the next financial year of a new United Kingdom Sports Council, separate from the Sports Councils for Scotland, Wales and Northern Ireland. The detailed mechanism which developed must be questioned in the light of the number of *seven* Government Ministers holding the portfolio of the Minister with the responsibility for Sport between 1992 and 1994, and also of the valuable cameo and insight into the dead hand of Government inaction which comes from one of the most unlikely of true sporting sources. Jemima Parry-Jones is a director of the National Birds of Prey Centre in Newent, Gloucestershire, and the daughter of Philip Glasier, one of the best-known falconers and author of a recognised classic in its field, *Falconry and Hawking*. Jemima Parry-Jones' own *Falconry: Care, Captive Breeding and Conservation* (1981) explains in relation to DoE inspections under the Wildlife and Countryside Act 1981, at page 179,

'Sadly the government system for running the Civil Service in general is now very outdated. It seems that as soon as someone in any governmental department gets to know and understand the system they promptly get moved to a different job and department [NB see list of junior Ministers, below]. Any business that was run in this way would be bankrupt very quickly. But this is the way the system works at the moment and so it has to be accepted'.

If Lord Hailsham's 1962 conception had existed in responsible form and structure from the time of the 1924 Wembley Stadium Committee Report's recommendation ignored for 50 years until the Safety of Sports Grounds Act in 1975 for a stadium licensing system and fire precautions, would 33 spectators have died at Bolton in 1946, 66 and Ibrox in 1971, 59 at Bradford and one schoolboy at Birmingham in 1985, and 95 at Hillsborough, Sheffield in 1989, apart from the thousands of others injured and bereaved during the same period? Parliamentarians and their acolytes who savour the flavour of hospitality tents and boxes at sporting events may ponder the question and answer during their next refreshment interval. Alternatively they may care to wait until they have read Chapter 5, *Public protection*.

COMPLETE LIST OF MINISTERS WITH RESPONSIBILITY FOR SPORT TO DATE (AS AT NOVEMBER 1999)

Minister	*Period*	*Constitutional status*
Rt Hon Viscount Hailsham	1962–1964	Minister with special responsibility for sport (1959–64; Minister for Science and Technology)
Rt Hon Lord Howell MP	1964–1969	Joint parliamentary under-secretary of State, Dept of Education and Science (with responsibility for sport)
	1969–1970	Minister of State, Ministry of Housing and Local Govt (with responsibility for sport)
Sir Eldon Griffiths MP	1970–1974	Parliamentary under-secretary of State, DoE Minister for Sport
Rt Hon Lord Howell of Aston Manor	1974–1979	Minister of State, DoE (responsibility for environment, water resources and sport)
Sir Hector Monro AE, JP, DL, MP	1979–1981	Parliamentary under-secretary of State, DoE (with special responsibility for sport)
Sir Neil MacFarlane MP	1981–1985	Parliamentary under-secretary of State, DoE (with special responsibility for sport for children's play, 1983–1985)
Richard Tracey JP, MP	1985–1987	Parliamentary under-secretary of State, DoE (with special responsibility for sport)
Hon Colin (now Lord) Moynihan MP	1987–1990	Parliamentary under-secretary, DoE (with qualified responsibility for sport)

Minister	Period	Constitutional status
Sir David Trippier RD, JP, MP	1987–1989	Parliamentary under-secretary, DoE (for Inner Cities and Urban Development with urban development grant-aided responsibility for sport)
Robert Atkins MP	1990–1992	Parliamentary under-secretary for State
Rt Hon David Mellor QC, MP	1993–1994	Secretary of State for National Heritage with responsibility inter alia for sport
Peter Brooke MP	1993–1994	
Rt Hon Stephen Dorrell MP	1994–	
Robert Key MP	1992–1993	Parliamentary under-secretary DNH
Ian Sproate MP	1993–	
Viscount Astor	1994–	
Ian Sproate MP	1995–1997	Minister of State DHH with responsibility for sport
Lord Inglewood	1995–1997	Parliamentary under-secretary DHH
Tony Banks MP	1997–1999	Parliamentary under secretary Culture Media and Sport
Kate Hoey MP	1999–	Parliamentary under secretary Culture Media and Sport
Lord McIntosh	1997–	Parliamentary under secretary Culture Media and Sport

GOVERNMENT DEPARTMENTS RELEVANT TO SPORT AND THE LAW EXCLUDING DEPARTMENT OF CULTURE, MEDIA AND SPORT

1	Attorney-General's Office	Crown Prosecution Service and appellate right against lenient sentences for criminally violent foul play
2	Ministry of Agriculture and Fisheries	Sport and recreation on agricultural and recreation land
3	Department for Education and Employment	School sport and physical education at local and higher education authorities
4	Department of Environment	Planning permission for school and physical recreation playing facilities
5	Department of Health and Social Security	Health and fitness through sport and physical education
6	Foreign and Commonwealth Office	Overseas issues including diplomatic associations
7	Home Office	Law and order, police powers and charities
8	Lord Chancellor's Department	Law Commission and Consultation Papers on public order and consent to criminal violence in sport
9	Department of Trade and Industry	Health and Safety Executive, health and safety legislation
10	Department of Transport	Transport and traffic in relation to sporting events
11	Treasury	Inland Revenue and VAT in relation to sport and recreation
12	Welsh Office [Parliament]	Local issues affecting Principality
13	Scottish Office [Parliament]	All matters affecting Scotland
14	Northern Ireland Office	All matters affecting Northern Ireland

ORGANISATION OF THE DEPARTMENT OF CULTURE, MEDIA AND SPORT FROM CIVIL SERVICE YEARBOOK 1998/99, AS AMENDED BY GOVERNMENT 1999

Secretary of State (1977)
Rt. Hon. Christopher Smith, PhD, MP

Special Advisors

Minister of State

Parliamentary Under Secretary of State

Historic Royal Palace Agency

Royal Parks Agency

Arts, Buildings & Creative Industries Group
Arts * Creative Industries * Buildings

Libraries, Galleries, Museums & GAC Group
Museums & Galleries * Cultural Property Unit * Libraries * GAC

Broadcasting & Media Group
Broadcasting * Media

Sports Tourism & Millennium Group
Sports * Tourism * Millennium

NLCB Section

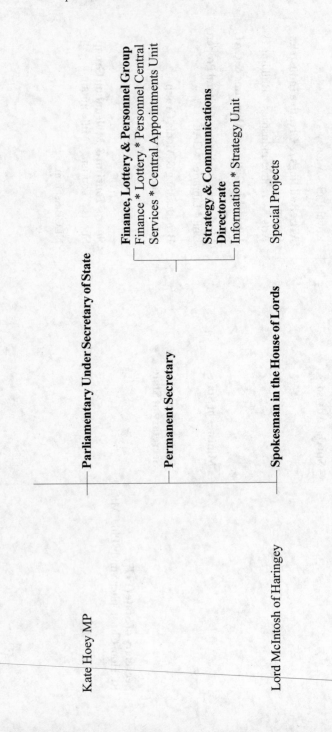

Kate Hoey MP

Parliamentary Under Secretary of State

Permanent Secretary

Finance, Lottery & Personnel Group
Finance * Lottery * Personnel Central
Services * Central Appointments Unit

**Strategy & Communications
Directorate**
Information * Strategy Unit

Special Projects

Lord McIntosh of Haringey

Spokesman in the House of Lords

SPORT & RECREATION DIVISION

Sport and recreation policy, sport for all, sponsorship of UK and English Sports Council, and Football Licensing Authority, Safety of sports grounds. Local authority and business sponsorship of sport. International matters.

Head of Division (Grade SCS)
S Broadley
Telephone: 0171-211 6078
GTN 211 6078
Fax: 0171-211 6149

SARD A
Sponsorship of the UK and English Sports Councils, National Lottery (sports aspects). PES co-ordination for sport. British Sports Forum/CCPR issues. Honours, Sports for Women, British Chess Federation.

Enquiries: 0171-211 6097
GTN 211 6097

Grade A(L)
G Holmes

Telephone: 0171-211 6093
GTN 211 6093
Fax: 0171-211 6149

SARD B
Sport: Youth Sports Unit; UK Sports Institute; Governing Body issues; International Matters; Drug abuse in Sport; Sport for People with Disabilities; Children's play.

Enquiries: 0171-211 6094
GTN 211 6094

Grade A(L)
S Ball
Telephone: 0171-211 6091
GTN 211 6091
Fax: 0171-211 6149

SARD C

Sports Ground Safety, Football Licensing Authority, Football Trust, Sports Ground Initiative, Football Policy Sportsmatch, Sports Sponsorship, Sports Broadcasting Rights, Local Authority issues, Playing Fields, Facility Provision Funding, Lottery Revenue Grants.

Enquiries: 0171-211 6075
GTN 211 6075

Grade A(L)
C Jones
Telephone: 0171-211 6086
GTN 211 6086
Fax: 0171-211 6149

NATIONAL LOTTERY CHARITIES BOARD & NEW OPPORTUNITIES FUND UNIT

Issues concerning sponsorship of the National Lottery Charities Board; establishment and sponsorship of the New Opportunities Fund; and Departmental Liaison for the Voluntary Sector.

Enquiries: 0171-211 6372
GTN 211 6372
Fax: 0171-211 6330

Head of Section (Grade A)
Mrs V Brand
Telephone: 0171-211 6371
GTN 211 6371

CHAPTER 3

Under Starter's Orders

INTRODUCTION

My response on behalf of the practising Bar of England and Wales to the invitation by Maurice Watkins, the solicitor director of Manchester United and Dr Ray Farrell of Manchester Metropolitan University to become Founder President of a British Association for Sport and Law on 6 February 1993, occurred symbolically on the 35th anniversary of the Manchester United Munich Airport disaster. It recalled inevitably the extended sensational conflict of legal liability between ice on the wings or slush on the runway dragging on for years. In turn it illuminates the starting point for understanding how complexities of *evidence* and conflicting interests on that occasion, between pilot or airport responsibilities, focused the simple legal issue, made difficult by the facts: where did the fault lie?

The absence of reported contested litigation relating to the tragedy does not detract from recognising and understanding how in those circumstances *Sport* and the *Law* merge with and interact upon each other. Also around that period of the Association's creation in 1993 the great Grand National Steeplechase starting tape fiasco, following the alleged tampered cricket ball imbroglio after the England versus Pakistan Texaco Trophy match at Lords in 1992, further illustrate the point. Independently each occasion with its international repercussions created a potential minefield for legal issues. The Grand National for negligence and/or breach of contract for any financial damage suffered from the loss of an indefinable period of preparation and training to attain peak level fitness for horse and rider on the great day; the Lord's Texaco Trophy Match ball accusations for defamation proceedings in London's High Court and revelations of alleged cheating by unfair and illegal ball-tampering, during the libel action *Nawaz v Lamb* ((1993) *Times*, 16–19 November). Since then, all on the same day in July 1999 while these pages were in preparation Bruce Grobbelaar's successful libel action against the *Sun* newspaper for alleged match fixing consistent with the Premier Football League's successful defence in London's High Court against the Office of Fair Trading, and Douglas Walker's clearance of drug offences by the decision of a Tribunal chaired by a QC after an earlier preliminary Tribunal had adjudicated and *publicly announced* that a prima facie case had been established. In the light of the uncertain pharmacological state of play at that time, justice, fair play and wisdom might have pointed to a deferment of such an interim announcement.

What may not be easily recognisable by the inexperienced practitioner and a superficial commentator is how the two disciplines of Sport and the Law demand different levels of understanding by lawyer and layman alike, and they differ in proportion to the different levels of involvement required by each of them. Therefore this chapter serves as an overview for all those who may not comprehend how the law intertwines with sport. It gives a bird's eye view of the subject as a whole and introduces the non-legal reader to some of the many overlapping issues as examples of what is often not recognised as a labyrinthine network of interlocking elements.

In sport, players are expected to know and play according to the Laws, penalties and sanctions for their enforcement of each game within which their performances occur. All participants, from coaches and trainers to doctors and physiotherapists within and without a commercially orientated competitive climate, are progressively required to recognise the demands of drug control and testing, together with the regulatory limitations upon personal medication. Administrators need to know the different legal categories applicable to their particular spheres of action. Secretaries should possess an awareness of the whole spectrum affecting their duties with the necessity to seek specialist advice whether exemplified by a simple sponsorship or insurance contract or a planning application, to name but a few; treasurers should have at least some basic familiarity with taxation and VAT and easy accessibility to specialist accountancy services relating to particular requirements. Finally, all lawyers concerned with legal practice in this minefield area, solicitors, counsel and judges, should also be expected to have an understanding of the available substantive law, and evidence and procedure applicable to the appropriate circumstances in issue in addition to the sporting subtleties and techniques, such as expert evidence relating to a particular situation. Profound experiences and precedent prove that this ideal is not always achieved, as these pages illustrate.

Transcending all such self-evident categories is the often overlooked or forgotten reality that the overwhelming majority of public and private domestic and international sporting controlling and governing bodies are part-time operators, some with a love for sport itself, others on an ego trip for self-aggrandisement, separate and apart from a full-time secretariat. Thus the Jockey Club and Aintree Racecourse authorities had ignored earlier warnings about the inherent defects in a flag-waving hand-start elastic tape control for initiating effectively the world's oldest and most celebrated steeplechase before a global television audience at a time when Wimbledon's All England Lawn Tennis and Croquet Club had progressed to electronic line out machines and the electronic eye had arrived to assist the cricket adjudication of the third umpire. Correspondingly, the suspect tampered Texaco Trophy Match cricket ball remained under lock and key at Lord's cricket ground without any attempt by the International Cricket Conference to allay the apprehensions in the public mind about the extent or prevalence of the practice in issue.

At Law, the procedural precedent blockage from a ten year-old Court of Appeal decision in *Law v National Greyhound Racing Club Ltd* [1983] 3 All ER 300 unseated the attempt by the Aga Khan's legal advisers to challenge the Jockey Club's disqualification on a disputed drug testing process of his filly Alysa's 1989 Epsom Oaks triumph, by the inapplicable judicial review route, instead of by breach of contract, explained in more detail in the pages of the Introduction and in the Judicial Review Appendix 14. Correspondingly the Football Association's Chief Executive at the time was allowed unchallenged by prosecuting Counsel and the trial Judge, to give arguably inadmissible and rebuttable evidence on the basis of his lack of expert knowledge of the technical issues relating to coaching and refereeing expertise involved in a criminal prosecution for grievous bodily harm, allegedly caused by an acquitted professional footballer against another in a criminal trial at Salisbury Crown Court, as criticised by me in various* legal sources† before the Introduction in this text (*R v Blissett* (1992); *Times*, 5 December).

Each of these examples illustrates the words of wisdom one of Britain's most revered jurists, F W Maitland, when he began his celebrated Lectures under the head of Dissertations:

'Let us remember one of Maine's most striking phrases: 'So great is the ascendancy of the Law of Actions in the infancy of Courts of Justice, that substantive law has at first the look of being gradually secreted in the intersteces of procedure'.

The constructive analysis of the Judicial Review procedural machinery prepared by Catherine Bond for what was originally Appendix 9 [now 14] in the 2nd 1994 edition demonstrates how this operates. Anyone wishing

---

*   *New Law Journal* 15 January 1993; *Solicitor's Journal* 2 July 1993.
†   *Legal Executive* July 1993; *All England Law Reports Annual Review 1992* (published 1993).

to explore 'substantive law' in greater detail than the limitations of space which these pages permits, for which a level of awareness alone has been attempted here, should refer to the 52 volumes of *Halsbury's Laws of England*. Each one contains material applicable to Sport and the Law.

Concurrently with Maitland's quotation from Maine is Lord Denning's favourite citation from Scotland's most celebrated legal chronicler and renowned historical novelist who was also a Writer to the Signet, Sir Walter Scott. He created for one his best known characters Counsellor Playdell in *Guy Mannering* the oft-recalled words:

> 'A lawyer without history or literature is a mechanic, a mere working mason; if he possesses some knowledge of these, he may venture to call himself an architect'.

2   HISTORICAL BACKGROUND

Against that background the manner in which Sport and the Law combine today is the result of the off-field story of post-Second World War public and professional British sport. One of persistent and sustained erosion of feudal controls by sporting governing bodies over their members evidenced by the table set out at the end of Chapter 11 at pages 415–417. Indeed, when Parker LJ more than a decade ago confirmed the plaintiff tennis player Ian Currie's right to pursue his appeal against Essex County Lawn Tennis Association, he explained, 'This is a developing area of the law' (*Currie v Barton and Rippon* (1987) *Times*, 29 July, p 42).

That erosion of feudalism for *public and professional sport* was spearheaded initially after the Second World War by James Guthrie's and later Jimmy Hill's politico-legal campaigns to emancipate professional footballers from their roles as the 'last bonded men in Britain', followed by Florence Nagle's successful challenge in the courts to the Jockey Club's refusal to grant racehorse trainers' licences to women in their own names.

Their ultimate triumphs created a better balance between the governance of public and professional British participants by their administrative controllers and their comparable social position in the world outside, beyond committee rooms and council chambers, as we shall see in Chapter 6, *Participation problems*. If the imagination, resourcefulness and will demonstrated by effective pioneers such as Guthrie, Hill and Nagle had been used more frequently to challenge 'decisions by the regulating bodies' (a judicially critical phase) before and after the Second World War, British sport's general development after it would not have been retarded in the manner exposed by comparisons in the international scene, especially in the high profile and publicised areas evidenced by cricket, rugby, soccer and lawn tennis.

Indeed, as we shall see in Chapter 4, *Parent, school and club partners*, parents and other guardians of children, sporting and physical education interests can rely upon Parliamentary and charity law, as a last resort, to challenge the decisions of local authorities, school governors and teaching staff if appropriate circumstances permit. In this way they can overturn obstructive and socially divisive decisions by sources which dispute the traditional existence of competitive games and playing fields to accommodate them. If the correct law is invoked to protect sport and its wider realm of physical education at this level then British sporting talent domestically and internationally will be in a position for the first time to realise its full potential, at present denied through a mixture of parental or general unawareness and obstructive socio-political attitudes alien to the nation's true sporting spirit and heritage.

For just as medicine demands doctors trained and experienced in their own disciplines for patients to be treated skilfully when they need and seek advice, so, too, does sport need the law to fill the gaps which sport itself cannot reach. Furthermore, sport needs an awareness in all cases to recognise when such a need arises, both at Parliamentary and litigation levels.

Judicial decisions have demonstrated an unawareness among lawyers and people in sport of the extent to which the law can help sport to benefit itself and the community it serves. In the years which have witnessed sport's explosion at the public level since the Second World War, planning and property, personal injuries, professional players' benefits and testimonials, charities, contracts, crimes, torts and tribunals have all illuminated this position through diverse and debatable judicial verdicts. Each of these conventional legal topics can create its own jurisprudential problems for practitioners without bedevilment by the imp which lurks within so many sporting contests out of court to create for litigation lawyers what is so well known as 'the glorious uncertainty of the game'. When this spills over into the legal arena, the consequences can be expensive and far-reaching not only for individuals and sporting organisations, but for society in general.

Examples will leap out from every chapter which follows. The extent to which they have accumulated during the last thirty or so years suggests that while tradition has preserved the conventional custom that sport is a relaxation and recreation from more pressing and heavily committed affairs of the day, it has often ignored or been totally unaware of the gravity of the burdens which have developed progressively while sport is obliged to fit into a general legal framework.

Within the last forty years the most popular of sporting activities in the United Kingdom have publicly or within the professional knowledge of the legal profession manifested the need to resolve differences of opinion among sporting administrators and their advisers and lawyers to a degree which demonstrates the need for that clear-cut awareness and understanding of the available substantive law, evidence and procedure applicable to the appropriate circumstances in issue.

This pattern of unawareness can be traced at the end of the Introduction in Part 5: 40 years on 1959–1999 in the outline of 251 years *In the Courts and Parliament*. It explains within the standard or level of burden of proof required for criminal trials, to a degree of satisfaction so that the reader or a jury can be sure, or sure beyond reasonable doubt, how the needs of society in the amoral climate of the last two decades of the twentieth century demand sport and the law, and the law and sport, to cooperate more effectively and efficiently than might be indicated by errors from the past that occurred through lack of care, thought and understanding of the evidential elements involved.

The categories which follow and are listed here were selected arbitrarily for the first-Butterworth edition in 1988 for a chapter headed '*Why Sport and the Law?*' when the need to justify their existence appeared necessary. That argument has never disappeared but the topics were retained for the second edition in 1994, and have been preserved here for two clear-cut reasons. For they illustrate (1) comprehensively and (2) separately (apart from individually applicable areas as taxation and VAT considered in Chapter 14 *No Fine on Fun*) areas which are most likely to affect the greatest number of participators within the 113 activities listed on Page 1 of the Preface.

Lord Denning flashed an oblique light on a generally unidentified problem area in the more recent of the two leading cricket-ball-out-of-the-ground cases from Linz in County Durham (*Miller v Jackson* [1977] 1 QB 966); (the Cheetham Cricket Club ground at Manchester providing the other sixteen years earlier (*Bolton v Stone* [1951] AC 850)). The ultimate decision considered in detail in Chapter 5, *Public protection* (infra at pages 117–122), was not relied upon in a later Court of Appeal verdict relating to noise nuisance from water-ski activities (*Kennaway v Thompson* [1980] 3 All ER 329). For present purposes, however, Lord Denning illuminated the existing lacunae in many minds and experiences more subtly than the clear-cut examples which follow here with an expression of surprise that opposition had not existed to a planning application (the arm of law which was flexed to block the asset stripping attempt on Fulham Football Club's Craven Cottage ground development scheme for residential accommodation in early 1987). For ease of reading in an ascending order of judicial and sporting complexities they will be illustrated in the following sequence. These examples are wide-ranging and apparently unconnected. The thread that runs through them is the subject of Sport and Law.

(1)   planning and property (Lord Denning's citation);
(2)   amateur rugby regulations (Court of Appeal);
(3)   crime (Newport Crown Court);
(4)   contract (High Court);

(5)   benefits (House of Lords);
(6)   charities and rating (House of Lords);
(7)   race relations and politics (House of Lords);
(8)   tribunals (High Court);
(9)   personal injuries (Court of Appeal);
(10) evidence (Court of Appeal);
(11) facts (Committee on Legal Education, House of Lords);
(12) Parliament.

Furthermore, as will be seen, in three instances (ie professional footballers' contracts, professional footballers' benefits, and charitable educational sporting trusts) the development of sport in general was retarded for respectively fifty, thirty and forty years because of inadequate and ill-considered applications or non-applications of the law to sport to an extent which would have changed the face and fate of British sport today if it had been properly served, as it clearly was not, by its administrators or by the advice they received; and in each of the above categories differences of judicial impressions required variations of earlier judgments by appellate courts, which might have been denied the opportunity for assessment if trapped by the flawed assumption of judicial infallibility built into the Denial of Justice explained earlier in the Preface through publication of the present Government's *Monitoring Justice*.

1   Planning and property

Miller v Jackson (supra) was a householder's civil claim against an adjoining local cricket club that cricket balls hit out of the ground created a physical and legal nuisance. A local High Court judge on circuit in his discretion granted an injunction. The Court of Appeal discharged it and approved in substitution an agreed amount of £400 damages for nuisance. The reasoning and also the result were not followed three years later by another Court of Appeal in a water-ski noise-nuisance case (*Kennaway v Thompson*, supra and infra, and in Chapter 5, *Public protection* at p 217). On that later occasion a £15,000 damages awarded by the circuit High Court judge was replaced by an injunction in qualified terms.

The significant subtlety commented upon by Lord Denning ([1977] 1 QB 966 at p 976) and referred to in a discerning note in the Modern Law Review, (Vol 41 1978 at pp 334–337) was,

'I must say that I am surprised that the developers of the housing estate [ie adjoining the ground] were allowed to build the houses so close to the cricket ground. No doubt they wanted to make the most of their site and put up as many houses as they could for their own profit. The planning authorities ought not to have allowed it.

The houses ought to have been so sited as not to interfere with the cricket. But the houses have been built and we have to reckon with the consequences'.

Lord Denning's stricture pre-supposed that an objection was made by the cricket club to the appropriate planning authority on behalf of the estate developers. The absence of any evidence during any of the judgments in the Court of Appeal or at first instance that such an objection had been lodged, or that any appeal had been made to the Minister under the provisions of the existing Town and Country Planning legislation, justifies the inference that no effective attempt was ever made to protect the club's position in the manner manifested by Lord Denning's surprise. The outcome of any such contemplated objection can never be guaranteed. On *appropriate evidence* and the burden of proof in civil cases (ie the balance of probabilities as distinct from the higher criminal burden of proof (supra)), it is at least arguable that Lord Denning's practical approach to the club's problem if operated at the correct time could have had at least modified or qualified, if not completely altered, the ultimate results, ie siting or with physical safeguards from protective netting to avoid the nuisance. Slough County Court during 1994 witnessed a comparable circumstance when His Honour Judge Nigel Hague QC refused an injunction to restrain cricket balls hitting an adjoining property (*Lacy v Parker and Boyle* (for Jordans CC) (1994) 144 New Law Journal 785 10 June). All of these are considered further at Chapter 5 *Public Protection*. Furthermore, while these pages were in their final stages of preparation, a complex inter-locking battle between competing and conflicting governing sporting bodies and commercial and public-funded interests for the future of Wembley Stadium, as a national sporting venue, were subject to the overriding planning jurisdiction of the local Brent council.

2   Amateur rugby regulations

More clear-cut and easily explicable than the contingencies of planning law objections are two relatively recent examples from the less simple form of football based on the Rules associated with Rugby School and the amateur game to which it gave its name as distinct from the professional Rugby League version from which the amateur Union administration is expressly dissociated. One concerned a Court of Appeal's decision that a High Court judge had not directed a jury with sufficient clarity in a civil libel action upon the correct interpretation of the Regulations relating to amateur status of the International Rugby Football Board, of which the Welsh Rugby Football Union was a constituent member. The other concerned a debatable and disputable direction by a Welsh Crown Court judge to a jury in the first-ever criminal trial for assault on a rugby field which resulted in a conviction.

During 1979 and by a libel action tried in 1982 the famous Welsh rugby union footballer, Dr J P R Williams (now Mr J P R Williams FRCS) complained that he and his amateur status had been defamed by two articles written in the *Daily Telegraph* by its then rugby football correspondent, John Reason. At a four-day trial the jury found unanimously that the plaintiff had been libelled and Russell J gave judgment for £20,000 in respect of two separate alleged libels, £12,000 for one and £8,000 for the other. In the Court of Appeal an application by the defendants for leave to adduce fresh evidence which had not been called during the trial was dismissed. It did accede, however, to an alternative submission and ordered a retrial on a separate and exclusively legal ground involving the game's administrative laws. For present purposes it suffices to explain that the regulations within the amateur rugby union game, both internationally and domestically, are complex. For the purpose of deciding whether or not to order a retrial once the issue of fresh evidence had been dismissed, the leading judgment of the Court of Appeal of Stephenson LJ explained in three separate ways how reluctantly it was obliged to direct the trial to take place all over again in the spirit that Lord Atkin once said (in *Res Behari Lal v The King Emperor* (1933) 50 TLR at p 2) in a Privy Council appeal from the Commonwealth: 'Finality is a good thing, but justice is better' (*Williams v Reason and Daily Telegraph* [1988] 1 All ER 262).

When introducing the issue of the basis for ordering a retrial in the earlier part of his judgment, Stephenson LJ explained (at p 264),

'The only grounds of appeal are that the judge misdirected the jury as to the true interpretation of the relevant regulation, or that, if he did not, he failed to put to the jury adequately the defendant's defence that the plaintiff was nevertheless in breach of the regulation'.

He continued (at p 271) that the judge left,

'to the jury both the interpretation of the [International Rugby Football Board] regulations (which he should not have done) and the decision of what evidence to believe and what inferences to draw from the oral and documentary evidence. But I have come to the reluctant conclusion with great regret that the trial went wrong, so seriously wrong as to require a new trial before another judge and jury, as I have already indicated'.

Finally, after explaining, also at p 271, that,

'The first issue in the case, the construction of the board's rules and regulations, was indisputably a matter for the judge. The law is stated as follows in 12 Halsbury's Laws (4th edn), para 1461 ...'

Stephenson LJ concluded with two separate passages at p 24, thus:

'[The judge] should have decided it conclusively. As it was, he left it to the jury to decide' (letter A).

... The judge himself should have insisted on determining the true meaning of the regulation himself. As he did not, this court has to consider and decide its true meaning. If the meaning which he invited the jury to give was wrong, we have no choice but to allow the appeal and order a new trial subject to O. 59 rll (2) [of the Rules of the Supreme Court]'

All three judges, Stephenson, O'Connor and Purchas LJ, agreed that the trial went wrong when the judge failed to address the jury about the appropriate regulations.

For reasons of expenditure no retrial was heard. On that point the real issue of defamation and the plaintiff's amateur status was never decided. It also illuminated the prohibitive cost of litigation and consequences of judicial error. Legal aid has never existed for defamation; and the range of public funding at all levels will dominate public debates for a long time after these pages appear. Legal aid is available however for malicious falsehood in which different levels of proof from defamation are required.

3   Crime

Before *Williams v Reason and The Daily Telegraph Ltd*, an earlier illustration of judicial error connected with Welsh rugby emerged during the first ever prosecution for a criminal assault on a rugby field, during 1977. The principles upon which an offence of that kind could be proved had existed for nearly a century and are dealt with more particularly in detail in Chapter 6, *Participation problems* (and see particularly *R v Bradshaw* (1978) 14 Cox; *R v Moore* (1898) 14 TLR 229 and reaffirmed more recently in *R v Venna* [1975] 3 All ER 788). Here it suffices to explain that deliberate and/or reckless tackling causing injury and particularly in breach of playing laws of any game prima facie creates an offence, both civil and criminal.

In *R v Billinghurst* (1977) Crim LR 553), the defendant had been charged in the Newport, South Wales, Crown Court with inflicting grievous bodily harm upon an opponent during the course of a game. Serious injury was caused, and, as the trial judge said in summing-up to the jury:

'where the line has to be drawn between that to which a person taking part in a rugby game is to be deemed to be consenting, and that to which he is not deemed to consent'.

In other words, taking into account what was an admitted assault, in an off-the-ball-incident with serious injuries, was it something to which the victim consented? The jury in its Welsh wisdom rejected this divergence from the correct legal concept.

The summing up was technically wrong because it conflicted with the laws of playing rugby football, which do not condone deliberate foul play. Indeed, the Law Commission Consultation Paper, 'No Consent and

Offences Against the Person' specifically refers in footnote 134 to paragraph 11 inter alia;

> 'Law 26(3) of the Laws of the Game of Rugby Football 1993/94 [which] forbids a wide range of dangerous play, including by sub-laws (3)(b)–(c), wilful hacking, kicking and tripping, and early, late or dangerous tackling'.

Furthermore, the summing up was also technically wrong in its conflict with the criminal law of the land. As the Court of Appeal explained in *R v Donovan* ([1934] 2 KB 498 at 507),

> 'If an act is unlawful in the sense of being in itself a criminal act, it is plain that it cannot be rendered lawful because the person to whose detriment it is done consents to it. No person can license another to commit crime'.

(See also generally *A-G's Reference (No 6 of 1980)* [1981] QB 715 and *R v Brown* [1993] 2 WLR 556.) If the error was understandable in 1977 because of the novelty at that time of such a prosecution, no similar mitigation exists in 1999. *Volenti non fit injuria* is one of the few well-known legacies of legal Latin jargon understood beyond the boundaries of the law courts and offices. It has no place in deliberate and/or reckless breaches of playing laws of any game, just as it has no place in the criminal law of the United Kingdom as cited above. This fact appeared to have been more immediately recognisable in late 1993 by the England rugby captain, Carling than by the visiting New Zealand All Black-tourists whom he condemned as 'mostly a dirty side'. Nonetheless, it was clearly a shock to local rugby playing school sources in Yorkshire when a former schoolboy was sentenced to 12 months in a young offenders' institution towards the end of 1998 for breaking another schoolboy opponents' jaw in breach of the laws of the game and the law of the land (*R v Calton* 29 September 1998 *Yorkshire Post*).

4 Contract

The simpler form of football, soccer, created its own complexities from two cases spanning nearly seventy years. In 1980 the club which is now AFC Bournemouth was able to rely on the traditional principle of an implied term of a transfer contract which had not been expressly formulated, that its transferred centre-forward, Ted McDonald would be given a reasonable opportunity to score sufficient goals in order to trigger an increased transfer fee (*Bournemouth v Boscombe Athletic Football Club Co Ltd. v Manchester United Football Club Ltd* (1950) *Times* 21 May). Before the First World War when the professional players combined to tackle employment restrictions, Harry Kingaby was the player nominated to challenge the contractual nexus between himself and Aston Villa, his employer club. This existed within a cartel-monopolistic system controlled by the confederation of employer clubs within the Football League competition and the overriding governing control of the Football Association which administered amateur as well as professional clubs and competitions. Aston Villa placed a transfer fee upon his services for his release to any other club, which prevented the free movement he desired.

As already explained at page 77 above in Chapter 1, *Genesis*, the trial judge, Mr Justice A T Lawrence non-suited the plaintiff and withdrew the case from the jury. He ruled there was no cause of action and confirmed the transfer fee to be permissible under the terms of contract of employment (*Kingaby v Aston Villa* (1913) *Times* 28 March).

So far as the two authorities, the Football League and the Football Association, were concerned, their restrictive employment system was apparently and complacently vindicated (see *The Story of the Football League* (1938) and *The History of the Football Association* (1953)). Dissatisfaction in society generally after the Second World War disturbed the pattern of conventional acceptability among all sections of the community and within the game. Under the aggressive chairmanship of James Guthrie, who had captained the last pre-war FA Cup winning team, Portsmouth in 1939, the Players' Union (formally the Association Footballers' and Trainers' Union) encouraged the restraint of trade issue in a county court action at Aldershot. One of their players who had played in the 1953 FA Cup Final for Bolton Wanderers against Blackpool and Stanley Matthews, desired a transfer. Aldershot imposed a requisite fee, and claimed possession of his club house. The defence challenged the possession claim to be vitiated by a tainted and unenforceable contract of employment in restraint of trade. It failed, but the judgment of Judge Percy Rawlins in granting a deferred possession order delayed for five months said:

> 'It may very well be, although I am not going to decide it, that as the defendant alleges, the rules of the Football Association place an intolerable burden upon some professional footballers.' *Aldershot Football Club v Banks* (*Aldershot News*, 4 November 1955).

Consideration was given to pursuing an appeal. Within a month, before a decision was concluded, the defendant had achieved his free transfer. The local chronicle commented:

> 'Until the whole complicated, outdated transfer system is overhauled, the Banks case will never be really closed.' (*Aldershot News*, 25 November 1955.)

Eight years later, it came nearer to closure with the well-publicised judgment of Wilberforce J in *Eastham v Newcastle United FC and The Football Association, The Football League and certain footballing personalities* ([1963] 3 All ER 139). The restraint of trade defence which had been abortively raised legally but with realistic results in the Aldershot County Court, and ignored before the First World War in *Kingaby's case*, was itself now vindicated.

Three years later it was extended to a more general right to work when Florence Nagle was permitted by the Court of Appeal to pursue her claim against the Jockey Club for authority to obtain a trainer's licence in her own name, in lieu of her head lad (*Nagle v Fielden* [1966] 1 All ER 689). By the time, therefore, in 1977, when Mr Kerry Packer arrived on the professional cricket stage, the law had moved a long way forwards in sporting industrial relations from the unsatisfactory state in which it had been allowed to remain unchallenged between 1912 and 1955. When England's cricketing establishment decided in 1977 to interfere with existing contractual relationships and impose positive restraints affecting the Packer 'rebels' there were many who recognized the twin torts of inducing breach of contract and restraint of trade which appeared inevitable for the five hour judgment of Slade J after 31 days of witness and advocacy submissions. The £250,000 bill of costs in many cricketing lawyers' eyes was avoidable with foresight at the time of legal conflict and not with the hindsight of wisdom after an event (see *Greig v Insole*). The well turned over *Bosman* ruling from the European Court of Justice establishing the free movement of workers within the Treaty of Rome and within the football entertainment industry and the public consciousness of it, was a decision awaiting judgment in line with the *Banks, Eastham* and *Packer*, progressions, unless, the Belgian authorities has followed the Banks - FA intervention explained at p 75 above in Chapter 2, *Genesis*, to activate his transfer wishes and thereby preclude the necessity for court action (*Union Royale Belgedes Societes de Football Association ASBL v Bosman* (1996) All ER (EC) 97).

An inevitable thought must cross many minds if the action by Harry Kingaby's ill-advised lawyers in 1912 for varied permutations which missed the open goal of restraint of trade is looked at in the light of the inexorable and inevitable consequences of the claims by *Banks* (1955), *Eastham* (1963), *Nagle* (1966), *Greig* (1978): how would modern British sport have developed in the intervening crucial formative years if the present established rights of contractual freedom had been established when the opportunity in 1912 was seen, and missed, by mis-reading the legal small print among the existing cases in the Golden Age of playing sport, but not advising upon it, before 1914?

The answer may be impossible to consider; but a similar question arises from two further examples of another missed open goal for football and a hit wicket for cricket at respectively the players' benefit and sporting educational charity levels. Both are affected by rulings from the highest judicial tribunal in the House of Lords; *Seymour v Reed* (infra) benefits, *IRC v McMullen* (infra) charities. Professional football players' benefits contain a story of either unawareness or apathy for over thirty years from

1927 until 1959 as already explained generally in the Preface and in greater detail in Appendix 1 hereafter. Finally, sporting education charities contain a story of another lost opportunity on the road to the Chancery Division of the High Court of Justice in London from the Sussex County Cricket Club's historic headquarters at Hove.

5   Benefits

One of cricket's happiest journeys in the law courts, although not without a struggle of Test Match proportions, was its ultimate achievement of tax-free benefits for professional cricketers; with a corresponding saga of more than thirty lost and wasted years while professional footballers sought an equality which eluded them through an apparent unawareness of their potential opportunities during the intervening years. The simple and clear-cut background legal story with a slightly more complex history is illustrated by the more recent and topical decision in London's High Court when Brightman J began his judgment in *Moore v Griffiths* ([1972] 3 All ER 399 at 403)

'In 1966 England won the association football World Cup for the first but not, one hopes, last time'.

The successful appeal by Bobby Moore, from the General Income Tax Commissioners, concerned a one-off payment by the Football Association to England's captain and his 21 playing colleagues for that triumph. It filled a legal gap which should have been plugged over forty years earlier if those who had been involved with professional footballers' affairs before and during the Second World War had understood properly the true legal nature of their own financial employment conditions by comparison with those which were known for professional cricketers.

Bobby Moore's bonus of £1,000 together with similar sums to his fellow squad members was held by Brightman J to have

'had the quality of a testimonial or accolade rather than the quality of remuneration for services rendered' (at p 409: b–c).

That was how the House of Lords in 1927 regarded the payments to the Kent County Cricket Club's opening batsman, James Seymour, on the occasion of the benefit match granted to him by the club committee for the traditional Canterbury Cricket Match against Hampshire in 1920 (*Seymour v Reed* [1927] AC 554).

Likewise, the principle enunciated by Brightman J was how the Special Commissioners of Income Tax in 1959 viewed the payments made to the

Peterborough United Football Club captain, Norman Rigby, in their decision (unreported excepted for the *Peterborough Citizen and Advertiser* 16 June 1959 and 24 July 1959). They discharged assessments made upon payments received by him and fellow Peterborough United players from two testimonial matches arranged during 1956 in circumstances directly analogous to those experienced by James Seymour at Canterbury in 1920. The time lapse of 32 years between *Seymour v Reed* and *Rigby v Inland Revenue Commissioners* is a classic example of the levels of unawareness.

In 1927, shortly after the House of Lords had overruled the Court of Appeal in *Seymour's* case to restore the judgment of an experienced and respected revenue authority, the same judge, Rowlatt J, was required to adjudicate upon the testimonial benefits paid to an Everton footballer, George Harrison. Because the payments were built in to the player's contract of employment via the Football League Regulations, Rowlatt J was obliged to differentiate the situation from Seymour's Canterbury Cricket Week match.

> 'He has earned this just as much as he earned anything else in the service of the club' (*Davis v Harrison* (1927) 11 TC 707 at 723).

Fourteen years later during the Second World War in 1941 the same fate was felt by three other professional footballers, Billy Dale and Billy Corbett of Manchester City and Alf Feebury of Notts County, when they applied abortively on the same contractual basis before Lawrence J (later Lawrence LJ, the Presiding Judge at the Nuremberg War Trials and then the first Lord Oaksey) (*Dale v Duff, Corbett v Duff, Feebury v Abbot* [1941] 1 KB 730 [1941] 1 All ER 312, 23 TC 763). There was no alternative but for the distinction between the contractual footballing element and the non contractual public subscription cricketing funding to be emphasised for the second time after the House of Lords judgment. Why nothing was ever done in the intervening years to attempt amendments to the Football League contractual regulations after the two abortive High Court attempts failed has never been explained.

As already explained above, after Peterborough United were elected to the Football League in 1960 the Football League regulations were amended to delete the contractual element in the professional footballers' benefits to equate them with the professional cricketers.

Cricket's own battle had lasted seven years while the Inland Revenue challenged the source of James Seymour's benefit funding from public and other donations. In due course it was invested by the beneficiary in the purchase of a farm.

The Revenue assessed it as income. The General Commissioners of Income Tax discharged the assessment; Rowlatt J upheld their discharge. His judgment was reversed by the Court of Appeal, who in due course were overruled by the House of Lords. The original contention and

Commissioners' conclusion as a personal gift were thereby confirmed finally in the highest tribunal.

6   Charities and rates

Fifty odd years later in 1980 a parallel procedural pattern emerged. As already explained briefly in Chapter 1, *Genesis*, a later unanimous House of Lords verdict overruled a Court of Appeal majority, a High Court judgment, and restored another ruling by Commissioners; on this occasion the Charity Commissioners' approval of the FA Youth Trust Deed, notwithstanding Inland Revenue objections. For in 1972 the Charity Commissioners registered it. Walton J upheld a Revenue objection to its charitable status. A Court of Appeal majority confirmed that judgment but in due course they were all overruled by the House of Lords, to restore the original registration and the Commissioners' conclusion for charitable status (*IRC v McMullen* [1981] AC 1). If the present Government's presumption of judicial infallibility under its *Monitoring Justice* concept had been activated to deny an appeal to the Court of Appeal for a final 'whitewash' in the House of Lords, the risk of a Denial of Justice for educational sporting trusts would be self-evident. Yet it is at least arguable that here is a further example of lost and wasted years in the development of British sport because of an unawareness and lack of understanding of the true manner in which the law and sport merge for the mutual advantage of each other. The factual foundation for this contention begins only six months after the House of Lords ruling in *Seymour v Reed* on 24 May 1927. For on 22 November 1927 a will made on that date by a testator in Hove, Sussex, gave a legacy value of £300

> 'To the Sussex County Cricket Club ... of Funding Loan in trust to pay the interest yearly to the Nursery Fund'.

Eighteen months later on 17 April and 15 May 1929 it was respectively argued and rejected as a charitable request (*Re Patten: Westminster Bank Limited v Carlyon* [1929] 2 Ch 276). Yet only four years earlier on 25 February 1925, the same judge Romer J had upheld as validly charitable a £300 bequest to form the nucleus of a regimental fund for the regiment, the 6th Dragoon Guards (the Caribiniers), of that particular testator,

> 'for the promotion of sport (including in that term only shooting, fishing, cricket and polo).' (*Re Gray Todd v Taylor* [1925] Ch 362).

The story of how the Sussex County Cricket Club and its advisers took the wrong route in their legal submissions before Romer J in 1929, and thereby missed the chance to steer sporting educational charities into general judicial approval fifty odd years before the House of Lords gave their blessings in the FA Youth Trust case during 1980 [*McMullen v IRC* supra] begins with a claim from two outstanding sporting legal academicians, in 1969 that,

'The chart of decisions on sport is erratic',

ie concerning charities (*Hanbury's Modern Equity*, 9th Edition by R H Maudsley. Cf my structure of chart in Appendix 12).

Professor Harold Hanbury was not only Oxford University's Vinerian Professor of Law among other academic honours. He was also Honorary Treasurer of the Oxford University Association Football Club for twenty-five years. Professor Ronald Maudsley was not only Professor of Law in London and American Universities. He had also been awarded Double Blues at Oxford for cricket and golf, and later shared the Warwickshire County Cricket Club captaincy with H E 'Tom' Dollery during Varsity vacations. They were therefore ideally equipped for their joint assessment.

It emerged from a sporting reading of the Parliamentary and judicial mixture which has shaped charity law in the United Kingdom to its present position in the late twentieth century. By 1929 a pattern had developed based upon the refinement given to charitable categories enacted in a Statute of Queen Elizabeth I, known generally as the Charitable Uses Act 1601, by a celebrated classification (per Lord Macnaghten: *IRC v Pemsel* [1891] AC 531) in 1891 which formulated four heads applicable today,

(1) relief of poverty;
(2) advancement of education;
(3) advancement of religion;
(4) general public good.

Four years later in 1895 a Court of Appeal upheld a judicial finding that a mere prize for yacht-racing was not validly charitable, see *Re Nottage* [1895] Ch 649. (Although today a Royal Yachting Association Trust is registered with the Charity Commissioners under the second head of education). The First World War witnessed a landmark decision which the House of Lords in 1980 warmly welcomed in its FA Youth Trust decision. This was the judgment of Eve J that bequests for building a fives or squash courts and an annual athletics sports prize for Aldenham School in Hertfordshire was validly charitable. It was based on the *mens sana in corpore sano* principle (*Re Mariette* [1915] 2 Ch 284, 288). Ten years later in 1925 Romer J applied it completely to the Carabiniers bequest by saying,

'One might equally say that no person can be trained to be an efficient and useful soldier unless as much attention is given to the development of his body as to the development of his mind'.

and he followed it with a specific citation from Eve J, of the self-evident advantages and benefits of physical education (*Re Gray* supra, at pp 368–369).

Another four years later in 1929 Romer J was primed for receiving similar arguments on behalf of the Sussex County Cricket Club Funding Loan bequest 'in trust to pay the interest yearly to the Nursery Fund'. What happened? As the judgment records at 389,

> 'As regards the trust for the benefit of the Nursery Fund of the Sussex County Cricket Club it was argued that the trust is one for the "supportation aid and help of young tradesmen, handicraftsmen and persons decayed" within the meaning of the statute of Elizabeth. In my opinion a professional cricketer is neither a tradesman, a handicraftsman nor a person decayed, and though undoubtedly, as a result of the administration of the fund, boys all of the working or lower middle classes and not well off financially may be embarked upon life as professional cricketers, it is, I think, reasonably clear that the object of the fund is the encouragement of the game of cricket and nothing else, and it has been held by authorities that are binding upon me that such a bequest is not charitable'.

Yet the evidence and legal precedents from different disciplines from sporting or educational charities or trusts all pointed in the opposite direction following the same judge's earlier finding for the Army. As his judgment explained earlier at p 386, it appeared on the evidence tendered before him that the Sussex County Cricket Club in the year 1908 established a special fund

> 'which has ever since been maintained by voluntary contributions and subscriptions for the purpose of teaching and coaching young cricketers in the game of cricket so as to enable them to earn their livelihood by becoming cricket professionals and of furthering the interest of cricket as a national game, such fund being known as the Nursery Fund. All the moneys received for the fund are spent in the payment of a professional cricketer in teaching and coaching young cricketers in the game of cricket and in paying the incidental travelling and other expenses incurred in connection with his employment. It is stated that during the past seven years thirty-one boys or thereabouts mainly between the ages of seventeen and twenty-one have by means of the said fund received instruction in the said game, and that about twenty-one of these boys are now being employed as professional cricketers by the Club or by other clubs and schools in the county of Sussex and other parts of the south of England, and Mr Godfree, who is a member of the Committee of the Club, says that the parents of the boys so taught are, he believes, all of the working or lower middle classes and not well off financially'.

The combined threads of teaching, coaching, ages of 17–21, schools, and 'not well off financially' point inexorably and inevitably to the established categories from 1891 of advancement of education and relief of poverty. A legacy for 'poor men of the trade of a tinplate worker' was held with 'no reasonable doubt [to be] a charitable legacy' (*Re White's Trusts* [1886] 33 Ch D 449 at 454). In *Roberts v Gray* ([1913] 1 KB 520), a contract claim concerning an apprenticed billiards player, the Court of Appeal unanimously followed established authorities in the words of the then Master of Rolls, Cozens-Hardy MR at p 525,

> 'education must not be taken in its narrow technical sense as merely meaning education to enable a man by the work of his hand to hereafter maintain himself as an artisan, but has a much wider meaning than that; it applies to education and instruction in the social state in which the infant [apprentice] is, and in which he may expect to find himself when he becomes an adult'.

With these citations, the available evidence and Romer J's own application of the Aldenham School judgment to the Army bequest in 1925 it is difficult to see how he would have failed to have been attracted by the argument that the apprenticed cricketers 'of the working or the lower middle classes and not well off financially' qualified for charitable status. The opportunity was lost and thus the dice were loaded against the serious attempts during the later 1950s to establish the joint Oxbridge FA *Amateur* Cup winning club Pegasus, with its object of advancing the game at university level, within the charitable educational setting after its Cup triumphs in 1951 and 1953.

The first Lord Oaksey in the City of Glasgow Police Athletic Association judgments of the House of Lords stood apart from his brother Law Lords with a strong dissenting judgment in 1953 when they distinguished the subject-matter from the Army Officers bequest upheld by Romer J in 1925 to reject its charitable status claim (*IRC v City of Glasgow Police Athletic Association* [1953] AC 380 at 397). A glimmer of light shone from the New South Wales, Australia, Equity Court in *Kearins v Kearins* (1957) when a bequest to Sydney University Rugby Football Club was upheld as charitable because of the Aldenham School judgment of Eve J; and in 1958 Parliament passed the Recreational Charities Act which widened the scene for social purposes as a charitable basis. No funds existed for Pegasus, a strictly amateur Oxbridge club, to fight a law-suit advised against the Inland Revenue during the late 1950s in the hope of preserving the profits from its two 100,000 Wembley Stadium crowd attendances and from the cup-ties leading up to them in 1951 and 1953. I reiterated their claim two decades later when responding to a commission for Sir Denis Follows to contribute a section on *Football and the Law* in the newly conceived *FA Manual of*

Administration. Written in 1971, edited by Sir Denis with his schoolmaster's pen, it appeared thus (at pp 154–155) in 1972;

'viii) Charities

One form of registration which hitherto has not troubled the football world and the world of sport is with the Charity Commissioners. This arises from basically a long established approach by the courts that sport as such is not a valid charitable object allowing it to qualify for charitable status and thereby charitable relief from taxation. House of Lords judgments have contributed to this thinking but Parliament by the Recreational Charities Act of 1958 has given fresh impetus to those who thought that the law had gone too far away from what should be the right approach to a highly technical and complex subject. Certainly sport associated with education and service discipline has been granted charitable status and any Old Boys' Club or others associated with educational foundations could claim to qualify. At one time thoughts existed in this direction for Pegasus FC after its FA Amateur Cup Final triumphs in 1951 and 1953; but as time went by the team's raison d'être and playing strength dwindled and the interesting reasoning behind this never fructified. The benefit, of course, is the very real one of freedom from the burden of income tax and the encouragement of bequests, grants and donations for this purpose. Any secretary or official sufficiently interested to pursue the matter further as a layman is advised to consult his local library or write to H M Stationery Office and study the House of Lords debate on the motion Charities and Charity Law as reported in Hansard (Parliamentary Debates): House of Lords: Wednesday 30 June 1971, columns 323–401. In one equally unknown and obscure realm of law freedom from income tax does exist in the football world: for certain players' benefits'.

In the same year (1972), Sir Denis registered the FA Youth Trust Deed. Eight years later the House of Lords followed and applied Eve J from 1915. The Lord Chancellor, Lord Hailsham of St Marylebone, did not specify Sussex County Cricket Club or its advisers when he explained ([1981] AC 1 at 17),

'I do not think that the courts have as yet explored the extent to which elements of organisation, instruction, or the disciplined inculcation of information, instruction or skill may limit the whole concept of education ... But it is clear to me that the decision in *Re Mariette* is not to be read in a sense which confines its application for ever to gifts to a particular institution'.

Sadly, *Re Mariette* was never mentioned in *Re Patten*, the Sussex case, and neither was *Re Gray*, Romer J's own decision. Yet even if Romer J had been persuaded to follow them for Sussex CCC, would sport have taken advantage of the possibilities it would have opened up? For when the Lord Chancellor, Lord Hailsham of St Marylebone, in the FA Youth Trust case thought the courts have not 'as yet explored ...', he was identifying the legal profession which services those courts, and initiates their intervention, rather than the judiciary who respond to chart the course of charities and other developing and emerging legal areas.

The comprehensive manner in which the House of Lords applied the concepts of physical recreation to the principles of standard charity law and practice, together with the absence of sufficient evidence on the issue of *recreation*, prevented the FA Youth Trust Deed judgments in any of the courts being able to consider the Recreational Charities Act 1958 (a state of affairs untouched by human legal hands until *Re Guild* [1992] and its application to the Sports Centre [then] in North Berwick, or 'some similar purpose in connection with sport'. This will be considered more appropriately in Chapter 14, 'No fine on fun'. So, too, will the ongoing battle at the time writing between Oldham Borough Council's wish to relocate the Clayton Playing Fields in that area of North-West Lancashire and the preservationists who are still fighting through the Chancery Division, the Court of Appeal and the local Council Chamber within the Charities Act 1960 (see *Oldham BC v Attorney-General* [1993] 2 WLR 224). Furthermore, Chapter 4, *Parent, school and club partners*, will explain the availability and applicability of charity law for rate relief to the advantage of sporting bodies, clubs, and the community generally. It will also emphasise the absence of any need for currently contemplated amending legislation when intelligent and imaginative application of the existing legal criteria should fulfil all required sporting social needs.

7   Race relations

Five years after the Youth Trust Deed judicial opinions, the House of Lords was again brought on to the sporting stage with legislation enacted during the reign of Queen Elizabeth II, as distinct from the charity legislation of Queen Elizabeth I, ie the Race Relations Act 1976 (*Wheeler v Leicester City Council* [1985] AC 1054). The relevance of this sensitive and developing area of law here is merely to emphasise the need for careful and thoughtful coordination of sport and the law. More appropriately it is considered in detail under Chapter 9, 'International interaction'. Here, it is mentioned solely to record the course it took procedurally.

The Leicester City Council sought to withdraw its facilities to the local rugby club for usage of its practice ground at Welford Road because players had exercised their free choice to tour South Africa with the England national representative team. An application for judicial review to Forbes J failed. So, too, did an appeal to the Court of Appeal (Brown-Wilkinson LJ dissenting). The House of Lords, unanimously overruled the Court of Appeal majority and Forbes J, and the Leicester City Council's decision. The conflict of judicial opinion here explains the manner in which sport and the law must be regarded as a developing rather than a static or contracting area. It is considered in greater detail in Chapter 9, *International Interaction* at pp 368-369, below. It can also be read in the light of the great West Indian cricketer Learie Constantine's High Court triumph 50 years ago during the Second World War, after American armed services personnel inspired discrimination against him at London's Imperial Hotel, Russell Square, as explained in Chapter 15, *Whither Sport and the Law* (below).

8   Tribunals

The House of Lords unanimity for soccer's charitable status in 1980 would have been some compensation for the FA's defeat a year earlier by Cantley J in 1979 in the High Court. He had expunged a disciplinary tribunal's suspension upon the former national team manager, Don Revie (*Revie v The Football Association* (1979) *Times*, 14 December) upon the principle of a likelihood of bias, which surfaced in the House of Lords through Lord Hoffman's judgment in the *Pinochet* proceedings (*Times* 18 January 1999). It is also the foundation for the Court of Appeal and House of Lords preserving Diane Modahl's claim against the regulatory athletic authorities for irregular drugtesting arrangements (*Modahl v British Athletic Federation* The *Times* 23 July 1999) which is dealt with more appropriately and in more detail under Chapter 11, '*Fair play and reason in court*'. The significance of that judgment here is that this was the third time within a quarter-of-a-century when decisions of soccer's ruling body's disciplinary tribunals had been reversed in the High Court. During 1962 from the north-east of England the High Court was called upon to reverse the FA's suspensions upon first the players and then officials and the club itself at Sunderland (*Elliott & others v the FA & others* (1962) *Times*, 12 April; *Ditchburn & others v the FA & others* (1962) *Times* 22 June). Cantley J's reversal of the ban upon the former England team manager Don Revie (*Revie v FA* (1979)) because of fundamental procedural tribunal errors (see Chapter 11) confirmed the need for care and caution in yet a further developing legal area essential to the efficient and effective administration of the world of sport. More recently, the Football Association of Wales Ltd was held in London's Chancery Division of the High Court to be in restraint of trade after administrative and tribunal decisions banned three minor league football clubs from playing on their own local grounds: *Newport AFC Ltd & Others v Football Association of Wales Ltd* (1994) 144 *New Law Journal* 1351, 7 October.

9   Personal injuries

That significant FA Tribunal year of 1962 also witnessed one of the rarer and perhaps more mundane necessities for the co-ordinating roles of sport and the law; the input and assessment of evidence. *Wooldridge v Sumner* ([1963] 2 QB 43) was a decision of great importance arising out of the White City National Horse Show of the Year. The claim was for personal injuries suffered by a photographer discharging his professional duties within the arena when he was injured by a competitive horse. Barry J awarded £6,000 damages against the competitor, but dismissed a claim against the organisers. The case is full of legal nuggets which will be more fully discussed and cited elsewhere (Chapter 5, *Public protection* and Chapter 6, *Participation problems*). Here it is important and relevant for a rarely recognised but none the less important area of judicial intervention. For the Court of Appeal reversed the trial judge's finding simply and solely on the ground that in assessing the evidence he had drawn the *wrong inference of fact* from it, and thereby had erroneously attributed negligence when the evidence pointed to error of judgment as distinct from negligence. As Sellers LJ said at p 52

'it provides a striking illustration and reminder of how uncertain can be the raw material of a court's inquiry, the evidence'.

Diplock LJ, at p 60 explained

'The relevant events took place in the course of a few seconds; all or some of them were seen by 12 different witnesses including the rider and the injured man, and, as is inevitable when honest witnesses give their recollections of what occurred in a very brief space of time, there were wide divergences in their respective accounts. In such a case an appellate court will not lightly disturb the findings of the trial judge as to what in fact occurred'.

On that occasion the appellate tribunal, after six days of forensic arguments and a reserved judgment running to over twenty pages, did feel obliged to disturb the trial judge's findings; but two decades later in *Condon v Basi* ([1985] 2 All ER 453) a later Court of Appeal applied an Australian precedent (*Rootes v Shelton* [1968] ALR 33) to extend the frontiers of sporting injury damages liability to common law negligence, and confirm the judgment of H H Judge Wooton in the Warwick County Court (see in Chapter 6, *Participation problems*).

More recently an unreported High Court judgment agreed a damages award of £30,557 of which £7,000 were general damages and the rest special damages for injuries received in a Karate practice session. Dr Michael

Davies began his judgment, leading to a finding of negligence as pleaded in the claims with my emphasis:

> 'I suspect that the judge in charge of the list was told that this was of great importance in the important world of Karate and involved great questions of principle. Having heard all the evidence I am totally confident it is nothing of the sort. No great question of principle arises. *There is a straightforward question of fact to be decided. The law,* which is found enshrined in one decision of the Court of Appeal to which I will refer, is, *in my view crystal clear* [ie *Condon v Basi,* supra]. The court has to find the facts, apply the law, and that is the end of it.' [*Champion v Brown* (1993) Unreported, 24 February.]

Thus the three high-profiled football cases of *Elliott v Saunders and Liverpool Football Club Ltd* (1994), *O'Neill v Fashanu and Wimbledon Football Club Ltd* (1994) *Times,* 14 October, *McCord v Swansea City* (1997) *Times* 11 February and *Watson and Bradford City Football Club v Gray and Huddersfield Town* (1998) were illustrative of the same *general* legal criteria. So too was the 16 year-old school boys successful claim against the Army, with an added element of the defending soldiers held to be liable, who were also adjudicated to have been acting *in loco parentis* (*Casson v MOD* (1999) *Bradford Telegraph and Argus* April 1999).

10   Evidence

The hard real world of admissible facts brings into play the crucial role and law of admissible evidence. For practical purposes it is often the decisive element in contested litigation. When Sam Weller tried to explain that

> 'the soldier said Ven they ordered him three hundred and fifty lashes.'

he was rebuffed

> 'you must not tell us what the soldier, or any other man, said, sir" interposed the judge: "it's not evidence".'

Textbooks from deservedly distinguished and eminent sources have continually analysed and assessed the juridical and admissible nature of evidence. Equally important for the litigant and the lawyer is the *collection* of it. Without intending to digress into the continuing contention about a fused or divided legal profession, the undisputed fact remains that collation and coordination of evidence is as essential and often difficult for operating a legal system as the ultimate presentation in court or advising on legal issues and preparing documents out of court. The *Williams v Reason and*

Daily Telegraph (supra) Court of Appeal conclusions which refused leave to admit fresh evidence in the Court of Appeal is one example of the desirability to get all the eggs together in the same basket at the outset of any contested issues before trials begin. The *Wooldridge v Sumner* (supra) verdict by the Court of Appeal because the trial judge drew the wrong inference of fact from the extensive evidence tendered before him is another example, this time of the need to try and assist the tribunal as much as possible with as much available and admissible evidence as can be achieved. Today this includes authentically proved video evidence.

A different version of extracting from evidence the wrong inference of fact occurred in an important action about a disputed will and codicil when the trial judge failed to sum up the essential facts correctly to the jury. The House of Lords at the end of 1958 reversed a majority Court of Appeal confirmation of the judge's summing up and found that this happened in a case which attracted much general attention at the time on 20 May 1957. It began in circumstances which created the original and more unorthodox sporting situation, tinged with a touch of undoubted criminality, known as the 'Colonel who debagged the Solicitor' (*Wintle v Nye* [1959] 1 All ER 552).

Purists who may object to its inclusion within a sporting legal context may be unaware of two sequels which do not appear in any law reports. Immediately after the House of Lords decision Lincoln's Inn barristers, dining in Hall in the presence of HRH Princess Margaret, drank a toast in honour of the Colonel and to his success. They also sent a jeroboam of champagne to him and to his ex-cavalry campaigner, ex-trooper Cedric (Spike) Mays who had helped his preparations, with a signed menu card inscribed 'for the successful amateurs to drink the health of the losing professionals'. Subsequently the serving colonel of their regiment, the Royal Dragoons, sent them both the regimental sports tie, dark blue, with golden eagles — the regimental badge. It was awarded only to those who represented 'the regiment in sporting events' (*Last Post,* Spike Mays (1974) p 81; *The Last Englishman,* A D Wintle (1986) p 283).

The key facts in the probate action for the estate of Colonel Wintle's cousin concerned a complicated will and codicil drawn up by the defendant solicitor. The testatrix had been nursed by the Colonel's sister for many years before she died. The sister was left far less interest in the cousin's estate under the will and codicil than what the solicitor received under them. Personal knowledge of his family convinced the Colonel that the testatrix had not appreciated or known the contents of either document when she signed them. He failed to obtain any satisfaction from the solicitor to redress the imbalance between himself and the Colonel's sister; but he could not sue because he was not linked legally to the estate and the signed documents. He therefore planned a campaign with military precision to place himself in the litigation riding seat.

A hoaxed invitation for tea effected a meeting between the two men. The Colonel ordered the solicitor to take off his trousers, ejected him on to the highway at Hove in Sussex, then

> 'exhibited the trousers in the trophy room of [his] club, telephoned the police, the Press and Nye's partner...and then went home and sat back with a large whisky awaiting results.' *Wintle*, (p 273).

They soon came. He was arrested later the same evening; charged with common assault, and appeared ultimately before Byrne J at Lewes Assizes, where he pleaded guilty. A six month's custodial sentence was imposed and served (in contrast to *R v David Bishop* (see p 35); one month reduced on appeal to a suspended sentence for punching on the head a defenceless rugby opponent lying on the ground). The worldwide publicity resulted in an assignment to Colonel Wintle of family interests under the will and codicil creating a right to challenge them in the Probate Division of the High Court of Justice. The only issue, per the Lord Chancellor, Lord Simonds ([1959] 1 All ER 557 C–D) was

> 'whether the testatrix knew and approved of the contents of (i) the will and (ii) the codicil'.

Neither fraud nor undue influence was alleged.

The jury answered 'Yes' to questions related to both elements after days of legal argument, evidence and a summing-up by Barnard J. A Court of Appeal majority rejected an appeal, after a further six days' argument with a reserved judgment on the seventh. The dissenting judgment of Sellers LJ was approved by the House of Lords reserved judgment after a further six days' argument on the basis (per Lord Simonds at p 557: G–H) that;

> 'The summing-up of the evidence substantially negatived the law which the learned judge had in terms enunciated'.

In brief, the House of Lords (p 559: G–H) agreed unanimously that the jury was not

> 'directed to view the [evidential basis of the] transaction with the vigilance and jealousy which the law requires'.

Its verdict was formally set aside, with consequential advantages to the Colonel's sister. Fifteen years later in *Wooldridge v Summer*, Sellers LJ was a member of the Court which reversed the trial judge on comparable circumstances of judicial error. That judicial mishap was an illuminating corollary to another and perhaps generally lesser known reason for erroneous verdicts and ultimate injustice: insufficient facts. The courts discourage litigation replays with additional facts which could have been obtained and used in evidence on a first hearing. This is why the Court of Appeal refused a retrial on the ground of additional evidence which it heard on behalf of the *Daily Telegraph's* appeal against the £25,000 damages libel award by the jury in favour of the Welsh international J P R Williams. It adjudicated that the additional evidence which it heard on oath could have been obtained for use at the original trial and thereby rejected a retrial on this ground, although it ordered one for the reason already explained in detail ie that the judge had failed to direct the jury correctly on the relevant rugby regulations about amateurism. No retrial ever took place, with the risks of costs as one of the matters leading to that position.

11   Facts

Against this background all readers both inside and outside the profession ought to know how a crucial but oft-forgotten *Report of the Committee on Legal Education* (Cmnd 4595), commissioned by Lord Gardiner, Lord Chancellor in 1967, and completed for his successor, Lord Hailsham of St Marylebone in 1971, under the chairmanship of Mr Justice (later Lord Justice) Ormrod, explained the realities underlying this aspect of the administration of justice, in para 91 at page 38, thus (with the author's own emphasis):

> 'The raw material of every *practising lawyer* is facts, and a great deal of his time will be spent, whether he is a judge or a barrister or a solicitor, *in finding the facts*. The law cannot be properly applied until they are ascertained. If the facts are wrong, the advice of the most learned lawyer will be, at best, worthless — and may be dangerous. Facts, therefore are of crucial importance to the practising lawyer at all levels, and his ability to *handle* facts is among his most essential skills. The *handling* of facts has many aspects. The practitioner must first *obtain* the client's instructions and the surrounding facts, and then *investigate* and *scrutinise* them for accuracy. Analysis of all the available data, to separate the *relevant* from the irrelevant and to perceive the relation between one set of facts and another and so to check reliability or expose errors, is an essential process in every case. In every case, also, he must *synthesise* his facts in order to present them lucidly and cogently, whether as an advocate, or as a pleader, or as a draftsman, or negotiator, or even as a letter writer. All stages of these processes will of course be controlled and informed by his knowledge of the relevant law, without which the exercise would be futile'.

The emphasis on italicised words here is made deliberately. To *find, obtain,*

handle, investigate, scrutinise and *synthesise* relevant facts is a process
in which both branches of practising lawyers depend upon other people
for providing the facts. The need to excavate for them, and also
corroborative witnesses in support, becomes more burdensome with every
passing decade as visual aid and television erosions of independent and
enquiring thought processes paralyse or inhibit the general public's
capacity to community coherently, and sometimes, too, the investigator's
ability to pursue with sufficient depth. The ideal of a Sherlock Holmes with
Dr Watson to eliminate the probable, or a Perry Mason's facility to whistle
up a Paul Drake-style assistant who can fly off to all corners of the globe
for information at a moment's notice, is hardly possible for practitioners
whose clients are tied to a legal aid budget, or even for those with no cash
limit. The client outside both of these categories, unable to afford legal
services, makes a mockery of Magna Carta: 'to no one shall we deny justice':
Colonel Wintle's triumph, recognised by Lincoln's Inn barristers and his
regimental Colonel, was to battle in the Court of Appeal and the House of
Lords, assisted only by ex-trooper Cedric (Spike) Mays (although he had
been represented by distinguished Counsel at the trial).

Thus, all who enter the lottery of litigation should somehow be primed
with the golden advice given in the presence of counsel and their client by
the late Simon Burns. He was the wise and skilled solicitor who steered the
appeal to the House of Lords of Reginald Woolmington to reverse the Court
of Criminal Appeal and quash a murder conviction when the Lord
Chancellor, Viscount Sankey LC, expressed the immortal words,

> 'Throughout the web of the English Criminal Law one gold thread is always
> to be seen, that it is the duty of the prosecution to prove the prisoner's
> guilt' (*Woolmington v DPP* [1935] AC 462 at 481 and 483).

He also had a knack of explaining to difficult and inarticulate clients in his
soft and slow Humberside burr,

> 'Mr Client. When you've fought the case and lost it, please don't come
> back to us and explain "If the barrister had only known about x, or y or z,
> we could have won the case." You must tell us, now, while there is still time
> to investigate, and evaluate, what you haven't told us so far'.

The chapters which now follow are relied upon for direct testimony as
evidence, as well as the inference of fact to be drawn from them; that those
who persist in believing that sport has nothing to do with law, and that law
can be divorced from sport, do so at peril to themselves and all whom they
seek to serve. No area of society is unaffected by legal issues. Sport is no
exception. The pattern and applicable legal areas selected for these pages
have been chosen from professional experiences and observation as being

most likely to affect and concern the widest possible readership to be interested. Every specialist sport and every legal speciality will doubtless expect far fuller treatment. That is not the purpose of this book. A level of general awareness is the aim for a gap which the ever increasing interaction and interrelation between sport and the law is almost daily proving to exist on daily published evidence.

Finally three examples from comparatively recent sporting injury cases illustrate the problems inherent in the selection and applicability of the appropriate evidence from specialist sources which is often required for establishing or rejecting liability:

1   *Smolden v Whitworth and Nolan* (1997) (*Times*, 19 April; *Times*, 18 December, 1996). Curtis J and the Court of Appeal respectively utilized the *defendant witness* referee's/specialist evidence in favour of the *plaintiff* of the Defendant's negligent scrum laws of the game.
2   *Fowles v Bedfordshire County Council* (1995) (PIQR P380). A gymnast who slipped on a mat claimed damages, established a one-third liability against the defendant council, but with a two-thirds contributory negligence reduction found against himself per, *inter alia*, Millett LJ in the Court of Appeal at p 388 who recorded how the plaintiff's own expert witnesses were 'stunned' by his 'utter foolishness'.
3   *Murray v Haringay Arena* [1951] 2 KB 529. This relatively old but nonetheless oft-cited leading case, to support the proposition that there is no obligation to guard against unusual dangers at sports venues, rejected a six-year-old's appeal from a claim for an eye injury at an ice-rink, Singleton LJ at pp 531–2 said: (as already cited in the Preface)

> 'The evidence given on the hearing was meagre. There was no evidence from anyone connected with the management; no evidence to show how long the rink had been in existence; no evidence to show the number of persons who normally attended matches; and no evidence to show whether there had been any other accidents there. In a sense this appears to be unsatisfactory, and yet it would seem that there are ways in which the plaintiffs might have obtained information on these matters.'

12   Parliament

The previous two chapters (*Genesis* and *Progressive perspective*), identified the extent to which Parliament as the United Kingdom's supreme law-making body is a source of legislation affecting sport; and further examples will emerge during the remainder of the text. What merits attention in this general survey is an often overlooked aspect of the position generally, explained in a little cited reference during Lord Hailsham's Carlton Lecture:

> '...in a free country it is a seldom cited but almost universal principle that an action is lawful unless prohibited by some positive rule of law or public policy, prescribed by statute or customary law'.

For controlling the excesses of personal and sporting misconduct and neglect Parliament has acted prohibitively during the later 1980s and early 1990s to a greater extent *in a short period* than during any earlier era of Britain's sporting and national history. It has begun also to act positively on fiscal issues to alleviate the revenue and VAT burdens which are annually the subject of pleas from sporting sources. Chapter 14, *No fine on fun*, explores some of them.

Thirty years ago, Professor Peter McIntosh in his most valuable but little-known *Sport in Society* (1963) summarised succinctly the first comprehensive chronicle of the British sporting scene, Joseph Strutt's *The Sports and Pastimes of the People of England*. McIntosh explained how Strutt's survey 'from the earliest period to the present time' [1801]

> 'classified sports under three broad headings:
> 'rural exercises practised by persons of rank",
> 'rural exercises generally practised" and
> 'pastimes usually exercised in towns and cities, or places adjoining them,"
> He [Strutt] was perhaps imposing upon the past those geographical and social distinctions which he drew from observation of the society at the end of the eighteenth century. Nevertheless he found it possible without distorting his evidence to notice in the sports of the Middle Ages these fundamental distinctions between rural and urban and between aristocratic and plebeian'.

These 'fundamental distinctions' explain the pattern of the extensive Parliamentary control of sport, leisure and physical education from medieval times to the beginnings of modern sport in industrial Britain and elsewhere a century ago. National security demanded the protection of archery by Parliamentary prohibitions on football and other pursuits which were diverting time from practising and preparing skills with bows and arrows. Concurrent with that pattern of legislation was the area described in 1962 a year before McIntosh's summary, as a

> 'complex hotch-pot of statutory enactments which have been built-up over the years',

namely, *The Game Laws of this country* (per Col James N Vallance OBE, TD, Chairman, Wildfowlers' Association of Great Britain and Northern

Ireland). That complaint echoed the immortal *Commentaries on the Laws of England* two centuries earlier where Sir William Blackstone recorded in 1765 (Book iv: pp 174–175)

'The statutes for preserving the game are many and various, and not a little obscure and intricate'.

He explained the offence

'of destroying such beasts and fowls, as are ranked under the denomination of game,'

to be one

'which the sportsmen of England seem to think of the highest importance; and a matter, perhaps the only one, of general and national concern; associations have been formed all over the kingdom to prevent its destructive process ...'.

That prevention to protect the species and the landed sporting property rights which accompanied it by criminal penal sanctions inspired the network of Game Law legislation which survives today. Blackstone explained, with a reflection of an enlightened eighteenth-century Oxford attitude from his chair as the first Vinerian Professor, which created the lectures on which his Commentaries were based before his leading judicial appointments, in the then Court of Common Pleas,

'the only rational footing, upon which we can consider it was a crime is, that in low and indigent persons it promotes idleness, and takes them away from their proper employments and callings; which is an offence against the public police [sic!] and economy of the commonwealth'.

The protection from that legislation shaped the gaming laws which created the ground rules between poachers and landowners and their gamekeepers, with Parliamentary and contractual permissions for licence holders to catch and sell game. Alongside, or because of this parliamentary control of rural sporting activities, landowners carved out their own areas of sporting rights and enjoyment within the framework of the property land laws. These created the exploitation of fishing, gaming and shooting rights through boundaries; easements, licences, profits a prendre and restrictive covenants which belong to the realm of real property and real estate law, where the detailed crucial creative conveyancing documents are found. Their protection comes from enforcement by the remedies of damages and injunctions of the civil wrongs of trespass (particularly against hunting and anti-hunt saboteurs), nuisance and negligence, together with conventional criminal offences of assault, malicious damage, and more specialised statutory offences in this legislative field such as the long-standing Night Poaching Acts, the Protection of Animals Act 1911, the Salmon and Freshwater Fisheries Act 1923 and more recently the Wildlife and Countryside Act 1981.

This blend of common law landed property rights and Parliamentary enactments which have catered down the years for protection and commercial exploitation of rural sports belong to the same legal stable which more recently has sired and applied to the commercial world of urban and industrialised sponsored sports the intellectual property rights found in copyright, franchising, media patents and trade mark laws, and considered in Chapter 13, *Sponsored gentlemen and players*.

Violent criminal elements more recently (and particularly since the acquiescence by light-headed and light-minded pseudo-intellectuals in a permissive society masquerading as a progressive or so-called civilised society since the 1960s) have poisoned certain urban and even rural sporting areas; and these have demanded special criminal sanctions. Accordingly, they have absorbed more concentrated Parliamentary time than any other period of Britain's sporting or social history. Thus, the Parliament which ended with the General Election of 1987 produced in its final year.

(1) Two Reports, Interim (Cmnd 9585) and Final (Cmnd 9710), from Mr Justice Popplewell on Crowd Control during 1985 and 1986.
(2) The Sporting Events (Control of Alcohol etc) Act 1985.
(3) The Public Order Act 1986.
(4) The Fire Safety and Safety of Places of Sport Act 1987.
(5) An improved Green Guide Code for sports ground safety.

Since then, four further statutes have been implemented to tackle the never-ending criminal element poisoning the soccer scene.

(6) The Football Spectators Act 1989
(7) The Football Offences Act 1991
(8) The Crime and Disorder Act 1998
(9) The Football (Offences and Disorder) Act 1999.

CONCLUSIONS

Looking back on this chapter, *Under starter's orders*, is there any message for practitioners, administrators, academics and others at whom the book is aimed? There is; because it has been, and throughout these pages it will again be necessary, to turn back the clock: to explain and examine procedural legal processes with their relevant evidence and try to demonstrate how verdicts are reached.

In that context they illustrate three basic elements which must provide a consistent legal and juridical thread or pattern throughout this book, and, it is suggested, for any understanding of how the law functions in practice and particularly within an emerging and not easily recognisable or identifiable area such as sport and the law — history, procedure and evidence, and appropriately admissible facts.

Sir Walter Scott focuses the *historical* setting. Maitland, quoting Maine, identified the *procedural* significance; and many within the law often forget the key role for ascertainment and excavation of the admissible *evidence and facts*. The extent to which this vital process is taught, if at all, in law schools is at present limited in scope, but beginning to be recognised by the professional governing bodies in harmony with University Law Schools. A similar question of equal importance concerns the extent to which, if at all, sport and physical education are taught in schools in Britain today.

That is why the relationships between a Parents, Schools and Club partnership must be considered together in the next chapter.

PART II

Personal Relationships

CHAPTER 4

Parent, School and Club Partners

THE PROBLEMS

Sir Bobby Charlton, CBE, and Will Carling could never have fulfilled their personal destinies and services to England in their different codes of football if their respective families' choice of schools (denied to so many) had not guided their talents ultimately to their most advantageous outlets. Charlton's scholarship at Ashington Primary School in Northumberland was switched from Morpeth Grammar School and a rugby tradition to Bedlington Grammar for soccer. Carling's parents chose Sedbergh with its rugby heritage in place of Shrewsbury's soccer successes. Yet in the United Kingdom at least, interlocking socio-political reasons and lack of any coordinated thought at Government, local authority, teaching and sporting administrative levels have created a legal mess, at least so far as the state sector is concerned.

In an opening paragraph to a survey on *Sport in the Curriculum* in Appendix 2 education specialist Dr Mary Malecka, a practising barrister, explains;

> 'The grassroots of sport are parched and shrivelled through lack of good provision from the top. There has been no will at government level in recent years to save sport in the state system of education. Notwithstanding a "Minister for Sport", there is no coordination between ministries as to the whole picture of decline in the availability of physical education to children and youth.'

Earlier in February 1999 Dr David Hempsall, headmaster of Queen Elizabeth's Grammar School, Blackburn, Lancs, told a forum of sports masters:

'Over the past two or three years, there has been clear evidence of an increase in indiscipline.

I have seen some pretty violent play myself, as well as referees being consistently hassled and insulted, I am now very concerned'.

Criticising the influence of Premiership soccer, Dr Hempsall said:

'There is a saying that the fish rots from the head down. Soccer at the top level presents a pretty unedifying spectacle.

My concern is that fair minded players will conclude it isn't worth the biscuit and drop out and that referees, fed up with the abuse, will also drop out. This will leave the field to the thugs and bully boys'. [*Daily Telegraph*, 5 February 1999.]

These attributions to abdication of the Rule of Law on the field are reflected by the absence of any coordinated harmonisation of policies for schools sport and its conduct off the field, both in the private, state and government areas.

Thus, in the later 1990's as the millenium approaches;

1. Mr Chris Hirst, headmaster, Sedbergh School, in his capacity as Chairman of the Independent Schools Sports section was obliged to publish a Code of Honour for School sport after two famous private sector Public Schools, Marlborough and Radley, had terminated inter-school cricket fixtures because of the unsporting and objectionable conduct of "sledging".

2. Mr David Hart, Secretary of the Independent Headmasters' Association issued a warning about the damages to school health from inadequate school sport activities replaced by the couch potato syndrome.

3. As explained in Dr Mary Malecka's Appendix on *Sport in the Curriculum* a Government appointed quango, The Qualifications and Curriculum Authority (QCA) under Section 21 of the Education Act 1997, has recommended alternative activities for 14–16 years-old pupils for physical education as part of their National Curriculum syllabus under level K4.

4. The potential decision to allow optional arrangements for such physical education would thereby subliminally accelerate the existing concern about unchecked sales of schools and recreational playing fields, with the consequential disastrous effect on health, education and sporting prowess. For this, not any member of either House of Parliament, or any one of the four Government departments concerned has ever attempted to control, ie education, environment, health, and local government. It would also have a potential disastrous effect on nurturing the talents of future Charltons and Carlings.

5. To draw attention to these socio-politico legal issues, affecting the health and welfare of the nation. A draft Act of Parliament for the *Preservation and Protection of School and Recreation Playing Fields* appears in Appendix 2(2) immediately following Dr Mary Malecka's *Sport in the Curriculum* survey.

Concurrent with these developments and with thoughts equally applicable today as they were at the beginning of the decade in a publication entitled '*Sport for All Into the 90s*', Sue Campbell then of the UK National Coaching foundation, now Director of the Youth Sport Trust, wrote as long ago as 1991;

> 'An area of concern is the ethics which underpin sporting performance. With the incessant demands to achieve higher standards, elite performers are being subjected to increasing pressure. Their behaviour provides the model for younger performers and creates a public image of sport. It is crucial that in every sense they represent the very best in sport. Coaches must therefore work to an ethical code (code of practice) which protects the athlete, the coach and the sport—'athlete first, winning second'. In Britain a full code of practice has been developed by the British Institute of Sports Coaches (BISC) whose members believe that sport is one of the most important 'tools' in helping to shape human development, and that coaches should be guided to use that tool skilfully and safely. If this type of code is neglected we are failing our athletes and failing sport'.

THE ISSUES

Previous generations may have ignored what Lord Howell in his Foreword to the First Edition described as 'the social and ethical considerations which sport presents in our everyday life'. Ethical considerations are relevant to sport at all levels. Parents now recognise that a career in professional sport, for the limited few with a potential talent capable of being nurtured and developed, can be as rewarding, profitable and self-fulfilling as any conventional and traditional trade or profession. Yet sporting talents may never achieve their full potential without adequate coaching, teaching and premises at school level provided from within the bureaucratic framework of the government Department for Education and Employment, as distinct from the portfolio attributable to a junior Minister in the Department of Culture, Media and Sport, associated with sport who has no formal, if any, direct affiliation with the three government departments associated with school sport: Education, Health and Environment.

Finally, for the great majority of sports participants, the natural enjoyment and fun to be shared require a need for facilities and coaching services. Thus, the integration of Parents, Schools and Clubs is as crucial for the personal happiness and self-fulfilment of all concerned with sport and recreation as it is for the ultimate performance of national representatives.

Accordingly, of equal importance to the safety element explained in the next chapter in the public protection of sport is the dimension of safeguarding the future of schools, school playing fields, playgrounds and competitive sport in schools. These demand even greater attention. No need exists for any who cares for British sport to explain or justify the contention. In this context, however, it is worth recalling how the founder of the modern Olympic Games based his own ideal upon the games ethic of the Victorian English public school system.

In *This Great Symbol: Pierre de Coubertin and the Origins of the Modern Olympic Games*, his biographer, Professor John J Macaloon, of the University of Chicago explains (p 79) how de Coubertin erroneously attributed to Dr Arnold of Rugby School the images of sporting emphasis created by Arnold's best known pupil there, Thomas Hughes, in *Tom Brown's Schooldays*, and how,

'In the memories of 1880's Englishmen, Arnold had indeed become associated with athletic games... Coubertin's identification of Arnold with education sport was an illusion in Freud's sense of the term: a deep and multiply determined wish fulfilled. Coubertin needed a link between school reform, social and moral education, and athletic games; and he needed that link embodied in a single, distant, exotic, kind and fatherly figure of patriotic and progressive genius to serve him as an image and the new France as a model. Because he needed Arnold to be this man, so he made him to be'.

Arnold's personal priorities were first religion, second character and moral leadership, and third intellectual excellence. His impact socially and educationally has been enduring, beyond the inspiration for de Coubertin's resurrection of the Olympic Games in 1896. A few years and also half-a-century later four unpublicised examples from renowned celebrities

    Osbert Sitwell
    Bobby Charlton
    Gary Lineker
    Will Carling

illustrate the significance of sport in education at different times and at different levels in the social hierarchy. These lead into section 76 of the Education Act 1944 now re-enacted substantially as section 9 of the Education Act 1996, a little known enactment which could have fundamental effects on British sport and physical education if parents and people concerned with and about the future welfare of British sport were aware of it. The under or non-usage of it to date confirms another level of unawareness.

PARENTS AND SCHOOLS

The younger generation of the Sitwell family, Sir Sacheverell, Sir Osbert and Dame Edith, were among Britain's literary leaders during the earlier part of the twentieth century. When Sir Osbert Sitwell's parents discovered 'that the headmaster was the most famous dribbler in England' (*The Scarlet Tree*) they were converted to their choice of preparatory school for his early education at the century's turn. The school was Ludgrove, then at Cockfosters near Barnet, Hertfordshire. It has now long been settled in its Second World War home at Wokingham in Berkshire. The headmaster was G O Smith, legendary amateur centre-forward for England on twenty occasions alongside the equally memorable professional players such as Steve Bloomer (Derby County), Ernest 'Nudger' Needham (Sheffield United), and John Goodall (Preston North End). Nearly half a century later, Bobby Charlton's grandfather, a member of the famous Northumberland Milburn family, persuaded the headmaster, Mr Hunter, at Ashington Primary School that his grandson's entry to Morpeth Grammar School after passing the eleven plus examination would deny his grandson the continued development of soccer because rugby was the school's traditional game; and, as Charlton himself recorded in *This Game of Soccer* (1967) 'Much to my relief I was switched to Bedlington Grammar - and soccer'.

Consistent with that pattern, during the later 1980s and early 1990s, it emerged that parental choice destined England's professional soccer captain, Gary Lineker, to attend the City of Leicester Boys School. This school had a soccer tradition as distinct from a more popular rugby-orientated tradition in the same city; and his rugby playing counterpart, Will Carling, was switched from Shrewsbury's great soccer heritage to Sedbergh and its rugby playing inheritance.

None of these profound choices needed or at their respective times would have been able to make use independently of Parliament's provision for such entitlements today under the Education Act 1944, enacted during the latter period of the Second World War.

Section 76 of that same Act [now s 9 of the 1996 Act] provides :

'In the exercise and performance of all powers and duties conferred and imposed on them by this Act (the Secretary of State) and local education authorities *shall have regard to the [1996: general] principle that, so far as*

*is compatible with the provision of efficient instruction and training and the
avoidance of unreasonable public expenditure, pupils are to be educated in
accordance with the wishes of their parents.'* [With my emphasis.]

Section 99 of that same Act (now s 497 of the Education Act 1996) contains
a limited sanction for enforcing this section. It creates a complaints
procedure to the Secretary of State, who 'may make an order' for such
enforcement of section 76 (now s 9) as is appropriate and practicable.
Furthermore, without resiling in any form and indeed by way of affirmation
the Education Act 1980 (now contained within the Education Act 1996)
provides under the heading (again with the author's emphasis).

6   Parental preferences
(1) Every local education authority shall make arrangements for enabling
the parent of a child in the area of the authority *to express a preference
as to the school at which he wishes education to be provided for his
child* in the exercise of the authority's functions and *to give reasons
for his preference.*
(2) Subject to subsection (3) below, it shall be the duty of a local education
authority and of the governors of a county or voluntary school to
comply with any preference expressed in accordance with the
arrangements.
(3) The duty imposed by subsection (2) above does not apply—
(a) if compliance with the preference would prejudice the provision
of efficient education or the efficient use of resources:
(b) if the preferred school is an aided or special agreement school and
compliance with the preference would be incompatible with any
arrangements between the governors and the local education
authority [made under subsection (6) below] or;
(c) if the arrangements for admission to the preferred school are based
wholly or partly on selection by reference to ability or aptitude
and compliance with the preference would be incompatible with
selection under the arrangements.

Section 76 [now s 9 of the 1996 Act]

It has been used in non-recreational circumstances on varied occasions
with varying success during the last four decades for situations ranging
from religion to policy making decisions about schools. Five may be cited
as illustrating a general approach.

Watt v Kesteven County Council ([1955] 1 QB 408) established that
section 76 laid down the generalities to be regarded along with other
considerations, including a power to make exceptions. If that basis for

action fails to motivate the local authority, then the practical availability of a complaint to the Minister to exercise his default powers under section 99 also exists. The Courts can still be used if he or the local authority exercise their Parliamentary powers capriciously or unreasonably (*Associated Provincial Picture Houses Ltd v Wednesbury Corporation* [1948] 1 KB 223); and *Cummings v Birkenhead Corporation* [1971] 2 All ER 881 confirmed that parental wishes are only one factor to be taken into consideration.

Both of these precedents come from the sensitive area of religious education. The more robust traditional sporting sphere, with its crucial impact on national health and fitness should and could have better results for sport and physical education if challenged on the right sporting and education issues and in the right circumstances of for example, unreasonable, illogical, and spurious egalitarian politically-motivated objections to sporting competition in schools. Thus, a school or teaching staff or governing body which denies pupils the undoubted advantages of competitive sport because of, for example, an unnatural or half-thought out social theory about egalitarianism or an equally debatable premise, could be justifiably and perhaps successfully challenged by parents under section 76 (now s 9). Further, if either local or national government officials were to ignore the forces of parental and public opinion, separate and apart from general national as well as sporting issues involved, there would be two further avenues available to parents:

(1)   a right of referral by complaint to the Minister under section 99 (now s 497), and

(2)   as a last resort, an overriding control of judicial review by the courts.

These provisions would have been available for the happy-go-lucky six-year-old schoolgirl certified as terrified of attending gymnastic classes but under threat of compulsion to attend by Suffolk County Council (*Daily Telegraph*, 16 October 1992). The capacity of parents to enforce the law depends, of course, upon the financial capacity to sustain litigation in addition to the will to pursue it. This was illustrated when parent-ratepayers objected to the London Borough of Enfield's proposals to change the system of education and character of schools within the borough. They brought an action to restrain the council from acting on its proposals. The parents succeeded in part with an injunction; but they were referred back to the Minister under section 99 of the Education Act 1944 (now s 497 of the 1996 Act) enforcing their rights under section 76 (now s 9) (*Bradbury v London Borough of Enfield* [1967] 3 All ER 434). Costs, however, were awarded in favour of the plaintiff parent-ratepayers.

Three recent cases since the first edition of 1988 also illustrate how this parliamentary machinery can be operated effectively, and significantly, because public bodies are involved, as distinct from private sporting governing institutions, by the process known as judicial review.

In *Harvey v Strathclyde Regional Council* (((1989) *Independent*, 6 July) the House of Lords upheld a decision of the First Division of the Court of Session (which had overruled the Lord Ordinary) to confirm that an education authority in the Paisley outskirts of Glasgow had in fact had regard to Scotland's equivalent under section 28(1) of the Education (Scotland) Act 1980 to section 76 (now s 9 of the 1996 Act) of the Education Act 1944 applicable to England and Wales for educating children in accordance with their parents' wishes. For it has consulted extensively with the parents and taken account of the parent representations before reaching a decision to discontinue a school even though the decision conflicted with the desires of most of the parents. The proceedings were initiated by a schoolgirl's mother who objected to the closure of the school and the transfer of pupils to another school.

A few months later the report of the London Queen's Bench Division having allowed an application for judicial review by school governors who opposed the local authority's policy which 'went against' the statutory duty under section 6 of the Education Act 1980 (now ss 411 and 413 of the Education Act 1996) to comply with parental preferences for a school for their child (*R v Greenwich London Borough Council, ex parte Governors of John Ball Primary School* (1989) *Times*, 16 November).

More recently, and again in a non-sporting context, section 76 of the Education Act 1944 and section 6 of the Education Act 1980 (both sections now part of the 1996 Act), for considering parental prejudices, were recognised as available in appropriate circumstances during the course of a successful application geared to section 55(4) of the Education Act 1944 (now s 509(5) of the 1996 Act) for judicial review relating to a legitimate expectation for consultation by a local education authority with parents in respect of travelling expenses outside the local education authority's district (*R v Rochdale Metropolitan Borough Council, ex parte Schemet* (1992) *Times*, 9 September, Roche J) and see also Butterworths *Law of Education*. Editors: Peter Liell, John E Coleman and Kenneth Poole.

Finally, in *R v Essex County Council, ex parte C* (((1993) *Times*, 9 December) the Court of Appeal dismissed an appeal from Jowett J who had refused a mother's application for judicial review seeking free transport under section 55 of the Education Act 1944 for a child 'with special needs' to facilitate his attendance at the school of his parents choice. In particular the Court explained that parental choice under section 76 of the 1944 Act was subject, inter alia, to 'the avoidance of unreasonable public expenditure'.

These are undoubted legal rights for enforcement under section 76 of the Education Act 1944 and section 6 of the Education Act 1980 created by Parliament and capable of enforcement through the courts. They were preserved intact by the monumental Education Reform Act 1988 (238 sections; 13 Schedules) which paid token lip service to physical education as a foundation subject within the National Curriculum under section 3(1)(a) and also by the Education Act 1993 (308 sections; 21 Schedules) which ignores physical education entirely. These two Acts have now been consolidated within the Education Act 1996: 583 sections; 40 schedules. They are all available to Parent Teacher Associations (PTAs) who have been concerned about extreme politically or socially debatable decisions to diminish or demolish competitive sports within and against other schools, without any apparent hope or means for challenging them. Local authorities, school teachers and governors who have hitherto considered their controversial attitudes to be immune from any effective challenge and decisions should be in no doubt about the potential parental capacity to attack successfully and to rout an intransigent enemy on this particular front. Finally, although the no less convoluted Statutory Instrument SI 1992/603 The Education (National Curriculum) (Attainment Target and Programmes of Study in Physical Education) Order 1992 provides in generally vague terms for such programmes and an attainment target, availability or rather non-availability of facilities for these purposes is not provided for them.

Another important sphere in schools is the equally contentious issue about preservation or sale of surplus school fields. The issue involves a mixture of local economic and political policies with some legal safeguards which are linked to planning law. Objectors to such policies are entitled to be vigilant for and alerted to action upon applications under the Town and Country Planning Acts by developers for change of use, particularly following a Domesday Book Register of school playing fields as explained on page 189 below.

(1)   Dual use of facilities

In 1983 the Environment Committee of the House of Commons was appointed to examine, inter alia, associated public bodies connected with the Department of the Environment, identifying expenditure, administration and policy. Its slender report and examination of evidence published in February 1986 on the Sports Council as an associated public body makes light reading compared with the erudite report from the Education, Science and Arts Committee of the House of Commons published in October 1982 on the Public and Private Funding of the Arts (HC 49). Nevertheless, at pages xxii in Paragraph 56, the Sports Council Environment Committee report did conclude:

> 56. Everyone is agreed that more dual use of school sports facilities would be desirable. There would be a net saving of public money and probably other benefits for all concerned. The way forward has been shown in many

places. The difficulties involved can be solved by officials if they are given a lead and persuaded to shed Departmental protectionism. What is needed is a greater firmness by Ministers on what is in the public interest. We were glad to hear that Mr Richard Tracey [then Under-Secretary of the DoE with responsibility for sport] thought the same and intended to have discussions with Ministerial colleagues in the DES. We strongly urge all Ministers concerned to bring these discussions to a successful and speedy conclusion and to place the public good before sectional Departmental interests'.

(2)   School playing fields and school games

The result of the Committee's 1986 recommendation for government ministerial coordination and cooperation was a joint seminar at the DoE organised by the two departments in December 1986. The conclusion was the establishment of a Forum of Commission. Yet throughout the proceedings no recognition was given at any stage by the conventional educational, environmental and recreational or Government sources in attendance that the present law suffices to provide answers for many of the clearly identifiable problems. It exists positively and negatively. Negatively, those same planning laws which were used in March 1987 by Hammersmith and Fulham Council to warn Fulham Football & Athletic Company's proposed asset strippers to 'keep off the Craven Cottage grass', are equally available to any group of local objectors in any part of the country to protest to local authorities who may be seduced by the financial offerings from similar property predators to local authorities for selling off school playing fields.*

No doubt, following from the Environment Committee's recommendation, a year later, March 1987, witnessed a joint Sports Council - Arts Council production entitled 'Getting it together: guidance on housing sports and arts activities in the same building' with a joint Foreword from the then respective Chairmen, John Smith, CBE and Sir William Rees-Mogg. Whatever resulted from such a guidance required further attention which was still unresolved at the time of the second edition in 1994, and the overall position still does not diminish the continued erosion of playing and recreational surfaces in a manner perpetually monitored without effective Government response by The National Playing Fields Association.

Thus while these pages were being prepared in late July 1999 on the eve of a Government change of Sports Minister, the Association was writing to its sympathisers

---

* See also the article by Gareth A. Davies in the *Daily Telegraph*, 3 November 1999 'Public can help to preserve playing fields', which lists school playing fields pending sale in October 1999.

68 School playing fields lost with the Government's consent since last October - ONLY ONE SAVED.

707 (at least) playing fields under threat since September 1996 when the then Government produced 'Sport: Raising the Game' which promised to protect playing fields.

The 1993 Register of Recreation Land managed by Sport England has not yet been updated.

There is still no statutory protection for recreation space and not even a hint that the present Government is minded to extend the NPFA's list of protected fields.'*

A Foreword from the then Minister for Sport, Robert Atkins, then housed in the Department for Education, in a 1991 publication entitled, 'A Sporting Double: School and Community' explained how a study entitled 'The Dual Use of School Sports Facilities' was published in June 1987 and this in turn led to the 1991 production,

'designed to help local education authorities, school governors and headmasters introduce or extend dual use provision in their schools. Recreation authorities and sports organisations will also find it useful in considering this possibility with their local schools'.

It concluded, at 1991 with the aspiration how,

'The guidance builds on the initiatives which the Department of Education and Science and the Environment (before the transference of government sports issues to the Department of National Heritage after the 1992 General Election), the Sports Council and others have developed over the years and as a result we hope that an increasing number of school sports facilities will be opened up for the benefit of the whole community'.

Unfortunately the wishes from the then Ministers for Sport and Education and Science at that 1991 date were overtaken by the conflict in Government circles which surfaced in July 1993. The Secretary of State for Education John Patten proposed that existing School Premises Regulations should no longer apply so far as minimum standards for teaching and recreation space were concerned. The then Minister for National Heritage housing the Government Sports Unit, Peter Brooke, was reported as seeing it

'as a cost-saving device with potentially disastrous results for team games and the ability to deliver the PE requirements of the national curriculum',

---

*   For anyone aware of a playing field under threat the National Playing Fields Association has a 'Land Loss Line' on 0171 590 4622 or e-mail at npfa.co.uk.

as provided for in the Education Reform Act 1988 (now part of the Education Act 1996).

This tension at Ministerial level in mid-1993 is wholly consistent with the administrative government indecisiveness which has followed from the House of Commons Environment Committee's conclusions in February 1986. It also contrasted with the claim made at the CCPR's Annual Conference in November 1993 by the House of Lords representative of the Department of National Heritage, Baroness Trumpington, that the 1993 Education Act with 308 sections allowed dual use partners such as the sports council and local authorities to enter into agreements with school governing bodies for the joint management of school facilities. Their implementation and application however, would be a matter for the Department of Education.

A classic example appears for preservation in Chapter 12, *Administrative advice* at pages 424-425 which was tracked by the *Daily Mail's* award-winning Ian Woolridge's 1987 campaign for preserving the War Memorial Recreation Ground at New Milton, near Brockenhurst and Southampton from the attempted transfer of 3.6 acres of oak fringed-grass with a car park for a supermarket.

The effect of such objection formalised under the Town and Country Planning Acts 1945–1971, would be to cause an inspector to conduct an enquiry, usually in public. This in turn would permit evidence to be called in support by any objectors, as well as for the applicants. The developer's plans would be scrutinised within the context of local, school and general environmental and social needs. The inspector would report formally to the Minister, in whose hands the overriding decision would be made: at the Government department which houses the so-called Sports Minister in his constitutional role as Under-Secretary at the Department of Environment (not, and never since Lord Hailsham's conception of the role, at the Department for Education and Science), and now in 1999 at the Department of Culture, Media and Sport.

All planning applications have to be advertised and notice given for the purpose of objections being lodged within a specified timescale. Accordingly, the rapes of school playing fields are subject to ministerial control under Parliamentary law and are controlled by the courts in the event of capricious or unreasonable ministerial misconduct. This is only if the victims are ready, willing and minded to operate the mechanisms advised by Lord Denning in *Miller v Jackson*, cited at p 141, infra.

Positively, section 508 of the Education Act 1996, contains provisions to facilitate recreation and social and physical training. Indeed, it contains a specific duty which is self-evident, namely,

'**508   Functions in respect of facilities for recreation and social and physical training**

(1) A local education authority shall secure that the facilities for primary,

secondary and further education provided for their area include adequate facilities for recreation and social and physical training.

(2) For that purpose a local education authority—

(a) may establish, maintain and manage, or assist the establishment, maintenance and management of,—
  (i) camps, holiday classes, playing fields, play centres, and
  (ii) other places, including playgrounds, gymnasiums and swimming baths not appropriated to any school or other educational institution,

  at which facilities for recreation and social and physical training are available for persons receiving primary, secondary or further education;

(b) may organise games, expeditions and other activities for such persons; and

(c) may defray, or contribute towards, the expenses of such games, expeditions and other activities.

(3) When making arrangements for the provision of facilities or the organisation of activities in the exercise of their powers under subsection (2), a local education authority shall, in particular, have regard to the expediency of co-operating with any voluntary societies or bodies whose objects include the provision of facilities or the organisation of activities of a similar character.'

That duty in substance creates a foundation and link for threading local education facilities with a community, whether through a club or not; and if any doubt or uncertainty could be raised it would be dispelled by the more recent provision under the Education (No 2) Act 1986, which received the Royal Assent on 7 November 1986. It was designed specifically to meet this particular problem of dual use facilities, and was announced for this purpose at the CCPR Annual Conference at that time, ie providing for the use of school premises outside school hours by members of the community served by the school. It is now contained within the Education Act 1996. Section 149 of the 1996 Act provides:

'149 County and maintained special schools: control of use of premises outside school hours

(1) The articles of government for every county and maintained special school shall provide—

(a) for the use of the school premises outside school hours to be under the control of the governing body except to the extent provided by any transfer of control agreement into which they may enter by virtue of paragraph (c);

(b) for the governing body in exercising control of the use of the school premises outside school hours—
  (i) to comply with any directions given to them by the local education authority by virtue of this sub-paragraph; and

(ii) to have regard to the desirability of the premises being made available for community use;

(c) for the governing body to have power to enter into a transfer of control agreement if their purpose, or one of their purposes, in doing so is to promote community use of the school premises outside school hours; and

(d) for the governing body, where they enter into a transfer of control agreement, to secure so far as reasonably practicable that the controlling body exercises control in accordance with any directions given to the governing body by virtue of paragraph (b)(i).'

It was implemented on 1 September 1987 (SI 1987/344 C8). How the section has been operated varies inevitably between local authorities. A comparable sanction to section 99 of the Education Act 1944, does not exist: and the ultimate power for enforcement may be required at ballot boxes during the period of local elections.

At the time of writing, uncertainty overshadows the extent of future usage because of financial restraints. A similar situation exists for the equally important potential nexus between clubs and schools sport. This in turn brings into focus again the significance of physical education as a charitable concept. Linked to the local Government Finance Act 1988, it contains the key for clubs which seek to fill the gap caused by teachers' strikes or reluctance to provide out of school facilities in their own time with club coaching facilities. Such legitimate substitutes to replace physical recreation arrangements abdicated by the teaching profession justify clubs to claim under the Local Government Finance Act 1988. There are advantages, mandatory or discretionary, which are dependant upon an application of the law relating to charities, now established by the House of Lords ruling in the FA Youth Trust Deed decision to extend to physical education for young people (*IRC v McMullan* [1984] AC1), and extended by the more recent House of Lords in *Guild v IRC* [1992] 2 All ER 10. These decisions absorb the 'interests of social welfare' criteria under the Recreational Charities Act, 1958 to include 'some similar purpose in connection with sport' related to a bequest 'to be used in connection with the Sports Centre [then] in North Berwick'.

(3)   Schools: club sport, schools and rates

Sections 47(1) and (2) and 48 of the Local Government Finance Act provide for rate relief by local authorities when premises are linked to charitable purposes; now as guided by the House of Lords.

This is consistent with the position for opposing planning applications on change of use for school premises, which is considered in detail under Chapter 12, *Administrative advice*, and, because it creates a form of local tax, also under Chapter 14, *No fine on fun*. In the context of school sport, however, the relevance of education and sporting charity law can be seen for clubs which structure their affairs and premises to provide the crucial coaching, teaching and training facilities in order to obtain the correct benefits.

A perfectly legitimate arrangement was recommended at a CCPR seminar in 1980 after the House of Lords judgment in the FA Youth Trust Deed case by a Senior Charity Commissioner, Mr Charles Weston. He advocated hiving-off a section of a sports club's premises and affairs to qualify for charitable purposes generally. This is equally applicable and available for rating purposes. Indeed it was validly established for VAT purposes when two sections of a bowls club at Watchet in Somerset successfully separated their indoor from their outdoor sections under the appropriate governing bodies (see Chapter 14, *No fine on fun*).

As we shall see in Chapter 12, *Administrative advice*, and 14, *No fine on fun*, the discretion has been operated advantageously in certain local authority areas and rejected in others. What may not be readily realised, which emerged by an omission from a valuable *Times* newspaper series during early December 1986, was recognition of the problem by the Wolfenden Committee Report on Sport in 1960 commissioned by the then CCPR. At the end of a detailed Paragraph 160, it concluded on page 64:

'We therefore would urge most strongly that local authorities should examine the claims of sports bodies for rating relief with the utmost sympathy and should treat them more generously rather than less generously than in the past. For the provision of maintenance of a facility for physical recreation on the part of a voluntary body may in a very real sense relieve the local authority of its own responsibility to provide such facilities, as laid down by various Parliamentary enactments, including Section 53 of the Education Act 1944'.

That section 53 cited at page 96 of the second edition of this book (and now section 508 of the 1996 Act) created a duty to provide 'facilities ... for social and physical training'. Thus, the wheel of history goes full circle. More than thirty years after the Report (which led ultimately to the Sports Council's creation), the need for its recommendations for rate reliefs ties in which the growing concern for the future of sport in schools and clubs. With the growing politicisation of sport generally, the ultimate sanction could yet be at local election times if the discretion allowed under legal remedies is not operated with 'the utmost sympathy' recommended as long ago as 1960. That sympathy was certainly recognised by the House of Lords judicial committee on a successful appeal after the majority judges in the High Court and Court of Appeal had failed to demonstrate it for charitable legal sporting status (*IRC v McMullan* supra, p 154), and again when overruling the Inner House of Scotland's Court of Session in *Guild v IRC* [1992] 2 All ER 10 (supra).

(4)   Physical education and charitable status and the courts

In 1980 the House of Lords judicial committee in *IRC v McMullan* ([1981] AC 1) confirmed that the Charity Commissioners' registration (eight years earlier in 1972) of an FA Youth Trust Deed was a validly registrable charity. This emphasised that physical education is legally regarded as educational for eligibility to charitable status. The taxation advantages for it are considered in Chapter 14, *No fine on fun*, and the consequences for rating of sports clubs are considered there, too, as well as below.

The real significance is seen in a cameo of dialogue between counsel and one of the two Court of Appeal majority judges overruled by the House of Lords in the interim journey from that 1972 registration to the 1980 winning post at Westminster:

> '*Appeal Judge*: Are you really saying that physical education is education like Latin and Greek?
>
> *Counsel*: Yes, my Lord'.

The Court of Appeal 2–1 majority, the first instance judge, and the Inland Revenue Commissioners, had all rejected the Charity Commissioners' registration of the FA Youth Trust Deed. The necessity for the House of Lords to be called upon to rule, as it did unanimously with all five judicial opinions, demonstrated vividly the gap between differing legal attitudes to this vital area of national interest. Physical education has always been linked to national health in the manner that sport and recreation legislatively and historically have been geared to the interests of national security in the United Kingdom, with priority given to archery over banned football in medieval times, and recognition of the need for national fitness built into the Fisher Education Acts of 1918 and 1921 at the end of the First World War; the Physical Training and Recreation Act 1937 in the years leading up to the outbreak of the Second World War; and, as we have seen above in the specific provisions of the Butler Education Act 1944, conceived and enacted during the peak years of the Second World War.

The final judicial score was 6–3 in favour of the FA Youth Trust. At half-time stage in the Court of Appeal ([1979] 1 All ER 588) it was 1–3 against the religion, education and general public good. During the interim period, while awaiting the result of the Court of Appeal's reserved judgment, I had commented 'Many consider that sport qualifies for them all, both realistically and cynically' (*Sport and the Law* (1978)). In a commercially oriented society lacking spiritual leadership that conclusion is reaffirmed here.

Indicative of the differing and limited attitudes are the thoughts contained in the leading House of Lords judgment delivered by the Lord

Chancellor, Lord Hailsham of St Marylebone, ([1981] AC 1) at page 17:

> 'I do not think that the courts have as yet explored the extent to which elements of organisation, instruction or the disciplined inculcation of information, instruction or skill may limit the whole concepts of education. I believe that in some ways it will prove more extensive, in others more restrictive than has been thought hitherto. But it is clear to me at least that the decision in *Re Mariette* [1915] 2 Ch 284 is not to be read in a sense which confines its application forever to gifts to a particular institution'.

Edgar Mariette was an Aldenham School housemaster who had made his will in 1908 containing bequests to the school he had served as boy and teacher, for building Eton fives squash rackets courts, and athletics prizes. Eight years later in 1915 when the casualty lists from the First World War battlefronts were extended by newsvendor placards at different ends of the Commonwealth announcing the deaths of Victor Trumper at the early age of 37 and W G Grace at 67, London's High Court in the Chancery Division heard contending arguments for and against the Mariette legacies. Mr Justice Eve had no reputation equivalent to the then recently retired Lord Chief Justice, Lord Alverstone, who had created a sporting track record as athletics Blue, administrator, and author; but he was a product of Exeter College, Oxford, where modern competitive athletics began in 1850. His judgment of less than two pages in the Law Reports ([1915] 2 Ch 284) was warmly endorsed by the House of Lords in the FA Youth Trust Deed case, ignored until then by many British sporting governing bodies, but relied upon in Australia after the Second World War to validate in December 1954 a bequest to the Sydney University Rugby Football Club (in *Kearins v Kearins* (1957) SR 286 (NSW)). It is reproduced *in toto* in Appendix 12. For present purposes the key passage of legal and educational sporting principles is contained in the following sequences, at pages 288—289:

> 'The object of this charity is the education, in the widest sense, of boys and young men between the ages of ten and nineteen. No one of sense could be found to suggest that between those ages any boy can be properly educated unless at least as much attention is given to the development of his body as is given to the development of his mind. It is necessary, therefore, in any satisfactory system of education to provide for both mental and bodily occupation, mental occupation by means of the classics and those other less inviting studies to which a portion of the day is devoted, and bodily occupation by means of regular organised games: to leave 200 boys at large and to their own devices during their leisure hours would probably result in their quickly relapsing into something approaching barbarism. For these reasons I think it is essential that in a school of learning of this description, a school receiving and retaining as boarders boys of these ages, there should

be organised games as part of the daily routine, and I do not see how the other part of the education can be successfully carried on without them'.

Forty-two years later McLelland J in the New South Wales Equity Court applied this precedent cf *Re Mariette* [supra] in *Kearins* (supra) to a bequest of £2,000 'for fostering the sport of Rugby Union at Sydney University'. Curiously it was not cited in any of the three court hearings of the FA Youth Trust Deed case, (although as we shall see later in the chapter relating to actionable sporting negligence in personal injuries Australian authorities are eminently persuasive citations for United Kingdom courts). As he explained:

'I cannot see any difference in principle between the provision of the means of bodily and physical development for school children or young men at school and such provision who attend the university who are, for the most part, young men and women. Participation in the sporting activities of the [Sydney] University has, I think, always been regarded as an important element in the development of men and women at the university, not only in respect of bodily and physical development but also as part of a well-balanced student'.

That attitude is consistent with Eve J's judgment before it and Lord Hailsham's opinion afterwards. The extension of the Recreational Charities Act 1958 'interests of social welfare' to include after a bequest 'to be used in connection with the sports centre [then] in North Berwick' also a concept of 'some similar purpose in connection with sport', creates a legal googly yet to be bowled to the whole world of sport and the law [*Guild v IRC* [1992] 2 All ER 10].

Nevertheless the Central Council of Physical Recreation's annual conference in November 1986 publicised the verdict of the Secondary Heads' Association that for British sport in schools;

'It is time to say there is a crisis in many parts of Britain. Not everywhere but in enough areas for us to be concerned as a nation'.

In March 1987 that general warning was particularised with a detailed report. For this chapter, it suffices to explain summarily how:

— 95 per cent of schools have suffered a 'rapid decline' in weekend and after-school sports fixtures in the past two years:
— 75 per cent of pupils have no opportunity to learn to swim at school;
— 40 per cent of schools have inadequate facilities for dance and gymnastics;
— so few schools employ groundsmen that nearly half of all playing fields are substandard by department of education and science criteria;

— only one teacher in 10 apart from specialist PE teachers helps out with school sports. In many schools help is non-existent;
— children aged 12–14 have on average only two hours of exercise a week and 65 per cent of sixth-formers can opt out of PE and games.

At the same time, the CCPR itself estimated that 547 school playing fields in whole or in part have been, or are about to be, sold. Subsequently, when a Domesday Book Register of School Playing Fields was published under the impetus of the Central Council of Physical Recreation, the National Playing Fields Association and Sports Council in October 1993, it showed that outside London 404 sites (about 1.75% of the total) were then currently under threat from development with planning permission either already granted or being sought: but it did not identify past playing field losses. The reasons for these unhappy developments are complex and are reflective of wider political and industrial problems surrounding the British educational picture, of which sport has always been a crucial segment the problem appears to have been insoluble, and any reasons it can be advanced for the overall position. For sport it may be suggested with confidence that the problems are concentrated on the following separate and interconnecting areas:

(a) industrial differences of approach to teachers' working conditions and pay between the profession, employers and Government;
(b) the conflict between traditional outside school hours recreational activities with developing family, social and industrial demands upon teachers;
(c) the novel attitude from different sources which challenges the authenticity and value of competitive sport in a nation which has given sport to the world;
(d) availability and preservation of school premises;
(e) dual use facilities for premises between schools and club industrial and social activities.

Finally at the end of a DoE and DES joint seminar in December 1986 hosted by the CCPR and the New Sports Minister Richard Tracey MP, I enquired of the senior DES representatives whether there existed within the Department a separate section for Physical Education: the cryptic answer was 'No. We also don't have one for maths and Latin. Why should we?' In 1991 a House of Commons Education, Science and Arts Committee endorsed the value of 'Sport in Schools' with special recommendations and in March 1994 the CCPR published a 'Charter for School Sport'.

One area which is never prayed in aid, however, is the only weapon which can be used effectively: the law. This illustrates another level of unawareness of the extent to which the law applies and is available when operated for the benefit of sport, and the society they both serve. Against a background of Parliamentary legislation and that overwhelming judicial approach to physical and sporting education in the United Kingdom, the wider more generally recognisable responsibilities within sporting education also need attention.

RESPONSIBILITIES

(1)   Introductory

Arrangements for facilities and premises which blend parents and schools with outside agencies simplifies application of the appropriate law. Parliamentary enactments and the common law and equity applied by the judges do not differentiate between different levels or categories of activities or disciplines. Schoolteachers, club coaches and both amateur and professional players are all subject to the same duties of care to guard against foreseeable risks, breaches of which causing damage, injury or loss, create the tort of negligence. Education authorities, clubs, governing bodies and promoters and entrepreneurs are subject to identical responsibilities for safety of premises and equipment; and all are equal and subject to liability under the criminal law. Different disciplines, recreation facilities and sporting situations must create differing examples. The principles are common to all of them. The illustrations cannot be exhaustive and others will no doubt occur and also apply to whatever results from extending the National Curriculum already referred to in this chapter and in Dr Mary Malecka's Appendix (p 539).

(2)   Supervisory

The supervisory roles of the teacher at school or the coach in sport or any form of physical recreation are identified in law, morality and spirituality. All generations in any civilised society are heirs to their own traditions and act in loco parentis to their successors. The teacher and coach positively assume an authority for which the law and society hold them responsible, legally and morally.

I recall enquiring of the wife of a Southern England Football League Club chairman, who had been a distinguished and prominent legal practitioner, whether any of her husband's director colleagues acted as a personnel adviser to young players who sought fame and fortune away from their northern homes. The incredulity with which the question was received suggested to me that this particular board of directors had never considered the point and the corollary may well be that the whole concept of acting in *loco parentis* as football directors and perhaps even to committee members is as alien to them as *mens sana in corpore sano*.

The law's approach is simple and clear-cut. Teachers, coaches, physical educationalists and all who act in loco parentis take on board the essential elements establishing the law relating to liability for civil negligence, ie:

(a) a duty of care
(b) to guard against foreseeable risks which
(c) if resulting in foreseeable damage
(d) creates a breach of duty
(e) with consequential liability for negligence.

Finally in the well-publicised rugby schoolboy drama of *Van Oppen v Clerk and the Bradford Charity Trustees* [1989] 1 All ER 273: affirmed [1989] 3 All ER 389 CA, Boreham J rejected (1) on the evidence a claim for alleged negligent coaching and (2) affirmed by the Court of Appeal, a claim for non-insurance on the basis that there was no higher duty on a school than on a parent to insure. On the evidence, however, a claim based on actionable non-disclosure appears to have been available, as explained in *New Law Journal* 1988 Vol 138 pp 532–533. What was not severally recognised at the time and indeed even now is relatively unknown was the initiative which recommended the compulsory implementation of insurance against injury in rugby playing schools. The sub-committee of the Medical Officers Schools Association (MOSA) was responsible. It demonstrates clearly the essential interaction between health, physical education and within the context of sport and society, its function within the Rule of Law, on and off the field.

The test of in *loco parentis* varies with different generations and age groups. It was applied by HH Judge Barry at Bradford County Court during 1999 in the case of *Casson v MOD* (infra). He succeeded as a schoolboy in establishing liability against Army personnel who caused personal injury and a broken leg during a work experience informal football match for which the *Affuto Nartoy v Clarke* (infra) and *Condon v Basi* (infra) principles were also cited in the reserved judgment. The changing attitudes to corporal punishment and the claims to chastise and censure are illustrative of this; and it may well be argued that conflicting opinions could exist about the level of care which is both blameworthy and blameless. Within this negligence formula the only guide must be the existing cases until the law is tested with special circumstances and developing disciplines such as hang-gliding or the martial arts, whose activities have yet to be considered in reported cases. Against this background, the most recent relevant and appropriate citations can be summarised in the manner considered in Chapter 5, *Public protection*. Closer analysis of these and other cases will disclose differing dicta from judges for defining different categories, ie coaches, supervisors, teachers. These must be tailored to any special identifiable situation, subject to any overriding House of Lords or Parliamentary guidelines which may yet emerge. For present purposes, the intention must be to sustain the theme throughout this book: a level of awareness.

Finally, in the context of *R v Hickson* (infra), when a former Olympic swimming coach was convicted and sentence for sexually abusing swimmers, at Cardiff Crown Court during 1985 a contribution in the *Journal of the British Association of Sports Medicine* [August 1999: vol 33 No 4] under the joint authorship of Rod Jaques and Celia Brackenbridge entitled *Child abuse and the sports medicine consultation* alerted sports medical practitioners to consider concealed signs of potential child abuse from physical education and coaching sources in *loco parentis* to their charges.

1932	Decision	Citation
Unprecedented striking in a school playground of golf ball which hit eye of fellow pupil inside a school building causing injury.	No liability **Principle** School and staff exonerated from responsibility which could not have been prevented even by supervision.	*Langham v Governors of Wellingborough School and Fryer* (1932) 101 LKJB 513, 147 LT 91: 96 JP 236: 30 LGR 276

1936	Decision	Citation
Schoolboy during vaulting horse gymnastic training at school landed in 'a stumble' suffering personal injury.	Local Authority liable **Principle** Lack of promptitude by games master to prevent stumble when or after vaulting created lack of care causing accident and negligence.	*Gibbs v Barking Corporation* (1936) All ER 115.

1938	Decision	Citation
Fee paying adult, participating in physical training class wearing rubber shoes, slipped on fairly highly polished floor (suitable for dancing but not for physical exercise) which caused personal injury.	Organising local authority council liable **Principle** (1) Council failed in duty to provide a floor which was reasonably safe in circumstances creating danger beyond usual degree of playing a game;	*Gillmore v London County Council* (1938) 4 All ER 331; 55 TLR 95, 159 LT 615.

(2) *volenti non fit injuria* defence rejected because of consent to risk of this added danger beyond ordinary hazard lawfully practised.

1939

Unanticipated action by child at swimming bath. Let go suddenly of a springboard to which she had been clinging, thereby disrupting preparation to jump from it by another child who suffered injury

Decision

No liability

Principle

Action not capable of anticipation, irrespective of adequacy of supervision, for which evidence was equivocal and not definitive.

Citation

Clark v Bethnal Green Corp (1939) 55 TLR 519.

1939

School pupil injured when fielding at cricket, under supervision of dual-role teacher also acting as umpire. Evidence conflict between: (1) Plaintiff (pupil's) — claim of placed at 'silly mid-on' (facing batsman)

(2) Defendant's (per the master) of 'square leg' location (at right angles to wicket) and moving close to batsman of own accord.

Decision

Liability proved

Principle

Umpire duties precluded exercise of sufficient supervisory care as master in charge. They conflicted with need to prevent boy to be very considerably less than 10 yards from wicket (as adjudged by court). This was a dangerous situation in the circumstances; and also in judgment of failure 'to exercise the care which the law required from a master in charge of pupils in these circumstances'.

Citation

Barfoot v East Sussex County Cl (unreported: *The Head's Legal Guide:* Para 3–111) [Croner Publications]. *Caught in Court:* 1989 John Scott p 221. NB Scott's industrious researches revealed that the trial judge, Humphreys J (Shrewsbury School XI) awarded damages for the Plaintiff Schoolboy after deciding 'with fear and trembling and with as much courage as I can assume', to disagree with the expert evidence testimony of the famous Sussex and England all-round player, Maurice Tate.

1947	Decision	Citation
School game of 'touch' played in room with insufficient space and one participant placed hand unwittingly through glass partition causing injury.	Liability proved. **Principle** Reasonable and prudent father would have contemplated possibility of such an accident.	*Ralph v LCC* (1947) 63 TLR 546 CA, 111 JP 548
1968	**Decision**	**Citation**
Horseplay during schoolbreak caused forseeable injury of eye from discarded elastic rope because of breakdown in usually adequate school supervision.	Liability proved **Principle** (1) Reasonable prudent parent principle (above) not applied to headmaster of school with 900 pupils. (2) Duty breached, to take all reasonable and proper steps to prevent injury between pupils, bearing in mind known propensities of boys or girls between ages 11 and 18.	*Beaumont v Surrey County Council* (1968) 66 LGR 580: 112 SJ 704
1981	**Decision**	**Citation**
12-year-old pupil with dislocated hip and unfit for physical training of which teacher advised. Wrongful persuasion that permission authorised and disability caused awkward movement resulting in injury.	Liability proved **Principle** Double failure: (1) to observe awkward movements. (2) to supervise properly within special category as disabled or crippled child.	*Moore v Hampshire County Council* (1981) 80 LGR 481 C.

1981

18-year-old gymnast injured when using trampoline facilities in gymnasium during period of supervision at gymnasium club.

Decision

Out of court settlement

Principle

No admission of liability on negligence allegation. Claim formulated for £350,000. Insurance policy ceiling at £250,000. Settlement of claim for £250,000, with denial on negligence liability that supervision inadequate.

Citation

Tracey Moore v Redditch and Bromsgrove Gymnast Club (unreported: but recorded for purpose of emphasising the value of insurance for victim and insured).

1984

15-year-old rugby playing schoolboy injured during school game by high tackle from schoolmaster during instructional period, without any unfair play issue.

Decision

Liability proved

Principle

Teacher momentarily forgot playing with young schoolboys of lesser and smaller physique than himself.

Citation

Affuto Nartoy v Clarke & ILEA (1984) *Times*, 9 February

1985

Former Olympic swimming coach sexually abused young swimmers

Decision

Conviction and custodial sentence reduced on appeal to 12 years

Principle

Breach of trust and charged in loco parentis

Citation

R v Hickson (1985) *Times*, 28 September, Cardiff Crown Court

1985

Soccer player injured by foul play in club match sued for wrongful assault and negligence in damages claim for broken leg.

Decision

Liability proved

Principle

Negligence proved and upheld in Court of Appeal because of duty

Citation

Condon v Basi (1985) 2 All ER 453.

owed by one competitor to another to play according to the rules was breached on this occasion by violent foul play.

1988	Decision	Citation
Schoolboy injured by rugby tackle but not insured	Negligence not proved and alleged failure to insure rejected	*Van Oppen v Clerk to the Bedford Charity Trustees* [1989] 1 AER 273 affirmed [1989] 3 All ER 389 CA.
	Principle	
	Evidence of no negligence. No duty to insure equivalent to non-parental duty to insure.	
1991	**Decision**	**Citation**
Schoolboy recovered damages against schoolteacher and governing body for broken neck in swimming bath injury	Liability proved	*Gannon v Rotherham MBC and Others Halsbury's Monthly Review* July 1991 91/1717
	Principle	
	Inadequate supervision and guidance	
1993	**Decision**	**Citation**
Disabled potential Paralympic archery candidate injured in training	Negligence proved	*Morrell v Owen and others Times*, 14 December 1993.
	Principle	
	Higher duty of care owed to athletes under disability than to able-bodied participants	
1996	**Decision**	**Citation**
Under-19 Rugby Union Colts player paralysed by collapsed scrum not regulated by referee in accordance with Laws of the Game	Negligence proved	*Smolden v Whitworth and Nolan* (1996) *Times* 18 December CA
	Principle	
	Failed in duty of care to apply Laws of Game appropriate to under-19 Colts - applying *Condon v Basi* (supra)	

1998	Decision	Citation
Pupil forced to join PE lesson notwithstanding injured ankle	Negligence proved **Principle** Known aggravation of pre-existing injurious condition exacerbated physically injured ankle	*Williams v Rotherham LEA* (1998) *Times* 6 August

1998	Decision	Citation
Broken jaw caused in schools Rugby Match	Conviction 12 months* Youth Offenders Institution **Principle** Criminal liability for school rugby assault	*R v David Calton Yorkshire Post* 29 September

1999	Decision	Citation
Schoolboy injured in work experience Army football game	Negligence proved **Principle** Breach of duty of care and in loco parentis	*Casson v MOD* *Bradford Telegraph v Angus* *Yorkshire Post* [April 1999]

*   Reduced to 3 months on appeal: [1999] 2 Cr App Rep (S) 64, CA.

In a valuable overview of the coaching and teaching field, under the heading 'Should coaches take care?', John Gardiner surveyed this supervisory scene from the widest possible perspective ((1993) *Sport and the Law Journal*, Nov, p 11; *New Law Journal*, 12 Nov, p 1598). The 1985 case citation is the natural link for the wider responsibilities, both criminal as well as civil, for the consequences of playing misconduct committed by one participant towards another. It was the first time that negligence in addition to civil or criminal assault was alleged in the United Kingdom courts, based upon an Australian precedent (*Rootes v Shelton* [1968] ALR 33). The principle applies to school as well as to adult activities. It is the appropriate stage to move on now to those wider responsibilities for playing participants beyond school and physical education per se, and also to wider public protection generally, with one final afterthought to be linked with Dr Mary Malecka's Appendix on *Sport in the Curriculum*, and the Genesis for this book, bred by *Corinthians and Cricketers* out of the then Association Football Players' and Trainers' Union (now the Professional Footballers' Association: PEA) and the joint Oxbridge soccer club Pegasus, coached by so many distinguished professionals of the early 1950s from

Tottenham Hotspur and clubs as explained earlier in these pages, and including Jimmy Hill OBE.

Half a century earlier, in 1904, the amateur Corinthians had defeated the then FA Cup holders full professional XI, Bury, in a Sheriff of London Shield fixture equivalent to today's annual FA Charity Shield opening season warm-up between the FA Cup Winners and Premier League Champions. The shock result of a 10–3 victory for the Corinthians was a landmark in their history. It was inspired by five goals from the previous season's Cambridge University captain Stanley Shute Harris. He progressed to six full England international appearances alongside Steve Bloomer and other legendary professionals before a Corinthians row with the FA over its amateur administrative representation prior to 1907 debarred any further Corinthians international selections, in the first World War of 1914–1918. Before he died prematurely in 1924 as a Preparatory School headmaster in Worthing, West Sussex, he wrote a book under the title of *The Master and His Boys* which experienced several reprints because of its successful reception. In his Foreword he explained:

'my object in writing these reflections is ......to put down a personal experience inthe hope that it may possibly be of use to some of those who read. My feeling is that there are many of us who do not realise sufficiently the immense trust which is given to us as schoolmasters, or the wonderful opening which lies ready to our hand ...... this little book, incomplete as it is, imperfect as it must be, at any rate has one merit. It deals with things as they are: it seeks to hide nothing, but endeavours simply and solely to visualise reality'.

That reality expressed barely twenty years after his sensational soccer career and five goals had destroyed the FA Cup holders, Bury (themselves record breakers with their 6–0 win against Derby County) included a chapter on *Games*. In turn, the extract cited below destroys forever the socio-politico humbugging ignorance which challenges the right of boys and girls to have the opportunities for self fulfilment otherwise to be denied with the dilution of competitive games in the National Curriculum. Today he would equate girls with boys, with what is here an everlasting expression of the Corinthian ideal in sport and recreation, from one of the all-time great Corinthians, of a later generation than C B Fry and G O Smith.

'The objects of athletics should be four-fold: (1) recreation for mind and body, (2) physical development, (3) training of character, (4) promotion of *healthy* competition and ambition. Having got these four principles into his head, the normal boy, be he naturally athletic or not, will do his utmost to become good at whatever games he plays, not simply because games appeal to him or because he thinks them more important than other things, but because the result of his training—as described in earlier chapters—will have been to imbue him with the determination to do his very best at *everything* he undertakes in order to fit himself to the utmost of his ability for his job in the world. It will be objected at once by many that no small boy can possibly be expected, while playing is games, to keep in mind an Utopian idea of this description. This is true, of course, but it is no less true that if such a idea *is* put into his mind and not infrequently recalled to his notice in reference to games, work and everything else that he *will* come eventually to have such an ideal ever present at the back of his conscious intelligence. He will feel within himself a consciousness that he is playing for a far greater stake than the mere winning of rewards and for that very reason he will play his games with a greater vigour, grit and enthusiasm than would be produced by any other motive. Moreover, with this ideal in view, we shall get far better results from the naturally unathletic boy than would otherwise be the case'.

Anyone who may consider these 1924 Corinthian thoughts from another age after seventy-five years, to be out-of-date, and unrelated to the last year of the twentieth century, should reflect upon how they read alongside the opinions from Michael Parkinson in the *Daily Telegraph* of Monday, 1 November 1999. He wrote on the morning after the French triumph against New Zealand in the Rugby World Cup and on the eve of the less than brilliant first match performance by the England cricket team on tour in South Africa (1st November 1999):

> 'There has never been a time in our history when the gap has been greater between the sporting haves and have-nots. At the pinnacle we have the Premier League luxuriating in untold wealth, neck deep in millions. At the bottom end we have kids without playing fields, impoverished, hopeless.'

They also raise a wider question: who speaks today for British Schoolteachers on the crucial questions concerning school sport and the problems which Michael Parkinson crystallises so clearly?

The British Association for Sport and the Law was created in 1993, forty years after the foundation for the British Association for Sport and Medicine in 1953: an historic sporting year. It is an echo from a golden past. England's Ashes against Australia; Stanley Matthews FA Cup Final winner's medal: Gordon Richards' only Derby success on Pinza, and Gordon Pirie's first of four world running records. Is it ever likely to occur again unless and until the world of teaching devoted to sport for its true meaning of health and education within the Rule of Law, as distinct from socio-political experimenting, learns to speak with one voice: to sing from a single hymn sheet as British Association for School Teachers in Sport?

CHAPTER 5

Public Protection

1 INTRODUCTION

When school and club partners in sport graduate as entertainers to attract spectators and spill over into environmental areas, the public interest and its protection become inevitable: this chapter therefore discusses the public protection of spectators and also participants in sport. Many disasters over the last few decades, often caused by both preventable misfortune and acts of God, have illuminated the issue.

Three national sports disasters within 20 years, Ibrox, Glasgow (1971), Bradford (1985) and Hillsborough (1989), after Bolton in 1946 a quarter of a century earlier, were followed by a judicial enquiry, litigation and legislation (except that no new legislation flowed from Bolton notwithstanding its Reports recommendations). These instances all point to three inevitable conclusions. One is the consistent knee-jerk reaction of horror at all levels of general social, sporting and political activity, too late for protection of the victims from the consequences of negligence by offending services. A second is the no less consistent application of Lord Hailsham's awareness now nearly 40 years ago as cited throughout these pages of the absence of any 'coherent body of doctrine, perhaps even a philosophy or government encouragement'. Third is perhaps the most disturbing and unnerving yet hitherto unmentioned element in any of the nine official reports spawned by successive Governments and judicial enquiries since the now historic first-ever Wembley Stadium FA Cup Final of 1923 between Bolton Wanderers and West Ham United; a pattern of potential sports crowd mishaps traceable through the Law Reports can be seen for more than a century and a quarter, with the warning shots across the bows of public ignorance and administrative apathy. How much more has been lost and unreported in the mists of time may now never be known.

On 13 April 1866 the collapsed section of a grandstand at the celebrated Cheltenham National Hunt Festival resulted in what every law student recognises as the starting tape for personal injuries liability in negligence by occupiers of premises: *Francis v Cockrell* [1870] 5 QB 501. Thirty years later in 1896 another grandstand collapsed at Ewood Park, Blackburn, home of the famous Rovers during a match against Everton. An incompetent contractor having been employed to repair it, the committee members of the then unincorporated association which constituted the club, were held personally liable and confirmed on appeal in damages (*Brown v Lewis* [1896] 12 TLR 455). A year later in 1897, Blackburn Rovers Football Club Limited was registered under the then Companies Act. More significantly as already cited in Chapter 1, *Genesis* at p 87,

> '—His Honour Judge Coventry in giving judgment said that committees of football clubs undertook a heavy responsibility in inviting the people to attend matches on their grounds. They made themselves responsible for the life and limbs of the people who went to the matches and used the stands. They knew that if the stands were not safe possibly hundreds of people might lose their lives or be maimed for life. It stood to commonsense that any football club which invited thousands of people to attend its matches incurred this responsibility. The law, which was generally—though not always—the impersonation of common sense, said that anybody who undertook such a heavy responsibility should see that these stands were as safe as it was possible to have them. In order to absolve themselves from liability, football clubs should show that they had done all they possibly could to secure the safety of the people. In this case he did not think this had been done.

> ### THESE IMMENSE 'GATES'

> had grown up, within his memory practically, and he thought that the football clubs in this district scarcely knew the responsibility they were incurring. To call in a joiner who had had no practical experience in regard to the construction of stands, and who probably did not know the right place to which to direct his attention in examining them was not, in his opinion, taking every precaution to ensure their safety. He must therefore find a verdict for the plaintiff for £25.' [*Northern Daily Telegraph*: 21 April 1896]

Five years later in 1901, the natural bowl of the old Crystal Palace ground, in the area of the present Natural Recreation Sports Centre in South London, was hewn out of nature to accommodate 110,820 spectators for the first FA Cup Final appearance of a southern team since Old Etonians lost to Blackburn Olympic in 1883: Tottenham Hotspur v Sheffield United. Members of the old Southern League outside the Football League, the now famous Spurs' attraction was sensational but free from any social disturbances in the absence of any irresponsible modern media mechanisms to incite it.

A year later witnessed yet a third grandstand collapse, with the gravest of consequences. At Ibrox, Glasgow, disaster struck within ten minutes of the kick-off for the then traditional Scotland versus England soccer international on 5 April 1902. A new stand had been built for the occasion which consisted of wooden planking upon steep uprights. The swaying of the crowd trying to follow an attack by the Scottish forwards caused seven rows of planking, 30 yards wide, to collapse. The 40 feet drop to the ground below killed 26 people and injured 587. Every damages claim was met, from the world wide donations as far flung as Japan and South Africa, *without* reported litigation, and the FA in London and Scottish FA in Glasgow followed the Blackburn Rovers precedent to become registered as the Football Association Limited in 1903. Yet no Government Inquiry was created. Instead, a prosecution for culpable homicide was brought against the timber merchant whose allegedly defective wood was used in the construction (*R v McDougall*: *Glasgow Herald* 10 July 1902). After a two day trial, the *Glasgow Herald* as cited above in Chapter 1 *Genesis* at p 88, followed His Honour Judge Coventry's foreboding for the future with a prophetic prescience

> 'THE verdict of 'Not Guilty' in the Ibrox case is probably what most people who have followed the course of the trial were prepared for. Whatever the amount of the responsibility resting upon the contractor for the ill-fated structure, it became increasingly obvious as the case for the Crown was unfolded that that responsibility did not lie exclusively with any single individual. A jury of ordinary intelligence and of fair mind were little likely therefore to make a scapegoat of the defender, more especially in view of the extraordinary conflict of evidence as to the true cause of the disaster. It is in this conflict of evidence, and not merely in the fate of the contractor, Mr McDougall, that the real interest of the case lies. The witnesses were mutually destructive to a degree that is not often seen in such trials, and the public are left in a state of complete bewilderment as to what chiefly conduced to the accident, and in doubt as to the means that should be adopted of preventing similar occurrences in future.
>   ....
> Unfortunately, the close of the case does not admit of the questions raised being dismissed from the public mind. The uneasy feeling remains that what occurred at Ibrox may occur again, and that at present there is no adequate means of preventing it. Obviously a stand such as that set up by the Rangers Club might be perfectly safe when occupied by a placid, orderly crowd, and yet become a source of terrible danger when filled by a mass of people labouring under the excitement invariably aroused by a football match.

As for the future, does the Ibrox disaster, with its sequel in the trial brought to a close yesterday, not point to the necessity for some very drastic regulations for the construction of the huge arenas required for the patrons of football? Surely modern skill and science should be equal to the production of something quite as stable as the ancient Roman circus'.

England's captain on that fateful day in 1902 was Steve Bloomer, succeeding G O Smith who had retired on Arthur Dunn's death to join W J Oakley as joint Headmasters at Ludgrove School for the next thirty years. With a sombre and uncanny foreshadow of events at Bolton in 1946 and Hillsborough in 1989 he recalled without video corroboration, as chronicled in Peter Seddon's splendid biography (already cited in Chapter 1 *Genesis* at p 66 on G O Smith's retirement) comparable impressions and circumstances with which present generations are all too familiar, visually and anecdotally.

'The following year, 1902, I reached the height of my ambition when I was elected captain of the English side. And how can I ever forget that day when it was the occasion of the most appalling disaster so far known in the annals of the game? It is known to this day as 'The Ibrox Disaster' and what a catastrophic tragedy it was. One minute the game was proceeding calmly and being keenly followed by the vast concourse; the next moment there was a terrible crash like the many peals of thunder in a great storm joining together in unison. The players stood as though rooted to the spot and there before our eyes we saw part of a huge stand, packed with people, crashing to the ground. The memory of that awful picture is still with me, with people crashing through iron railings as if they were so much matchwood. The groans, cries of fear and the uproar which followed beggars description.

Of course, the game was stopped while the killed and wounded were removed and attended to. The officials assembled inside our dressing-room and, though some asked for the game to be abandoned, the Football Association chairman Mr J C Clegg* was firm in his advocacy that the game should be finished as most of the crowd did not realise the enormity of the disaster and he feared a panic if they were told. After a time we got on the field again but to do so we had to pass long rows of dead and terribly injured. I remember one of the reports of the game said: 'Bloomer captained the England team but was overweighted with responsibility, seeming inconsistent and irritable'. Well I'll tell you, it was the hardest moment of my life to continue playing after threading my way through those rows of dead and dying... maybe that's why I was inconsistent and irritable. I believe 26 people were killed and hundreds injured... and it was due to some unsound

---

*   Later, as Sir Charles Clegg, primarily responsible for Sir Stanley Rous' appointment as Secretary of the Football Association in 1934, and founder of Clegg and Sons, Solicitors, Sheffield.

Russian timber on the wooden terrace being unable to withstand the strain...
when it collapsed people just fell through the gaping hole. The game didn't
count in the records and we later played a 2–2 draw at Birmingham and the
Scots won the championship. With all my international successes it seems
remarkable that such a disaster should have occurred on the one and only
day I captained England against Scotland'.

Twenty years after Ibrox, 1902 version, the release of tensions after
World War One and the era of Bright Young Things and the Jazz Age
carried public entertainment sport along with it. A new Wembley Stadium
was constituted within the complex of a new British Empire Exhibition. Only
the second Southern Club after Tottenham Hotspur in 1901 to reach an FA
Cup Final, on this occasion, West Ham United, also from London should
have alerted the authorities to recall the 114,815 crowd at Crystal Palace
two decades earlier. Consistent with the paralysis and/or incompetence
which is the hallmark and trademark of traditional British sporting
maladministration, nothing was prepared for a near disaster, averted
primarily by the famous Policeman and his white horse: the arrival of HM
King George V, and concentration on the game, won by Bolton Wanderers,
2–0. An estimated 200,000 crowd officially recorded as 126,000 overflowed
into a stadium equipped for less than 100,000. Miraculously no fatalities
and a (relatively) mere 1,000 injured appear to have completed the casualties
chronicled in a memorable contemporary essay from Robert Lynd entitled
'The Battle of Footerloo'.

'It would, perhaps, be an exaggeration to say that Wembley Park was turned
into a battlefield: but as the stretcher-bearers bore the seeming corpses one
after another through the crowd and out of the ground, it looked considerably
more like a battlefield than like a football field'.

The outcome was a Government Report in 1924 under a former Home
Secretary, Edward Shortt, KC, to whose committee the FA did not attend.
It contained recommendations ignored for half-a-century until the Safety
of Sports Grounds Act 1975, following the second Ibrox Stadium disaster
in 1971. The absence of any major sporting crowd tragedy at football
grounds where the cluster of current crowd disasters have occurred is a
reflection of the sporting social good behaviour between 1919 and 1939
while ground records were established in the inter-war years (as recorded
in Appendix 5) by Harry Grayson.

When the Second World War ended in 1945, followed by the Bolton
Wanderers fatalities (33) in 1946 and the consequential Government Report
in 1947 there began a sequence of events which ended with Lord Justice
Taylor in 1990 beginning his Final Report on the Hillsborough, Sheffield
disaster with

'It is a depressing and chastening fact that mine is the ninth official report covering crowd safety and control at football grounds ... why were [so many] recommendations and others not followed? I suggest two main reasons. First, insufficient concern and vigilance for the safety and well-being of spectators. This was compounded by a preoccupation with measures to control hooliganism. Secondly, complacency which led all parties to think that disaster as had not occurred on previous occasions it would not happen this time. But there is no point in holding inquiries or publishing guidance unless the recommendations are followed diligently'.

Legislation, litigation and four editions of a Green Guide Code for Safety have proliferated alongside the inevitable compensation claims following each national disaster identified already above and in the following pages. Furthermore, concurrent within the national calamities were the spiralling number of accidents at theme parks, leisure centres and general activity holiday centres, of equal concern for victims and their families as those from more publicised occasions, especially from daily road traffic battlefields and their casualty consequences, which continue with even more depressing and chastening facts than those traced by Lord Justice Taylor.

During 1986, the Consumers Association *Which* magazine, the Sports Council's *Sport and Leisure* bi-monthly journal and the *Guardian* newspaper (3 August 1987, p 28) all advocated an inspectorate system of control: and the British Activity Holiday Association (BAHA), which was formed for cohesive control, was unable to discover which government department would or should be stirred to act. Once more, Lord Hailsham's absence of any 'coherent body of doctrine, perhaps even a philosophy or Government encouragement' became apparent.

2   TOWN AND COUNTRY TIES AND DIFFERENCES

In less dramatic contexts, however, Parliament at different times has been concerned with public protection in differing ways from time immemorial, alongside common law and equitable remedies, especially within a rural sporting perspective. Thus Peter McIntosh's assessment in 1962 of Joseph Strutt's antithesis from 1801 becomes appropriate once more when he contrasted

'rural exercises generally practised'

with

'Pastimes usually exercised in towns and cities or places adjoining them'.

Lord Hailsham's awareness in 1962 of the absence of any 'coherent body of doctrine, perhaps even a philosophy of government encouragement', led to his concept of a 'focal point under a Minister'. That absence means that modern legislation reacts to ad hoc situations without any underlying principles or pattern uniting the disparate sporting recreational and leisure interests. The following modern illustrations emphasise the point.

Date and Source	Purpose/Object	Origins	Sponsor
1999 Football (Offences) and Disorder Act	Control Hooligans	Private Member	Home Office
1998 Crime and Disorder Act	Further control disorder	All-Party	Home Office
1995 Activity Centres	(Young Persons' Safety)	Safeguard Risk dangers - Lyme Regis Tragedy	Private Member
1991 Football (Offences) Act	Control of disorderly behaviour at football matches	Taylor Report	Home Office
1989 Football Spectators Act	Supervision of local authority functions under Safety of Sports Ground Act 1975	Taylor Report	Home Office
1986 Public Order Act	Public protection from violence	Social and football crowd hooliganism	Home Office
Sporting Events (Control of Alcohol etc/Act 1985	Liquor control		Home Office
1984–1987 Tall Ships Race	Inquiry headed by Richard Stone QC	19 lives lost: 67-year-old barque: *Marques*	Department of Transport

Date and Source	Purpose/Object	Origins	Sponsor
1984 Occupiers Liability Act	Protection of landowners to permit warning notices for recreational visitors but excluding liability	Pearson Commission (Cmnd 7054–1, paras 1546–50) Law Commission Report (Cmnd 6428)	Lord Chancellor Lord Hailsham of St Marylebone
1981 Wildlife and Countryside Act	Protection of environment and natural rural sources	Consolidating legislation	Ministry of Agriculture, Fisheries and Food
1979 Fastnet Yacht Race Report (Mr Justice Forbes)	Inquiry Report and Recommendations	15 lives lost: 24 boats abandoned	Royal Yachting Association and Royal Ocean Racing Club
1975 Salmon and Freshwater Fishes Act	Pollution Control	Protection of Fisheries and Fishing Rights Report	Ministry of Agriculture Fisheries and Food

3   RURAL AND WATER SPORTS

Such modern plurality is entirely consistent with the earliest legislation primarily affecting rural sporting and proprietorial interests recorded by the English legal system's most traditional jurist and historian. Blackstone's eighteenth-century commentaries (Bk IV, Ch 13, p 174) identified gaming laws sanctions

'constituted by a variety of acts of parliament: which are so numerous and so confused, and the crime itself [killing game even upon their own estate] of so questionable a nature, that I shall not detain the reader with many observations thereof'.

Nearer our own time, Sir William Holsdworth's monumental *History of English Law* traced back to Richard II a fragmentation comparable to our own period when he wrote under the head of *Hunting and Game* (Vol 4, p 505):

'The legislation on this subject proceeded on many different principles. Sometimes it proceeded on the principle that assemblies for the purpose of hunting and sporting gave opportunities for riot and disorder; sometimes on the principle that hunting and sporting ought to be the privilege of the landowners, and that other classes ought to employ themselves in a manner more suited to their condition in life; and sometimes on the principle that it resulted in the wanton destruction of game. We can see all these principles underlying Richard II's statute on the subject [13 Rich II St 1 Ch 13] and they appear clearly enough in the various statutes of this period'.

Those different principles, objectives have a common legal denominator which echoes today's legislative examples above and is rooted in realty and intellectual property law: the licence principle. It originated with the Royal prerogative recognised by Blackstone from its creation after the Norman Conquest and the parcelling out of Forest Laws and survives today as an example in Hampshire's New Forest. It has been perpetuated for centuries by Parliament with an ebb and flow of restrictions and authorities for defining, preserving and killing different species of game; and it is structured to provide individual property ownership protection through the laws of civil trespass, criminal damage, poaching and the Public Order Act 1986.

For lawyers, surveyors, agents and other associated professional practitioners, the conveyancing machinery of freeholds, leaseholds, contractual licences, deeds of grant, easements, profits à prendre and incorporeal hereditaments are a staple diet. For lay readers, or the non-property-orientated lawyer, a former editor of one of the leading sporting journals *The Field*, Wilson Stephens, summarised the position succinctly in the *Guinness Guide to Field Sport* (pp 215–216) during 1974 thus:

'The difference between British law on the right to sport in its rural context, and that which applies over much of the rest of the world, is the application of the principle of separate enjoyment. This means that to own land, to farm the land or exploit it in other ways, and to shoot, or catch the game and fish upon it, are three different usages and may possess separate identities. He who owns the land, may, if he does not wish himself to farm it, let it to somebody who does. Similarly, if he does not wish to exercise his right to the sports it provides, he may let them, or sell these rights. Alternatively, he may sell the land and retain the sporting rights; or sell the land to one buyer and the sporting rights to another.

Elsewhere in Europe the right to sport has gone with the ownership of land, in most cases being inseparable from it. A consequence has been that the well-being of game, and inevitably of other wildlife, has varied with the interest of individual landowners in sport. There has been no monetary incentive, as there is in Britain, for a non-interested landowner to maintain the environment in a condition favourable to game in order to let or sell at an enhanced price to those who are interested. Nor is there the incentive for buyers or lessees to do likewise in order to obtain the best results from what they are paying for ...

Fishing rights are held and traded in exactly the same manner as shooting rights. In English law a river is regarded as land which happens to be covered by water. There is no right of property in the water itself, but the owner of the land over which it flows is entitled to the natural benefits which it brings, and is protected against disturbance of this entitlement by pollution, diversion, or alteration of flow upstream. This lays upon him the responsibility of ensuring that no acts of his, or of his servants, disturb the enjoyment of these benefits by those downstream'.

Protection of those rights exists through a mixture of Parliamentary and common law and equity developments. Within the present limited context of establishing a level of awareness, public protection can most conveniently be seen through the better known sporting interests of hunting, shooting and fishing, and the contrasts and conflicts with watersports.

Hunting

At present no statute, with one qualification, prohibits or encourages the highly profiled foxhunting (other animals are served statutorily for closed and open seasons or periodic control, eg Badgers Act 1973; Deer Acts 1963, 1980 and 1987; and many varied statutes for salmon and other fishing). Hunts and their members until recently were generally believed to be protected only by their readiness to enforce the civil law of trespass. Now they have the general advantages of the Public Order Act 1986. The one qualification is the rarely used section 1(1)(a) of the Protection of Animals Act 1911. It creates a statutory exception to the offence to torture, infuriate or terrify a captive animal. This can include foxes, although proof of the offence may be difficult, and the protection here is for animals and animal lovers.

The Public Order Act 1986 was designed for wider social problems than anti-hunt saboteurs. Sections 4 and 5 and also section 39 purport to extend police powers where hitherto they had no power for acting against misconduct on private land. The criminal common law was also invoked during 1986 in original and unusual circumstances after activists had desecrated the grave of the 10th Duke of Beaufort on Boxing Day 1984, ten months after he had died aged 83. Two offenders were charged and convicted at Bristol Crown Court on two counts of conspiracy at common law for attempting to dig up the Duke's remains. They were each imprisoned cumulatively for three years (*R v Curtin and Anor* (1986) *Times*, 12 June).

In the previous year the civil common law was operated against the Master of a West Country Hunt for a successful claim in damages and injunctions for hunting too close to land where its hounds were not welcome and it could be inferred that inadequate steps were taken to prevent them (*League Against Cruel Sports v Scott* [1985] 2 All ER 489). Over a century before that judgment it was established that hunt members entering land without permission, orally or by written licence or other authority, committed a trespass (*Paul v Summerhays* [1878] 4 QBD 9). Consistent with these remedies the Peterborough-based Fitzwilliam Hunt obtained an injunction against a hunt saboteur who had blown a trumpet and imitated hunt cries to mislead hounds, taking them out of the control of their owners and thereby causing a trespass to goods (*Fitzwilliam Land Company v Cracknell* (1993) *Peterborough Evening Telegraph* 9 September, 4 November). Subsequently a local authority's ban on hunting on ethical grounds was held to be unlawful in a judicial review as ultra vires its statutory powers (*R v Somerset County Council, ex p Ewings* (1994) QBD 9 Feb, [1994] 6442 NLJ 461; and a potential national government ban is fluctuating on and off the political agenda.

Shooting

By contrast, any sport with built-in lethal products as its raison d'être is regulated by Parliamentary control, separate and apart from property licences to shoot on land not owned by the firearm possessor. The Firearms Acts 1968 and 1982 and statutory Rules specified in the first edition have since then been extended by the Firearms (Amendment) Acts 1988 and 1997 and the Firearms (Amendment) Regulations 1992, made under section 2(2) of the European Communities Act 1972 pursuant to Council Directive No 91/477/EEC, Cumulatively they regulate the control, acquisition and possession of firearms and shotguns generally. (See generally *Archbold* 1998 Edition, paragraph 24, et seq.) Game licences for sporting rights owned or hired or purchased are required under the Game Licences Act 1860, which contains a built-in framework for forfeiture or suspension when the basis for the grant is breached, eg poaching, itself subject to a network of statutory provisions capable of ensnaring the unwary or careless country sportsperson. A responsible gundealer, gunsmith or a specialist publication such as *Gun Law* by Godfrey Sandys-Winsch, *The Law Relating to Firearms* by P T Clarke and J W Ellis or *Fair Game* by Parkes and Thornley should be consulted for any uncertainty.

Fishing

With splendid irony for the present text, Izaak Walton's sporting literary classic *The Compleat Angler* contains the opinion that there is,

'No life so happy and pleasant as the life of a well-governed angler, for when the lawyer is swallowed up with business, and the statesman is preventing or contriving plots, then we sit on cowslip banks, hear the birds sing, and possess ourselves in the quietness of silent silver streams'.

Of all sporting participants, none is as well served with legal literature and guidelines as those who throw a fishing line. Parliament has legislated extensively with substantial statutes from the Fisheries Act 1878 to the Salmon and Freshwater Fisheries Act 1975 and the Salmon Act 1986; and the courts have been ready to protect the sport and its participants and thereby the fish with injunctions against pollution, eg *Pride of Derby Angling Association v British Celanese* [1953] 1 All ER 179, which also included orders against Derby Corporation and the British Electricity Authority on the grounds of nuisance (see also *Nicholls v Ely Beet Sugar Factory* [1936] Ch 343).

More recently in a landmark test case decision at Swindon County Court in Wiltshire, £10,000 damages with £2,750 interest and costs were awarded by Judge Dyer for negligence and nuisance caused by a trout farm which was alleged to have let thousands of rainbow trout escape into a prime stretch of the River Kennet near Marlborough in Wiltshire. The complaint by the Savernake Fly Fishing Club against the former owners of the trout farm was that the voracious farm-reared rainbow trout had ruined 40% of the 1990 angling season because they pestered fishermen who were attempting to catch the more wily brown trout, and thereby damaging their sporting interests for which club membership cost £500 a year. The Anglers' Co-operative Association welcomed the decision as a precedent for similar cases in other parts of the country: *Broderick and Brown* (on behalf of the *Savernake Fly Fishing Club v Gale & Ainslie Ltd* (1993) *Times*, 30 March).

Furthermore, injunction proceedings have succeeded by anglers against unauthorised canoeists (*Rawson v Peters* (1973) EGD 259); and this raises the most significant and crucially important issue for the future of rural sport: How are the conflicting interests to be balanced to satisfy the needs of land and water users? The Sports Council and CCPR published a joint National Water Sports Code sub-titled 'Some behaviour recommendations for water recreational users' towards the end of the 1970s; and more recently during the early 1980s the Sports Council with the cooperation of the National Anglers' Council, the Water Space Amenity Commission and the British Canoe Union has published *Angling and Canoeing Statement of Intent*. Clearly the problem will not go away.

Indeed, without restraint on both sides it can only get worse in a violence-orientated society, notwithstanding Izaak Walton's idyllic tranquillity. Furthermore, it conveniently leads on to another aspect of the consequences of water sport activity: not merely to anglers on the banks, but householders too. This is the problem of noise, a common law private nuisance. It was highlighted by the successful claim in 1981 against the Cotswold Motor Racing Club which resulted in a Court of Appeal reversal of a £15,000 damages award by the trial judge, and replacing it with a modified and complex injunction (*Kennaway v Thompson* [1980] 3 All ER 329). It thereby returns the lawyer and the sporting participants to the general problem of public protection within the tiny space available for fun for 55 million British people. The issue falls into place conveniently under two separate headings, public protection outside sports premises, of which *Kennaway v Thompson* is one startling example, and public protection inside sports grounds and premises, clearly illuminated by the Bradford City tragedy. No less a tragedy was the canoe disaster at Lyme Regis Bay in Dorset resulting from grossly inadequate supervision, control and preparation. The controlling company and one director ULL Ltd and Peter Kite were convicted of manslaughter and in due course the Activities Centres (Young Persons Safety) Act 1995 was implemented.

4   PUBLIC PROTECTION OUTSIDE SPORTS PREMISES

Here the law is embedded exclusively in judicial precedents applied to the differing facts of differing games. In rural communities space problems create fewer difficulties than urban areas demonstrate. There the need to sustain a balance between public recreational and private proprietary interest has created regular judicial headaches in applying the common law of public and private nuisance. Understandably the cases fluctuate around the most popular ball games of cricket, football, golf and tennis.

Golf first entered the law reports in the early 1920s, cricket in the 1950s, football in the 1960s and cricket again in the 1970s. Watersports emerged too, as these pages show. Three leading cases explain the legal position. They deal with domestic rights in conflict with sporting occupancies for public protection. Miss Bessie Stone, Mrs Miller and Miss Kennaway are all enshrined in perpetuity throughout the law reports and text books as their problems required judicial clarification of a developing law to new situations.

Nuisance and negligence are the areas concerned. None of the ladies obtained what she had claimed: not because of any male chauvinism but because the vagaries of litigation must always depend upon special facts, differing human judicial attitudes and, in the celebrated summary of the great American judge and jurist, Mr Justice Oliver Wendell Holmes: 'The life of the law is not logic: it is experience' (*The Common Law* (1881) p 1). In brief,

Miss Stone

failed to persuade a trial judge (that cricket balls hit out of a ground to adjoining land can be a remedy in civil law), succeeded in the Court of Appeal but lost her claim in the House of Lords;

Mrs Miller

(with her husband) obtained from a trial judge an injunction but lost in the Court of Appeal with a substitution of damages;

Miss Kennaway

failed to get a full injunction (for noise comprising a nuisance in law created by a boat and water ski races) but on appeal from a trial judge obtained a restricted injunction in addition to damages.

How did this all arise? The answer requires an explanation briefly of the applicable legal principles, the differing facts, and the enigma of judicial variation. For the present context, the difference in law between nuisance and negligence must be recognised.

Legal nuisance involves an interference with the use of enjoyment of land. It can be public, which involves criminal law processes and sanctions; or private, which the sporting examples here illustrate on the initiative of an aggrieved complainant. Negligence, too, can involve criminal elements. Here the context concerns civil liability with three essential elements:

(i)   a duty of care recognised by law;
(ii) breach of that duty by failure to apply foreseeable standards, and
(iii) damage from that breach which is not too remote.

Against that legal background a sporting journey from Cheetham Cricket Ground near Manchester across the Pennines to another cricket ground at Linz, County Durham, and then down to Gloucestershire to a water-ski and motor boat course, illuminates the problems.

1947 was a vintage year for English cricket. Compton and Edrich broke all records and postwar crowds hit new peaks. On 9 August Miss Bessie Stone had stepped from her garden gateway on to the pavement of the highway when she was struck on the head by a cricket ball hit out of the adjoining Cheetham Cricket Ground by a visiting player, causing her injury. She sued for damages against representative club members (an accepted procedural practice against an unincorporated club membership which will become apparent in Chapter 14, *Administrative advice*). Her claim therefore was based correctly on the two known allegations available to her in the law of civil wrongs known as torts:

(i)   negligence,
(ii) private nuisance.

At the trial before Mr Justice Oliver, at the then Manchester Assizes, in December 1948, negligence was rejected and nuisance dismissed; in the learned judge's opinion a single isolated act causing direct damage could not properly be brought under the head of nuisance to a highway: but if he was wrong, the damages were provisionally assessed for £105. An appeal to the Court of Appeal confirmed the judge's reasoning and conclusion on negligence, but a reversal by a 2–1 majority on nuisance. The cricketing authorities were understandably concerned at the consequences beyond Cheetham and the Court of Appeal. A successful appeal was argued to the House of Lords by counsel specially instructed — Sir Walter Monckton, not only King Edward VIII's personal adviser at the time of the Abdication crisis, but also a distinguished school and club cricketer, future President of MCC and the Surrey County Cricket Club and guide to James Guthrie on the restrictive professional footballers' contracts as explained in *Genesis* Chapter 1 above; and also Mr W A Sime, then captain of Nottinghamshire County Cricket Club and a future Crown Court Recorder. Juristically their Lordships ruled that the evidence of only six hits outside the ground in 28 years meant that the risk of repetition was not sufficiently foreseeable for negligence liability (*Bolton v Stone* [1951] AC 850). Lord Oaksey, as Lord Justice Oaksey, the civilised world's Presiding Judge at the Nuremberg Trial of War Criminals, and father of the *Daily* and *Sunday Telegraph's* John Oaksey, explained:

> 'the standard of care in the law of negligence is the standard of an ordinary careful man, ... He takes precautions against risks which are reasonably likely to happen'.

Distinguishing the facts from a golfing liability where subsequent interferences were proved (*Castle v St Augustine Links* (1922) 39 TLR 615), Lord Oaksey concluded (1951) AC 863),

> 'There are many footpaths and highways adjacent to cricket grounds and golf courses on to which cricket and golf balls are occasionally driven, but such risks are habitually treated both by the owners, committees of such cricket and golf courses and by the pedestrians who use the adjacent footpaths and highways as negligible and it is not, in my opinion, actionable negligence to take precaution to avoid such risks'.

More significant than the negligence result itself, however, was the manner in which the nuisance issue was considered by the House of Lords. Lords Porter (at p 860) and Reid (at p 868) considered that Miss Stone's counsel admitted that nuisance fell with the dismissal of negligence, although Lord Reid significantly said;

> 'I find it unnecessary to deal with the question of nuisance and reserve my opinion to what constitutes nuisance in cases of this character'.

With this specific reservation by the most revered and respected of modern Law Lords, any euphoria for cricket and the general sporting world should be tempered not only with the knowledge that the issue could be re-argued on different facts, but also by a note from one of the most distinguished of modern commentators, and by a usually unrecognised footnote to legal history.

Professor (Sir) Arthur Goodhart, who edited the *Law Quarterly Review* for 50 years, was described by Lord Denning in the centenary issue (1984) at page 514 as 'Beyond doubt the greatest jurist of our time'. In a contemporary analysis over his familiar initials, 'ALG' in Volume 5 (1951) at pages 460–464 under the title 'Is it cricket?', he began

> 'one cannot help feeling sympathy for Miss Stone',

and ended

> 'As the present case has given rise to some misunderstanding in the popular press it is to be hoped that it will be made clear to those responsible for cricket clubs, whether these are situated in a town or in the country, that they are under a duty to take reasonable care not to injure those persons who may be passing outside their ground and that the degree of care must depend on the facts of each particular case. It is, as we said at the beginning of this note unfortunate for Miss Stone that the facts in her case were on the borderline, and that it was necessary for three separate courts to consider them'.

Monckton's biography from the pen of F E Smith's son, the second Lord Birkenhead: *Walter Monckton, The Life of Viscount Monckton Brenchley* (1969), at page 267, commented on the position concerning nuisance issue with a reference from Miss Stone's plaintiff counsel, the late Mr H I Nelson KC.

> 'The outcome brought immense relief to all concerned with cricket clubs, but not to Mr Nelson who had represented the plaintiff with such conviction of the justice of her case. Although Lord Porter said that it had been conceded on behalf of the plaintiff that if the claim in negligence failed the claim in nuisance must also fail, Nelson had made no such concession, as Walter Monckton was afterwards to confirm.

It must seem strange (said Nelson) that to shoot with a gun, or a bow and arrow, or even, as has been held in one case, to permit a piece of beef fat to fly out of a butcher's doorway in the course of chopping meat, may render the perpetrator liable in nuisance to any user of the highway injured thereby, whilst a cricketer may deliberately hit cricket balls into the highway with impunity. Possibly at some future date a cricket ball so hit may cause a major disaster, and the whole question of liability be reopened. The cricket ball case certainly made the headlines. To associate the sacred game of cricket with nuisance was regarded by many as something akin to blasphemy'

(Mr H I Nelson to Lord Birkenhead).

Thirty years after Miss Bessie Stone's misfortune, cricket balls again hit the law reports as well as a complainant. The victims on this occasion were a local neighbourhood and Mr and Mrs Miller whose property adjoined the long established Linz Cricket Ground in County Durham. Balls hit out of the ground caused consternation and Mr Justice Reeve at Durham granted them an injunction against the club as well as modest damages. On appeal to the Court of Appeal the injunction was discharged to be replaced by an agreed damages award of £400. Yet again, it would be unwise for any cricket or sporting buffs to be overjoyed with the result. The appeal judges were not united in their approach, the academic lawyers criticised it, and a later Court of Appeal dealing with similar legal issues concerning different facts and a different sport emphatically refused to follow it (*Miller v Jackson* [1977] 3 All ER 338, not followed by *Kennaway v Thompson* [1980] 3 All ER 329).

The former Lord Chief Justice, Lord Lane, as Lord Justice Lane, was ready to uphold the injunction after delaying it to give the club time to accommodate the circumstances, and Lord Justice Cumming-Bruce, while not going that far in the remedy, agreed that negligence had been proved because there was a foreseeable risk (as distinct from the failure to establish this point against the Cheetham Club of injury to adjoining occupiers). Hence, the £400 agreed damages for negligence. Lord Denning, however, in a judgment which he has extracted without critical comment at the end of his publication *Landmarks in the Law* (1984) rejected both negligence and nuisance and would have dismissed the claim for damages. In particular did he rely upon the fact that plaintiffs were authors of their own misfortune in coming to the nuisance.

Three years later a different Court of Appeal was required to consider a damages award by Mr Justice Mais to a householder who complained about the noise from power boats and water-ski activities adjoining her property near Fairford in Gloucestershire. She, too, came to the nuisance, but the court held that the degree of noise overrode the public interest in the club's undoubtedly important sporting activities of an international nature. The injunction was limited in scope, and *Miller v Jackson* was specifically rejected as a binding precedent.

The most significant thread which binds both judgments is Lord Denning's built-in warning to all sporting organisations adjoining land potentially ripe for development. He said:

> 'I am surprised that the developers of the housing estate were allowed to build the houses so close to the cricket ground .... The planning authorities ought not to have allowed it. The houses ought to be so sited as not to interfere with the cricket. But the houses have been built and we have to reckon with the consequences'.

Similar considerations emerged in *Lacy v Parker and Boyle (for Jordans CC)* already discussed at page 59.

Lord Denning's realistic approach to the key practical sporting legal focus begs the question as to whether or not anyone ever objects to that particular form of planning application. Nevertheless, he identified what must become a more a more urgent problem in a tightly packed urban community encouraged by the Sports Council campaign, 'Sport for all'.

The cases which follow are merely illustrations and many others are to be found in the standard textbooks:

1922

Golf ball played from 13th tee parallel with Sandwich Road, Kent, much frequented by motor cars and taxi cabs, into which road golf ball was hit. Windscreen of passing taxi cab hit by ball and splintered glass, causing loss of driver's eye (*Castle v St Augustine's Links Ltd* (1922) 38 TLR 615)

Decision

Golf Club and player jointly liable for £450 damages and costs.

Principle

Tee and hole were public nuisance from the conditions and in the place where they were situated. No precedent for different facts: but slicing of ball into roadway not only a public danger but was the probable consequence from time to time of people driving from the tee.

1949

Stamford Bridge, Chelsea Supporters overflow into neighbouring garden properties after exclusion from Moscow Dynamo match in 1945 (*Munday v Metropolitan Police Receiver* [1949] 1 All ER 337)

Decision

Compensation against Receiver, Metropolitan Police.

Principle

Award under Riot Damages Act 1886 (still in force). Elements of riot proved under applicable law as at 1945–1949.

1950

Noise from Speedway track surrounding football ground disturbed occupiers of residential properties surrounding stadium (*Attorney General v Hastings Corporation* (1950) 94 Sol Jo 225)

Decision

Injunction against speedway noise obtained.

Principle

Nuisance to private interests overrode public interest in speedway competition.

1951

Cricket ball hit from Cheetham CC, Manchester to roadway on rare occasions. (*Bolton v Stone* [1951] AC 850)

Decision

No liability.

Principle

No negligence or nuisance. Remote risk of injury not reasonably to be anticipated.

1951

Widow of deceased motor car race marshall sued organisers of race in Jersey and executors of the crashed car driver who also died (*O'Dowd v Frazer-Nash* [1951] WLR 173)

Decision

No liability.

Principle

Organisers had taken all reasonable precautions. No negligence by driver for brake failure.

1961

Footballs kicked out of field by young children (from green used frequently for recreational purposes) on to adjoining roadway. Motorcyclist thereby caused to swerve fatally (*Hilder v Associated Portland Cement Manufacturers* [1961] 1 WLR 1434)

Decision

Field owners liable for negligence.

Principle

Failure to take reasonable care from reasonably anticipated danger to road users.

1968

Pedestrian walking along narrow public lane injured on head by golf ball (*Lamond v Glasgow Corporation* (1968) SLT 291)

Decision

Liability established for negligence.

Principle

Although no previous history of any accident, 6,000 shots a year played over fence should have created forecast of foreseeable happening.

1977

Cricket balls hit out of 70-year-old cricket club ground into adjoining gardens prevented occupants who had recently purchased house from using garden in summer (*Miller v Jackson* [1977] 1 QB 966)

Decision

Injunction discharged on appeal by Club, but £400 agreed damages for nuisance.

Principle

On appeal Club guilty of nuisance and negligence; but Appeal Court's discretion discharged injunction because public loss of cricket prevails over hardship from individual non-use of garden (see also pp 58–59 above for building development consent creating problem under Town and Country Planning laws).

1981

Power-boat racing noise upset neighbour who built a house adjoining watersports lake usage (*Kennaway v Thompson* [1980] 3 All ER 329)

Decision

Damages award by trial judge of £15,000 discharged on appeal by householder.

Principle

Courts do not approve the concept of wrongdoers purchasing potential to continue by merely paying for the injury. Injunction in modified but none the less effective terms to modify noise.

1994

Lacy v Parker & Boyle (for Jordans CC) (1994) 144 NLJ 785

Decision

Injunction refused.

Principle

Plaintiff came to the nuisance to which he objected when cricket balls damaged adjoining property.

5   PUBLIC PROTECTION INSIDE SPORTS GROUNDS AND PREMISES

A pattern of precedents can be seen which show how victims of accidents at sporting or recreational occasions have claimed for injuries, some successfully, others not so successfully. The codification under the Occupiers' Liability Acts 1957–89 to create the common duty of care avoided thereafter the need to consider any implied term in a contract of entry to premises. This had been one of the legal arguments upon which the injured victim in the first seriously recorded report of a claim for damages due to defective sporting premises was able to recover damages, *Francis v Cockrell* (1870) 5 QB 501. On that occasion a grandstand collapsed at Cheltenham Races and the promoter was held liable for the default by the contractor of which the promoter was innocent. The other legal argument was the currently applicable basis for a claim of negligence.

This is in an area where the well-known legal concept of *volenti non fit injuria* comes into operation. It cannot apply to unlawful violent foul play on the field. It also does not apply to the ordinary hazards of attending sporting occasions. For unusual experiences which could have been foreseen a breach, then the 'common duty of care' can override the *volenti* position.

The reported cases which explain how the law operates in this area of public protection within the grounds and premises disclose two particular trends which run throughout this text. One is the crucial question of fact which is the first base to all live legal issues, both litigious and non-litigious. The other is the appellate structure which enables findings of fact to be disturbed on appeal. Three important cases illustrate features in each of the two categories under consideration. For the first, of protection within, they are as follows:

(1)   *Whitby v C J Brock* (1886) 4 TLR 241,
(2)   *Hall v Brooklands Auto-Racing Club* [1933] 1 KB 205,
(3)   *Wooldridge v Sumner* [1963] 2 QB 43.

The first, *Whitby v Brock*, may be said to be on the fringe of sport with its location and subject-matter: the old Crystal Palace (before the fire in 1936), and bona fide fireworks (before being used in sporting metaphors). An injured visitor successfully obtained a damages award for injury by a firework on a jury's verdict. The judge, however, gave judgment for the defendants, and the plaintiff appealed successfully. During the course of the appeal hearing, the Master of the Rolls, Lord Esher (at page 242) observed;

'Surely there was negligence in letting off fireworks in such a way as to strike the Plaintiff'.

Counsel's response summarised the *volenti* principle:

'At a cricket match a spectator struck by a ball in the course of a game has no right of action, as he takes the risk on himself when he goes to a match'.

Over fifty years later in *Hall v Brooklands*, as we shall see below, the Court of Appeal extended this more elaborately.

In *Whitby v Brock*, however, the Court of Appeal unanimously decided that the jury's verdict was justifiable on the evidence and should be restored. Yet fifty years later in *Hall v Brooklands* the converse occurred which caused critical comments contemporaneously to be made of the ruling, and makes it a valuable source for citation of general principle but as a verdict, one of which must be regarded as having been decided on its own special facts.

At the famous Brooklands race track near Weybridge in Surrey, a car hurtled over a crowd barrier and hit a spectator who claimed compensation. A jury, assisted by specialised engineering evidence, found for the plaintiff.

A strong Court of Appeal, Scrutton, Greer and Slessor, LJJ, read the evidence and its inferences differently and reversed the jury's finding (the converse to what happened in *Whitby's* case). The points which are more significant for the professional and lay reader than the actual conclusion on the particular facts are the principles applicable to this important area of spectator sport which have stood the test of time and specify when the *volenti* principle does and does not apply to spectators at sporting events. When they were applied thirty years later in the case concerning the White City Horse Show, *Wooldridge v Sumner* (supra) already considered in Chapter 3, *Under starter's orders*, above p 157, the Court of Appeal decided that the experienced trial judge had drawn the wrong inferences of fact from the evidence. Once again it reversed a finding on this occasion to the disadvantage of the plaintiff, in whose favour the trial judge had awarded damages. It decided that an error of judgment rather than negligence caused the accident to a photographer inside the competition area when he was hit by a competitor's horse. The claim was against the rider and the show organisers, who were initially exonerated. Sellers LJ in the context of this claim against a competitor explained succinctly at page 56 the general proposition concerning liability to spectators by participants with words which are equally applicable to promoters operating the now statutory 'common duty of care':

> '... provided the competition or game is being performed within the rules and requirements of the sport by a person of adequate skill and competence the spectator does not expect his safety to be regarded by the participant'.

If these words are adapted to promoters as well, then the more detailed and elaborate explanation below from the earlier Court of Appeal judgment in *Hall v Brooklands* can be recognised more readily. Sellers LJ would have been equally accurate and consistent if he had been required to adjudicate, for example, after the Bradford City fire disaster and had said:

> '... provided the competition or game is being performed within the rules and requirements of the sport [or particular organising activity] by a person

[or organisation] of adequate skill and competence the spectator does not expect his safety to be regarded by the participant [or organiser, save in 1986 by the Bradford City legal requirements]'.

Against those summaries of the cases the principles laid down in *Hall v Brooklands* and their applicability to a sequence of cases summarised in tabulated form can be read as a condensed understanding of this general area today, always to be qualified by the Bradford experience.
Scrutton LJ explained the position thus;

'The question of the liability of the Brooklands Company raises questions which are of general application to any cases where landowners admit for payment to their land persons who desire to witness sports or competitions carried on thereon, if these sports may involve risk of danger to persons witnessing them. A spectator at Lord's or the Oval runs the risk of being hit by a cricket ball, or coming into collision with a fielder running hard to stop a ball from going over the boundary, and himself tumbling over the boundary in doing so. Spectators at football or hockey or polo matches run similar risks both from the ball and from collisions with players or polo ponies. Spectators who pay for admission to golf courses to witness important matches, though they keep beyond the boundaries required by the stewards, run the risk of the players slicing or pulling balls which may hit them with considerable velocity and damage. Those who pay for admission or seats in stands at a flying meeting run a risk of the performing aeroplanes falling on their heads. What is the liability of the person taking payment for permission to view these various sports?'

Here the liability of the person taking payment was the sole issue on appeal. In a later passage Lord Justice Scrutton in effect answers his own question after extracting the principle involved from earlier precedents, as

'... a promise to use reasonable care to ensure safety. What is reasonable care would depend on the perils which might be reasonably expected to occur, and the extent to which the ordinary spectator might be expected to appreciate and take the risk of such perils. Illustrations are the risk of being hit by a cricket ball at Lord's or the Oval, where any ordinary spectator in my view expects and takes the risk of a ball being hit with considerable force amongst the spectators and does not expect any structure which will prevent any ball from reaching the spectators. An even more common case is one which may be seen all over the country every Saturday afternoon, spectators admitted for payment to a field to witness a football or hockey match, and standing along a line near the touchline. No one expects the persons receiving payment to erect such structures or nets that no spectator can be hit by a ball kicked or hit violently [ie in those far off 1930s the learned judge had in mind "violently" within the playing laws of the game, eg of the cannon ball shooting epitomised by Ted Drake, or Eric Houghton or hitting of the Jim Smith/Arthur Wellard style; not today's ill tempered, dissenting, lawless, physical mobile body contact violence] from the field of play towards the spectators. The field is safe to stand on, and the spectators take the risk of the game'.

Lord Justice Greer, in words which also are still applicable, gave another approach to the same test with examples which are equally of value, referring to spectators and the promoter and/or occupier of premises.

'... both parties must have intended that the person paying for his licence to see a cricket match, or a race, takes upon himself the risk of unlikely and improbable accidents, provided that there has not been on the part of the occupier a failure to take usual precautions. I do not think it can be said that the contents of the contract made with every person who takes a ticket is different. I think it must be the same, and it must be judged by what any reasonable member of the public must have intended should be the term of the contract. The person concerned is sometimes described as "the man in the street", or "the man in the Clapham omnibus", or, as I recently read in an American author, "the man who takes the magazines home, and in the evening pushes the lawn mower in his short sleeves". Such a man taking a ticket to see a cricket match at Lord's would know quite well that he was not going to be encased in a steel frame which would protect him from the one in a million chance of a cricket ball dropping on his head. In the same way, the same man taking a ticket to see the Derby would know quite well that there would be no provision to prevent a horse which got out of hand from getting amongst the spectators, and would quite understand that he was himself bearing the risk of any such possible but improbable accident happening to himself'.

A representative pattern of cases for over a century, including those decided before the codification by the Occupiers' Liability Acts to create the 'common duty of care' illustrates the difficulties in establishing liability for injuries where no exceptional dangers or hazards were established.

1870

Collapsed Grandstand at Cheltenham Races (*Francis v Cockrell* [1820] 5 QB 501)

Decision

Judgment for spectator.

Principle

Negligently constructed stand for which promoter vicariously liable.

1886

Firework injury at (old) Crystal Palace (*Whitby v CJ Brock* (1886) 4 TLR 241)

Decision

Judgment for visitor.

Principle

Negligence proved.

1896

Collapsed grandstand at Blackburn Rovers (*Brown v Lewis* (1896) 12 TLR 455)

Decision

Judgment for spectator.

Principle

Negligent construction. Club committee members made personally liable.

1902

Ibrox stand collapses *R v McDougall Glasgow Herald* 10 July

Decision

Acquittal culpable homicide

Principle

Insufficient evidence

1932

Polo player on pony ran through a hedge at Ranelagh injuring a spectator (*Piddington v Hastings* (1932) Times, 12 March p 4)

Decision

Judgment for owners of premises.

Principle

No failure by premises owners to use reasonable care.

1932

Motor race track. Contact of wheels at 100 mph between two Talbot racing cars caused one apparently to leave the track and go over rails at side of track (*Hall v Brooklands Auto-Racing Club* [1933] 1 KB 205)

Decision

Judgment for owners of premises and competitors.

Principle

No evidence per Court of Appeal that owners or competitors had failed to take reasonable care.

1946/7

Blackshawe v Bolton Wanderers Football Club and Howarth

Decision

Damages for deceased estate

Principle

Negligent stewardship

1949

Ice hockey players stepped out of or broke off from hockey game to fight, injuring spectator with stick (*Payne and Payne v Maple Leaf* (1949) 1 DLR 369 (Canada))

Decision

Players liable.

Principle

No consent to breach of rules.

1951

Ice hockey puck hit six-year-old rink-side spectator (*Murray v Harringay Arena* [1951] 2 KB 529)

Decision

Judgment for owners.

Principle

No lack of safety. [See earlier citation Ch 3 *Under Starters Orders* for inadequate litigation preparation]

1962

Photographer at horse show injured by winning horse (*Wooldridge v Sumner* [1963] 2 QB 43)

Decision

Judgment for organisers and competitor.

Principle

No lack of safety.

1971

Spectators injured at motor-cycle scramble meeting (*Wilkes v Cheltenham Home Guard Motor Cycle and Light Car Club* [1971] 3 All ER 369, CA)

Decision

No liability.

Principle

Almost inexplicable accident. Competitors and organisers exonerated from negligence. Competitor entitled to strain to win if not foolhardy.

1974

Spectators at 1971 Ibrox disaster (*Dougan v Rangers Football Club* (1974) *Daily Telegraph*, 24 October p 19)

Decision

Judgment for representatives of deceased victims. Glasgow Rangers liable.

Principle

Failed to exercise sufficient care to spectators in egress and handrails prior to 1975 Act.

1976

Discus hurled from practice net on athletics ground ricocheted from guy-rope and hit spectator standing well behind the net (*Wilkins v Smith* (1976) 73 LS Gaz 938)

Decision

Judgment for owners.

Principle

Duty fulfilled by keeping spectators out of the area of foreseeable deflection.

1987

Bradford City Fire disaster (see below)

Decision

Judgment for victims.

Principle

Negligence by Club and local Fire Authority.

1987

Sheffield United Special Police

Decision

£51,699.54 liability to club to South

Services (*Harris v Sheffield United Football Club Limited* [1987] 2 All ER 838)

Yorkshire Police Authority.

Principle

Special police services for soccer crowd problems chargeable for beyond normal public duty to maintain law and order.

1991

Cunningham v Reading FC Ltd (1991) *Times*, 20 March

Decision

Judgment for injured Police Officers from hooligans on Football Club premises.

Principle

Crowd law negligence and Occupiers Act 1957, s 2(1), (2) established because of prior knowledge of club about a violent element among particular visiting supporters.

1991

Alcock v Chief Constable of South Yorkshire Police [1991] 4 All ER 907.

Decision

Judgment for Defendant against Hillsborough claimants.

Principle

Only those present in stadium and not those watching on television qualified to claim disaster damages.

1992

Hicks and *Paul v Chief Constable of South Yorkshire Police* [1992] 65

Decision

Parents of deceased daughter Hillsborough spectator failed to provide evidence of physical injury prior to death.

Principle

Onus of proof question of fact not satisfied for Court.

1993

Cook, Cochrane, Hampson v Doncaster Borough Council (1993) *Sporting Life* 16 July

Decision

Judgment for jockeys and racehorse owner for injuries resulting from open hole or underlying void in racetrack on occasion of 1989 St Leger autumn meeting.

Principle

Defendant corporation controlling owners of the racetrack surface liable for unsatisfactory conditions creating negligence liability.

1998

Frost v Chief Constable of South Yorkshire Police [1998] 3 WLR 1509

Decision

No evidence to damages for psychiatric injury suffered by Hillsborough Police Officers

Principle

No extension of duty and breach to protect therefrom.

These judicial pronouncements emphasise the vital and crucial difference between consenting to the normal risks of sporting events, and where no such consent occurs or can be inferred; and in the ongoing saga of the Hillsborough litigation readers seeking more considered analysis beyond the scope of this publication should be assisted 9 July 1999: 115 LQR 345. *Psychiatric Injury and Rescuers* from Stephen Todd, University of Canterbury, New Zealand.

Furthermore, in *Cunningham v Reading FC Ltd*, Drake J (1991) *Times*, 20 March adjudicated that the exoneration by a one-day FA Commission of Inquiry of any culpability by the Defendant Club was irrelevant and of no value to his own judicial investigation into liability under common law negligence and the Occupiers Liability Act, for which the issues and evidence were entirely different. Substantial damages of £250,000 were awarded to five police officers who had been injured during an Association football match at Reading Football Club's ground when supporters of the visiting team rioted using concrete broken off from the terraces as weapons.

The position concerning public protection within grounds and premises can be summed up as follows. The spectator has no protection against a promoter who regulates his affairs safely or the player who performs within the rules of a particular game. On the other hand, the promoter or organiser who arranges negligently or the player who performs recklessly is at risk for a claim in negligence. Where the protection of the spectator outside sporting premises is concerned, the position here is covered by nuisance as well as negligence. Nuisance involves acts which affect adversely the public at large and negligence a duty of care to one's neighbours which is breached with consequential and foreseeable damage.

Negligence was the basis on which Sir Joseph Cantley brought his wealth of experience as Chairman of the Summerlands Isle of Man fire disaster Inquiry and the High Court trial judge in the dispute between England's former football manager Don Revie and the Football Association when he adjudicated in favour of the victims during test cases following the Bradford City fire disaster. He concluded that the club was two-thirds to blame for failing in its duty of care to spectators; and the local West Yorkshire Metropolitan Borough Council as the local fire authority had failed in its duty under the Fire Precautions Act 1971, and was one-third to blame

(*Fletcher & Fletcher: Britton v (1) Bradford City Association Football Club (2) Health and Safety Executive, (3) West Yorkshire Metropolitan Council*) (Leeds Crown Court: 23 February 1987: *Times, Daily Telegraph,* 24 February 1987).

The unprecedented Parliamentary action upon urban and national sporting issues which followed so swiftly after the Bradford disaster ran concurrently with the urgent progress of the litigation. This emphasises the sharp contrast with the pattern of legislation for rural sports from their Norman Conquest origins in the Forest Laws attribution to a royal prerogative. Indeed, Stephen J's authoritative *History of the Criminal Law of England* claimed in 1883;

> 'Between 1389 and 1832, or 443 years, about twenty acts were passed relating to game; and these collectively constituted the game laws when the present statute, 1 & 2 Will 4, c 32, which replaced all but one of them, was passed into law'.

Until 1937, with its Physical Training and Recreation Act, Parliament had never entered *directly* on to the *public* sporting scene. It was that scene which caused Lord Hailsham to explain during 1962

> 'recreation generally presented a complexity of problems out of which modern Government was not free to opt'.

It had opted out after its own crowd safety reports in 1924 and 1946 following the Wembley Stadium and Bolton Wanderers eruptions respectively. Spurred by the late J L Manning's justifiable accusation of an unfilled gap in the public interest two years before the 66 fatalities at Ibrox, Glasgow, 1971, there was thereafter no alternative to further action. Lord Wheatley has described in his memoirs *One Man's Judgment* (p 177) how he was invited to report on the events and conclusions from them (not dissimilar from the post-Wembley and Bolton reports) which led directly to the Safety of Sports Grounds Act 1975 and the Green Guide equivalent to the Highway Code for crowd safety. These in turn proved inadequate as Bradford demonstrated, on the same day, when a 14-year-old schoolboy died during an imbroglio amounting to a riot between the notorious visiting Leeds United crowds and home team supporters at Birmingham City's ground. The Prime Minister, Mrs Thatcher, responded to the national sense of urgency. Mr Justice Popplewell, a former Cambridge University cricket blue and noted games player and former practitioner in Queen's Bench personal injury cases, was commissioned to report. Within a year he had produced an Interim (Cmnd 9585) and a Final Report (Cmnd 9710), and Parliament subsequently enacted three new laws:

Sporting Events (Control of Alcohol etc) Act 1985
Public Order Act 1986

Fire Safety and Safety of Places of Sport Act 1987
and responded to Mr Justice Popplewell's recommendation for a new Green
Guide.

BRADFORD, HILLSBOROUGH AND BEYOND

The Interim and Final Reports of Mr Justice Popplewell's Committee of
Inquiry into Crowd Safety and Control at Sports Grounds (Cmnds 9585
and 9710) were based on evidence from over 200 oral, written and inspection
sources. They contain all the factual and legal elements which are essential
for understanding what is required for the belief expressed in the
Introduction to the Final Report (para 13, page 2)

> 'that the paramount need is to protect the public by improving safety
> standards, and thereby restoring confidence among those who attend sporting
> events. This means that effective steps should be taken quickly. In this
> belief I commend my findings and recommendations for your consideration'.

The date of that Introduction is November 1985. Nearly a year later in
November 1986 the litigation (*Fletcher & Britton v Bradford City
Association Football Club & Others* (supra)) which followed from the facts
presented in the two Reports, as two test cases to establish liability,
emphasised and confirmed the key recommendation in paragraph 3.52 at
page 23 that

> 'one authority must be given the responsibility for security structural safety
> at undesignated sports grounds and stadia'.

During the course of counsel's opening speech for the plaintiff at Leeds
Crown Court a similar 'Departmental interest clash or overlap' to that
described in the House of Commons Environment Committee's complaint
concerning governmental confusion over dual use of school playing fields
emerged.

The four statutes concerning 'structural safety at undesignated sports
grounds and stadia' cited below and in force at Bradford were enacted at
different times over a span of fourteen years in isolation from each other.
The Home Office was the Whitehall department concerned with the Fire
Precautions Act 1971, the Safety of Sports Grounds Act 1975 and the
Building Act 1984, delegating operation of all statutes to local authorities.
The Department of Employment was concerned with the Health and Safety

at Work Etc Act 1974, with its implementation delegated to HM Factories Inspectorate. Current Regulations in 1994 made under the Act in 1992, implementing an EC Directive (EEC 69/391) in the UK relate inter alia to risk assessment and protective measures.

The relevant detailed provisions *at the time of the Bradford City disaster*, summarised here for convenience in comprehensible form, functioned in the following way:

Fire Precautions Act 1971 s 10	Discretion to complain to a magistrates' court if premises subject to the Act cause the appropriate 'Fire Authority (to be) satisfied that the risk to persons in the case of fire' is so serious that prohibition or restriction ought to be imposed until remedied.
Safety of Sports Grounds Act 1975 s 10	Identical discretion to complain to magistrates' court where 'the risk to spectators at a sports ground is so great' that, similarly, prohibition or restriction ought to be imposed until remedied.
Health and Safety at Work Etc Act 1974 ss 3, 18, 21.	Obligation on employers and self-employed persons to ensure that 'persons not in their employment are not ... exposed to risks to their health and safety' with enforcement powers available to HM Factories Inspectorate.
Building Act 1984 s 77	Discretion to complain to magistrates' court in respect of overloaded building (eg the collapsed Ibrox grandstand at the time of the 1971 disaster).

As Mr Justice Popplewell's Final Report explained in Paragraph 3.47 at page 23;

'It appears that there are three authorities who have the power to deal with breaches of structural safety at undesignated sports grounds (*ie overwhelming majority of those outside the publicised professional and leading amateur stadia which are subject to special designated Government orders*]: the Health and Safety Executive (under section 3 of the Health and Safety at Work Etc Act 1974); a county council (under section 10 of the Safety of Sports Grounds Act 1975); and a district council under section 77 of the Building Act 1984)'.

The Building Act 1984 did not arise during the Bradford City litigation, but the overlap of jurisdictions from the other three enactments caused Counsel in opening the trial for the representative plaintiffs to observe

'The general state of decay ought to have placed any regulatory authority on its guard'.

The claim against the club briefly was that it ignored notices of risk from those regulatory authorities: and against them was alleged lack of vigilance. The functional and operation difficulties in action or by concern in pursuing their knowledge of risk on an enforced avoidance of those 'regulatory authorities' were graphically expressed in the subsequent paragraphs of that Final Report, Paras 3.48–3.50 (inclusive at page 23) leading to the Recommendation for an integrated control.

'3.48 It is also clear that while these authorities have the power to enforce provisions of their respective Acts, they have no duty to inspect the premises to ascertain whether there have been any breaches. This difficulty was highlighted by the events at Bradford referred to in my Interim Report [NB it also emerged during the judgment of Sir Joseph Cantley sitting as Deputy High Court judge on the Bradford City litigation].

3.49 It is in my view essential that one authority, and only one authority, should have the responsibility for the structural safety of undesignated sports grounds and stadia [ie those outside the limited Orders by statutory instrument made for the leading Football League and other nationally known stadia].

If not, there will not only be a duplication of efforts and waste of resources, but also a risk that no one will in fact inspect these grounds and stadia.

3.50 The necessary inspection must depend on the perception of risk, particularly having regard to other buildings within the jurisdiction of the particular authority. But a duty to inspect and ensure compliance with reasonable standards of safety is necessary.'

The absence of such a specific statutory duty did not preclude the claim for negligence against the three defendants in the special circumstances leading to the Bradford City fire disaster. The initial claim against the club for lack of reasonable care was founded on general common law negligence principles incorporated in the fifth of the seven statutes identified at the outset of this chapter, ie the Occupiers' Liability Acts 1959–84, with additional claims based on failure to observe the Green Guide. Of that document the Interim Popplewell Report recorded in Paragraph 2.28 at page 10,

'Had the Green Guide been complied with this tragedy would not have occurred'.

In accordance with accepted litigation procedures, the Club brought within the action as additional parties:

(1) the West Yorkshire Metropolitan Council and

(2) the Health and Safety Executive

for breaches of their respective operations under their respective applicable enactments. They in turn alleged failure by the Club to respond to notices which it had received from regulatory authorities so that within this circuitry the claim on behalf of and by innocent victims of the disaster revolved around what will be the logical corollary to both Popplewell Reports. They found the facts and made recommendations. The judge, Sir Joseph Cantley, was concerned with liability and blame.

Further developments in addition to the Bradford City litigation have occurred since the Final Popplewell Report published in early 1986 and the Final Taylor Report in 1990.

(1) Three new revised Guides to Safety at Sports Grounds have been published by the Home Office and Scottish Office resulting from recommendations in the Interim as well as the Final Popplewell and Taylor Reports. The current edition in 1997 claims to

> 'meet the common goal: that is the safety, comfort and welfare of all spectators at all games, at all times and in all situations'.

Like its precedent its contents comprise in effect a good housekeeping guide to sports ground safety, based upon sound building, construction and engineering principles. Ironically, and sadly, its principles are consistent with the evidence given to and the recommendations made by the Wembley Stadium Committee Report in 1924 (Cmnd 2088). Thus Paragraph 40 of more than sixty years antiquity stated

> 'We have been somewhat surprised to find that in many cases little or no precaution is taken against the risk of fire in stands. We do not suppose that either the risk or the consequences of fire would be so serious in an open stand as in a closed building, but we consider it most important that adequate arrangements should be made to deal with any outbreak which might occur'.

Chapter 15 of the new 1997 Guide spells out the details for prevention. Alleged breaches of the old Guide formed a substantial section of the claim for negligence against the Bradford City Club.

(2) The Sporting Events (Control of Alcohol etc) Act 1985 received the Royal Assent on the day after publication of the Interim Popplewell Report in July 1985. Its implementation has given extended power of closure and search, in addition creating offences in connection with

alcohol on coaches and trains - and it will be further considered in Chapter 12. '*Administrative advice*'. It was passed to meet the social problems of soccer hooliganism, in the same climate which created the Public Order Act 1936 in response to Mosley's marches in London's East End before the Second World War. That enactment, and in particular section 5, has been substantially repealed and extended by the Public Order Act 1986. The Public Order Act 1986 gives discretionary (not mandatory) powers to the Courts to ban offenders from attending sporting matches.

(3) The current legislation is now an additional weapon in the legal armoury in the war against football hooliganism. It also has built in to it powers of extension by the Home Office, if, as already has been evidenced to the world at large on television, as well as to sporting observers, the danger signals from potential crowd explosions at boxing, cricket, and racehorse meetings are not defused sufficiently by longer-standing statutory powers or adverse consequences. Existing examples illustrate the point from the association football world. One from the Heysel Stadium experience in May 1985; the other from the riots at the Luton Town versus Millwall FA Cup tie a few weeks earlier, and a third from Europe generally.

(a) Heysel Stadium Extradition proceedings in Belgium were instituted against football followers from England on the initiative of Belgian authorities, after a three-tiered extradition ladder in London, from Chief Stipendiary Magistrate, Divisional Court to the House of Lords. A Belgian Parliamentary Commission of Equity cited in the Final Popplewell Report emphasised criticism of UEFA and Belgian footballing and other footballing authorities, against whom proceedings were initiated;

(b) Britain's former Minister with responsibilities for Sport, Mr (now Sir) Neil MacFarlane, criticised the FA in London for a lenient sentencing policy on the clubs associated with the violence at the Luton Town versus Millwall Cup Tie in early 1985 before the Bradford, Birmingham and Brussels disasters a few weeks later;

(c) *European Convention on spectator violence and misbehaviour at sports events and in particular at football matches* was cited in the Final Popplewell Report with ten key points geared to a coordinated teamwork structure with the comment in paragraph 1.47 (page 9):

'This is a blue-print for European football, which has lessons for our domestic game'.

All the circumstances emphasise that sporting authorities are in a position to regulate their affairs. Three examples from within the domestic English game, at Bristol, Brighton and Derby, prove this.

(4) The Fire Safety and Safety of Places of Sport Act 1987 was among many statutes enacted before the General Election in June 1987. By a Commencement Order (SI 1987 No 1762) its principal provisions did not come into force until 1 January 1988. It contained 40 sections and five schedules, and therefore is too long to reproduce here. On its second reading in the House of Commons, Mr Douglas Hogg MP, as the Minister concerned, explained: 'Despite the complexity of the Bill ... its purpose is simple: to provide more effective protection from the dangers caused by fire and to ensure a higher standard of public safety may exist' (HC Hansard: 30 March col 813). The impact of this enactment upon sporting and local authority recreational administration will clearly be formidable. The key substantive point for sport is the requirement of a safety certificate for a permanent stand which provides covered accommodation for 500 or more spectators at any category of sports ground. Procedurally, local authorities will be able to serve enforcement notices without an initial court application, as under the 1975 Act.

(5) The Football Spectators Act 1989 received Royal Assent two years later on 16 November 1989, seven months and one day after the Sheffield Wednesday Hillsborough Stadium disaster on 15 April 1989. It was enacted just two months before Lord Justice Taylor's Final Report (Cm 962) was presented to Parliament on 10 January 1990 (with its basic proposals for all-seater stadia and rejection of non-sports comprehending Prime Minister Mrs Thatcher's unrealistic and unworkable so-called membership scheme; in essence a dog or motorist licensing scheme). This Act created a Football Licensing Authority and replaced the provisions of the Public Order Act 1986 for restriction and exclusion orders which the author had been advocating analogously to road traffic offences since the Appendix 2 to the first edition initially published in the 1978 *Sunday Telegraph Sport and the Law*.

(6) In 1991 the Football (Offences) Act was enacted to implement three of the many specific recommendations of the Final Taylor Report, namely throwing of missiles, racialist chanting and going on to football pitches without lawful authority or excuse. In due course by Statutory Instrument it was extended to UEFA and FA Premier League fixtures.

(7) In 1999 the Football (Offences and Disorder) Act came into effect as from 27 September 1999 while these pages were in preparation. It extends the concept of banning orders contemplated in all previous *Sport and the Law* Appendices during 1978/1988 and 1994 to the International stage and also prohibits indecent or racist chanting and unauthorised ticket sales.

For the great majority of the 43,000 registered clubs at the Football Association's 16 Lancaster Gate headquarters, or those who meet Ian Wooldridge's brilliant criteria, cited in the Preface here from Cliff Morgan's BBC *Sport on Four* radio programme, that sport exists at

> 'Village cricket, soccer on Hackney Marshes, Old Boys rugger teams getting legless afterwards, point-to-pointing, county golf, darts leagues in Dorset'.

Lord Justice Taylor's 76 recommendations in that Final Report may have no direct *administrative* application or significance. It contained 427 paragraphs, 8 appendices and nearly 120 pages and photographs. Nevertheless, the First Aid, Medical and Ambulance recommendations in paragraphs 64–68 inclusive, will be ignored by many at their peril in the context of current inevitable injuries off, as well as on, the field of play.

Before leaving the Taylor Report, which justifiably may be said to have changed the face of British football and sport generally, one significant lacuna was observed in the *British Journal of Sports Medicine* (September 1998, Vol 32 p 198) from F W Smith at Woodend Hospital, Aberdeen. He noted the Report's silence on a need for separate docotrs for teams and crowds. It contains a warning that should not be ignored.

Two crucial sections in it applicable to subsequent events at the time of writing the second edition in early 1994 created a common thread throughout the whole sporting world which embraced athletics (and the Norman-Temple suicide inquest and published prelude scenario); cricket (and ball-tampering surfacing in Allan Lamb's libel action); horse racing (and the Grand National starting fiasco); rugby union football (and its rejection of the realities of semi-professionalism alongside an apparent ignorance of violence) and soccer (with its Chief Executive's testimony in court acquiescing in violence). All of these as assessed by David Miller in the *Times* before and after Christmas/New Year 1993–94 and Alan Hubbard in the *Observer* during early 1994 qualify for Lord Justice Taylor's strictures in his chapter 1 under the heading of 'Poor Leadership' in paragraph 55 and in chapter 2 at paragraph 132 under the heading 'Leadership and Example'.

The first of these at paragraph 55 demonstrates an understandable unawareness, as a pupil from a distinguished Northumberland rugby-playing school, of the Corinthian Casuals' retention of traditions at their own ground, Tolworth, near Kingston-upon-Thames, Surrey.

> '55. Then there is what happens on the pitch itself. Long departed are Corinthian Casual standards; accepting decisions of the referee without demur; affecting a modest diffidence on scoring a sensational goal. For many years now referees' decisions have been regularly challenged by spread arms and entreaties; even an unsensational goal has caused the scorer to be hugged and embraced all the way back to the centre spot. The cool self-control of

Corinthian Casuals will never return. Perhaps we should not lament its departure since there is no harm in a reasonable show of joy in success. But, more recently, things have gone further. On scoring a goal a player nowadays often rushes straight towards the perimeter fencing and either affects to climb it or, with fists raised and shaking, goes on his knees to excite response from supporters. Little has been done to stop such demonstrations which are calculated to hype up the fans into hysteria'.

Subsequently he brought a refreshing touch of judicial realism to explain the consequences to all sporting participating offenders when he reported in paragraph 132 with words and thoughts of general application four years later in 1994:

'132. It is in the first instance up to the players themselves, then the referees, the managers and the club directors to stop both incitement and violence by players whether on or off the ball. The referees, managers and directors have power to do this. If and when they fail to use it, the FA must take a firm disciplinary line using their very full powers to fine those involved including the clubs and to penalise the clubs in points. If all else fails, there is no reason why violence on the pitch should have any immunity from the law of the land or from police action'.

Indeed, all of this was corroborated by his brother Law Lord, Lord Griffiths of Govilon in the County of Gwent, a former Cambridge University and Glamorgan county cricket bowler, President of MCC and the Royal and Ancient (St Andrews), in a London *Evening Standard* interview (14 December 1993) after the New Zealand rugby tourist experiences:

'the law may be usefully employed to stop some of the excessive brutality in contact games ... I absolutely deplore stamping. I don't mind a bit if the law is employed so that people have it brought home to them that this is not part of the game'.

Such sentiments are echoed by the Law Commissions Consultation Paper No 134 on *Consent and Offences against the Person*.

Furthermore, even before Parliament felt forced to intervene on a national level, certain admirable local efforts identified immediately hereafter were made, notwithstanding the pathetically inadequate and surprising attitudes expressed to Lord Justice Taylor as reported in paragraph 52 of his Final Report, which related to the administrative periods of the late Mr Croker at the Football Association and his successor Mr Kelly at the Football League:

'52. The FA and the FL have not seen it as their duty [in the past] to offer guidance to clubs on safety matters. In their written submission they said:

"Of course, both The FA and The Football League are concerned to ensure that crowd safety standards are the highest reasonably practicable. It is felt, however, that neither of these authorities should be charged with the responsibility of setting detailed safety standards or enforcing them'".

Accordingly, the gaps left by that abject abdication of public responsibility were filled by some at least of the professionally administered company-clubs in the fullest way.

The Bristol City Case (*Bristol City v Milins* (1978) *Daily Telegraph*, 31 January)

The Bristol City Football Club company demonstrated the private control of public places by seeking and obtaining an injunction in its local Bristol County Court restraining a 17-year-old supporter from entering or attempting to enter its Ashton Gate ground.

He had created a 'substantial' disturbance involving fighting during at least two City home games in 1977. After the first he was convicted in the magistrates' court of a Public Order Act offence. The Club sent his father a letter stating that he was banned from the ground for the rest of the current season. He later defied the ban by attending and being ejected from another match. Hence the injunction order.

The Brighton and Hove Albion Case (*R v Clark and Ors* (1985) *Daily Telegraph*, 10 April)

Easter Monday, 8 April 1985 witnessed a coastal fixture at Fratton Park, Portsmouth between the home club and Brighton and Hove Albion. Five Brighton followers from the East Sussex area near the famous Goldstone, Hove, ground were convicted with varying sentences of 14 days' imprisonment, 28 days' detention and £100 fines, for various Public Order Act offences of a conventional kind. Immediately after the sentences, from which no appeal was lodged, all five were banned for life from the Brighton ground. The Secretary of the Brighton & Hove Albion Club, Mr Ron Pavey, was reported as having said,

'We don't want these people at our ground. We declared that anyone convicted would be banned for life from the Goldstone ground and we will stick with that policy'.

Derby County (1986)

The Board now bans any supporter who misbehaves in the ground for five years. A letter is sent threatening an injunction against them if they come into the ground in breach of the ban. Anybody who is convicted of a criminal offence within the ground is now banned automatically for life.

Any doubts that the Public Order Act applies to premises which ordinarily could be regarded as private were dispelled in *Cawley v Frost* (supra) by Queen's Bench Divisional Court of the High Court of Justice (per Lord Widgery LCJ, Melford Stevenson J and Caulfield J). The facts and extracts from the judgments may assist professional as well as lay readers to explain what may appear to be a paradox or conflict between private and public elements.

After an evening match between Halifax Town and Preston North End in 1976 about 200 supporters of each club were prevented by police intervention from clashing on the speedway track between the stands and pitch. Among the arrests was one for using threatening words or behaviour in a *public* place whereby a breach of the peace was likely to be occasioned, contrary to section 5 of the Public Order Act 1956 (as amended).

The point was taken and upheld at a lower court that part of the playing area or speedway track was sufficiently distinguishable to lose the character of a *public* place. The High Court rejected this and three judges led by the Lord Chief Justice of England in the Divisional Court of the Queen's Bench Division, Lord Widgery LCJ, laid the law down thus:

> 'Where you have an establishment which is set up to provide for the public, such as the Halifax Town Football Club or Wembley Stadium, one ought to approach it on the basis that it is a public place in its entirety.' (*Cawley v Frost* (1971) 64 CHR 20.)

Surprising as this decision and these pronouncements may be to the non-lawyer, they were recognised within the legal profession at least three years earlier. Anti-apartheid disrupters of a men's doubles match on No 2 Court at Wimbledon between Davidson and Bowrey and Pilic and Drysdale were required to obtain a House of Lords ruling that the local Wimbledon justices had rightly dismissed the charge against them for lack of sufficient evidence that they had been guilty of insulting behaviour (a High Court ruling having disagreed with the lay bench), and for the purposes of the House of Lords appeal it was conceded that No 2 Court at Wimbledon was a public place.

The legal process was initiated by a Metropolitan Police officer in the period long before the present Crown Prosecution Service began, involving the legal profession at all levels. (This was distinct from the time when police officers acted in a quasi-legal capacity by formulating charges and also the charges at the magistrates' court proceedings.) The defendant had entered the playing area to interrupt play for political and non-sporting exploitation. The House of Lords confirmed the local Wimbledon law justices' conclusion that the behaviour of interruption was not *insulting*. No argument was pleaded at any effective stage that the conduct was *abusive*. Yet on the basis that entrance to the ground was legal, either by invitation or by paid ticket, the status of entry created licence and licensee. It was abused by misconduct. Thus the charge of *abusive*, as distinct from *insulting* behaviour consistent with the provisions of section 5 of the Public Order Act 1936 whereby a breach of the peace was likely to have been occasioned would have been justified on the facts and at least arguably likely to have resulted in a conviction which would have been upheld by the higher courts. The ruling is therefore no more than an authority for (a) the facts of the particular case, (b) a confirmation of the construction approach to the meaning of insulting, and (c) for the agreement that private sporting premises are a public place (*Brutus v Cozens* [1973] AC 854).

One final set of enactments which require attention from the Popplewell complex of seven [now eight] identifiable and applicable statutes to sporting premises are the Occupiers' Liability Acts 1957–84. Passed initially in 1957 to codify the previous common law cases into a 'common duty of care' they were extended by the Act of 1984. This was enacted following two Royal Commission Reports in order to protect ramblers and recreational users of land from being treated as trespassers in rural districts.

Finally, during November 1993 in a different legal dimension an enterprising Bury, Lancashire, solicitor, Bernard Clayton, obtained an award of £101.75 damages and costs against Oldham Athletic Football Club from the Deputy District Judge in Bury County court, after he had been kept out of the ground with a valid ticket, when Manchester United were playing, because the defendant club had inadvertently admitted so many with forged tickets. The claim comprised not only a refund for the cost of the ticket, but also damages for wasted travelling expenses, unnecessary child-minding expenses, and loss of enjoyment, for which £25 was awarded, consistent with the Court of Appeal decisions applying developing recognised principles transcending any possible claim for a sportslaw jurisprudence in *Jarvis v Swans Tours Ltd* [1973] QB 233, [1973] 1 All ER 71 and *Jackson v Horizon Holidays Ltd* (1974) *Times*, 6 February. (*Daily Mail*, 16 November 1993.)

PERSONAL AND CROWD SAFETY CONCLUSION

Facts and evidence always are the only practical yardstick by which a situation can be assessed and judged legally. There are so many different situations which have given rise to injunctions and damages: a regatta, fairs, fire-works, circus, and noise from Earl's Court sideshows.

There are weapons in the legal armoury which have yet to be involved extensively in the struggle which has developed between a public suffering from uncontrolled crowd violence or other abuses and promoters, clubs and other organisers of sporting events who in the past have given an impression of failing to recognise their responsibilities beyond the narrow confines of their own backyards. The civil remedies initiated by proprietorally interested parties cited here demonstrate one potential level of action. Another has been the creation of a Football Safety Officers Association. Its object under its Rules

> 'would be to improve safety at football grounds, promulgate best practice, enhance the role of safety stewards and continually develop safety officers' expertise'.

Only planned coordination between Parliament and all those ready to recognise responsibilities for public protection can prevent repetition of past disasters. Its necessity on a permanent basis appeared confirmed on the eve of the last football season of the century, 1999–2000, with the news from the National Police Intelligence Unit that the hooligan elements, whether outside or inside stadia had not been eliminated. The shadows of World Cup 1998 and Marseilles cannot be ignored or forgotten, and the apprehensions which have arisen as a result of the resurrection of England v Scotland crowd rivalries for competitive fixtures are self explanatory. Thus after a week of manic media coverage of two association football matches notorious for lack of skill between the two national sides Adrian Lee wrote an article in the *Times* on Friday 9 November 1999:

> 'They fought street battles in Glasgow, screamed racist abuse inside Wembley and marauded through London's West End seeking an outlet for their hatred, yet the behaviour of England supporters won praise from two police forces – deploying about 3,000 officers at vast public expense – after their team's fixtures against Scotland.
>
> Such is the infamy of the national team's followers that anything less than a repeat of the mayhem during the World Cup finals is now tolerated. Such is the anxiety of the Government and the football authorities that almost any excess is ignored in their anxiety to make a successful bid for the 2006 World Cup.'

Crowd violence and hooliganism are the fall-out or pay-off from a permissive society cheerfully hailed thirty years ago with thoughtless abandon by the Chancellor of the Exchequer, Roy Jenkins MP, to be the 'civilized society' (*Times* 21 July 1969 as already cited) of which football is a mere victim of exploitation. This practical coordinated solution is offered to try at least to contain and even perhaps eradicate what is a social as well as a sporting evil. Its direct relevance to playing as well as spectating emerges from Chapter 6, *Participation problems*.

Participation Problems

1 INTRODUCTION

Participants in sport have no less claim to public protection than anyone else concerned with it: and within the context of these pages participation in sport means how a person approaches and plays the game. The concept of 'participation' involves a complexity of social issues which include the sportperson's amateur or professional status and the consequences arising out of this distinction. The requirement to obey the Rule of Law, however, demands the same standard of conduct, whether competing or indulging in any way at all within an amateur or professional environment.

Behaviour in sport reflects behaviour in society generally. Thus, a violence-orientated society will inevitably create violent elements in sport and this chapter accordingly deals with the criminal and civil liability of offenders in sport. It also demonstrates that all participants in sport are always at risk if they break the law of the land in the course of play. It also illuminates the reluctantly recognisable reality developing within sport that the law of the land does not stop at the touchline or boundary.

Participation touches the law at every point of the sporting compass and for all ages. For in the same spirit which caused the late Mr John Hislop, in a memorable *Times* feature article during early 1987, to claim how it is often forgotten that without horses there would be no racing of the equine kind, correspondingly without participants there would be no sport of any kind.

The table produced at the in the Preface from Derek Casey's initiative at the Sports Council (now Sport England) in March 1999 identified 30,920,000 participatory adults and children within a formal framework of 421 National Governing bodies.

In an earlier summary at the time of preparing the first 1988 edition of this book a former Director-General of the Sports Council, John Wheatley, explained to the CCPR Annual Conference in Bournemouth during November 1986 how the then lesser number of

'approximately 390 governing bodies of sport which exercise some measure of control or guidance in the form of committees of the United Kingdom... reflect various backgrounds and produce a pattern of management of sport which demonstrates the vast range of interest and has some important consequences'.

One of the most important of those consequences explained by John Wheatley was recorded a quarter-of-a-century earlier in the Wolfenden Committee Report on Sport, *Sport and the Community* (1960), established by the CCPR. This led to the Sports Council's creation under Royal Charter in 1972, as we can see in Chapter 2, *Progressive perspective*. The preceding years had led to a revolution in the nature and structure of the participatory role in sport *qua* amateur and professional. The Wolfenden Report in 1960 was faced with the dying days of the social and artificial antithesis between the professional and amateur status. Three years later (in 1963) the MCC abolished the formal distinctions between Gentlemen and Players. In turn before Wimbledon went 'Open' in 1968, the Wolfenden Committee had already endorsed (page 69, para 172):

'genuine amateurism which is worth preserving, namely, the wish to play a game for straightforward enjoyment, without any thought of money or of indirect financial gain. This is the element which is uppermost in the attitude of millions of humble games players; it is not snobbery or class distinction, nor does it imply any rebuke to those who perfectly legitimately play games for a living'.

Anachronistic as such thoughts may appear in the money mad media dominated Sportsworld of 1999, this last contemporaneous comment identified the lingering social stigma which had clung to paid performers until money sport monopolised the public sporting scene from the mid-1960s onwards, notwithstanding the first professional sporting knighthoods to Sir Jack Hobbs and Sir Gordon Richards in the Coronation Honours list of 1953, followed by Sir Leonard Hutton in 1956 and subsequently Sir Stanley Matthews CBE in 1965, and the millionairess winners of the Wimbledon Ladies Tennis Championships. It also reaffirms the great Steve Bloomer's recollection cited in Chapter 1 *Genesis* of the contrasting attitudes towards professional footballers generally at the turn of the century and that of the gentlemanly Corinthian G O Smith. The Wolfenden majority concluded.

'There seems to be no reason why difficulties about the status of a very small number of players should lead to a solution which would prevent the millions who just want to play something from being amateurs, in the full sense of the word.'

Nearly four decades later, the difficulties have persisted, notwithstanding the refreshing readiness to recognise the charade of trust funds in public athletics. They still preserve the title 'amateur' in national and international governing bodies (eg the International AMATEUR Athletic Federation) and 'boot money' existed in amateur rugby until it faced reality and embraced professionalism. In October 1985, a Scottish schoolboy athlete initially lost his amateur status upon receiving a 10p bag of sweets as a prize for winning competitively, until public ridicule caused his reinstatement. At the present time of writing in mid-1999 the International Rugby Board members and the four home United Kingdom Rugby Unions — England, Scotland, Wales and All Ireland — have compromised the amateur and professional status. The Unions have ceased to argue that 'amateurism' has been preserved while players are allowed to earn money from associated activities 'connected' with rugby union as distinct from professional Rugby League football. Ironically, perhaps the last bastion of *bona fide* amateurism to justify retention of the description in its title is the British AMATEUR Rugby League Association (BARLA).

Throughout the later 1980s and early 1990s the gap between playing standards of rugby at the televised entertainment levels and school, club and other grass-roots categories has widened with each passing year. Yet what is often ignored is the comparable position where the *professional* stage and theatre function on a different plane qualitatively and quantitatively from the countless *amateur* thespians and choral, musical and operatic societies which flourish throughout the land. The amateur status and ethos merit and doubtless voice the wish of a great majority of rugby union players and club members for preservation as much as those whose skill and sacrifices in time and family and employment situations deserve compensation for the entertaining pleasure and value they provide for millions.

During the Second World War, Profession D W Brogan, writing for the American public in *The English People: Impressions and Observations* (1943), claimed correctly at the time (page 69):

'Professional football is by far the most important game from the spectator's point of view but it is only the cream of a very deep milk jug'.

With successive generations *all* sport perpetually gushes forth fresh sporting talents from a very deep well of milk; but money sport sours the cream at the top and frequently curdles it into unlawful social and commercial conduct, as we shall see throughout this chapter.

Every sporting participant initially carries an amateur sporting status. The majority millions retain it. Relatively few become paid professionals:

and even fewer can afford to remain amateurs at the public participatory level as sporting heroes, or heroines, with professionally developed skills and techniques. Classic examples at different ends of the century are the immortal C B Fry, and the American banker, Charlie Fenwick, who rode the 40–1 outsider, Ben Nevis, to win the 1978 Aintree Grand National, or HRH The Princess Royal, competing for Great Britain in the Olympic Games of 1976, and winning the first race of the prestigious Diamond Day afternoon at Ascot on 'Ten No Trumps' at 9–1, in the Dresden Diamond Stakes ladies race in July 1987.

Economically the two worlds of *bona fide* amateurs and commercial professionals do not and cannot co-exist on the playing fields, notwithstanding the great volunteer British traditions administratively, without which sport and recreation could not survive. The antithesis which has replaced them now revolves upon a showbiz-grass roots axis.

Against this background and perspective of the two participatory amateur and professional sporting categories, it must be emphasised that none can escape the applicable law, with its inevitable overlapping elements. Obvious areas for duplication include sporting responsibilities, civil and criminal misconduct, *off* as well as *on* the fields of play, and certain paradoxical situations. These can be seen especially in relation to income tax (*Jarrold v Boustead* [1964] 3 All ER 76), with its tax-free compensation for loss of amateur status when entering rugby League's irreversible professional status, and reputation involving defamation (of an amateur golf champion) (*Tolley v Fry* [1931] AC 333), both of which with splendid irony, protect the amateur status commercially.

A valuable report from a CCPR Enquiry under the Chairmanship of Charles Palmer OBE into Amateur Status and Participation in Sport, published in 1988, highlighted the differentiations in attitudes with different governing bodies towards a status preserved in many circumstances by trust funds which many would consider incompatible with tradition and understanding. Towards the end of 1994, a Sports (Discrimination) Bill introduced in the House of Commons by Wakefield's Labour MP, Dennis Hinchcliffe, aimed to undermine the artificial differentiations. It illustrates how Sport and the Law functions in Parliament, without any member of either House attempting to take on board the insidious erosion of loss of recreational playing fields, at that time or in the intervening five years since leading up to this third edition.

2   PARTICIPATORY SPORT AND THE LAW

'It is as much in the interests of the Plaintiff himself as of any other contestant that there should be rules for clean fighting and that he should be protected against his adversary's misconduct in hitting below the belt or doing anything of the sort.'

With these oft forgotten and rarely recalled words already cited in the Preface, one of Lord Denning's predecessors as Master of the Rolls, Lord Hanworth, in 1933, and the Court of Appeal reversed Mackinnon J's judgment and thus rejected a claim by the then 18-year-old Irish heavyweight boxer, Jack Doyle, against the proprietors of the now demolished White City Stadium and the British Boxing Board of Control (1929) (*Doyle v White City Stadium Ltd* [1935] 1 KB 110). His professional boxing licence was suspended for six months, and his £3,000 purse was forfeited under the small print of the fight contract after the referee had disqualified Doyle for foul fighting in a contest for the heavyweight championship of Great Britain. This was against the late Jack Petersen, who subsequently became the President of the British Boxing Board of Control. Doyle's lawyers had argued, because of their client's legal status as an infant, that forfeiture was a penalty which was contractually disadvantageous and thereby not beneficial to their client. The test then as now, since the Infants Relief Act 1874 and more recently under the Minors' Contracts Act 1987, has been that infants' contracts must be for beneficial necessaries.

The Preface citation from Lord Hanworth has already explained how the Law Report headnote and title is incomplete because it omits the Board of Control against which judgment was initially obtained when exonerating the White City Stadium defendant. The successful appeal did not require to experience the present government's Denial of Justice concept in its '*Monitoring Justice*' false premise.

Of equal significance as distinct from Michael Watson's successful judgment (now subject to appeal) was the judicial basis of Doyle's case that it concerned an infant's contract with its criteria for beneficial necessaries. Thus, although the forfeiture within the rules was to cause financial loss the rule was enforceable beneficially within Lord Hanworth's criteria. Michael Watson's judgment against the Board transcends sporting administrative as well as medical areas, which become apparent in the next chapter *Sports Medicine and the Law*.

Twenty years before Doyle's case an earlier Court of Appeal had upheld a trial judge's ruling about a different form of an infant's sporting contract. They had allowed a claim by a leading international billiards player, John Roberts, for breach of contract against the infant defendant who obtained advantages from the agreement arising out of a form of touring apprenticeship experiences. This was adjudged to be beneficial for necessary instruction and education towards future playing proficiency (*Roberts v Gray* [1913] 1 KB 520). It had been available but never used for the advantage of cricket apprentices as legatees in the mishandled charity claim by Sussex County Cricket Club's advisers already discussed above in Chapter 3, *Under starter's orders* (*Re Patten* [1929] 2 Ch 276).

Doyle's Court of Appeal appearance is cited extensively in all leading practitioners' and student text books for the many-sided legal principles with which it bristles, concerning not only infants' contracts, but also the non-necessity to imply a contractual term for giving notice of alterations in administrative rules comprising the small print of the particular contract. As already cited, all are silent, however, about Lord Hanworth's citation extracted above. So, too, are the memoirs of Doyle's celebrated leading counsel Serjeant Sullivan, *The Last Serjeant*. This was also the title to his status in legal rank, now extinct, but commemorated in the area known as Serjeant's Inn, just off Fleet Street. They do dwell extensively on one of Sullivan's even better known and non-sporting clients, Sir Roger Casement. He was hanged for treason. Lord Hanworth's words threading the true spirit of sport with law, and the law with sport, should also be 'hanged', as a warning against sporting treason, in every schoolroom, dressing room, changing room, committee room, board room and club room throughout the land.

Such an ideal will not happen because of the conflicting commercial, criminal and personality interests which fluctuate through the varying layers of fun, healthy competition, professionalism, entertainment, internationalism and terrorism which comprise the pyramid structure which forms sport in the latter part of the twentieth century. As a reflection of the Law in Sport it transcends the rules and laws of all games. It is also illuminated most vividly the extent to which the criminal and civil law of the land have had to be wheeled on to the playing battlefields throughout the 1970s and 1980s for protection of players and the sport itself. The principles of control by the courts were first established in 1878 (*R v Bradshaw* (1878) 14 Cox 83 and *R v Moore* (1898) 14 TLR 229) and subsequently gathered dust in musty leather bindings on library shelves for nearly a century after. They were reaffirmed more recently in a wider and non-sporting context by a more modern Court of Appeal Criminal Division in 1975 (*R v Venna* [1975] 3 All ER 788). The significance of *Venna*, which is particularised at page 156, below, is that it fills the gap left by Lord Mustill in the sado-masochistic case of *R v Brown* [1993] 2 All ER 75 at 109h–i, [1993] 2 WLR 556 at 592H–593D, and cited in extenso in the Law Commission Consultation Paper No 134 (on Consent and Offences Against the Person) when he is reported as saying after a survey of 'contact' sports, ex cathedra of *Bradshaw* (after no practitioner before him referred to *Venna*):

> 'This accords with my own instinct, but I must recognise that a direction at nisi prius, even by a great judge, cannot be given the same weight as a judgment on appeal, consequent upon full argument and reflection. The same comment may be made about *R v Moore* (1898) 14 TLR 229'.

These principles, broken down into language comprehensible to a jury and thus to any man, woman or child on the terraces, were first used in the 1978 *Sunday Telegraph* edition of this book. Repeated in the first ever British Sport and the Law conference at the University of Birmingham in July 1978, they have stood the test of time with extended usage and application since then. They are repeated here as a warning to all potential violent sporting offenders and those who would encourage them.

'From 1878 to 1978 the British, and, in particular, English and Welsh [NB since then, Scottish, too] Courts have sustained the same principles of reckless and deliberate violent action for players as they have applied to protecting spectators in deciding what are the consequences of rough and illegal play. Tackle fairly and there is no problem. Tackle foully but accidentally, eg slipping in the mud or on canvas, and there would be no legal liability; but tackle foully or hit below the belt with deliberation and/ or recklessness and there is no doubt what the consequences would and should be: a criminal prosecution and claim for damages. If these thoughts are regarded as fanciful, consider the following examples.'

Those examples which followed in 1978 consolidated both the criminal and civil liability illustrations at the time. Since then the violent acts in the course of play in so many different disciplines, but primarily at both traditional football codes, have caused an annual pilgrimage to all courts. This has occurred at every level: High Court, Crown Court, County Court, Magistrates' Court, Coroner's Court and Compensation Board. The easily available remedy of civil assault has been extended by a concurrent claim for negligence which was upheld by the Court of Appeal in *Condon v Basi* [1985] 2 All ER 453.

Sadly, the optimism for self-regulation within sport itself which was expressed when I first raised the possibilities of involving the courts'' powers has not been fulfilled.

In a *Police Review* article in 1969, I first explained the reality of criminal conduct built-in to deliberate and reckless tackles following the prosecution for manslaughter of a player who killed an opponent with a blow struck during the course of a soccer game (*R v Southby* [1969] *Police Review*, 7 February, vol 77, p 110). In friendly terms the need to involve the courts was rebutted by a member of the FA staff, the late John Carvosso, in a contribution to the *FA News* (March 1969, p 288).

He claimed the absolute power on the field of the referee to be 'sufficient ... to deal with every contingency'. Ironically in the same issue, now more than twenty-five years ago, a need for action to control criminal foul play was crystallised by a more modern Corinthian and Cricketer than my own schoolboy heroes, C B Fry and G O Smith. At page 297 an article entitled '*A Bad Example*' was written under the authorship of A H Fabian in his capacity as a former Cambridge University (captain), Corinthians, Derby County and England amateur player, and a frequent co-author with Tom Whittaker, Arsenal's trainer and later manager. He also played cricket for Cambridge University and Middlesex and was a master at Highgate School. He suggested 'that it should be brought home to the star professional footballers that a responsibility they carry is the example they set to the young boys who will be the players of the future'.

In October 1986 when the Court of Appeal heard the Welsh Rugby International, David Bishop's appeal, it echoed those words: 'Local heroes have a responsibility to the game, their fellow players and to the public'. They were spoken by a former pupil at Highgate School during Fabian's mastership there, Lord Justice Brian Neil.

A decade after that *Police Review* initiative, in 1980, when another Welsh rugby international player, Paul Ringer, was sent off the field at Twickenham for striking an opponent outside the laws of play, letters to *The Times* from disparate sources concerned with the law and order confirmed the referee's verdict. Manchester's Chief Constable, James Anderton, explained the criminality; the master in charge of games at St Edward's School, Oxford, reiterated the bad example for boys, and an 80-year-old supporter voiced his concern for the future by comparison with the standards of the past. By the time of the Bishop affair in 1986, such outstanding Welsh International Rugby players as Clem Thomas in *The Observer* and Wilfred Wooller in the *Sunday Telegraph* were condemning selection committees and coaches for any field offences; and as we shall see, the legal consequences of their inactivity could be considerable. By the end of the decade the sentencing tariff for vicious criminality has descalated to 18 months immediate custodial imprisonment (*R v Lloyd*: *Times* 24 January 1989). A rugby hooker aged 28 who kicked the head with great force of an entirely innocent opposing winger who was lying on the ground (in a minor club game) after having released the ball on being tackled while the referee was watching the ball, appealed against his sentence at Bristol Crown Court. While dismissing the plea against sentence, in the Court of Appeal Criminal Division, Pill J explained:

'the game was not a licence for thuggery... what the appellant did had nothing to do with rugby football or the play in progress. The Recorder's description of the appellant's action that it was a vicious barbaric act was justified. The sentence [of 18 months] was appropriate.'

This and many other cases cited below appear in the Law Commission's Consultation Paper No 134 (supra) at paragraph 10.13: and footnote 93 to paragraph 10.11 contains the following extract from both codes of football:

[93] 'A wide range of dangerous acts is specifically forbidden by Law XII of the Rules of Association Football; the particular conduct in *Bradshaw* would seem to be outlawed by sub-laws (*c*) and (*d*), the "Advice to Referees" appended to which (1993 edition, p 35) says "Jumping at an opponent and not jumping for the ball is a foul; there is no such thing as accidental jumping

at an opponent". Law 26(3) of the Laws of the Game of Rugby Football 1993/94, similarly forbids a wide range of dangerous play, including, by sub-laws (3)(b)–(c), wilful hacking, kicking and tripping, and early, late or dangerous tackling.'

Accordingly, for ease and convenience of reference, the case summaries and illustrations of the basic principles outlined briefly below will be broken down into their own subdivisions of:

(1) Criminal liability and;
(2) Civil and compensatory liabilities.

Other chapters deal with the more commercially orientated aspects of participation problems, namely:

(i)   Status, reputation and compensation;
(ii)   Contracts;
(iii) Finance.

Criminality and civil liability are the key to keeping participants within the rules of play when adequate penal playing laws, eg the sin-bin principle (long-established for the potentially violent ice-hockey and water-polo, and introduced since 1982 to professional Rugby League Football) or the will to enforce and punish the existing laws against offenders, do not exist and fail to deter.

Criminal liability

The judicial principles applying the common law which have been sustained repeatedly for over a century from *Bradshaw* (1878) via *Moore* (1898) down to their reaffirmation in *Venna* (1975) did not appear to require application to the sporting scene until the violent explosion which publicly at least can be traced to the Bulgarian and Portuguese players' assault upon the Brazilian, Pelé, in England during the World Cup in 1966. The same principles were applied to the £4,000 damages award in 1970 by Rees J for a broken leg injured in a foul tackle in a local Sussex amateur game (*Lewis v Brookshaw* (1970) 120 NLJ, p 413). They could have been applied also to two notorious field dismissals by referees while the 1970s unfolded. In 1974, during the FA Charity Shield match at Wembley Stadium the referee sent off two international soccer players for fighting on the field, ie assaulting each other: Kevin Keegan (Liverpool) and Billy Bremner (Leeds United) witnessed by millions of TV viewers. In 1977, at Cardiff's National Stadium, in the Wales versus Ireland rugby international game, for similar mutual assaults, the referee, Norman Sansom, dismissed Geoff Wheel

(Wales) and Willie Duggan (Ireland). No really effective action was taken condemning such conduct within the course of that game, which was also witnessed extensively on television. A less charitable view, culminating in the comments of the England Rugby Captain, Will Carling, was taken of the New Zealand players' actions towards the end of 1993 during their tour of Britain.

Any mistaken belief that mobile body contact sport contained a built-in licence to commit crime, however, was soon to be dispelled. An amateur South Wales rugby player during early 1977 had the double misfortune during the course of a game (1) to break the leg of an opponent (2) who was a Borstal prison officer. The victim's principals were not content to lose his valuable professional services without an attempt to let similar offenders realise the consequences. That was how *R v Billinghurst* (supra) became the first ever rugby footballer to be prosecuted and ultimately convicted of the offence of assault occasioning actual bodily harm. The case was extensively reported in the popular and professional legal sources. By the time David Bishop, the Welsh international player, punched an opponent on the ground away from the ball during a club rugby match in South Wales neither he nor his club could claim that they were unaware of the legal consequences. No move was made by Bishop's club committee to discipline his conduct privately within the club membership's own internal capacity to regulate its own affairs. Accordingly, the prosecuting authorities had no alternative but to act upon the evidence and the complaint which led to the player's plea of guilty to the charge of common assault and ultimate prison sentence. This was varied on appeal from an immediate to a suspended sentence of one month, in abeyance for a year. His concurrent suspension by the Welsh Rugby Union, the game's governing body, was no different from experiences of any other practitioner such as a dentist, doctor or lawyer disciplined by his peers for a serious offence in a graver category than, for example, an isolated and single road traffic offence of speeding.

The legal principles applied when the South Wales prosecuting authorities prosecuted in 1977, *R v Billinghurst*, and 1985, *R v Bishop* were laid down with unequivocal clarity by two eminently respected and experienced Victorian criminal trial judges: Bramwell LJ who later became Lord Bramwell, and Hawkins J who is now recalled as Lord Brampton.

In *Bradshaw's* case ([1878] 14 Cox CC.83), a jury acquitted a footballer in a friendly game on a manslaughter charge after evidence had been given from one of the two umpires then in charge of the game that no unfair play occurred. During prosecuting counsel's opening speech to the jury, Bramwell LJ interrupted a reference to the game's rules to say (at p 48)

'whether within the rules or not, the prisoner would be guilty of manslaughter if while committing an unlawful act he caused the death of the deceased'.

His summing-up (at p 85) to the jury included these words:

> 'If a man is playing according to the rules and practice of the game and not going beyond it, it may be reasonable to infer that he is not actuated by any malicious motive or intention, and that he is not acting in a manner which he knows will be likely to be productive of death or injury. But, independent of the rules, if the prisoner intended to cause serious hurt to the deceased, or if he knew that, in charging as he did, he might produce serious injury and was indifferent, and reckless as to whether he would produce serious injury or not, then the act would be unlawful. In either case he would be guilty of a criminal act and you must find him guilty; if you are of a contrary opinion you will acquit him'.

On the evidence the jury returned a verdict of Not Guilty.

Twenty years later in *Moore's* case ([1989] 14 TLR 229) the evidence was that the accused jumped with his knees against the victim's back. This threw him violently against a knee of the goalkeeper, causing an internal rupture and ultimate death, a few days afterwards. He, too, was charged with manslaughter; and on this occasion the verdict was Guilty. Hawkins J's summing-up to the jury explained (at pp 229–230)

> 'the rules of the game were quite immaterial' and 'it did not matter whether the prisoner broke the rules or not. Football was a lawful game, but it was a rough one and persons who played it must be careful to restrain themselves so as not to do bodily harm to any other person. No one had a right to use force which was likely to injure another, and if he did use such force and death resulted, the crime of manslaughter had been committed'.
>
> 'If a blow were struck recklessly which caused a man to fall, and if in falling he struck against something and was injured and died, the person who struck the blow was guilty of manslaughter, even though the blow itself would not have caused injury'.

Nearly a century after *Bradshaw's* case in *R v Venna* ([1975] 3 All ER 788), a more recent Court of Appeal dismissed appeals against convictions for assault occasioning actual bodily harm and Public Order offences in a non-sporting context. The reserved judgment after two days of legal argument included the following significant sentence (at p 793 f–g),

> '*R v Bradshaw* (1878) 14 Cox CC 85 can be read as supporting the view that unlawful physical force applied recklessly constitutes a criminal assault.'

What constitutes 'recklessly' has been the subject of such subsequent gymnastics by the higher judiciary in the House of Lords that they moved the learned Editors of the leading practitioners' 'bible' in the criminal courts,

Archbold, in their Preface to the 41st Edition [1982] at page v, to describe them as 'a challenge even to the most gifted of Her Majesty's trial judges'. (Since then, the current 1998 Edition spans 22 pages in paras 17–50 and 17–61 for discussing 'Reckless' — 'Recklessly', while preserving the *Bradshaw* test in Para 17–82.) 'Wildly impulsive' is the definition in *The Oxford Mini-dictionary*. Disregarding the consequences is the yardstick used by practitioners. For present purposes it would be advisable for each citation from Bramwell LJ, Hawkins J and the Court of Appeal in *Venna* to be hung alongside Lord Hanworth's words in *Doyle's* case in the places mentioned above.

Before illustrating the application of these principles to prove criminal violence committed in the name of a game, it is appropriate to identify two developments which have occurred since this treasure trove of judicial wisdom has surfaced down the years. One is the corruption inherent in the bastard expression 'professional foul'. The other is the little known or cited revelation from the Government-funded Criminal Injuries Compensation Board.

The vice contained in the corrupting use of the term of professional foul is three-dimensional, or to adapt the standard sporting metaphor, it creates a corrupting hat-trick. *Archbold* (42nd Edn 1985, at p 2256 in para 27–156) explains:

'This word corrupting means dishonestly but purposely doing an act which the law forbids.'

Accordingly, the professional foul corrupts in three concurrent ways:

(1)   the law of football, rugby or soccer;
(2)   the law of the land, criminal and civil;
(3)   the profession of playing games according to both sets of laws above.

It may also be said to be a corruption linguistically for all three reasons; but that debate need not be considered here. Suffice it to say that it should be expunged from the vocabulary of every self-respecting sportslover and condemned except to explain that what has been called a professional foul in the past is in reality an actionable criminal and civil assault.

The Criminal Injuries Compensation Board was created in 1964 to administer a compensation scheme for victims of violent crimes after public opinion brought pressure through a vigilant press campaign amidst a growing tide of violence demanding it. The scope is complex, but its jurisdiction certainly can cover both field and crowd violence from sporting activities in appropriate circumstances. Even the traditional legal age limitations for young offenders and victims can be modified, too. Regional centres exist and enquiries are best made first to the Criminal Injuries

Compensation Board (England: Whittington House, 19 Alfred Place, London WC1E 7LG; Scotland: Blythswood House, 200 West Regent Street, Glasgow G2 4SW). By 1980 the tide of sporting violence had reached a sufficient level for inclusions of two paragraphs headed 'Football violence' in its Annual Report (paras 29 and 30).

Paragraph 30 concluded with a reminder of the devastating effect all too easily forgotten that criminal violence, which corrupts and poisons the sporting scene, *has upon the victims.*

> 'While there is not considerable public awareness of the existence and extent of football violence, we doubt whether the public is aware of the catastrophic effects which result from such criminal acts. The Board frequently deals with cases of people scarred for life, sometimes with cases of people seriously and permanently maimed and occasionally with people who are killed. We welcome the efforts which the courts, the police and many sporting organisations are taking to attempt to lessen the number of such crimes.'

The extent to which 'sporting organisations' are taking or encouraging attempts 'to lessen the number of such crimes', both off and on playing fields, is debatable. The ambivalence of many rugby playing sources, for example, regrettably, in South Wales towards the prosecution of David Bishop, is paralleled only by the Football League's expulsion of Luton Town from its Littlewoods Cup Competition for attempting to exclude violent visiting supporters from its terraces, and stands.

Paragraph 29 explained the Board's developing involvement and the principles upon which it operates. It began with a general statement, and then provided an example which failed to meet its criteria. That required standard requires a civil standard of proof on the balance of probabilities. Since the example cited in the report, the civil law of liability for injuries as explained by the Court of Appeal in *Condon v Basi* has now extended the tort of negligence specifically to the playing in a field in a manner which leaves the Board's example from 1980 open to a fundamental reassessment and review. The Board is concerned with criminal injuries. The level of proof in criminal courts is certainly to a degree of sureness or satisfaction beyond reasonable doubt. The proof required by the Compensation Board is on the balance of probabilities: ie the civil burden of proof, the level or degree of proof required in civil cases. Because of the developments contained in extending the law of civil negligence explained below at page 174, to sporting violence, this example provided in Paragraph 29 has been overtaken by events and is deliberately omitted here to avoid any risk of confusing the reader. Paragraphs 29 and 30 with the concluding sentences cited above of now nearly 20 years antiquity but still relevant today included with the author's own emphasis in the concluding paragraph reads as follows:

'Football violence

29. Public attention has been focussed recently upon the increasing pattern of mindless violence amongst both players and spectators. It results in injury to police and other people who are trying to keep the peace, to players and also to innocent bystanders. The phenomenon is not confined to professional soccer; amateur football, both association and rugby, is by no means immune and there are disturbing signs that the cricket field has growing problems in this respect. In our view, there is no doubt that a major contributory factor is the excessive consumption of alcohol amongst young spectators.

We are making an increasingly large number of awards to police officers who have been injured when attempting to restrain or arrest troublemakers, and to those we have referred to as innocent bystanders who are injured by bottles, beer cans and bricks indiscriminately thrown inside and outside the stadium.

We are also getting more and more applications arising out of alleged crimes of violence on the field of play itself. There is little problem when there is a proved "off the ball" incident: what raises far more difficulty is the alleged vicious or wild tackle. Here the alleged victim must prove either that there was an intention to injure him as opposed to a mere over-zealous desire to get the ball, or, and this is a very difficult matter in what is necessarily a heat of the moment situation, that the alleged assailant was guilty of "recklessness" within the meaning of *R v Venna* [1975] 3 All ER 788, [1976] QB 421, 61 Crim Ap R310; and other authorities.

30. Police, players, or spectators are not the only victims of injury arising out of sporting activities. In one recent case a full award was made to a referee who sent off a player for misbehaviour in a Sunday football match. The player returned onto the field of play and butted the referee with his head on the nose as a result of which the referee was knocked unconscious and sustained injury in the area of the nose.

Of course, the Board receives many applications from spectators assaulted on their way to and from football matches, often only because they are wearing a scarf or other emblem which indicates that they are supporters of the club playing against that "supported" by the assailant.

The wider problem of violence is one for the law-makers, the law-enforcers, and the clubs and associations concerned. There are signs that the clubs and associations are taking measures to cope with a problem which unfortunately shows no sign of going away.

While there is not considerable public awareness of the existence and extent of football violence, *we doubt whether the public are aware of the catastrophic effects which result from such criminal acts. The Board frequently deals with cases of people scarred for life, sometimes with cases of people seriously and permanently maimed and occasionally with cases of people who are killed. We welcome the efforts which the courts, the police and many sporting organisations are taking to attempt to lessen the number of such crimes'.*

Whatever efforts were made they clearly did not suffice to prevent a return to this area seven years later in the Annual report for the year-end 31 March in 1987. It was presented to Parliament by the Home and Scottish Secretaries in December 1987. The then CICB Chairman Michael Ogden QC, began a section with the above citation against a marginal note at page 13 headed *Violence connected with sport.*

'37. For many years the Board has received a large number of applications from spectators assaulted at or in the vicinity of sporting events, notably as a result of violence at or near football grounds. In the last few years, the Board has received an increasing number of applications arising from violence among players, particularly during rugby or football matches.'

Also at page 14 it concluded;

'We consider that it is in the interests of everyone that people who commit criminal offences on the playing fields should be prosecuted. Anyone who considers that an injury upon him was caused by a criminal offence should draw the attention of the police to it. If he does not do so, he is unlikely to receive compensation from the Board'.

This last qualification identifies para 6(a) of the Scheme, which provides for withholding or reducing compensation for delay, non-disclosure to the police and other inhibitory factors.

Since that date in 1987 the Board has continued to make awards regularly without returning to the general commentary of its 1980 and 1987 Annual Reports. Yet notwithstanding such an authoritative source a continuing claim persists that the courts are not the forum for discussing criminal or civil liability (see *Solicitors' Journal* 1993 Vol 137 No 25 page 628: Simon Gardiner, and No 27 page 693: Edward Grayson and Catherine Bond). Furthermore, on 26 November 1991, the full Criminal Injuries Compensation Board at Nottingham granted a £15,000 interim award to a fully qualified physical education teacher who lost an eye in a third fifteen so-called friendly rugby game from a proven deliberate assault upon it, (CICB: *Mark Johnson* (1991) NLJ p 1725: *Halsbury's Laws* MR 92/594: *All ER Annual Review* 1992: p 313). Finally, while these pages were being prepared, criminal proceedings for unlawful killing on a North London rugby field were initiated and on a self-defence plea resulted in an acquittal; and the Law Commission Consultation Paper No 134 (supra) contains in paragraph 46.4 a graphic summary of the level of tolerance to be considered in the following way:

'46.4 The process of participating in sport might be said to involve a certain amount of give and take; but, at the same time, there is a limit to the extent to which criminal sanctions can or should be withheld because of the attitude of the victim. We may give an example. Fast bowling in modern professional cricket is potentially extremely dangerous. To avoid or greatly minimise that danger batsmen are permitted, though not obliged, to wear a variety of protective clothing, particularly helmets. A batsman who declined to protect himself in that way would undoubtedly be creating a situation where a bowler bowling normally would be creating a significant risk of causing serious injury. That is, in the first place, a question for the cricket authorities; but the implication of the scheme that we provisionally propose is that a bowler who continued in his usual way and injured the batsman would be risking criminal liability, because above a certain level of hazard the consent or connivance of the victim is no defence. Similar considerations will apply, with increased force, if very fast, dangerous bowling is permitted in cricket at a lower level than the modern first-class game, particularly if the batsman's ability to cope with very fast bowling is obviously limited.'

This in turn recalls a valuable cameo captured by David Frith, the former editor of *Wisden Cricket Monthly* in his valuable book *The Fast Men* (1975). At pages 139–140 he refers to the injured Sri Lankan batsman Sunil Wettimuny and the account

'related by Peter Marson of *The Times*, who wrote the following dialogue surrounding Wettimuny's arrival in hospital: "What happened to you?" "I was hit playing cricket." "Where?" "At The Oval." "Who did it?" "Thomson." At this point, and with the timing peculiar to officers of the law, a police sergeant who had chanced to be within earshot of the conversation interjected: "Do you wish to prefer charges?"'

David Frith commented (as at 1975),

'It raises an interesting point. A fast bowler who has written that he aims to hit batsmen could find himself in the position of an American ice hockey player who has recently faced a criminal charge of assault with a dangerous weapon (a hockey stick) during a match. The penalty, if convicted, is three years' jail'.

Just over a decade later in a Canadian citation referred to in *R v Brown* (supra) and also in the Law Commission Consultation Paper No 134:

'In *Regina v Ciccarelli* (Ontario Prov Ct 1988), Minnesota North Star Dino Ciccarelli was convicted of assault for his part in an incident which took place on 6 January 1988, in a National Hockey League game in Toronto, Ontario ... Ontario Provincial Court Judge Sidney Harris said, "It is time now that a message go out from the courts that violence in a hockey game or in any other circumstances is not acceptable in our society". Ciccarelli was sentenced to one day in jail and ordered to pay a £1,000 fine'.

Finally, in a little known publication but highly relevant to United Kingdom activities from America, *PROS and CONS* (1998) two investigative reporters, Jeff Benedict and Don Yoeger, posed what their book jacket back cover from Time Warner Books state is

> "the ultimate question: Is winning football games more important than upholding society's standards of the law? You read the stories, and then you be the judge".

The front jacket flap cover citation cannot be ignored, allowing for the greater population radius from which to draw a conclusion which is at least worthy of United Kingdom apprehensions:

> "They're America's heroes. They drive expensive cars. They live in the biggest homes. Darlings of television sports and role models to millions of kids everywhere, National Football League players have come to personify the American dream. But there's a dark side to this hero worship, a seamy element that's rarely addressed by the league itself or the public. In a recent sampling of NFL players, it was estimated that *one out of every five players has been charged with a serious crime.* That includes such criminal offences as rape, kidnapping, assault and battery, weapons possession, drug dealing, driving while intoxicated, domestic violence and, yes, even homicide".

The percentage may be higher, but some of the offences are sadly not unknown sadly to British sport heroes.

SAMPLE SUMMARY ONLY OF CRIMINAL PROSECUTIONS FOR SPORTING VIOLENCE ON THE FIELD OF PLAY: 1878–1994

[NB Almost daily and frequently weekly referrals come the author's way from all parts of the United Kingdom to illustrate the increasing and sickening sequence of field violence which sadly inspired the London *Evening Standard's* publication under its title *Sporting Spite: Rebels and Rebellion in World Sport* (1991), cited above. The examples which follow could be multiplied countless times over to reflect a basic thread and principle.]

1878

Leicester Assizes

Prosecution for unlawful soccer tackle: manslaughter charge (*R v Bradshaw* (1878) 14 Cox CC 83)

Decision

Acquittal.

Principle

Deliberate and/or reckless tackle not proved to jury. Rider by jury to tighten up tackling rules.

1882

Berkshire Quarter Sessions

Bare-knuckle prize fight. Prosecution of spectators for aiding and abetting in such fight (*R v Coney* (1882) 8 QBD 534)

Decision

Conviction quashed for defective summing up.

Principle

Blow struck in prize fight clearly an assault, but playing with single sticks or wrestling does not involve an assault, nor does boxing with gloves in the ordinary way. Consent of illegal prize-fighters to interchange of blows no defence.

1898

Leicester Assizes

Prosecution for unlawful soccer tackle: murder (*R v Moore* (1898) 14 TLR 229)

Decision

Guilty. Manslaughter.

Principle

Deliberate and/or reckless tackle outside laws of game proved.

1901

Central Criminal Court: Old Bailey

Test case prosecution against National Sporting Club for illegality or legality of Queensberry rules boxing competition (*R v Roberts and Ors* (1901) *Daily Telegraph*, 29 June)

Decision

Acquittal.

Principle

Boxing within the rules as distinct from boxing until exhausted not unlawful. See pp 172–173 below.

1969

Maidstone Assizes (transferred from Chelmsford)

Prosecution for murder after death from niggling blow in Essex amateur soccer match (*R v Southby* (1969) *Police Review*, 9 February, vol 77, p 110; NLJ vol 120, p 413)

Decision

Guilty. Manslaughter.

Principle

Deliberate and/or reckless blow outside laws of game proved.

1977	**Decision**
Lyons, France	Conviction (reversed on appeal).
Prosecution of rugby international for field assault (unreported)	**Principle**
	Deliberate and/or reckless foul play on field equals criminal conduct.

1978	**Decision**
Newport Crown Court	Conviction (not to be appealed).
Prosecution for broken jaw in rugby tackle	**Principle**
	As above — deliberate and/or reckless foul play on field equals criminal conduct.

The French connection deliberately inserted here has no binding authority on the English courts. Because the prosecution was supported by the French Rugby Union against one of its international players later selected to play against England in the International Rugby Tournament, the citation is inserted deliberately and non-recklessly to remind all aggressively minded players and their belligerently minded friends in the Press Box, as well as all other home sporting national bodies, of the potential and ultimate consequence of violent and unlawful conduct on sporting fields.

1980	**Decision**
Croydon Crown Court *Court of Appeal*	Immediate custodial sentence (six months).
Prosecution for three fractures to face in rugby tackle: Guilty plea (*R v Gingell* [1980] Com L Rev 661)	Confirmed in principle, reduced to two on appeal because first precedent (quaere: why only six: why not more?).

1980	**Decision**
Wolverhampton Crown Court	Jury acquitted in spite of evidence.
Prosecution for gouging out eye in rugby tackle (*R v Doble* (unreported) Stafford Cr Ct, 8–10 Sept 1980)	**Principle**
	Judge recommended victim to approach Criminal Injuries Compensation Board.

1982	**Decision**
Scottish Sheriff's Court	No evidence offered against one. Other pleaded guilty: suspended sentence.
Prosecution of two opposing rugby captains: prosecuted on advice of Procurator-Fiscal (unreported)	**Principle**
	Action at last: against punch-up on field (hitherto not pursued by abdication of prosecution responsibilities and also by victims for younger generations).

1985

FA Tribunal

Complaint by one professional footballer of assault by another within framework of bringing game into disrepute under FA Rule 35(a) (unreported)

Decision

Not proven, but deposit returned to complainant on establishing prima facie case.

Principle

Action at last: recognition of existence of potential offence at professional level.

1985

Dursley, Gloucestershire, Magistrates' Court

Private prosecution for broken leg in soccer tackle (unreported)

Decision

Guilty: £180 fined with costs.

Principle

Action at last: by victim on own initiative.

1985

Clacton, Essex Magistrates' Court

Prosecution against woman footballer for breaking opponent's jaw in women's friendly soccer match

Decision

Guilty: £250 compensation and costs.

Principle

Female of species can be as deadly as the male!

1986

South Wales

Process initiated against Welsh International rugby player for alleged assault in club match

Decision

Guilty plea to common assault.

Principle

Action at last, long overdue, against alleged offenders at public level. First prosecution against international in United Kingdom.

1985–86

Newport Crown Court and Court of Appeal

Concussion from punch in off-the-ball rugby union incident (*R v Bishop* (1986) *Times,* 12 October)

Decision

Guilty plea to common assault. Sentence: One month's custodial imprisonment reduced without reasons to one month's suspended imprisonment.

1986

Cardiff Crown Court

Ear bitten after tackle in police rugby union match. (*R v Johnson* [1986] 8 CAR (5) 343) Inflicting grievous bodily harm with intent contrary to s 18 Offences against the Person Act 1861

Decision

Convicted. Six months' custodial imprisonment. Confirmed on appeal.

1988

Swindon Magistrates' Court

Decision

Guilty plea. Inflicting grievous

Broken jaw by professional soccer player in tunnel after match (*R v Kamara* (1988) *Times*, 15 April)

1988

Bristol Crown Court

Broken cheekbone caused by amateur rugby player in club match kicking opponent on ground during course of play (*R v Lloyd* (1988) *Times*, 13 September)

1988

Wood Green Crown Court

Broken jaw by amateur soccer player in 'friendly' match (*R v Birkin* (1988) *Enfield Gazette*, 7 April)

1989

St Albans Crown Court and Court of Appeal

Concussion from kick on head to player on ground by soccer opponent (*R v Chapman* (Court of Appeal Criminal Division transcripts))

1991

Ct In Cum Bd

Eye gouged out from Rugby Union foul play in line-out (1991) NLJ 1725, Hals Laws MR 92/54)

1994

RN Plymouth Court Martial

Broken nose from Rugby Union foul play (*RN v Russell* (1994) *Times*, 23 February)

1994

Court of Appeal Criminal Division

Facial fractures admitted

Probation and Compensation Order [See also Ch 15, whither Sport and the Law? Pp 425–426] (*R v Piff* (1994) *Guardian*, 2 February)

bodily harm contrary to s 20 Offences against the Person Act 1981. £1200 fine £250 compensation and costs.

Decision

Conviction: grievous bodily harm 18 months' imprisonment.

Decision

Actual bodily harm.

Decision

Grievous bodily harm. Eighteen months' custodial sentence. Confirmed on appeal.

Decision

Criminal liability admitted though offender not identified. £15,000 interim compensation award.

Decision

4 months detention. Reduced ranks.

Decision

Attorney-General's reference to Court of Appeal Custodial Sentence substituted. Compensation Order cancelled.

1999	**Decision**
Sheffield Crown Court	12 months Youth Offenders
Schoolboy breaks opposing	Institution *
schoolboy's jaw in school rugby *R v*	
Carlton (Yorkshire Post 2	
September 1998)	

* Reduced to 3 months on appeal: [1999] 2 Cr App Rep (S) 64, CA.

Criminal liability: vicarious liability and responsibility

One final area of criminal liability for sporting violence which to date has not yet arrived in court is the question of ultimate and final responsibility. Responsibility vicariously for civil liability would certainly exist against coaches, committees and selectors with proof of appropriate evidence of known violence. It has also been confirmed by the American case of *Tomjanovich v California Sports Inc* No H–78–243 (SD Tex 1979). A similar response equating criminal with civil liability and responsibility, subject to the variations in the degree or level of evidence and proof required, has yet to be tested in the courts for this particular sporting penalty area. Nevertheless there is now appropriate precedent available from the associated world of entertainment which I suggest can support the positive response to the referee's question. This guidance is provided from *Wilcox v Jeffrey* [1951] 1 All ER 464, that if the appropriate evidence can exist of knowledge of proven violent sporting offences and encouragement to persist is given by further selection with no contrary warning of discouragement; then vicious criminal liability can arise, in the circumstances discussed immediately below.

In 1949 a greatly admired United States musician and citizen Coleman Hawkins, a jazz saxophonist, was granted permission to enter the United Kingdom under art 1 (4) of the Aliens Order 1920, subject to a limitation against taking any employment, paid or unpaid. The owner of a monthly magazine, *Jazz Illustrated* was convicted at Bow Street Magistrates Court under art 18 (2) of the Order, of aiding and abetting a breach of the condition of entry by encouraging a concert performance given by Coleman Hawkins. The appeal against conviction was heard by a strong Divisional Court in the King's Bench Division comprising the Lord Chief Justice, Lord Goddard, Humphreys J and Devlin J (as he then was). The facts included circumstances of active and more significantly negative encouragement which Lord Goddard explained in his characteristically robust and colourful style when rejecting the appeal against conviction (at p 466):

'The appellant [Wilcox] clearly knew that it was an unlawful act for him [Coleman Hawkins] to play. He had gone there to hear him, and his presence and payment to go there was an encouragement. He went there to make use of the performance, because he went there, as the magistrate finds and was justified in finding, to get "copy" for his newspaper. It might have been entirely different, as I say, if he had gone there and protested, saying:

> "The musicians' union do not like you foreigners coming here and playing and you ought to get off the stage".'

At that period, international mutual exclusivities among musicians unions operated as keenly on both sides of the Atlantic as the recent differences between the national acting unions manifested in the dispute about the wife of Sir Andrew Lloyd-Webber, Sarah Brightman, performing in America. Lord Goddard continued:

> 'If he [Wilcox] had booed, it might have been some evidence that he was not aiding and abetting'.

More than 40 years on in the 1990s, the concept of a Lord Chief Justice recommending booing as a form of discouragement at a public performance is both indicative of the shift in social attitudes and also the change in climate surrounding light entertainment. Furthermore, Lord Goddard was not unfamiliar with the sporting scene. During the vintage Corinthian era he had obtained his running Blue for Oxford versus Cambridge in the Annual Athletics Inter-University Sports at Queen's Club in 1898 and for many occasions when the fixture was resumed in 1946 in the year of his appointment as Lord Chief Justice he was seen to be officiating near the winning post at the White City. The point was made clearly in *Wilcox v Jeffrey* that negative as well as positive encouragement can comprise aiding and abetting; and although that ruling may one day be challenged the undoubted fact is that it is still cited in the leading practitioners' and academic books as an authentic authority, ie Glanville Williams, *Textbook of Criminal Law* (1983, 2nd edn, p 250), Smith & Hogan, *Criminal Law*: Part I. General Principles (1983, 5th edn, pp 122, 125); *Archbold* (42nd edn p 2308 at para 29.5). Accordingly, until it is overruled or distinguished by any court of comparable status, sports, coaches, committees, and direct participating supporters of the selection of known violent playing offenders cannot say that they have not been warned of the full criminal consequences if their choice persists in offending by committing criminal offences, albeit misguidedly, in the name of a game. To what extent the same principles could apply to the selection of offenders with known violent proven criminal convictions outside sport is a further question which may yet have be considered in the future if current violent sporting tendencies continue unabated. An admirable step in the right direction was the peremptory and public action by the Rugby Union executive in March 1987 to exclude from selection for the next rugby international players who had been associated with violent play during the Wales versus England international at Cardiff forty-eight hours earlier.

Finally separate and apart from these physical offences against the criminal law are others which happily are rarer in apparent extent, but none the less have to be recorded. Mr Simon Inglis followed his own valuable and learned architectural and historical survey of *The Football Grounds of England and Wales* with no less a salutory reminder of the extent to which sport reflects society, in the later publication *Soccer in the Dock*. The chapter 'Power to the People' recalls the assistance of campaigning newspapers to uncover financial (as distinct from physical) corruption within the professional game during the 1960s. Resulting from these and other energetic concurrent pursuits from additional sources, prosecutions of a different kind from those analysed above were mounted. They may be summarised thus:

1963

Doncaster Magistrates' Court

Prevention of Corruption Act 1906. 3 players charged with attempting to fix a 3rd Division Football League match.

Decision

Fined maximum £50 each.

Principle

FA ban permanently from football and football management.

1963

Rochdale Magistrates' Court

Agent charged with offering bribes to footballers.

Decision

Fined £60.

Principle

Tip of iceberg during investigations.

1964

Mansfield Magistrates' Court committal proceedings

Nottingham Assizes

Conspiracy to corrupt.

Decision

Guilty and custodial imprisonment for international footballers.

Principle

International footballers not above the law.

3 CIVIL LIABILITY

Introduction

The corollary to the criminal process for broken limbs on sporting fields at any code is clearly a damages claim, with the corresponding burden of proof in civil claims geared to a balance of probabilities. That is distinct from the degree or level of satisfaction beyond reasonable doubt or satisfaction of sureness required for the necessary burden or proof in criminal trials.

Unlike the criminal liability lineage beginning in 1878, injury inflicted in the course of play by participants, as distinct from those caused by land occupiers or promoters, do not appear to have entered court reports until the beginning of the century, and particularly during the interwar years, 1919–39. In the Court of Appeal decision of *Wooldridge v Sumner* arising out of the White City National Horse Show of the Year, Diplock LJ (later Lord Diplock) said:

> 'It is a remarkable thing that in a nation where during the present century so many have spent so much of their leisure in watching other people take part in sport and pastimes there is an almost complete dearth of judicial authority as to the duty of care owed by the actual participants'.

Albeit, as he concluded,

> 'to the spectators'.

In that particular case, a professional photographer was the injured plaintiff. Twenty-odd years later in *Condon v Basi*, the Master of the Rolls, Sir John Donaldson, commented in the early part of this judgment:

> 'It is said that there is no authority as to what is the standard of care which governs the conduct of players in competitive sport generally and above all, in a competitive sport whose rules and general background contemplate that there will be physical contact between the players, but that appears to be the position. This is somewhat surprising, but appears to be correct'.

What was 'said' on the occasion to the Master of the Rolls, was incomplete. On four earlier occasions one of the most self-disciplined of all sporting activities, golf, threaded a pattern of liability from which 'a standard of care which governs the conduct of players in competitive sport can be gauged' was clearly identifiable; and Diplock LJ's comment is explicable from six interlocking sources:

(1) the absence of any legal aid until 1950 to assist litigants of slender-means for civil claims;

(2) notwithstanding the existence since 1950 of that limited legal aid capacity, private litigants as distinct from institutions, multi-national organisations or sporting governing bodies can hardly run the risk of costs involved; indeed, even the FA was justified in asking the Sports Council and the CCPR to join their quest for charitable status on behalf of the rest of sport for the potential expense of its appeal to the House of Lords in 1979–80;

(3)   the absence at present in 1999; of any wish to contemplate an American-style contingency fund system for legal costs, which has at last been floated in outline form by the solicitors' governing body, the Law Society;

(4)   the general reluctance in more leisurely days to bring the law courts onto the playing fields before professional sport and commercial sponsorship created a conventional climate for litigation;

(5)   a continued reluctance generally to recognise that sport cannot be above the law, and that however magical and dramatic it may be, the ordinary rules of life and the law of the land are never suspended at any time of its existence;

(6)   the lesser quantum of persistent and sustained sporting field violence before 1962 compared with its progression permanently since then.

Boxing

One particular activity fuses the civil and criminal liabilities into a combined focus: boxing. This self-proclaimed Noble Art of Self-Defence contains in that descriptive title a legal issue common to both civil and criminal litigation (*R v Palmer; R v Turner, Lane v Holloway*). Today the legality or illegality of boxing depends exclusively upon whether or not the evidence produced before a court creates a condition of sparring or prize fighting, from which modern boxing has evolved. So far as the Law Commission Consultation Paper No 134 (supra) is concerned, paragraphs 10.21 and 10.22 state:

'10.21 The only explanation of injury and death continuing to be caused in boxing with complete impugnity, at least as far as the criminal law is concerned, is that the immunity of boxing from the reach of the criminal law is now so firmly embedded in the law that only special legislation can change the position. We do not consider further in this Paper whether such legislation should be introduced, for two reasons. First, as we have already pointed out, the legality of boxing is a clear anomaly in the context of the general rules applying to sports and games that are described above, or in the context of any general rules for sports and games that might emerge from the study conducted through this Paper. Second, we fully recognise that whether or not boxing should continue to be legal is a hotly contested issue, already much-debated, that is not going to be resolved by any sort of appeal to the general law.

10.22 Therefore, it is in our view for Parliament to take an entirely separate decision, in the light of the material sedulously put before it by the British Medical Association and others, as to whether boxing should continue to be lawful. We merely note that, in the event of boxing continuing to be lawful, and there being comprehensive legislation on offences against the person, it will be necessary specifically to provide in any such legislation that it is not criminal to kill or intentionally severely to injure another person in the course of a boxing bout'.

More realistic and meaningful in the welter of commentary after the death of the young super bantamweight boxer Bradley Stone on 2 April 1994 have been the recommendations of some of the British Boxing Board of Control's doctors and Neil Allen, the London *Evening Standard's* boxing and athletics correspondent from his knowledge of all the competitions' drug-testing regulations. These are spot-check weight-tests during pre-title fight training to avoid dehydration and other health-damaging practices. In brief, a prize fight exists, and is illegal, if parties meet intending to fight until one gives in from exhaustion or injury is received whether gloves are used or not. A mere exhibition of skill in sparring, demonstrating the Noble Art, is not illegal (*R v Orton* (1978) 39 LT 293, 43 JP 72J). The liability judgment of Kennedy J in Michael Watson's negligence claim against the British Boxing Board of Control recorded at the outset of this edition in the Preface (now subject to appeal) for lack of appropriate medical skills and facilities raises a wider issue which would not have been, immediately available in its aftermath. This results from the various declarations *On principles of Health Care for Sports Medicine* formulated in 1981, 1987 and most recently in 1993 by the World Medical Association. It is an independent confederation of professional medical associations from approximately 70 different, of which the British Medical Association is a founder member. It has drafted and recommended in number 13

'ethical guidelines for physicians in order to meet the needs of the sportsmen or athletes and special circumstances in which medical care and health guidance is given'.

The final thirteenth guideline has a direct interconnection between sports medical physicians and the law with its requirement

'The participation of a sports physician is desirable when sports regulations are drawn up'.

The full transcript in *Watson v British Boxing Board of Control* does not identify how far this particular guideline was activated in the circumstances of this case. Nevertheless the emergence of sports medicine as a speciality in which knowledge of the various differentials in prevention and/or restrictions of injury, and many that could have been foreseen for protection of Michael Watson in 1991 after his fight with Chris Eubank raises permutations which all governing bodies and their medical and legal advisers would do well to consider. The Guidelines do not yet have the force of the evidential impact of a Highway Code in relation to road traffic affairs. Nevertheless, their existence and particularly Guideline No 13 cited above could well provide prima facie evidence pointing towards a duty of care with a foreseeable risk of injury, to be ignored at peril.

A quintet of legal rulings over half a century from 1866 to 1911 demonstrates the differing degrees of evidence for the legal status of boxing, which in Britain has never been formally legalised. Nevertheless, one of the many valuable judgments from Australian courts has come as close as anything can be traced judicially for legitimising its existence. For in the Supreme Court of Victoria Mr Justice McInerney in *Pallante v Stadiums Property Limited* (No 1) [1976] VR 331 rejected a procedural application to strike out the statement of claim by a boxer who had received eyesight injuries when boxing under Australian Boxing Alliance Rules. He sued all persons other than his opponent, namely the promoter, his trainer, the matchmaker and referee. (See also Lord Mustill in *R v Brown* [1993] 2 WLR 556 at 592 F–G.)

The summary of the judgment at [1976] VR 332 vindicated boxing as 'not an unlawful and criminal activity so long as, whether for reward or not, it was conducted by a contestant as a boxing sport or contest, not from the motive of personal animosity, or at all events not predominantly from that motive, but predominantly as an exercise of boxing skill and physical condition in accordance with rules and in conditions the object of which was to ensure that the infliction of boxing harm was kept within reasonable bounds, so as to preclude or reduce, so far as is practicable, the risk of either contestant incurring serious head injury, and to ensure that victory should be achieved in accordance with rules by the person demonstrating the greater skill as a boxer'.

The ultimate result of the claim was never disclosed, and in the absence of contrary information, should be treated as having been settled. Two commercial cases in the English courts for events outside the boxing ring concerned management contracts and procedural remedies. In *Warren v Mendy* [1989] 3 All ER 103 injunctions were refused; *Watson v Prager* [1991] 3 All ER 487 concerned a stay of a restraint of trade action which resisted effectively an arbitration agreement tarnished by invalidity.

Finally, it is appropriate to identify a perspective which appears in a valuable American publication, *Boxing and Medicine* (1995) edited by the leading sports related neurologist, Robert C. Cantu. Its Preface begins:

"Boxing is a controversial sport that has drawn criticism from physicians since its inception around 800 B.C. There is no doubt that boxing is a dangerous activity that can result in death or brain damage - but is it any more dangerous than any other risky sports? For example, the chance of fatality in boxing is 1.3 per 100,000 participants. This is a fraction of the risk seen in other socially accepted sporting pursuits such as college football

(3 per 100,000), motor cycling (7), scuba diving (11), mountaineering (51), hang gliding (55), sky diving (123), and horse racing (128) - citing some high risk sports, *Sporting News* 1980 Aug 16".

Such statistical assessments must always be variable and challengeable, with fluctuations at different periods of time and levels of activity. Cantu's contribution to sports medicine and his dedicated team of contributors are recognised and admired worldwide for their attempts to benefit from their medical experiences an activity which in its ideal form is more than a cliché titled 'Noble Art of Self-defence'.

The English cases are summarised below.

1	1866	After a trial following a boxing
	R v Young [1866] 10 Cox 370	fatality, fighting with gloves in a
	held by Bramwell B at 373	private room, supported by medical

fatality, fighting with gloves in a private room, supported by medical evidence that the sparring with gloves is not dangerous, thereby did not create a breach of the peace or result in a manslaughter verdict. However, it had occurred to him that

'supposing there was no danger in the original encounter, the men fought on until they were in such a state of exhaustion that it was probable they would fall and fall dangerously, and if death ensued from that it might amount to manslaughter'.

2   1878

R v Orton (1878) 39 LT 293

Court of Crown Cases Reserved (forerunner of Court of Criminal Appeal, now Court of Appeal Criminal Division) confirmed a jury's verdict which had considered evidence of the contest, including examination of the gloves used:

Kelly CB: 'No doubt the contestants wore gloves; but that did not prevent them from severely punishing each other.'

Danman J: 'The jury having examined the gloves and having the fact proved that the contestants severely mauled each other, they found rightly that this was a prize fight. The question was entirely one for the jury.'

3	1882	Court of Crown Cases Reserved confirmed

R v Coney [1882] 8 QBD 534

(1) a prize fight is illegal;

(2) all persons aiding and abetting are guilty of assault (although the evidence before the court did not qualify for a conviction);

(3) consent of the persons actually engaged in fighting the interchange of blows does not afford any answer to the criminal charge of assault (which is the *volenti non fit injuria* principle applied to criminal law: (see also *R v Donovan* [1934] 2 KB 498; no one can consent to crime).

4	1901	Central Criminal Court (Old Bailey).

R v Roberts & Ors Daily Telegraph & other sources: 29 June 1901

Prosecution for manslaughter following fatal accident after head injury during gloved contest at fashionable National Sporting Club in London.

Grantham J's summing up to jury explained that

'he thought the weight of evidence went to show the fatal blow was caused not by a knock-out blow inflicted by Roberts, but by a fall on to the rope in the effort of the deceased victim, by throwing himself back, to avoid a blow.'

The jury's verdict in answer to specific questions formulated by the trial judge was (1) accident; (2) boxing match; (3) not guilty of manslaughter.

The decision was limited to the facts and did not extend the principle which contrasts illegal prize fighting with lawful sparring and boxing. It is wrongly cited in sporting and social texts as legitimising boxing, a technical status which has never positively arisen. Hence the ruling on the limited special facts: not illegal.

5   1911

R v Driscoll and Moran
[*British Boxing Year-book
1985*: p 12]

Birmingham Magistrates' Court:
Jim Driscoll and Owen Moran were
summoned to show cause why they
should not be bound over to keep
the peace on the eve of a
featherweight title fight. Both were
bound over and the contest was
delayed for two years, before it was
promoted and ended as a draw at the
National Sporting Club premises at
King Street, Covent Garden in
London.

The last weapon in the legal armoury originates from a mixture of common law and statute, the Justices of the Peace Act 1361. Its availability to protect the peace of the realm applies not only to participating contestants but also to the public at large. Thus it can be used against boxing promoters' arrangements for stewarding the developing problems of crowd conduct comparable to football hooliganism. Against that background of British boxing's law court appearances, the affinity with civil liability and damages can be assessed. The issue of consent as defence to a civil claim for damages was considered fully by the Court of Appeal Civil Division during a civil claim of assault in *Lane v Holloway* ([1968] QB 379). It applies equally effectively to the more frequently utilised remedy for claiming civil damages against an offending participant of negligence; and also to a lesser extent when the remedy provided by the law of nuisance can be applied (ie by coming to the nuisance).

There are three separate heads under which damages can be recovered for playing field injuries caused by participants:

(1)   assault and battery, technically trespass to the person;
(2)   negligence;
(3)   nuisance.

1   *Assault and Battery (or trespass to the person)*

This basis for a compensation award of civil damages is illustrated by a colourful case arising out of a domestic dispute (*Lane v Holloway* [1968] QB 379). The two most effective claims were for broken legs resulting from foul football play before *Condon v Basi* (supra), namely *Lewis v Brookshaw* (1970) 120 NLJ 143 and *Grundy v Gilbert* ((1978) *Sunday Telegraph*, 31 July, p 31). The contrast and legal difference between civil assault and negligence is explained clearly in separate passages from the section on tort in Volume 45 of Halsbury's Laws of England (4th Edn) and an extract from one of Lord Denning's judgments.

Civil assault distinguishable from negligence. The Tort section in Halsbury's Laws, under the joint editorship of the late Professor Harry Street and Professor N E Palmer explains (para 1310 at p 602):

'Assault is an intentional offer of force or violence to the person of another';

and a footnote to this citation comments,

'There appears to be no decision in which mere negligence has been held sufficient to constitute an assault'.

Lord Denning in *Letang v Cooper* ([1965] 1 QB 232 at pp 239–240) explained that if an offender

'does not inflict injury intentionally, but only unintentionally, the Plaintiff has no cause of action in trespass. His only cause of action is negligence and then only on proof of want of reasonable care ... if intentional it is the tort of assault and battery. If negligent and causing damage, it is the tort of negligence'.

Battery is the actual as distinct from the intentional striking, and usually implies a prior assault. The form of pleading in court documents for the damages claim ideally includes 'assaulting and beating' (*Lane v Holloway* at p 380). *Condon v Basi* extended the frontiers of negligence to define a duty of care against causing foreseeable dangers owed by one participating competitor to another. The judgments were based on this plea. It also included in addition to negligence, a claim for assault and battery in the county court particulars of claim, which had begun the action *Lane v Holloway* ([1968] 1 QB 379).

The Court of Appeal was concerned with three separate legal issues arising out of a domestic punch-up at Dorchester in Dorset, where Judge Jefferies had dispensed his own brand of rough justice two centuries earlier. The facts concerned the consequences of retaliation by a young man's over-reaction with a violent blow causing serious injury and damage to a more elderly man after his insulting remarks. Each of the three legal issues has an importance generally and for sport particularly.

(1) Damages quantum, increased six-fold from £75 to £500.
(2) Consent to an injury (*volenti non fit injuria*).
(3) Claims based upon an unlawful act, ie fighting, cannot sustain a remedy (*ex turpi causa non oritur actio*).

Lord Denning dealt with that last legal point by explaining at page 386:

'Even if a fight started by being unlawful, I think that one of them can sue the other for damages for a subsequent injury if it was inflicted by a weapon or savage blow out of all proportion to the occasion';

and with the second by agreeing

'that in an ordinary fight with fists there is no cause of action to either of them for an injury suffered. The reason is that each of the participants in a fight voluntarily takes upon himself the risk of incidental injuries to himself. *Volenti non fit injuria*. But he does not take on himself the risk of a savage blow out of all proportion to the occasion. The man who strikes a blow of such severity is liable in damages unless he can prove accident or self-defence'.

Salmon LJ at page 388 said of them

'There are recondite topics about which there is much learning';

and at page 399:

'To say in circumstances such as those that *ex turpi causa non oritur actio* is a defence seems to me to be quite absurd. Academically of course one can see the argument, but one must look at it, I think, from a practical point of view. To say that this old gentleman was engaged jointly with the defendant in a criminal venture is a step which, like the judge, I feel wholly unable to take'.

Winn LJ at pages 395–396 cited two of 'the great criminal judges' in *R v Coney* (supra), Sir James Fitzjames Stephen and Hawkins, J, concluding that Hawkins J in *R v Coney* said;

'It is always a question for the jury in case of an indictment, as it was for this county court judge.
    ...So within the limits of his findings of fact it is for this court. I do not, having regard to those findings, regard what happened as a fight to which the plaintiff [victim] consented, to which he was *volens*. I regard it as a case where this young man [defendant] went down to thrash the other, older man'.

The actual citation by Winn LJ from Hawkins J and the prelude to it, are of sufficient significance to justify reproduction here as a classic statement of the common law which has stood the test of time for more than a century with approbation, and in principle, is applicable to both civil as well as criminal liability.

Hawkins J in *R v Coney* ([1882] 8 QBD at pages 554–555) explained:

'Nothing can be clearer to my mind than that every fight in which the object and intent of each of the combatants is to subdue the other by violent blows, is, or has a direct tendency to, a breach of the peach, and it matters not, in my opinion, whether such fight be a hostile fight begun and continued in anger, or a prize-fight for money or other advantage. In each case the object is the same, and in each case some amount of personal injury to one or both of the combatants is a probable consequence, and, although a prize-fight may not commence in anger, it is unquestionably calculated to rouse the angry feelings of both before its conclusion. I have no doubt then, that every such fight is illegal, and the parties to it may be prosecuted for assaults upon each other. Many authorities support this view. In *Rex v Ward*, the prisoner was tried for the slaughter of a man whom he had killed in a fight to which he had been challenged by the deceased for a public trial of skill in boxing. No unfairness was suggested, and yet it was held that the prisoner was properly convicted. To the same effect is the case of *R v Lewis*, in which Coleridge J, said "When two persons go out to strike each other, each is guilty of an assault". See also *R v Hunt*, per Alderson B, *R v Brown*, by the same learned Baron, and by Bramwell B, in *R v Young*.

The cases in which it has been held that persons may lawfully engage in friendly encounters not calculated to produce real injury to or to rouse angry passions in either, do not in the least mitigate against the view I have expressed; for such encounters are neither breaches of the peace nor are they calculated to be productive thereof, but if, under colour of a friendly encounter, the parties enter upon it with, or in the course of it form, the intention to conquer each other by violence calculated to produce mischief, regardless of whether hurt may be occasioned or not, as for instance, if two men, pretending to engage in an amicable spar with glove, really have for their object the intention to beat each other until one of them be exhausted and subdued by force, and so engage in a conflict likely to end in a breach of the peace, each is liable to be prosecuted for an assault: *R v Orton*. Whether an encounter be of the character I have just referred to, or a mere friendly game, having no tendency, if fairly played, to produce any breach of the peace, is always a question for the jury in case of an indictment, or the magistrates in case of summary proceedings'.

Nearly a century later these principles were applied in substance to claims for damages for broken legs arising from foul tackles on soccer fields in *Lewis v Brookshaw* in 1970 and *Grundy v Gilbert* in 1977 as cited below. I am also indebted to Hayden Opie, President of the Australian and New Zealand's Sports Law Association and a senior lecturer in Law at

Melbourne University for drawing attention to their application as long ago as 1971 in *MacNamara v Duncan* (1971) 26 ALR 584.

	Decision
1970 *Lewes Assizes*	Decision
Civil action for damages for assault for broken leg in Sussex soccer match	£5,400 damages and costs.
	Principle
(*Lewes v Brookshaw* (1970) 120 NLJ 413)	Deliberate and/or reckless foul play outside laws of game.
1971 *Supreme Court of Australia Capital Territory*	Decision
Civil action for assault (trespass to the person) for head injury from intentional blow outside rules of play	A\$6,000 damages and costs.
	Principle
(*MacNamara v Duncan* (supra))	Intentional blow to which no consent, even though probability of such acts known to occur.
1977 *Bodmin Crown Court*	Decision
Civil action for damages for assault for broken leg in Cornwall soccer match (*Grundy v Gilbert* (1977) *Sunday Telegraph*, 31 July, p 31)	Almost £4,000 damages and costs.
	Principle
	Deliberate and/or reckless foul play outside laws of game.

James Condon suffered a broken right leg from a foul tackle by Gurdaver Basi in Leamington, Warwickshire, in a local league soccer match on Sunday 30 March 1984. The referee sent off the offender for serious foul play and the victim's lawyers were ready to sue not only, as pleaded in the form Particulars of Claim, for assault and battery, but also in the tort of negligence. To this we now turn.

2 Negligence

The essential elements from a developing lineage include not only the factors identified by Lord Denning in *Letang v Cooper* (supra) of

(1) unintentional injury;
(2) proof of want of reasonable care comprising breach of duty; but also the third element of:
(3) reasonable foreseeable risk of injury or damage.

Reliance was placed on Australian authorities where the remedy had been applied for recovery of damages suffered by one participant arising from a water-ski accident against another, notwithstanding that there was 'no authority as to what is the standard of care which governs the conduct of players in competitive sports generally'. Golf had provided a pattern on four occasions and ice hockey and motor rally driving among others. In two of the golfing cases the duty was owed to fellow participants: in two others to the wider public by a participant, and in a fifth under the law of public nuisance. Save and except for the nuisance example, the negligence cases in which liability was established by one competitor against another or beyond may be summarised as follows, with an asterisk against the fellow competitor/participatory victim precedent.

1927	Decision
Cleghorn v Oldham (1927) 43 TLR 465	Player liable.
	Principle
Golfer not in course of play swings club during demonstration and injures person standing by.	Not in course of play. Defence rejected of consent to negligent act not unfair or vicious in recreation. Negligent misconduct actionable in recreation as in any other activity.
1949	Decision
Payne & Payne v Maple Leaf Gardens Ltd (1949) DLR 369 (Canada)	Players liable.
	Principle
Ice Hockey players stepped out of or broke off from hockey game to fight, injuring spectator with stick.	No consent to breach of rules.
Pre-1962	Decision
Unreported decision of Seller LJ on South Eastern Circuit (see [1963] 1 QB 43 at 55) Golfer in four-ball hit into rough, losing the ball. Said 'Out of it' and encouraged better players to proceed. Resumed after finding ball, causing injury as victim turned round at defendant's cry of 'Fore'.	Player liable.
	Principle
	Conduct outside the game; unnecessary for it; showed complete disregard for safety of those he knew were in line of danger from being hit from an unskilled instead of lofted shot over their heads.
1968	Decision
Pedestrian walking along narrow public lane injured on head by Golf ball (*Lamond v Glasgow Corporation* (1968) SLT 291)	Occupier liable for negligence.
	Principle
	Although no previous history of any accident, 6,000 shots a year played over fence should have created forecast of foreseeable happening.

1981/82

Harrison v Vincent [1982] RTR 8

Passenger in sidecar during motor
cycle and sidecar combination race
injured.

Decision

Motorcycle rider competitor and
also race organisers liable.

Principle

Rider and employers failed in duty
to take care of condition of
competing vehicle.

1982*

Bidwell v Parks

Lewes Crown Court (unreported,
except newspapers) French J.

Golfer in tournament injured by ball
hit from fellow competitor without
warning.

Decision

Fellow competitor golfer liable.

Principle

Dangerous for 24 handicap golfer to
take shots which could have gone
anywhere without warning.

1983

Hewish v Smailes

Epsom County Court (provided by
Court archives by H H Judge John A
Baker DL)

Decision

Head butt causing broken nose and
black eyes to 38-year-old local
player in local league match.

Principle

Civil assault (trespass to the person)
damages claim: £400 general
damages and £5.80 proved special
damages and costs.

1989

Vermont v Green (provided by Mr
Oliver Sie, Barrister) Basingstoke
County Court

Decision

Kick during course of play to
opponent causing two nights in
hospital adjudicated to have been
deliberate on spur of moment.

Principle

Civil Assault (trespass to the person)
damages claim: £400 general
damages; but claim for aggravated
damages refused.

1989

*Thomas v Maguire and Queen's
Park Rangers* [1989] *Daily Mirror*,
17 February, High Court, London

Damaged ligaments to professional
footballer (Tottenham Hotspur)

Decision

Negligence claim based on illegal
tackle.

Agreed damages £130,000 settled
out of court.

1990

May v Strong

Decision

£10,000 damages to 19-year-old

Teesside Crown Court

(Halsbury's Laws MRE 92/62 All Eng AR (1991) p 313)

semi-professional footballer (£6,000 pain, suffering and loss of earnings: for compound fracture of tibia and fibula, £4000, special damages for net loss earnings for 9 months.

Principle

Serious foul play and violent conduct sent off field by referee

recklessness held by judge as assault.

1994

O'Neill v Fashanu and Wimbledon Football Club Independent 14 October, High Court, London.

Settlement of claim without admission of liability

Decision

Negligence claims bases on alleged illegal tackle.

Principle

£70,000 agreed out-of-court settlement of claim without admission of liability after plaintiff's case and first defendant's disciplinary record admitted in evidence by Collins J.

1996

McCord v Swansea City High Court, London

Facts Professional football negligence claim against injuries, based on illegal tackle

Decision

£250,000 damages award.

1996

Smolden v Whitworth and Nolan Under 19 Colts

Facts Rugby injury

Decision

Referee liable.

Principle

Failed to observe laws of the game for under 19 colts players.

1997

Hedley v Cuthbertson (unreported)

Mountaineering death from guide's failure to take adequate safety precautions when proceeding with a manoeuvre.

Decision

Guide liable.

Principle

Lesser standard effected than one expected when overstating danger posed by a rockfall.

1998	Decision
Pearson v Lightning [Tues 30 April]	Liability upheld on appeal.
Golfer liable for injury caused by ball deflected from bush.	Principle
	Risk of causing injury small but sufficiently foreseeable to create liability.
1998	Decision
Watson and Bradford City v Gray and Huddersfield Town, Times 29 October, Leeds High Court: Newcastle High Court May 1999	£900,000 damages.
Professional football negligence award for mistimed tackle breaking opponent's leg. Claim for alleged interference and contractual relations rejected.	
1999	Decision
Casson v MOD	Negligence - £3,000 interim award
Bradford Telegraph and Argus, April 1999	
Army work experience broken schoolboy's leg. In loco parentis	

The non-citation of any of those sources before 1985 to the Court of Appeal in *Condon v Basi* [1985] could not prevent it from reconciling the test *defining* a competitor's duty of care owed to another competitor which was formulated by the Australian court in *Rootes v Skelton* (supra), with the differing formulae which can be extracted from comparable citations concerned with a competitor's duty to a bystander or spectator. Thus, in *Wooldridge v Sumner* ([1963] 2 KB 43) which contained Sellers LJ's citation (1962) of his own finding of negligence by the golfer in the four-ball competition, the same learned appeal judge in that case also formulated a test for negligence by a competitor against a spectator which was considered without dissent in the finding of negligence by a motor cycle competitor towards his sidecar passenger in *Harrison v Vincent* (supra). Furthermore, in *Elliott v Saunders and Liverpool FC* [*New Law Journal*, 5 August 1994] Drake J rejected an obiter in *Condon v Basi* elevating a higher duty owed between professional footballers to each other, when he held generally that;

> 'an intentional foul or mistake, or an error of judgment, may be enough to give rise to liability on the part of the defendant, but whether or not it does so, depends on the facts and circumstances of each individual case'.

After John O'Neill's agreed £70,000 out-of-court settlement of claim a few weeks later the *Independent*, 14 October 1994, explained in greater detail how the courts are generally continuing to award damages against players as they have since at least 1927 in the United Kingdom and also the Commonwealth by application of the traditional trilogy of

(1) duty of care which has been breached;
(2) by reason of failing to heed a foreseeable risk;
(3) resulting in injury or damage.

Indeed the New South Wales Supreme Court Common Law Division of Lee CJ, after an award of A\$68,154.60 with costs against not only an offending player who broke an opponent's jaw in a professional rugby league match, but also the employer club (*Rogers v Bugden and Canterbury Bankston Club* (unreported) 14 December 1990 and see All ER Rev (1991) p 246), was subsequently affirmed on appeal with an increase for aggravated damages [1993] Australian Torts Rep 181–248 CA (NSW).

Furthermore, in *Johnston v Frazer* (1990) 21 NSWLR 89 the New South Wales appeal court upheld the trial judge's A\$121,490 damages award for a broken thigh and back injuries caused by one horse crossing in front of two other runners under the guidance of a jockey held to have failed to have taken reasonable care for the safety of a fellow jockey in the relevant circumstances.

There remains, however, one final head of claim against a player participant which overlaps here, as it has overlapped already in an earlier chapter: nuisance.

3   Nuisance

The third golfing claim cited above from 1968 in which liability for negligence was established contains the flavour of a nuisance claim: for the injury was received when walking along a narrow public lane. Because it was argued and accepted judicially that the risk was foreseeable, the claim succeeded in 1968 in negligence against Glasgow Corporation, the occupiers of the links from where the ball was played. Nearly fifty years earlier, a taxi driver, George Thomas Castle, familiar to every law student, lost an eye when a golf ball from the St Augustine's golf links in Kent splintered his windscreen on 18 August 1919, when he was travelling along the highway adjoining the golf course. He claimed and recovered £452 damages against the golf club on the ground of nuisance (*Castle v St Augustine's Links Ltd* [1922] 39 TLR 615).

The claim was formulated and argued on the basis that the source of injury interfered with his enjoyment of the public thoroughfare bisecting the links. Sankey J (later Lord Chancellor) was satisfied that the location of

'the tee and the hole were a public nuisance under the conditions and in the place where they were situated'.

Because of the public element this remedy of nuisance was available to the injured plaintiff. It was a weapon in the legal armoury used successfully for the complainants in the cricket ball case of *Miller v Jackson* at Linz County Durham (supra) and the noise from the powerboat racing in *Kennaway v Thompson*. It will be recalled in the former case that after Reeve J had granted an injunction the Court of Appeal discharged it and an agreed sum of £400 was settled for the nuisance damages. In the latter case the damages award by Mais J of £15,000 for nuisance was replaced by a limited injunction, on a structured basis to restrain limited future nuisances. (More recently see *Lacey v Parker and Boyle (for Jordans CC)* (1994) 144 NLJ 188).

Damages

The permutations of principles and formulae which are available for assessment of damages awards are generally outside the scope of this work. They will be found extensively in the specialist sources: *MacGregor, Ogus* and Halsbury's Laws (4th Edn) Volume 12. In one respect, however, the courts have recognised that a sporting participant may require special consideration, separate and apart from the general recognition already available as explained by the Criminal Injuries Compensation Board (supra) for innocent victims of criminal violence.

In 1968 Thompson J in *Mulvain & Another v Joseph & Another* (infra) explained that the injury arising out of a road traffic accident to an American club professional golfer who was playing on a European tour raised novel and interesting questions of law. The injury to his hand impeded his opportunity to enhance his anticipated experience, publicity, prestige and money prizes from the tour. It required his return to America without completing his programmed tournaments. Damages were awarded under numerous special heads relating to the particular sporting profession:

(1)   loss of opportunity of competing in tournaments;
(2)   ensuing loss of experience and prestige which might have resulted in his becoming a tournament professional in America;
(3)   loss of a chance of winning prize money.

The limited report in the *Solicitors' Journal* of 22 November 1968 (*Mulvain & Another v Joseph & Another*) of Thompson J's judgment concludes

> 'The figure was bound to be speculative, but he would award under that head [broken down as numbered above] £1,000 damages against the taxi driver and owner [the defendants], including damages for disappointment felt by the plaintiff through the frustration of his plans'.

Additional damages for the usual head of pain and suffering were the significantly lesser amount of £140.

Accordingly, the fouling footballer who causes injury to an opponent in breach of the game's laws, and using the formulae available of *Condon v Basi*, an injured plaintiff could involve himself and/or an employing club in damages which could be substantial. Authority for *general* damages in sporting injuries is scarce, but see *Girvain v Inverness Farmers Dairy* (NLR, 19 Feb 1994, and Kerrigan's Appendix). Furthermore, while these pages were being processed, a Criminal Injuries Court Board awarded a 31-year-old disabled athlete *fit to carry on his sport* but proscribed in the job market £70,000 general damages for pain, suffering, loss of amenity and loss of future earnings, applying the *Smith v Manchester City Council* (1974) 118 Sol 50 397, 17 KIR ICH) formula for assessing general damages. Consistent with vicarious liability and responsibility at criminal law, this leads on naturally to a similar assessment for civil liability.

Civil liability: vicarious liability and responsibility

The civil law's concept of vicarious liability contains different elements and angles of approach from those in the criminal law. The distinction may not be self-evident to a layman, but it is easily recognised by lawyers through two separate strands resulting in an ultimate individual responsibility for clubs, directors, committee members or coaches, and potential individual financial liabilities.

(1)   *Respondent superior*, 'let the superior person answer', is the common law liability for acts done during the course of employment and direct contractual relationships.

(2) Agency opens up fields of liability which can be linked through three separate sources in the light of the undoubted existence of a negligence liability for personal violent foul play.

(i) *1896: Brown v Lewis* (1896) 12 TLR 455, Blackburn Rovers Football Club committee were held liable for their own personal negligence in having employed an incompetent person to repair a stand: and a year later in 1897 the club converted its legal status into that of a limited liability company.

(ii) *1919: Williams v Curzon Syndicate Ltd* (1919) 35 TLR 475. Defendant proprietors of a residential club employed an old and dangerous criminal as a night porter, one Lister, who stole the plaintiff's jewellery from a safe in the club manager's office. The plaintiff alleged that the defendants were negligent in employing such a man without taking proper care to ascertain his record. Because they were found not to have used due care in engaging an old lag, they were liable to make good the plaintiff's loss.

(iii) *1943: Bradley Egg Farm Ltd v Clifford* [1943] 2 All ER 378 at 386. The Executive Council of an unincorporated poultry society were held to be personally liable for the damage caused by a servant of the society who performed a contract negligently. Because the society were unincorporated and there was no legal or factual principal on whose behalf the council members could act (a position which will be explained more comprehensively in Chapter 14, *Administrative advice*) only those council members (as in the case of the Blackburn Rovers committee members) would be liable. Other members of the society were not liable.

(iv) *Thelma (Owners) v University College School* [1953] 2 Lloyd's Rep 613, where a pupil acting as cox for a school eight was held to be the school's agent and the governors were liable for his negligence through defective steering on River Thames.

(v) *1979:* In *Tomjanovich v California Sports Inc* No H–78–243 (SD Text 1979), the injured player, Tomjanovich, did not sue the other player, Kermit Washington. However, a lawsuit was brought against Washington's employer for injuries received when Washington punched Tomjanovich in the face during the professional basketball game. Substantial damages were awarded by a jury, and settled on appeal: but liability was proved on the principle of the employer's failing to curb the offender's 'dangerous tendencies' of what is known as 'enforcer' in the National Basketball Association.

(vi) *1981: Robitaille v Vancouver Hockey Club Ltd* [1981] DLR (3rd) 288 British Columbia Court of Appeal upheld the Judge's damages award because of medical neglect of medical staff within control of the club citing *Monen v Swinton* and *Pendlebury Borough Council* [1965] 2

ER 349 at 351 (see also Chap 7 *Sports Medicine and the Law* (infra) and Grayson: *Ethics, Injuries and the Law in Sports Medicine* (1999).

(vii) *1990: Rogers v Bugden and Canterbury Bankstown Club* (unreported) 14 December 1990 and see All ER Review (1991), p 246. In Australia, however, as explained at page 181 above, the New South Wales Supreme Court Common Law Division of Lee CJ is en route to appeal after an award of A$68,154.60 with costs against not only an offending player who broke an opponent's jaw in a professional rugby league game, but also the employer's club.

Accordingly, whereas the ultimate liability for vicarious criminal liability and responsibility is penal, the parallel result civilly is financial. The scope of potential compensation is explicable factually in human equations by the Criminal Injuries Compensation Board survey and when considering commercial compensation. Thompson J's judgment in *Mulvain v Joseph* (supra) gauges the measure of loss suffered by the American golfing professional prevented by injury to his hand from competing his European experiences and tour. To adapt the Lord Chancellor Lord Hailsham of St Marylebone's words in *IRC v McMullan* (supra), the courts and thereby the profession have not as yet begun to explore with any depth the scope for compensation flowing from playing field violence. Thus clubs, committees and coaches have been put on notice of the full financial consequences concurrent with the warning at page 166 above about the full criminal consequences through the selection of known offenders against the laws of the game, whether or not there has been a conviction against the laws of the land.

Ancillary awards

In addition to compensation claims for unlawful foul play are the remedies which exist at common law for protection of reputation and compensation through defamation damages, and Parliamentary provisions for industrial and insurance awards. The first two, defamation and industrial awards are more appropriately located in the comprehensive Chapter 14, *Administrative advice*. National Insurance payments are a logical corollary to the heads of damages known to the common law.

The Courts' approval here can be seen in *R v National Insurance Commission, ex parte Michael* [1977] 1 WLR 109 (referred to in *Faulkner v Chief Adjudication Officer* (CA on appeal from Social Security Commissioner) unreported 18 March 1994), where a policeman's claim for a football injury was rejected — 'it was not part of his employment to play in this game of football': a preamble to the cases listed below.

National Insurance

Compensation

National Insurance (Industrial Injuries) legislation has existed since the 1946 Act implemented in 1942 wartime Beveridge Report, replacing ultimately the late nineteenth century Worker's Compensation enactments. Social Security (formerly National Insurance) Commissioners adjudicate under a complex network of appellate procedures, but, in the industrial injury areas, they cover a pattern of precedents illustrating the fine legal distinctions essential for awarding state benefits to victims of industrial accidents.

Initial claims are dealt with by insurance officers working out of local offices of The Department of Health and Social Security. Their decisions against a claimant are appealable to local National Insurance Tribunals covering the country and, thereafter, to the Social Security Commissioners sitting in London, Edinburgh, Cardiff and Belfast.

Their decisions (which, for England, Scotland and Wales, are reported at the discretion of the Chief Commissioner) include cases where claims have been allowed and disallowed, and the Clerk to each local tribunal has a set of these reports, which may be consulted by claimants and their representatives. (The style of citation appears below.)

The legal test for entitlement to benefit is that an employer earner should have suffered 'personal injury ... by accident arising out of and in the course of this ... employed earner's employment'. Sport arises thus:

National Insurance *(Industrial injury Claims)*	Circumstances
	Allowed
Football R (1) 13/51	Male nurse at mental hospital performing duty as employee in charge of patients able to play football. Injured during course of duty and, therefore, employment.
Cricket R (1) 3/57	Male nurse at mental hospital injured while duty working as member of cricket team for pleasure of patients and assisting recoveries. Employed as such.
Volleyball R (1) 68/51	London Fire Brigade fireman injured at volleyball during compulsory fitness training period; refusing to play creating liability for disciplinary action. *Held*: employed to play.

R (1) 13/66

Fireman employed at Royal Radar Establishment injured when playing volleyball during recreational period including long period of waiting, and for which required to be and remain physically fit.

Held: part of employment.

R (1) 3/81

Police cadet injured when the police personnel carrier in which she was returning to training school after representing her cadet force in the Cadets National Swimming Championships was involved in an accident.

Held: Entitled Participation in the championships was a training exercise which commenced and concluded at the training school.

R (1) 7/85

Police officer normally worked as a finger-print officer. On day of accident was to have undertaken duties as a sailing instructor at a location 40 miles from normal place of work. Before setting out he telephoned the police station (from his home), as he was required to do, to confirm that no fingerprinting duties had arisen.

His employer reckoned his employment to have started from that time. On the journey to the sailing centre, riding his own motor cycle, he was involved in an accident.

Held: (by the Court of Appeal, reversing the Commissioner). At the time of the accident the claimant was in the course of his employment. (Note: The Court of Appeal judgment appears in an appendix to the report of the Commissioner's decision which presently features in the loose leaf folder of 1985 printed decisions.)

Disallowed

Football

Policeman injured in representative

R (1) 57/51

match played during duty hours. No compulsion to play. Not part of employment.

R (1) 2/69

Laboratory technician injured during game in employed hospital grounds in lunch hours.

Temporary cessation of employment; thereby precluded claim.

R (1) 5/75

Police officer held by Court of Appeal not employed when injured in representative match.

R (1) 2/80

Fireman attending (under orders) a residential course at the Fire Service Technical College in Gloucestershire. Injured playing football in a match organised by the students which took place in the college grounds after the instructional sessions had ended.

Held: Not entitled. He had finished his work for the day — and was playing for his own pleasure and recreation.

R (1) 4/81

Airline stewardess suffered accident (at Dacca) whilst playing tennis in a 'stop-over' period at a time when she was on call. It was contended, inter alia, that airline crews were required to participate in sporting activities in order to keep themselves fit.

Held: Not entitled. Not required by her contract of employment to play tennis. No 'in course of' employment (R (1) 13 fireman at volleyball) distinguished.

The legal refinements and distinctions which create these different decisions belong to a legal textbook and journal rather than the intended guidelines here. They indicate an area where the public are more likely than not to become involved with a legal claim. Within this context the Italian doctors' death certificate issued for the Italian professional boxing champion Angelo Jacopucci after his knockout by Britain's Alan Minter

becomes recognisable with its tragic description: 'an accident at work'.
A schoolteacher out of class hours injured during school activities playing
games would be eligible for an award; whereas a member of a works' team
for fun probably not.

4   CONCLUSION

The principles of common law and statutory provisions set out above are
of universal application. Sadly they are needed now to an extent which
was non-existent in the days of a more stable and less violent society. The
criminal law was generally quiescent for football field offences at soccer
until 1969 (*R v Southby* (supra)) and in rugby until 1977 (*R v Billinghurst*).
In 1930 the distinguished Cambridge don, Sir Percy Winfield, delivered his
classic Tagore Law Lectures in the University of Calcutta (1931, *Cambridge
University Press*). He was obliged to say at that central period between
the two World Wars about the application of the doctrine of *volenti non
fit injuria*

> 'to unlawful sports, operations, or processes, or to unlawful incidents in
> sports, etc, which are lawful'.

That

> 'The reported cases and *dicta* are scanty'.

Apart from the above citations within this chapter there are many more
which have been excluded and which illustrate the principles involved
without developing them, which is the editorial basis upon which the law
reports are compiled. Nevertheless, neither reported cases nor dicta on
the subject today can be considered scanty. Indeed, practitioners' and
students' textbooks now consciously and self-consciously include specific
sections for sporting issues and particularly consequences of violent play
when hitherto they were ignored or absorbed into the general text.

Furthermore, each particular sport has its own self-determining internal
regulations and rules exclusive to its own discipline which do not require
attention of the courts unless they conflict with the law. This has occurred
frequently in the past at the level of disciplinary tribunals. These will be
dealt with in depth at Chapter 11, *Fair play and reason in court*. In
particular, at the time of Winfield's Tagore lectures and especially before
the First World War the balance of sporting literature quantitatively and
in anthologies tilted towards the traditional moneyed classes' areas of
indulgence in field events, 'huntin', shootin' and fishin''. Each required
an awareness of either property laws, firearms law or game laws, linked by

a common thread of Parliamentary or contractual licensing, in the manner explained at the beginning of Chapter 5, *Public protection*, above.

With the leisure explosion and the need to balance conflicting sporting interest in a mixed urban-rural community within the framework of international competition, the amount of law outside the general principles identified here must vary within each particular sport. For illustration purposes only, a representative selection can be summarised below, indicating topical issues but also matters of permanent concern to the actual discipline involved and its participants.

Horse Racing	Rule 180 (ii) of the Jockey Club's Rules of Racing empowering discretionary disqualification for banned substances, even from innocently used substances contained in chocolate Mars Bars!
Motorcar Racing	FIA (Fédération Internationale de L'Automobile) regulations controlling designs of vehicles to prohibit excessive skirting of car bodies for additional road surface grip. [In 1994 more controversial and debatable mechanical requirements were under surveillances, at the time of the deaths of Ayrton Senna and Roland Ratzenberger] and in 1999 Simon Barnes with understandable acerbity explained in relation to a miniscule mechanical measurement which had overshadowed Formula One's season's ending in *The Times* [1 November 1999] "The independent court had decided that the measuring equipment that had been used all season was inadequate for the measuring of a matter on which so much money had depended ... So the Malaysian rule-breakers of Ferrari were reinstated and it was game on ..."];
Hunting	Animals Act 1971 consolidating and codifying common law obligations and remedies, of general application to keepers of all non-dangerous animals.
Shooting	Firearms legislation generally for national security and game law licenses.
Fishing	Parliamentary and Common Market legislation for protection of offshore and Inland Waterways fishing.

The last category exemplifies the need for the level of awareness among not only participants in the most numerically popular of all participatory sports: angling. It also demands a concurrent awareness among simultaneous participants: water-sport activities whose boats can conflict with fishing lines, and offshore commercial operators in breach of national and common market quotas.

If notwithstanding the contents of this chapter anyone should still doubt the nature and extent of the problems for participants and their administrators, coaches and managers and all others associated with sport, they should reflect upon the following citation from the *Daily Telegraph* sports column 'Sport Around the World' for Monday 15 July 1991. It contained the crucial following paragraphs:

> 'The worst violence in sport occurs on suburban club playing fields, according to a university survey in Australia — and the biggest problems are not restricted to the macho world of rugby league, rugby union, and Aussie rules.
>
> One of the most violent sports is men's lacrosse, and there are also many injuries in men's and women's soccer. Kicking is most common-place in water polo, and elbowing is a problem in netball.
>
> Almost a third of all players felt the level of violence in their sport, including verbal abuse, was excessive, Prof Ray Vamplew, of Flinders University tells the *Sydney Morning Herald*. And more than half the spectators thought violence was excessive in the sport they were watching.
>
> "One of the worst problems", says Prof Vamplew, "is when you get down to the C and D grades, where players said umpires were biased and incompetent. Lots of umpires agreed with that. Professional sport was the best controlled by match officials and this was a key buffer against violence"'.

Professor Vamplew has since transferred his Professorial Chair to be the first in the United Kingdom for Sports History at the Simon de Montfort University, Leicester. More specifically, however, his 1991 opinion and evidence were corroborated in the London *Times* of 13 April 1991 by the celebrated writer and former editor of *Punch*, Alan Coren, with eye-witness testimony:

> 'Last Saturday I watched a really cracking football match ... Utterly professional. Totally committed. Prodigiously physical. Impressively cynical. Above all, unstintingly competitive, and not a player on the field over 12 years old ... sport has changed, and competition has changed, and it is too late to change either of them back.'

For how long such faith in the control of match officials will be justified, only time and the integrity and intelligence of professional administrators will tell. Time will also tell how much longer, too, the artificial attempts to construct a jurisprudence of so-called sportslaw out of 113 different VAT exempt non-profit-making activities listed in the opening pages and exemplified above here will last the course.

Against all of that background the next chapter follows logically: 'Sports medicine and the law'.

CHAPTER 7

Sports Medicine And The Law

1 INTRODUCTION

The Preface to the last edition of *Sport and the Law* explained,

'Sport, with medicine and music, like Tauber's song, goes round the world'.

They each create an international language recognised throughout the world linked to the regulations of global International Sports Federations. They transcend the jungle laws of commerce to emphasise an arguably true meaning of sport as health and education within the Rule of Law. Its theme is crystallised in the Preamble to a Working Paper as long ago as 1980 on a Code of Ethics for Sports Medicine for the World Medical Association with a global membership from approximately 70 different countries it identified

'the distinction between sport as a recreation, and competitive sport as practised by professionals, for the doctor specializing in sports medicine has a fundamentally different role according to which of these his patient engages in'.

It is also the medical measure of the contrast between entertainment and grass roots sport at a time when the medical fall-out from violence, drugs and over-use and stress at all levels for participants in sport has highlighted Sports Medicine as a speciality within medicine, which is rapidly approaching the same status as other medical specialisations.

Indeed, less doctors concerned with sport are progressively pursuing the recognition that Sports Medicine has equal value to other identifiable medico-legal categories. Inevitably, the evolution of Sports Medicine must invoke the law as a close ally for the health of sport and the community. The National Sports Medicine Institute of the United Kingdom at St Bartholomew's Hospital, the British Association of Sport and Medicine and the Association of Chartered Physiotherapists in Sport are each recognised as an acceptable unit of medicine within society generally and the medical services particularly: and the Academy of Medical Royal Colleges in the United Kingdom have now established a new Intercollegiate Academic Board to develop sport and exercise medicine in the United Kingdom and to develop high standards in this area of medical care to benefit all participating in sport and exercise.

Two of the most important subjects in Sports Medicine and the Law are the unlawful use of violence and drugs. Cheating by drugs can have lethal consequences. Correspondingly, too, can cheating by violent foul play. When sports performers break their respective participatory laws or regulations to cheat by violence or drug absorption proved by medical or pharmacological evidence to a level of criminal or civilly actionable liability, the action and sanction from sporting governing bodies with their blazer suited part-time amateur administrators and unprofessionally qualified officers is relatively minimal, with such violations sometimes even being ignored. When armed services personnel or practitioners in the standard *professional* calling of the clergy, law or medicine breach their codes of conduct or practice, they know the score and the ultimate sanction of expulsion.

The great Brazilian footballer Pele was brutally and criminally assaulted out of the 1966 World Cup on English playing fields without any sanction or effective action taken against the named Bulgarian and Portuguese offenders identified in his book *My Life and the Beautiful Game* cited at page 258. After the Canadian sprinter Ben Johnson was stripped of his Olympic Games title for drug abuse offences he was reinstated as if his misconduct had been condoned. It was only when he re-offended some five years later that a life ban could have been imposed. Ultimately, Johnson retired before this sanction was implemented.

The medical evidence for proving such serious and socially disastrous sporting situations is crucial provided that the medical role is recognised and identified. Dr Malcolm Bottomley, the Medical Officer to the British Athletics team and Medical Officer to the Bath University Medical Centre and also the Distance Learning course there for Sports Medicine, explained in 1990, writing in *Medicine, Sport and the Law* (Blackwell Scientific Publications) at page 165:

'There is no question that high levels of physical activity lead to physiological changes and patterns of illness and injury that are unfamiliar in the general practice of medicine. Sports Medicine is a speciality. It is to be hoped that its present struggles lead it to a mature status where it is recognised as a speciality in its own right and can fit into the conventional framework of medicine. Until then the present unsatisfactory state, where athletes' medical care is fragmented, uncoordinated and, unfortunately, sometimes contradictory, will continue'.

An example of how that 'present unsatisfactory state' exists within the framework is that two of the crucial issues which were identified at the end of Chapter 15 to the first edition, *Whither Sport and the Law* and still remain as two of 'Sport's Four Vices' Violence and Drugs. To the more general pattern of Sports Medicine I now turn.

2   SPORTS MEDICINE GENERALLY

Bobby Moore's CBE status as England's World Cup-winning captain in 1966 means that he cannot be ignored when he wrote in the Foreword to a different kind of sports book, Dr Muir Gray's *Football Injuries* (1980):

'It has always been a bone of contention of mine that not enough has been, or is being done, to alleviate or treat injuries at the lower levels of football'.

No less renowned in football circles is Andy Gray, who became the only recipient ever of both the Player of the Year and Young Player of the Year awards in the same season from the Professional Footballers Association in 1977. His travels took him around the world with Dundee United, Aston Villa, Wolverhampton Wanderers, Everton and Scotland. His words, too, cannot be ignored when he wrote during 1986 in *Shades of Gray* at page 96:

'It's often said in dressing rooms that horses have better treatment than humans, and it's true as far as some football clubs go ... Happily, most clubs, especially first and second division sides, have tightened up on their medical care in recent seasons. But I could still name you a team of class players whose careers have been finished early because they were abused so badly'.

Happily, too, medicine in sport has progressed since those passages were written. Nevertheless, it is at least arguable that such progression has not been far or fast enough. Since Gray's elegy the Football Association National Rehabilitation and Sports Injuries Centre has been opened at the National Sports Centre in Lilleshall, Shropshire; HRH The Princess Royal, as President of the British Olympic Medical Centre, officiated at the opening of Northwick Park Hospital and Clinical Research Centre in Harrow on the outskirts of North London; a London Sports Medicine Institute which had been opened on the campus of St Bartholomew's Medical College in 1987 was converted into the National Institute of Sports Medicine in April 1992 and the Royal Society of Medicine in 1994 initiated a specialist sports section under the presidency of Sir Roger Bannister. Yet Dr Dan Tunstall Pedoe, the former medical director of the London Institute and medical adviser to the London Marathon explained to the *Daily Telegraph* (23 December 1986):

'Sports medicine has had virtually no official recognition or support from the health service. The average struggling athlete, let alone the serious amateur, is less well served here than in other countries, where there is government money for injuries and where there may be well-established sports clinics'.

This message was anticipated when Mr Donald A D Macleod FRCS, Honorary Surgeon to the Scottish Rugby Football Union, wrote in his contribution to Dr Tony Dunnill and Dr Muir Gray's *Rugby Injuries* (1982) (the companion volume to Muir Gray's *Football Injuries*):

'there is a strong argument in favour of all responsible sporting bodies ensuring that the common injuries associated with their particular sport are identified and minimised, wherever practical, by legislation and education in conjunction with informed coaching. However, we must not lose sight of the fact that sport must retain a sense of advantage and achievement, essential components in the challenge of participation in sport'.

Not surprisingly, against this background, the National Sports Medicine Institute has three main objectives: the establishment of clinical services throughout the UK; the establishment of a tiered education system in sports medicine for doctors, medical undergraduates, paramedical staff, coaches, trainers, and members of the public who are involved in sport; and the establishment of a national research programme. It is the logical corollary to the conception 25 years ago in 1969 after a Royal Society of Medicine assessment of the general sporting injury scene, of Mr W E Tucker MVO, FRCS, a former rugby international and the leading sporting orthopaedic practitioner of his era who was also one of the founder members of the British Association of Sport and Medicine. He said that there should be an orthopaedic surgeon in each town which had the privilege of looking after the local football team. The Royal Society had estimated the social impact of sporting injuries within the UK at that time and had calculated 1,500,000 sporting injuries annually, with two outstanding consequences. Sufferers were unable to continue with their respective sports, and 10 per cent of the injuries caused absence from work (*Daily Telegraph*, 24

September 1969). This occurred before the Sports Council's creation and grant of a Royal Charter in 1971, with its later policies of 'Sport for All' and 'Ever Thought of Sport?'

Complete statistics are never available for this type of survey, partly because sport straddles every aspect of social behaviour for all generations, and so many different Government departments are involved, spanning health, education, environment, foreign affairs, public order, trade and industry (see Chapter 2, *Progressive perspective*). A more recent comment in the London *Times* (2 March 1984) under the heading of 'Medical Briefing' explained,

> 'With alarming frequency sportsmen are dropping dead as they play. Those who enjoy especially stressful games — squash for example — seem to be particularly vulnerable to unexpected heart attacks'.

It confirmed what I was told around the same time by the Professor of Cardiovascular-Surgery at Oxford University:

> 'Those who play squash to keep fit often forget that it is more likely necessary to get fit to play squash!'

More recently, in 1990 the British Athletic Board's Director of Coaching, Frank Dick, assessed in a discussion paper leading to the National Institute's foundation, that 25% of Britain's medal-winning potential is lost through illness or injury and that 5%–10% of attendance at casualty departments of hospitals are caused by sports injuries. Yet in medical training the treatment of soft tissue injuries is inadequately taught. Furthermore, even before then he cited during 1989 the European Coaches Association's view that 'stress-related injuries were going to cripple European nations'. In that dimension the legal consequences have hitherto never been contemplated.

At that same period in the early 1990's, as explained in *Ethics, Injuries and the Law in Sports Medicine* (1999), a British Sports Council's Sheffield University commissioned survey concluded in its 'Summary of the injuries and exercise main report—national study of the epidemiology of exercise related injury illness':

Six million new sports injuries require treatment each year. Accident and Emergency departments are well equipped to deal with the more serious injuries, but family doctors may be less familiar with the management of sports injuries. To help reduce costs and improve effectiveness, the way in which sports injuries are managed should be reviewed. NHS Sports Injury Clinics may be needed to fill the gaps.

Six years later, a leading article in the *British Journal of Sports Medicine* from Robin Knill-Jones (June 1997 at pp. 95–6) recorded that:

Sports related injuries form a significant part of the workload of the National Health Service. Patients with acute injuries account for between 3.9% and 7.1% of total attendances at casualty departments, and a higher proportion of attendances — 28% by children. An unknown proportion of these injuries go on to become chronic or recurrent problems which later involve orthopaedic clinics or general practitioners. Clearly, there is an unmet need for expert advice and treatment, for which, for whatever reason, NHS resources are unavailable.

Thus, it may be argued that sports medicine (and its ethical criteria), with its uniquely complex and rarely recognized general and specialist multi-disciplinary requirements, which are rarely understood within both sport and society and medicine generally, stands apart from other medical and paramedical areas. This also reflects the clear division between sport as a branch of the entertainment industry and sport in its health and education role, with or without a competitive framework.

Closer to medical and clinical circumstances, the therapeutic value of the Sports Council's 'Sport for All' campaign can never be over-emphasised. A belief in sport for the disabled was a logical outcome of Sir Ludwig Guttman's conviction after the Second World War that work and recreation of all kinds greatly improved the mental, psychological and physical rehabilitation of spinally-injured patients. This was a logical sporting corollary to the late Sir Archibald McIndoe's earlier therapy in a non-sporting context at his world famous plastic surgery unit at East Grinstead's Queen Victoria Memorial Hospital in Sussex for the Second World War airmen whose burnt and shattered faces were re-structured to accelerate a return to normal life. His brilliant ancillary service to his surgical team for the mental, psychological and physical rehabilitation of his patients was to surround the wounded with the most beautiful and graceful nurses available, many of whom married their patients.

Parliament has attempted to keep pace with Guttman's initiatives through two little known and perhaps under-used enactments. Section 4 of the Chronically Sick and Disabled Persons Act 1970 requires public undertakings to provide access, parking and toilet facilities (including those relating to sport and recreation) which are practicable and reasonable for disabled persons needs. Section 5 of the Disabled Persons Act 1981 imposed duties on those who grant planning permission under section 29 of the Town and Country Planning Act 1971 (now section 76 of the Town and Country Planning Act 1990) to draw attention to section 4 and other provisions of that 1970 Act for the benefits required for the disabled. Perhaps there are many centres, including the USA, which have in the past overlooked the needs and sporting requirements of the disabled.

Section 19(f) of the Disability Discrimination Act 1995 logically progresses towards prohibition against discrimating against a disabled person with 'facilities for entertainment, recreation or refreshment'.

These essential initiatives also demonstrate a healthy move towards understanding the practical and realistic requirements for the less fortunate minorities in the community. All the plaudits for the apparent financial triumph and profitability from the commercially-dominated Los Angeles Olympic Games of 1984 ignored the disgrace which should shame its admirers for deciding that the 1984 Wheelchair Olympics, the Paralympics, failed to obtain any share of the bounty which was earned from the able-bodied Californian Olympics.

The Spirit of Stoke Mandeville: the story of Sir Ludwig Guttman by Susan Goodman (1986) recorded (at p 140) how;

> 'The United States was the Olympic country in 1984 and it was anticipated that the Paralympic Games would be held there also. An appropriate site was located, and approved, at the University of Illinois in Campaigne. Then in April, to the dismay of everyone involved and particularly the competitors, it was announced that funds necessary to hold the Games could not, after all be raised in the United States. Joan Scruton, as Secretary General of the International Stoke Mandeville Games Federation, remembers a hastily convened meeting at the sports centre which was attended by representatives of foreign member nations. That day the decision was taken to mount the seventh Paralympics at Stoke Mandeville. The Games would not be cancelled; the hundreds of athletes who had trained hard towards this goal would not be disappointed; the Olympic flame would be lit for them as for the able-bodies'.

As Susan Goodman went on to record (at pp 140–141);

> 'Appropriately, those seventh World Wheelchair Games — but the first in the "World" category to be held in Britain in the Games' twenty-four years of existence — were dedicated to [Ludwig Guttman's] memory and to his vow: "We will build a sports stadium and an Olympic village so that the disabled athletes of the world will always have their own Olympic facilities here at Stoke Mandeville when other doors are closed to them"'.

Guttman had allowed disabled competitors to fulfil their potential as athletes. Contrarily, some able-bodied athletes are knowingly destroying themselves by using dangerous substances to improve their performances. There are genuine problems which will be identified later in the chapter, 'International interaction', and will be further considered here, for reconciling lawful medically-prescribed drugs which breach sporting regulations and outlawing a blatant form of cheating. That is the essence of sport's drug issue, irrespective of the health hazard. Thus, in the definitive study of this dilemma, *Foul Play: Drug Abuse in Sports*, Tom Donohue and Neil Johnson (1986) explain that beta-blockers (at p 85);

'are widely used to treat high blood pressure and certain cardiac disorders such as "angina pectoris", a pain over the heart brought on by excessive exercise ... Theoretically, beta-blockers could be used by marksmen to reduce pre-competition tension; but owing to their potentially harmful effects and possible use as doping agents, the International Shooting Union placed beta-blockers on its list of banned substances'.

The wiser and vital legal problem for sports and, indeed, society in general which these developing areas create was crystallised comprehensively and advantageously for this chapter by the Sports Council's Medical Adviser, Dr Martyn Lucking, at a Sports Council Symposium on 'Drug Abuse in Sport" for sporting governing bodies held at King's College, London, on 27 March 1985. He explained:

'There is ignorance amongst a lot of medical practitioners in prescribing to athletes. A lot of them, even those in charge of major sports teams, do not know what is going on. It is very important that doctors are made terribly aware of the type of drugs which are banned and to be careful when prescribing to participating athletes not just at the event but during the training period. The Sports Council has been discussing at meetings white lists and black lists which are being drawn up. They will be circulated. The athletes themselves should be aware of this situation and know what drugs they can take and what they cannot take without contravening the laws of their sport'.

Fourteen years later in 1999 while this edition was being prepared, the internationally publicised drug offences before and after the Barcelona Olympic Games demonstrated how little has changed generally.

That charge of ignorance among medical practitioners by the Sports Council's own medical advisers brings the law in medicine directly into line with the law in sport. Yet medicine in sport mirrors the law in applying conventional professional standards and concepts to sporting situations. It also exposes the chaos which followed the claim by the President of the International Olympic Committee, Juan Antonio Samaranch when commenting in an interview with a Spanish daily newspaper and recorded in the London *Daily Telegraph* (26 July, 1998) and the BBC World Service that 'substances that do not damage a sportsman's health should not be banned'.

The reverberations from this bombshell were seen and heard worldwide. A week later the Head of the International Olympic Medical Commission, Prince Alexandre de Merode, was recorded in the *Independent* (18 August, 1998) to have been 'appalled' after Samaranch was reported to have said he saw no harm in athletes taking certain drugs as long as they were not a threat to health.

I don't understand,

he said

> people who want to reduce the list of banned drugs are those who want
> doping to continue. President Samaranch has always been against doping
> and he has always supported the action taken by the medical commission.
> I know where these ideas have come from — doctors who have forgotten
> their professional ethics.

The World Medical Association at its Ottowa Congress in October 1998
considered the issues ethically and an IOC congress at Lausanne in
February 1999 brought on stage government as well as sporting sources
to tackle with clear-cut conclusions a global legal medical sporting and
ethical dilemma which continues to defy definitive solutions. The
forthcoming Olympic Games in Australia offer a ray of hope with the
robustness and realism which characterises that sports loving nation.

As recorded in the *Guardian* for 17 September 1999

> 'Olympic athletes caught trying to smuggle performance-enhancing drugs
> into the country before next year's Games could face life imprisonment.

> Anyone caught illegally importing anabolic steroids or the blood-
> boosting drug EPO faces a maximum fine of Aus$50,000 (£21,000). A person
> caught trafficking a commercial quantity of the same goods would be liable
> for a life sentence.

> It is a major victory for the Australian Olympic Committee, who in a
> detailed submission made to the Prime Minister John Howard last year,
> called for the manufacture, trafficking and illegal possession of sports drugs
> to be subject to the same restrictions and penalties as social drugs'.

The rest of the world should adopt this precedent.

3   SPORTS MEDICINE WITHIN THE LAW

To date, sports medicine within the law and a need to open up levels of
awareness can be identified under three overriding general categories.
Specialist sub-divisions can doubtless be found. Current developments
fit neatly into the following three divisions:

(i)   violence;
(ii) negligence;
(iii) drugs.

The first and last are not only clear-cut and self-evident: their prevention is essential for the general health of sport. The first has been considered in depth in Chapter 5, *Public participation* and Chapter 6, *Participation problems* for its legal consequences. The last, which goes to the root of so many social evils within modern societies, will be an appropriate note on which to end this chapter. The second has the more easily and readily recognisable links with the law. It is also the most complex of all. Yet they all three interact within and upon each other. How they relate to each other has been shown already by the general observations cited here above on the sporting medical scene from England's World Cup-winning soccer captain and two leading orthopaedic surgeons involved with inherently violent play regulated by the Laws of the Game for rugby football. It is an appropriate note on which to begin examining in depth the inter-relationship between Sports Medicine and the Law.

(i)   Violence

This subject is discussed in detail in the previous Chapter 6, *Participation problems*. In the Sports Medicine and the Law context it takes on an important significance as the results of violence are inextricably linked to medicine.

The *Sunday Telegraph* edition of *Sport and the Law* appeared in 1978, with its confirmation of the 1977 series of articles explaining how deliberate and/or reckless violent foul play created criminal and civilly-actionable liabilities. Shortly afterwards the social impact of those malpractices was illuminated by two learned papers from different points of the playing and geographical compass in the British Medical Association Journal for 23 December 1978. The distinguished rugby international player, as Dr J P R Williams (now Mr J P R Williams, FRCS), wrote from clinical examinations at his surgery then at Bridgend in South Wales. These established from his medical evidence based upon his rugby playing experiences that the playing tactic of collapsing the scrum at rugby football caused cervical spinal injuries. In the same issue, two practitioners closely associated with the Guy's Hospital Athletics injuries clinic, Dr John Davies and Dr Terence Gibson, explained how 30 per cent of their referrals of rugby injuries were directly attributable to deliberate and/or reckless foul play.

In early 1992, the Arsenal and England team doctor, John Crane, disclosed after an address given to the London (now the National) Institute of Sports Medicine at St Bartholomew's Hospital in London that he and his Arsenal and England physiotherapist colleague, Fred Street, established that 18 per cent of the injuries they identified in the Arsenal dressing room were attributable to foul play.

Neither medical source specified, or perhaps neither knew, that the medical evidence it had adduced created prima facie breaches of the law justifying, on admissible evidence in court, criminal or civil process in the United Kingdom courts. The century-old principles had been established in *R v Bradshaw* ((1878) 14 Cox CC 83) and later confirmed in *R v Venna* ([1975] 3 All ER 788) (and as explained in Chapter 6, *Participation problems*).

Yet one beneficial result of the South Wales analysis was its impact on the law-makers within the rugby union game. The injurious effects of such a collapsed scrum sufficed to cause a change in the playing laws of the game to identify and outlaw this particular offence. No parallel change in the playing laws could legislate for the more general deliberate and/or reckless violent play. Yet more effective administrative penal laws have fluctuated with varying degrees of discipline to suspend or ban players from national to village green status to meet the Honorary Scottish Rugby Union's consultant surgeon's advocacy to 'minimise [injuries] wherever practical, by legislation'. Such action within a game such as rugby union football, can be as effective as any attempted Parliamentary sanction. Indeed, no better description of the limits to sporting legislation was given than the following judicial words of the then Montague Shearman, later Shearman J (who had the sombre task of sentencing Edith Thompson in 1922 as the last British woman to be hanged before Ruth Ellis, following the well-known Thompson-Bywaters murder trial):

'All that a governing body of sport can be expected to do is to keep order and punish open offences against its laws, and it can no more render its subjects good sportsmen and amateurs than an Act of Parliament can render citizens virtuous'.

(*Athletics and Football: The Badminton Library* (1887) Athletics Government p 227.)

Doctors practising or interested in the sporting scene can provide medical evidence which identifies areas where the sporting laws may require a reassessment as contemplated in Mr Donald A D Macleod's citation above.

Finally, the legal practitioner familiar with personal injuries claims and cases will be aware of what the average sportsperson suffering from, or concerned administratively with, sporting issues may not know: that the medical evidence could be crucial in establishing or rejecting claims for compensation on violent foul play. Medical evidence assisted the awards in the three leading reported civil damages awards for broken legs in Chapter 6, *Participation Problems*.

(1) *Lewis v Brookshaw* (1970) Sussex, £5,400.
(2) *Grundy v Gilbert* (1978) Bodmin, £4,000.
(3) *Condon v Basi* (1985) Warwick, £4,900.

It was also important for evaluating the contemporary and concurrent 1999 awards of Gordon Watson against Kevin Gray and Huddersfield Town of £900,000 and the interim £3,000 award for the schoolboy Maxwell Casson explained and listed in Chapter 6, *Participation Problems* above.

The level of quantum in these awards may appear capricious, or inadequate when compared with the Canadian citations referred to below. That problem raises separate and difficult legal questions extraneous to this chapter. What they prove is that on appropriate medical evidence, linked to equally appropriate and admissible general evidence, broken limbs can at least be compensated, and medical testimony in the form of agreed medical reports between the litigating parties, or oral medical evidence in court, is a crucial factor merging sports medicine with the law. It is even more significant in the realm of sporting medical negligence, to which this chapter now turns.

(ii)   Negligence

The English courts to date had been free from sporting medical negligence claims until Michael Watson's judgment against the British Boxing Board of Control identified early and throughout these pages (although the thrust of the claim and judgment were targeted towards the administration arrangements for what proved to be inadequate medical arrangements). This does not mean that no allegations of malpractice have ever been made. None so far has progressed to judgment; and even if such an event were to occur, the facts would have to result in a sufficiently novel point of law, or an illumination of any existing one with sufficient originality to merit an arrival for posterity and future citation in the appropriate Law Report. There is also a three-fold suggested explanation for the comment by Lord Diplock (as Diplock LJ) in *Wooldridge v Sumner* ([1963] 22 QB 43) about 'the duty of care owed by the actual participants to the spectators';

> 'It is a remarkable thing that in a nation where during the present century so many have spent so much of their leisure in watching other people take part in sports and pastimes there is an almost complete dearth of judicial authority'.

This is arguably explicable because of:

(1)   general reluctance to recognise sport cannot be above the law;

(2)   absence until 1950 of legal aid to assist litigants of slender means;

(3)   general reluctance in more leisurely days before professional sport entered the big money leagues to bring the law courts into the playing fields.

As the sporting scene explodes socially and athletic injuries demand specialist forms of medical attention, the present 'complete dearth of judicial authority' which Lord Diplock believed to exist could well diminish as the duties of care owed by the medical profession to sporting practitioners and administrators develop within the traditional foreseeability test, plus the causal connection with consequential damage, to create an alleged negligent medical act.

For the general legal as well as medical scenes the categories of negligence are never closed, however, as the Court of Appeal under Sir John Donaldson MR illustrated in *Condon v Basi* ([1985] 2 All ER 453). Furthermore the five outline Parts 1–5 inclusive, spanning 251 years in the Courts and Parliament, provide a survey which was not presented to Lord Justice Diplock or within his judicial knowledge, notwithstanding his personal reputation as a proficient Point-to-Point horseman, when expressing his unawareness of the time position as cited above in *Woodbridge v Sumner*.

It applied Australian judicial rulings to uphold a county court award of £4,900 damages for a leg broken in a foul soccer tackle, on the basis of breach of the duty of care in negligence owed by one player to another. This development occurred notwithstanding that the established facts were equally consistent with, and indeed also pleaded as, a civil assault. The categories of medical negligence have been most valuably and conveniently identified under the following eight separate headings by Professor J K Mason and Dr Alexander McCall Smith in the first edition (1981) of *Law and Medical Ethics* at Chapter 10 pages 126–142. Their equally valuable fifth edition published in 1999 does not require any adjustment from their Chapter 9 where the following structure re-adjusts to fit Chapter 7 here:

(a) *vicarious liability*
(b) *the reasonably skilful doctor: the usual practice: the custom test*
(c) *mis-diagnosis*
(d) *negligence in treatment*
(e) *the problem of the novice*
(f) *protecting the patient from himself*
(g) *res ipsa loquitur*
(h) *injuries caused by drugs* (the third main overriding category here linking sports medicine and the law).

Can they be applied to sport? Of course they can. The legal principle underlying every aspect of negligence with its duty of care-breach-foreseeability-causing-damage structure is constant for every different set of circumstances. All that sport does, as in every situation where the legal requirements appear for the first time, is to create a new level of awareness.

(a)   Vicarious liability

The purely legal issues involved in vicarious liability and sport, the antithesis between general culpability and exclusion of liability for negligence both general and medical, emerged dramatically in 1958 during the Munich air crash disaster which destroyed the famous Busby Babes and the official travellers with the Manchester United football team's party. The conflict of legal liability causation between ice on the wings, or slush on the runway, dragged on for years. The vicarious liability there was contested between whether the air*port* and/or the air*craft* authorities were responsible ultimately in law for their officials' contribution to one of international sport's most poignant fatal disasters before the 1985 crowd tragedies in Europe and England. This dispute contrasted with the devoted attention and facilities and staff at the Munich hospital where Sir Matt Busby and his fellow victims were admitted. They demonstrated to the world how general medical care and skill responded in traditional style to an acute emergency, and earned universal acclaim and admiration.

Those experiences illuminated the overlapping legal areas as a result of the expansion of international sport and the higher frequency of travel. In the United Kingdom, vicarious liability for medical negligence at hospital level has suffered from near immunity because of the frequent charitable elements involved in funding hospitals to complete application (see *Roe v Minister of Health, Woolley v Minister of Health* [1954] 2 QB 66, [1954] 2 All ER 131; *Razzall v Snowball* [1954] 3 All ER 429 and *Higgins v North West Metropolitan Regional Hospital Board* [1955] 1 All ER 414). After that flurry of judicial activity, administrative arrangements were made between the various medical defence societies and the appropriate Government departments for apportionment of damages awarded and costs but since January 1990 the entire costs of negligence litigation are borne by the National Health Service (see generally Mason and McCall Smith: *Law and Medical Ethics*, 5th edn, page 221).

An example of the vicarious liability principle to non-hospital medical malpractice emerges vividly from the facts and awards by the British Columbia Court of Appeal. It upheld the trial judge on a claim by a 28-year-old Canadian professional ice-hockey player, Mike Robitaille, against his former employer hockey club, Vancouver, known as the 'Canucks' (see *Robitaille v Vancouver Hockey Club Ltd* [1981] DLR (3rd) 288).

Sustained complaints to various club officials and doctors of developing injuries suffered in play were rejected in what were found judicially to be arrogant and high-handed forms of conduct. The neglect proved resulted in considerable personal and professional losses and suffering. The doctors' nexus with the club to establish a relationship involving vicarious liability as there was a level of control and involvement comprised a relatively modest bonus of $2,500, season tickets, free parking and access to the club lounge. The appeal court upheld the trial judge's evidential findings that:

> 'the measure of control asserted by the defendant over the doctors in carrying out their work was substantial. The degree of control need not be complete in order to establish vicarious liability. In the case of professional person, the absence of control and direction over the manner of doing the work is of little significance: *Morren v Swinton and Pendelbury Borough Council* [1965] 2 All ER 349, 351'.

Also confirmed were the trial judge's damages awards:

(1) $175,000 for loss of professional hockey income;
(2) $85,000 for loss of future income other than from professional hockey;
(3) $40,000 for the traditional pain, suffering and loss of enjoyment of life.

Of equal significance for all sportspersons was a concurrent approval by the appeal court of the trial judge's conclusion about the plaintiff's contributory negligence. He was held to be:

> '20% at fault because his failure to take any action [ie, to complain] to protect his own interest was less than reasonable. There was evidence upon which Esson J could find that Robitaille was negligent ... the trial judge correctly distinguished cases ... which dealt with factory workers ... dealing here with a highly paid experienced modern day professional athlete and not a factory worker responding to the mores of olden times'.

The plaintiff's contributory negligence assessment by the Court of not pursuing his medical complaints to agencies outside the negligent club's control earlier than he did was possibly harsh. Nevertheless, the trial judge heard extensive oral evidence, and his final awards, which included aggravated and exemplary damages, demonstrated his ultimate awareness of the plaintiff's overriding and justifiable grievance for medical neglect which created a clear-cut vicarious liability.

This case should be contrasted with *Wilson v Vancouver Hockey Club* (1983 5 DLR (4n) 282 (BC SC) affirmed 22 DLR (4n 516), CA). The Ontario Court of Appeal affirmed the trial judge's decision that the doctor in the case was an independent contractor on the facts of the case and the club was exonerated from liability. This was because the evidence indicated that the doctor made his decision on treatment without advice from the management of the club, and because the doctor felt he served the interest of the players exclusively and that his primary obligation was to them as servants of the hockey club.

Finally, as explained in detail during analysis of the anomalous position of boxing generally in Chapter 6, *Participation Problems*, the position of any medical practitioner associated with a governing body, where foreseeable risk elements exist, should at the present time be alerted to World Medical Association Guideline for Practitioners in Sports Medicine number 13 'the participation of a sports physician is desirable when sports regulations are drawn up'. The full transcript of Kennedy J's decision in *Watson v British Boxing Board of Control* confirm this places on sports regulatory bodies a duty to their sport and any patients under their care in the context of Robitailles case. Although this guideline 13 does not appear to have been pleaded its desirability clearly emerges from Mr Justice Kennedy's comprehensive judgment.

(b)   The reasonably skilful doctor: the usual practice: the custom test

No other professional discipline can be more readily aware of the universal search for progressive treatment to alleviate suffering than medicine. The general public's and layman's awareness, too, cannot ignore the onward march of new frontiers: from Simpson with chloroform; Madame Curie with radiology; Pasteur and immunology, down to our own century and Banting, Best and Macleod with insulin, and the triumph of Chain, Florey and Fleming with penicillin.

In sports medicine, too, anyone who followed the public interest during the 1950s will recall the tension surrounding the fate of Mr Denis Compton's kneecap. Mr W E Tucker FRCS extracted it with his mixture of orthopaedic skill and international rugby playing experience (both functions inherited from an equally distinguished paternal practitioner in both activities). This allowed his patient to continue playing Test and County cricket with success and public acclaim. Mr Compton had already retired from an active professional football career with an FA Cup winners' medal and wartime international honours; and the novelty of the nature of this surgery was not concerned with his winter game (in which Paul Gascoigne's self-induced injury has commanded comparable current attentions). Nevertheless, the intervening years have witnessed contractions in periods of time from when a conventional cartilage operation for a footballer incapacitated the patient for weeks, to modern remedies which can return a player to training within days.

Against this background of inevitable mobility in thinking and equipment, what is the norm to apply? Each specialist area of medicine, more so than the law, has its own levels of knowledge with interdisciplinary connections. A trainer or physiotherapist would not be expected to have the same level of skill as an experienced physician or surgeon. The courts have moved on even since the first edition of Mason and McCall Smith:

Law and Medical Ethics appeared in 1981, with three landmark House of Lords decisions on medical duties. It ruled on warning of risks (*Sidaway v Board of Governors of the Bethlem Royal Hospital and Maudsley Hospital* [1985] AC 871, [1985] 1 All ER 643) and conflicting medical opinions (*Maynard v West Midlands Regional Health Authority* [1985] All ER 635, [1985] 1 WLR 634). Yet on this basic issue of what is the usual or customary level of skill to apply, Lord Scarman and their Lordships reiterated long-established principles from the 1950s in two passages appropriate for citation here. For a detailed discussion of the debate about the quality and level of evidence for assessing medical liability generally see Kennedy & Grubb: *Medical Law*, 2nd edition 1994 at pages 465–468.

In *Sidaway* at page 649 he referred to a jury direction by McNair J in the leading case of *Bolam v Friern Hospital Management Committee* ([1957] 2 All ER 118, [1957] 1 WLR 582):

> 'as a rule that a doctor is not negligent if he acts in accordance with a practice accepted at the time as proper by a responsible body of medical opinion even though other doctors adopt a different practice. In short, the law imposes a duty of care; but the standard of care is a matter of medical judgment'.

In *Maynard* at page 638 he said:

> 'I do not think that words of the Lord President (Clyde) in *Hunter v Hanley* [1955] SLT 213 at 217 can be bettered: "In the realm of diagnosis there is ample scope for genuine difference of opinion and one man clearly is not negligent merely because his conclusion differs from that of other professional men ... The true test for establishing negligence in diagnosis or treatment on the part of a doctor is whether he has been proved to be guilty of failure as no doctor of ordinary skill would be guilty of acting with ordinary care"'.

More recently these criteria have been applied and re-affirmed by the House of Lords with an emphasis on the levels of logical evidence and causation required in *Bolitho v City and Hackney H.A.* [1997] 4 AER 771 citing at 776b 'a doctor is not guilty of negligence if he has acted in accordance with a practice accepted as proper by a responsible body of medical men skilled in that particular art ... Putting it the other way round, a doctor is not negligent, if he is acting in accordance with such a practice, merely because there is a body of opinion that takes a contrary view'.

In Australia, however, a decision of the High Court upholding the appellate and New South Wales courts in *Rogers v Whittaker* [1992] 109 ALR 625 [1992] 4 MedL.R.79 (HC of Aust) with the robustness characteristic of its sporting culture has rejected the English Court's traditional deference to medical opinions epitomized in *Bolam* and *Bolitho*, and asserted the decision of the court itself as a matter of law in adjudicating whether a defendant's conduct has conformed to the standard of reasonable care demanded by the law, and not by the standard of the medical profession or some part of it.

One unreported example of undoubted medical neglect for which the my own legal infancy and paternal restraint against litigation blocked the ultimate writ for neglect was cited here in Chapter 1, *Genesis* in the same spirit as Lord Haldane of Cloan's account in his posthumous memoirs of the Irish appeal case to the House of Lords. A novel point of real property law was argued extensively. Judgment was reserved; but as the first Lord Chancellor in a Labour Government explained (*Richard Burdon Haldane: an Autobiography* (1929) page 66):

> 'Unluckily, the next day was Derby Day, and the lay clients met on the racecourse, and were said to have settled the case there, so judgment was never delivered'.

My leg broken by accident in the Oxford University soccer trials resulted in treatment from a local hospital which included advice to walk upon the broken leg while the plaster was setting. In due course the broken limb lost its alignment, and an ulcer was created inside the plaster. Maternal wisdom caused a transfer to a London hospital, more specialised treatment and prevention of more serious consequences. Clearly the Oxford medical staff were legally negligent by today's judicial standards, and, indeed, by the standards of that particular period before Lord Scarman's citations appeared during the mid-1950s. The combination of personal legal infancy; the absence of legal aid; and parental advice, all merged to inhibit the justifiable proceedings for medical negligence against the appropriate Oxford hospital sources.

Furthermore, the Oxford University sporting authorities who had control of the Iffley Road ground where the injury occurred had no first aid or treatment facilities of any description. They too were, in my opinion today, also guilty of vicarious negligence. In the spirit of Lord Haldane's experience, however, judgment was never delivered, although perpetuation of this medical lacuna anywhere could well fill this particular legal gap at some time in the future.

(c)   Mis-diagnosis

The potential danger for this category of negligence must be realised by all concerned with athletic injuries in every sport where judgments have to be made under pressures of time and circumstances, eg TV cameras and a crowded arena. *Mason and McCall Smith* explains:

'A mistake in diagnosis will not be considered negligent if [the usual degrees of dealings with patients] standard of care is observed but will be treated as one of the non-culpable and inevitable hazards of practice'.

They cited in a footnote a judicial observation,

'unfortunate as it was that there was a wrong diagnosis, it was one of those misadventures, one of those chances, that life holds for people (*Crinon v Barnet Group Hospital Management Committee* (1959) *Times*, 19 November)

Canada, however, again provides a direct example of liability which was established, this time in the Ontario Court of Appeal. A 41-year-old tool and dye worker broke his right *ankle* when playing soccer with his young son. A negligently erroneous X-ray prescription for attention to the right *foot* was compounded by a cascade of consequential errors involving more than one medical practitioner, who successively consolidated earlier mis-diagnosis. This resulted in the appellate court's confirmation of the trial judge's ruling that 'one negligent doctor could be liable for the additional loss caused by the other'. The appeal court also upheld the damages award of $50,000 for the general damages, which included $34,465 for loss of income up to the date of trial. The successive mis-diagnoses proved very expensive for the doctors, who included a radiologist, as well as painful for the patient (*Price v Milawski, Murray and Castroyan* (1978) 82 DLR (3d) 130).

(d) Negligence in treatment

The examples above of the professional ice-hockey player, my own personal Oxford University experiences and the 41-year-old soccer-playing father, all illustrate negligence in treatment. A grey area or border line exists between negligence and error of judgment. It was illuminated by the extensively reported judgments on the baby whose delivery was forced by being pulled out too hard with forceps and wedged, with resulted asphyxia and brain damage. The House of Lords refined Lord Denning's distinction between negligence and error of judgment when the trial judge's damages award of £100,000 was overturned on the basis that he drew the wrong inferences of fact from the oral and documentary evidence (*Whitehouse v Jordan* [1981] 1 All ER 267, [1981] 1 WLR 246, HL). Lord Fraser in the House of Lords explained at page 281:

'The true position ... depends on the nature of the error. If it is one that would not have been made by a reasonably competent professional man professing to have the standard and type of skill that the defendant holds himself out as having, and acting with ordinary care, then it is negligence. If, on the other hand, it is an error that such a man, acting with ordinary care, might have made, then it is non negligent'.

In *Whitehouse v Jordan* a conflict of medical testimony caused the Court of Appeal and the House of Lords to adjudicate that the very experienced trial judge had drawn the inferences of fact from the conflicting medical evidence. In sports medicine as a developing science and discipline, with varying levels of experiences for different sports and different parts of the anatomy, the possibilities of conflicting and genuine specialist opinions could exist. Speculation without real example cannot prophesy here. The legal formula has been laid down by the House of Lords in *Whitehouse v Jordan* and affirmed in the later opinions of *Maynard* and *Sidaway*. Sports medicine must lie with it until tested in the fire of evidenciary battles.

(e)   The problem of the novice

Every professional is at first an amateur. The beginner must be guided by instructions. The standard laid down by the House of Lords (see *Sidaway*, above) 'accepted at the time as proper by a reasonable body of medical opinion' is comparable to the fledgling athlete and games player projected into action with veterans. Public allowances of limited sympathy for youth alongside maturity will not include forgiveness for sub-standard performances. The law does not differentiate either. If liability arises it could be vicarious for any employer or controller of a practitioner associated primarily or secondarily with medical services, whether as a doctor, physiotherapist, trainer or traditional sponge man. The amateur club which permits an unqualified member to act as an ad hoc first aid assistant without any practical experience resulting in any serious or actionable injury is as much at risk as the hospital committee allowing an inexperienced practitioner to carry out complex operations usually reserved for the maturer staff (see *Brown v Lewis* (1898) 12 TLR 455 for committee member's liability when negligent sub-contracting causes liability).

(f)   Protecting the patient from himself

This particular category in the reported cases is concerned with suicide attempts and tendencies. An analogy can apply to excessively enthusiastic athletes seeking performance enhancement from drugs or striving to return to action when not fully fit. Without firm medical guidance, emphasising the harmful consequences of the zest for play overriding the consequences of such medical advice, then a liability for negligence could well arise. The demands and stresses of competitive professional sport are particularly vulnerable in this category.

(g)   Res ipsa loquitur

This penultimate stage in *Mason and McCall Smith's* classification of medical negligence has veered between extreme critical and literal commentaries upon it in the House of Lords (*Ballard v North British Railway Co* (1923) SC (HL) 43 at 46). Lord Shaw of Dunfermline said in 1923:

> 'If that phrase had not been in Latin, nobody would have called it a principle ... The day for canonising Latin phrases has gone past'.

Lord Denning brought it all into focus as Denning LJ in a hospital negligence case (*Cassidy v Ministry of Health* [1951] 2 KB 343 at 365, [1951] 1 All ER 574 at 588, CA) with the judgment that the plaintiff in the case before him on appeal was entitled to say:

> 'I went into hospital to be cured of two stiff fingers. I have come out with four stiff fingers and my hand is useless. That should not have happened if due care had been used. Explain it if you can'.

Lord Normand in 1950 (*Barkway v South Wales Transport Co Ltd* [1950] 1 All ER 398 at 399) explained that it is:

> 'no more than a rule of evidence affecting onus. It is based on commonsense, and its purpose is to enable justice to be done when the facts bearing on causation and on the care exercised by the defendant are at the outset unknown to the plaintiff and are or ought to be within the knowledge of the defendant'.

Earlier, in an English Court of Appeal decision, Kennedy LJ explained:

> 'The teaching, as I understand, of that phrase ... is this, that there is, in the circumstances of the particular case, some evidence viewed not as a matter of conjecture, but of reasonable argument, which makes it more probable that there was some negligence, upon the facts as shown and undisputed, than that the occurrence took place without negligence.
>
>   The res speaks because the facts stand unexplained, and therefore the natural and reasonable, not conjectural, inference from the facts shows that what has happened is reasonably to be attributed to some act of care under the circumstances ... it means that the circumstances are, so to speak, eloquent

of the negligence of somebody who brought about the state of things ... more consistent, reasonably interpreted, without further explanation, with your negligence than with any other cause of the accident happening'.

Finally, Canada provides one more graphic example which would have horrendous consequences for any athlete. The plaintiff entered hospital for treatment for a fractured ankle and left with amputated leg. No explanation existed. That evidence on applying the principles cited above pointed in one inevitable direction: negligence (*MacDonald v York County Hospital Corporation* [1972] 28 DLR (3d 521)).

(h)   Injuries caused by drugs

'Compensation for injury by drugs is now regulated in the United Kingdom by the Consumer Protection Act 1987. This derives from the European Directive on product liability (Council Directive 85/374/EEC), the aim of which was to create strict liability for most injuries which were caused by defective products; this policy had long been advocated by commentators on compensation for personal injury. Under the terms of the Act, strict liability is borne primarily by the manufacturer of a defective product although the suppliers will also be held liable if they cannot identify the manufacturer'.

Thus did Mason and McCall Smith highlight an area illuminated with the widest general publicity through the Thalidomide tragedy. For sportspersons, and sports medical practitioners, however, the social evil inherent in the drug trade raises legal, medical and sporting administrative issues which were crystallised by two leading sports personalities in a manner discussed in Chapter 9, '*International interaction*'. This crucial social as well as sporting problem cannot be emphasised too strongly for sport as one which extends beyond the level of medical injuries caused by incorrectly or negligently prescribed drugs into the wider and equally significant career injuries suffered by the sports patient's lawfully prescribed drug treatment under national legislation which conflicts with the sporting legislation of a sporting governing body.

Two examples which are cited in that paper (Ron Angus (from judo) and William Johnston (Football)) identified not only a developing area which has yet to be thought through between the three interlocking worlds of sport, medicine and the law: they crystallise and illuminate the revolution which has projected sport from a healthy, fun loving competitive and educative element to a ruthlessly commercialised sector of a high profile entertainment industry containing within it seeds of destruction for health, sport and society. They raise questions for the future which have yet to be acknowledged and faced by sport and society for which an answer can be provided only in part by the law. They are the reason why this chapter concludes with the questions they pose and why the heading comes at the end of this division of Sports Medicine and the Law into Violence, Negligence and Drugs.

The foundation for the claim that 'an answer can be provided only in part by law' was confirmed on St Leger Day, Doncaster, Saturday 12 September 1987. The Home Office announced that it had asked the Advisory Council on the Misuse of Drugs to consider whether steroids should be included in the Misuse of Drugs Act 1971. Nine years later in 1996 it was implemented. A bulletin entitled '*Drugs in Sport, a Reappraisal*' from the Institute of Medical Ethics under its Director, Dr Richard Nicholson, claimed to raise two main questions:

(1) is it unethical for a sportsman to take drugs?
(2) is drug-taking so serious a problem that the governing bodies of sports need to draw up rules to prevent it, with punishments for contravention of the rules?

The premise on which the questions were posed challenged and canvassed within a sporting context wider issues that the health hazards beyond sport identified in *Foul Play, Drug Abuse in Sports* by Tom Donohue and Neil Johnson cited at page 221 below, or in Dr Ellen Grant's *The Bitter Pill: How safe is the 'perfect contraceptive'?*, referred to in Chapter 8, '*Women in Sport and the Law*'. Finally, the August 1987 edition of the authoritative *Pacemaker International* journal, in a feature article entitled 'The Ugly Mask of Drugs' (page 50), explained the dangers for the breeding side of racing, that Bute and Lasix which are permitted under rules in most American racing states, 'may mask congenital deficiencies in horses that will later be passed on to their offspring, thus having a detrimental effect on the breed'. Indeed, in the context of this trespass upon nature and God's own territory, it is pertinent to enquire: are two-legged animals different from four-legged ones?

This important trio of publications prove the complexity of the subject and the need, perhaps in Britain at least, for an in-depth assessment based upon authentic evidence to the level and degree of quality which produced both celebrated Reports to which Sir John Wolfenden gave his name. Furthermore the debate which has surfaced during the autumn of 1999 about the possible nexus between food substances and the positive tests on athletes relating to a banned substance mandrolene have so far ignored one celebrated precedent from the world of horse-racing. Hill House and Ryan Price. A positive dope test, over thirty years ago now posed the question crystallised in Peter O'Sullivan's autobiography *Calling the Horses*:

'whether level of Cortisol to which Hill House reacted was self-created or administered'.

In due course, as O'Sullivan anticipated correctly

'The latest tests on Hill House at Newmarket are likely to confirm the findings of one eminent diagnostician. Namely then the elements traced in the horse are part of his natural organism'.

The Report in the *Independent* newspaper for 17 September 1999 that

'UK Sport is consulting the Department of Agriculture and Fisheries over the use of steroids in farming as a possible source of the existence of the drug [mandroline] in athletes';

suggests that this one will run and run and that assistance from the legal world's advisers may benefit those who can speak and plead their own case.

(iii) Drugs

The symposium mounted in 1985 by the Sports Council at London University's King's College occurred when the Sport's Council's campaign for drug testing among sporting governing bodies was backed by a formidable body of oral, documentary and visual evidence. This explained graphically the adverse health consequences of rule breaking by cheats indulging in drug-taking throughout the sporting world at all levels, internationally and domestically. It was concerned primarily with the inter-relationship between the health and ethical sporting problems. It was not concerned directly with the wider legal aspects which are illuminated immediately below to expand sport's own conflict of laws situation, considered generally in Chapter 9, *International interaction*.

January 1984 witnessed a *Sunday Telegraph* announcement from the British Judo Association that a dope test on Ron Angus, winner of the under 78 kilo category in the All-England Championship in December 1983, had proved positive. A sample contained traces of a stimulant, pseudo-Ephedrine.

Angus, who had dual Canadian-British nationality, claimed that the substance must have been contained in a sinus decongestant which he had taken under a lawful medical prescription by his Canadian doctor. Because he had breached the Association's requirements he was banned for life from competing in British championships.

Five months later, after he had taken legal advice, the *Daily Telegraph* reported that the High Court in London had lifted the ban with the

Association's consent. It admitted that the absence of a hearing for Angus to explain his position breached the rules of natural justice, and the life ban was duly rescinded. The Association's rules have now been tightened to place the onus on competitors, and by implication, therefore, on their *personal doctors* to ensure that lawful medication does not contain banned substances (*Daily Telegraph*, 15 June 1984).

Even wider publicity was suffered by Scotland's international outside-left Willie Johnston, sent home in alleged disgrace from the 1978 FIFA World Cup. From the facts explained in his book *On the Wing* and in the medico-legal opinion expressed at the Sports Council Symposium, he appears to have suffered a gross injustice which should never have occurred.

His own *English* Football League club doctor had lawfully prescribed Reactivan pills for his nasal condition. The *Scottish* FA doctor had warned Johnston about drugs; but the footballer patient had not realised that his pills contained a stimulant called Fencamsamin, of which traces were found after a positive dope test, in breach of FIFA rules. His international football career was blighted without any apparent personal culpability on his part.

No complaint appears to have been made to FIFA by anyone on Johnston's behalf, and the fact that FIFA's registered office is in Switzerland takes it outside the United Kingdom Courts' jurisdiction. Thus Johnston could not directly have made a similar claim in Scotland against the disciplining governing body, FIFA, to that made successfully by Ron Angus against the British Judo Association, unless he had emulated John Cooke's claim and sued his own Scottish FA (see Chapter 9, *International interaction*).

Nevertheless, on the facts summarised above from Johnston's own account, he was undoubtedly innocent of any offence under the principles of British criminal law. Indeed, section 28(3)(b)(i) of the Misuse of Drugs Act 1971, says that any accused person shall be acquitted of a drug offence 'if he proves that he neither believed nor suspected nor had reason to suspect that the substance or product in question was a controlled drug' ie one of which the use is controlled by the Act, and thereby unlawful generally.

That sub-section, and others comparable to it in principle as laid down by Parliament, illustrates the problems which face sports participants who require drugs lawfully for medicinal purposes.

(1) *How* are athletes and their personal doctors to know when a breach or potential breach of a sporting governing body's rules against drug abuse occurs?

(2) *How* are sporting governing bodies to know that a failure to meet their own stringent rules for the protection of a particular sport does or does not arise from a lawful medicinal prescription?

(3) *How* are lawyers to balance the interest of the sport in which they

advise administrators with the need to respect the rights of individual competitors?

(4) *What* is the patient to do when faced with what may become a conflict of personal health interests against the undoubted right in a free society to participate in healthy competition?

These questions cannot be shirked and have to be thought through within the framework of what lawyers recognise, usually in the international legal field, as a conflict of laws situation. Furthermore, with the explosion of international sport, and the concern of the World Health Organisation as well as international governing bodies about the problem, there is the added issue of international harmony for approaching solutions.

As sport becomes more commercially competitive within a TV-regulated global coverage, the necessity to keep sport within a healthy framework for itself and its participants demands a coordinated effort from everyone concerned along the lines suggested below. Without such a concord, recourse to the courts or some form of legal investigation would be bound to follow.

Doctors who treat patients competing athletically must familiarise themselves with the requirements of the particular sport in question, both at domestic and international level — and pass on this information to their patients.

Lawyers who advise administrators must see that any regulations to prevent cheating do not either transgress natural justice rules and the opportunity to be heard, or contravene the spirit of the British parliamentary defence that ignorance of the facts can be a defence in a drugs case.

Administrators should try, with doctors, pharmacists, lawyers and drug manufacturers, to attain a balance between the sport's rules and the individual's medicinal requirements, in the interests of fair play, health and the avoidance of cheating.

Competitors must familiarise themselves with their own medical requirements within the rules laid down by their particular sport.

The breakdown of this union has heralded a spate of sensational situations which are only the tip of a wider and deeper iceberg. Thus, after Ben Johnson was caught using steroids in the 1988 Seoul Olympics, the problem of the widespread use of steroids within sport was highlighted and the floodgates for legal consequences and liabilities were opened. Shortly after Johnson's positive test of the steroid stanozolol, the government of Canada appointed the Honourable Charles L Dubin to lead the *Commission of enquiry into the use of drugs and banned practices intended to enhance athletic performance.* This has been the most detailed and innovative legal report which has been published on this subject and the Canadian Government merits praise for instigating this. Chief Justice Dubin said of the problem in the report, 'the evidence shows that banned performance-enhancing substances and in particular anabolic steroids are being used by athletes in almost every sport, most extensively in weightlifting and track and field.'

Robert Armstrong QC, a member of the Canadian Bar Association and Commission Counsel to the Dubin Inquiry, stated at an International Symposium on sport and the law held in Monaco in 1991 that Canada had lost its innocence as a sporting nation in Seoul. The Dubin Inquiry showed that the use of drugs within sport had no national boundaries and after the report was published it was seen that most athletic countries of the world had lost their innocence. Dr Robert Kerr, a doctor practising in San Gabriel, testified before the Dubin Inquiry that he had prescribed anabolic steroids to approximately twenty medallists in the 1984 Olympics. Pat Connolly, a coach of the women's track team at the US Senate Judiciary on steroid abuse in the US, estimated that five out of ten gold medallists in the US men's Olympic track team used anabolic steroids at Seoul.

The most common forbidden performance-enhancing techniques include taking steroids, human growth hormone and blood doping. Blood doping is where the athlete takes blood out of his own body and then re-injects it a few weeks later, days before the event in order to increase his oxygen carrying capacity, thereby improving performance. It must be constantly borne in mind that whilst these athletes are cheating themselves and the public, they are also preventing other athletes from achieving success. These banned practices are obviously adopted frequently by a significant number of athletes and only one deterrent exists which is in- and out-of-competition testing.

The Sports Council in London governs the dope testing in Britain with an accredited IOC Laboratory and has implemented one of the most stringent programmes in the world. In 1992 over 4,000 samples were taken from athletes in 53 different sports, with a higher number than ever before coming from out-of-competition testing. It is difficult to assess how effective dope testing is as a deterrent. Taking as a touchstone Ben Johnson, who was tested positive for the second time in March 1993 after suffering so much humiliation following the Seoul Olympics, it is apparent that for some athletes it is not an effective deterrent.

The prohibited use of steroids within sport has resulted in much litigation in recent years. Many athletes challenge bans imposed on them after a positive test. For example, a 25-year-old Swiss athlete, Sandra Gasser, who had attained international standard in the 800 metres and the 1500 metres, appealed to the Chancery Division of the High Court after she was suspended for two years from eligibility to enter athletics competitions held under IAAF rules, following a positive test of the metabolite of methyl testosterone at the 1987 World Championships in Rome. An Arbitration Panel of the IAAF affirmed the decision. Scott J refused declaratory relief by writ (not by the usually misconceived judicial review procedure) that the suspension was unreasonably in restraint of trade (although he accepted that the restraint of trade principles applied to the facts of the case).

More significantly, however, in his unreported judgment he made two observations to suggest that a different approach by the plaintiff's lawyers (as so often happens) might have had different consequences. First, he found in relation to one of the two tested samples of urine: 'The Panel might have found that the other explanation was too conjectural to be accepted. But no evidence to incline them to the view had been put before them by the plaintiff or the SLV'.

Second, he explained that the Panel:

'accepted the other explanation. They may have been wrong in doing so. They may have been wrong in regarding the identified procedural failure as not material. But unless they exceeded their jurisdiction, exceeded, that is to say, their terms of reference, the Plaintiff is stuck with their conclusions. Any remedy of appeal to the High Court under the Arbitration Acts is long since time-barred'.

Furthermore, Robert Armstrong QC, at an international symposium said that 'basically Dubin recommended that in order to have a fair right of appeal, athletics should be in a position to be able to test the scientific validity of the test results'. The question therefore remains, could *different evidence* in the *Gasser* case of the kind contemplated specifically by Scott J have produced a different result? For that reason the decision and reliance upon it as a binding precedent must always be challenged as based upon a debatable foundation because of apparent inadequate or insufficient preparation *in the eyes and mind* of the trial judge for reliance upon it by those who wish to challenge tribunal practices in this area.

Katrin Krabbe, from Germany, has successfully overturned one IAAF ban for drug abuse but in November 1993 appealed on legal technicalities unsuccessfully to an IAAF arbitration panel against a ban imposed on her for the alleged use of the drug Clenbuterol. Andrew Saxton and Andrew Davies are the two British weightlifters who were sent home from the Barcelona Olympics in 1992 for being tested positive for Clenbuterol. Davies and Saxton have argued that their use of the substance did not justify disqualification as the drug was not on the IOC's list of banned substances at the time of competition.

The British sprinter, Jason Livingstone, was also sent home from the Barcelona Olympics as he was tested positive for the drug methandianone in a random out-of-competition test before the Olympics. He appealed to the British Athletic Federation Appeals Panel which dismissed his appeal by a 2–1 majority in April/May 1993. In the appeal, there was some doubt cast over the positive test as, in fact, a metabolite of methandianone had been found, not the actual substance. Livingstone argued that just because a metabolite of the substance had been found, this was not conclusive proof that he had actually used methandianone. This view was supported by the evidence of Professor Arnold Beckett, previously a member of the IOC's medical commission. However, the majority of the panel felt that the evidence which was before them put beyond reasonable doubt that Livingstone had taken the drug and had indeed cheated.

In December 1992, Harry ('Butch') Reynolds obtained judgment in a Court in Ohio against the IAAF for damages for $27.3m for wrongfully banning him from athletics. Following a competition in Monaco in August 1990, Reynolds was randomly tested and it was found that he had traces of the anabolic steroid nandrolone in his urine. The IAAF did not seek to defend the proceedings and subsequently argued that the Ohio Court had no jurisdiction over the IAAF and chose to ignore the judgment. It should be noted that the Ohio court accepted everything that Reynolds said in his complaint as correct since the proceedings were not defended. The award of damages therefore is not a result of conclusions based on evidence heard from *both sides* on the merits of the case and as such this massive award should not be taken as a measure of how such damages will be assessed in the future, or, indeed that the disqualification in the particular circumstances was invalid. Furthermore, in May 1994, the Ohio court judgment was successfully appealed on the basis of no jurisdiction over the IAAF, with yet further appeal to the American Supreme Court (equivalent to the House of Lords) reportedly being contemplated by Reynold's advisors (*Daily Mail*, 21 May 1994), without any ultimate effect.

Another contentious example to illustrate the problem emerged after a rugby international between France and Wales in Paris during 1992. Anthony Clement and Jean-Baptiste Lafond were allegedly tested positive for the use of prohibited drugs. In due course, it emerged that Malcolm Downes, the Welsh Rugby Union honorary surgeon, had prescribed Clement drugs for sickness and dysentery. Lafond had been administered with Pholeodine for a cough by a French doctor.

In due course each player was exonerated, but what emerged is that the Welsh Rugby Union uses the same list of banned substances as the International Olympic Committee, which differs from the list adopted by the French Rugby Union. Correspondingly, after an international conference in Bermuda of rugby doctors (which I attended to give legal guidance) had recommended criteria for drug testing, the International Rugby Board, which was not renowned for its consistency over discrepancies in financial compensation for loss of time from normal employment, required reminding of the necessity for creating sanctions for findings of positive tests.

Thus the battle against cheats who perform with forbidden performance-enhancing techniques will probably rage on into the next millenium. The detrimental side-effects of the use of steroids must be constantly stressed in order that sportspeople who are tempted to use them will understand that a better performance is not the only effect of this practice.

When yet another sportsperson is tested positive, the public become resigned to the view that certain sports are not 'clean' and subsequently suspect that innocent participants may themselves be cheating. Undoubtedly, the real victims of this crime are the competitors who choose to compete using their own natural resources and refuse to compromise their own integrity in order to be better, stronger or go faster.

On that issue an argument has been formulated that any proven loss by a competitor downgraded with consequential financial sponsorship disadvantages would have a cause of action for negligence giving rise to damages (see the *Independent on Sunday* and Bath University Distance Learning Course for Doctors). It can also be extended, at least within the United Kingdom, to the criminal liability of obtaining a pecuniary advantage by deception under section 15(1) of the Theft Act 1968.

Mr Justice Dubin's Report concluded:

'Cheating in sport, I fear, is partially a reflection of today's society. Drugs and the unprincipled pursuit of wealth and fame at any cost now threaten our very social fabric. It is little wonder the immorality has reached into sport as well. Of course, cheating as such is not a new phenomenon in Olympic competition, but the methods used to cheat have become more and more innovative and more pervasive. Moreover the use of drugs as the method of cheating has reached epidemic proportions'.

If there is a solution, then what better remedy can be found than the end of Hubert Doggart's Appendix on The Corinthian Ideal:

'Three groups whose efforts could be harnessed to stop the rot and ensure the survival, relatively intact, of the Corinthian ideal.

First, the doctors, whose Hippocratic oath can be construed as an upholding of the Corinthian ideal in medicine. Secondly, the lawyers, who once played without a thought that their services qua lawyers would be needed, but cannot now be sure. And, thirdly, school teachers, whose raison d'être could be called "the upholding of the Corinthian ideal in body, mind and soul"'.

Finally, because drug abuse is a national and international health hazard, the British Government surely cannot opt out of taking an interest here, just as it is no longer ignoring its need to become involved with the problems of sporting crowd violence.

As a start, consideration could be given to whether the lethal and recognised use of any known sporting drug substances, in addition to those which are already prohibited, should be outlawed alongside LSD, heroin, cocaine and other evil substances. The proposals announced by the Home Office (on 12 September 1987) that anabolic steroids were under consideration for being added to the lists of prohibited drugs were clearly a step in the right direction. They took nine years for implementation in 1996 under the Misuse of Drugs Act 1971 (modification Order 1996) and the Misuse of Drugs ((Amendment) Regulations 1996): in the interests of health and fair play, which in the end is what sport, in and out of court, is all about.

Within that professional context the British Association of Sport and Medicine at its Annual Congress in 1998 recommended to the General Medical Council that practitioners associated with drug related offences in sport should be subjected to professional sanctions. The response may well exist at the time of this publication and if delivered will be short.

CHAPTER 8

Women in Sport and the Law

1 INTRODUCTION

Coincidence and/or comity of editorship combined in August 1999 to produce from both sides of the Atlantic special *Women in Sport* editions of their respective Sports Medicine journals. Neither dealt specifically with identifiable legal issues, nor was it required to. For women and sex in sport is as explosive a topic as its wider gender importance dominates the dying years of the 20th century. Yet if any one act were required to identify the impact which women in sport have had on its development in history I would at least be ready to advocate the potential legal consequences, which the local Epsom police were considering, if Emily Wilding Davidson had not died from her injuries on 8 June 1913 without recovering consciousness, after she brought down the horse owned by HM King George V in the Epsom Derby, Amner, seriously injuring its jockey, too, Herbert Jones.

Forty six years later in 1959 and forty years ago from today the memoirs of Dame Christabelle Pankhurst, one of the leading militant suffragettes, edited by the Rt Hon Lord Pethick-Lawrence in *Unshackled: The Story of How We Won the Vote* recorded:

> 'Emily Davidson paid with her life by making the whole world understand that women were in earnest for the vote. Probably in no other way and no other time could she so effectively have brought the concentrated attention of millions to bear upon the cause'.

Today, women around the world are still relishing the feast of international football climaxed when USA beat China 5–4 before a 60,000 crowd televised globally. The Marlebone Cricket Club (MCC) voted to open its doors to lady members for the first time since its foundation in 1787, and Susan Hawthorne, Executive Director of The [American] *Physician and Sports Medicine* wrote in her *Editor's Notes*: Vol 27 No. 8 August 99: p 7 after citing statistical figures of growth athletic USA activity:

'What distinguishes these phenomena from the old feminism is the underlying *assumption* of equality. A generation ago, feminists had to work to establish that assumption. Now, phrases like "run with the boys" are passé not because women have achieved all we plan or need to—we haven't—but because competing with "the boys" is not the main concern. The point is the achievement, whatever that may be. In the realm of sports, this means that women's teams and athleticism are no longer considered just curiosities or pale copies of men's sports. Instead, they are intrinsically worthy as examples of the pursuit of excellence in the context of intense competition.

In sports medicine, researchers and clinicians are responding to the growth in women's athletics by studying gender-related differences in injury rates and examining positive and negative aspects of physical activity and health in women, such as osteoporosis prevention and the female athlete triad. A number of such developments are reflected in this issue'.

If anyone could doubt today that sport is entwined essentially with health as well as education, the emancipation from the days of Emily Davidson's self sacrifice is irrefutable evidence in rebuttal. Nevertheless, while the English Football and the fans have welcomed Wendy Toms and her women colleagues to officiate in public competitive games, the male dominated Professional Footballers Association refused the only registered women's FIFA agent Rachel Manderson to seek the Central London Courts adjudication and a £2,500 damages award and costs on the basis that she had been the victim of unlawful discrimination contrary to the Sex Discrimination Act 1975 when barred because of gender from their Annual Dinner Awards. For as Domhnall Macauley has written in his Editorial for the *British Journal of Sports Medicine* 1999 August vol 33: No 4, page 225

'Competitive sport evolved in the mid-Victorian era when men were men and women stayed at home. Sport was designed for men, and the nature of most sports reflects predominantly male traits of strength, size, and shape. Indeed, many sports evolved from the celebration of the physical attributes of the successful soldier in battle. But, while the world has changed, sport has remained in times past and although we see increasing opportunities for women in sport, these simply reflect extensions of male sport rather than the introduction of sport to which women would be particularly suited. The rules, regulations, and values of sport thus remain rooted in a different era and can cause conflict between our idealised female role model and the demands of top sport'.

Thus during a House of Lords debate on Sport and Active Recreation on 24 April 1991 Baroness Hollis of Heigham told the House of Lords

'Baron Pierre de Coubertin — the founder of modern Olympics — fought all his life to exclude women from sport. I understand that Mrs Pankhurst threatened to disrupt the 1908 London Olympics in the same inimitable and intimidating fashion in which she was interrupting the political meetings of Lloyd George and Churchill in order to get women admitted to the sports of tennis, archery and skating in those Olympics'.

She was able to tell the House, however, that

'By 1988 in Seoul, one-third of the competitors were women but they are still excluded from the triple jump, judo, the pentathlon and the pole vault; yet women have climbed Mount Everest and regularly beat men in marathon races'.

By 1990 the percentage of women over the age of 16 participating in sport (excluding walking) had increased from 52% in 1987 to 57%. This compared with an increase in men's participation from 70% to 73% in the same period. Furthermore, women's participation in indoor sports has increased faster than men's and the gap between them was marginally closed.

Inevitably, therefore, there are certain outstanding legal issues which affect women in sport. These include sex discrimination which manifests itself in many different forms, including whether men who had undergone a sex change can ever be classed as a woman in a sporting context, and the use or effect of the contraceptive pill within sport. The interaction and interrelation with health issues is inevitable as the frontiers of chemical and pharmacological research are pushed forward with athletic acceleration and the special edition on "*Women in Sport*" of The *British Journal of Sports Medicine* [August 1999 vol 33, no 4] contained an in-depth *clinical* seven pages assessment of the effects of the oral contraceptive pill (OCP) on skeletal health, soft tissue injury and performance in female athletes, without commenting on the potential legal issues flowing from them yet the manner in which those frontiers have been re-defined is landmarked for sport and society in well-known precedents, to be detailed further below, which have reached the courts on both sides of the Atlantic. In 1977 Dr Renee Richards, the guide, philosopher, friend and intermittent coach over many years to the Wimbledon champion Martina Navratilova, was obliged to obtain injunction relief in New York against the United States tennis authorities. She succeeded in preventing their reliance on a sex-chromatin test for determining that she was a female after surgical sex-change treatment before which she had been Dr Richard Rasskind, a New York opthalmic surgeon. In 1960, London's High Court was required to adjudicate on a similar medico-legal phenomenon in a non-sporting context in *Corbett v*

Corbett (ors Ashley) ([1970] 2 All ER 33) and it is now public knowledge how, unknown to many outside family circles, a distinguished writer (around that latter period), James Morris, underwent similar surgery to become Jan Morris.

Concurrent with these medical revolutions there has emerged in recent years the climax to a social revolution which can be traced generally to John Stuart Mill's celebrated essay on the *Subjection of Women*, written in 1861 and published in 1869. It involves many issues embracing women's rights within sport and the law. Emily Wilding Davison's fatal collision with His Majesty King George V's horse, Amner, at Tattenham Corner during the Derby Stakes at Epsom in 1913; Florence Nagle's High Court triumph over Jockey Club intransigence and chauvinism in the Court of Appeal during 1966; and the Parliamentary sex equality legislation of 1970 and 1975 which flowed directly from Britain's entry into the Common Market pursuant to the European Communities Act 1972, and the consequential commitments under the Treaty of Rome.

All this is a far cry from the days when Mrs Martha Grace at Downend, near Bristol, bowled her three sons, E M, G F, and W G Grace, to cricketing immortality in the mid-1850s. Sex-chromatin tests and Parliamentary legislation for eligibility to play games would hardly have been contemplated as necessary. Nearly a century later in the days before the Second World War they would have been equally regarded as fanciful when Mrs Selina Blanchflower captained Belfast Ladies soccer team, while her two sons, Robert Daniel, and Jackie, at their mother's knee, learned the skills which projected both into soccer's history books with Northern Ireland's World Cup soccer teams and club triumphs respectively with Tottenham Hotspur and Manchester United in the later 1950s and early 1960s.

Furthermore, Barbara Cartland, in her foreword to the biography of the mother of Jackie Blanchflower's Manchester United colleague, Bobby Charlton, 'Cissie', explained how they owed as much to their mother's influence and encouragement as to their own undoubted talents.

Significantly one of the unexpected and unanticipated yet most welcome surprises from the development of women in sport has been the contrast in examples between women and men at the public entertainment level. It is universally recognised that the standards of behaviour by women in the sporting field surpasses that of men. How many women can the reader name who have smashed their tennis rackets down on the grass at Wimbledon in temper, sworn at the umpire and/or crowd in sheer frustration or provided such a poor example of behaviour that a parent would not wish his or her child to attend the world's greatest tennis tournament to see them play?

Yet a mere twenty-five years after the Blanchflower brothers' Celtic glories from over the water, sex legislation from Britain's Parliament had become essential. It was used most emphatically to expose and compensate for proven sexual discrimination within the crucial sporting area of Physical Education at the other source of Britain's Celtic pride, over the borders in Scotland.

An Industrial Tribunal, sitting in Glasgow during three January days in 1986 adjudicated on its reserved judgment dated 28 February 1986 in an unreported decision under the Sex Discrimination Act 1975 in *Miller v Strathclyde Regional Council* (Case No S/2582/85). It held,

(1) unanimously that the respondent Council had unlawfully discriminated against a superbly professional and experienced qualified applicant by not placing her on the short list of candidates to be interviewed for the position of Principal Teacher of Physical Education at Grange Academy, Kilmarnock; for which the Tribunal found it just and equitable to award the applicant the sum of £1,000 as compensation for injury to her feelings, and

(2) by a 2–1 majority, that the respondent Council had further discriminated against the applicant on the ground of her sex by not appointing her to that post; and, as compensation for her loss of earnings as a result of not being appointed to the promoted post, an additional £1,600 was ordered to be paid by the Council.

The total compensatory award was £2,600.

The full reasons for the Tribunal's verdict and awards comprise fifteen single line spaced typescript sheets. They included the following significant conclusions for the future of sporting administration excellence and physical education in the United Kingdom (Transcript pages 14 and 15),

'Having considered all of the evidence the Tribunal had no hesitation in holding that the reason why the applicant was not put on the short list to be interviewed for the post of Principal Teacher of Physical Education at Grange Academy was because of her sex. There was no doubt in the mind of the Tribunal that the applicant's qualifications and breadth of experience and range of interests were greater than any other candidate on the list of candidates and that she should have been on the short list';

and;

'The majority of the Tribunal in this case ... take the unusual view after careful thought, that the applicant would have been appointed to the post had it not been for the sex discrimination'.

Within the sporting sphere, separate and apart from the wider social implications generally, the full impact and value of these verdicts cannot be overstressed. Indeed, the important Final Report of the Recreation

Management Training Committee published in 1984 by the Department of the Environment included in its Recommendation for 'the establishment of a single professional institution for leisure managers' (paragraph 7.41 at page 98), amongst its specific proposals that 'The institute should appoint an education committee', and additionally,

'The education committee should include in its membership representatives from the education field who are familiar with academic requirements' (Paragraph 7.43 at page 98).

Furthermore, the Government's Response to the House of Commons Environment Committee noted 'an imbalance between men and women on the Sports Council will be borne in mind when future appointments are made' (1986: No 504).

The consequences of unlawful sexual discrimination to circumscribe the scope for implementing such an important recommendation are self-evident. At a time when sporting prowess, physical fitness and communal health are matters of acute national concern and interest, these disclosures from a country with such great sporting pride and traditions as Scotland inherits, should alert all who profess an association with the national future in these areas of the hidden traps and dangers which may lurk undetected. This concealment would have continued but for the legal power granted by Parliament under the impetus of the Common Market and its Treaty of Rome. How this came about is a further mixture of social, economic and legal history which intertwine in clearly definable strands.

2   UNITED KINGDOM SEX DISCRIMINATION LAW GENERALLY

How the present law emerged and what it means today are summarised with Lord Denning's customary conciseness in *The Due Process of Law* (1979) at page 245, thus:

'... there is growing apace the move for equality. We have the Equal Pay Act 1970 and the Sex Discrimination Act 1975. These were the direct result of our joining the Common Market. They were passed so as to fulfil our obligations under the Treaty of Rome. Whenever a woman does work of equal value to a man, she is entitled to pay equal to his. Whenever there is a job which she can do — she is entitled to apply for it and to get it on equal terms with a man. There must be no discrimination against her because she is a woman. Likewise there must be no discrimination against a man because he is a man. This was invoked when a bachelor Mr Jeremiah claimed that he was put on to dirty work when the women were not. I said in *Jeremiah v Ministry of Defence*: [19 October 1979: ultimately reported in [1979] 3 All ER 833 at 836]

"Equality is the order of the day. In both directions. For both sexes.
What is sauce for the goose is sauce for the gander'".

Clearly the complex ingredients which comprise the sporting sauces inevitably create a pot-pourri of issues and elements which are still taking shape within the pressure cookers of a rapidly changing society. The legal starting point today, however, must be the Common Market, and the Treaty of Rome to which the United Kingdom became inextricably tied by the European Communities Act 1972.

It was established as the European Economic Community (EEC) on 25 March 1957. In turn it had evolved from the European Coal and Steel Community (ECSC) first announced publicly in Paris on 9 May 1950, by Robert Schuman, the French Foreign Minister. Three years earlier in 1947 *The Character of England* had been published under the editorship of Sir Ernest Barker, Oxford University's Professor of Political Philosophy. In a chapter entitled 'Homes and Habits', the fashion historian James Laver explained: 'Women are now emancipated to a degree which would have frightened the pioneers of Feminism' (page 479). Yet nearly forty years later, *Miller v Strathclyde Regional Council* demonstrated the limits to that emancipation during the last decade and a half of the twentieth century. How they exist within the *sporting* legal framework is as always a mixture of statutory and judicial interpretation; and on this occasion they form a legacy of pioneering sacrifices and spirited independence and creativity which should never be forgotten; illustrated representatively by Emily Wilding Davison before the First World War, Florence Nagle after the Second World War, and Mrs Margaret Stack and her daughter Prunella Stack, and Phyllis Colson, between the two World Wars.

3   PIONEERING WOMEN IN SPORT AND THE LAW

Emily Wilding Davison may mean little to many of the modern generation. Eighty odd years ago she merited a near state funeral when her coffin travelled to its last resting place in Morpeth, Northumberland, after her death in Epsom General Hospital on Sunday 8 June 1913. At the Derby Stakes four days earlier on the traditional Wednesday afternoon she broke away from the crowd and ducked under the double rails at Tattenham Corner, running onto the racecourse as the horses raced down upon her. She dodged under the head of Agadir, ridden by a skilled jockey (and future trainer), Walter Earl, and threw up her hands to grab deliberately the horse owned by H M King George V, Amner. It turned a complete somersault, falling upon and injuring seriously its jockey, Herbert Jones. (Four years earlier for its owner's father, King Edward VII, Jones had won the race on Minoru.) Emily Wilding Davison died four days later on 8 June

1913 from the injuries she received without recovering consciousness. Until she died the local police, who had arranged for her urgent arrival at the hospital, were considering her legal responsibilities.

At the Epsom coroner's inquest on Tuesday 10 June 1913, the jury returned a verdict that her death was caused by a fracture of the base of the skull, being accidentally knocked down by a horse through wilfully running on to the course during the progress of the race. The coroner recorded a verdict of death by misadventure.

Dame Christabelle Pankhurst, as already cited at page 325 above, one of the leading militant suffragettes has recorded in her memoirs *Unshackled: The Story of How we Won the Vote* (edited by the Rt Hon Lord Pethick-Lawrence in 1959),

'Emily Davison paid with her life by making the whole world understand that women were in earnest for the vote. Probably in no other way and no other time could she so effectually have brought the concentrated attention of millions to bear upon the cause'.

If a similar action were to occur before the television cameras in 1999 no spark of imagination can contemplate its impact. Retrospectively what happened in 1913 was clearly explosive.

Five years later with a post-war General Election in focus, Lloyd George's Government ended a 50-year campaign with the right to vote, for women over 30, enshrined in the Representation of the People Act 1918, and the right to become an MP under the Parliament (Qualification of Women) Act 1918. A year later the Sex Disqualification Removal Act 1919 unlocked universally all university and legal professional doors until then barred to women, to complete a legislative hat-trick which Emily Davison's supreme sacrifice undoubtedly precipitated. (Many women, and perhaps men, too, would not understand the true significance of sport in not only men's and boy's lives, but also the national psyche. They may not realise how much the women's liberation movements' inheritance today from the suffragette campaigners for social and economic emancipation owes to Emily Wilding Davison's awareness of the vital impact which sport can have in changing the law.) Those three statutes are a permanent memorial to the use she made of sport so dramatically, and tragically, and, indeed, unlawfully, for law reform and accelerating the march of history.

During the 1930s at a time of national unease and an awareness of the gap in the nation's physical culture structure, acknowledged by Parliament through the Physical Recreation and Training Act 1937, already explained in Chapter 2, *Progressive perspective*, three women left indelible footsteps in the sands of time with their visionary administrative creation. In 1935 Prunella Stack developed to a national stage, as a preamble to the

Government legislation two years later, the foundation laid five years earlier by her mother, Mrs Mary Bagot Stack, the Women's League of Heath and Beauty; and in that same Silver Jubilee Year of the reign of King George V and Queen Mary, a physical education teacher, Phyllis Colson, single-mindedly conceived the idea of a nationally coordinated 'umbrella' of sporting governing body organisations. Thus in 1935 was born the Central Council of Physical Recreation, whose crucial role as a forum for Britain's sporting governing bodies and for initiating vital projects and campaigns in the national interest has already been outlined in Chapter 2, *Progressive perspective*.

The Second World War's absorption of women into every level of service and social life shattered any obstacles to recognising their capacity to cope with almost any role to challenge their talents. Women's rights campaigns which followed it concerned themselves with wider targets than sporting fields. Yet the racing world once more set the scene for a happier, but no less significant, breakthrough than that provided by Derby Day 1913, half-a-century later in 1966.

Florence Nagle had trained racehorses for many years before the mid-1960s in southern England. The limitations and fiction imposed by the Jockey Club's monopoly over controlling British horse racing caused licences to be granted to women trainers through their 'head lad' (often a man of middle age). Chapter 11, below, *Fair, play and reason in court*, explains how she was able, with her advisers, to avoid the *procedural* hurdles found before the Master in Chambers and single Judge on appeal, when the Court of Appeal comprising Lord Denning MR, Danckwerts and Salmon LJJ, gave her an uninterrupted ride (by reversing the orders of the earlier decisions, from which she had appealed). The Master and Judge had struck out her Statement of Claim which contained a declaration and injunction reliefs for the grant to her personally of a trainer's licence. The appeal court judgments which gave her leave to proceed with her claim extended the procedural issues of permission to carry on with her action into a landmark decision concerning the right to work, for all genders and for all generations. One often forgotten consequence from it appeared in 1983 when Mrs Jenny Pitman, in her own name, was able to train Corbière to win the Grand National as the first-ever woman trainer's triumph in that great event. Another consequence was the election of women members to the Jockey Club and the male bastions were further breached when the Jockey Club amended its Rules of Racing to accept women jockeys officially, or as they are now known, jockettes.

Four years later Parliament enacted the first stage of its anti-sex discriminatory legislation to bring Britain into line with Article 119 of the Treaty of Rome via the Equal Pay Act 1970. Thus the scene was set for the ultimate legislative confirmation with the Sex Discrimination Act 1975.

4   PARLIAMENTARY INTERVENTION

In a Court of Appeal decision, *Shields v E Coomes (Holdings) Ltd* [1979] 1 All ER 456, which must be explained more particularly in its correct chronological context below, Lord Denning illuminated the interlocking complexities of this new dimensional legislation thus at page 463:

> 'The English statutes are plainly designed so as to implement the EEC Treaty and the directives issued by the Council. They are the Sex Discrimination Act 1975, to which is scheduled the Equal Pay Act 1970, as amended. All came into force on 29 December 1975. They must all be taken together. But the task of construing them is like fitting together a jig-saw puzzle. The pieces are all jumbled up together, in two boxes. One is labelled the Sex Discrimination Act 1975; the other, the Equal Pay Act 1970. You pick up a piece from one box and try to fit it in, it does not. So you try a piece from the other box. That does not fit either. In despair you take a look at the picture by the makers. It is the guide issued by the Home Office. Counsel on behalf of the Equal Opportunities Commission recommended especially para 3.18, which he says will show the distinction between the two Acts. Even that will not make you jump with joy. You will not find the missing pieces unless you are very discriminating'.

In considering selective discrimination within the present perspective of Women in Sport and the Law, it is sufficient to direct attention here to Article 119 of the Treaty of Rome [now Article 141 of the Treaty of Amsterdam]; the preludes to British Parliamentary legislation, and how the statutes generally and specifically control the present legal structure.

Article 119 [141] has been described as dealing with two issues:

> 'First it places an obligation on member states to do certain things with regard to equal pay. Second it tries to define what equal pay actually means. On both counts the wording of Article 119 and its implication have aroused controversy'.

This controversy has not been directly concerned with sport. Indeed, only one particular section from this network of enactments, namely section 44 of the Sex Discrimination Act 1975, specifically identifies sport; but the philosophy and interaction behind the various legislative pieces must be recognised for any attempted understanding of them.

The full text of Article 119 [141] reads as follows:

> 'Each member state shall during the first stage ensure and subsequently maintain the application of the principle that men and women should receive equal pay for equal work.

For the purpose of this article, "pay" means that ordinary basic or minimum wage or salary and any other consideration whether in cash or in kind which the worker receives, directly or indirectly, in respect of his employment from his employer.

Equal pay without discrimination based on sex means:

(a) that pay for the same work at piece rates shall be calculated on the basis of the same unit of measurement.

(b) that pay for the same work at time rates shall be the same for the same job'.

When the then Home Secretary, Mr Roy Jenkins, introduced the legislation at the Second Reading in the House of Commons, he explained,

'Nothing in Part 1 itself makes a discrimination unlawful ... It is only where a person discriminates in a situation dealt with subsequently in the Bill that discrimination is unlawful'.

Thus sex discrimination per se is not unlawful. What creates actionable consequences is discrimination in a welter of identifiable situations which may be conveniently categorised for the present limited purpose under the following headings set out in the statutory arrangement of sections at the commencement of the Sex Discrimination Act 1975:

(1) Employment
(2) Specified bodies such as trade unions, and various agencies
(3) Education
(4) Goods, facilities, services and premises
(5) Special conditions or arrangements and advertisements.

Employment including pay disputes under the Equal Pay Act are heard by industrial tribunals, with a right of appeal to an employment Appeal Tribunal. All others are tried in county courts with appeals to the Court of Appeal.

Section 44 of the Sex Discrimination Act as mentioned above contains the sole section identifying sport in a very limited manner. It comes within Part V of the Act under a general heading alongside other categories including charities, insurance and other circumstances nominated as 'General Exceptions from Parts II to IV' (ie those covering employment, education and other unlawful discriminatory areas). It stated thus:

'Nothing in Parts II to IV shall, in relation to any sport, game or other activity of a competitive nature where the physical strength, stamina or physique of the average woman puts her at a disadvantage to the average man, render unlawful any act related to the participation of a person as a competitor in events involving that activity which are confirmed to competitors of one sex'.

The key concepts here, of course, are the antithesis between 'the average woman' and 'the average man', and also 'competitors'. Both have been considered in the reported decisions of the tribunals and the courts. Both will doubtless have to be considered again. In a survey of the first decade's operation of the legislation from its inception on 31 December 1975 in *The Financial Times*, 3 January 1986, Lady Howe, the Equal Opportunity Commission's first deputy Chairman wrote,'

'The legislation was neither perfect nor comprehensive'.

No reference was made to section 44. If it had been, the comment would have been justified that the first decade reflects an exploratory experience with a stop-go pattern. The reported cases illustrate a gradual move towards its beneficial application to sportswomen with the inevitable hiccups en route. Furthermore, a valuable survey by Dr Alice M Leonard for the Equal Opportunities Commission of the *First Eight Years* (1976–1983) (summarised in the *New Law Journal* 31 January 1986) of the tribunal referrals identifies in its fuller text sport alongside 'Literary, artistic' in the applicants' occupations for claims under both the 1970 and the 1975 Acts; and for men as well as women only 1% of those who utilised the legislation are logged under these three comprehensive categories.

With such scant material no definable pattern can yet be traced; but the recorded cases in the various reported sources manifest a tentative approach bedevilled by the unrealistic delineation between 'the average woman' and 'the average man'. Women no less than men in sport demonstrate talents and qualities well above average which the slightest reflection can easily recognise. Indeed, this Parliamentary injection into sex legislation of the commercial shipping language of averaging suggests that the draftsman of the section and Parliament not only did not understand women in sport but could not have understood the above average skills which are the hallmark of true athleticism. A grandstand survey of some of these skills among women will explain and emphasise the point.

5   ABOVE AVERAGE GRANDSTAND VIEW

No legislation or litigation was ever needed for an adoring tennis public to share and enjoy the qualities demonstrated before, between and then after two World Wars. First through the Mesdames Lottie Dodd, Suzanne Lenglen, Helen Wills Moody, Betty Nuthall, Dorothy Round and Kay Stammers until the outbreak of the Second World War. Then after it, with the more publicly exposed televised performers such as Maureen Connolly, Louise Brought, Christine Evert, Ann Jones, Virginia Wade, Martina

Navratilova, Steffi Graff, Monica Seles, and more recently Martina Hingis.

Likewise, the athletics world and a wider public rejoiced at the Olympic triumph of the Dutch housewife and mother, Fanny Blankers-Koen, who won four Gold medals at London's Wembley Stadium in 1948, Northern Ireland's Mary Peters' victory in 1972, and Fatima Whitbread's 1987 success. Many will also recall how, before the Second World War, Marjorie Pollard followed masculine footsteps to represent England's women cricket and hockey elevens before writing regularly for the *News Chronicle*, a tradition carried on more recently by Rachel Heyhoe Flint with cricket and the *Sunday Telegraph*. When England's lady cricketers won the Ladies World Cup Final at Lord's in 1993, the trophy was presented on the grass outfield as ladies were then still excluded from certain areas of the Lord's pavilion: an echo of 30 years earlier when the Indian golf champion 'Papwa' Sewsunker Sewgolum won the Durban Open golf championship and received his prizes outside in the pouring rain while his white competitors watched inside.

Laura Davies today follows a tradition when ladies' golf produced its inter-war years champions who played mixed foursomes on equal terms with their men golfing partners: Diana Fishwick and Joyce Wethered come readily to mind. After the Second World War Jeanne Bisgood became England's Ladies' Golf Champion while practising as a barrister from the Lincoln's Inn Chambers at 5 New Square, where she was succeeded as a tenant in the sport of practising tax law by Margaret Hilda Thatcher.

Amy Johnson flew into airspace and international public imagination before disappearing over the Thames Estuary on war service. Many differing generations will know how Sonia Henje, Jacqueline du Bíef and Esther Williams respectively skated and swam from their particular sporting disciplines into wider audiences at the cinema.

On horseback the women (and their horses, too) have produced their own fan clubs. From Pat Smythe and her Olympic and European successes on Flanagan to Virginia Leng, Lucinda Green and The Princess Royal as eventers, with The Princess Royal actively effective as a winning jockey and President of the British Olympic Association. Furthermore, Alison Dean's devotion in looking after the record-breaking classic colt, Reference Point, throughout his career, leading to the racecourse in triumphs in 1987, was a crucial factor in the superb teamwork organised at Henry Cecil's training stables at Warren Place, Newmarket. Also within the Olympic setting, women's fencing was the springboard from which Mary Glen Haig was elected to succeed the late Lord Burghley, Marquess of Exeter, to the much coveted position of one of Britain's two members on the International Olympic Committee.

Such examples as these can be multiplied by any sporting afficionado. (Apologies are extended herewith to all other ladies omitted solely for reasons of space. Each one mentioned, and so many others who merited inclusion, illustrate the antithesis between their own achievements and 'the average woman'.)

6 JUDICIAL INTERVENTION

What is the 'average woman' and what is the 'average man' in *this* context has yet to be fully investigated by the courts. A tentative approach to it was made in the unreported decision of the Court of Appeal which was concerned with whether or not a 12-year-old schoolgirl was discriminated against playing football with boys of her own age (see *Bennett v The Football Association Ltd and The Nottinghamshire FA* Court of Appeal transcript: No 591 of 1978). Tentative, because the issue and evidence called before the county court and accepted in the Court of Appeal was directed towards comparing and differentiating medically between boys and girls of 12 years of age, below and above the age of puberty. The conclusion was that the circumstances of the case proved existence of a disadvantage (the Act being silent on age levels).

The playing merits do not appear to have been argued of the 12-year-old plaintiff-contender for a place in the boys' team for which she had been selected. Yet Lord Denning (at page 2 of the transcript: No 591 of 1978) said 'She ran rings around the boys'; and a witness as recorded in the *Daily Telegraph* report of the county court hearing said she was 'a vicious tackler and once tackled a 15-year-old so hard he had to be supported and taken from the field'. This pointed, of course, to this particular plaintiff not being put 'at a disadvantage, to the average boy'! Concentrating on what appeared to be a diversion in evidence from doctors about puberty, and without apparent arguments on above average skills, the Court of Appeal overruled the Deputy County Court Judge who had adjudicated and awarded £250 in favour of the 12-year-old 'vicious tackler' of a '15-year-old'. The trial judge had held that prior to puberty there is little difference in stamina between males and females and therefore the exception under section 44 did not apply. The Court of Appeal reversed this particular decision saying that 'woman' for the purposes of the Act was defined as a female of any age.

Two years later in *Greater London Council v Farrer* ([1980] ICR 266), the Employment Appeal tribunal at page 272 C–D per Slynn J said, of *Bennett's* case,

'we read the decision of the Court of Appeal as applying to the particular facts before it'.

Certainly the imbalance between the medical evidence concerned with puberty and the apparent absence of argument on the evidence tending to prove the existence of above average athletic talents which did not disadvantage the female plaintiff leave this decision without any general guidance for further disputes in the manner stated above. Any schoolgirl footballers not caught through average talents by the exclusion clause in section 44 can at least consider their chances on different evidence and arguments of a replay. Furthermore, the Football Association have modified their restrictions and emulated the Jockey Club by admitting to its Council a representative of the Women's Football Association, and with women refereeing on the field, even the FA here has moved with the times.

More generally, the Employment Appeal Tribunal in *GLC v Farrer* said of section 44 at page 272 C–D:

> 'it seems to us that this section is dealing with a situation in which men and women might both be playing in the same game or taking part in the same event. It is in that situation that the disadvantage of the woman because of physical strength, stamina or physique would become a relevant matter. It does not seem to us that this section is dealing with the situation where it is desired that a girl should play a game against a girl, or where teams of girls are to play teams of girls'.

Indeed, the circumstances of that particular case threw up the relevance of a specifically exempting section within the Sex Discrimination Act 1975. Section 51(1) exonerates any acts done under a statutory authority passed before the 1975 legislation. This applied to the London Government Act 1963. Schedule 12 of the Act created a right to impose restrictions on wrestling licences. It was invoked to prohibit women's wrestling. An industrial tribunal allowed an appeal by a woman wrestler, who was equipped physically and professionally to be licensed, against a promoter's rejection of her services because of the 1963 prohibition. The Employment Appeal Tribunal reversed the industrial tribunal.

Practical realities were the reason for the Amateur Swimming Association's rejection of the Oxford University woman waterpolo coach to play in the annual inter-Varsity men's match with Cambridge University. The precedent created by Sue Brown who coxed the Oxford University crew in the annual Boat Race was the basis of the claim for that plea. Rowing, of course, is a non-body contact sport. Waterpolo is not. Those who have experienced its rigours will respect and understand the reasons for discrimination against the Oxford University female coach:

> 'Waterpolo is a physical contact sport and Fiona [the coach] is involved in hard tackling. It's like Rugby in a pool'.

(See *The Daily Telegraph*: 4 March 1983.)

This may be contrasted with the selection by Oxford University in 1986 of another Fiona, Macdonald. She became the first woman to gain a golfing Blue. The only surprise in this example is that it has taken so long for this award to arrive (although the traditional competition for academic honours with the men has perhaps traditionally concentrated attention on the University's Schools comparisons rather than those at Iffley Road and Oxford's other games playing areas).

A more clear-cut pattern of decisions unfolded under the Sex Discrimination Act 1975 which did not involve the concept of the average woman in arriving at decisions.

In 1977 the first fully reported decision in this subject area concerned, appropriately, a professional solicitor sufficiently skilled to apply for a post as woman golf professional. The applicant armed with this double qualification failed to prove before an industrial tribunal, and on appeal to an Employment Appeal Tribunal, that a local authority had disregarded her professional golfing qualifications in competition with male applications for a local council coaching post.

Both Tribunals considered as an issue of fact and thereby concluded that no discrimination had existed when rejecting contentions that

(1)   certain interview questions
      and
(2)   confusion about interview arrangements for an appointment she was
      unable to attend

were discriminatory on the grounds of her sex (*V Saunders v Richmond-upon-Thames BC* [1977] IRLR, Vol 6, 362).

Also in 1977, however, a 22-year-old snooker player did satisfy a Sheffield County Court judge that a publican discriminated unlawfully against her sex when he refused to allow women in his premises to play snooker because

(1)   too many wanted to do so
      and
(2)   women ripped the snooker table cloths (*Rice v Chatteron* (1977) *Times*,
      29 June). She obtained a nominal damages award of £10 and costs.

Two years later a similar result was achieved in Belfast under comparable Northern Ireland legislation on appeal from a county court judgment to the High Court. The Belfast YWCA banned young women from its snooker tables because of

(1)   alleged inexperience with snooker cues and consideration that they
      would be more likely than young men to make a tear in the cloths of
      the snooker tables, which were very costly to repair, and

(2)   talking and laughing to disturb the necessary silence for concentrating by other players.

One of the arguments justifying the discrimination by the Belfast YWCA was that private membership excluded the discriminatory legislation. The established facts proved that the snooker room and its facilities were open to temporary membership with no more selection requirements than an acceptable standard of behaviour and witness to enter the premises, as distinct from the more usual exclusivity created by club memberships. Notwithstanding prima facie sound reasons for the discrimination, it was held unlawfully in breach of Article 30 of the Sex Discrimination (No 1) Order 1976 which reflected the 1975 Act. Nominal damages of £25 and costs resulted (*Bateson v Belfast YWCA* (1980) NI 135).

Sandwiched between these two legal snooker table victories, for complainants about discrimination against playing that particular game, were Theresa Bennett's FA tackle and also the peripheral but sportingly connected decision of the Employment Appeal Tribunal and Court of Appeal concerning equal pay for a woman among many men counterhands in betting shops, already cited for general principles above (*Shields v E Coomes (Holdings) Ltd* [1979] 1 All ER 456). A claim for equal pay was rejected by a 2–1 majority of an industrial tribunal on the basis that differences of quality of work-loadings justified the inequality of which complaint was made. Particularly significant was that in troublesome areas the man counterhand worked longer hours in a protective role. The Employment Appeal Tribunal allowed an appeal by the woman complainant. When the respondent company appealed to the Court of Appeal it failed to obtain a reversal to the original tribunal's finding. The variation in pay was held to be discriminatory and not due to a material difference other than difference of sex, which would have justified the distinction within section 1(3) of the Equal Pay Act 1970. As Bridge LJ concluded at page 473:

'if the company had employed persons specially trained as security guards who were recruited from either sex [to operate the protective function], entirely different considerations would arise, but that is certainly not the case'.

The following year, 1979, witnessed one step forward and another step backwards for the battle by the woman wrestler Sue Brittain, in her married name of Marjorie Farrar, for a licence. It failed as explained above because of the pre-1975 escape clause section 51(1) which was properly operated by earlier legislation in 1963 (*Greater London Council v Farrar* [1980] ICR 266).

In 1980 and 1981 the breakthrough arrived with Mrs Belinda Petty, an experienced judo referee. She took on the British Judo Association at another industrial tribunal after she was banned from refereeing the All-England's *men's* contest, although still allowed to referee all-male club and area events and the *women's national* event.

The Association claimed, inter alia, that women did not have the strength to separate two hefty male fighters, and even arranged a demonstration as part of its evidence at the tribunal hearing to try to prove this. Indeed, one of the demonstrators said in testifying: 'I wouldn't feel happy on the mat with a woman refereeing. I think I would find the physical aspects of a woman controlling two hefty men on the mat a little degrading'. The tribunal rejected this and other arguments as an unlawful discrimination, and in October 1980 ruled that Mrs Petty's qualifications should be considered on her merits. The Employment Appeal Tribunal confirmed this decision in June 1981, stressing that it failed to see how provisions for refereeing related to the participation of competitors.

The Employment Appeal Tribunal found in its judgment [1981] ICR 660 at pages 665–6 per Browne-Wilkinson J:

'It is common ground that judo is a sport in which men and women ought not to compete one with the other. Section 44 saves from being unlawful "any act related to the participation of a person as a competitor in that activity," ie judo. Mr Beloff submitted that the "act" referred to (ie preventing women from refereeing men's events) was "related to" the participation of men as competitors. He said that the words related to" were wide words — unnecessarily wide if all that was meant to be covered was a provision preventing competitors of both sexes from competing. In our view this is not correct. We cannot see how provisions as to referees relate to the "participation" of the competitors in the contest. They might, at a stretch, be said to relate to the sex of the competitors but not to those competitors' participation in the contest. We think that the words should be given their obvious meaning and not extended so as to cover any discrimination other than provisions designed to regulate who is to take part in the contest as a competitor. Any other construction would lead to great uncertainty: for example, would the section be extended to discrimination against the lady in the box office at a football ground? For these reasons we consider the decision of the industrial tribunal to be correct and we dismiss the appeal'.

Mrs Petty's successes in 1980 and 1981 were in effect the top score for sportswomen at half-time in the first decade which followed implementation of the 1975 Act. As the second decade got under way, at the time of writing the first edition during 1987, further developments were anticipated to occur to confirm the social revolution reflected in the exploding sporting scene.

In 1988 Sandra Priestley challenged the Social and Recreational Club (in *Priestly v Stork Margarine Social and Recreational Club*) at her place of work for operating an unwritten 'men only' rule in the snooker room.

She maintained that the club was not private and therefore could not be exempted under section 29 of the Sex Discrimination Act 1975 which relates to discrimination in the provision of goods, facilities or services. Her case was upheld in the Birkenhead County Court by HHGP Crowe, QC on 24 June 1988 (unreported) because the club did not have a selection procedure, and any employee of the company to which the club was linked was automatically qualified to join. Furthermore, in 1992 the Leeds Industrial Tribunal judged that Susan Thompson, a top amateur pool player, had been discriminated against on the grounds of her sex; and further, that she had been victimised in her rejection for membership by the Professional Pool Players Organisation (PPO). The tribunal observed that her rejection had been under 'the old pal's act' and that it seemed to be the case of the best woman player being regarded as good as the worst man (23 March 1992: unreported). In due course at the 1992 AGM of the PPO her application for membership was accepted.

The full fall-out from Mrs Miller's triumph over Strathclyde Regional Council (see paragraph above) has yet to be assessed, if the result itself has yet percolated through the various layers of inter-disciplinary sporting knowledge to those who would be expected to wish to know of it. For so far as the author is aware, above average sportswomen who compete professionally in the sporting market-place alongside men for lucrative commercial prizes, such as darts or in the eventing fields, have yet to chance their arms or risk their costs or those of the Equal Opportunities Commission before tribunals. Lady Howe's comment that 'The legislation was neither perfect nor comprehensive' can be extended with ever grater force to Women in Sport for its application. It may well be that the best is yet to come from these statutory innovations, stimulated by the global progress internationally spanning all generations.

Finally, attention to the social engineering of the EEC-inspired legislation should not divert attention from other equally important areas which can be overlooked for Women in Sport and the Law. One is a recent development at local club level, another is the conventional or standard legal scene: finally there is the impact of medicine and science.

7   WOMEN AND 'MALE' PRIVATE CLUBS

The Sex Discrimination Act 1975 effectively allows discrimination against women in private sporting clubs. Section 29 allows single sex clubs, or unequal membership rights in private clubs. Between 1976 and 1988 the Equal Opportunities Commission received some 2,000 complaints about the lower status and treatment of women members of private sports clubs. Private sports clubs such as some major golf clubs of national significance. The Marylebone Cricket Club in contentious and indeed acrimonious circumstances ultimately succumbed to considerable external pressures while others still insist on excluding women from their membership. In *Priestly v Stork Margarine Social and Recreational Club* (supra), Mrs Priestly succeeded in becoming a member of the snooker club at her place of work because the club was not private. Significantly some major golf clubs and the MCC are private clubs per se, but have a public role in society: indeed it has been said of them, 'a private role with a public face'. Time alone may decide when generally accepted social attitudes will permeate such old-established institutions and force them to admit women as members.

In 1993 a tangential decision affecting women's club membership rights took place when the West Kent Golf Club made a routine application for renewal of its liquor licence to the Club's bar under section 3(1) of the Licensing Act 1964. Local magistrates rejected the claim, which was affirmed on appeal in the Croydon Crown Court, because women were excluded from the bar. There is no binding precedent among lower court decisions, but as a persuasive weapon in the campaign for sporting and social equality among local clubs it could accelerate the pace comparable to the women's progress in track and field athletics (see *Daily Telegraph*, 25 May 1993, page 3). Since then, the threat of losing out on National Lottery grants has forced many clubs to lift restrictions on women members. These have included full voting rights, committee membership, unrestricted use of courses and access to the inner sanctums of club bars.

8   STANDARD LEGAL SCENE

The novelty of acclimatising to the new dimensions for women's rights within the sporting as well as wider social setting should not divert attention from the continued application of traditional legal remedies and liabilities with a sporting flavour. Nothing in the legislation considered above affects them in any way whatever. As if to emphasise this position during the latter half of the first decade of this new era, the following five court appearances have concerned women in sport within a mixture of commercial, criminal and family contexts.

Commercial

1   During 1982/3 a dispute between the Women's Professional Golf Association and its then executive director landed both in the High Court on injunction proceedings until settled out of court in a customary way (*Edwards v WPGA; APP Publicity Promotions Ltd v CM Walker and others* (1982) *Times/Daily Telegraph*, November).

Criminal

2   In 1985 a woman footballer who broke an opponent's jaw in a woman's friendly (sic!) match on May Day was convicted of assault and ordered to pay £250 compensation by Clacton Magistrates (*Baker v Bridger*, (1985) *Daily Express*, May)

3   1986 recorded from America, in circumstances which would have been treated similarly in the United Kingdom, namely a fight between two women jockeys. One bit the arm of another who then required a tetanus injection. The Stewards imposed a £30 fine for 'causing a disturbance in the jockey's quarters', a TV room (*Calder Race Course, Miami*, (1986) *Daily Express*, 1 July).

Family

4   1981 witnessed divorce proceedings which doubtless are repeatable. A wife petitioned effectively on the ground of her husband's unreasonable behaviour based upon an excessive obsession with cricket, both participatively and statistically (Wolverhampton Divorce Court: *Rowley v Rowley*, (1981) *Times/Daily Telegraph*, 26 August).

5   1987 saw 'Golf was his mistress' when a wife petitioned successfully in the High Court Family Division (*Lane v Lane*, (1987) *Daily Telegraph*, 4 June).

Therefore nothing in the recent legislation suspends or qualifies in any way whatsoever the operation of the general law applicable to women whether in sport or outside it. What the legislation has tried to do with varying degrees of success is to outlaw sexual discrimination in certain proscribed situations, with sport singled out together with other limited areas under section 44 of the Sex Discrimination Act. This is yet to have further judicial treatment. Treatment of a more recognisable kind is perhaps the most appropriate note on which to end this never-ending development of sport and the law.

9   MEDICAL INTERVENTION FOR WOMEN IN SPORT AND THE LAW

London's High Court in 1960 witnessed a then unique claim to annul a marriage because of a sex change operation, when medical evidence proved that the female party to the marriage had been born a man. In *Corbett v Corbett (ors Ashley)* [1970] 2 All ER 33 Mr (later Lord Justice) Ormrod, himself trained as a doctor before being called to the Bar, was asked to adjudicate on this then unprecedented condition. In acceding to it he held that the party who had undergone a sex change operation

'is not a woman for the purpose of marriage but is a biological male and has been since birth'.

As we have already seen at the outset of this chapter unknown to many outside family circles as a distinguished writer, too, around that period, James Morris, underwent similar surgery to become Jan Morris; and almost a decade later sport caught up with this new medical phenomenon in the year Parliament passed the Sex Discrimination Act during 1975. Dr Richard Rasskind, a New York opthalmic surgeon, and a skilled tennis player, received similar surgical treatment to become after the operation Dr Renee Richards. Inevitably, the question emerged: what were the tennis authorities going to do about it?

For the next two years Dr Renee Richards shunted between various US tennis tournaments which were sufficiently enlightened to accept her entries with the knowledge of her transsexuality. Those which were not either rejected her outright, or conditional upon chromosome tests being factually or conveniently satisfied. The world-wide International Tennis Federation invoked Olympic Games tests which the doctor was unable to satisfy. When the locally based tennis authorities also required such stringent limitations upon entry the New York jurisdiction was invoked. In an action against the United States Tennis Association, the US Open Tennis Championship Committee and the Women's Tennis Association Inc, during 1977, Dr Richards claimed relief as a professional tennis player who had undergone sex reassignment surgery which had allegedly changed her sex from male to female. She sued for a preliminary injunction against the organisations

(1) to prevent reliance on a sex-chromatin test for determination of whether she was female and thus
(2) to permit her participation in the Women's Division of the US Open tournament.

The legal foundation of the action was that the condition breached the anti-discriminatory code built into the New York State equal opportunities legislation. After hearing a battery of conflicting medical and tennis evidence, Judge Alfred M Ascione held

'when an individual such as plaintiff [sic], a successful physician, a husband and father, finds it necessary for his own mental sanity to undergo a sex reassignment, the unfounded fears and misconceptions of defendants [sic] must surely give way to the overwhelming medical evidence that the person before him is now female'.

Accordingly, a requirement that the Plaintiff pass the sex-chromatin test in order to be eligible to participate in the tournament was grossly unfair, discriminatory and inequitable, and violated the Plaintiff's rights under the New York Human Rights Law, and granted the injunctions (*Richards v US Tennis Assn & Ors* 1977: 400 NYS (2nd) 267).

Similar reliefs would have been available to Dr Richards at that time under British law if she had been subjected to similar conditions for a United Kingdom tournament. Not only could the Sex Discrimination Act 1975 have been invoked; as a result of the Court of Appeal's decision which acknowledged matrimonial sterilisation in *Bravery v Bravery* [1954] 3 All ER 59 (where a wife failed to obtain a cruelty degree because the majority of the court held that she had consented to her husband's vasectomy), Dr Richards could have argued that the condition to undergo a sex-chromatin test would comprise an incitement to commit or to attempt to commit a battery.

By the time Dr Richards arrived in Britain, however, she came with an entirely different professional tennis status; as coach and adviser to the future Wimbledon champion Martina Navratilova in 1977. This lasted for five years until Dr Richards retired from professional tennis and returned to her other profession, opthalmic surgery. By then, in 1982, English courts had begun to consider 'the average woman'.

Ten years later in April 1993, also from the USA *The Times* reported, 10 March 1993:

> 'A 16 year-old-girl who hopes to become an Olympic boxer is at the centre of a sex-discrimination lawsuit filed on Monday by the American Civil Liberties Union (ACLU). The lawsuit, filed in Seattle on behalf of Jennifer McCleery, claims she is being prevented from boxing violation of state anti-discrimination laws. She trains under the name Dallas Malloy. "Since I started boxing, I realized how much I love it," she said. "It's like any other sport to me and I feel it's my right to be able to compete with others." Kathleen Taylor, executive director of the ACLU of Washington, said the girl was only seeking the right to box against other women'.

In Britain the barriers have come down in this area: and while matters of taste dictate attitudes to women's involvement, the law has not been invoked to prevent it.

Finally, in a crucially important feature in the *Guardian* of 31 December 1993 under the headline *Women runners pay price of overwork*, Duncan Mackay reflected the most important issue for the future of *all* sport at the public entertainment level in relation to women in particular when he wrote with a sub-title 'on the growing casualty list of a crowded cross-country programme':

'Britain's selectors will be anxiously scanning the results of tomorrow's women's race in the County Durham international cross-country at Beamish for signs of fresh talent.

With the approach of the world cross-country championships in Budapest on March 26 they have seen the country's best runners falling faster than needles off a Christmas tree.

Liz McColgan, Andrea Wallace, Lisa York, Gillian Stacey, Suzanne Rigg and Hayley Haining are long-term victims of injury or illness and Andrea Whitcombe has been unable to handle the huge expectations of her after she twice won the English national senior title as a teenager. All would have been strong candidates for places in Budapest.

The most alarming aspect is the age of some of them: York is 23, Whitcome 22 and Stacey and Haining 21. In addition Sharon Murphy, who was 21st in the 1992 world junior cross-country championships as a 16-year-old, has not raced this winter because of illness. Paula Radcliffe and Jenny Clague, Britain's best young prospects, have also suffered from viruses and injuries and they are barely out of their teens.

Bud Baldaro, the national cross-country coach, is resigned. "I thought we would have a great team this year but now it is looking pretty thin", he admitted. His one consolation is that Jill Hunter, injured for the past year, should return.

Like Frank Dick, the national director of coaching, Baldaro believes that far too much stress is being imposed on runners expected to perform over country, track and road the year round. "Athletes are being pulled all over the place. If it is like this now, what is it going to be like in 1994 when the programme is even worse?"

The cross-country season has expanded rapidly in recent years with the introduction of an international Grand Prix circuit and next December, the first European championships.

The British Athletic Federation has not helped by adding events to the calendar. This season there are British and national championships and a separate UK world cross-country trial.

Baldaro is also concerned that there is still not enough medical back-up for elite athletes who break down. Fiona Truman, for example, was once Britain's best teenage runner and a member of the senior team that won silver medals in the 1988 world cross-country championships. But when she was injured she had to pay £1,000 for physiotherapy that was to no avail: her Achilles injury forced her to retire.

Britain's women distance runners are often trapped in a vicious circle. If they want to reach world class they need to run more than 100 training miles a week. But with sponsorship opportunities limited, especially for women — even McColgan found trouble finding a shoe contract before she won the 1991 world 10,000 metres title — they also have to race regularly to support themselves. This over-activity stretches their bodies to breaking point and increases the chances of injury or illness.

The recent gain in form of runners from China has heaped further pressure on the home runners. Many coaches in Britain find it hard to believe that the Chinese could handle the huge training loads they are reported to undertake — around 170 miles a week — without resorting to performance-enhancing drugs.

Leading athletes treat a thin line between training hard and over-training. Unfortunately for Britain, too many women are on the wrong side of it'.

10   CONCLUSIONS

In retrospect a number of illustrations of the artificiality of 'the average woman' and 'average man' concepts in this chapter cannot be ignored. All are fundamental and inconclusive, but must be recognised.

The law which has been considered here and throughout the book is essentially Anglo-Saxon for traditional common law and equity-orientated legal systems. Overseas and particularly totalitarian and all those countries with government-funded and supported sporting systems which approach sport with a different traditional and practical standpoint from that recognised throughout the United Kingdom and by the inheritors of its attitudes cannot be ignored. There is also a differential in their approach to women. Lightheartedly but nevertheless significantly it was treated with depth and subtlety by Peter Ustinov in his satire, *The Love of Four Colonels*. Produced in 1951 and reflecting the Four-Power occupation of Germany by Great Britain, France, Russia and the USA it portrayed with that author's customary perception the different national characteristics built in to the title. How far and to what extent comparable different national attitudes to Women in Sport and the Law will become relevant is an issue which must surface at some time in the future. Its form could well emerge in the final illustrations with which this chapter began.

Baron de Coubertin in his dogmatic male chauvinism cited by Baroness Hollis of Heigham, defined the modern Olympic Games as being

'The solemn and periodic exultation of male athleticism with internationalism as a base, loyalty as a means, not for its setting, and female applause as regard'.

The Olympic Charter still retains the words:

'No discrimination is allowed against any country or person on grounds of race, religion or politics'.

Notably, the word 'gender' has been omitted and it is indeed true that there is still discrimination against women within the Olympic movement. They are still excluded from many events, for example, ice-hockey, modern pentathlon, baseball, wrestling, waterpolo and some track and field events.

Football on the other hand is moving towards potential inclusion, with FIFA taking initiatives within the IOC to include women's football in the

Olympic movement. The inaugural Women's Football World Cup took place in England in 1991, England's women won the Women's Rugby Union World Championship (*Times*, 3 May 1994). FIFA are keen to encourage the women's game in order to achieve Olympic Games status and while these pages were being completed the USA and China attracted global media coverage for their women's World Cup Final in Pasadena's famous Rose Bowl Stadium.

Nevertheless, in spite of all the progress made administratively, legally, politically and socially it would be idle and indeed unrealistic to pretend that the last has been heard of developments for women in sport and the law and indeed women in sport and medicine. It is appropriate to conclude this chapter with the end of Domnhall Macauley's Editorial in the *British Journal of Sports Medicine* (supra) at page 224

'Sport and sports administrators are used to straight-forward principles that winners are first, results are the arbiter, and categories are determined by a test. The irony is that, although women may now compete with men in many sports, we must seek means to prevent men competing in women only sports. Now that athletes can have sex change operations and take appropriate hormones, sporting organisations have the difficulty of deciding who should compete in single sex category sports. This is not an easy decision and they must now arbitrate on complex issues of sex. Testing for sex is fraught with difficulty and we have seen the test change from a visual inspection to a clinical examination, and from identifying Barr bodies to formal chromosome analysis. We still have not found the solution. We may begin to wonder if a chromosome or outward appearance should define sporting category. If a man takes female hormones and has surgery to change his sexual characteristics is (s)he male or female? Similarly, if a woman takes male sex hormones, which change her body shape, how do we define his/her sex? Is sex really an issue of body or mind? What if a man feels he is from Venus and a woman from Mars? It all used to be so simple. Rats and snails and pupply dogs tails—the Y chromosome'.

Returning to my Preface and the law relating to sport is simple; on this occasion it is the gender and sex which make it difficult.

Finally, the active participation of women in boxing can now no longer be ignored. The 13th International Amateur Boxing Association (IABA) congress in Beijing in November 1993 sanctioned women boxing for participation in their international competitions. In May of that same year, three women were appointed to judge the heavyweight title fight between Riddick Bowe and Jesse Ferguson, namely Patricia Johnson, Sheila Holmon-Martin and Eugenie Williams; and in the United Kingdom Jane Couch, known as the 'Fleetwood Assassin', has established her licensed right to fight under the aegis of the British Boxing Board of Control.

PART III

International Sport

CHAPTER 9

International Interaction

1 INTRODUCTION

Three international cultures span the world: medicine, music and sport; and three different levels of comprehension and understanding know no boundaries in any land and any language. Sporting competition, medicine and music create a universal form of communication. Each has differing rules or forms of practice, but sport alone cannot exist in any structure without a rule book. The Rule of Law applies to sport around the world. By adapting the 113 activities listed in the Preface to an international stage, the never ending scope and scale for an international dimension to sport becomes self evident. International law for sport is gaining an ever-increasing importance and significance due to the impact of modern travel and television. Television viewers in the UK seem to be interested not only in watching the sides they support play abroad, but also television has opened up interest in many foreign sports which are either not played in the UK or played to a very limited extent. These sports include American football, Australian rules football, sumo wrestling and baseball.

Britain's practising lawyers in *general domestic practice* outside sport, burdened with clients' problems *need* not be troubled *generally* in their daily grind with issues of an international flavour. The lawyer and any man or woman involved *with sport today* cannot dare to ignore them, or at least be unaware of their potential applicability.

Air transport, satellite and cable television and the BBC World Service have shrunk the globe in a style comparable to the impact with which a century ago the road and rail networks facilitated the sports explosion in the United Kingdom shared by every other country experiencing similar developments. While trains spread their network and the populace for creation of new towns and sporting centres, William Clarke took his All

England Cricket XI to spread that game's gospel throughout the land. Professional football proliferated within the framework of the Football League, formed in 1888, the year in which Gladstone's Local Government Act created the earliest structured county boroughs, and horse race tracks were opened up to punters beyond local heaths and town moors. Now television brings the Sports Council's 'Sport for All' campaign to an international spectator and participatory level from stadia and arenas throughout the world.

Consistent with that development no one throughout the world concerned with whatever meaning can be given to sport is potentially unaffected by any one of the many areas which could be primed to adapt in a dramatic and effective fashion. Two current practical examples from within the United Kingdom come immediately to mind. One has an existing and immediate national Parliamentary source. The other has a potential litigation liability. Each can doubtless be multiplied around the world, but they suffice to illustrate the point which can apply to only one of the 30,920,000 participants functioning within and without the 421 National Sporting Governing Bodies identified by the Sports Council, now Sport - England. Beyond these two practical Parliamentary and potential litigation liability sources, which can touch the hem of anyone who activates their function, it is possible in a single chapter to select only arbitrarily certain areas which can attempt to demonstrate how the law can be shown a role to play in the interests of all who are concerned with the international sporting community. There can be many enigmatic or differently selected variations on this theme and I have chosen those which it is hoped will be recognised by anyone who would wish to be aware of how he or she can be affected by this uncharted global dimension.

2   INTERNATIONAL SPORT AND LAW GENERALLY

(1) Parliamentary
(2) Potential litigation liability

3   PUBLIC INTERNATIONAL LAW

Public legal issues which transcend that domestic law but could still be interlinked with it.

4   PRIVATE INTERNATIONAL LAW

Domestic sports related international issues soluble only by law transcending sport.

5   ADMINISTRATIVE SPORTING ACTION

Remedies for results when initiative action is required.

Inevitably there must be an overlap with areas as fluid as the state of play in a hard fought sporting contest. All that they can aim to achieve at this explosive period in sporting legal history is to alert readers to the areas which can be identified, for which no claim for exclusivity and comprehension is made, and then see how far they can be appropriate or identifiable or recognisable for each reader's particular interest.

2   INTERNATIONAL SPORT AND LAW GENERALLY

(1)   Parliamentary

The Football (Offences and Disorder) Act 1999 received the Royal Assent on 27 July 1999 and came into effect two months later on Monday 27 September 1999, in time for the bulk of the remaining months of the current season and thereafter. The structure of the Statute is in line with earlier legislation aimed to curb without even expecting to achieve abolition of a sporting social phenomenon which excited my own entry into the area twenty years ago with a draft Safety of Sports Persons Act. It appeared in an Appendix to all three earlier editions of the *Sunday Telegraph* (1978) Butterworths 1988 and 1994 and, for comparative purposes is repeated here. What it did not anticipate at any stage was a perverse continuity what erupted during the 1998 World Cup Competition in France and thereby inspired section 1 of the new Act.

International football banning orders

The powers are self explanatory in section 1(2), (3) and demonstrate the willingness of Parliament to tackle a problem which has proved resistent to all the remedial palliatives proposed for it so far. What will become self-evident is that those for whom it is targeted will be unaware of its existence until in breach of its provisions, consistent with the playing offenders against the Laws of a Game, whether at soccer or rugby, who does appear aware of the potential civil or criminal liability.

(2)   Potential litigation liability

At the time of writing on the day when the '*International banning orders*' came into force, the well reported threat from overseas to a well known United Kingdom professional footballer for an alleged foul tackle causing serious cruciate ligament injury to an opponent on an overseas ground, outside the immediate jurisdiction of the English Courts has been publicised exhaustively. The threat may never materialise, but it throws into focus for the wider international dimension what has emerged from the message which has been sustained throughout these pages and in all previous editions.

Sport knows no universal sporting Parliament comparable to the CCPR in London and the other home countries' equivalent bodies in Scotland, Wales and Northern Ireland as a debating forum and/or meeting ground. Certainly no democratically elected body exists universally to legislate for sport. Each particular discipline has its own world governing body, some democratically elected, others existing as self-perpetuating oligarchies. The law affecting international sport therefore comes from the traditional domestic and international layers already identified in Chapter 1 *Genesis* and Chapter 2, *Progressive perspective*

(1) playing
(2) playing penal
(3) administrative
(4) national

} laws

extended by this international dimension to two more widely embracing areas of

(5) international governing body
(6) overseas national

} laws

The first four above-listed categories in the United Kingdom do not differ when considered in an international context. David Bishop's prosecution by the South Wales police authority for assaulting an opponent, followed by his suspension by the Welsh Rugby Union, was the appropriate action for the harm done. Equally, equivalent action should have been implemented against the Bulgarian and Portuguese footballers on English football fields as they were in breach of soccer's playing and British national criminal laws during the World Cup competition in 1966. The Brazilian visitor to these shores, Pele, was the victim. He identified the offenders, who were witnessed by millions of TV and video watchers, in *My Life and the Beautiful Game* (Pele, 1977 with Robert L Fish), cited extensively below.

They each breached

(1) playing
(2) playing penal
(3) national
(4) international governing body
(5) overseas national law

} laws

but no effective administrative action was taken under category (3) administrative laws above by the English or FIFA authorities in the manner which would inevitably exist today.

The referees and/or linesmen who saw all fouls and thus assaults did not dismiss the offenders from either game. The FIFA off-field administrators took no comparable action to that of the Welsh Rugby Union against David Bishop, as they clearly could have done, by suspending each player for the remainder of the tournament. On the other hand, other countries have enforced their own laws against British citizens. The extradition proceedings by the Belgian government to return the British citizens who committed criminal offences in the Heysel Stadium disaster is an example of how international law can apply to the international sporting scene (*Government of Belgium v Postlethwaite* [1987] 2 WLR 365).

A different international sporting legal problem, which is more appropriate to Chapter 7, *Sports medicine and the law*, is emerging through the sophisticated process developing with drug deceptions which reflect a wider medical problem for society generally. It arises when a conflict exists between prescribed lawful medical treatment for the use of drugs prohibited by domestic and international sporting governing bodies, and their medical justification. In one well publicised situation, an English Football League club professional footballer playing for Scotland, Willie Johnston in the World Cup competition during 1978 in South America was found guilty of breaching the world governing soccer body's (FIFA's) drug regulations. The available factual evidence points to a conflict or confusion of communication between the patient and his club or national team's medical advisers about any awareness that this lawfully prescribed drug was a prohibited substance under the FIFA drug regulations. Six years later in 1984, an All England British Judo Association champion with dual British/Canadian nationality was prescribed a lawful drug by a Canadian doctor which breached the Association's rules.

More recently in 1992 two rugby union international footballers were allegedly tested positive for the use of prohibited drugs after France played Wales in Paris. It emerged that the Welsh Rugby Union honorary surgeon had prescribed drugs for sickness and dysentery suffered by Anthony Clement and the French doctor had administered Pholeodine to Jean-Baptiste Lafond for a cough.

All of these four cases are dealt with in medical detail in Chapter 7. Here they illustrate the principle more widely recognised in international legal circles as a conflict of laws situation. Humiliation resulted in all cases. For the professional footballer a publicised return to Scotland f administrative sports offence to which section 28(3)(b)(i) of the M of Drugs Act 1971 would have provided a defence in a British c court

'If he proves that he neither believed nor suspected nor had reason to suspect that the substance or product in use was a controlled drug'.

It was not a defence available to Willie Johnston before the court of world football's ruling body, and it does not appear to have been known to him or any advisers for use in mitigation of his sentence (punishments which should have been inflicted upon the players who criminally assaulted Pele but were supinely not implemented by that same world governing football body in 1966). For the British Judo Association, the humiliation resulted in a High Court retraction of a life ban from competing in the British championships. This was for the breach of a natural justice principle also experienced by the Football Association in its unjudicial administrative treatment of its former national team manager, Don Revie. These two cases are referred to in more detail respectively in Chapter 7, *'Sports medicine and the law'* and Chapter 11, *Fair play and reason in court*. Humiliation also resulted for the French Rugby Union which then operated a list of banned substances different from the Welsh Rugby Union's use of the International Olympic Committee's list.

These conflicts between lawfully prescribed drugs for authentic medicinal purposes and desirably prohibitive sports drug laws will not disappear, if at all, until a harmonisation formula can be devised between participants, doctors, administrators and lawyers. Until such an ideal occurs, these examples will illustrate sport's own special conflict of laws situation. The Canadian Government's 'Commission of Inquiry into the use of drugs and banned Practices intended to increase Athletic Performance', which produced the Report of Mr Justice Dubin after Ben Johnson was disqualified in the 1988 Olympic Games, analysed the problem. It could not and did not devise any effective remedial and/or ameliorative action.

Correspondingly, the undefended civil litigation, on its merits, by the IAAF against Harry 'Butch' Reynolds, explained towards the end of Chapter 7, *'Sports medicine and the law'* has its decidedly international flavour, indicative of the global village, dominating International Sport today. Reynolds commenced proceedings in his home town court of Columbus, Ohio, USA. Rightly or wrongly the IAAF considered that it did not see what this had to do with Ohio and, in any case, did not think that justice could have been obtained in Reynolds' home town courts. It also considered the remoteness of Ohio from the realities of the situation when recognising how the drug sample in dispute was taken in Monte Carolo; the IAAF headquarters at the time were based in England (see *Reel v Holder* [1981] 3 All ER 321 for the jurisdiction point); the factual witnesses in the case were from France, and expert witnesses were German and English.

In the future, however, one simpler resolution to such problems (as explained by the author in the *New Law Journal* for May 3 1991) may lie with a little known jurisdiction which has existed since 1983, but surfaced to a wider audience during early 1991 at two separate international gatherings geared to sport and the law. The first, organised by a group of progressive Australian counsel from Selborne Chambers, Sydney, NSW, was held on the Olympic Committee's doorstep in Switzerland, and the other by the charitable arm of the IAAF, the International Amateur Athletic Foundation in Monaco. Each was enlightened by the developments disclosed by Dr Gilbert Schwaar, the then Secretary-General of the Court of Arbitration for Sport (CAS).

CAS was conceived by the President of the International Olympic committee, HE Snr Juan Antonio Samaranch, the former Spanish Ambassador in Moscow, in 1983 just before the 1984 Los Angeles Olympiad, when a wave of litigation — nearly all of it unsuccessful — brought the Olympic movement under severe pressure. The idea was to set up an arbitration institution which would deal with disputes directly or indirectly linked with sport. Although created by the IOC, which covers its running costs, the members are completely independent of the IOC in the exercise of their duties. They comprise a panel of 60 international jurists with a working knowledge of sport, selected equally from the IOC; international federations such as FIFA; the Association of National Olympic Committees; and by the President of the IOC from outside the other three areas.

The jurisdiction is open to sports bodies, individuals practising or teaching sport, businessmen, corporate bodies, public or private, who may all refer to the CAS with a view to attempting to settle any conflict by arbitration, provided the dispute has a bearing on private interests. Any problems of a technical nature arising during the practice of a particular sport, such as the competence of a referee's or umpire's decision, would remain within the jurisdiction of the appropriate international federation or domestic organisation concerned. Thus, the capacity to play at appropriate times which brought amateur basketball players (*R v The British Basketball Association ex p Mickan and Cheesman* [1981] March 17 CAT 0111) or an amateur tennis player (*Curry v Barton & Rippon* (1987) *Times*, 27, 28 March and 29 July) before the English courts, could lie within the jurisdiction of CAS, *if equal funding resources would exist for all parties before it.*

At the time of preparing these pages in July 1999 the 69 paragraphs of statutes contain a recognisable procedural code designated in R 44

'identifying written submissions and an oral presentation'.

Although the usual pre-condition for costs is contained in the statutes (R 64), they are silent on the crucial question of legal aid or assistance for submission and particularly by an individual in conflict with a governing body to the CAS authority. When Dr Schwaar was questioned, at each of the conferences about this, his responses on both occasions were unequivocal. In the appropriate circumstances the equivalent of legal aid or assistance would be forthcoming. Nevertheless that silence continues to this day, with a significance and consequence which are self-evident. For the resources of a sporting governing body with access to direct or indirect funding and resources can easily *place an individual adversary at a disadvantage professionally and create a clear-cut injustice position.* Dr Gilbert Schwaar recognised this. Until activated to create equal professional access and resources, any such system must not only lack credibility; it also justifies suspicion towards attempts for denial of justice to anyone eligible for an audience in a public Court of Law.

As travel and television contract the globe to bring international sport into every living room, the concept of an International Court of Arbitration for Sport on circuit need not be a fanciful one. National and international sport have travelled a long way since Florence Nagle caused the Jockey Club to re-assess its attitude to women trainers. At one time, India's judiciary has been invoked to consider the existence of that country's equivalent of the Britannic Assurance County Championship, the Ranji Trophy, and the Argentine international footballer Diego Maradona was contemplating an appeal against a world-wide ban against him for alleged drug abuse. The Court of Arbitration for Sport with its 60 sporting jurists would have been an appropriate tribunal for both cases, subject to *funding on an equal footing for all parties associated with any issue.*

The extent to which any international jurisdiction will be effective must depend upon the extent to which IFs [International Federation's] regulations so permit or with their prior agreement and the capacity of any potential attendee to afford the facilities for travel and legal services in the absence of any funding assistance.

One other harmonisation area in international sport which affects the United Kingdom is a corollary to the VAT conflict of laws area considered in Chapter 14, '*No fine on fun*'. It will be recalled there how the Celtic Football & Athletic Football Club Ltd and the Football Association Ltd were able effectively to rely upon UEFA competition regulations obliging them to reciprocate hospitality to opposing sporting competing bodies in order to refute HM Commissioners of Customs & Excise rejection of their claims for allowable entertainment input expenses under the appropriate VAT regulations. Now the Inland Revenue has entered the same area of international fiscal consistency.

The Financial Secretary to the Treasury, the Rt Hon Norman Lamont MP, responded with the following information in a written Parliamentary answer on 25 March 1987 to a question about information he had available as to what level of payment countries other than the UK formally levied the commencement of taxation (HC Written Answer, 25 March 1987, Hansard: Vol 113 col 212):

'Countries which have withholding arrangements include the USA, Canada, France, Germany, Australia, New Zealand, Belgium, Switzerland, Portugal, Spain, Finland, Norway and Sweden.

Generally, tax is withheld on all payments subject to the effect of the relevant double taxation agreement. For example, the UK-United States of America convention exempts the visiting entertainer or sportsman from liability where the gross receipts do not exceed $15,000 (or their sterling equivalent) in the tax year concerned'.

Consistent with this universality, Regulations were laid in the House of Commons the following day, 26 March 1987, containing details of the new rules for the withholding of tax at source on payments to non resident entertainers and sportsmen. They were introduced under SI 1987/1530 as a withholding tax to take effect from 1 May 1987 and consolidated in sections 555–558 of the Income and Corporation Taxes Act 1988 and SI 1987/530. For this purpose a Foreign Entertainers Unit was set up to administer the new scheme on 5th Floor, City House, 140, Edmund Street, Birmingham, B3 2JH (telephone 021–200–2616).
Notwithstanding the universality of this position, the overriding tax burdens on British Sport generally (see Chapter 14, *No fine on fun*) resulting in early 1991 in John Lister, Honorary Treasurer of the British Athletic Federation, who explained in the international sporting context,

'The athlete withholding tax, the proper title is foreign entertainers tax, is particularly disliked because as you would imagine we get no sympathy at all from the likes of Mr Said Aouita or a variety of Kenyans when we tell them well we are very, very sorry, but we have to deduct 25 per cent British income tax from their appearance money. We get a very short answer and the result is inevitably that we pay the tax which then becomes an added cost to us. So we in sport in Britain are very much on our own.' [See generally Chapter 14, *No fine on fun*.]

Such aims for uniformity and consistency lead to three other areas where a pattern of principle can be discerned in which sport can be said to have been identified and recognised internationally in law; and how it is always necessary to keep a level of awareness well in mind. One concerns intervention by the English courts; another the arrival of Common Market law at its legislative and litigation levels, and the third concerns the never ending struggle by sport to prevent invasion into its territory by alien trespassers seeking to exploit its existence for naked political purposes.
For the first, Chapter 6 unfolded in its earlier pages the table of English court decisions against international sporting governing bodies which had

failed to realise how the judges will assist victims of injustice and unlawful actions committed by sporting governing bodies. Soccer (FIFA), cricket (ICC), badminton (IBA) and athletics (IAAF) all received their come-uppances in the courts when acting contrary to the restraint of trade laws so far as soccer and cricket were concerned, and contrary to their own regulations in the badminton and athletics cases. They were all relied upon and identified by the *Daily Telegraph* racing editor, Tony Stafford, in a warning to the Jockey Club at Portman Square about the consequences of its reported intention to enforce the Royal Western India Turf Club's ban on an English jockey, Kevin Darley. He had been disciplined for his riding of the horse Sweet Success in Bombay. The incident turned sour when he complained that the Indian administrative procedures did not comply with the rules of natural justice. Past precedents within the international racing fraternity pointed to an international agreement which had allowed the automatic application of riding bans which had been imposed overseas to apply to the UK.

Tony Stafford pointed out the capacity of English courts to rule against unlawful actions by international sporting governing bodies; citing in particular Foster, J in the case of (*Cooke v The Football Association* (1972) *Times*, 24 March). Here the judge ruled FIFA's regulations to be in restraint of trade and also told the FA to withdraw from FIFA if the world body would not alter its rules 'to accord with the principles of English law' relating to restraint of trade. Stafford also reminded the Jockey Club of its own downfall in the Court of Appeal during 1966 at the persistence of Florence Nagle and her experienced legal advisers to establish women's rights for a trainer's licence in their own name (*Nagle v Fielden*, supra). Instead of automatically implementing Darley's three months' riding ban from India at Darley's behest the Jockey Club suspended it pending Darley's appeal in England to allow him to continue riding. When the Jockey Club ultimately confirmed the ban in a London hearing of the appeal to its own jurisdiction, three weeks alone were left of the original ban. If there had been an implementation of the full three months under an automatic suspension pursuant to the relevant international agreement there could well have been a re-run of the FA's further downfall experienced in 1979 when it was adjudged to have breached a natural justice principle in its treatment of its former national team manager (*Revie v The Football Association* (supra)). The Jockey Club's refusal to apply the Indian suspension automatically was another step on the road to fair play in sport and justice in the law at international level.

The second pattern of principle to be observed is the creeping encroachment of European Community law upon the European sporting scene. A free market for the participants in professional sports under Articles 48–51 of the Treaty of Rome [now Articles 39–42 of The Treaty of Amsterdam] overshadows the traditional planning for team structures in

British professional football. In three landmark cases of Dutch cyclists (*Walgrave and Koch v Union Cycliste Internationale* (c 36/74) [1974] ECR 1045 (ECJ): *Dona v Mantero* (c 13/76) [ECR 1833 (ECJ) and Bosman's *cause célèbre: Union Royale Belege de Societes de Football (ASBL) v Jean-Marc Bosman* (c 415/93 [1995] ECR1–4921: [1996 1 AER (EC) 97. the European Court of Justice has accepted jurisdiction for disputes concerning *professional* as distinct from amateur sport as an economic activity under Article 2 of the Treaty [now Article 2 of the Amsterdam Treaty].

Finally, and by no means least, the European principle in Bosman reflects the impact of English rugby players arguing that they should have unqualified freedom of movement. The Leicester Rugby Football Club lived up to its nickname of 'the Tigers' when it pursued the Leicester City Council through the High Court, the Court of Appeal and ultimately to the House of Lords to gain a unanimous verdict that the Council had improperly operated the Race Relations Act 1976. It had purported to suspend and ban the club from use of the council's own Welford Road Recreation Ground because three of its players had exercised their freedom of choice to accept an invitation from the Rugby Union at Twickenham to represent England on a rugby tour of South Africa (*Wheeler and others v Leicester City Council* [1985] 1 AC 1054).

In a general internationally mobile sporting world it can be seen from this summary and overview that the tentacles of international sport and law are gradually and almost inevitably creeping into the British domestic sporting scene. Notwithstanding their diversity they can still be fitted into the traditional legal framework of international law, namely,

(1) Public
(2) Private } laws
(3) Conflicting

3   PUBLIC INTERNATIONAL LAW

Convention and tradition confines this area to relationships between states. Lord Radcliffe, a Lord of Appeal for fifteen years and Director General of the Ministry of Information during the Second World War, took a broader view when he spoke upon The Rights of Man after that war to the Grotius Society (1950, Vol 36, p 5), founded in 1915 to promote the ideas of international law:

'I do not know what international law is: but at least I am confident that, if it is to have any power over the hearts and minds of men, it cannot be just the body of rules that sovereign States are prepared from time to time to recognise in their dealings with each other. If it is to bind the conscience of mankind, it must be felt to have behind it the sanction of some less mundane authority. The protection that we can expect to get is indeed a matter for experts: but it is the protection that we ought to get that we dwell upon in our distress'.

Protection was the last thing that the outstanding international footballer, Pele, received from referees, or football received from its sovereign body, FIFA. There was no effective punishment of the offenders for Pele's 1966 World Cup distress expressed thus in *My Life and the Beautiful Game* (1977, Pele with Robert L Fish on pages 144–145)

'... against Bulgaria ... I had been the target of merciless attacks from Zechev of Bulgaria throughout the entire game. Zechev did everything he could physically to cripple me, and the referee, Jim Feeney* gave neither me nor any of the others on our team the protection we had a right to expect from an official in a game.'

...

'Morais, of Portugal, had a field day fouling me, eventually putting me out of the game. He tripped me, and when I was stumbling to the ground he leaped at me, feet first, and cut me down completely. It wasn't until I actually saw the films of the game that I realised what a terribly vicious double-foul it was. The stands came to their feet screaming at the foul, but the English referee, George McCabe allowed Morais to remain on the field, although again, even in the most inexperienced league in the world, he would have been thrown out for either of the two fouls, let alone both. Dr Gosling and Mario Americo came to help me from the field, and Brazil went on to play with ten men and ended up eliminated from the tournament'.

Those impressions of what the films showed for Pele have been confirmed by my own viewing of the official film of the 1966 World Cup Competition, *Goal*, by its scriptwriter and the then *Sunday Times* football correspondent, Brian Glanville, and also by *The Times'* senior sportswriter, David Miller. The six legal consequences as set out previously at page 356 could be considered in turn insurance if implemented. They were all repeated fourteen years later during the semi-final of the 1982 World Cup competition in Spain. The West German goalkeeper Schumacher assaulted the French defender, Battiston, in a manner condemned internationally by the sporting press. Yet as David Miller recorded in his book on the 1966 World Cup, *The Boys of '66: England's Lost Glory* at p 21,

---

* NB Jack Rollin, football's leading statistician and author of the *Guinness Book of Soccer Records*, in his *World Cup Triumph 1966* records the referee as Her Tschenscher of West Germany. Pele's text is as cited above.

'Any dignified sport would have suspended for life the West German goalkeeper for his atrocious foul in the 1982 semi-final, which shamefully handicapped the French. From FIFA there was no more than a murmur'.

Battiston's 1982 West German experience and Pele's Portuguese and Bulgarian experiences in the 1966 World Cup created a classic combination of circumstances which could and should have demonstrated — but did not — how all six legal layers at p 356 can be acted upon. These fouls merited the following sanctions:

(1) playing — sending off from field;
(2) playing penal laws — in breach of Law 12 of Association football — violent conduct or serious foul play;
(3) administrative — suspension or dismissal from competition in the manner suffered by Scotland's star winger who was sent home from the 1978 World Cup in Argentina following a positive drugs test in breach of FIFA rules but lawfully prescribed under Parliament's Misuse of Drugs Act 1971 (see Chapter 7, 'Sports medicine and the law', infra);
(4) national — prosecution under Section 47 of the Offences Against the Person Act, 861, for assault occasioning actual bodily harm;
(5) international governing body — as in (2) above with censure upon referees and FIFA noted by David Miller for abdicating responsibilities;
(6) overseas national laws as in (3) above, with the precedents from other violent visitors or criminal offenders to United Kingdom shores.

In fact nothing at all ever happened. Furthermore, many participants of *all* sporting codes would argue that a comparable position existed towards the end of 1993 in what the England rugby union captain, Will Carling, described as 'dirty play' by the New Zealand tourists.

The offenders escaped back to their native lands without any effective punishment for their undoubted criminality. The reluctance of the prosecuting authorities in the Liverpool area (covering Goodison Park, where the Pele assaults occurred) to take action could conceivably have resulted from diplomatic sensitivities. Since then, in the next World Cup, at Mexico City in 1970, England's captain, Bobby Moore, was intimidated by a false charge of alleged theft in the Colombian capital of Bogota; and as the world knows, twenty years later, the South Wales prosecuting authority charged a Welsh international amateur rugby footballer with the offence identified and suffered by Pele. To those who supinely and irresponsibly say 'It's all part of the game', Pele's beautiful game and that of others — the game of ballet without music — there is one question to be answered. What should happen to any member of a dance routine chorus whipping the feet from under the legs of Fred Astaire and Ginger Rogers?

Punishment or condonement? For 1994, FIFA's red card sanctions at last redress the balance which had been out of kilter in 1966.

Sustaining Lord Radcliffe's yardstick for international law sanctions as 'the protection we ought to get that we dwell upon in our distress', it was granted by Foster J in the Chancery Division of London's High Court in 1972. A Sheffield-born former Manchester United player, John Cooke, found that his proposed transfer back to the County Palatine for service with Wigan Athletic, then outside the Football League, from Sligo Rovers in Eire, was blocked. This was due to FIFA's insistence on upholding the restrictive practices built in to the Republic of Ireland's FA and Football League provisions of a kind which Wilberforce J had declared to be in restraint of trade and unenforceable and thereby unlawful in the celebrated Eastham Case in 1963 (supra). FIFA's control covers the FA in London, the custodians of English soccer, with whom Wigan Athletic was registered. The FA were bound by contract and loyalty to FIFA to obey the world body's refusal to register the transfer from Sligo Rovers to Wigan Athletic: Cooke's employment contract was subject to Irish restrictions of the kind outlawed by Wilberforce J. With FIFA's registered offices in Switzerland outside the jurisdiction of the English courts, there was only one course open to Cooke's English lawyers at the time of commencing proceedings in advance of the judgment during 1972. They sued the FA for declarations attacking the FIFA overriding restrictive articles and confirming the Irish prohibitions. Foster J unshackled Cook from his Eire and FIFA bonds in the spirit of Guthrie's campaign to free soccer slaves from being the last bonded men in Britain (*Cooke v The Football Association*: (1972) *Times*, 24 March). Four days later (28 March 1972) a letter to *The Times* from Mr David Green commented on FIFA's Article 14 which was held to be unlawful with its references to contracts subject to national Rules 'no matter how harsh the terms of the contract may be,' under English common law,

> 'And is it not, to adapt the words of Mr Justice Wilberforce in Eastham's case, incongruous to the spirit of an international sport, that any rule of an international governing body should be drafted in the revolting terms of Article 14'.

Pace David Miller, 'From FIFA there was no more than a murmur'.

International cricket also acted unlawfully when the ICC unwisely combined with the TCC in restraint of trade. They attempted to block the Packer assault on professional cricket's limited economic employment terms by interfering with Packer's contractual relationships with his contracted players (*Greig v Insole* (supra)); and so, too, was the FA of Wales prohibition on the three junior league clubs, Newport AFC, Caernarfon Town and Colwyn Bay, against playing on their home grounds in the Principality (*Newport AFC Ltd and Others v FA Wales Ltd* (supra)).

4 PRIVATE INTERNATIONAL LAW

The other cases, listed at the beginning of Chapter 3, *Under starter's orders*, dealing with international governing bodies were concerned with the construction of governing body regulations. The purpose of the regulations was to meet Lord Radcliffe's criteria of 'the protection that we ought to get that we dwell upon in our distress'. On both occasions, the courts confirmed membership for Taiwan's governing sporting body of respectively the International Badminton Association and the then International Amateur Athletic Association (today more realistically an International *Trust Fund* or *Trustee* Athletic Association) (*Shen Fu Chang v Stellan Mohlin* (unreported (1977) QBD, Goff J, except at [1981] 3 All ER 324g–h; *Reel v Holder* [1981] 3 All ER 321).

In the athletes' case Lord Denning MR said at page 323c;

> 'I put on one side any thought of international politics. In international law Taiwan's claim is not recognised.'

Referring to the badminton case and Goff J's judgement Lord Denning confirmed at page 324g-h

> 'These courts can and should make a declaration in favour of Taiwan [of wrongful exclusion from IAAF membership in 1978] to that extent. We do not think this should give rise to any international complications. We are making a declaration on the meaning of the rules according to English law, which is the governing law'.

Five years later the Commonwealth Games Federation arrived in London's High Court to end with the ex cathedra obiter dictum of the Vice-Chancellor in the Chancery Division, Sir Nicholas Browne-Wilkinson. He was concerned, without citation to him of the Court's emancipation of participants from feudal sporting bonds explained in Chapter 11, *Fair Play and Reason in Court*, only for a claim by a South African born participant to swim for England whose alleged English residence and domicile had been disputed. He ruled after a rushed interlocutory hearing that the Federation were right

(1) to give the word 'domicile' in article 34(3) of its constitution the ordinary popular meaning of the word and,
(2) not to apply the legal meaning which would ordinarily be given to it under the English law of domicile.

He also ruled that even if the law of domicile's traditional legal meaning in tax and family law precedents, concerned with the effect of the legal location or base for a litigant, was the correct test, the full evidential requirements for proving the criteria making England the domicile of choice had been satisfied (*Cowley v Heatley and others* (1986) *Times*, 24 July). Once more, as in *Reel v Holder* (supra) the case turned on the true meaning of the rules, according to English law. His general gratuitous strictures as cited below and based upon traditional judicial unawareness of how law today is essential for the health of sport, ie

> 'sport would be better served if there was not running litigation at repeated intervals by people seeking to challenge the decisions of the regulating bodies'

become more inappropriate as every passing year demonstrates. This third edition emphasises how the law provides solutions which governing bodies and the judiciary and many members of the legal profession and lay public cannot, or will not see.

5   ADMINISTRATIVE SPORTING ACTION

The decision of Leicester City Council to ban the Leicester Rugby Club from using its practice ground at Welford Road, Leicester, for twelve months must be evaluated in this administrative context. The decision was taken under the Race Relations Act 1976. Why? Three Leicester Rugby Club amateur players had exercised their right to tour South Africa with the England national rugby team; these three players held the view that their sporting activities were not relevant to the political situation in South Africa at that time. Mr Justice Forbes upheld this administrative local authority decision. So, too, did a Court of Appeal majority, Lord Justice Browne-Wilkinson (who later succeeded Sir Robert Megarry as Vice-Chancellor of the Chancery Division) dissenting. On appeal the House of Lords unanimously reversed the earlier rulings (*Wheeler v Leicester City Council* (supra)).

The Race Relations Act 1976 contained in section 71 a duty upon local authorities to carry out their functions with the need to promote good relations between persons of different racial groups, which existed in the Leicester City Council's territory. The existence, scope, interpretation and implementation of this section was the key legal issue. Lord Justice Browne-Wilkinson posed the contending antithesis in this section from his dissenting judgement:

> 'on a point of fundamental principle. The case raises a conflict between the two basic principles of a democratic society: viz, on the one hand, the right of a democratically elected body to conduct its affairs in accordance with its own view [ie Leicester City Council] and, on the other, the right to freedom of speech and conscience enjoyed by each individual in a democratic society';

and he ultimately reached

'the conclusion that the decision of the council is unlawful since legally irrelevant matters were taken into account.'

In the House of Lords, to use a popular rugby metaphor, its judicial grand slam of five Law Lords' unanimous ruling was based on two fundamental premises:

(1) the council's ban on the club's use of its practice ground at the Council's recreation premises was unreasonable and unfair and amounted to procedural impropriety within the now familiar principles set out in *Associated Picture Houses v Wednesbury Corporation* [1948] 1 KB 223,

(2) the Council's use of its statutory power was a misuse of power because the Council intended to and did in fact punish the club when they had not broken any law.

Just as the rugby players established they had not broken any laws, some cricketers could have argued this in 1982 when the Test and County Cricket Board banned England's Test cricketers who had earned their living professionally in South Africa. *Wisden's* Notes by the Editor (1983 Edition at page 80) recorded of those events how

'The Prime Minister ... Speaking in Parliament, Mrs Thatcher said "We do not have the power to prevent any sportsmen or women from visiting South Africa or anywhere else. If we did we would no longer be a free country"'.

Correspondingly Lord Roskill said when delivering one of the two leading House of Lords opinions with words equally applicable to the arguably unlawful ban on the cricketers as they were to the undoubtedly unlawful ban on the Leicester Rugby Club's use of its Welford Road ground, (at p 1076)

'It is important to emphasise that there was nothing illegal in the action of the three members in joining the tour. The government policy recorded in the well known Gleneagles agreement has never been given the force of law at the instance of any government, whatever its political complexion, and a person who acts otherwise than in accordance with the principles of that agreement, commits no offence even though he may by his action earn the moral disapprobation of large numbers of his fellow citizens'.

A year later, the New Zealand Rugby Football Union was less effective in protecting its tour to South Africa in 1985. Here a complex network of interlocutory procedures ultimately resulted in a High Court injunction being granted with sufficient timing prior to the departure date to prevent the tour from taking place (*Finnigan and Another v New Zealand RFU*

[1985] NZLR 185). An appeal to the Privy Council was academic and rejected. If time had been on the Union's side, it is arguable that the decision could have been reversed for, two individual plaintiffs with no connection with the NZRFU other than that they happened to belong to rugby clubs, were held to be entitled to challenge the decision of the latter body to send a representative team to South Africa. The New Zealand Court of Appeal took the view that, although the law recognised a distinction between private and public law decisions (especially in relation to an individual's right to challenge them) and although the decision in question was by a private and voluntary sporting association, the decision of the NZRFU was one of 'major international importance' such that 'a sharp boundary between public and private law [could not] realistically be drawn' and court intervention was permissible.

Since these dramatic and explosive legal issues were considered in controversial contexts the South African sporting scene has shifted with the legal dismantling of apartheid. Readmission to the community of international sport has now followed and the earlier texts from the first edition of this book dealing with the debatable interpretations of the so-called Gleneagles Agreement, the Commonwealth Declaration on Apartheid in Sport, may now be considered both otiose and obsolete. Certainly there are many who would consider that the sporting boycott imposed internationally on South Africa, whether legal or not, contributed to a wider and deeper national political change of scene and climate within South Africa. Furthermore, if the ultimate result has been to integrate blacks into South African sport and therefore society generally, then retrospectively the end may be said to have justified the means.

Finally, for New Zealand and its international rugby experience, defeat by South Africa in the 1999 World Cup third place match, following its shock result against France five days earlier, created a new dimension for a perceived national sporting disaster. The BBC World Service's admirable information sources, on the eve of the third place encounter with South Africa, reported [4 November 1999], in detail from Palmerston North Massey University's campus, where the famous All Blacks trained in preparation for the competition:

"Believing the defeat may have a crushing effect on this rugby-crazy nation's collective psyche, it has released a list of experts willing to help those struggling to cope with the defeat, which has been received as a national disaster ...... Dr Graeme Bassett, of the School of English and Media Studies saw the defeat as a major blow to the self-esteem of a large segment of the population.

"It is as if the team represents the self-worth of the country. People say "it's only a game" but emotionally it isn't only a game for a lot of people",

Bassett said.

> "Even the most intellectually reserved and critical minds can be moved
> by the passion and spectacle of it all."

Bassett said New Zealand had a fragile sense of its own identity, and the worth of the country seemed to be tied up with sporting achievements. An additional BBC World Service report also recorded concurrently from the players "A nervousness about going back and facing the general public".

On a less sombre note, from a less media intense era a decade ago, it is appropriate to end this chapter with its never ending march into the future with the words of one of the world's greatest and best loved international athletes of all time, Emil Zatopek from Czechoslovakia, in a BBC Radio 4 *Sport on Four* interview (Saturday 27 June 1987), reproduced here with the permission and assistance of the producer Peter Griffiths and its presenter Cliff Morgan. Zatopek began by saying in an interview with Ian Dark;

> 'As a schoolboy I have had the good teachers who told us: England is the
> cradle of modern sport and I came to London, like, in to the cradle of modern
> sport'.

He ended with what should be a beacon for sports lovers throughout the world to ensure all those who are prepared to identify and fight the evil spirits outside sport waiting to destroy it as fun and joy.

> 'I esteem sport activity as really activity for good conditions, good health
> and happy life ...
>   Sport activity: it is giving really a pleasure; by travelling; by meeting; by
> this friendship. It is greater than the victory. All the world, sportsmen are
> like brothers';

and as a contemporary of Fanny Blankers-Koen, he doubtless intended to include the sisters, too.

So long as international sport continues to be the catalyst which enables so many people to make new international friends without, it may be hoped, the need to resort to the law in court, Zatopek's ideal may be sustained at grass roots levels even if the commercial and competitive pressures in the showbiz framework renders it today more than an ideal nostalgic dream.

CHAPTER 10

Single European Market and UK Sport

1 INTRODUCTION

The British Parliament's European Communities Act 1972 legislated (on 17 October 1972, to take effect on 1 January 1973), for Britain's entry into the Common Market, created by the Treaty of Rome. The Lord Chancellor in Britain's government at the time was Lord Hailsham of St Marylebone. He had already created the role of a Minister with responsibility for sport. Forty years earlier during the winter of 1932–33, his father Viscount Hailsham had been MCC President at the time of the so-called Bodyline crisis, when Test Matches between England and Australia dominated the international cricket scene. Sixty odd years before that, at Kennington Oval in South London in 1870, his grandfather, the first Quintin Hogg, and founder of the Regent Street Polytechnic, participated in the earliest traceable international soccer match between Scotland and England players. Today's sporting world sees that historic fixture lost in the mists of time and the traditional Ashes series are part of a world-wide International Cricket Council framework, within an exploding and expanding European political, sporting and legal scene.

2 COMMON MARKET SPORT AND THE LAW PERSPECTIVE

Two separate and different dimensions dominate any realistic approach to this chapter within the United Kingdom:

(1) What is the true nature of sport and
(2) Whether or not Lord Hailsham's heterogeneous concept corroborated

by the 113 different activities cited at Preface Page 1 is accepted, the 30,920,000 grass roots participants from 421 national governing bodies are less likely to be affected than their showbiz competitors in an active sports context with a single market essentially based on the'economic policies of member states' confirmatory under Article 2 of the Treaty.

A touchstone can be seen through the well publicised and generally well recognised European Court of Justice judgment in the *Bosman* case. Article 48 brought his freedom of movement as a worker economically in line with the road from *Banks* at Aldershot in 1945; *Eastham* at Newcastle in 1963, and *Packer* at Lord's in 1978. It does not directly concern the commercial economic activities of the 43,000 grass roots and other football clubs registered with the Football Association at Lancaster Gate, irrespective of the untold numbers at Hackney Marshes or village greens throughout Britain. Nevertheless, because the legal thread connecting these pioneers is contractual the picture is even more clearly illustrated by applying Lord Denning's favourite citation from Scotland's more renowned lawyer and Writer to the Signet, already cited at p 138:

'The lawyer without history or literature is a mere working mason. With them he may venture to call himself an architect'.

Bosman's dash for freedom, in his case under unlawful restraints, is also in line with an attempt by England's professional goalkeeper a century earlier to free himself from a contract he signed with the then Burslem Port Vale Club a year after the Football Association authorised professionalism in their mainly amateur game during 1885. In 1886 William Rowley signed for their then neighbouring Stoke Club in breach of his Burslem Port Vale agreement. He was injuncted and adjudicated under the contract to pay £5 liquidated damages by HH Judge Jordan in the Burslem County in circumstances which have an echo for today as recorded:

'Mr Baddelley: "This man Rowley, to the great discredit of the Stoke Football Club has been seduced from his own club in the face of this agreement."

His Honour: You charge the Stoke Club with seduction (Laughter).

Mr Baddelley repeated the Stoke Club has seduced the Defendant, Rowley, from Port Vale'.

His phraseology is equally applicable in current circumstances [*Staffordshire Sentinel* 9 November 1886]

3 COMMON MARKET CATEGORIES

The single European Act was signed in Luxembourg on 17 February 1986 and at The Hague on 28 February 1986. It came into force on 1 July 1987: and Article 4 of The Treaty created for The Community four separate institutions;

(1) a European Parliament, with elected representatives from the Common Market countries;
(2) a Council, of Government Ministers, one from each member state, the principal decision making body;
(3) a Commission, of 17 members nominated by Government agreement, acting in the EC's interests, and not their nominating country, proposing policy and administration;
(4) a Court of Justice of 13 judges, including one from each state, with the power to interpret EC Law.

Lord Denning has explained, almost symbolically in the present Sport and the Law context, in his volume entitled *What Next in the Law* (pp 295–296):

' ... the principle of the supremacy of Community law. The Treaty, its Regulations and Directives, take priority over any of our English law. If there is any conflict or any inconsistency between Community law and English law, then Community law is to prevail'.

He expanded this in a judgment in *Bulmer v Bellinger SA* where he explained with his renowned colourful simplicity [1974] Ch 401 at 411

' ... the Treaty (of Rome) concerns only those matters which have a European element, that is to say, matters which affect people or property in the nine countries of the common market besides ourselves. The Treaty does not touch any of the matters which concern solely England and the people in it. These are still governed by English law. They are not affected by the Treaty. But when we come to matters with a European element, the Treaty is like an incoming tide. It flows into the estuaries and up the rivers. It cannot be held back. Parliament has decreed that the Treaty is henceforward to be part of our law. It is equal in force to any statute ...'.

Clearly Lord Denning was referring to the Community law laid down by the Common Market Parliament in Brussels and the European Court of Justice at Luxembourg. It is a hybrid straddling both conventional national law and the two conventional forms of international law, public and private. Furthermore, although twelve years have passed since July 1987, the full impact of Europe on *grass roots* sport and the Law in the United Kingdom cannot *at present* be appreciated or anticipated, particularly because the nature of the Common Market's purpose and philosophy is structured *economically* within its legal framework. For the bulk of the 30,920,000 million British participants, associated with 421 national general bodies Chapter 6, *Participation problems*, are drawn from the non-profit making voluntary sector. Accordingly the manner in which British sport *outside the high profile commercially orientated branch of the entertainment* industry will be affected by this new dimension to the English legal system cannot be assessed with any element of or accuracy or, indeed, confidence. This is exemplified by the Customs and Excise correction of its omission to operate the EEC Directive since 1990, as explained hereafter in Chapter 14, *No fine on fun*.

This uncertainty is also easily identifiable within Sport and the Law's own development within the United Kingdom. A full century elapsed between the judicial common law establishment of criminal liability for football field violence in *R v Bradshaw* (1878; supra) and its extension to Rugby Union in *R v Billinghurst* (1978; supra). Restraint of trade had to wait from its emergence in *Mitchell v Reynolds* (1711) 11 p Wms 181 and *Leather Cloth Co v Larsent* (1869) LR 9 Eq 345 before being pleaded and argued in *Aldershot Football Club v Banks* (1955 supra) and later in the *Eastham* (1963) and *Greig v Insole* (1978) cases, having been ignored in the *Kingaby* saga (1912; supra). Finally Mr Justice Eve's landmark *mens sana in corpore sano* sporting educational charity decision in *Mariette* (1915 supra)) which was ignored in the arguments vainly seeking similar status for the Sussex County Cricket Clubs Nursery Fund in *Re Patten* (1929; supra), had to wait for its resurrection in 1957 for the Sydney University Rugby Club in *Kearins v Kearins* (supra) before achieving the highest accolade from the House of Lords in the FA Youth Trust affirmation of it in *IRC v McMullan* (supra).

Add all of that to the number and names of the occasions in which the House of Lords has overruled lower courts in 75% of its referrals on sporting legal issues, and any confidence in applying EC law to UK sport when appropriate in the future must be muted. For another reversal of a lower court decision albeit on a *non*-sporting context, see *Marshall v Southampton and South-West Hampshire Health Authority (Teaching) (No 2)* (explained at p 379, below).

For present purposes, the level of awareness which is the leitmotiv throughout these pages is the most that can be aimed for here. More detailed assessment must await events which have to happen, apart from certain guidelines in the existing cases to date identified below.

4   COMMON MARKET SPORT AND LAW

Furthermore, Community law's supremacy over English, or in the special context which is being considered here, British law, is not confined to Brussels and Luxembourg. Chapter 14, *No fine on fun*, will show how the competition rules of the European Football Association, UEFA, enabled Scotland's Celtic Football Club and the Football Association in London to win their battles with H M Customs and Excise over whether or not business entertainment expenses of hotel accommodation should be allowed as recoverable input tax (*Celtic Football & Athletic Co Ltd v Customs and Excise Commissioners* [1983] STC 420, and LON/VAT Tribunal 83/484).

The basis for the Scottish Court of Session's and London VAT Tribunal's respective rulings was built into the UEFA competitions' respective rules. Those for the UEFA European Cup in Celtic's case, and those of the UEFA Youth Cup for the FA, both obliged the host country to provide accommodation which would be reciprocated on a return fixture. Thus, what would otherwise have been regarded as a non-claimable VAT input was justified by UEFA's administrative football law. The respective court and tribunal rulings resulted in favour of the two national football associations, resolving a conflict between UEFA law and Britain's VAT law as enacted by the British Parliament (under the then Finance Act which had created it in 1973, after Britain's Common Market entry, by the European Communities Act 1972).

Although this example of sport's administrative laws was not within Lord Denning's purview cited above, it illuminates the principle to be operated when their mandatory nature collides with a Parliamentary enactment, (or, perhaps it could be argued, a Customs and Excise interpretation of it). In the present context of Common Market considerations, this collision between sporting European law and sport's administrative law is coincidental. An equally vivid illustration could come from FIFA or any other supra-national governing sporting body. It assists as a prelude to Lord Denning's more formal judicial explanation, in a fully reported case on the fringes of sport concerning a woman betting shop employee, *Shields v E Coombes Holdings Ltd* ([1978] 1 WLR 1408 at 1415). The woman succeeded in a claim for equal pay with male counterhands under Britain's Equal Pay Act 1970. The then Master of the Rolls developed the supremacy of Community Law when he applied Article 119 of the Treaty of Rome [now Article 141 of the Treaty of Amsterdam] which creates an equal pay principle for men and women:

'It arises whenever there is a conflict of inconsistency between the law contained in an Article of the Treaty and the law contained in the internal law of one of the member states, whether passed before or after joining the Community. It says that in any such event the law of the Community shall prevail over that of the internal law of the member state'.

A similar experience occurred in *McCarthys Ltd v Smith* [1979] 3 All ER 325 [1980] ICR 672 at 692 affecting pay differential between men and women as a warehouse manager. Having failed before an industrial tribunal the complainant found support from Lord Denning, but a Court of Appeal majority, being less certain, caused a reference to the Court of Justice of the European Communities for a direct ruling under the provisions of Article 177 of the Treaty of Rome [now Article 234 of the Treaty of Amsterdam] concerning that particular procedure.

As Lord Denning has explained in *What Next In the Law* (Butterworths: 1982 at p 299) of the European Court at Luxembourg:

'They adopted my view. The case came back to us — when we held that the woman manager was entitled to equal pay with her predecessor. I said (1980) ICR 672 at 692:

"The majority of the court felt that Article 119 [now Article 141 of the Treaty of Amsterdam] was uncertain. So this court referred the problem to the European Court at Luxembourg. We have now been provided with the decision of that court. It is important now to declare and it must be made plain that the provisions of Article 119 of the EEC Treaty take priority over anything in our English statute on equal pay which is inconsistent with Article 119. That priority is given by our own law. It is given by the European Communities Act 1972 itself. Community law is now part of our law: and, whenever there is any inconsistency, Community law has priority. It is now supplanting English law. It is part of our law which overrides any other part which is inconsistent with it. I turn therefore to the decision given by the European Court. The answer they gave was that the man and the woman need not be employed at the same time (which had been argued against the woman in the case). The woman is entitled to equal pay for equal work, even when the woman is employed after the man has left. That interpretation must now be given by all courts in England. It will apply in this case and in such cases hereafter"'.

A decade and more after that landmark decision, in the wake of Sally Gunnell's claim that she is entitled to the same amount of payment as Linford Christie for her athletic appearances as a Barcelona Olympic Gold medallist, differentials and distinctions may well be argued successfully to exist because of different sponsorship agreements and crowd drawing power capacities. Nevertheless, the existence of these decisions from the

English Court of Appeal and the European Court point the way ahead for sport to recognise the potentialities which the European umbrella can unfold.

More recently, in 1993, the European Court ruled that the English Parliament's compensation ceiling under the Sex Discrimination Act 1975, as amended, section 65(2) for wrongful dismissal, was in a breach of Community Law and decided in effect that consequences will require amending legislation in the UK Parliament (*Marshall v Southampton and South-West Hampshire Health Authority (Teaching) (No 2)* [1993] 4 All ER 536, [1993] 3 WLR 1054 ECJ and article 6 of Council Directive (76(20) EEC)).

Finally, in the wider, more commercially orientated area of articles 85 and 86 [now Articles 81 and 82 of the Treaty of Amsterdam] dealing with restrictive commercial agreements, one case at least with a sporting flavour concerned the service of coin operated amusement machines for public houses in what used to be known as the East Riding of Yorkshire, now known as Humberside. An interim injunction was extended until the trial of action for what the evidence established was a serious issue to be tried, based on Article 85 of the Treaty [now Article 81 of the Treaty of Amsterdam], for which damages would not have been an adequate remedy in accordance with the well established principles in *American Cyanamid Co v Ethican Ltd* [1975] 1 All ER 504, per Sir Neil Lawson sitting as a judge of the High Court in *Cutsforth v Mansfield Inns Ltd* [1986] 1 All ER 577.

If ever the inevitable question is therefore asked — whatever has this got to do with sport — the answer is simple: everything. For just as rugby football and other mobile-body-contact sport players erroneously believed that they were above the law and immune from prosecution in the British Courts for violent foul play until the South Wales police put the prosecutor's boot into them dramatically in a conviction in 1977 (*R v Billinghurst* (supra)) so, too, could there be a corresponding belief of immunity from Community law. British sport, however, is affected by crucial decisions of the European Court of Justice.

The Common Market test for this purpose under Article 2 [now Article 2 of the Treaty of Amsterdam] relates to 'the economic policies of member states' and therefore applies only to professional and not to amateur participants. This coincides with the English courts' attitude which limit the restraint of trade doctrine to professional sportspersons and not amateurs, who have no trade (formally and official, at least) to protect in sport, irrespective of whatever may be their activities outside it (*R v The British Basketball Association, ex p Mickan and Cheesman*, (1981) 17 March, CAT No 01116), although no universally comprehensive definition of amateur has yet been created. In *Gasser v IAAF* (supra) relating to a woman athlete's two year suspension for alleged drug offences, Scott J held that restraint of trade could apply to athletes in receipt of trust funds under the IAAF regulations (a body often realistically referred to as the International Trust Funds Association), but held on the facts that the restraint was reasonable in all the circumstances.

5   EC SPORT AND LAW DECISIONS/JUDGMENTS

The Common Market decisions of the European Court of Justice about sport appear in a number of judgments. One concerns 'pacers', the racing cyclists' equivalent to pacemakers in the horse racing or athletic worlds, in a Dutch cycling contest (*Walgrave and Koch v Union Cycliste Internationale* case 36/74, ECR [1974] 1405, [1975] 1 CLMR 320). The other originated from an Italian Court's reference to the European Court from a commercial dispute about payment for services to discover players outside Italy to play for a local Italian club, Rovigo (*Dona v Mantero* case 13/76, ECR [1976] 1333, [1976] 2 CLMR 578). They both established without any qualification the important principle that the practice of *professional sport* is subject to Community Law and the jurisdiction of the European Court in so far as it constitutes an economic activity within the meaning of Article 2 of the EEC [now Article 2 of the Treaty of Amsterdam], ie

'It shall be the aim of the Community, by establishing a Common Market and progressively approximating the economic policies of Member States, to promote throughout the Community a harmonious development of economic activities, a continuous and balanced expansion, an increased stability, an accelerated raising of the standard of living and closer relations between its Member States'.

The Dutch cyclists' case arose because the international governing body controlling the sport made a new rule that in the world championships to be held in Spain (which was then not a member state),the pacer and the stayer had to be of the same nationality. The Court confirmed its jurisdictions over professional sporting issues but ruled that in spite of EEC Articles prohibiting discrimination (Articles 48–66 [now Articles 39 to 55 of the Treaty of Amsterdam]) national teams could be selected on the basis of harmony of nationality. The Dutch national team accordingly was not competing in breach of Community law. Correspondingly, England's national representative sporting sides are justifiably able to discriminate on playing merit against potential candidates who play in England but are not English nationals (although the curious anomalies of registering South African-born cricketers to play international cricket for England are too well known to be repeated here).

The Italian professional football commercial dispute arose because the employing club chairman claimed that the plaintiff agent acted prematurely in signing players whose registrations were prohibited under a rule of the Italian Football Federation. This limited registrations of non-Italian national players within the Italian domestic competitions. This restriction was held to be prohibited by the anti-discriminatory EEC Articles and referred back to the Rovigo tribunal for further adjudication on the facts. Of equal significance was confirmation by citation of the Walgrave precedents that jurisdictions existed to adjudicate on matters concerning professional sport as an economic issue under Article 2 (supra).

A third precedent has emerged between a Belgian National Football coach wishing to coach a French football team. The French football authorities insisted on a French qualification. The European court to whom the issue was referred decided that any refusal to permit continuation of such work required stated reasons of authenticity, of which absence would be a breach of the Treaty, *Heylens v Union Nationale des Entraineurs* (1987) ECR 4097.

The majority of the domestic British sporting administrators are all now aware of these crucially important judicial decisions. In addition to the Bosman ruling which progressed *Banks', Eastham's* and *Packer's* pioneer progress for contract freedom in commercial professional entertainment sport. They may not have time to consider an Opinion from a different Advocate General [Lenz] whose opinion in Bosman's led to the judgment Alber on 22 June 1999. He has advised that staggered dealings for transfers in the professional Basketball circuit can be compatible with the freedom of movement of *workers* under certain conditions [*Lehtonen and Castors Canadian Dry Namur-Braine v Basketball Feds.* Case C-176/96.

On a wider basis than Article 48 [now Article 39 of the Treaty of Amsterdam], Article 86 of the Treaty [now Article 82 of the Treaty of Amsterdam] was invoked by the Commission to which the Independent Television Association (ITVA) on 5 April 1989 had referred a purported granting by the Football Association at Lancaster Gate in London of exclusive permission to the BBC and a complex of companies, BSB, for televising football matches for which it owned the rights, and expressly excluding any other UK broadcaster at the Commissioner's request. The exclusivity clause is not only in breach of the competition Article 85(i) [now Article 81 of the Treaty of Amsterdam] but also an abuse of the FA's dominant position under Article 86 [now Article 82] — see official Journal of the EC 3 AW 1993 (93) c 94/06).

A year earlier on 10 June 1992 in another television dispute the Scottish Football Association succeeded before the European Court of Justice in having annulled an earlier EC Commission decision requiring the broadcasting of peremptory information relating to alleged interference with Argentine Football Association matches (SFAC EC Commission [Official Journal EC: 10:7:98 ref 92/C 174(2)]). Also in 1992, a licensed French private television company also succeeded with the European Court of Justice in challenging an EC decision to refuse an injunction against the European Broadcasting Union *La Cinq SAVEC Commission (European Broadcasting Union intervening)* Case T–44/90 [1992] 4 CMLR 44.

CONCLUSION

Such economically orientated EC decisions are as relevant and applicable as they would be in more recognisable domestic jurisdictions. They illuminate how wide the range of sporting legal issues can be when different national legal issues converge, but must be regarded in a different light for considering what value, if any, they have for *grass roots* UK sport.

Finally, Lord Denning's incoming tide conceals icebergs which are beyond the scope of these pages, but include particularly in a commercial context such depths as diplomas for coaching, lotteries, animals, ocean-going sailing yachts (even used for sporting purposes concurrently with commercial enterprises: see Chapter 14, *No fine on fun*, p 483) and VAT which will remain in the United Kingdom for only commercial and no longer for non-profit making sporting sources. This accords with Customs and Excise and H M Treasury developments to meet European requirements. Like the celebrated *Ole Man River*, Lord Denning's tide will keep rolling along, but for Sport and the Law, into territories undreamed of in the past, and of questionable significance *qua sport* for the grass roots 30,920,000 UK participants within 421 national governing bodies.

PART IV

Administration

CHAPTER 11

Fair Play and Reason in Court

1 INTRODUCTION-GENERAL

Michael Watson's judgment award against the British Boxing Board of Control in London's High Court on 25 September 1999 for negligent failure to protect his health in 1991 after his World title fight against Chris Eubank belongs more appropriately to Chapters 6 and 7 respectively on *Participation Problems* and *Sports Medicine and the law*. It is included here for three reasons.

First, because of the Defendant's status as a governing body, and the erroneous suggestion that it was the first time such liability had been established against a national sporting governing body, at least in the United Kingdom. Second, because such a development disclosed to generations unfamiliar with the past has been hailed as a messianic revelation in the manner already explained in the Introduction after Mrs Justice Ebsworth's judgment against the Welsh Rugby Union in 1997 (on that occasion for breach of the rules of natural justice).

Third, because of the incompetence among National Governing Sporting Bodies and their legal advisers there is a movement towards exclusion of the jurisdiction of the Courts against them in favour of arbitration and away from the Courts. Such a shift of venue would not lessen expense, and would also sweep under carpets away from public scrutiny and exposure culpable misconduct of the kind experienced by Michael Watson. His circumstances of alleged disastrous administrative incompetence now subject to appeal were not dissimilar from the injuries caused to Wendy Morell by the British Les Autres Association during her preparation for the 1992 Barcelona Paralympics. Training in a leisure centre for an archery selection she was injured severely by a discus thrown against a net and *not* a safety curtain (see *Morell v Owen* supra). Furthermore, the British Boxing Board of Control was also on the receiving end of a money judgment against a boxer's claim, but reversed in its favour on appeal, where its name does not appear in the reported title by the action in *Doyle v White City Stadium Ltd* [1935] 1 KB 110.

2 INTRODUCTION-SPECIFIC

By the nature of his claim and judgment, Michael Watson was entitled to seek justice and obtained it. The purpose and thrust of this chapter concentrates on initial denials of justice and attempts, some successful and others not so successful with Courts. Furthermore the story which unfolds here is a classic example of an enlightened judiciary, inevitably led by Lord Denning's vision to meet the needs of the changing scenario in this dynamic growth area where the tensions on the field of play are often reflected in the Committee room or board room off it. Through abortive claims for libel and ultimately successful claims for restraint of trade, an accepted and acceptable awareness of the correct criteria has been established for dispensing justice on the appropriate evidence in the interests of not only the victims of physical injury and administrative oppression but also of sport itself. They are delineated at the end of this chapter; and having been cited and/or recycled frequently at seminars and other publications they are identified here as the yardstick to be borne in mind throughout this chapter and the basis for the title to it:

(1) avoid any risk of pre-judgment or prejudice or likelihood of it;
(2) formulate and notify clearly, preferably in writing, any assertions needing reply;
(3) notify clearly, and preferably in writing, any date for investigation or hearing;
(4) act intra vires, within the rules, and not ultra vires, outside them;
(5) remember the right to be heard in defence of any allegation;
(6) in cases of difficulty or complexity, consider carefully, any request for legal representation.

Consistent with the gradual fusion of Parliamentary, common law and equity and EEC developments within sport, sport has attempted with varying degrees of success and failure to create its own mechanisms, jurisdictions, rules and regulations for controlling its administration.

The courts of law become the last resort for victims of maladministration and oppression to obtain justice when their application does not conform to common law or the equity rules of natural justice. This chapter therefore discusses how sporting governing bodies and those whom they purport to control forced the courts and judges to recognize the roles they have to play when fair play and reason in sporting committee rooms and council chambers flies out of their windows.

Notwithstanding that final goal, however,

> 'Justice can often be done in domestic tribunals better by a good layman
> than by a bad lawyer'.

That was how Lord Denning explained the court's general reluctance to intervene in such proceedings. This also reflected the fact which is often forgotten, overlooked or, ignored, that nearly 100% of contested criminal matters in the United Kingdom are concluded either by lay justices guided on legal matters by professionally trained court clerks, or by juries directed on matters of law by the trial judge (the only exceptions being the legally qualified stipendiary magistrates adjudicating in densely populated communities). Lord Denning continued:

> 'This is essentially so in activities like football and other sports, where no
> points of law are likely to arise, and it is all part of the proper regulation of
> the game.' (*Enderby Town Football Club v The Football Association* [1971]
> 1 All ER 215).

During 1989 Lord Denning's words were illuminated by a coincidence of administrative and legal experiences involving Swindon Town Football Club, the International Cricket Conference, the Test and County Cricket Board and HH The Aga Khan. Each particular situation was well publicised at the relevant time. The connecting thread between them demonstrates the necessity for a level of awareness, the achievement of which is the object of this book.

Swindon Town Football Club was demoted from the First Division of the Football League to the Third Division in 1990 because of Boardroom financial irregularities. After a tentative High Court action was abandoned due to a realistic risk of high costs, the directors of the Club with great communal support exercised their right *within the Football League Regulations* to attend before an Appeals Committee of Football Association Councillors. An impeccable hearing conducted by Lord Denning's concept of 'good laymen' resulted in a preservation of Swindon Town's Second Division status based on sound legal principles. Ironically, a spokesman for the Football League had expected the Football Association to support the Football League. In fact the Football Association Appeals Committee did not support the Football League because they considered the penalty it had imposed to be too oppressive. As one of the Counsel representing Swindon Town, I pointed out in the sports correspondence columns of *The Times* (18 July 1990) the Football League's bizarre and unsporting attitude. I also questioned without any response or rebuttal, the fitness of the Football League to administer its competition when such an attitude exists. More recently Jacob J in London's Chancery Division of the High

Court held the Football Association of Wales to have acted in restraint of trade when prohibiting three minor league football clubs from playing in their home grounds (*Newport AFC Ltd and Others v FA of Wales Ltd* (1994) 144 NLJ 1351) [1995] 2 All ER 87. In arriving at this conclusion, and contrary to opposing arguments granting an interlocutory injunction, he also adjudicated that contrary to opposing arguments a declaration is a sufficient cause of action (see also Grayson: *Sport and the Law: All England Law Reports Annual Review* 1995).

Earlier in 1989 the former Secretary to the International Cricket Conference and MCC, Jack Bailey, published a book he entitled *Conflicts in Cricket*. In revelatory pages 101–2, he wrote of the Packer litigation which had been fought out in 1977 and 1978 in the same Chancery Division of London's High Court as thirteen years earlier Mr Justice Wilberforce had applied the long-standing common law principles and equitable reliefs associated with restraints of trade to the professional football world. (*Eastham v Newcastle United Football Club Ltd and the Football Association* [1963] 3 All ER 139.)

> 'The cricket authorities had lost on every point of law involved, although they had emerged with some credit from a moral standpoint. Had it all been worth it? Or rather had we anything to show for the damages and costs awarded against us, amounting to some £250,000* (later shared equally between ICC and TCCB) apart from a vast amount of publicity for cricket all over the world?
>
> Well, for one thing, it had been a lesson. It had taught the cricket authorities that good intentions, if not paving the road to hell, are not enough when it comes to the law of the land ... A contract was a contract and if certain players were required they would have to be issued with legally binding contracts for a twelve-month period or longer.
>
> We also learnt the law regarding inducement of breach of legal contract and what was reasonable in the cricket world, both to protect established cricket and to prevent unlawful restraint of trade.
>
> ...
>
> During the case, and at a comparatively early stage, our counsel had entered a defence that ICC and TCCB were employers' associations and as such immune, as were trade unions under current law, from the charges against them. The rules and prime activities of both bodies were not held to constitute them as employers' associations, but almost as soon as the case was over TCCB set about amending their rules and constitution to enable them to qualify'.

*   And later passed on to the unfortunate MCC and County Cricket Club members in increased subscriptions, any one of whom could have told the then legal advisers of the ICC and TCCB that they were batting, bowling and fielding on a likely losing legal wicket from the start: and at least one solicitor county cricket club executive, Stanley Allen, MBE, from Sussex, did!

It was not the fault of the 'good layman' who was the nominal defendant, Douglas Insole, that his experiences as a distinguished Corinthian-Casual amateur footballer, former Cambridge University soccer Blue, and ultimate representative of his University on the FA Council, had not prepared him for expensive professional advice resulting in that disastrous legal result fifteen years after the football landmark decision in the *Eastham* case during 1963.

Correspondingly, it was not surprising that HH The Aga Khan battled in vain against the Jockey Club's disqualification of his filly Alysa, after winning the Epsom Oaks in 1989, by use of the judicial review machinery, when he and his legal advisers were trapped by a precedent of the Court of Appeal in *Law v National Greyhouse Racing Club Ltd* [1983] 3 All ER 300 that the judicial review procedure is not applicable to private sporting governing bodies. His legal advisers had chosen to argue his claim on this basis instead of the route recommended by the Court of Appeal by way of a writ for breach of contract earlier. As I have written in the *All England Law Reports Annual Review* for 1992, after he had lost on this inevitable ground in the Court of Appeal,

'It left him and his advisers with a recognition of his breach of contract remedies — and, in the absence of any application for leave to appeal to the House of Lords, or of any apparent intention ever to have tested this particular climate in the House of Lords — with the question, why on earth the traditional contract route had been ignored in favour of a procedure trapped by binding precedent (*R v Disciplinary Committee of the Jockey Club exp The Aga Khan* (1992) *Times*, 9 December)'.

A careful analysis of how and why this has occurred appears in Catherine Bond's Appendix 14. It emphasises the warning of Woolf LJ (as he then was) at the Divisional Court level in the All England Review [1991] *Sport and the Law*, pp 313–314 that there was 'no relief which the court can provide on application for judicial review until the law is either changed by a higher court or by statutory intervention', with the Aga Khan's ultimate withdrawal of his support for British racing from the United Kingdom to France and Ireland for five years between 1990 and 1995.

3   LIBEL

Twenty-two years before *Enderby Town* in 1971, Lord Denning had prepared the ground for those conclusions as stated above with a prophetic foretaste of what lay ahead, given through a judgment concurring with the better known words of Tucker LJ, in the sporting libel action of *Russell v Duke of Norfolk* ([1949] 1 All ER 109, [1949] 65 TLR 225). It was the last of many unsuccessful attempts in the years 1919–39 between the two World Wars to use this particular remedy of defamation before a judge and jury to challenge sporting disciplinary tribunal decisions. Domestic tribunal decisions can easily have adverse effects upon those who are subject to their verdicts. Thus, as this chapter explains, they emerged in the last fling of the Gentlemen v Players era through sensational libel actions at the time from the two sporting spheres where unashamed and unconcealed financial interests and investments predominated in two of the most high-profile professional sports, horse racing and association football.

Today libel has been replaced by declaratory judgments through an exclusively judge-made route identifiable in its own category of administrative law. Within the world of sport there is now an overlap between the general common law of economic torts which protect interference with employment and contractual relationships and the correct procedural remedies. Because mistakes by administrators and practitioners still continue as illustrated through the last thirty years from the worlds of football (*Eastham* and *Revie v The Football Association*), cricket (*Packer*) and racing (*Nagle* and the *Aga Khan*), an explanation of how the modern route was carved, which also highlights the errors made before it began and along the way, is the most suitable and helpful form of narrative, as guidance in avoiding similar disasters in the future.

Lord Denning's path to natural justice in the world of sport began with one of those many libel actions which appeared to pre-Second World War practitioners to be the most effective and, indeed, only, remedy for protecting reputations and clearing the name of victims defamed or otherwise harmed by debatable domestic tribunal disciplinary or administrative decisions. In the *Russell v Duke of Norfolk* trial the Court of Appeal considered a racing trainer's licence which was found to have been withdrawn after a properly conducted inquiry by the sport's ruling body, the Jockey Club. It decided that a drug had been administered to a horse named Boston Boro, trained by James Russell, which ran in the John O'Gaunt Plate at the Lincoln Spring meeting of 1947, the race before the traditional Lincolnshire Handicap (which is now run at Doncaster).

The finding of fact was to the effect that the trainer was guilty of negligence in not preventing the drug's administration. When the decision was published in the Racing Calendar that negative conclusion was omitted. It thereby allegedly created a contrary implication, namely, that the plaintiff himself was a party or privy to the more serious inference of active administration of the drug (per Asquith LJ [1949] 1 All ER at 118, 55 TLR at 231). The libel action failed on two conventional grounds:

(1) publication was privileged, and
(2) the plaintiff had consented to it contractually via the Rules of Racing, by which he was undoubtedly bound.

4   NATURAL JUSTICE AND RESTRAINT OF TRADE

In the Court of Appeal, however, Lord Denning took the first step on the road which has led to the modern law of natural justice in sport. It not only encourages, but also on the appropriate facts, enforces challenges to unjust and thereby unfair decisions by domestic sporting tribunals and their governing bodies. He explained the following pre-conditions ([1949] 1 All ER at 119–120, [1949] 55 TLR at 231–232).

(1) 'Common justice requires that before any man is found guilty of an offence carrying such consequences [as taking away his livelihood] there should be an enquiry at which he has opportunity of being heard'.

(2) 'The Jockey Club has a monopoly in an important field of human activity ...' [a point to which he was to return on more than one occasion, and particularly in the landmark decision of *Nagle v Fielden* [1966] 2 QB 633.

(3) '... whether the enquiry was held in accordance with the essentials of justice. That, in my opinion, is the conclusion of law ... It would be no easy matter for a jury to distinguish between the question whether there was a proper inquiry and the question whether the decision of the stewards [of the Jockey Club] was right or wrong; whereas a Judge is able to put aside the correctness of the decision as irrelevant. On this question I am entirely in agreement that there is only one conclusion possible on the evidence — namely, that the enquiry was in accordance with the principles of natural justice'.

That conclusion of law is summarised neatly in Halsbury's Laws of England [4th Edn] Volume 1, paragraph 64 at page 76, where justice in the law is married with fair play in sport by the following two sentences.

'Implicit in the concept of fair adjudication lie two critical principles, namely, that no man shall be a judge in his own cause (*nemo judex in causa sua*) and that no man shall be condemned unheard (*audi alteram partem*). These two principles, the rules of natural justice, must be observed by courts save where application is excluded expressly by necessary implication'.

Nevertheless, Lord Denning explained in *The Discipline of the Law* (page 150) in 1979, precisely thirty years after he first laid the trail in *Russell v Duke of Norfolk*, with the following paragraph under the head of 'Powers against own members' at the outset of the section 'Abuse of "group" powers'.

'During the last 30 years, the Courts have done much to protect the individual member against injustice by the association itself. They have condemned

Rules that are in unreasonable restraint of trade and held them to be invalid. They have overthrown the decisions of domestic tribunals which were unjust. They have interfered with the discretion of committees when exercised unfairly. They have, in accordance with their long tradition, upheld the weak and put down the "oppressor's wrong"'.

The observant reader will note in that citation the additional road alongside the path of natural justice by which judges have protected the victims of administrative group oppression. In addition to surveillance of domestic tribunals by the courts he identifies injustice by the association itself and condemnation of 'Rules that are in unreasonable restraint of trade and held ... to be invalid'.

When he wrote in 1979 that extra dimension of unreasonable restraint of trade was fresh in every sporting lawyer's mind as well as in Lord Denning's, resulting from his twin offices of Master of the Rolls and President of Whitchurch Cricket Club. In the preceding year of 1978 Slade J had adjudicated in London's Chancery Division of the High Court against cricket's establishment in the celebrated *Packer* litigation. He upheld complaints through representative proceedings by three well-known players via procedural remedies of declaratory judgments that:

(1) the International Cricket Conference (ICC) intended changes retrospectively of qualifying rules, and
(2) the Test and County Cricket Board's proposed ban was both ultra vires and unlawfully in restraint of trade.

Concurrent with these judgments were further rulings brought by Packer's World Series Cricket Pty. Limited against the same governing bodies that their conduct was also an unlawful inducement to the contracted players concerned to break their contracts with the Australian-based management (*Greig v Insole* [1978] 1 WLR 302).

Coincidentally, in 1979 Cantley J in London's Queen Bench Division of the High Court adjudicated against the rejection by the Football Association of the plea made to it by the legal representatives of its former national team manager, Don Revie. A disciplinary tribunal of the FA had earlier spoken critically of Revie and thereby demonstrated a likelihood of bias thus breaching the elementary rules of natural justice. The tribunal banned Revie from football management activities for ten years. As Revie's leading counsel, Mr Gilbert Gray QC, has explained to the author, the disciplinary tribunal was formed by FA officers who were purporting to adjudicate on his client's conduct after he had withdrawn from his England team management contract. The High Court judgment expunged the ten-year ban which had been imposed on Revie because he had established the likelihood of bias (1979) *Times*, 14 December).

The link between the two judgments of *Greig v Insole* and *Revie v The FA*, coming so close together in time and connecting the two national games, was the economic consequence of taking away a man's livelihood which had been recognised by Lord Denning initially in *Russell v Duke of Norfolk* in 1949, and crystallised by him in *The Discipline of the Law* in 1979. They had the following effect upon a sporting practitioner's livelihood of:

(1) a governing body, by creating restrictive practices for working conditions and acting unreasonably in restraint of trade which can curtail or limit or even exclude the right to work, which Lord Denning, Danckwerts LJ and Salmon LJ identified in *Nagle v Fielden* [1966] 2 QB 633, and

(2) a disciplinary tribunal purporting to impose periods of suspension and acting unfairly in breach of natural justice which can be equally damaging to that right to work.

Ironically, for the FA, its *Official History* published a quarter-of-a-century earlier to celebrate the ninetieth anniversary of its foundation in 1953, contained the following citation from the charge to the trial jury in *Russell v Duke of Norfolk* by the trial judge, the Lord Chief Justice, Lord Goddard. It was approved by the Court of Appeal, with a significant commentary on it by the author, Geoffrey Green, the distinguished *Times* Association Football Correspondent for many years and a former Cambridge University soccer blue. At p 349, he cited Lord Goddard to have directed the jury:

'Did Mr Russell receive a fair and honest hearing before the Stewards? Was the inquiry before the Stewards conducted fairly? Domestic tribunals, such as the Jockey Club, were not bound by procedure such as governed the courts of law, but in holding an inquiry into the conduct of a person they must act fairly and give the person to be brought before them a fair notice of the charge of, or complaint against him and an opportunity to defend himself'.

Green commented with much prescience for a non-lawyer in the light of subsequent judicial affirmation,

'The parallel between the Football Association and the Jockey Club in this matter is important since all Football Courts of Inquiry, all Commissions and Disciplinary Boards are domestic tribunals qualified to act under the Rules of The Football Association. The importance of strict adherence to the procedure laid down by the FA is, therefore, paramount'.

That passage was available to the FA's legal advisers when two sets of procedural errors were committed only a few years after Green wrote in

1953. During the later 1950s and early 1960s two Commissions of Enquiry purported to adjudicate upon the alleged irregularities about the affairs of the Sunderland Football Club and its officials and players. Public acknowledgement of administrative errors with appropriate costs was duly made twice during 1962 in two separate statements made in separate High Court actions brought by the players in one, and the club and officials in another, before two different judges in the Chancery Division of London's High Court, as we shall see below. It was still available to the different generation of FA Tribunal members twenty-five years later in the *Revie* case when the High Court was required to intervene in circumstances epitomised by the opening citation at the commencement of this chapter from Lord Denning in his judgment in one of the FA's happier court appearances when defending against *Enderby Town*.

How the law has developed in this crucial area for the victims of oppression from authoritarian sporting regimes is a classic example of the protection created by the courts without Parliamentary intervention when they are activated effectively by the correct procedural remedies operated by practitioners selecting the right and not the wrong legal remedies. It also illustrates once more how sport reflects a wider and more general development of the law not only for the benefit of sport itself but also for society generally, with the application to the narrow world of sport of the developing legal process from the larger world outside it. It is a process which the inadequacies of incompetent governing bodies and their equally inadequate advisers seek to avoid by excluding the jurisdiction of the Courts.

5   THE JUDICIAL ROAD TO SPORTING JUSTICE

(1)   Between two World Wars: 1919–39

In the years before, between and immediately after the two World Wars the feudalism inherent in the Gentlemen and Players amateur-professional dichotomy, based upon its economic and social class distinctions, dominated the administration and much of the playing of British sport, particularly the two most professionally and commercially orientated and popularly practised pursuits, horse-racing and professional football. Indeed, at the time of writing in the late 1990s some would say that so far as a practical and practising gap between amateur administrators and professional practitioners is concerned, the divisions still exist in both areas in nearly all participatory sports. The need for a full-time paid director-general or secretary need not necessarily bridge these divisions if the administration is still subject to committee control.

Before 1939, with money and reputations at stake, and the control and remedies of the kind considered here available in the courts but unrecognised and unused by the practitioners instructed by victims of sporting administrative oppression, each sport inspired the inevitable litigation with ineffective results in the examples cited below as we have seen earlier. Professional footballers' advisers before 1919 had failed to choose the correct legal remedies to tackle the restraint of trade transfer system in *Kingaby v Aston Villa* during 1912 (supra); after 1919, in *Davis v Harrison* [1927] 43 TLR 623, they failed to equate professional cricketers' tax-free benefits with footballers, because the professional footballers' terms of employment incorporated a discretionary benefit claim by contractual ties instead of the non-contracted public appreciations, which contrasted with professional cricketers in the saga lasting from 1920 until the House of Lords final judgment in *Seymour v Reed* [1927] AC 554. Racing, too, had its revenue problems in the same year when a professional jockey's appreciation from a grateful winning owner was held to be liable to tax (*Wing v O'Connell* [1927] IR 84); and both sporting sources witnessed unsuccessful libel actions against the two ruling bodies, the FA and the Jockey Club, with a foretaste of what might have been if the correct procedural and substantive remedies had been considered.

Professional football was concerned with irregularities allegedly committed during the 1920s against the FA's own internal Rules and the Football League's parallel Regulations by the then Board of Directors of the Arsenal Football and Athletic Company Limited. The story is told in similar general terms without legal analysis by the former Arsenal *amateur* international player Bernard Joy in *Forward Arsenal* (1952) at pages 49–50, and by Geoffrey Green in *The History of the Football Association* (1953) before the passage cited above equating the FA's domestic tribunal procedures with the Jockey Club (page 285).

The FA's investigation into Arsenal's affairs resulted in suspensions of certain directors, including Mr G W Peachey, Mr J M Humble, the Chairman, Sir Henry Norris, and the club itself was censured. As Bernard Joy wrote of the Chairman,

'It was unfortunate that his soccer interests ended on such an unhappy note, because he did as much as anyone to put Arsenal on the map by instigating the move from Woolwich to Highbury' (in 1913).

Two separate sets of proceedings were launched — one by Mr Peachey for company law relief in the Chancery Division of the High Court; the other by Sir Henry Norris in the Queen's Bench Division for libel and impugning the investigation. All were unsuccessful in circumstances which prima facie might have been handled differently to produce more advantageous results, ie they should have proceeded by the breach of natural justice route which was available even at that time instead of the by then conventional and almost obsessive faith, with adverse results, in defamation. The following examples illustrate how the governing bodies should and could have been taken to the courts, but were not.

Peachey's action was brought against the company-club to prevent the surviving directors implementing the FA's directives to the Board that the condemned men should 'not be permitted to continue in their positions as directors or to take part in the management of the club'. Injunctive relief was sought against the mechanism of the club's company meetings and share transactions. In the end he withdrew his claim against the club upon payment of his costs. For present day practitioners, however, the significance lies in the concession made by Peachey's Counsel as reported at the time:

> 'he did not think the findings of an outside body like the Football Association would be appealable against in that Court, or could scarcely be appealed against in any way. He should imagine that the Football Association could only be proceeded against by way of libel action ... The decision of the Football Association in a matter of this sort was not a judicial position that could be against in that Court ... The Football Association purported to dismiss Mr Peachey from the board of directors ... The only ground alleged against Mr Peachey was that he had been remiss in his duty. This Mr Peachey denied, and although he attended the meeting of the Commission he was not asked a single question on the point ... Mr Peachey had acted in the way he had [ie of suing the club] because he was dissatisfied with the original finding by the Football Association ... He felt he was being hounded out'.

(*Daily Telegraph*, 17 November 1927, page 14.)

That revelation of 'not being asked a single question on the point' on the attendance by Mr Peachey at the Commission contained a prima facie complaint of a breach of natural justice. It was never pursued. Ironically in the same Chancery Division of the High Court the then MP for the Govan division of Glasgow, Neil Maclean, was commencing proceedings by a writ alleging that he had been wrongly expelled by a trade union committee. He argued that the Trade Union had acted *ultra vires* its own rules and thereby unlawfully, and also that they were in breach of natural justice. Although the claim failed, Maughan J, later Lord Chancellor as Lord Maughan, reiterated in early 1929 in language appropriate to this text:

> 'the principles of fair play so deeply rooted in the minds of modern Englishman that a provision for an inquiry necessarily imports that the

accused person should be given his chance of defence and explanation. On that point there is no difficulty'.

(Maclean v The Workers Union [1929] in Ch 602 at 625).

The idea expressed by Peachey's counsel that 'the Football Association could only be proceeded against by way of a libel action' was clearly shared by Sir Henry Norris's advisers. At the same time that Maughan J was hearing evidence and argument which led to his judgment (supra) during early 1929 in the Chancery Division of the High Court, Sir Henry Norris pursued the first of his two Queen's Bench Division actions against the FA. It was for libel based upon an imputation of alleged dishonesty for having received relatively small amounts of money from Arsenal FC in breach of the appropriate domestic rules and regulations.

The opening address by the eminent and experienced practitioner Sir Patrick Hastings KC to the then Lord Chief Justice, Lord Hewart and the jury, contained these ominous words:

'A Commission was set up which was remarkably appointed and amazingly conducted, but whether it was properly constituted and conducted did not affect the question of the alleged libel'.

Equally amazingly, however, after the libel action was lost, he told the court about a further action between the same parties which was in the court list which sought to impugn the appointment and proceedings of the commission appointed by the FA:

'in view of what had happened in the first case he felt that no useful purpose could be served by proceeding with the [second] action'.

Again, a prima facie breach of natural justice would appear to have existed at least for the purposes of argument and evidence, in the manner which later succeeded against the FA after the Second World War (twice during 1962 in the circumstances concerning the two formal Commissions of Inquiry into Sunderland Football Club, a third time on behalf of Don Revie in 1979). On each occasion in 1927 and 1929 affecting Arsenal the available procedural route for obtaining an effective judgment against the FA appears to have been unrecognised or needlessly rejected.

Shortly afterwards during 1931 and 1932 Hastings was again concerned in a sporting libel action which was a forerunner of the *Russell v Norfolk* claim in 1949. *Chapman v Lord Ellesmere* ([1932] 2 KB 431), is cited extensively in all the leading practitioners' and students' textbooks on issues of privilege and damages. Here it is noteworthy principally for three reasons:

(1) consistent with the Jockey Club's practice in *Russell's* case, no criticism was, or appears likely to have been, made of the conduct of the domestic proceedings to create a complaint about natural justice;
(2) the Jockey Club's conclusion that the trainer had been negligent in not safeguarding the admittedly doped horse was published in the Racing Calendar and elsewhere in a manner which could have justified readers in a belief of personal involvement: yet there was in fact no personal involvement in this case and the trainer was not given the opportunity to establish his innocence;
(3) Hastings himself wrote in *Cases in Court* that the libel claim:

> ' ... was the only method by which Mr Chapman could free his character from the implication placed upon it, and establish once and for all that he was completely innocent ... The public attention drawn to his unfortunate position by the overwhelming verdict of a jury must have gone a long way to wipe away the stigma of his warning-off notice.' [page 83].

It is a nice academic point in 1999 whether the same result might have been achieved for both Chapman in 1932 and Russell in 1949 today. If they had sought declaratory judgments identifying the discrepancies between the published Racing Calendars' version of the tribunal findings and the truth they could possibly have been successful in clearing their names. Had similar circumstances arisen today a claim against the publisher of the Jockey Club's rules for negligent misstatement would be justified under the Civil Law of negligence (as distinct from the Jockey Club rules), based on the landmark decision of the House of Lords in *Hedley Byrne & Co Ltd v Heller & Partners Ltd* [1964] Ac 465.

One difference between the *Chapman* (1932) and *Russell* (1949) decisions which justified Hastings' comment 'to wipe away the stigma' was that at the trial Chapman succeeded initially against three sets of defendants: the Jockey Club, its agents Weatherby & Sons, who published the *Racing Calendar*, and *The Times* and other newspapers. The Court of Appeal reversed the jury's findings against the first two defendants (the Jockey Club and Weatherby) on the ground that the proceedings and publication respectively were privileged (consistent with the *Russell v Duke of Norfolk* findings). A retrial was ordered on the excessive damages awards against *The Times* and other news agencies (who were then not privileged but today would also be privileged under the Defamation Act 1952, Schedule 11, paragraph 8 (c)). Hastings' biographer, H Montgomery Hyde, wrote: 'No new trial took place as the parties came to terms'. Romer LJ

[1932] 2 KB at page 477 noted that Hastings' forensic skills at the height of his advocacy powers had excited 'the jury [who] became "furious" and "hysterical"' before awarding the damages which were ruled on appeal to have been excessive.

The remaining seven years after *Chapman's* case, leading up to the outbreak of war in 1939, were free from challenges to the jurisdiction of sporting governing bodies, with one exception: this was *Doyle v White City Stadium Ltd* [1935] 1 KB 110 (see pages 149–50) (supra). There, the Court of Appeal overturned the trial judge and a plea for leniency on behalf of a disqualified boxer, pointing out that 'rules for clean fighting' were in his own as well as 'any other contestant's interests!': a lesson and moral overlooked by many modern ball game administrators at all levels. Indeed, the public attention drawn to *Chapman's* case as recorded by Hastings could also have contributed to this absence of sporting disciplinary disputes. As Hastings also wrote in *Cases in Court*:

> 'At the same time the action may have done some good in the racing world by establishing, even more firmly than before, the absolute authority of the Jockey Club'.

Thus, other sporting bodies and the general public could understandably have misled themselves into the belief of the infallibility of all sporting governing bodies. If this belief existed, the post-war years should have dispelled it.

(2)   After two World Wars: 1945 onwards

A year before the Second World War ended, in 1944, Mr A T Denning KC, a survivor of the First World War, was appointed to the High Court bench. In 1948 he was promoted to the Court of Appeal. In 1952, three years after *Russell's* case, he took the first step along the widest possible road (beyond the narrow sporting scene) for the courts' control over power based bodies on which sport has been obliged to travel. It is traceable through

(1) the well-known and much canvassed Court of Appeal judgments in *Abbott v Sullivan* ([1952] 1 All ER 226); *Lee v The Showman's Guild of Great Britain* ([1952] 2 QB 239) and many others through to the Vice-Chancellor, Sir Robert Megarry's comprehensive survey in *McInnes v Onslow Fane* ([1978] 1 WLR 1520) in the tribunal lane; and

(2) also through the parallel economic pathway of restraint of trade and interference with the right to work stimulated by the little known county court action *Aldershot Football Club v Banks* (*Aldershot News*, 4

November 1955): Wilberforce J in *Eastham v Newcastle United* [1964]
Ch 413; the Court of Appeal in *Nagle v Fielden* [1966] 2 QB 633; *Cook
v FA and FIFA* [1972] 24 March, p 8 down to the *Packer* litigation in
1977 (interlocutory) and final judgment of Slade J (supra) in 1978, and
many others, too, including, more recently, *Newport AFC Ltd and
Others v FA of Wales Ltd* (1994) 144 NLJ 1351, 7 October.

Today, there *should* be few sporting bodies and sportspersons of all ages,
sexes, denominations or disciplines unaware of the courts' overriding
surveillance in these fields. Nevertheless, the extent to which the message
has not yet been received was demonstrated towards the end of 1986 and
1987 by yet another dimension to the David Bishop rugby common assault
saga. His Crown Court conviction and custodial sentence of one month,
varied by the Court of Appeal Criminal Division to a suspended sentence
of one month's imprisonment for two years, was followed by an 11 months'
suspension imposed on him by the Welsh Rugby Union. Complaints that
this was a needless intrusion by the sport's governing body overlooked
the double jeopardy to which any practitioner in the learned professions
or services is also subjected by his or her peers if convicted of serious
criminal as distinct from minor offences.

The length of the Welsh Rugby Union's suspension of 11 months was
also challenged. Bishop complained that it had been imposed without his
having had an opportunity to be heard personally at the time when the
suspension was imposed. His amateur status did not deprive his entitlement
to natural justice. After reported proposals to challenge the initial decision
in the High Court, the Welsh Rugby Union provided for a personal hearing
attended by legal representatives. This sequence of events suggested that
initially a denial of natural justice could have occurred on the occasion of
the original decision to suspend the player, ie he was not present or
represented or heard in his defence or aware of the nature of the disciplinary
(as distinct from the court) charge against him.

In due course, the first finding was confirmed after a full and represented
personal hearing. As soon as the result was known, Bishop's advisers
once more complained of injustice and again announced an intention once
more to seek High Court intervention. On this occasion, the only apparent
complaint could have been directed to the composition of the investigating
tribunal itself on the lines laid down by Cantley J in *Revie's* case, or against
the actual conduct of the proceedings within the four walls of the hearing.
The earliest published reports recorded that the proceedings begun in the
Cardiff High Court Registry had been discontinued because of an
irregularity. This would be consistent with the published statement of
Bishop's advisers wishing to seek judicial review of the second and
confirmatory verdict. In *Law v National Greyhound Racing Club Limited*
[1983] 3 All ER 300, the Court of Appeal emphasised earlier decisions that

the emerging procedural jurisdiction which the courts have evolved (known as judicial review) is confined to the review of activities of a public nature as distinct from a purely private or domestic nature. (See Appendix 14 for full discussion of this case.)

Thus the Leicester Rugby Club's successful challenge all the way up to the House of Lords concerned a public activity. The challenge was brought under the judicial review procedure against the purported ban by its local public authority, Leicester City Council, upon the club using council playing fields property, because the Club allowed its players to exercise their freedom of choice to wear England's white rugby shirt in South Africa. The Welsh Rugby Union's disciplinary committee decision on David Bishop, although concerned with a public issue, does not apply. Traditional High Court remedies suffice. That was how the post-war pattern began to unfold two years after *Russell's case in 1949.*

Abbott v Sullivan (supra), which occupied the Court of Appeal for five days in 1951, was the starting gate for the courts to enter an arena in attempting to dispense justice among domestic tribunals purporting to act in disciplinary circumstances. This was the first time that domestic tribunals had been investigated in depth and there was a subsequent impact on sporting tribunals. Ultra vires conduct was established successfully against a disciplinary committee which caused a corn porter employed to remove grain from ships in London Docks to be removed from a register of corn porters. He could not obtain damages for it from a trial judge or from a Court of Appeal majority. Claims for defamation and procuring a breach of contract were dismissed. Lord Denning who dissented, however, considered it to be:

'not an ordinary contract case. It is a claim in an uncharted area on the border land of contract and tort';

and he thought the court 'should entertain the claim for damages' on the footing of contract.

Four months after *Abbott v Sullivan*, a different court in *Lee v The Showman's Guild of Great Britain* [1952] 2 QB 329 unanimously upheld the trial judge's verdict that a ruling by a disciplinary committee purporting to fine and ultimately expel a member on the basis of alleged unfair competition was ultra vires and void. Arguments that the committee had exclusive power under its rules to interpret them to the exclusion of the courts were dealt with by Lord Justice Romer saying:

'The proper tribunals for the determination of legal disputes in this country are the courts, and they are the only tribunals which by training and experience, and assisted by properly qualified advocates, are fitted for the task. The courts jealously uphold and safeguard the prima facie privilege of every man to report to them for the determination and enforcement of his legal rights'.

Two years later, in 1954, a sporting governing body's rules for the first time received the same treatment, albeit in a commercially based dispute as distinct from its disciplinary jurisdiction. Commercial claims in tort against certain officers of the British Amateur Weightlifters' Association by members were defended procedurally (as distinct from on the merits). This was consistent with the Court of Appeals principles set out in the *Showman's Guild*, Mr Justice Lynskey followed through by saying:

'The Parties can, of course, make a tribunal or council the final arbiter on questions of fact. They can leave questions of law to the decisions of a tribunal, but they cannot make it the final arbiter on questions of law. They cannot prevent its decisions being examined by the courts.'

(*Baker v Jones* [1954] 2 All ER 553 at 558–559.)

In the following year, 1955, the emphasis in court shifted for the first time from disciplinary proceedings to administrative oppression by a governing body's restrictive rules. James Guthrie was the constructively aggressive Chairman of the then Professional Football Players' and Trainers' Union (now the Professional Footballers' Association (PFA)). He had captained Portsmouth at Wembley, the last pre-war FA Cup-winning team, against Wolverhampton Wanderers, and he revived the players' fight for contractual freedom forty years after it had been thoughtlessly forfeited in the misconceived action during 1912. On that occasion it will be recalled how Harry Kingaby's claims against Aston Villa for damages for (1) loss of employment because of the transfer fee charged and also (2) maliciously charging an excessive transfer fee, were nonsuited by AT Lawrence J on the basis that (1) there was no cause of action and (2) no evidence of malice was proved. Guthrie now placed his union behind defending a claim in Aldershot County Court for possession of club premises against one of its players, Ralph Banks.

Banks had been transferred to Aldershot for £500 from Bolton Wanderers after he had played left-back against Stanley Matthews in the 1953 Coronation Cup Final in a dramatic finish which witnessed Matthews' team, Blackpool's 4–3 victory. At Aldershot he disputed a wages offer from Weymouth who were unable to afford Aldershot's wish to recoup their £500 transfer fee. Although his contract of employment for 12 months from 30 June 1954 to 30 June 1955 had terminated at the date of the court action in October 1955, his Football Association registration permitted Aldershot's retention of his services under the FA Rules. The county court Judge, HH Judge Percy Rawlins, who had just been transferred to the

Aldershot County Court circuit from his west country circuit base, refused leave for Banks to join the FA as a defendant to a counterclaim and plead that the club's possession claim was based upon an unenforceable contract in restraint of trade and thereby tainted with illegality; but he ordered the FA to attend through counsel and a representative to assist him on the contractual arrangements.

A possession order was made with effect five months from the date of judgment on 28 October 1955; evidence was provided by a future FA deputy secretary, Douglas Hawes, in answer to a question by the judge that Banks was under a 'penalty'. (A 'penalty' in this context of the retain and transfer system was equivalent to a perpetually renewable lease built into the football governing body rules to which the professional players' contracts were tied.)

In his judgment HH Judge Percy Rawlins said,

'It may very well be, although I am not going to decide it, that as the defendant alleges the rules of the Football Association place an intolerable burden upon some professional footballers. But it may well be that as the Football Association says, the rules were necessary for the protection of footballers because the Football Association exists to some extent to protect footballers and to prevent their exploitation'.

(*Aldershot Football Club v Banks*, (1955) *Aldershot News*, 4 November.)

An appeal to the Court of Appeal was under consideration when as Guthrie in his own version (*Soccer Rebel* [1976] page 74) explained: 'Aldershot, perhaps under guidance or orders, gave Banks a free transfer'; to the club he wished to join, Weymouth. Seven years later Wilberforce J in 1962 converted that 'penalty' testified by the FA's representative and HH Judge Rawlin's impression of an 'intolerable burden' (arising out of the FA's feudal retention of a player's services after his employment contract had expired) into the category of an unenforceable restraint of trade (*Eastham v Newcastle United Football Club, Football Association and Football League* [1964] Ch 413).

Three months into the year following *Aldershot v Banks* [1955] the scene shifted back to disciplinary proceedings in the Queen's Bench Division of the High Court. Pilcher J adjudicated that the Stewards of the National Hunt Committee had acted ultra vires their own rules on three grounds.

(1)   They had disqualified and warned off a livery stable keeper for 'training and running' a horse under their jurisdiction which the Plaintiff had undoubtedly trained but did not run;

(2)   their indefinite disqualification breached their own rule requiring a specified time scale, and

(3)   the actual offences alleged were not subject to Regulations relied upon.

(*Davis v Carew-Pole* [1956] 2 All ER 524.)

By now the first decade of post-war sport had ended after a sports-starved nation had sustained its morale on the home front throughout the war years with substituted competitions for the traditional fixtures, which had resumed with a more intense and commercially organised combative spirit among administrators and players. The long-standing soccer rivalries in the north-east of England between Newcastle United, Middlesbrough and Sunderland with maximum-wage ceiling restrictions inspired the Sunderland club into alleged irregularities and ultimate conflict with football's authorities reminiscent of the Arsenal Club's difficulties half-a-century earlier. In the year after Pilcher J's decision in *Davis v Carew-Pole*, a joint FA-Football League Commission of Enquiry was established in 1957 to investigate allegations that the club and many of its players and officials had allegedly side-stepped the archaic maximum-wage ceiling structures with 'under-the-counter-payments' which were outside the game's administrative laws. Draconian sentences of varying levels of severity were imposed by the Commission on the Directors, Manager and Players for alleged offences against the game's financial prohibitions. By the time when the joint FA-Football League Commission of Enquiry adjudicated ultimately, the players concerned had benefited from the legacy of union and legal organization left behind by Guthrie. He had been dismissed by his union in circumstances which caused the distinguished sporting MP for Huddersfield East, J P W Mallalieu, himself a former Oxford Rugby Blue, champion in Parliament for professional footballers, and son-in-law of Portsmouth's single FA Cup-winning manager, Jack Tinn, to write in 1976 at the beginning of *Soccer Rebel* under the heading of *A Single Minded Man*:

'I consider that Jimmy Guthrie did more than any other individual to improve the working conditions of professional footballers. I also consider that professional footballers have treated Jimmy Guthrie with gross ingratitude'.

When the FA-Football League Commission of Enquiry adjudicated, the Sunderland Club's own legal advisers were equipped to recognise the developments which created a different sporting legal climate from when the Arsenal advisers failed to use the weapons available to their clients in the legal armoury even in 1927 and 1929. Thus, in 1962 on two separate occasions the FA had to admit grave errors of procedure through counsel on two separate hearings in actions brought first by the players and then by Sunderland FC and its officials. These procedural errors required that all disciplinary punishments were expunged from the record. The fallacious belief of counsel in 1927 that 'the findings of an outside body like the

Football Association would [not] be appealable against in court', and of Sir Patrick Hastings in 1929 that 'no useful purpose could be served by proceeding with the action' impugning disputed FA proceedings at that date, were now dead and buried along with the *Gentlemen v Players* fixture which MCC terminated during 1963. The courts were now more than ready to act if called upon to rectify the miscarriages of sporting maladministration of any kind, and the pattern of development unfolded rapidly.

A classic example occurred midway through the five years spanning Sunderland's saga of soccer injustice when professional Rugby League Football was similarly ruled offside, in early 1960. During a cup-tie on 13 February one of Keighley RFC's players, Jack Holmes, was sent off the field. On the following day, 14 February, the referee submitted his report to the appropriate disciplinary committee in accordance with the rules. On 15 February the committee met to hear the case, and suspended the player. Summary justice could not have acted more swiftly and summarily. On this occasion it was summary injustice.

No notification had been given to the club or to the player that the case was going to be considered. The referee's report was not received by the club until some time on 15 February; and it was not brought to the attention of Mr Holmes at all. Accordingly the club and player had no alternative but to go to court for 'a decision clearing him of the odium the suspension had naturally caused' (per Mr Ingress Bell QC). Mr Justice Danckwerts in the Chancery Division granted against members of

(1)   the disciplinary committee, and
(2)   the appeals committee of the Rugby Football League that
    (i)   the suspension was not valid, and
    (ii)   they had no jurisdiction to hear the case further.

As *The Times* newspaper law report recorded, with the Judge's words which are as applicable today as they were more than three decades ago, in 1960:

> 'In his Lordship's view the hearing, or absence of hearing, by the disciplinary committee on 15 February was so unfair that it could not be treated as a valid decision. On the ground of natural justice it was the duty of a body like this to hear the player, and it should be the onus of the committee to notify him that the case would be heard on a certain day'.

> (*Keighley RFC Ltd & Anor v Cunningham & Ors* (1960) *The Times*, 25 May, page 5.)

The year after the FA's capitulations in 1962 to Sunderland FC's claims witnessed Wilberforce J's landmark decision in the *Eastham* case (supra) during 1963. (This outlawed the retain and transfer system attacked on the wrong battle lines in 1912. It confirmed the first shots fired effectively against it, appropriately in sight of the Aldershot military barracks, on behalf of Ralph Banks under Guthrie's generalship in 1955.) Three years later came the next landmark decision with the Court of Appeal's creation of the right to work in *Nagle v Fielden* (supra). The Court's decision was obtained on a procedural stage of the action after first the Queen's Bench master and then the Queen's Bench judge in Chambers had each ruled that the plaintiff, Florence Nagle's, statement of claim disclosed no cause of action (on different grounds which ultimately succeeded in the Court of Appeal). The far-reaching consequences were in substance as effective as if the action had been fought at trial with witnesses. The ultimate advantages for women's rights are considered in Chapter 8, '*Women in Sport and the Law*'. The Jockey Club conceded defeat after resisting the claim until the Court of Appeal's unanimous reserved judgment. In a fascinating cameo published twenty years after in an interview given by Mrs Nagle to Sue Montgomery in *The Sporting Life* during 1986, she explained how, after the judgment, a number of Jockey Club members explained how they had been on her side all the time, although they had omitted to express support to her before the verdict. It is as easy to back litigation winners as it is to choose winning horses after the contest has concluded!

Sandwiched between those two landmark decisions of 1964 and 1966, Scotland came on stream with another example of unnatural justice in 1965. The Scottish Football Association failed, as the Jockey Club were to fail a year later, to obtain a procedural abandonment at half-time before a final judgment whistle on a claim against it in court by the St Johnstone Football Club. The Association had purported to censure and fine the Club £25 for arranging a benefit game for one of its players without formal authorisation. No notice was given of the intention to publish or even to attend on its disciplinary pronouncement. Lord Kilbrandon had no difficulty in applying the appropriate principles of natural justice to grant a declaration against the Association in Edinburgh's High Court, known as the Outer House (*St Johnstone Football Club v The Scottish Football Association Ltd* [1965] SLT 174).

By contrast with the decisions from the ball games and race track council chambers, the more cerebral world of contract bridge produced a text book example of how to conduct an investigation after the Executive Committee of the World Bridge Federation in 1965 announced alleged irregularities by British bridge players during the World Bridge Championship in Buenos Aires, South America. An Enquiry was established by the British Bridge League under the joint chairmanship of Sir John Foster, QC, MP, and General Lord Bourne. After a lengthy in-depth investigation attended by counsel instructed by solicitors, with the right to cross-examine witnesses, the charge of cheating by allegedly having used 'finger signals' was rejected, and the full account of the blueprint for such an ideal procedure appears in *Story of an Accusation* (1966) by one of the acquitted accused, the celebrated bridge practitioner and chronicler, Terence Reece.

By the end of the 1960s the fallacy of sporting administrative immunity from the due process of law had been fully illustrated. The FA, Scottish FA, Rugby Football League, Jockey Club and National Hunt Committee had all been scrutinised by the courts and found wanting in either their quasi-judicial or administrative capacities, and, in the case of the Football Association at both levels. The scene was therefore set for a review judicially by Lord Denning of the process he had identified in *Russell v Duke of Norfolk*. The opportunity arrived in another industrial case concerned with a trade union's expulsive conduct cited in the next paragraph. On the facts and evidence he dissented from his fellow appeal judges and the trial judge who was upheld by the Court of Appeal majority. The Court, apart from Lord Denning, was strongly criticised for its decision in the *Journal of Public Law*. Nevertheless the principles which Lord Denning summarized should be regarded (with one further refinement by the Vice-Chancellor, Sir Robert Megarry, eight years later in *McInnes v Onslow Fane* [1978] 1 WLR 1520), as the general and overriding guideline for all sporting governing bodies and tribunals with power to act fairly or unfairly, judicially or unjudicially.

In *Breen v AEU* ([1971] 2 KB 175 at pages 189–190), Lord Denning explained the position in clear terms which equates the court's control over private bodies with that over statutory authorities (subject always to the distinction identified in *Law v National Greyhound Racing Club Limited* (supra) that the process of judicial review is available against public but not private activities, in which latter category the courts place domestic sporting activities. The latter are regulated and controlled by the declarations and injunctions which are referred to by Lord Denning as 'the modern machinery for endorsing administrative law' (at the end of the following citation). Neither of Lord Denning's dissentient appeal judges dissociated themselves from his general survey. It began with a backward glance to the 'last 22 years', and thereby *Russell v Duke of Norfolk* (supra):

'there have been important developments in the last 22 years which have transformed the situation. It may truly now be said that we have a developed system of administrative law. These developments have been most marked in the review of decisions of statutory bodies: but they apply also to domestic bodies.

Take first statutory bodies. It is now well settled that a statutory body, which is entrusted by statute with a discretion, must act fairly. It does not matter whether its functions are described as judicial or quasi-judicial on the one hand, or as administrative on the other hand, or what you will. Still it must act fairly. It must, in a proper case, give a party a chance to be heard: see In *re HK (An Infant)* [1967] 2 QB 617, 630 by Lord Parker CJ in relation to immigration officers; and *R v Gaming Board for Great Britain, Ex parte Benaim and Khaida* [1970] 2 QB 417, 430 by us in relation to the gaming board. The discretion of a statutory body is never unfettered. It is a discretion which is to be exercised according to law. That means at least this: the statutory body must be guided by relevant considerations and not by irrelevant. If its decision is influenced by extraneous considerations which it ought not to have taken into account, then the decision cannot stand. No matter that the statutory body may have acted in good faith; nevertheless the decision will be set aside. That is established by *Padfield v Minister of Agriculture, Fisheries and Food* [1968] AC 997 which is a landmark in modern administrative law.

Does all this apply also to a domestic body? I think it does, at any rate when it is a body set up by one of the powerful associations which we see nowadays. Instances are readily to be found in the books, notably the Stock Exchange, the Jockey Club, the Football Association, the innumerable trade unions. All these delegate power to committees. These committees are domestic bodies which control the destinies of thousands. They have quite as much power as the statutory bodies of which I have been speaking. They can make or mar a man by their decisions. Not only by expelling him from membership, but also by refusing to admit him as a member: or, it may be, by refusal to grant a licence or to give their approval. Often their rules are framed so as to give them a discretion. They then claim that it is an unfettered discretion with which the courts have no right to interfere. They go too far. They claim too much. The Minister made the same claim in the *Padfield* Case, and was roundly rebuked by the House of Lords for his impudence. So should we treat this claim by trade unions. They are not above the law, but subject to it. Their rules are said to be a contract between the members and the union. So be it. If they are a contract, then it is an implied term that the discretion should be exercised fairly. But the rules are in reality more than a contract. They are a legislative code laid down by the council of the union to be obeyed by the members. This code should be subject to control by the courts just as much as a code laid down by Parliament itself. If the rules set up a domestic body and give it a discretion, it is to be implied that the body must exercise its discretion fairly. Even though its functions are not judicial or quasi-judicial, but only administrative, still it must act fairly. Should it not do so, the courts can review its decision, just as it can review the decision of a statutory body. The courts cannot grant the prerogative writs such as *certiorari* and *mandamus* against domestic bodies, but they can grant declarations and injunctions which are the modern machinery for enforcing administrative law.'

(*Breen v AEU* [1971] 2 KB 175 at 189–190.)

As the 1970s and 1980s unfolded, Lord Denning's assessment in *Breen's* case of the progress since 1949 in the readiness of the courts to operate, and their example to be followed, become recognisable. In 1985 the jockey John Francome, who had been disciplined in 1979 for indiscreet disclosure to a bookmaker friend, explained in his recollections, *Born Lucky*:

> 'As with most private clubs the Jockey Club makes its own rules and then judges and penalises anyone who breaks them accordingly. Except for the fact that no press reporters are allowed, their enquiries are run on much the same lines as a normal court of law, with the Jockey Club Disciplinary Committee acting as judges, with solicitors who put their case and the defendants with solicitors put theirs'.

This account of natural justice at the Portman Square Headquarters of horse racing's ruling body satisfies the courts' own standards and anyone aggrieved by Jockey Club justice has a direct route to the High Court if it uses the correct contract foundation and not the erroneous judicial review mechanism experienced by the Aga Khan's case..

Variations exist of the pattern which is now recognised by those who understand the relevant court requirements of judicial control over domestic tribunals. Examples of this emerged during the decades following *Breen v AEU*. In *Machin v The FA* [1983] Bristow J's ruling against a referee's report allegedly incorrectly recording a foul tackle was overruled by a Court of Appeal majority, on this occasion in favour of the FA. Lord Denning and Lawton LJ preferred to uphold the finality of a referee's factual finding, with Buckley LJ dissenting on the basis that the court was justified in drawing inferences of fact where an apparent perversity existed. More significantly, and for more permanent usage, all judges now accept unequivocally the use of television and video recording evidence. In 1987 the Charlton Athletic management did not appear to be aware of this. It protested publicly against such evidence when one of its players was disciplined and later exonerated for an alleged offence against a referee, recorded on camera but not witnessed by any FA official.

In 1978 Sir Robert Megarry, Vice-Chancellor, in *McInnes v Onslow Fane* ([1978] 3 All ER 211) rejected the grievances of an unsuccessful applicant to the British Boxing Board of Control for a promoter's licence. The lengthy reserved judgment absorbed the pattern of precedent which by then had developed in the nearly 40 years since *Russell v Duke of Norfolk* and structured the potential circumstances into three separate categories for which natural justice could or could not apply. He identified: (1) forfeiture situations such as deprivation of livelihood, for which judicial fair play rules must always apply; (2) application cases of the kind comparable to joining a club for which the rules of natural justice were not applicable (notwithstanding the right to work established in *Nagle v Fielden*), and (3) expectation cases such as renewal of a licence, where natural justice rules could apply ([1978] 3 All ER at 218). Certain observations in which he gratuitously echoed the sanctimonious words of the then Vice-Chancellor,

Sir Nicholas Browne-Wilkinson in *Cowley v Commonwealth Games Federation* during 1986 (Tuesday 24 July), railing against the intervention by the courts against sporting governing bodies, were clearly made without any awareness of the National Hunt, Rugby League, *Sunderland* and *Eastham* for football and interlocutory *Packer* cricket precedents cited above, protecting sporting victims of oppressive maladministration.

By the 1980s, South African sporting associations brought the law on a stage highlighted by the House of Lords judgments in *Wheeler v Leicester City Council*. These are considered more appropriately in Chapter 9, '*International interaction*'. As already explained, because a public activity was involved, the judicial review procedure was implemented. In 1986, when the Commonwealth Games Federation in Edinburgh rectified an earlier omission to ban the South African-born swimmer, Annette Cowley, by giving her an opportunity to be heard, they reconvened a meeting to remedy this earlier omission. The ultimate High Court hearing before Sir Nicholas Browne-Wilkinson, V-C, was concerned with issues of rules construction and the meaning of domicile within their provisions as distinct from any natural justice elements which had been implemented at the reconvened administrative meeting dealing with that issue (see *Cowley v Healey* (supra)). Four years earlier in 1982 the Test and County Cricket Board was surprisingly unchallenged when it banned celebrated England cricketers for three years. They had toured and played as a team in South Africa. Notably they had admittedly broken no national or cricket law, or even the notoriously wrongly called Gleneagles Agreement. This, too, is considered more appropriately in Chapter 9, *International interaction*; but it raised profound issues of conduct allegedly justifying procedural questions in restraint of trade; and if pursued to court the judgments in the *Eastham* and *Packer* cases of respectively Wilberforce J and Slade J would have been assessed within a new and different international context.

The international position was considered by Foster J in the Chancery Division of London's High Court, as we have already seen in Chapter 9, *International interaction*, (*Cook v The Football Association* (1972), *Times*, 24 March, page 8). On that occasion the FIFA rules were held to be in restraint of trade because the rules purported to repeat the Banks-Eastham registration restrictions preventing the Plaintiff transferring from Sligo Rovers in the Republic of Ireland to Wigan, then outside the Football League. The learned judge also directed that if the international body would not be bound by English law, then the FA as the representative defendant should leave the world body. Furthermore as Chapter 10, *Single European Market and UK Sport*, also explains, Common Market law transcends, regrettably many may consider, traditional common law rules/principles; and Article 48 [Article 39 of the Treaty of Amsterdam] creates a mandatory right for 'The free movement of workers' which has already been brought to the notice of all European football authorities.

Since January 1988 when the first edition of this work was published, Scott J (as he then was) has rejected two applications commenced by writ, and the Divisional Court and Court of Appeal have explained on more than one occasion that judicial review is not available against sporting governing bodies so long as *Law v The National Greyhound Racing Club* remains a binding precedent, namely, unless and until it is overruled by the House of Lords or legislation. As I have explained in Butterworths All England Law Reports Annual Review 1992:

> 'It would appear that there is a death wish or hypnotic eye which seduces sporting litigants into this no man's land of legal procedure with for them, fatal and doubtless costly, results',

unless prepared to challenge the procedure in the House of Lords.

In *Currie v Barton and anor* (1988) *Times*, 12 February, the Court of Appeal upheld Scott J's refusal to find that the denial of a personal hearing by an Essex County Lawn Tennis player banned for three years after a dispute with his non-playing captain was in breach of natural justice, because he had written a letter explaining his side of the story; and the House of Lords was never given an opportunity to consider whether this decision could have been added to its catalogue of reversal of lower court decisions summarised in Appendix 10. Indeed in *Memoires of a Libel Lawyer* my instructing solicitor on the appeal, Peter Carter-Ruck said 'We lost the case and I felt, and still feel, my client had suffered an injustice.' [Chapter 41, p 263.]

Four months later in an unreported but well-known decision in sporting administrative circles, Scott J refused to disturb an IAAF Arbitration Appeal Board's confirmation of a two-years ban on a 25-year-old Swiss athlete, Sandra Gasser, after she had been tested positively for anabolic steroids. The value of the judgment must be qualified because he explained that the Arbitration Panel:

> 'held that "the B sample was not tested in a proper and efficient manner according to normal laboratory practice" ... The Panel might have found that the other explanation was too conjectural to be accepted. But no evidence to incline them to that view had since been put before them by the Plaintiff or the SLV [The Swiss Federation] ... The Plaintiff is stuck with their conclusions. Any remedy of Appeal to the High Court under the Arbitration Acts is long since time-barred.' (*Gasser v IAAF* (1988) 15 June (unreported))

It should also be noted that Scott J accepted the Plaintiff's claim that restraint of trade was an appropriate cause of action, but he refused relief on the basis that the suspension had been reasonable in the circumstances. Four years later in 1992 the IAAF found itself on the receiving end of a

Columbus, Ohio, USA court judgment in a case brought by an American track athlete Harry L 'Butch' Reynolds for injunctive relief and substantial damages, on the basis that he had been wrongly suspended after a positive drug test. The judgment was successfully appealed in the American Courts. For reasons of costs and absence of assets against which a judgment could be enforced the action was undefended and judgment was obtained in default of defence, and not on its merits and a further appeal to the Supreme Court was reportedly contemplated. At an international symposium organised by the International Athletic Foundation, Counsel for the Canadian Government Dubin Inquiry, Robert Armstrong pointed out it

'Basically recommended that in order to have a fair right of appeal, athletes should be in a position to be able to test the scientific validity of the test results'.

In the *Gasser* case Scott J inferred that this had not been exhausted by the complainant-plaintiff's evidence and may yet be taken to the Supreme Court. In the *Reynolds* case the IAAF had not contested the merits. Hence the limited value of both decisions.

Of greater significance in 1991 and 1992 were the abortive attempts to use the judicial review route to judicial relief. Rose J in *R v Football Association Ltd, ex parte Football League Ltd* [1993] 2 All ER 833, found that the FA was a domestic body whose powers arose from and duties existed in private law only. In *R v Disciplinary Committee of the Jockey Club* [1993] 2 All ER 853 the Court of Appeal unanimously held that any correct remedy was in contract by writ.

In a valuable Foreword to a series of essays in honour of Lord Denning: *The Judge and The Law* edited by Professor J L Jowell and J P W McAuslen [1984], his distinguished contemporary, Lord Devlin, has written:

'When Tom and I were young during the 1920s the law was stagnant. The old-fashioned judge looked to the letter of the statute and for the case on all fours. He knew that he had to do justice according to law. Either he assumed that the law when strictly applied would always do justice or else he decided that, if it did not, it was not his business to interfere. Today this is not the idea. No statement of the law, be it a precedent or a statute, is ever final; it is to be read in its context and its context can change'.

During the course of a procedural application in the Court of Appeal to proceed out of time in *Currie v Barton and Rippon* (supra), Parker LJ said, confirming the leave given by the Court of Appeal's Mr Registrar Adams, words which confirm Lord Devlin and are relevant to the themes of this chapter,

'The particular field of law which is here involved is a developing field. It is a field in which decisions have been made which would have been unthinkable a few years before they were made'.

(*Currie v Barton and Rippon*, (1987) *Times*, 29 July page 42.)

No context is changing more rapidly within society at the public level with a mixture of public interest and private activity than the whole world of sport. How sporting bodies have been brought to court during the 1970s, 1980s and 1990s is summarised below. As a summary, it is not offered as a comprehensive survey. Nevertheless it charts a pattern of which, within the purpose for which this book has been written, many may not be aware.

The *Revie* (1978) and *Cowley* (1986) Commonwealth Games examples demonstrate this. In *Enderby Town v FA* from which the opening citation of Lord Denning at the head of this chapter was extracted, legal representation was refused at the tribunal hearing but upheld by the Courts. For Revie, Cowley, and indeed, ultimately David Bishop, the tribunals allowed the lawyers to attend. In today's changing sporting scene even 'the good laymen' would be wise to be assisted by the services of a good lawyer if natural and, indeed, any justice is to be guaranteed for sport and its proper administration according to law. The common laws of tort relating to restraint of trade and breach of contract with which the Packer team bowled out cricket's establishment required more than just a good layman. That standard or level of excellence can suffice without any further assistance to operate the rules of natural justice and fair play if the following sound elementary rules of common sense extracted from the cases are implemented:

(1) avoid any risk of pre-judgment or prejudice or bias or likelihood of it;
(2) formulate and notify clearly, preferably in writing, any assertions needing reply;
(3) notify clearly, and preferably in writing, any date for investigation or hearing;
(4) act intra vires, within the rules, and not ultra vires, outside them;
(5) remember the right to be heard in defence of any allegation;
(6) in cases of difficulty or complexity, consider carefully any request for legal representation.

If these principles require illuminating or consolidation for the lay reader, and some lawyers, perhaps, too, no better source exists outside of sport than Sir Terence Rattigan's renowned dramatisation of *Archer-Shee v The King* (1910) in *The Winslow Boy*. The true story has become well-known from the stage and film versions. It is told fully in the biographies of the

great Irish advocate, Carson, by Edward Majoribanks (1932) and H
Montgomery Hyde (1953), and in Rodney M Bennett's definitive study,
The Archer-Shees Against the Admiralty (1973).

Carson led a personal as well as a professional crusade against the
Admiralty to expunge a false accusation that a 13 year-old cadet had stolen
a five shilling (25p) postal order from a fellow pupil at the Royal Naval
College, Osborne, on the Isle of Wight. He had been expelled after
investigations at which he had no opportunity to defend himself properly.
When a bureaucratic blockade, lasting nearly two years, against a proper
investigation of the facts was breached in the High Court, Carson's cross-
examination of the Judge Advocate of the Fleet who was also Recorder of
the former Oxford Quarter Sessions (prior to the controversial Beeching
Reforms under the Courts Act 1971), concentrated on a single point:

Q.   You said you were Recorder of Oxford.

A.   Yes.

Q.   I suppose if you were to try a boy for theft as Recorder of Oxford you
      would give an opportunity for both sides of being heard.

A.   I would not do otherwise.

On the following day the Admiralty surrendered. They had been exposed
for failing to operate fair play and reason behind closed doors.

SUMMARY OF SOURCES CONFIRMING CITATIONS IN CHAPTER 11

Date	Sport	Issue/ Principle	Decision
1971	Soccer	Claim for legal representation.	Court of Appeal Refused on facta and construction rules.
1973	Soccer	Claim that offence of foul tackle different in referee's report from evidence on admitted television evidence: alleged breach of natural justice.	Court of Appeal by 2–1 majority reversed experienced trial judge and held sufficient opportunity to know offence and deal with it at tribunal.
1977	Cricket	Industrial issues overlapping. Attempt to ban players because of Packer innovations.	Court held in restraint of trade and unlawful inducing breach of contract. TULRA 1974 not applicable after late pleading amendment allowed.
1979	Horseracing	Bookmaker banned for 3 years	High Court confirmed no breach of natural justice.
1979	Soccer	England team manager's protest about constitution of tribunal imposing 10 years' ban because of adverse attitudes to him personally expressed by tribunal members: objections overruled.	Court held tribunal hearing contrary to natural justice because of likelihood of bias among tribunal members.

Date	*Sport*	*Issue/ Principle*	*Decision*
1983	Soccer	Brighton & Hove Albion FC captain challenged ineligibility for FA Cup Final because of points total totting up for disciplinary offences.	Court refused intervention on basis no breach of natural justice or other unlawful act.
1984	Judo	Life ban because of positive drug test challenged on basis that lawful prescription conflicted with sporting governing body rules [NB: see also Ch 7: 'Sports medicine and the law'.]	High Court Consent Order rescinding ban and restoration of licence membership: Consent Order precluded detailed reasons, but natural justice breach arguable.
1985	Rugby Union	Schoolmaster spanning amateur rugby union and professional rugby league threatened with forfeiture of status as amateur and administrative school sport committee membership.	Retraction upon Counter-threat by schoolmaster to Rugby Union of legal action; anticipated restraint of trade, interference with contract and potential libel.
1985	Soccer	Attempt to life ban by UEFA (European football authority) on British clubs competing after Brussels disaster.	High Court refuse application as ultra vires power of defendant English FA to enforce application outside jurisdiction.
1987	Tennis	Court of Appeal leave to appeal when time had expired.	Leave granted. 'The particular field which is here involved is a developing field.'
1990	Soccer	Internal Appeals machinery operated effectively and	Appeal against oppressive demotion allowed

Date	Sport	*Issue/ Principle*	*Decision*
		successfully under Football League Regulations.	by FA Appeals Committee.
1993	Disabled wheelchair archer	Negligent organisation	Liability established
1994	Soccer	Restraint of trade prohibiting right to play on own territory	Declaratory judgment and injunction granted
1999	Boxing (subject to appeal)	Negligent medical organisation	Liability established subject to appeal

CHAPTER 12

Administrative Advice

1 INTRODUCTION

(1) Background

The 30,920,000 participants who are listed with the 421 National Sporting governing bodies and analysed in the Sports Council's (now Sport England's) citation in the Preface here, embrace the Central Council of Physical Recreation for England and Wales. It deservedly enjoys a membership of 268 national organisations, 2 British-based and 66 constituted with a responsibility for England. Each governing body in turn has its own constituent members, which form a mass of sporting groups beyond accurate numerical assessment. The CCPR's former Treasurer, Sir Denis Follows, claimed towards the end of his 1983 Philip Noel-Baker Memorial Lecture, 'Whither Sport, the true nature of sport':

> 'sport ... remains with the masses. And this goes for all forms of physical recreation. There isn't enough money available to turn us all into professionals. So let us be generous: Say 1% of participants receive any financial reward for practising sport. It is with the remaining 99% that we should concern ourselves'.

Then he posed the crucial question and supplied the answer:

> 'Where is sport going? I say that at the top level it has ceased to be sport — it has become a branch of the entertainment industry. Whether it should go that way or not is for those in control of its destinies to determine, but for 99% of the participants, we, the devotees of sport and recreation, have a responsibility to ensure that the young of this country are brought up to

observe the basic principles of fair play and sportsmanship — a respect for others and for authority: A recognition that in any sporting contest there must be losers as well as winners and that while we honour the winners, we applaud the efforts of the losers. This is essentially an educational process in which we all have a part to play'.

Sir Denis Follows, not everyone may know, was an educationalist by heart, and by training. He began his professional life as a schoolteacher. So, too, did his no less distinguished predecessor, Sir Stanley Rous. So, too, did the immortal C B Fry, G O Smith, Harry Altham, John MacGregor Kendall-Carpenter and so many other admired examples of the scholar-athlete remained schoolmasters all their lives. Therein lies the key to the crucial problem which faces British, and, indeed, international sport today, a problem which is so rarely recognised, or understood, in a world of public sport dominated by market forces and commercial predators: how to shift the balance of administering and controlling sport back to leaders and teachers of their calibre, and away from the political activists and money men, and women, too, who use and abuse sport and prostitute its real values, spelt out by Follows, as a medium for quick profits or spurious political purposes at domestic and international levels.

It also is reflected in the problems cited at the conclusion of the Preface and the need for that

'99% of the participants, the devotees of sport and recreation — to ensure that the young of this country are brought up to observe the basic principles of fair play and sportsmanship — an educational process in which we have a part to play'.

Self-evidently that educational process must begin in the home; be carried on at school and thereafter in the sporting and recreational context, be carried on at higher education through university and club structures. For preservation of those situations it is essential for their administrators to be advised with comparable levels and qualities of expertise which are more easily available to Follows' reference to 'That branch of the entertainment industry'. How such comparable levels can be obtained for the complex and different layers of activity among the 113 'heterogeneous list of pastimes' from the VAT non-profit making list must depend on differing levels of enthusiasm and availability of resources in different parts of the country. There can be no doubt that they exist, and three experiences establish this. One was cited in the *Introduction* to my second edition; another comes from a hitherto unfashionable professional football club on the South Coast of England, and a third from less fashionable days than one enjoyed today by the embodiment in football of Follows' branch of the entertainment industry'.

As I wrote in the second edition in 1994 (Pages xli–xlii) how

'The understandable battle to preserve rugby union's amateur status alongside its emergence as a world-wide televised branch of the entertainment industry nevertheless appears to ignore or be unaware of the long-established precedents from the traditional theatre and film industry. The [then] thousand or so regular fee-earning Equity card carrying, professionals in the United Kingdom are swamped numerically by the amateur Thespians who tread the boards for fun in a comparable pattern experienced by amateur musicians and singers who never intend to join the professional ranks. In the same cultural seam of communal activity, the distinguished *Sunday Times* internationally renowned rugby union correspondent Stephen Jones identified in his 1993 award winning Sports Book of the Year, *Endless Winter: the Inside Story of the Rugby Revolution*:

'Millions of the lovely beaverers — who vividly demonstrate their affection for the game and its ambience by spending every leisure minute in the exhausting process of providing the fitting backdrop for players at all levels to come out on the rugby field and play. They still do, these heroes. Every week for nothing'.

It is possible that the understandable defenders of the faith for the time spirit of amateur rugby have failed to recapture those precedents for preserving its integrity while allowing the talents and sacrifices of time and family and employment commitments by the relative handful of players involved at the high profiled and globally televised entertainment level to be rewarded for the pleasure they give to millions and also the funding for salaried administrators, and stadia developments'.

In that same spirit a London based solicitor already acknowledged and identified in the Introduction, Trevor Watkins, took up the battle for survival of AFC Bournemouth when it was minutes away from commercial and football extinction under financial commitments to the Inland Revenue, HM Customs and Excise and Lloyds Bank. In his inspirational book with Ivo Tennant, *Cherries in the Red* (1999), he tells the fairy tale justifiably crystallised on its dust-jacket

'How one football fan saved his club and became chairman',

during the late 1990s.

Nearly seventy odd years earlier in 1931 many people outside North-West England and also a younger generation brought up with Henry Ford's alleged canard, 'history is bunk' may not be aware how Manchester United faced a similar crisis, with 'a crippled Club unable to fulfil its remaining fixtures and resigning from the Football League'.

(The Gibson Guarantee 1994: Page 13)

To the rescue came James Gibson a clothing manufacturer to whom the dedication of the text says simply

'to James Gibson, the Chairman and President of Manchester United 1931–1951. His passion for the Club shone like a beacon — his inspiration and energy must never be forgotten'.

It certainly was not by his successor, the local solicitor, Harold Hardman, who steered the then Matt Busby and his Babes into Europe before the Munich tragedy of 6 February 1958, after gaining Olympic Games gold and FA Cup winning and losers medals with Everton as an amateur alongside the great professionals of the day. Today, however all is apparently forgotten as the present chairman Mr Edwards creates a Monopolies and Mergers Commission Government Enquiry, and in as yet unresolved factual circumstances compounded by Government interference devalues the FA *Challenge* Cup Competition traditions by leading his team to Brazil for reasons still blurred with ambiguities at the time of writing in autumn 1999.

There may never be another Harold Hardman, but for Trevor Watkins and, James Gibson there will always be others to save the day for clubs in peril for whom this chapter has been prepared.

Accordingly, this chapter will embrace the difference between clubs and companies, charities and trusts, although to some extent these differences have emerged already within the earlier chapters. It will concentrate on summarising and emphasising what has already been identified, the need to control sport by the proper administrative reins which are held by the masses and their representatives. It will also explain briefly those areas of organisation where some accountancy, legal and medical and other professional disciplines' advice should be expected. For if any group of persons administering sport at any level, whether it be domestic or national, expects to do so without legal advice at least, then will they please consult the governing bodies at Lord's, Lancaster Gate, Portman Square and Twickenham.

There are also gaps which exist between public and private levels within sport which require special attention. Sport needs space to be played; and needs participants; parents share their children's development with the schools; schools in turn can benefit from liaising with clubs and local authorities should show deeper recognition of clubs' crucial role in filling the gaps left by teachers' wider problems as already explained in Chapter 4, *Parent, school and club partners*.

This chapter will deal first with the rights of individuals who comprise the masses; then with the collective rights of clubs and companies and finally, with some of the extras which often make the difference to a cricket score. These final points could add a level of awareness which might otherwise be overlooked.

2   INDIVIDUAL SPORTING RIGHTS

(1)   Playing Fields Planning
(2)   Parents
(3)   Schools
(4)   Rate Reliefs

(1)   Playing Fields Planning and Land

Without space, organised outdoor sport could not exist. For at least a decade, the Central Council of Physical Recreation and the National Playing Fields Association have combined their attempts to prevent school and industrial playing fields rendered surplus by local authority and commercial policies from being sold off and destroyed as recreational outlets. Their need for support from every member of the community, 'the masses', was evidenced publicly by two dramatic experiences during 1987.

The Craven Cottage football ground in West London where Fulham have played since 1896 has many romantic sporting associations apart from its approach through Bishop's Park, its riverside site and the location for Edward Bulwer-Lytton's writing of *The Last Days of Pompeii*. To the property marketeers it was a prime site for redevelopment and the Last Days of Football at the Cottage. A network of transactions too complex for and irrelevant to this text had prepared the route for an orthodox deal. Its operators had overlooked the surprise expressed by Lord Denning in *Miller v Jackson* (supra) that the planning application for development outside the Linz, Co Durham cricket ground, had not been opposed. On this occasion the local authority's Planning Committee was alerted sufficiently by meetings at the local Hammersmith Town Hall and public opinion generally. The public pressure resulted ultimately in deferment of the planning application and renegotiation of the ground's ownership through a business consortium to preserve the ground for its more than ninety years usage for football purposes. The issues ended in London's Court of appeal during 1992 when the trial judge was reversed. He had declared that the Club's directors and principal shareholders were entitled to give evidence to a public enquiry supporting a compulsory purchase order, although their testimony would be contrary to certain undertakings that they had given in an agreement under seal. The enquiry came within the witnesses (Public Enquiries) Protection Act 1892 and prohibiting testimony was argued and held to be contrary to public policy. A reserved judgment in the Appeal Court found there was no rule of public policy whereby a football club could ignore the undertakings given by the club's directors not to give evidence at the local council enquiry to support the council's compulsory purchase order at the enquiry and there was no rule of public policy rendering such an agreement illegal or unenforceable (*Fulham Football Club and others v Cabra Estates plc* (1992) *Times*, 11 September; All ER Annual Review p 364).

Further south, on even more romantic territory bordering on Hampshire's ancient New Forest, another property operator cast its covetous eyes on the War Memorial Recreation Ground at New Milton, near Brockenhurst and Southampton. The intention of the London-based property company was to transform the 3.6 acres of oak-fringed grass into a car park for a supermarket. Its misfortune (or that of its market researchers) was an unawareness that, as Ian Wooldridge explained in the *Daily Mail* on St Leger Day, Doncaster, Saturday 12 September 1987,

> 'I learned such sports as I have ever been able to play there because New Milton is my home town'.

After he announced in August 1987 the proposed development through the pages of his celebrated inside sports column, which has more than once brought the Sportswriter of the Year Award, the story had moved over to the front page within a month. The director in charge of the project was quoted as saying, 'We are disappointed that emotion clouded the issue'. Wooldridge wrote,

> 'It certainly did. The emotion of a local population finally roused to the spectre of losing a town-centre recreation area bought by public subscription to honour its war-dead was such that a dithering town council met in special session on Wednesday evening [9 September] to reassess the issue.
>
> Seventeen of the 18 town councillors turned up. They talked for only 15 minutes. They then voted 13–4 to send the developers packing. And by yesterday the developers acknowledged they had been beaten'.

Wooldridge continued with a most significant and heartwarming paragraph:

> 'Let Britain take note. It can be done. No issue in *Sportsmail's* pages over the past 25 years — be it soccer hooliganism, the antics of Mr McEnroe or even Zola Budd — provoked such angry and prolific responses as the test-case of New Milton's little public recreation ground.
>
> Letters arrived from all over Britain saying:

'The same is happening here'.

Hundreds wrote offering to add their signatures to New Milton's public protest petition organised by two local freedom fighters, 52-year-old Doreen Fernie and 79-year-old Bob Gates.

We had letters from former New Milton residents in Australia where the story was re-printed and from the Falkland Islands.

They came from people who had spent holidays in the friendly little town and had fond memories of enjoying a rare facility — a green lung with shady trees and bench seats right in the village centre.

Above all, we had letters from ex-Servicemen, some of whose relatives are commemorated on the Recreation Ground's war memorial'.

With citation of further sources from Second World War survivors and a tribute to Mrs Fernie and Mr Bob Gates, both awaiting hospital treatment, Mr Wooldridge ended thus:

'They fought certainly on emotional grounds, to preserve a small patch of British Heritage and protect the huge right of the British people to resist cynical land development by those who will never need the facilities they destroy. If the *Daily Mail* assisted in that campaign then we are very proud.

All over the country, sports ground and public parks are in similar peril.

Many just disappear, the victims of public apathy as much as sharp-suited avarice'.

New Milton, Hampshire, has shown the national way.

The way is clear for all who are ready and willing to attack the twin enemies of sporting land; apathy of their neighbours and local authorities on the one hand and the 'sharp-suited avarice' on the other. Section 29(2) of the Town and Country Planning Act 1971 marks the route. This enables any member of the public to make representations to the local planning authority within 21 days of the publication in the local press of any applications. If sufficiently orchestrated it could have the results explained by Wooldridge. No less attention was generated in North-East England when Newcastle United's commercial coordinators contemplated a removal to the City's 700 year old open space Town Moor. A comparable campaign to the fight in support of the New Milton War Memorial Recreation Ground again repelled the potential invader.

Even one objector can suffice to create a public enquiry by a Department of Environment Inspector. This was the experience of the Littlehampton Town Football Club who play in the Unijet Sussex County League. Their application for their playing area adjoining the then home of a local solicitor was to the appropriate planning authority, the West Sussex County Council, in 1964. Permission was sought to build a new dressing room and gymnasium accommodation in a corner of a sports field which the football club shared with the local archery, cricket, croquet, hockey and tennis clubs under a Queen Victoria Diamond Jubilee gift in 1897 from the then Duke of Norfolk. The trustees who administer the ground faced the opposition to the point of a formal Enquiry by the then Minister's government Inspector. At that time the application could have been abandoned, in the manner experienced at New Milton. The trustees pursued it, evidence was called, and ultimately the planning consent was rejected. The Inspector's report dismissing the appeal made it clear, however, that a fresh application signed or a different part of the ground would be favourably received.

In due course a fresh application was made successfully. Today a magnificent two storeyed structure built by private enterprise on a part of the ground authorised by the trustee-owners and also by the local authority justified the original application which, in effect, succeeded on a replay. The final result is a valuable example of the two dimensional use of the national planning laws in a local context. The beneficiaries of the planning permission granted for the Littlehampton Sports Field are the whole community and their visitors to that salubrious part of Sussex in an area administered now by Arun District Council for Sir Denis Follows' sporting 'masses'.

(2) Parents

The precedents from Bobby Charlton's grandfather and primary school headmaster: Sir Osbert Sitwell's parents, section 76 of the Education Act 1944, and the Enfield School litigation, were all set out in Chapter 4, '*Parent, school and club partners*'. They are referred to again here solely as a reminder and in the spirit of New Milton's victory over its property predators. Local authority bureaucrats and teaching ideologists are no less enemies of the nation's sporting heritage when the battle has to be fought for parental rights as laid down by Parliament in R A Butler's 1944 Education Act.

An individual parent, with sufficient private means to the extent which enabled Florence Nagle to take on the Jockey Club to the Court of Appeal in *Nagle v Fielden*, may not be stirred sufficiently to raise the battle flag alone against anti-competitive sporting school staffs and their local authorities. Parliamentary rights and recourse to the courts are available to Parent Teacher Associations and Parent Associations per se. They should re-read Ian Wooldridge's message and consider how far it applies to their own children's and grandchildren's futures for jousting with those who challenge at school level the national sporting heritage in Sir Denis Follows' message:

'This is essentially an education process in which all have a part to play'.

(3)   Schools

Here, too, the precedents were set out in Chapter 4. Section 53 of the Education Act 1944 (now amended as section 508 of the Education Act 1996) implements a duty on 'a local education authority' to provide for adequate facilities for recreation and social and physical training (thereby of sport) for persons receiving primary, secondary and further education; and since the first edition was published section 42 of the Education (No 2) Act 1986 has been implemented by SI 1987 No 344 with effect from 1 September 1987 and its provisions are now contained within section 149 of the Education Act 1996. This at least opens the doors to statutory authorisation for dual use of facilities

'(when not required by or in connection with the school) for use by members of the community served by the school'.

New Milton's spirit should be used to claim it as Paradise regained.

(4)   Rate Reliefs

This area shades into the next section dealing with clubs. The formal legal status of clubs in relation to unincorporated associations is, except for taxation purposes, unknown to the law; but they function administratively only through their duly elected officers and trustees. Thus, each individual member can stir his or her club committee and officers into lawful and regrettably unlawful action.

Rate reliefs under the local Government Finance Act 1988 and the operation of section 47 in the light of the House of Lords guidelines for sporting educational charities (in the FA Youth Trust Deed and Recreational Charities Act decisions) were mentioned in Chapter 4. Not every local authority would necessarily adopt the enlightened attitude shown by the Arun District Council in the past (as so shown in Chapter 14, *No fine on fun*) towards the Worthing Rugby Football Club and the Bognor Regis Town Football Club. Each of these sources provides coaching and thereby physical education for school children outside school hours. This is of course of benefit to the local community. Indeed, Worthing RFC claims to organise the biggest annual mini-rugby festival in the world with 1,000 young players participating on the day. Each club's coaching satisfies the education criteria for charitable status established in the Alderham school case of *Re Mariette*. (See Appendix 12). This was affirmed by the House of Lords in the FA Youth Trust Deed case of *IRV v McMullen* [1981] AC 1. Furthermore, when the concept of rate reliefs for sports clubs was floated at the Sports Council Recreation Management Seminar Conference in Harrogate during early 1986 and later at the joint DOE-DES Sport in Schools Seminar later that year, the reaction from other local authority sources was less than favourable.

In the last resort, however, for any local authority as well as for national government, power is with the people: the masses, at the ballot box. Those who care sufficiently should recognise their right which they hold in trust for all present and future younger generations. Above all, they should remember New Milton, Doreen Fernie, Bob Gates, Ian Wooldridge, and the Daily Mail, as they all took up the cudgels on behalf of the local community against commercial predators.

Before then, an earlier landmark decision took Arsenal Football Club to the House of Lords. A local litigant in person ratepayer challenged its rating valuation because of environmental interference with private residential property engendered by the footballing ambiance: and won (*Arsenal Football Club Ltd v Ende* [1977] 2 WLR 944). This does not always please its neighbours, as an echo of Littlehampton Town: and neighbouring attitude contrasts particularly with the more recently published opinions expressed in *Fever Pitch* by a dedicated Arsenal follower, Nick Hornby.

3   COLLECTIVE RIGHTS: CLUBS AND COMPANIES

(1)   General

Any reader and his or her associates who consider the time has come for the natural and normal progression towards treating clubs as companies will be following a precedent identified in the citation at pages 37–38 of Chapter 2, *Progressive perspective* from Montague (later Mr Justice) Shearman's chapter 'Athletic Government' in his classic century-old sporting textbook in the Badminton Library: *Athletics and Football*. The initial discussion would be the form or structure which that collective action should take: club and company limited by shares, limited by guarantee, incorporation by royal charter, or friendly societies under recent legislation.

(2)   Clubs

As a legal entity clubs are unknown to the law, except for the artificial formalities equating them with companies as corporations under revenue laws (see for example, *Worthing Rugby Football Club Trustees v IRC* [1987] STC 273).

The legal basis for a club is the contract which each member makes with another on joining the unincorporated association which remains (See Day J and Court of Appeal in *Steele v Gourlay* (1886) 3 TLR 772).

Because of this personal relationship, liabilities follow which usually are shared among the members either collectively or upon an indemnity basis. For example, the committee members of the Blackburn Rovers Football

Club employed a negligent contractor. Personal injury was suffered due to a collapsed grandstand (see *Brown v Lewis* supra). The committee members were held personally liable and subsequently the club was converted a year later into an incorporated company which removed this liability. The company has a separate legal personality or identity from those who own it, a principle established by the House of Lords in 1897, the year in which Blackburn Rovers converted (see *Salomon v Salomon* [1897] AC 22). Consistent with that overriding negligence principle, the courts have recently progressed to recognition of a duty of care owed to a fellow member by an officer or member of a club performing a task on behalf of other members if he becomes aware of circumstances giving rise to the risk of injury. Thus a local sports club chairman (who had been warned when reserving an indoor five-a-side football pitch on local authority premises that it was in a dangerous condition creating a risk of injury to fellow members, but failed to warn them of it) was liable to a fellow member for loss suffered by him: *Jones v Northampton Borough Council* (1990) Times, 21 May; (1990) *Independent*, 25 May.

(3)   Company limited by shares

Incorporation as distinct from an unincorporated status shifts the legal responsibility from individual members and committee members to the legal personality of the company, avoiding the personal liabilities of the kind experienced by the Blackburn Rovers committee in *Brown v Lewis* (except in extreme circumstances when company directors also can create a personal liability). Correspondingly Judge Brian Appleby QC has explained to the author that after his period as Chairman of the Nottingham Forest Football Club Committee, he was able to persuade its members that the risk of personal liabilities more than merited the surrender of its unique unincorporated association status within the Premier Football League. Thus it fell into line with all the other company/club structures.

The change of status also shifts control to the shareholders. Articles of Association can restrict transfers of shares and therefore control of the company. This emerged during litigation over a take-over bid that failed for control of Tottenham Hotspur during its doldrum years in the mid-1930s (*Berry and Stewart v Tottenham Hotspur Football and Athletic Co Ltd* [1935] Ch 718): and subsequently in the 1993 action replay of *Venables v Sugar* (May 1993). (*Edennote Plc, v Tottenham Hotspur Plc, Alan Sugar and Amstrad Ltd*, 14 June 1993).

Conversely, after the Second World War, when a minority shareholding in the Bristol Rovers Football Club Limited became dissatisfied with the affairs of the organisation, it instituted one of the first recorded inquisitions into any company's affairs under the then new provisions of section 164 of the Companies Act 1948. The company and commercial issues were complex but one of the passages locked in time after nearly forty years has this insight into football club administration with this comment in the Board of Trade Report into the Inspection of Bristol Rovers Football Club Limited in 1951:

> 'in the Inspector's view too many members of the Board gave absorbed attention to the Team Manager's sphere of interest, to the exclusion of the legal, financial and administrative affairs'.

(Report of A Frank Ward, FCA, Inspector appointed by Board of Trade:
page 34)

Plus ça change, plus c'est la même chose?

As more and more shareholder supporters of football clubs have become dissatisfied with directors' administration of club affairs, the legal tussles between the shareholders have become more common-place. Indeed, the other Bristol club, City, was the cause of a 16-day High Court action in July 1978. Its former chairman failed to upset a resolution to increase the club-company's increased share capital but one of his supporters was awarded damages for improper voting use of 500 shares at a rate of £2.50 per share (*Hobbs & Leadbetter v Castle, Bristol City Football Club Ltd and others,* (1978) *Times,* July 1978, page 2).

More recently in *Western Counties Construction Ltd v Witney Town Football and Social Club* (1993) Times, 19 November, Morrit J on appeal from Oxford County Court confirmed rejection of a winding-up petition by creditors who failed to bring the club on the construction of its rules within section 220 of the Insolvency Act 1986 as an unregistered company; and the creditors' remedy lay against the individuals with whom their contracts had been made, and the appeal would accordingly be dismissed.

For clubs with limited financial resources one of the problems flowing from conversion to corporate liability status is the annual expenditure of filing the statutory documentary returns with the companies Registry and the formalities which require a working knowledge or awareness of company law, and the need for frequent legal and accountancy services. Furthermore, as the sample case histories here demonstrate, company formation gives power to the majority shareholders and so far as they co-exist, with the directors. An unincorporated association club structure leaves power with the members who appoint and dismiss the committee and trustees according to the rules, which ideally should be sufficiently clear to avoid differences of interpretation.

Conversely, it can be convenient for a local club with a friendly membership to form a company for a limited purpose, eg for the purpose of holding a lease of club premises to avoid the necessity of executing a succession of documents in the event of changes through social mobility, deaths or other departures of trustees in whom all club land must be vested for clubs under the Law of Property Act 1925, sections 34–36.

(4)   Company limited by guarantee

This form of company is traditionally funded from group sources, subscriptions or fees and is progressively used by many professional, trade research, and other similar bodies. It is also increasingly used by governing sports bodies. In addition, it qualifies for exemption under section 35 of the Companies Act from use of the word 'limited' if its objects are

'the promotion of commerce, art, science, education, religion, charity or any profession and anything incidental or conducive to any of those objects'.

Sport per se is significantly absent from that list although it is arguable that sport is conducive to art, science, education or charity.

Accountancy and corporate information disclosure are less stringent than the requirements for a share company; and important differentials exist between the two types of company on member's liabilities in the circumstances of a winding-up. Potential candidates for this category could hardly be expected to contemplate it without specialist legal and accountancy advice.

(5)   Company incorporated by royal charter

The source is a royal prerogative founded in common law. The word royal is not necessary for the title; and it does not appear in many corporations structured in this way, exemplified by the Sports Council and the Jockey Club. The qualifying standards for consideration must be self-evident from the standpoint of public interest.

(6)   Friendly societies

This established structure with a benevolent philosophy has been revamped under the Friendly Societies Act 1992 to harmonise with UK insurance and company legislation and where applicable EC directives, with the concurrent creation of a Friendly Societies Commission. The starting point for enquiries should be 15 Great Marlborough Street, London, W1V 2AX.

4   EXTRAS

All areas of law affect administrators. The following topics have been chosen arbitrarily for discussion as they are the subjects which are most applicable to the administration of sport. This list can never be exhaustive because the needs of every individual, participant, club or company must differ dependent upon individual demands and requirements. specialist textbooks will be found on every topic in every reasonably stocked public library; and such a source in any event should have on its shelves the comprehensive volumes of Halsbury's *Laws of England*, 4th Edn; Halsbury's Statutes, 4th Edn; The Digest, including Continuation Volumes and Reissue Volumes. The following are the most pertinent subjects.

(1)   Land, lease and licenses;
(2)   Liquor licences;
(3)   Lotteries, betting and gaming;
(4)   Libel, slander and copyright;
(5)   Insurance;
(6)   VAT refund.

(1)   Land, lease and licences

Consistent with the theme which must have become apparent throughout this text, sports clubs have no privileges when buying, selling or owning property. For real estate, and present purposes, the most significant subjects must be (i) ownership or title; (ii) easements or restrictive covenants; (iii) landlord and tenant and licence relationships.

(i)   Ownership or title

All evidence of a company's or club's right to play on its ground whether a freehold, leasehold, peppercorn rental title or merely a licence, must be recorded in documents. In the beginning the services of a solicitor are essential and they would be no less necessary if points of dispute were to arise. Even freehold title today does not provide absolute right for owners to treat it indiscriminately.

(ii)   Easements and restrictive covenants

Easement such as rights of way or rights to light or other equivalent legal privileges and restrictive covenants (which are in effect a form of negative easement) can be troublesome and frequently expensive irritants if not understood with clarity and handled expertly.

Restrictive covenants involving limitations and restrictions on land and building development are found more frequently in urban as distinct from rural areas. Parliament has laid down a procedural and substantive code for applying to various jurisdictions, and for this purpose the services of an architect and surveyor familiar with the local requirements would be essential.

(iii)   Landlord and tenant licences

Parliament has imposed on ancient common law and equitable provisions complex legislation and formulae for which expert professional advice would be needed at some stage. The Football Association in the early 1950s after a number of court decisions clarified the position for its clubs, whereby agreements for occupiers and the hirers of property satisfied the requirements of a lease to invoke the protection of the Rents Act, whilst others failed to do so and thereby qualified for the lesser category of a licence with loss of Rent Act protection.

Those cases from the early 1950s which inspired the FA's initiative (*Errington v Errington* [1952] 1 All ER 149 and *Facchini v Bryson* [1952] 1 TLR 1386) excited much professional interest at the time. They sustained their drama with the House of Lords approval of some of the dicta in them when it delivered judgment in *Street v Mountford* [1985] 2 All ER 289.

Company and club premises can produce special headaches, and for business, by way of contrast with domestic accommodation, recent legislation has produced considerable commercial and professional legal problems. For example, when Newcastle United applied for consideration as a potential World Cup venue in 1966, it found itself involved with the local corporation over the terms of renewal of the lease on which St James Park has always been held. A lawn tennis club registered as a society under the Industrial and Provident Societies Act 1983 has been able to claim status as a business for protection under the Landlord and Tenant Act 1954 (*Addiscombe Garden Estates Ltd v Crabbe* [1958] 1 QB 513). Furthermore, in appropriate circumstances, the Landlord and Tenant Act 1954 provisions can be excluded by specific agreement (*Tottenham Hotspur Football & Athletic Co Ltd v Princegrove Publishers Ltd* [1974] 1 All ER 17.) Conversely, in 1982 the more than century old Rossendale United Football in North-West England was able to rely upon the Act to overturn, in the then County Palatine Court in Manchester an expulsion notice in the local Rossendale County Court and preserve its occupancy of the ground at Dark Lane in Rossendale since 1898. On that occasion a combination of local solicitor services from the Cheshire County League and London counsel combined to achieve a settlement to preserve continuity for now more than a century *Rossendale Free Press*: 20 Feb 1982.

(2)   Liquor Licences

Any practitioner familiar with the current edition of *Paterson's Licensing Acts*, containing over 1700 pages of text and appendices, will recognise the impossibility of attempting to embrace here any part of it. Different types of certificate exist for registration as well as different types of licences; supper, occasional, special or extended hours, together with the transfers of licences. One particular segment for which the then Lord Chief Justice, Lord Parker, said

'there have been a mass of authorities dealing with what can and cannot be a special occasion for the purpose of the Licensing Acts' (s 74(4), 1964) (*Lemon v Sargent* [1971] 3 All ER 936 at p 937).

Unfortunately, much seems to depend on the attitude of the local police and local justices. In Wales the local Chief Inspector failed in a High Court appeal against the grant of the justices to a hotelier who had obtained a special order of exemption under s 74(4) Licensing Act 1964 extending by one hour the permitted licensing hours for the match on Saturday 9 October 1971 so that refreshments might be supplied to the players and officials from the local football club following a home match. The justices held that the occasion in respect of which the application had been made was 'a special occasion'. The Divisional Court confirmed the justices' finding that this particular football match was quite independent of the activity of the hotelier. However, it was noted to be a borderline case (*R v Llanidloes (Lower) Justices, ex parte Thorogood* [1971] 3 All ER 932).

In Kent, a local golf club succeeded in the High Court against a refusal by the local justices to grant a special occasion licence. The key, as so often happens and in this jurisdiction particularly, is the relationship of the facts to the particular organisation and the local police approach. Thus in the Leicester courts, the local sporting clubs were trapped by a policy decision to oppose progressively increased applications by organisations not only including sport; and when Leicester City Football Club appealed to the High Court against a refusal to grant a special licence at their Filbert Street ground, before the match, during half-time and after the final whistle, in accordance with the practice over the previous seventeen years, Kennedy J held that on the evidence he was unable to intervene and overrule the justices; findings that the First Division matches were not 'special', although it appears the judgment included the recognition by the justices that an important fixture such as an FA Cup semi-final, might be treated differently (*Leicester Mercury*, 9 February 1985).

Since then, of course, Parliament has intervened with two interconnected enactments which in turn cross-refer in effect to two others. The Sporting Events (Control of Alcohol Etc) Act 1985, as amended by the Public Order Act 1986 under section 40(1) and Schedule 1, creates a network of prohibitions for England and Wales against transporting and consuming alcohol at sporting events.

Section 30 of the Public Order Act 1986 gives courts the discretionary power to impose an exclusion order upon convictions for offences connected with football. This extends generally a principle which had been created six years earlier in 1980 for licensed premises generally, and also for Scotland, under two statutes of that year: the Licensed Premises (Exclusion of Certain Persons) Act 1980 and the Criminal Justice (Scotland) Act 1980, Part V, sections 68–77. It surely cannot be unfair to enquire how this lack of co-ordination at Whitehall and Westminster occurred. Was it because of the 20% limitation of time imposed upon a junior Parliamentary Under-Secretary or an unawareness at the Department of the Environment of the problems involved?

(3)   Lotteries, betting and gaming

Consistent with the identification of the current edition of *Paterson's Licensing Acts* it is appropriate here to refer to the first edition of the *Law of Betting, Gaming and Lotteries* by Colin Milner Smith QC and Stephen Philip Monckom. Their volume contains 777 pages of text and appendices, and demonstrates the futility of any attempt to condense it here. The House of Lords, at the end of a procedural exercise straddling the Commercial Court with criminal procedure during 1980, laid down guidelines for identifying the requirements for a lawful lottery under legislation passed by Parliament four years earlier in the Lotteries and Amusements Act 1976 (*Imperial Tobacco Ltd v A-G* [1980] 1 All ER 866).

That enactment provided for three separate types of lottery with which event organisers and treasurers should be familiar.

Section 3: Small lotteries incidental to exempt entertainments

Under this section sporting or athletics events are included in the exemptions which exist, but among other conditions the most crucial are that,

(i)   no money prizes are permitted, and
(ii)   tickets can be sold or issued and the result declared at the place and on the occasion concerned.

Section 4: Private lotteries

Private lotteries can only exist within the framework of a private organisation. The only people who are able to purchase tickets are the members of the club or organisation and only they themselves can appoint the promoter. The club or other private organisation alone can benefit and only the winning ticket purchaser will receive a prize.

Section 5: Public lotteries

This section specifies 'participation in or support of athletic sports or games or cultural activities'. Among other conditions it includes the total value of tickets (as amended by Statutory Instrument) to be £10,000 or less; registration with the Gaming Board; and the lottery is promoted on behalf of a club or society registered with the local authority.

The House of Lords in *Imperial Tobacco Ltd v AG* (supra) emphasised the essentiality of a distribution of prize by lot or chance and that the chance of winning was secured by a payment, contribution or consideration by those taking part.

Two years after the 1976 Act the *Royal Commission on Gambling* under Lord Rothschild's chairmanship reported in its *Conclusions* published in July 1978 (Cmnd 7200).

'Despite the good work being achieved through many lotteries, the situation we have discovered is scandalous. There is wholesale disregard of the law which is inadequate and confused, commercial exploitation to a totally unacceptable degree, gross lack of security and, we suspect, a good deal of plain dishonesty'.

(Paragraph 12.134: page 194.)

How far this Conclusion can be sustained or rejected nearly twenty-one years later would depend upon evidence similar in quantity to that which appeared before the Commission. What it contains, however, is a built-in warning to avoid pitfalls, be careful and take professional guidance or advice.

Section 6: National Lottery

Chapters 12 and 13 in Volume 1 of the *Royal Commission on Gambling* (above) explained respectively at pages 163–164 and subsequently at page 227 the background to what was passed by Parliament as the National Lottery Act 1993 on 21 October 1993:

'12.5   All lotteries must be considered from two aspects — as a form of fund-raising and as a form of gambling. It is commonly supposed that lotteries are an infallible means of raising funds with very little trouble. The truth is otherwise and there have been some costly failures through poor administration. The Isle of Man lottery in the 1960s was one example and there have been more recent cases, on a smaller scale, in Britain.

12.6   Attitudes to lotteries as a form of gambling have varied over the years. There was a time when it was commonly thought immoral that anyone should be able to gain a large sum of money at the expense of his fellows and without the exercise of any skill or effort on his part. This view is less common today [ie as at 1978] ... One reason for this change of attitude is the generally more tolerant attitude towards gambling under proper control that exists throughout the world today. Most Governments take the view that lotteries are a harmless form of gambling and also provide harmless entertainment ...

12.9   State lotteries in Britain have had a long history extending from 1569 to 1826....

13.64   We conclude that there should be a single national lottery for good causes run by a National Lottery Board....

13.65   The good causes to benefit from the national lottery should not be defined in terms of organisations but of objectives which should be:
(i)   Sport.
(ii)   The Arts.
(iii)   Other Deserving Causes.
Nothing more elaborate is required'.

The Act extended the 'Other Deserving Causes' to comprise charities, national heritage and the Millennium Fund projecting local and national restoration schemes within the widest environmental range towards the year 2000. A Director-General, Peter Davis, was appointed by the Secretary of State for the Department of National Heritage, and as he explained in an interview with *Leisure Management* in December 1993, his first task was to produce a Draft Invitation to Apply (ITA) and Draft Licence to Run the National Lottery under the two-tier system for its administration under sections 5 and 6 of the Act. (See also pages 391–395.)

(4)   Libel, slander and copyright

Once more the standard text books on the subjects indicate the scope of the areas which these topics cover: *Carter-Ruck on Libel and Slander*

(7th edn Butterworths 1997); *Copinger and Skone James on Copyright; Gatley on Libel and Slander.*

There has been a cascade of writs issued for defamation in recent years, most of which are settled before they reach court. No general distinction in law affects the sporting scene. Only the relevance of the particular facts triggers any legal issue here, as in all other areas. Thus at the time of writing, the mystery of the alleged tampered cricket ball during the 1992 Lord's Texaco Trophy between England and Pakistan (now locked away in Lord's Pavilion) continued. Defamation proceedings due to Allan Lamb's comments concerning the state of the ball were begun and withdrawn after disputed evidence alleging breaches of cricket's laws 42.4 and 42.5 and consequential damage to the image of the game and integrity and romantic idealism at the *public* level.

Within the context of Sport and the Law there are two levels where organisers should be careful. One is ordinary administration. The other is conventional publication. In general it is essential to realise that programme criticisms, record announcements and every form of communication can create risk situations; libel for the written and slander for the word. A wrongful expulsion by a secretary resulted in judgment against officers and committee members responsible for the secretary's errors (*Birne v National Sporting Club Ltd & Ors* (1957) *Times*, 12 April, page 13).

In the 1930s one of the great anomalies arising out of the curious role of the amateur sportsman resulted in an award of damages to a famous amateur golf champion for a libel which had been published gratuitously, which expressed knowledge of the risk that payment and thereby professionalism could be inferred. Cyril Tolley claimed that a commercial advertisement in a national newspaper had impugned his amateur status by a cartoon depicting him with a chocolate bar sticking out of his trousers coupled with the caption:

'The caddie to Tolley said, Oh, Sir,
Good shot, Sir That ball, see it go, Sir,
My word how it flies,
Like a cartet of Frys,
They're handy, they're good, and priced low, Sir'.

(*Tolley v Fry* [1931] AC 333).

Procedurally the House of Lords ordered a retrial on the issue of damages; and the action was settled. The libel principle, however, was established on that occasion more than 60 years ago, to preserve a reputation and its amateur status; by today's commercial cultural standards, a near unbelievable exercise.

Nevertheless, the more recently publicised golfing libel action in Nottingham Crown Court, had a century-old echo with it for preserving a reputation for fair play and honour and rejecting cheating assertions (*Buckingham v Rusk and Dene* (*Independent*, 28 April 1994)). Thus in 1890 a distinguished nobleman and friend of the Prince of Wales and future King Edward VII, Sir William Gordon-Cumming, was accused of cheating at cards during a house party on the eve of the Doncaster St Leger Race meeting, the oldest classic horse race in the world. He sued for slander; called the Prince of Wales as a witness on his behalf, with harmful effect; and heard a biased summing-up by the Lord Chief Justice, Lord Coleridge, after a trial which lasted six days. He lost the action which he ought to have won. The procedural problems are reported in *Gordon-Cumming v Green and others* [1980–1] 7 TLR 409–410; and the full story was told in the *Royal Baccarat Scandal* by Lord Havers, Edward Grayson and Peter Shankland when it was first published in 1977. More recently the former Liverpool goalkeeper Bruce Grobbelaar cleared his name in London High Court defamation libel proceedings with an £85,000 damages award after he had survived Winchester Crown Court jury trials verdicts for alleged corruption when juries could not agree on verdicts (*Grobbelaar v Sun Newspaper* Tuesday 29 July 1999).

Finally, to protect the organiser completely against any copyright infringement from musical entertainment at sporting occasions, whether from gramophone records or other forms of reproduction, then consultation should take place with the Performing Right Society Limited of 29 Berners Street, London, W1 (Tel: 0181–580 5544) and the Phonographic Performance Limited Company at 14 Ganton Street, London W1 (Tel: 0181–437 0311). An injunction was obtained against Rangers FC Supporters Club Greenock, for breaches of copyright under this head (1974, Scots Law Times 151); but if the amount charged is excessive a right of reference exists to the Performing Right Tribunal (*Performing Right Society Ltd v Aristidou*, (1978) *Times*, 6 July, page 12).

(5) Insurance

Normally there should be no difference from the normal everyday type of policy required for normal domestic or household needs. For the essence of good administration demands good housekeeping.

The usual type of household policy, tailored to the specialist sporting requirements, will cover property, theft and liability for personal injury; and the governing body of the appropriate sport will be the best source for such enquiry.

No limit for compensation need exist, subject to the amount of premium, for which cover can be obtained. Thus, pluvius policies for cricket benefit matches will be required whereas they will not need to be considered for indoor boxing tournaments where the risks of cancellation from training or other circumstances create liability to spectators and contestants involving different insurance elements. No limits exist to the potential permutations of cover, but the nature and wording of the insurance policies must be precisely thought out and formulated. The following points merely illustrate the needs of sporting policy holders; and a graphic example of the need for precision can be seen below after an unsuccessful claim in London's High Court for an alleged failure to insure against theft in respect of the disappearance of the Aga Khan's record-breaking 10 lengths Derby winner, Shergar, on 9 February 1983.

(a)   Property insurance

To rebuild a grandstand or building after destruction by fire almost inevitably demands the expenditure for architects', surveyors' and similar consultants' fees and a suitable clause to cover these expenses can be added. Also a further example or experience occurred at Littlehampton. Although the ground and buildings were comprehensively covered by policies, a fire which burned down an old pavilion, housing all the club's kit and equipment, disclosed that the kit and equipment remained uninsured.

(b)   Theft

Apart from conventional cover against chattels, a fidelity policy to protect club or company property against defaulting employees would also provide an additional safeguard via the insurers' enquiries about the bona fides of staff likely to handle valuables and cash; and while Mr Justice Rattee's High Court decision on Shergar in April 1994 was bloodstock related, the principle behind it had a wider lesson. The available reports from racing sources [*The Sporting Life: Racing Post* 27 April 1994] point to the Plaintiff co-owners of shares in the stallion, Coolmore Stud, Co. Tipperary, and others, believing that

(1)   as 'theft was exceedingly unlikely to happen' and
(2)   they had given no thought to insuring the Derby winner against theft and
(3)   the risk was considered so slim in the insurance world that theft cover was available as an 'extra goody' in many policies at no additional premium and
(4)   there was no implied terms that 'theft cover was included in the invitation to the bloodstock agents to obtain' 'morality cover'.

Accordingly, the cover asked for in the Lloyd's open market had been obtained, and in the absence of the theft cover asked for there was no breach of duty to create negligence.

(c)   Legal liability

This provides the widest scope for cover and costs. While the courts decide the law and quantum of damages for assessment of injury, whether to life, limb or reputation, the insurance companies track the decisions for evaluating the ultimate costs for assessing risks.

Hence, the majority if not all the cases listed under chapters 4, 5 and 6 would have been contested under the umbrella of an insurance policy; and further areas of legal liability into which sport and recreation may stray for attracting insurance move outside the self-imposed restraints in these pages of participation and spectatorship, where individuals or groups participate in activities away from spectator involvement: namely, such outdoor or supervisory worlds as playgrounds, potholing, rock-climbing and skateboarding.

Here, the disparate facts which are the key-note to litigation plot a zig-zag course of liability and non-liability; and skateboarding, which created such ambivalent reactions about whether it is a sport, a form of transport or a social and public menace during the later 1970s, formed its own Skateboard Association under the aegis of the Sports Council but was forced to go to Holland for adequate insurance facilities.

Finally, five other separate points need stressing.

(1)   All clubs should have a 'Public Liability' insurance in force, and it ought to include liability when the ground is loaned or hired for any purpose other than normal use, such as a religious crusade or a boxing tournament. Club activities outside the ground and overseas tours should also be covered.

(2)   To insurance a club's liability to its employees, a separate policy is usually required. The premium is calculated at a rate per cent on the total wages and salaries, and this cover is additional to any benefits that can be obtained under the National Insurance Scheme (see Employers' Liability (Compulsory Insurance) Act 1969).

(3)   As so many clubs take part in overseas tours, secretaries should ensure, that, before they travel abroad, some sort of cover for medical expenses has been arranged. The cost of having a comparatively minor operation in some foreign countries is enormous, and there is no equivalent of our National Health Service in many areas.

(4)   Two complementary situations which can appeal to clubs and members collectively or individually are (a) group insurance schemes and (b) personal insurance which many participants obtain in particularly violent or physical pursuits supplementary to any other cover.

(5)   Finally, a club committee and officers may find it prudent either by insurance or provision in their club rules to provide for general or specific indemnities. One example, and there could be countless others,

where claims for damages arise, is in the field of defamation. More surprising was the disclosure during Michael Watson's judgment against the British Boxing Board of Control on 25 September 1999 that notwithstanding its professional expertise among its well-known named Stewards insurance cover did not exist.

(6) During the judgment of Mr Justice Drake in *Elliott v Saunders and Liverpool Football Club* in 1993 he posed the question of potential comprehensive insurance within the professional game. Nothing has progressed since then and for general specialist purposes in the World of Sport I am indebted to the Appendices from Mr Andrew Deans, Solicitor, head of the sport and leisure liability team, and Mr Justin Claydon, of Hextall Erskine. Solicitors to the Insurance Industry and also Mr Tony O'Brien of Perkins Slade Insurers to the Central Court of Physical Recreation.

CONCLUSION

What emerges from this chapter is the complexity inherent in administering sport at any level: school, club or national institution. Furthermore, consistent with different areas of legal practice, sport, too, demands a knowledge by practitioners of the myriad minefields which can trap the unwary. Thus the litigation lawyer who slavishly believes that judicial review is a procedural avenue open to his or her client in sport should study the fate of the Aga Khan's abortive claim against the Jockey Club, and Catherine Bond's analysis in Appendix 14.

PART V

Commerce

CHAPTER 13

Sponsored Gentlemen and Players

1 INTRODUCTION

In 1983 *The Howell Report* from The Central Council of Physical Recreation's Committee of Enquiry Trust Sports Sponsorship which had which had been created in 1981 explained

'The jargon of sponsorship and associated activities is extremely confusing for the uninitiated. Indeed, the distinction between very different activities which are usually lumped together under the heading of 'sponsorship' [as patronage and philanthropy] is not understood by many people who have a responsibility for the government of sport, much less by members of the general public'.

By 1999 almost every level of sporting administration today , domestically and internationally, looks to sponsorship for full or shared funding for its sustained existence. Sponsorship has an ever increasing importance within sport at both public and domestic levels. Sponsors seek out sport as it purports to promote a healthy and clean lifestyle for their products. Sport itself requires the money from sponsorship in order to invest money back into itself and also to reward the successful competitors. Sponsorship of major sporting events is keenly sought to the extent that modern day sport at the public entertainment level would be unimaginable without certain companies attaching themselves to the Olympics, cricket, soccer and horse-racing, to name but a few. Correspondingly many sporting school trips abroad would be unthinkable without parental and other sponsorship sources.

As a modern phenomenon, it has been around for longer than many may know, without delving back into ancient history, where its earliest roots can be found. The Howell Report explained at Page 8.

'Much of the early support of sport as well as the arts belonged in the category of patronage. How could it be otherwise? The modern tools of commercial sponsorship particularly television did not exist. Yet two cricket events in the early 1860's provided pioneer examples of sponsorship — rather should they not be called 'marketing' — for gain.

One was the backing of England's first tour of Australia in 1861 by a catering firm who made a profit of £11,000 from their investment. The other was the decision in 1863 by a Worcester sports outfitter, John Wisden by name, to underwrite the publication of *The Wisden Cricketers' Almanack*.

This world famous 'bible' of cricket reference and record, 130 plus years on, is still a must on the book shelves of enthusiasts of the sport. Yet 'Wisden', a name now synonymous with cricket rather than the [then] still in business founding firm, provides a perfect illustration of a modern sponsoring danger, that of the marketing tool becoming better known than the company or product'.

A century after Wisden's pioneering initiative of 1864 the Gillette toiletry company innovated modern cricket's first knock out Cup Competition. By 1991 it was so successful as a cricket brand image that history repeated itself by a withdrawal in a mutually appreciative atmosphere, now being continued in the frame of the NatWest Bank Trophy.

Sponsorship has no traditional legal status. Like sport itself, it leans more to description than delineation. There is no sponsorship statute, and no private civil sponsorship case law per se exists at present independent of conventional commercial law of decisions (as distinct from VAT tribunal and High Court judgments).

As a factual phenomenon which has arrived on the sporting scene in particular, and the arts-leisure-recreation stage generally, sponsorship has now been recognised in the form of an important HM Treasury Memorandum of evidence. Consistent with the Howell Committee's narrative development this was submitted to the Education, Science and Arts Committee of the House of Commons (supra, appointed under SO No 86A (Eighth Report 1982) HC 49–11) under the title of *Taxation in the Context of Private Sponsorship and of Gifts of Art Objects to Public and Private Institutions*, and thereby formally acknowledged authoritatively its existence. HM Customs and Excise have also recognised the existence of sponsorship in its VAT Leaflet No 701/41/95, 1 July 1995. Entitled 'Sponsorship' it provides specific guidance on 'how VAT applies to sponsorship where this is in the form of money, goodwill services'.

Each of these two authoritative sources has a crucial role to play in the functional operation of sponsorship. It qualifies in the appropriate circumstances acceptable to the Commissioners of Inland Revenue under the conventional tax laws and practices for tax reliefs. It is subject to VAT burdens and practices. These fiscal sources therefore point to sponsorship for what it is: a business-commercial concept used by the sponsor as a key promotional marketing tool.

In the frenzied climate of media manipulation, it is easy to forget how sponsorship's existence is vital for sport at regional and local as well as at national and international levels. It is also necessary to distinguish sponsorship from its associated ancillary advantages to sport and the arts-leisure-recreation scenario through the more familiar philanthropic and patronage methods of funding. Sponsorship is a legitimate taxation expenditure within a corporate or personal budget and as such it is distinguishable from the personal indulgence or whim of an enthusiastic benefactor. Indeed, according to the Central Council of Physical Recreation's associated body, The Institute of Sports Sponsorship, by 1989

> 'Currently over one thousand commercial companies in the United Kingdom between them subscribe over £200 million in various sponsorship schemes — a clear sign both of how important sport has become as a means of promoting commercial interests and how greatly organised sport now relies on commercial backing'.

When Barclays Bank Plc replaced the *Today* newspaper as sponsor for the Football League's centenary season of 1987–88 to create the Barclays League, the then chairman of Barclays Bank, Sir John Quinton, explained that he was a season-ticket holder at Tottenham Hotspur, but that the sponsorship deal was,

> 'a decision made for hard-headed commercial reasons with clear business objectives in mind'.

Those objectives were stated with the claims;

> 'We believe that the Barclays League Championship is an ideal promotional vehicle for us for a number of reasons. It appeals to youth — and young people are a key recruitment area for the bank. It involves clubs from throughout the country — and Barclays has at least one branch in every town where a league club is located. It is an event which is of interest to all ages and all sociological groups — and Barclays is keen to increase its market share in a number of target sectors. It offers more matches during a longer season than any other sports event in the UK, has 14 live televised matches during this season and offers enormous scope for our local branches and branch staff to become involved.
>
> Having said all that, football is also rather special in this country. Whatever its problems in recent years, it remains our national game and the local League club remains a vital part of the community. We are pleased our sponsorship

can help to ensure the continued health of the game and indeed encourage its rebirth as a great family entertainment'.

These thoughts and attitudes from one of British soccer's highest profile sponsors were consistent with the approach from the Gillette toiletry company seen by some as the modern pioneers of nationally recognised sports sponsorship in the United Kingdom. The late Gordon Ross, who was involved closely at its inception in 1963 with the famous cricket competition The Gillette Cup, explained the mutual benefits from this ideal liaison between sport and commerce in his book *The Gillette Cup: 1963 to 1980*.

The trophy was inaugurated in the year the artificial distinctions between Gentlemen and Players were abolished in 1963 by MCC, prior to its own surrender of authority (apart from continued control of cricket's Laws) to the Test and County Cricket Board and the National Cricket Association for all aspects of the amateur game, during the later 1960s, as we have seen in Chapter 2, *Progressive perspective*. Initiated, as Ross wrote 'rather too much of a mouthful for the sports pages of the newspapers', as 'The First-Class Counties Knock-Out Competition for the Gillette Cup', it was simplified in the press as 'the KO Cup'. Ultimately it was titled formally 'The Gillette Cup', which, after eighteen finals, because of its outstanding success, led ultimately to its demise.

Ross wrote of the relationship between Gillette and cricket:

'The manner in which Gillette acted, in the lowest possible commercial key and with meticulous care and responsibility, produced a confidence which established a happy marriage between cricket and the sponsor. Sponsorship in cricket grew gradually as a result of this sensitive approach, but few could have anticipated its final ramifications in the form of Packer's brash and gimmicky mass-media promotion'.

In his closing pages under the chapter heading of 'Reflections', Ross wrote interrogatively with words which have a message for all sponsors who wish to follow the impeccable trail blazed by Gillette's sponsorship. This trail has since been littered with less mutually beneficial results to sport and commerce,

'People may ask, "What did Gillette derive from the Gillette Cup and why [sic!] they get out of it?"

This is a question that can only be answered if it is broadened to ask, "Why do companies sponsor sport — or the arts for that matter?"

Obviously the prime reason for doing so is the publicity which is given to the company name. There are two ways of looking at that. First, the company wishes to project a good image of itself by association with a well regarded national event; in Gillette's case the advantage of association with a clean, masculine game is beneficial for its products. But the second consideration carries limitation with it and is the more important: the use of the company's name is only really valuable when the name is the same as the trade mark under which its products are sold, or in the case of a company not selling goods, is the same as the business name under which it trades.

Thus the multifarious activities of the Unilever organisation would probably render a Unilever Cup worthless, but the Cornhill Tests must be of considerable value. In Gillette's case two things happened as the eighteen years went by: the number of its products sold under trade marks other than Gillette increased with the company's diversification: and research showed that the public was beginning to associate the Gillette Cup less and less with products using the trademark Gillette, or even with the company itself. The competition was becoming a national institution set apart from the company's business. Exact measurement of such things is impossible but that seemed to be the trend'.

Ross continued with an example from the horse-racing scene in illustrating what he called 'The other reason for sponsoring is the altruistic one' which, as we shall see, is more accurately a form of patronage. He explained,

'In days gone by, wealthy individuals were able to sponsor sporting events (Lord Derby is a good example in the horseracing world). In today's economic climate, and with the growth of national events and the media, sponsorship by individuals is virtually impossible and their place as generous citizens is now take by large companies. It is a proper activity for them and one from which they can derive credit. This was originally why Gillette came in.

In the famous offer letter of 4 September 1962 [which clinched earlier negotiations] they wrote of the company's "general desire to identify itself with the promotion of British sport and to make some tangible contribution to the future of first-class cricket".

That is the way it went, and Richard Burton [initially the company's legal adviser and subsequently Chairman] echoed this at a BBC television interview the night before the last final when he said:

"It cannot be measured in advertising terms. The memory I would like to leave is one where both sides, cricket and Gillette, had a very happy partnership."'.

Ross concluded his chapter and the book with a prophetic last paragraph:

'In leaving cricket, Gillette knew that they would not be inflicting any damage on the game itself. What they had created, with the help of cricket's administrators, was an extremely valuable commercial proposition, and its attraction was very quickly appreciated by a number of companies who competed for it when it became known that the competition was on the market. The altruistic motive had been fulfilled — and the Gillette Cup will remain always an historical landmark in the folklore of cricket'.

So the wheel of history had turned full circle almost a century after cricket's earlier 1861 pioneering precedent for what in effect was an international sponsorship. As this 20th century ends, and the commercial mutuality which is at the heart of the sponsorship relationships becomes more intense, the jargon jangling within and outside the sponsorship arenas, which the *Howell Report* recognised, takes on a cliché riddled flavour of value for money and performance related pay, and particularly in the frenetic intensity of international competitive sport world-wide. Thus the disappointing results of the England international cricket XI during 1999 produced thoughts about non-renewal of at least one major sponsorship: and the bizarre mystery surrounding Manchester United's disruption of football's greatest tradition, outside perpetuation of the common spirit within the game, by withdrawal from their defence as holders of The Football Association *Challenge* Cup Competition, has caused its current sponsors, Axa Insurance, to question publicly the level of their commercial investment. Within that commercial setting it is essential to recognise the legal basis for modern sponsorship, and its distinction, with well-known examples, from closely associated categories with which it can easily be confused, namely philanthropy and patronage.

2   LEGAL AND FACTUAL FOUNDATIONS AND DISTINCTIONS

The essence of an effective sponsorship arrangement must be the sponsorship contract. A simple example from the professional football world is published at pages 464-465 below, with permission of the Aston Villa club, together with a check list of the nuts and bolts of a sponsorship contract which was contained in evidence published in the most valuable Howell Report from the CCPR towards the end of 1983. See pages 462-463 below.

Additional associated legal categories which constantly arise involve copyright, licensing, passing-off, patents, trusts, and others in addition to taxes and VAT. For example in 1990, the BBC failed in a claim for exclusivity and breach of copyright under section 16 of the Copyright, Designs and Patents Act 1988 when British Satellite Broadcasting Ltd used short excerpts from the BBC's live broadcasts of soccer World Cup matches to show highlights of matches in its sports news programmes. After six days of evidence and legal argument, Scott J in a reserved judgment held that this amounted to 'fair dealing ... for the purpose of reporting current events' and was therefore protected by section 30(2) of the 1988 Act because the World Cup matches were current events and inter alia the material was used in genuine news reports, (*BBC v BSB Ltd* [1991] 3 All ER 833).

Because space within this chapter alongside others in this book proscribes the aim to provide a general level of awareness and as such only an outline and overview with easily recognisable illustrations can be attempted here. Indeed, sponsorship has become a growth area to such an extent that since the year of England's World Cup Soccer triumph in 1966, taken as a well-known and identifiable starting point, nearly a dozen in-depth authoritative studies have surfaced to which reference will be made at various stages in this chapter.

For an in-depth analysis of the comprehensive legal issues involved, the reader is referred to *Sponsorship of Sport, Arts and Leisure: Law, Tax and Business Relationships* (1984 Stephen Townley and Edward Grayson), the only exclusively *legal* survey of the sports sponsorship scene published to date in the United Kingdom. In 1987, Iain C Baillie, a member of the New York Bar and a Chartered Patent Agent published *Licensing: A Practical Guide for the Businessman* and in 1989 and 1990, Deborah Fosbrook and Adrian C Laing published two volumes of *The Media Contracts Handbook: A Master Contract Reference Book* for use within the Media Industry. Cumulatively they provided 75 specimen precedents, with a warning in their Introduction to Volume 2 under the heading of 'Sponsorship Generally'.

> 'There is no standard type of sponsorship deal. We have chosen particular circumstances which commonly involve the advancement of money by a commercial company to an individual, agent, or association in return for media exposure of the sponsor's product, name, trademark or logo'.

Within the present survey for this particular chapter, three fundamental differentials which are frequently ignored, overlooked or unknown, must be recognised.

(1) Sponsorship can be as important for local and regional institutions and their activities as the often overvalued national and international sources.

(2) Sponsorship can be applied and accepted for legitimate tax deductible purposes in six different circumstances or levels, ie
   (i)   Personal individuals or team groups (eg Torville and Dean by Nottingham Corporation or Watford Football Club by Iveco);
   (ii) Governing bodies (eg Football League by Barclays Bank Plc);
   (iii) Events (eg NatWest Bank Trophy in succession to the Gillette Cup);

    (iv) Product (eg Brylcreem by Denis Compton or tennis equipment by individual performers at Wimbledon or elsewhere);

    (v) Long-term or one-off within time limits;

    (vi) Local, Regional or National in scope and range.

(3) Sponsorship is not

    (a) Philanthropy;

    (b) Patronage.

Terminology and definitions

The significance of each of these three different elements above will emerge during this chapter, but the last two concepts will be dealt with first because of the confusion which can be caused by not understanding the distinction between philanthropy and patronage. The border-line between philanthropy and patronage can be blurred, but they are both to be distinguished sharply from sponsorship. That distinction was explained conveniently in a second *Economist Intelligence Unit* (EIU) *Special Report on Sponsorship* (1980/81) by Jean Simkins at p 5. Distinguishing the sponsorship concept from that of patronage, the point is made there that

'the terms are sometimes interchanged and it is not unusual to refer to patronage by individuals (as opposed to organisations) as sponsorship, as in the case of sponsored walks for charity. In general, however, the term patronage in connection with commercial enterprises is applied to financial or material assistance given without the expectation of any return even in the form of publicity'.

Then the contrast is rightly made with

'Sponsorship [as being] essentially a business deal, which is intended to be for the advantage of sponsor and sponsored. If successfully designed and carried out, with properly defined objectives, sponsorship arrangements can be of real benefit to both parties and, at the same time, be of benefit to the community in providing events and facilities which would otherwise not be available. It is desirable to keep a clear distinction between sponsorship and patronage ventures, and to regard them as quite separate activities to which different criteria apply'.

The framework for such successful design, carrying out and properly defined objectives is always contractual. Barclays Bank Plc stepped into the breach left by a dispute over the contractual arrangements between the Football League and *Today*. The review of the 1986 Commonwealth Games at Edinburgh under the title *Unfriendly Games: Boycotted and Broke* (1986) by Derek Bateman and Derek Douglas, two experienced Scottish journalists, identified an assessment of the management of organisation by the distinguished consultants Coopers and Lybrand, commissioned by Mr Robert Maxwell. They recorded at page 43;

> 'He must have been astonished [on reading the consultant's report] at the incompetence which led to "uncertainty as to whether contracts and in particular contracts that are part of a wider sponsorship arrangement have actually been signed, and the contents of those contracts".'

Contractually styled documents are not essential for philanthropy or patronage: indeed in law they are inconsistent with such bounty (*Balfour v Balfour* [1919] 2 KB 571). Nevertheless in the current economic and social climate about disputed rights, clarification and certainty in documentary form are always desirable. Alternatively, symbolic or inferred inscriptions would suffice. Two classic sporting examples suffice, and demonstrate differences from sponsorship.

(a)   Philanthropy

Philanthropy describes the act of donation without the expectation of receiving any form of gain in return. It is illustrated by a direct link between one of Fleet Street's landmarks in London which continues to survive time's ravages and the departures to Docklands and elsewhere of its newspaper associations. The sign of the Three Squirrels, outside the branch of Barclays Bank Plc, at No 19, represents how it is known and labelled and listed in the telephone directory as Goslings Branch.

For over three hundred years it has served the legal, literary and journalist professions, with its proud saga of two families, Gosling and Sharpe, who dominated the branch until the amalgamation with the Gurney, Backhouse and Barclay families to form the present structure in 1896. The best-known member of the Gosling family beyond the banking fringe was Robert Cunliffe Gosling who died prematurely after surgery in 1923 aged 53.

In the last decade of Queen Victoria's England he had been a double cricket and soccer Blue at Cambridge, and when only three soccer home international matches were played each season, he was capped five times on merit as an amateur forward alongside such renowned professionals as Bassett (West Bromwich Albion), Bloomer (Derby County), Goodall (Preston North End), Spikesley (Sheffield Wednesday), to name a few. C B Fry wrote in *Life Worth Living* of R C Gosling, that he was a

> 'magnificent forward ... very fast, skilful and unselfish. Otherwise he was an MFH with a princely income, and played in perfectly valeted brown boots which must have cost him a fiver. He aided the Corinthians in their

reputation up North as a team of toffs. We were suspected of being Guards officers and young squires'.

Gosling was part of the Essex county squierarchy, later President of the County Cricket Club, a JP and High Sheriff, and mourned deeply by his tenant farmers and retainers when he died in 1923. In 1902, after the early death aged 41 of his fellow Old Etonian Arthur Dunn, founder of Ludgrove School (mentioned in Chapter 4, *Parent, School and Club Partners*), Gosling donated a trophy. It is inscribed

'In Memoriam'

The Arthur Dunn Challenge Cup

It has been played for annually, except for interruption from two World Wars, enthusiastically and by Old Boys XI's from the leading public schools. The donation by Gosling in memory of his friend had no sponsorship or patronage strings attached. It was a gift. It was philanthropy. The Arthur Dunn Challenge Cup, unknown to many, is the second oldest knock-out soccer cup competition in the world after the FA Cup, the FA having faced reality in 1974 to abolish its Amateur Cup Competitions created in 1894.

(b)   Patronage

Patronage is a step beyond philanthropy where donors do not expect to achieve gain, but allow their name to be associated with the subject matter of a donation.

In the year before Gosling's gift of the Arthur Dunn Cup during 1902, professional boxing had survived its trauma recorded in Chapter 6, *Participation problems*, of the jury's acquittal at the Central Criminal Court of defendants charged with manslaughter following a death in the ring at the National Sporting Club, which claimed to be the headquarters of professional boxing at its premises in King Street, Covent Garden (*R v Roberts and ors* [1901] supra). The Club's limited finances also placed it at a disadvantage for competing with commercial promoters and boxers' managers for services of the leading fighters to entertain Club members and their guests. Something more tangible than a naked commercial reward was required to redress this financial imbalance. For at that stage at the beginning of this century, no equivalent honour or trophy existed for professional boxing at any weight equivalent to the FA Challenge Cup Competition, which was conceived in 1871, from the precedent of Harrow School's Cock-House knock-out competition. Indeed after a mere thirty years it attracted a crowd of 114,815 to the Final tie at Crystal Palace in 1901, albeit with a London club, Tottenham Hotspur (then in the Southern League) from outside the Football League playing Sheffield United.

The National Sporting Club's active President was a celebrated all round sportsman and sports lover, the 5th Earl of Lonsdale. He provided generous donations and presided over the administrative structuring for the different weight divisions, into which boxing had been organised. The proposal to award a belt in honour to the winner of each National Sporting Championship fight at the appropriate weight, with the winner on three occasions at the same weight becoming the property owner of the prize, was adopted. After the demise of the Club in the later 1920s and establishment of the British Board of Boxing Control (1929) the Board took over the award of what are now known throughout the world as the Lonsdale Belts. The Board's first award was to the British flyweight champion from Scotland, Benny Lynch in 1936. The Club's first award was made in 1909 to the British lightweight champion Freddie Walsh. A conflict of evidence exists in boxing sources about the formal title of the original belts before the Board's present designation with the name of their donor who undoubtedly paid for the original foundation during his active Presidency of the Club. He patronised it with his presence as well as his bounty and sought no reward beyond his sporting satisfaction.

Lord Lonsdale's indulgence was the converse of the circumstances which stirred Dr Johnson's rebuff in 1754 to Lord Chesterfield ten years after rejection of support for the doctor's Dictionary preparation

> 'Is not a patron my lord, one who looks with unconcern on a man struggling for life in the water, and when he has reached ground encumbers him with help? The notice which you have been pleased to take of my labours, had it been early, had it been kind — but it has been delayed until I am indifferent, and cannot enjoy it; till I am solitary and cannot impart it; till I am known, and do not want it'.

3 SPONSORSHIP ORIGINS

Barely a century after Dr Johnson's patronage commentary the first example of modern sponsorship appeared in 1861, in turn almost a century before the Gillette initiative in 1962. *Sponsorship of Sport, Arts and Leisure*, by Stephen Townley and Edward Grayson, explains in its opening pages under the heading 'Historical Perspective' how cricket provides the precedents from its early growth as a public sport in the nineteenth century, via the personality cult clinging to Dr Grace and his exploitation of cricket while retaining his amateur status, down to the subsidised amateurism, during the years between two World Wars, from entrepreneurs enthusiastically devoted to cricket such as Sir Julien Cahn, ready to employ the Gentlemen to facilitate their continuing as subsidised amateur Players on the county championship circuit.

In 1861 expatriate Englishmen, Felix Spiers and Christopher Pond, had established substantial catering contracts for their supply of refreshments to the Melbourne and Ballarate Railway. To publicise their enterprises they sent an agent to England. Charles Dickens was invited to provide a series of public readings as a method of advertisement. When these failed to materialise the then finest and first ever English cricket team to tour Australia was arranged. It was assembled through the organisation of Surrey County Cricket Club's Secretary, William Burrup, and captained by H H Stephenson, also of Surrey. It succeeded on and off the field to such an extent that during the Australian winter Messrs Spiers and Pond returned to Britain to create a famous catering company until its ultimate absorption by the Express Dairy Group.

About the same time other enterprising cricket sponsors, John Wisden and James Lillywhite, conceived the idea of advertising their sports goods, shops and equipment through annual publications. The name of one survives in print, the other in London's lights as a store; and the dusty sporting bookshelves confirm this pattern from Gamages and Spalding to other examples from our own times. In 1895 the professional doctor, W G Grace, playing cricket as an amateur, surprisingly retained that status with Gloucestershire and England while also retaining £9,073 8s 3d from three separate sources. During that forty-eighth year of his life Grace scored his hundredth first-class hundred and for the first time (by any batsman), he also scored 1,000 runs in May. As Graham Parker's *Gloucestershire road: A history of Gloucester County Club* (published in 1983 in association with National Westminster Bank Plc) records:

> 'The *Daily Telegraph* launched a National Shilling Testimonial which brought him £4,281 9s 1d. There were others. GCCC added £100, £1 for each century perhaps, but a scant reward for his formidable contribution to their affairs. The Club was in the throes of a financial crisis. However, they did give him a Century of Centuries Dinner at the Victoria Rooms, Bristol on 24 June. The total of all the donations came to £9,073 8s 3d. Some amateur!'

In 1981, two years before Parker's county history, Eric Midwinter's biography *W G Grace: His Life and Times* noted

> 'A shrewd cartoon showed WG thanking Sir Edward Lawson [the *Telegraph* proprietor and later Lord Burnham] who is saying, "Don't mention it, doctor, look what you've done for my circulation"'.

In the following year of 1896 he captained the Gentlemen against the Players for each match played, at Lord's and the Oval. He also captained England, as an amateur of course, in the three Test Matches against the visiting Australians captained by G H S Trott.

Another modern sporting historian, Gerald Howat, has been equally forthcoming over the mystery which once shrouded the overnight conversion of Grace's memorable Gloucestershire all-rounder successor during the winter of 1937 from Hammond, WR, professional cricketer and former professional footballer with Bristol Rovers, to Mr W R Hammond, amateur in 1938. This created his eligibility to captain England against the Players, and Gloucestershire in the County Cricket Championship (unsponsored) during the summer of 1938, and England in South Africa during the winter of 1938–39.

Howat explains with candour how Hammond was invited to join the Board of Directors of an expanding firm of motor tyre suppliers which had begun after the First World War, namely Marsham Tyres.

'Hammond's value to Marsham Tyres lay in the contacts he was able to make. Bill Pope, a fellow-director and subsequently managing director after the second world war, remembered the contribution he made to the firm:

"Whether on cricket tours or playing in England, on the golf course or at some dinner, he brought us business. He had an easy manner, a memory for names and, of course, great prestige. In the continuing growth years of 1938 and 1939, despite the European political uncertainty, he was involved as our firm's main outside 'contact' man"'.

Howat explains that

'Pope admitted that the glamour of bringing in business appealed to Hammond more than the routine of following it up, but his job remained clear — to get the orders. He was popular with the firm's representatives and surviving photographs show him smiling at golfing functions and office gatherings. In attracting to their ranks one of the best-known figures in England, Marsham Tyres had done themselves a service. By 1939, an expansion programme which some had felt to be too ambitious had proved over-modest. New production facilities could scarcely meet increasing demand'.

During that summer of 1938 television cameras were at Lord's when Hammond scored his unforgettable 240 against Australia on Friday 24 and Saturday 25 June. The Pavilion rose to grant the standing acclamation given intuitively at the end of only the most specially styled innings. Very few at the time were aware that on the evidence now adduced by Gerald Howat's biography it is at least arguable that it had been sponsored by Marsham Tyres.

When the war ended, a more public but subtle form of sports sponsorship developed whereby the manufacturers of Brylcreem used the unnamed and unidentified photograph of Denis Compton, taking advantage of his cricketing image in 1948, with bat and head and shoulders, fully aware also of his reputation as a war time international footballer. Sales increased enormously and as Peter Hunt, Director of Public Affairs for Coca-Cola's Northern Europe Export Corporation explained,

> 'from Compton it was an obvious thing for Brylcreem to do something for cricket itself. And so appropriately, the County Cups were inaugurated. They were named after the manufacturing company, which was then County Laboratories'.

Ultimately it became part of the Beecham group, but after a similar experience to Gillette's success and perhaps ambivalence in the public mind and eye between sport and the initial nature of the sponsored product, Brylcreem and the parent group, Beechams, withdrew from cricket. Significantly, Hunt commented when he spoke and published in 1966, in the fourth year of the Gillette initiative,

> 'It also became known that Gillette were intending to spend a fair amount in introducing their own awards in cricket and it was felt there was no room for two such sponsorships unless Brylcreem were prepared to invest a considerably increased amount of money'.

That potential conflict between two competing sponsors in the same field leads directly back to the succession of Barclays Bank Plc to the *Today* newspaper at the beginning of the Football League Championship Centenary season, and the nature of the contractual row which exploded because of the publicised disagreement over the terms of the Football League contract with the *Today* newspaper. A contract is the key to all sponsorship arrangements, as it must be to all intelligent and validly intended and binding commercial arrangements.

4   SPONSORSHIP CONTRACTS: THE KEY TO SUCCESS OR FAILURE

Barclays Bank's arrival on the football sponsorship scene during August 1987 deflected attention from the dispute which erupted publicly during the withdrawal by the *Today* newspaper of its sponsorship of the Football League Championship competition. In October 1986, through its then parent company News UK, it had hurriedly replaced Canon (UK) Ltd after the start of the 1986–87 soccer season as the competition's sponsor. On Monday 3 August 1987 the *Today* columns announced that it had '"told the Football League that it is proposing to end its sponsorship contract with them".

This follows the League's failure to live up to its side of the agreement despite five months of complaints from *Today*.

The League immediately announced it would seek legal advice. The deal was signed last season by News UK, the owners of *Today*. Since then the paper has become part of News International'.

The charges and counter-charges between the respective parties of repudiation can be assessed only by reference to the contract terms. Only if the dispute arrives in court will a final judgment be possible. Within the present context of avoiding conflicting sponsorship investment, however, and with the Brylcreem-Beecham policy in mind it is significant that the *Daily Telegraph* recorded the conflicting sides of this key issue on Monday 3 August 1987 at page 21 through its football correspondent Colin Gibson, thus:

'The major grievance ... voiced at meetings with League officials regularly since the signing has been the introduction of a sponsor for the centenary celebrations, though the League refute the charge. *Today* claim that they were never told that Mercantile Credit were to be allowed to sponsor the centenary events for £250,000.

Graham Kelly the League Secretary (and subsequently Chief Executive of the Football Association) said yesterday

"The centenary events are a separate matter entirely. *Today* are the sponsors of the League Championship. The centenary celebrations are seven or eight special events and we hoped that the two sponsorships [ie for the championship sponsored by *Today* and the centenary game applicable here] would complement each other"'.

That hope would certainly appear to have more chance of fulfilment with the replacement by Barclays very swiftly after the *Today* withdrawal in the week after the centenary celebration game at Wembley Stadium. Its then chairman, Mr (now Sir) John Quinton, announced at the time when the objectives stated at the commencement of this chapter were explained:

'As you know, our subsidiary company Mercantile Credit led the way with its sponsorship of the League's centenary celebrations. I know that they are well pleased with the sponsorship and I am sure that Barclays' sponsorship of the League Championship combined with Mercantile Credit's involvement with the centenary will give the Barclays Group a unique double and a unique opportunity for cooperation'.

The closer nexus between the two banking companies than that between a newspaper and an unconnected merchant bank is self-evident.

Significantly, the point about shared sponsorship recognised by the Brylcreem-Beecham awareness of Gillette's arrival on the cricket scene is one of the many specified in the contract check list published in the CCPR's *Howell Report* provided for it by the sports sponsorship consultant David Way and reproduced in full here on pp 462-463 (*Howell Report,* 31, Chapter 5, *Governing Bodies*).

For under the subheading of 'Contracts' at that page in the Report the comment is made with an almost prophetic anticipation of the current football conflict:

'In this modern sporting world, governing bodies will find themselves involved in sophisticated contractual negotiations which are crucial to their financial stability. The need for watertight contracts and the employment, if necessary, of sound professional advice cannot be over-emphasised'.

Indeed, the same guidance is applicable to everyone entering into a sponsorship deal which goes beyond the simple clear-cut provisions of the Aston Villa styled situation which is also reproduced at pages 464-465.

Point 14 of the contract check list emphasises with prescience for the Football League-*Today* dispute,

'Shared sponsorships should be avoided, but if an event has more than one then arrangements concerning all sponsor benefits must be agreed beforehand. This applies especially to identification in the title, print and television bannering'.

It is also arguable that sponsors of individual sponsored beneficiaries, such as for the multiple sandwich board atmosphere which permeates professional lawn tennis players at Wimbledon, will also have such guidance in mind at their negotiation and contract signing stages.

Associated with and ancillary to this overriding need for thoughtful planning is the further example in the Howell Report of 'the importance of proper, legal contracts and the need to protect the rights of individuals and teams' demonstrated by the All England Women's Lacrosse Association (AEWLA). The Association explained to the Committee of Enquiry how a properly drawn legal contract helped to prevent a commercial sponsor from interfering either with the technical conduct of a major event for its own marketing ends and it also ensured payment of the sponsorship fee. The event was the first World Tournament for women, held at Nottingham in 1982.

An American company manufacturing plastic lacrosse sticks wanted to accelerate the conversion from wooden to plastic sticks by creating a brand-name link with the international federation. After payment of the first sponsorship instalment fee the American manufacturing company threatened to withdraw as sponsor unless all players used their sticks even though there was no contractual obligation to do so. After negotiations the manufacturing company realised that it could not enforce this requirement. The result was an amendment to the International Women's Lacrosse Federation constitution. A clause was inserted to ensure that no company can have a monopoly on sponsorship or any influence over the use of equipment.

That example of purported interference and control of sport by commercial interests raises a cascade of moral questions concerning the operation of sponsorship. The Howell Report investigated this position thoroughly, which is discussed in its Chapter 13, under the title 'Ethical Considerations'. It concluded with a recommendation, which has yet to be implemented, that the Government should refer to the Office of Fair Trading for full examination of the relationship between important sporting events in the United Kingdom and whether any monopoly situation exists.

This Recommendation was fulfilled when it went to Court over the FA Premier League's control of television rights and notwithstanding its failure to outlaw the monopoly, the European Commission has now announced its own investigation for purposes of breach of its Competition Laws, Articles 85 and 86 [now Articles 81 and 82 of the Treaty of Amsterdam]. In the years since the Report was published, commercial involvement has hardly decreased; and another angle was aired in Sir Denis Follows' Philip Noel-Baker Memorial Lecture on the theme, 'Whither Sport?'

It extracted this section when Follows said:

'Nearly every top level performer has his agent. If he is an individual performer, his agent contracts his appearance. As a result in certain sports, the governing body has ceased to govern. The agent or the entrepreneur cracks the whip assisted by the television producer. We have now reached the stage where the sport at the top level has become almost completely show business with everything that one associates with show-biz — the cult of the individual, the desire to present the game as a spectacle, more money, less sportsmanship, more emphasis on winning'.

The role of agents rumbles on almost daily, irrespective of Rachel Anderson's discrimination award against the Professional Footballers' Association because of her gender, and notwithstanding her popular and professional regard in the eyes of her many eminent football playing clients (see also — above). Here, too, however, 'the need for water-tight contracts and the employment, if necessary, of sound professional advice' cannot be overemphasised. It was illustrated vividly when one of G O Smith's successors as England's centre-forward and captain and now the current England team manager, decided to go to court during the period after the

SPECIMEN SPONSORSHIP CONTRACT:
Checklist (from the Central Council of Physical Recreation:

The Howell Report) 1983
[450 supra]

Table 5.1 Contract Checklist

From David Way (sports sponsorship consultant)

1. Title: The precise title of the event and the degree of emphasis given to the sponsor should be agreed. Will they, for instance, receive 'equal billing' in the title?
2. Duration: The precise duration of the sponsorship with start-finish dates.
3. The Event: Details of the event/competition should be included.
4. Fees: Details of fees and dates when payments become due must be covered. If the fee is linked to the RPI then specify the month when new figure will be taken.
5. Option to Renew: The first option to renew the contract should be given to the current sponsor(s). State deadline. If existing sponsor(s) declines then the event should not be offered to another potential sponsor at terms which are more beneficial without the existing sponsor being given first option on those better terms.
6. Governing Body's Authority: Is the governing body authorised to sign on behalf of participating clubs/teams' players? State position clearly.
7. Information: Organisers to keep sponsors informed, in advance if possible, of any changes affecting the event. Copies of all sponsor press releases to go to sponsor.
    Sponsors to keep organisers informed of any press releases, information, developments affecting the event. Copies of all sponsor press releases to go to organisers.
8. Cancellation: Sponsor may withdraw support. How much prior notice required? Payments required? These payments will probably be linked to involvement of a new sponsor.
9. Promotion: Sponsor's use of competition/event/competitors for promotion and publicity purposes. Any limitations?
10. Conflict of Interests: Should there be any restrictions concerning competitive products?
11. Television Cover: Clearly the situation regarding television covers companies, channel, duration, live or highlights. Firm commitments

are to be avoided but television companies will usually state their 'intention' to cover.

The financial consequences (if any) of loss of television should be covered in the contract.

12. Television Boards: If television boards are to be used their size/precise location should be given. The use of imprecise terms like 'prime sites' should be avoided.

13. Sponsor's Facilities: Will free/reduced price tickets/passes/seasons be available?

    Will entertaining facilities be available for company personnel/ company guests?

14. Shared Sponsorships: Shared sponsorships should be avoided, but if an event has more than one then arrangements concerning all sponsor benefits must be agreed beforehand. This applies especially to identification in the title, print and television bannering.

15. Problem Products: Both sides should try to anticipate possible problems related to products — drink/tobacco/gambling and young people, for instance.

ASTON VILLA FOOTBALL CLUB

SPONSORSHIP CONTRACT

Between Aston Villa Football Club plc and:

Company Name:

Address:

Telephone Number:

Invoicing Address (if different from above) ....

....

Please reserve the ***   FOR THE:

Aston Villa versus   match

To be played on

Number of Guests in Sponsors Party

SPONSORSHIP COST   V.A.T. will be added where applicable.

DEPOSIT PAID

Signed ....

Name ....

Position ....

Date ....

Signed on behalf of Aston Villa Football Club ....

Name ....

Date ....

World Cup competition of 1982 over a commercial contract indirectly associated with sponsorship contracts.

Kevin Keegan sued his former public relations and promotion company Public Eye Enterprises Ltd in breach of contract, in Leeds Crown Court, after the World Cup had ended. He had begun the action with two claims. One was for damages that Public Eye Enterprises had not performed sufficiently a representation and oral terms of a written Agreement dated 16 November 1972 that it would guarantee him £30,000 over the next two years. The other was that the company held £3,714.79 on his behalf, but that it had failed and refused to hand it over. The case lasted over six working days, including evidence and legal argument. McCowan J's judgment delivered on 27 October 1982 covers 38 pages of typescript, and the Court of Appeal transcript judgments number 12.

Yet one key issue went to the heart of the case. Keegan admitted in evidence that he had wrongly believed a written agreement for five years lasted for only three.

At the trial and during evidence nothing was heard further about the claim for damages, which Keegan's counsel told the court was not to be pursued. The other claim was amended to £4,709.81, and was admitted, subject to set-off under a counterclaim by Public Eye Enterprises Ltd. This amounted also to two claims. One was that Keegan had broken his agreement with the company and entered into numerous commercial contracts of a nature deemed to be controlled by the written agreement of 16 November 1972. The other was that a former director of the company, Harry Swales, had induced Keegan to break his contract with it and damages were claimed against both of them.

The judge was not unfamiliar with the football field in court. He had acted as counsel for the wounded plaintiff in *Lewis v Brookshaw* (see Chapter 6, *Participation Problems*) at Lewes Assizes and in London's High Court during 1969 and 1970 when Rees J had awarded £4,000 for deliberate violent foul play creating a civil assault. On this occasion he made three crucial findings on what was a commercial agreement which were not challenged in the Court of Appeal (which was concerned solely with technical financial issues).

(1) The written agreement dated 16 November 1972 was a sole agency agreement. This gave Public Eye Enterprises Ltd exclusive control over the off-field and non-sporting contractual activities it covered, during the five-year operation until 16 November 1977.

(2) Keegan was in breach of contract because he entered into contracts without the prior knowledge and approval of Public Eye Enterprises Ltd before that five-year period had expired.

(3) If Keegan had been correct that the written agreement lasted for only three years and not five it would have terminated on 16 November

1975 and not in 1977; and in those circumstances Keegan would have been free to enter into contracts without obligation to Public Eye Enterprises Ltd as soon as the three-year period ended. The judge's verdict after hearing evidence and examining documents during the six days' hearing ruled against this; and he made an order against Keegan for an account and against Keegan and Swales for damages to be assessed (*Keegan v Public Eye Enterprises Ltd* (by original action) and (by counterclaim) *Public Eye Enterprises Ltd v Keegan and Swales* (1984) CAT No 84:575; (1982) *Times*, 28 October; *Yorkshire Post*, 21 October 1982).

The uninitiated may be assisted to know that Sir Patrick Hastings, the leading advocate with Norman Birkett during the years between the two World Wars, and afterwards for a period, used to say: There is a bull point in every case. One of his regular junior counsel, Theo Matthew, immortalised the profession in his classic *Forensic Fables,* under the pseudonym 'O', with a moral at end of each Fable. The moral which is to be extracted from the *Keegan* case is an addition to the CCPR — David Way contract check list. Read and remember what has been signed; and do not omit to check it when a row erupts about it.

Annexed to the page in the CCPR Howell Report on which that check list appears is a comment under the heading Integrity of Sport. The paragraph records,

> 'Throughout this Report, one main area of concern is the preservation of the integrity of sport. The fears voiced by Victor Head (author of *Sponsorship: The newest marketing skill:* cited in Chapter 2 'Growth of Sponsorship') that "sport could soon be run for the benefit of the promoting company and not primarily in the interests of sport itself" are understood by the Committee'.

On the other hand, promoting and sponsoring companies are in a powerful position to benefit sport when sport fails to benefit and protect itself. David Miller in *The Times* on the opening day of the new Barclays League football season wrote on 15 August 1987,

> 'I wish that Barclays, with their vested interest, would have conditional clauses written into the prize money benefits which penalise bad behaviour on and off the field'.

Perhaps one day they and others will, and thus steer sport into a foul-free fund dimension once more. During the summer of 1999 certainly the professional cricketing skills of the England and national team, and Manchester United's mystery shrouded decision *NOT* to defend their title as holders of the FA Cup Challenge Cup Competition, have caused the respective sponsors concerned in the appropriate competitions to be apprehensive about potential future involvement.

Analogous to the well-known off-field legal concept applied often to easement, negligence and nuisance: the sponsorship categories are never closed. Alongside its phenomenal growth the Sports Council established in 1982 a Sports Sponsorship Advisory Service, with the services of a consultant, Mr Derek Etherington; and in November 1985 the CCPR implemented one of the 73 Recommendations of the Howell Report, to

'encourage the establishment of an Association of Commercial Sponsors of Sport in order to further the interest of sport itself and sponsoring companies'.

Under the presidency of HRH the Duke of Edinburgh the Institute of Sports Sponsorship was launched by the Central Council of Physical Recreation in 1982. Its guide published in 1989 under the title of *The Search for Sports Sponsorship* covered in general terms what are particularised in the 75 specimen precedents contained in the two volumes of Fosbrook and Laing (supra at page 451 above), ranging from agency, via exclusivity to the video and non-theatrical market. One developing area not covered by either is what has become known as Ambush Marketing. This is the trespassing and hijacking of existing sponsored rights without authority, ie a classic example being purported use of the Olympic Games symbol licensed to users whose exclusivity is infringed by copying of it.

In a reverse situation based on footballers' picture cards with shirts incorporating the Three Lions Logo of the Football Association the confectionary company, *Trebor Bassett Ltd v FA Ltd*, successfully obtained a High Court declaration against the Football Association under s 21 of the Trade Marks Act 1994 and kicked into touch a cross action against it by the FA. They established *in evidence* for Mr Justice Rattle's satisfaction that their products did not comprise 'uses' to infringe the FA's registered trade marks ([1993 FSR p 211). The evidence and arguments in the case illustrate clearly how differing levels of contentious sports related activities require expert guidance, which inevitably will differ among those 113 listed at the commencement of the Preface.

Licensing

The licensing of intellectual property rights in connection with sport and sporting events is becoming an ever more popular phenomenon. Copyright, logos, patents and trade marks are licensed to persons or organisations who wish to exploit a name, reputation, event or personality and thus, the merchandising of national and international sports events, emblems and mascots and personalities is now the norm for many major sporting events. Merchandisers may take licenses of these emblems or mascots and put them on their products so that the product may be associated with the particular event.

For example the Barcelona Olympics produced the mascot 'Cobi' based on a Catalan mountain dog. More than 1,200 products were licensed with this symbol. The international Olympic rings are also licensed for commercial exploitation on a grand scale. The governing body of European football has an emblem for each of its events and a mascot 'Bernie' which is available for merchandising purposes, and Eric Cantona was required to litigate and settle after challenges to infringements of his registrations relating to his personal reputation and goodwill These are just four examples of many which illustrate the extent of sports licensing.

As Iain C Baillie explains in the Introduction to *Licensing — A Practical Guide for the Businessman* under the heading

> 'What is licensing'
>
> Licensing is a branch of the law of contracts. The contract is a specific form of agreement and strictly speaking embodies a licence; ie permission from an owner of a right to another to use part of that right. The other side of the contract is the obligation assumed by the receiver of the permission (ie the licensee) in return for the permission.
>
> ... it is the contract which defines the obligation of the parties. The "right" backs up the contract and can be used separately for enforcement if there is a breach. The "weaker" the right the weaker the contract and its back-up enforcement.
>
> As in most areas of the law, licensing has no exact boundaries but a useful definition is a revocable right to do or secure that which you otherwise cannot do or secure.'

Together with those formal structured developments, that growth is evidenced by the in-depth studies which have emerged during the two decades since England's success in the 1966 World Cup. Without claiming the list to be exhaustive, the following may assist readers wishing further guidance.

1	1966 Peter R Hunt MCAM, FIPR	*Public Relations Aspects of Sponsoring Sport*
2	1972 The Sports Council	*An Inquiry into Sponsorship*
3	1981 HM Treasury Memorandum (of evidence to House of Commons Committee)	Taxation in the Context of Private Sponsorship and of Gifts of Art Objects to Public and Private Institutions

4	1981 *Economist* Intelligence Unit Ltd: Jean Simkins	Sponsorship 1980/81
5	1983 The Central Council of Physical Recreation	*The Howell Report*
6	1984 Stephen Townley and Edward Grayson	*Sponsorship of Sport, Arts and Leisure: Law, Tax and Business Relationships*
7	1987 Iain C Baillie	*Licensing: A Practical Guide for the Businessman*
8	1988 Victor Head	*Successful sponsorship*
9	1989 The Central Council of Physical Recreation	The Search for Sports Sponsorship
10	1989 Deborah Fosbrook and Adrian C Laing	*Vol 1 The Media Contracts Handbook*
11	1990 Deborah Fosbrook and Adrian C Laing	*Vol 2 The Media Contracts Handbook*
12	1998 Hayley Stallard	*Bagehot on Sponsorship, Merchandising* and *Endorsement*

5   SPONSORED TAX LAWS

Introduction

The developing nature of this area means that conflicts of attitudes will inevitably arise. Thus the valuable EIU *Special Report on Sponsorship 1980/81* claims

'Sponsorship is not the same thing as advertising. Although for some companies sponsorship expenditure comes out of the same budget as advertising, it is important to be aware of the division of the two'.

Irrespective of that division in economic or marketing circles, so far as the Inland Revenue is concerned, the equally valuable HM Treasury Memorandum of Evidence to the House of Commons Education, Science and Arts Committee identified for allowable tax deductible expense explains:

'in computing business profits for tax purposes ... the business purpose — generally advertising — must be the sole purpose for which the purpose is made'.

Ordinarily these issues would fall into the next chapter, Chapter 14, *No fine on fun*. However, since this particular aspect of fiscal policy and practice commanded the specific attention of the Treasury-Revenue evidence to the House of Commons Committee with an emphasis on private sponsorship, it is convenient to conclude this chapter with an awareness of the authoritative guidance given from such a source.

That awareness in reality for those among the 30,920,000 participants within the framework of the 421 National Governing Bodies, who *do not* have *in-house services*, should extend to such *professional guidance* appropriate for the particular sponsored occasion, as advertising, events, individual rights and televising and broadcasting territorial requirements. Local sponsorships do not differ from national ones in quality criteria for advice and guidance.

6   SPONSORED TAX LAWS

Taxation in the Context of Private Sponsorship and of Gifts of Art Objects to Public and Private Institutions is the title of a joint HM Treasury — Inland Revenue Memorandum comprising of documentary evidence submitted during 1981 to a relatively little-known but crucially important House of Commons Education, Science and Arts Committee on the Public and Private Funding of the Arts (Session 1980–81 (1982) HC 49–11 at pp 291–292). It did not identify Sport in any way at all; but the taxation principles which it summarised clearly for that Committee's guidance are equally applicable to sport.

The same may be said of the evidence given to the Committee by a former Chairman of the Arts Council, Lord Goodman, who was also Chairman of the Association of Business Sponsorship and the Arts (ABSA), and, also, of the statement made by the then Norman St John Stevas MP, a former Minister for the Arts during an interview with Victor Head, the author of *Sponsorship: The newest marketing skill*, both during 1981. The questions posed an issue which is relevant equally to both spheres, and so, too, are the answers (today as correct as they were when given in 1981).

[*Question*]

Much heat is generated over the question of changes in tax laws to encourage more sponsorship. Do you feel that perhaps not enough emphasis is placed on the fact that sponsorship expenditure can be regarded as a form of advertising promotion and so qualify for tax

[*Answer*]

Since it took office in 1979, the Government has reduced the minimum qualifying period for covenanted payments to charities from over six years to over three years and introduced tax relief on the higher rates of income tax in respect of covenanted payments by *exemption in the appropriate way (eg 52% for companies paying corporate tax)?*

individuals up to an annual ceiling of £3,000. [NB Further increased to £5,000 from 6 April 1983, s 23(2).] These concessions were designed to ease the position for donations, and the arts benefit considerably as most arts organisations are registered charities. There are signs that they are not widely enough known and used.

That part of the answer that 'most arts organisations are registered charities' creates a prima facie differential from sport, save and except that the concluding sentence is equally applicable to sport, ie 'There are signs that they are not widely enough known and used'. For whereas sport per se is not yet recognised as a valid charitable concept, sport qua education has qualified charitably for over seventy years without full advantage ever having been taken of this position, either intellectually or practically (see Chapter 1, *Genesis*, Chapter 2, *Under starter's orders*).

The former Minister, as Mr Norman St John Stevas, concluded thus:

[*Question*]

[*Answer*] (concluded)

'You mention the provisions under section 130 of the Incomes and Corporation Taxes Act 1970 (now section 74 of the Income Tax and Corporation Taxes Act 1988) whereby *revenue expenditure* [NB author's emphasis] incurred "wholly and exclusively" for the purposes of a trade can be offset against tax. The Inland Revenue has instructed its Inspectors to advise companies at the outset whether sponsorship deals should qualify in this way, so there is now every opportunity for companies to frame their proposals so as to get the maximum tax relief. I hope businesses are aware of this concession by the Inland Revenue.'

Identical advice was tendered by Lord Goodman in his own evidence testified at about the same time in 1981 to the House of Commons Education, Science and Arts Committee which was cited by me in the chapter entitled 'Tax, VAT, Hope and Charity' in *Sponsorship of Sort, Arts and Leisure: Law, Tax and Business Relationships* [1984] by Stephen Townley and Edward Grayson at page 261. In the present context, and with words which are equally applicable to sports sponsorship, Lord Goodman told the Committee (HC 49–11, pp 291–292 at para 742) inter alia.

'There is some recognition needed of the Inland Revenue. There is a lot of discussion about whether there should be more generous terms made available for subsidies to the arts... In fact, taxation relief for companies is pretty adequate. You can get taxation relief for any activity that bears a relationship to what you are doing. You can get taxation relief from any payment under a covenant. So it is a thin excuse for people to say there is no tax relief.

There is one very important matter that the head of the Inland Revenue made. He agreed they would notify all their Inspectors of Taxes to tell companies in advance if they inquired whether a particular contribution would be tax deductible or not. I do not think that is sufficiently generally known. If a company has any doubt, therefore, Somerset House has instructed the Inspectors of Taxes that they should advise whether that doubt is real or not'.

'Company' in that context, of course, is interchangeable with any other identifiable legal persona. Clubs which are legally identifiable as unincorporated associations and known technically and realistically only through their members are nevertheless trapped within the statutory definition of 'company' for all tax purposes. Indeed, although at common law, in equity, and under property legislation they hold land only through trustees, for direct tax purposes, the club itself as an unincorporated association is the chargeable person (*Worthing Rugby Football Club Trustees v IRC* [1985] STC 186; *Carlisle & Silloth Golf Club v Smith* [1913] 21 CB 75).

With this crucial caveat, and against the background of the authoritative sources cited above, the joint HM Treasury-Inland Revenue Memorandum takes on an almost familiar ring for taxpayers generally. Under the subheading of Evidence to the House of Commons Education, Science and Arts Committee of Note by H M Treasury the Memorandum begins with an explanation of how

'It sets out the position on sponsorship and gifts under present taxation arrangements and has been prepared in conjunction with the Inland Revenue'.

Summarised here is the sequence of published headings:

Private sponsorship

(i)   Covenanted payments: which bring into operation the whole range of charity law.

(ii) Business expenses: the conventional and traditional legitimate allowances of a revenue (as distinct from capital) nature

Gifts (which are more usual in the Arts than the Sports scene), ie

> CTT (Capital Transfer Tax)
> CGT (Capital Gains Tax)

When the Memorandum expands into details, the sub-heading *Business expenses* inevitably develops Mr Norman St John Stevas' well-known 'wholly and exclusively' text in the following way, with words which are equally applicable to sponsored sport:

> 'A sponsorship payment will normally be a deductible expense in computing business profits for tax purposes if it is of a revenue nature (ie not a capital payment) and is incurred wholly and exclusively for the purpose of trade. The first condition means that no deduction is allowable for any lump sum donation towards, for example, the building or modernisation of a theatre, or the purchase of a work of art. The second condition means that the business purpose — generally advertising — must be the sole purpose for which the payment is made. The expenditure will not be admissible if it is incurred for a dual purpose — eg both promoting a business and promoting a charitable or benevolent object'.

The contrast between revenue and capital payments is of particular significance and importance in the sporting world, with its special developing problems under the volatile climate of safety of sports ground proposals following from the Interim and Final Reports of Mr Justice Popplewell and Lord Justice Taylor and their respective enquiries into Crowd Safety and Control at Sports Grounds. See Chapter 5, *Public protection*, pp 201–241.

Neither the Inquiry nor its reports was concerned directly with financial methods for implementing its Recommendations. Sport's own dramatic tragedies during 1985 which culminated in the fatalities at Bradford and Birmingham, in England, and later at Brussels, highlighted the Safety of Sports Grounds Act 1975 which followed the Ibrox Stadium, Glasgow, deaths in 1971, ten years before the Committee's Report in 1981. It also exposes the limitations built in to that 'first condition [in the Treasury — Revenue Memorandum] ... that no deduction is allowable for any lump sum donation towards, for example, the building or modernisation of a theatre'.

Successive Finance Acts have been prepared to treat for *capital* allowance purposes certain expenditure, on buildings, as being plant (unless a deduction can be made elsewhere) to which safety certificates apply under the sports ground safety legislation (see here the retrospective effects of section 40 of the Finance Act 1978, upon section 49 of the Finance (No 2) Act 1975) and ultimately section 119 of the Finance Act 1989 now all consolidated with the Capital Allowances Act 1990, sections 55, 69, 70, following recommendations in the *Final Hillsborough Taylor Report* paragraph 115 [cm 962, January 1990].

The national awareness of the need for some form of financial assistance to modernise antiquated sports stadia also merits assessing how far the debatable decision of the Burnley Football Club's grandstand tax disallowance should be re-argued. Mr Justice Vinelott's different interpretation of crucial *sporting evidence* overruled the factual findings of the distinguished Special Commissioners. Presided over by the late H H Monroe QC, together with his successor, Mr R H Widdows, they held on the evidence before them that the then new building structured before the 1975 safety legislation did qualify for a repair allowance, although it was disallowed under the head of plant. (See *Brown v Burnley Football and Athlete Co Ltd* [1980] 3 All ER 244, [1980] STIC 424, and also *Tax 'Anomaly'*: para 115, page 19 *Final Hillsborough Taylor Report* (supra)). As pointed out earlier and below, the perverse reversal by Vinelott, J of the Special Commissioners adjudication on the evidence, which qualified the new stand structure for a repair allowance, is inconsistent with the Queen's Bench Divisional Court's conclusion by Lord Widgery LJ and Melford Stevenson and Caulfield, J, that a football stadium 'is a public place in its entirety'.

The judge disagreed with their actual findings. This was inconsistent with the recent re-emphasis by the House of Lords in *Cole Brothers v Phillips* ([1982] STC 301) that the crucial importance of commissioners' conclusions on admissible evidence will not be overturned lightly. The detailed care with which the experienced Special Commissioners assessed the evidence relating to the Bob Lord stand's location within the famous Turf Moor ground at Burnley emerges from the law reports and raises the query why the club did not adapt the precedent from the game's ruling body at Lancaster Gate for its House of Lords charity appeal to seek financial assistance from the Sports Council and the CCPR, and challenge the divergence of judicial opinion at least in the Court of Appeal.

The Howell Report (p 39) stressed

'It is the responsibility of sports organisations to limit tax liabilities in respect of sponsorship income ... They must always obtain proper professional advice concerning taxation'.

So, too, should sponsors and potential sponsors. In particular the borderline between business and entertainment issues, which is easily blurred and therefore capable of entering the disallowed areas under traditional tax law and practice, needs only to be mentioned for demanding specialised and practical professional advice. A classic and well-reported trap is the sponsor which attempts to indulge in racehorse ownership under sponsorship colour. Recreation is disallowed; legitimate advertising accepted. Accordingly, the Jockey Club changed the Rules of Racing to permit company ownership, and thereby sponsorship, through the advertising of horses in training and thus complement the long-standing sponsorship of famous races. How many people outside the racing fraternity know that the celebrated European Champion, Moorstyle, before it was retired to the National Stud at Newmarket, was sponsored by a Yorkshire-based furniture company, whose fortunes were not hindered by the local and international success of its four-legged investment?

7   CHARITY

No less in need of specialist advice is the lamentable story of sport's neglect of its opportunities to take full advantage of the manner in which sport as an education concept has been open to development for over seventy years. In 1976 the valuable *Report of the Goodman Committee*, published by the National Council of Social Service on *Charity Law and Voluntary Organisations*, recommended, inter alia, that

> 'the encouragement of sport and recreation should be recognised as an independent charitable object provided the necessary element of altruism and benefit to a sufficient section of the community are present. In so far as the existing law does not make this clear it should be amended'.

At the time when these thoughts were formulated the FA Youth Trust Deed case was en route from Mr Justice Walton via the Court of Appeal to the House of Lords. We know now from earlier citations in this text how the concept of an educational sporting charitable trust confirmed Mr Justice Eve's landmark decision in *Re Mariette* ([1915] 2 CH 284), where he held that a gift for providing squash courts in an Aldenham School was charitable on the ground that sport was part of the curriculum of such an establishment.

When the joint Treasury — Revenue Memorandum on Arts Sponsorship explained at the outset of its explanation that,

> 'A payment in sponsorship of the arts may qualify for tax relief in one of two ways'.

it prefaced the Business expenses category with Covenanted payments. The opening sentence under that latter heading proclaimed

'Many of the bodies which promote activities in the field of the arts are
established charities'.

In the FA Youth Trust Deed decision of the House of Lords (*IRC v
McMullen* [1981] AC 1 at 17), Lord Hailsham of St Marylebone explained,

'I do not think that the courts have as yet explored the extent to which
elements of organisation, instruction, or the disciplined inculcation of
information, instruction or skill may limit the whole concept of education.
I believe that in some ways it will prove more extensive, in others more
restrictive than has been thought hitherto'.

For 'courts' should be read Sport and the Law together. Amateur
administrators and professional lawyers have been jointly guilty of the
omission inferred by the Lord Chancellor, who, as Chapters 1 and 4 explain,
when Minister for Science and Education in 1962 under Mr Macmillan's
premiership, created the role of a Minister with special responsibility for
Sport. Indeed, so too was the House of Lords itself which resisted the
temptation to tackle the Recreational Charities Act 1958 during its own
deliberations because of inadequate evidence in the FA Youth Trust case.
This had to await *Guild v IRC* [1992] 2 All ER 10. On that occasion an offer
to the House of Lords from the Irween House of the Court of Session duly
resulted in the 'interests of social welfare' criteria contained in s 1(1) [of
the 1958 Act] being upheld after a bequest 'to be used in connection with
the Sports Centre [then] in North Berwick' to include also a concept of
'some similar purpose in connection with sport'. Bearing in mind the
problems for defining sport, as I wrote in the *New Law Journal* 15 January
1993 'whenever this legal googly will bowl the courts, as some day it will,
watch this space for another potential entrant to the House of Lords Sport
and Law lottery'.

The establishment of charitable status would have four clear advantages
for any sporting organisation, namely,

(1) statutory exemption from most forms of direct taxation;
(2) covenanted payments which, as the joint Treasury — Revenue
    Memorandum explained, enables a sponsored recipient to obtain
    repayment of the tax deducted by the Inland Revenue from a
    sponsoring company;
(3) mandatory 80 per cent rate relief under the Local Government Finance
    Act 1988, 547, for sporting organisations registered with the Charity
    Commissioners;
(4) discretionary 100 per cent rate relief for non-registered sporting
    organisations effectively executing charitable functions, such as

evening and weekend sporting education facilities, to schools whose playing fields and gymnasia are closed outside normal school hours.

The practical methods of achieving these desiderata are spelt out more emphatically in Chapter 14, *No fine on fun*; but it is noteworthy at this stage to explain that the green light for progress was shone for sport by Mr Charles Weston, the Charity Commissioner who was responsible for the Trust Deed's registration in 1972, at a CCPR seminar organised after the House of Lords FA Youth Trust decision. He advised the hiving-off process, whereby a section of a club or organisation can be separated from its main body administratively for specific educational purposes. The FA's own school at the National Sports Centre at Lilleshall in Shropshire, sponsored by General Motors, is a classic illustration. The Midland Bank sponsorship of the Metropolitan Police five-a-side youth soccer tournament is another; and the Lloyds Bank Masters Chess Tournament is on all fours with Vaisey's judgment in *Re Dupree's Will Trusts* ([1945] Ch 16) that a chess tournament for young people in Portsmouth was ideally educational. As I explained at the end of his contribution to the British Association for Sport and the Law's *Sport and the Law* journal for November 1993 (p 90) on the *Guild Case*, a Home Office publication entitled *Voluntary Action* has thrown doubt or at least begun a debate on the future existence of current charity structure and the law: and the ongoing saga of the Clayton Playing Fields in North West Lancashire is a classic example of local initiatives dealt with hereafter in Chapter 14: *No Fine on Fun*.

8   VAT AND SPONSORSHIP GENERALLY

Value Added Tax replaced Entertainment Tax and Selective Employment Tax as an administrative headache for British sport, as well as the remainder of the leisure industry, resulting from Britain's entry into the Common Market under the European Communities Act 1972. For sponsorship purposes it applies to those services supplied by businesses which meet the registrable turnover limits established at the time of writing at £51,000. The business element at the heart of sponsorship inevitably creates a potential taxable supply.

The absence of that key business factor destroys the need for registration within the VAT tax band. England's High Court confirmed this when it upheld an appeal to a VAT tribunal by a country landowner against a Customs and Excise assessment in respect of shooting rights to friends and relatives for a fee. A supply of services was admittedly provided; but was it for a business? The Customs and Excise commissioners said it was. The documentary and oral evidence tendered by the landowner and his accountants satisfied the tribunal and the High Court that no advertisement or other commercial insignia existed (*Customs and Excise Commissioners v Lord Fisher* [1981] 2 All ER 1). The position of Sporting Rights generally is now regulated by H M Customs and Excise leaflet No 742/2/92.

When the business element exists, and the statutory ceiling of £51,000 is reached, then sporting organisations carried on commercially charge VAT at the standard rate of 17.5 per cent on taxable supplies; and generally they can deduct any VAT charged on supplies to them, except on business entertainment.

9 VAT AND SPORT GENERALLY

The Aston Villa specimen sponsorship contract reproduced above includes VAT in its charges for services supplied; and the developing dimension of this new kind of tax alien to traditional Anglo-Saxon commercial and legal sources demands a mixture of specialist legal and accountancy services at every level of activity. Three further illustrations demonstrate this from the standpoint of organisation or administration, sporting competition rules, and the EEC itself.

1   *Organisation or administration*

Sport's special constitutional structure should always be recognised and considered. The Watchet Bowling Club in Somerset was assessed by the customs authorities liable for registration. They ignored the sporting and accounting realities that two separate sections existed affiliated to the two national bodies, indoors and general: the English *Indoor* Bowling Association (EIBA) and the English Bowling Association (EBA). The supplies of each unit individually was below the registrable VAT threshold, although together they qualified within it. The VAT Tribunal confirmed that neither was registrable as a taxable person (*AG Hayhoe (on behalf of Watchet Bowling Club and Watchet Indoor Bowling Club) v Customs and Excise Commissioners*, VAT Tribunal ref LON/80/341, 13 January 1981).

2   *Sporting competition rules*

The Union of European Football Associations (UEFA) regulations mandatorily required competing clubs and associations to reciprocate hospitality during competitive fixtures. Thus they were upheld by the Scottish Court of Session and a London VAT Tribunal respectively as recoverable input tax which the customs authorities had disallowed for the Celtic Club and the Football Association (*Celtic Football & Athletic Co Ltd v Customs & Excise Commissioners* [1983] STC 420; *Football Association Ltd v Customs & Excise Commissioners London VAT Tribunal/83/484*).

3   *The EEC*

A hotel sale to a North Wales fishing club was exempt from VAT. The Tribunal applied a little known paragraph (h) under Article 13 of the Sixth EEC Council directive concerning land which had not been built on, in that case a river bed and adjoining land comprising supply of a fishery and fishing rights (*Parkinson v Customs & Excise Commissioners* (1985) *Times*, 8 November).

In an authoritative manner comparable to the joint Treasury — Revenue Memorandum, HM Customs & Excise Commissioners published a VAT Leaflet, No 701/41/90 and more recently VAT Leaflet 701/41/95. They contained specific guidance for Sponsorship Rights in what was formerly No 701/5/81, the leaflet entitled *An Annex*.

The most recent VAT Notice 701/41/95 poses the crucial question and answers it as follows: with my own emphasis at the end:

'*What is sponsorship?*

'Sponsorship is the term commonly used for financial or other support in the form of goods and services given by business or members of the public to sports, arts, education, charities, etc. The sponsor receives something in return, for example, advertising, free or reduced priced tickets, hospitality etc.

You will be making supplies if there is a written or oral agreement of understanding that, in return, for a sum of money, goods or other services, a sponsor will secure from you some publicity or other form of benefit. It makes no difference if the sponsorship is called something else. *What matters is the agreement or understanding between the parties*'.

Thus, all and each of these elements has to be calculated, assessed and taken into account by all parties to a sporting sponsorship agreement if appropriate to the particular sponsorship transaction. Comprehensive analysis here can never cover all contingencies, just as no medical textbook can provide for every prognosis. Awareness of potentialities is the most realistic target which can be contemplated.

Indeed, that awareness becomes more acute each day with the Parliamentary Question and Answer as recorded in Hansard for 22 July 1993 relating to 'the liability to VAT of amateur sports and cultural activities in the public sector' from Mr Roger Gale MP (North Thanet).

Treasury

C — North Thanet

439 *Mr Roger Gale*

'To ask Mr Chancellor of the Exchequer, what plans he has to change the liability to VAT of amateur sports and cultural activities in the public sector'.

Sir John Cope
'I am discussing with my Rt Hon Friend the Secretary of State for National
Heritage a VAT exemption for the supply of certain services by non-profit
making organisations and local authorities to persons who take part in sport
or physical education. This would be a limited exemption to be introduced
by Treasury Order. The precise scope of the exemption would be determined
after we have discussed with the representative sports bodies the services
and sports to be included.

 We shall also be holding discussions with a view to examining the case
for exempting certain cultural services and associated goods supplied by
public authorities'.

In due course publication of the Value Added Tax (Sport, Physical
Education and Fund Raising Events) Order 1994 was laid before Parliament
and came into effect from 1 April, 1994 as SI 1994/68. Its general significance
in addition to fiscal benefits to the non-profit-making organisations
identified has been relied on throughout this text in support of Lord
Hailsham's 'heterogeneous list of pastimes'.

10   CONCLUSIONS

It is appropriate that the last word on this technical but nevertheless
crucially important area of sports sponsorship within the framework of Sport
and the Law should come from the Howell Report. In the section dealing
with tax implication, Chapter Seven under the heading of 7.8 *Corporation
Tax* it states (p 41):

 'Any sporting body which at the end of an accounting period has a liability
 for the payment of corporation tax may well question whether their affairs
 have been ordered to their best advantage ... We believe this approach to be
 more realistic to this problem than expectation of any early government
 policy to provide special exemption for sport or its sponsors'.

Such pessimism may now soon be overtaken by events in motion to occur
after publication. In substance it is not far removed from Lord Goodman's
evidence to the House of Commons Education, Science and Arts Committee
(at page 472, supra). Not for the first time the two worlds merge on common
ground for the community's cultural benefit.

CHAPTER 14

No Fine on Fun

(Changing laws for sport beneficially
and charitably)

1 INTRODUCTION

No Fine on Fun: The Comical History of the Entertainment Duty (1957)
was the title of a polemical publication from Sir Alan Herbert, barrister,
author, one-time MP, librettist, humourist, satirist and lone campaigner.
Lawyers and laymen still admire his many *Misleading Cases* and his
Uncommon Law. Laymen and lawyers still enjoy his partnerships with
Vivian Ellis and their melodies from *Bless the Bride* and *The Water Gypsies*.

No Fine on Fun crystallised and climaxed his sustained attacks upon
the Entertainment Duty imposed by Parliament on a target area built-in to
its title imposed as a temporary pretext as a patriotic First World War
contribution from all amusements during 1916. Alan Herbert's campaign
destroyed it.

Today sport has been replaced with equally crippling fiscal burdens.

Sir Denis Follows died in 1983. Before then, in Sir Alan Herbert's
tradition, he left this message with that Philip Noel-Baker Memorial address
at Loughborough College in March of that year, part of which has already
been cited in Chapter 2, *Progressive perspective* supra at p 106:

> 'For years I have been shouting from the roof tops against the iniquitous
> taxation system of this country so far as sport is concerned. When I tell
> you [1983] that of the £888,000 raised by the British Olympic Association
> in 1980 to send out teams to the Olympic Games, to maintain the sporting
> prestige of this country, we paid £176,000 in tax, you can understand my
> indignation and concern. Any sports organisation in this country which is
> a non-profit distributing body should be relieved of all forms of taxation
> of the revenue it raises; and for good measure no sports body should be

required to pay 15 per cent VAT on the admission charges to sports gatherings.

In 1957 [the year of *No Fine on Fun*] a Conservative administration abolished entertainment tax because the tax was killing sport and entertainment. How much more vital is it in 1983 that entertainment tax in the guise of VAT should be taken off the back of sport? We in sport have long argued that if the Government did not take so much out of us in taxation we should not be crying out for so much to put back through the Sports Council and local government'.

A decade later a partial alleviation was established with a successful Special Tax Commissioners Appeal by the British Olympic Association against Inland Revenue assessments to corporation tax for four years prior to 1993 in relation to sponsorship income raised for preparing and sending teams to Olympic Games and from exploitation of its logo. The Special Commissioner Mr T H K Everett was persuaded on the evidence before him that

'BOA was not merely exploiting its logo. Its activities were far wider and were so entwines as to form a melange and — on the facts BOA's activities as a whole were uncommercial and did not constitute a trade'.

(*BOA v Winter (Inspector of Taxes: (SC 3124/94)* per *Simon's Weekly Tax Intelligence* 5 May 1995 p 734.)

It has not been appealed and an acceptable basis has been achieved for accounting on this basis.

At about the same time, belatedly, after a sustained CCPR and National Playing Field Association campaign, VAT for non-profit-making Sport, Physical Education and Fund-Raising Events has been alleviated as from 1 April, 1994 with retrospective effect as explained earlier in Chapter 13, *Sponsored gentlemen and Players*.

The significance of the CCPR in this context is that as long ago as a CCPR Taxation and Sport Seminar, held in London during 1986, Richard Baldwin's B Com FCA, AR11, one of the co-authors with Richard Hanney ACA of *Tax and Financial Planning for Sportsmen and Entertainers*, explained

'I recently reviewed the audited accounts of six governing bodies and these appeared to indicate that all six were treated slightly differently from a corporation tax viewpoint'.

Nearly seven years later, again, Richard Baldwin was associated with a Report from his specialist football industry accountant firm, Touche Ross, entitled 'The Taxman Cometh! The importance of PAYE to football clubs'.

The Guardian for 26 July 1993 as reported by Don Atkinson explained;

> 'An Inland Revenue crackdown is set to close dozens of football clubs unless they put their tax affairs in order, Touche Ross, the accountancy firm, has warned';

and he concluded by citing

> Richard Baldwin, a Touche partner said:

>> 'Not only do clubs have to collect and account for PAYE and National Insurance on payments to employees, they also have to complete the paperwork required by the Revenue.
>>   This is often a minefield for staff who may not have the time or expertise.
>>   In particular, allowances and expenses should be supported by documentary proof'.

More recently in a CCPR 'Strategy for Sport' presentation to the Government Richard Baldwin's fun as Deloitte Touche is quoted

> 'The Treasury receives approximately four times more money from sport in taxes than it returns through central and local government'.

Such considerations at National Government and CCPR levels can be of little direct concern to the 30,920,000 participants comprising 67% of the population, and the greater number of 421 National Governing Bodies, identified in the Sports Council's (now Sport England's) March 1999 survey cited in the Preface. Furthermore the reference to 'six governing bodies' being treated slightly differently from a corporation tax viewpoint, — in the context of the 421 total number of National Governing Bodies qualified in the Sports Council's Report, points to the impossibility here of attempting to do more than identify in the broadest possible spectrum those aspects of tax and VAT collection and assessments which are most likely to affect the 67% and any particular number of the 421 National Governing Bodies without access to specialist fiscal services of the kind available at National Government and internationally orientated organisations such as the British Olympic Association and any other comparably high profiled target for taxation and able to afford the level of fees required by such an internationally orientated organisation as Deloitte Touche.

Accordingly, the purpose of this chapter within the scope of this particular book's comprehensive range can be only to highlight those areas for which professional experiences, instructions and observations have demonstrated since the first edition was published in January 1988, a need for general attention and comment. Any specific requirements not covered by such a general approach would merit possible professional advice.

2   TAXATION PRACTICE GENERALLY

Effective practice and operation of the law tax for the public generally and the sporting world particularly demand two levels of awareness whether acting personally or representatively through a governing body or professional trade union or association. One is the traditional barrister-solicitor-accountant expertise. The other is knowledge of attitudes adopted by an ever-increasing army of tax and VAT commissioners and inspectors and charity commissioners, all battling for or against the taxpayer in the middle. This leads on accordingly to one oft-forgotten reality which cannot be ignored, whether in sporting or wider social spheres.

As a branch of law, taxation affects everyone of the 30,920,000 participants and the 421 National Governing Bodies journeying from the cradle to the grave, and even there, too (see Clore Estate litigation: *Stype Investments v IRC* [1984] STC 609: [1985] STC 394). Only traffic laws, touching pedestrians as well as vehicle users, equal this in range of regulatory control. Nevertheless, even this similarity is differentiated by one crucial and fundamental operation. Symbolically for sport and the law it has been summarised graphically by the future Master of the Rolls, Sir John Donaldson, as Lord Justice Donaldson, before he succeeded Lord Denning, where he said in *IRC v Garvin* [1980] STC 296 at 313:

'There is a certain fascination in being one of the referees of a match between a well-advised taxpayer and the equally well-advised Commissioners of Inland Revenue, conducted under the rules which govern tax avoidance. These rules are complex, the moves are sophisticated and the stakes are high'.

Sadly, but realistically, this equation can concern only a litigation Superleague. The available services are not always 'equally advised'. Indeed, more often than not the balance between the payer and the Revenue is decidedly unequal at the level where fairness is required most urgently, ie at the lowest litigiously contentious, but, for the practitioner, most significant level: the General or Special Commissioners, where the hard factual evidence to which so much tax law is related must be adduced.

Thus, on the one hand, the United Kingdom courts have repeatedly refused to accept evidence on appeals to judges from tribunal levels not produced at the earliest possible Commissioner hearing. They also have repeatedly emphasised how findings of facts before Commissioners have to stand unaltered on appeal, unless there is no supporting evidence for them (*Cole Bros Ltd v Phillips* [1982] 55 TC 188). Yet no legal aid exists for any professional assistance of any kind at those levels to taxpayers, many of whom cannot afford representation of any description if they wish or need it. On the other hand, however, the House of Lords, since both Sir John Donaldson's sporting image in *IRC v Garvin* (supra) and the Cole

Bros Ltd ruling, has berated the Revenue for not being represented professionally at that earliest possible level in *Reed v Nova Securities Ltd* (1984) STC 124. The House of Lords thus confirmed the principle applied by the Court of Appeal in J P R Williams libel action, when it rejected the Daily Telegraph's fresh evidence, available but not relied upon at the initial trial. For it attempted to use that evidence for seeking a retrial (which it obtained on the different ground of the judge's misdirection to the jury about the amateur rules of Rugby Union football), after Dr (now Mr) J P R Williams' libel damages award, as already explained in Chapter 6, *Participation problems*. Evidence on appeal which could have been obtained with diligence at an earlier hearing is usually too late for use as a second bite at a cherry, even if it could tip the balance of judicial digestion for a verdict, on the principle that there must be an end to litigation.

Another illustration of a potential costs injustice is where the Football Association funded the initial stages of its Inland Revenue battle to confirm the Charity Commissioners' registration of its Youth Trust Deed. The final round of appeals in the House of Lords was affordable only with support from the Sports Council and CCPR. Sport therefore does not differ from any other fiscal sphere whereby different circumstances demand differing levels of collective or individual advice and funding of a professional nature. The tax and VAT problems of sport and recreation are as diverse and varied as countries and individuals who all create separate and contrasting, although frequently overlapping, fiscal issues. Furthermore, the growth of international sporting competitions and prizes means that double taxation issues and separate taxations in different countries must be considered closely, with a further awareness of what Richard Baldwin differentiates in treatment 'from a corporation tax viewpoint'. Throughout this chapter the reader is credited with the personal knowledge of the usual tax charges, ie

(1)	Personal	Income Tax
		Capital Gains Tax
		Inheritance Tax
		Rating Taxes
		Value Added Tax
(2)	Clubs	As above and also
(3)	Companies	Corporation Tax

Accordingly, the structure of these pages will follow the pattern of chapters dealing with active action within sport, namely

Chapter 4, 'Parent, school and club partners';
Chapter 5, 'Public protection';
Chapter 6, 'Participation problems'.

3   PARENT, SCHOOL AND CLUB PARTNERS

(Chapter 4)

(1)   The bracketing of clubs with companies stems from the author's professional experiences, instructions and observations since the first edition manuscript was completed in October 1987. This is that notwithstanding the now 86-year-old and unchallenged precedent of *Carlisle and Silloth Golf Club v Smith* [1913] 3 KB 75, uncertainty still persists how, for fiscal purposes, the sources and existence of unincorporated associations are the artificial creation of statute within the definition of 'company' for the purpose of the Income and Corporation Taxes Act 1988 and Taxation of Charitable Gains Act 1992, and thereby accountable for corporation tax on any income or chargeable gains which may be obtained.

Any doubts or questions about the fact of an unincorporated association not having a separate legal entity (and being recognised in law only through its individual members or representatives) were dispelled in the network of various appeals involving the Worthing Rugby Football Club during the 1980s. The Club's unsuccessful appeal against a Development Land Tax Act ruling and the Revenue's successful appeal relating to capital gains re-affirmed the Carlisle Silloth Golf Club principle that it is the *association* and *not* the *individual* members who are liable to tax, despite the fact that an unincorporated association does not have a separate identity. This position contrasts sharply with the potential personal liability in contract and tort as illustrated by the Blackburn Rovers collapsed grandstand case on *Brown v Lewis* (1896) 12 TLR 455; *Carlisle and Silloth Golf Club v Smith* [1913] 3 KB 75 (income); *Worthing Rugby Football Club Trustees v IRC* [1985] 1 WLR 409 (capital gains); *Frampton v IRC* [1987] STC 273 (Development and Tax) Value Added Tax Act 1983, s 31(3). An unincorporated association must still be represented by counsel and not a member before the courts (although not the commissioners) because it is not a litigant in person — *Animal Defence and Anti-Vivisection Society v IRC* (1950) 66 TLR (Pt 1) 1112.)

(2)   As already explained in Chapter 4, *Parent, school and club partners*, sections 47(1) and (2) of the Local Government Finance Act provided for rate relief by local authorities when premises were linked to charity status, now as guided by the House of Lords in its two landmark decisions a decade apart from each other in 1981 and 1992 respectively. The FA Youth Trust case of *IRC v McMullan* [1981] AC 1 and the *North Berwick Sports Centre* decision in *Guild v IRC* [1992] 2 All ER 10. Each has given bona fide claimants for charitable status with a sporting flavour an authentic foundation: the FA decision re-affirmed the then 65-year-old decision of

Re Mariette [1915] 2 Ch 384 that physical education is as validly charitable as the teaching of Latin or Greek; and the *North Berwick* judgment extended the 'interests of social welfare' contained in section 1(1) of the Recreational Charities Act when considering a bequest to 'be used in connection with the Sports Centre (then) in North Berwick' to include also a concept of 'some similar purpose in connection with sport'. How to define 'sport', for that purpose in the context of that litigation (as distinct from Lord Hailsham's philosophical and philological approach recorded at the outset here on page 1 of the Preface) as others and I have questioned in these pages and in the *New Law Journal*, 15 January 1993, can yet await a House of Lords hat-trick on sporting charitable decisions.

(3)   For present purposes, however, a mandatory relief of 80 per cent of the rate levied on premises occupied by a charity wholly or mainly used for charitable purposes can be obtained from the appropriate rating authority. It can also be granted a discretionary relief to 100 per cent for the first of the following three categories specified in section 47(2) of the Local Government Finance Act 1988, namely

(i)   charities;
(ii)   organisations not established or conducted for profit and whose main objects are charitable or are otherwise philanthropic or religious or concerned with education, social welfare, science, literature or the fine arts;
(iii) clubs, societies or other organisations not established or conducted for profit and whose premises are wholly or mainly used for the purposes of recreation.

At present politically, attempts to extend the mandatory relief area to all non-profit-making organisation have failed. Thus, during a House of Commons debatable initiated by the then Mr Denis Howell, MP on Sports Facilities during late November 1991, the Labour Party spokesman Tom Pendry explained that Government sources had told him in respect of an earlier written answer

'about the total number of sports clubs that received rate relief in 1991, but what they refused to tell me — despite an explicit request on my written question, although I have since discovered the answer as a result of pressing other departments — is that the survey showed that 1,136 voluntary sports clubs applied for rate relief in 1991 under the present system but were denied'.

Subsequently, in the early summer of 1993 the CCPR Annual Report for 1991–92 recorded how its own 'survey reveals a bleak picture. Findings based on returns from 3,200 clubs revealed that 24.5% of clubs received no rate relief whatever. 33.5% of clubs receive less than 50% rate relief. Only 31.5% of clubs receive 50–100% rate relief'.

(4) By 1999 little had changed substantially. One mechanism for attempting to qualify for charitable rate relief stems from the wise advice given at an earlier CCPR Taxation and VAT conference at London's Waldorf Hotel in 1980. On that occasion the principal Charity Commissioner, Mr Charles Weston, whose encouragement for registration of the FA Youth Trust Deed in 1972 was endorsed ultimately by the House of Lords in *IRC v McMullan*, recommended an administrative mechanism for attempting to achieve authentic charitable educational sporting status: hive off a section of a club or other organisation, administratively and physically. This method and result were achieved by a bowls club at Watchet in Somerset extraneously to charitable issues and intentions. It emerged during a successful appeal to a VAT Tribunal against a Commissioners of Customs and Excise assessment upon the club for VAT purposes (*AG Hayhoe (on behalf of Watchet Bowling Club and Watchet Indoor Bowling Club) v Customs and Excise Commissioners,* VAT Tribunal ref LON/80/341 13 January 1981 (unreported)).

The Club was structured in two separate sections, and affiliated to the two national governing bodies under its two separate sections, indoors, and general: the English Indoor Bowling Association (EIBA) and the English Bowling Association (EBA). Proof by oral and also detailed documentary accounting and administrative evidence of the two separate club sections satisfied the VAT Tribunal and the Customs and Excise assessment on the club as a registrable VAT unit was discharged. Neither of the two separate entitles was compulsorily eligible for that tax.

Questions have been raised about the practical and legal implementation of Mr Weston's guidance. Thus, if the physical accommodation can be provided in the manner that clearly existed at Watchet, trustees who hold properties in accordance with traditional land law concepts, transcending the artificiality produced by the Court of Appeal in *Worthing Trustees v IRC*, could be appointed to more than one unit without creating any conflict of interest or legal objections to Mr Weston's concept.

(5) Finally a more esoteric and subtle aspect of sports related charitable activities was omitted from the second edition in 1994, partly through inadvertence but also because of its elusiveness. Accordingly, it does not appear in any of the other publications which have faithfully followed the text. It concerns an area in North-West Lancashire known as the Clayton Playing Fields. It is a saga which is ongoing, with the Oldham Corporation locked in battle for ten years with the local objectors against its wish to

sell or relocate. The legal issues under section 13 of the Charities Act 1960 and the cy près doctrine can be found in *Oldham Metropolitan Borough Council v Attorney-General* [1993] 2 All ER. The battle continues in the Oldham Council Chamber with the objectors heartened by a recent House of Lords decision in *R v Oxfordshire County Council and others, ex parte Sunningwell Parish Council* [1999] 3 CO LR 160. An appeal was allowed against a Court of Appeal's refusal to a village glebe as a village green in the public interest.

4   PUBLIC PROTECTION (CHAPTER 5)

Two contrasting decisions impinging upon the issue of public protection illuminate the artificial and arcane world in which taxation law is administered and practised, separate and apart from legislative links today with EC law directives, outside the mainstream of ordinary legal life and experience. One concerns the famous Burnley Football Club. The other demonstrates how a little-known tennis coaching property in the Midlands with which it will be more convenient to begin was foot faulted because of an absence of professional advice. It also illustrates the problems created by he limitations to Sir John Donaldson's fascination in *IRC v Garvin* (supra) when a taxpayer in person does not qualify for his standpoint of being a

> 'referee of a match between a well-advised taxpayer and the equally well-advised Commissioners of Inland Revenue, conducted under the rules which govern tax avoidance'

where the

> 'rules are complex, the moves are sophisticated and the stakes are high'.

(1)   Thus, *Thomas v Reynolds and Broomhead* ([1987] TC No 3080: (1987) 119 Taxation 77) may be of concern to more people in sport than the actual taxpayers associated with the result, because of the general taxation pitfalls which it parades.

Walton J in London's Chancery Division of the High Court described it as 'a rather unfortunate little case', for the taxpayers. It could also be unfortunate for sport generally, although concerned immediately with tennis coaching. Through no fault at all of the learned judge, it may also be unfortunate for the image of the law. For it emphasises the imbalance caused by the House of Lords attitude in recommending revenue representation before the Commissioner while legal aid does not exist for taxpayers at the crucial level. No detailed formal report of the judgment in the official Tax Cases appeared until June 1987 (TC No 3080), although a valuable commentary in the weekly journal *Taxation* from which a citation is taken below was published on 24 April 1987.

The Inspector of Taxes had appealed against a ruling of the General Tax Commissioners at Scarsdale in Derbyshire. It had favoured the taxpayers, Messrs Reynolds and Broomhead. They traded in a partnership business as qualified tennis coaches. In order to provide winter services to their pupils they had bought during their tax year ending 31 March 1982, an inflatable cover of high-grade polythene, together with the necessary equipment to inflate it, and a hut for storage when the cover was not in use. By personal appearance without representation they claimed a first year capital expenditure allowance under section 41(1) of the Finance Act 1971. Subsection (1)(a) provides its availability where;

> 'a person carrying on a trade incurs capital expenditure on the provision of machinery or plant for the purpose of trade'.

The General Commissioners found in favour of the taxpayers. The Revenue appealed, represented by solicitors and Counsel experienced in taxation affairs, challenging the Commissioners' decision. The key issue was how the General Commissioners in accordance with correct judicial principles had applied the relevant law to the facts provided before them by the taxpayers. Because Parliament has never defined either machinery or plant, the Courts have been obliged to define this particular gap themselves. A cluster of reported cases, including *Brown v Burnley Football Club* (infra), culminating in the *Cole Bros v Phillips* (supra) in the House of Lords differentiates between 'plant' and the 'ambience' or 'setting' for carrying on the business concerned. Their Lordships decided that the ultimate conclusion is essentially a question 'of fact and degree for the Commissioners to decide' ([1982] TC 307 at 307 (j)).

Two practical questions which Walton J had to decide were

(i)   whether the inflatable cover

> 'is plant, because quite clearly, although the machinery by which the balloon is inflated is machinery it is by no means obvious that the cover itself, the air balloon, is plant'

(ii) also

> 'whether upon the facts found in the Case Stated by the General Commissioners the air cover has any direct part to play in the business carried on'.

Apparently the facts found by the General Commissioners based on the information supplied by the taxpayers resulted in finding that the inflatable cover's primary function was to provide shelter. Before Walton J the taxpayers, appearing in person, added valuable

> 'various facts which are certainly not covered in the Case Stated ... unfortunately I can pay no attention although I have not the slightest reason to suppose that they are untrue'.

The learned judge was trapped by the House of Lords ruling in *Cole*'s case that any appellate court would be bound by the General Commissioners' findings. The principle which arises is clear: there must be an end to litigation.

The draconian imposition of the principle as the stage between Tax Commissioners and the High Court is inconsistent with other procedures with which litigants, and especially those unable to afford High Court representation and ineligible for legal aid, could be familiar. Appeals from magistrates' courts to Crown Court, and many interlocutory/interim appeals in civil proceedings at County Court, High Court, and even Court of Appeal levels, permit additional evidence not available or used at an initial stage. The exclusion of this practice from revenue appeals creates an injustice and inconsistency which so far has failed to excite reforming zealots warmly concerned with human rights yet less concerned with the public's rights of evidence in tax litigation.

The additional facts which Walton J felt constrained to reject for his judgment related to beneficial lighting conditions, dipping outside floodlights, and general coaching advantages: all directed to meeting the legal criteria for 'plant'. *The Taxation* journal under a main headline 'Winners lose' claimed in its 'Commentary' paragraph:

> 'The inference is that Mr Justice Walton considered that the taxpayer should have won their case, but he was bound to hold in favour of the Revenue because they had not put the correct facts to the General Commissioners'.

Even if the taxpayers had been served by professional assistance there is no guarantee that the limitations of human communications would have disclosed the material facts at the crucial initial stage: a situation which the late Mr Simon Burns, defence solicitor in Woolmington (supra), cited anecdotally in Chapter 3, at p 79, would have recognised. (with his advice to disclose *ALL* facts before trial and not leave them for aterthoughts).Nevertheless, the circumstances leading to Walton J's inevitable judgment are unsatisfactory, as indeed is this whole legal taxation sporting area. It must await another set of comparable facts, and opportunity to consider Vinelott J's judgment on the Burnley case in the Court of Appeal or even the House of Lords.

During the Chancellor of the Exchequer's autumn budget proposals for November 1993 it was announced that buildings and structures would not thereafter qualify as plant for tax reliefs although this would not affect expenditure for those purposes already qualified, and also the 'repair' circumstances considered below in the *Burnley Football Club* case.

(2)   At Burnley the famous football company club directors decided in 1969 on architectural advice that the part of their playing area premises at Turf Moor known as the Brunshaw Road stand which had been built in 1912 could no longer be regarded as safe, and consequently arranged for its demolition, at a replacement cost of £209,365. In due course that sum was argued as a basis for deduction from the company club's profits for corporation tax purposes as either

(a)   a 'repair of premises' allowance under section 130 of the Income and Corporation Taxes Act 1970 or
(b)   capital expenditure on the provision of plant for the purposes of the Club's trade under section 41 of the Finance Act 1971.

Before the Presiding Special Tax Commissioner, Hubert Monroe QC and his successor, R H Widdows, the club failed to establish its claim for plant, but succeeded to establish, with the author's emphasis,

> '*On the facts we find the Stadium to have been the profit-earning entity,* the premises being occupied for the purposes of the Club's trade to which paragraph (d) section 130 refers. The actual playing field together with the surrounding stands and terraces was where, to use a colloquialism, it all happened: the spectators paid their money to occupy the stands and terraces so that they might watch the players on the field and, as spectators and supporters, participate in the matches put on by the Club. *We find the stadium, as we have defined it, to be the premises and the stand to be physically, commercially and functionally an inseparable part.* On that footing it seems to us that the replacement of the Brunshaw Road stand qualifies as "repairs of premises" and we so hold'.

In accordance with the appellate procedure in revenue cases the Crown declared its dissatisfaction with that finding as 'being erroneous in point of law'. Vinelott J adjudicated, again with the author's emphases,

> 'The question "What is the whole, the entirety, the entity which is said to have been repaired by replacement of part?" cannot be answered by any one yardstick or rule of thumb. It must, in the words of Lord Reid, "be answered in the light of all the circumstances which it is reasonable to take into account" (see *Regent Oil Co Ltd v Strick* [1965] 3 All ER 174 at 179, [1966], AC 295 at 313).

Application of the principle enunciated in para 9(11)(3) of the case [stated] would not, as it seems to me, have pointed to the playing field and the surrounding stands and terraces which the Special Commissioners take in [it] to constitute the entity or premises which were repaired. The profit-earning undertaking comprehended also a car park, changing rooms, baths and, more remotely, a gymnasium. All were, as I see it, equally part of the "profit-earning entity" ... It may be that, for instance, a sports stadium designed and built as a single building would constitute separate "premises", and that replacement or renewal of a part, more or less extensive, would be a repair of the premises as a whole, though it is not easy to see why, in such a case, a car park, baths and changing rooms forming an integral part of the structure should not be as much part of the stadium as the spectators' seats and the ground itself. However, in the recent case the premises occupied by the club comprised a number of distinct structures. It was not designed, far less built, in accordance with a single plan. For instance, the Cricket Field stand was added in 1969. Each separate part of the whole had its own distinct function. *No part, except the football pitch itself, was necessary to the performance of the club's central activity of arranging professional football matches as a spectacle. The club could have continued its activities without affording covered seats for those of its supporters prepared to pay for that amenity.* It could have leased a part of its ground to another prepared to afford that or other amenities, as I believe is sometimes done by racecourse owners.

In my judgment, therefore, the erection of the new Brunshaw Road stand *was not* a 'repair' *of any larger entity*, whether identified *as the whole* premises *occupied* by the club for the purposes of its business or as the field and surrounding *stands* and *terraces* alone'.

As I have reached the clear conclusion that the erection of the new stand was not a repair, the further question whether, if it had been a repair, it could nonetheless have been expenditure of a capital nature does not arise for decision. It is also a question which can only be asked on the hypothesis, in my judgment false, that the erection of the new stand was a replacement of part of some larger whole. It would I think be undesirable that I should express any opinion whether, if the hypothesis had been well founded, the expenditure would have been expenditure of a revenue or capital nature, having regard to the interval between the erection of the old stand and the erection of the new stand, and to the enduring nature of the new stand. (*Brown (Inspector of Taxes) v Burnley Football and Athletic Co Ltd* [1980] 3 All ER 244 at pages 255–256.)

That judgment was delivered after the Ibrox Stadium disaster of 1971 and Lord Wheatley's Report on it which led to the Safety of Sports Grounds Act 1975. The Bradford City and Hillsborough Sheffield disasters with their respective reports from Mr Justice Popplewell (1985) and Lord Justice Taylor (1989 and 1990) with their consequential legislation were yet to come, and the impact which the tragedies on those occasions made on the judicial and public consciousness did not exist when Mr Justice Vinelott reversed the experienced Special Commissioner's fact findings to hold

> 'No part, except the football pitch, was necessary for the performance of the club's central activity of arranging professional football matches as a spectacle. The club could have continued its activities without affording covered seats for those of its supporters prepared to pay for that amenity'.

The artificiality of this ruling from the leafy lawns of Lincoln's Inn is emphasised when it is set against the Divisional Court decision in *Cawley v Frost* (1976) to find that the Halifax Town stadium was a public place in its entirety for public order offences.

Nevertheless it is difficult to ignore the opinion that if the Burnley Football Club had appealed to the higher courts either a *Wooldridge v Sumner* finding in which the learned judge drew the wrong inferences of fact from the evidence would have resulted, or an echo would have been heard of Viscount Dunedin's House of Lords view of the Court of Appeal in the *Seymour v Reed* (1927) AC 554 tax-free cricketers' benefit landmark decision at pages 560–561,

> 'honestly, had it not been for the fact that honourable judges, whose opinions I respect, have come to another conclusion, I would have thought the contention was quite preposterous'.

Parliament and the Government have since those crowd disasters and subsequent successive legislation (see Chapter 5, 'Public protection') attempted to alleviate the financial inhibitions caused by this reversal of the very experienced Special Commissioners' careful factual conclusions. First the Finance (No 2) Act 1975, s 49 prior to the Burnley decision and consistent with the Safety of Sports Grounds Act 1975 amended the capital allowance rules to provide for tax relief when safety certificates existed: and ultimately section 119 of the Finance Act 1989, now all consolidated in the Capital Allowances Act 1990 s 69 and 70, following recommendations in the Hillsborough Taylor Report. For clubs and stadia owners whose premises do not qualify for football ground tax reliefs, the judicial Burnley blockage remains unless and until attempts are made to reverse it on a further appeal, if necessary to the House of Lords as experienced in *Seymour v Reed* and ultimately in the FA Youth Trust and North Berwick Sports Centre charity (supra cases), where earlier decisions were reversed by Britain's court of last resort. The FA Youth Trust experience of supporting funding from the Sports Council and the Central Council of Physical Recreation could encourage such a course, and a valuable and practical critique of the position generally appears in the *British Tax Review* (1990) No 11 at pages 329–334.

5   PARTICIPATION PROBLEMS (CHAPTER 6)

Seymour v Reed (supra: [1927] AC 554, already considered in earlier pages is inevitably the starting point, with its reversal of the Court of Appeal majority and restoration of the eminently experienced tax judge, Rowlatt J who had affirmed the General Tax Commissioners' decision. This was that the proceeds of James Seymour's benefit match at the traditional Canterbury Cricket Week in 1920 were a gift or donation from an appreciative public subscription and not assessable to tax as income. More recently history's wheel turned full circle after the transfer from Nottingham Forest to Southampton of the England international goalkeeper, Peter Shilton. On that occasion in early 1991 the House of Lords again reversed the Court of Appeal to establish on this occasion that a £75,000 payment to him from Forest to encourage his transfer and thus reduce its wage bill was not as claimed, and argued, a golden handshake. It was held to have been an emolument from his employment under section 181(1) of the Income and Corporation Taxes Act 1970 and thereby liable to tax (*Shilton v Wilmshurst* [1991] 3 All ER 148, [1991] STC 88). A beneficial constructive critique of the decision appears from John Tiley, Cambridge University's Professor of the Law of Taxation in the Taxation section of the *All England Law Reports Annual Review* (1991) at pages 346–347 and more generally in my own Sport and the Law pages at page 309 and in the 1990 volume at pp 245, 248.

In the years between these pages in Chapter 1, 'Genesis', I have already explained how advisers to the Professional Footballers Players' and Trainers' Union hopelessly tried to equate the footballers' discretionary but contractually tied benefit payment position with the cricket circumstances (see *Davis v Harrison* (1927) 43 TLR 623: *Dayle v Duff: Corbett v Duff: Feeburg v Abbott* (1941) KB 730 and pages supra), until my articles in the *Football Association Bulletin* (April 1953) and *Rating and Income Tax* (1953) led to the Peterborough United non-Football League experiment in *Rigby v IRC* ((1959) *Peterborough Citizen and Advertiser* 16 June, 24 July) and the ultimate deletion of all contractual elements from professional football players contracts. Thus the Football Association's appreciation to its World Cup winning players in 1966 with a £1,000 bonus payment outside the match fee was held by Brightman J to have had 'the quality of a testimonial or accolade outside rather than the quality of remuneration for services rendered' *Moore v Griffiths* [1978] 3 All ER 309 at page 409 (b–c) consistent with the *Seymour v Reed* tax-free cricketers' benefit principle and thereby not assessable to tax.

No appeal was lodged by the Revenue against either of these Peterborough United and 1966 World Cup decisions based upon the *Seymour v Reed* precedent. Two further appeals, however, reversed High Court rulings in the Court of Appeal.

In *Moorhouse v Dooland* [1955] 2 All ER 93 the Professional League cricketers' *contracted* benefit was equated with the old-styled footballers' contractual regulated payments and was thereby held subject to tax. A decade later, a trend for *amateur* rugby union players to move over into professional rugby league which has been doubtless encouraged by the Court of Appeal's decision in *Jarrold v Boustead* [1964] 2 All ER 76 can be seen from its decision that inducement payments to amateur rugby union players to become professional players under rugby league professional rules were treated as once and for all capital payments and not subject to income tax. Of this decision in relation to *Shilton v Wilmshurst* (supra), Professor Tiley's *All England Law Reports Annual Review 1991* commentary says it 'was not cited but presumably remains in place' because the House of Lords decision 'leaves intact the tax-free status of the compensation for giving up a senior position' (*Pritchard v Arundale* [1971] 3 All ER 1011).

A final example of the manner in which tax laws today are entwined with high-profile and high-earning sportspersons appears from an interest-free loan from Arsenal Football Club to its Republic of Ireland International, David O'Leary, of £266,000 repayable on demand to a Channel Islands Trustee for the benefit of the employees. The loaned money was invested in a Jersey Bank, and interest accrued to the employee. A Special Commissioner's conclusion was upheld on appeal in the High Court that the income arising from the settlement arrangement stemmed from the employment source and was chargeable under Schedule E and not from the bank deposit under Schedule D, Case V, *O'Leary v McKinlay* (1991) *Tax Journal*, 7 March [1991] STC 42.

Since 1987 rules have existed for withholding of tax at source on payments to non-resident entertainers and sportsmen for which a special Foreign Entertainers Unit was set up to administer the new scheme at 5th Floor, City House, 140 Edmund Street, Birmingham B3 2JH (telephone 0121 200 2616). The burden of collection lies upon the organiser or arranger of the circumstance creating the occasion. The significance of this development was highlighted and recorded in *Hansard* for 21 May 1993 Vol 225, No 184, col 286 and in *Taxation* for 3 June 1993, that the amount of tax and interest (taking repayments into account) obtained from foreign entertainers and sportsmen by the Revenue's specialist unit has steadily increased. In the first year of operation, 1987–88, the unit brought in £6,921,507 plus £3,178,043 tax and interest from the previous year. For 1992–93 the unit received £19,953,506 plus £508,569 relating to the previous year.

Finally, no picture of fiscal revenue matters in relation to Sport and the Law would be complete without sadly recording how the circumstances leading to the Swindon Town Football Club's experiences before the High Court and the FA Appeals Committee resulted directly from Football League investigations into financial irregularities which ended ultimately with a criminal trial and Crown Court conviction and jailing of the former chairman. Payments had been made to players without deduction of tax and a prosecution was brought for conspiracy to defraud the Inland Revenue. In due course the sentence of 12 months was halved on appeal *R v Brian Hiller* (1992) *Times*, 30 July, 11 December. Furthermore, at the time of writing seven years later, similar circumstances cannot be discounted.

6   VALUE ADDED TAX GENERALLY

(1)   The proposed intention of

'a VAT exemption for the supply of certain services by non-profit-making organisations and local authorities to persons who take part in sport or physical education',

as announced by the Paymaster-General in the House of Commons on 22 July 1993, does not detract from the application of this particular European impact on British cultural life and all other sporting areas since the tax came into operation in the United Kingdom on 1 April 1973 with the passing of the Finance Act 1972 which became law on 27 July 1972.

(2)   A decade later it was subsequently consolidated in the Value Added Tax Act 1983. Statutory instruments, EC directives, VAT leaflets and VAT tribunal and High Court ruling all the way up to the House of Lords added to the 51 sections and 11 Schedules contained in the 1983 Act.

(3)   Accordingly, within the context of attempting to create a level of awareness within these pages, a sample selection of three precedents from the cases, and a fourth example of the impact from a sporting political lobby, must suffice to demonstrate how this particular law is operated and practised within a sporting context.

(4)   For more detailed guidance in addition to specialist advice the reader is referred to the Customs and Excise leaflets which are readily available from all of their offices under their titles of Value Added Tax, VAT Notices:

Youth Clubs No 701/35/90: 1 July 1995
Sponsorship No 701/41/95: 1 July 1995
Letting of facilities for Sport and Physical Recreation No 742/1/90: 1 March 1990
Clubs and Associations No 701/5/90 1 June 1990
Non Profit Making Club Exemptions VAT/701/45/94

7　VALUE ADDED TAX CASE EXAMPLES SPECIFICALLY

((1)　*Customs and Excise Commissioners v Lord Fisher* [1981] 2 All ER 147 was a High Court decision upholding a VAT Tribunal that although shooting rights of a family, established where pheasants supplied ample targets, were organised in a business-like way, and guests contributed to the cost, they did not convert pleasure and socially enjoyable activities into a business. Accordingly, they were not concerned with the making of taxable supplies for a consideration and thereby assessable for VAT.

(2)　*Celtic Football and Athletic Club Ltd v C & E Commissioners* [1983] STC 470 and *Football Association v C & E Commissioners* (1985) VAT Tribunal Reports 106 established that the contractual obligations imposed by the Union of European Football Associations (UEFA) requiring reciprocal hospitality arrangements for home and away competition fixtures excluded the services provided by the host association from qualifying as a business entertainment which would ordinarily have been excluded as a deductible input tax.

(3)　*Customs and Excise Commissioners v Professional Footballers' Association (Enterprises) Ltd* (1992) *Times*, 11 March, the House of Lords, Court of Appeal majority all upheld a VAT Tribunal finding that an awards dinner including trophy presentations was for a consideration rather than a supply of goods for no consideration and therefore not assessable for VAT.

EC Council Directive 77/388 (Sixth Directive, art 9(2)(d)) [itself deleted by Tenth Council Directive 84/386, art 1] resulted in a European Court of Justice judgment that ocean-going sailing yachts, even if used for sporting purposes concurrently with commercial enterprises must be regarded as forms of transport (*Hamann v Finanzamt Hamburg-Eimsbuttel* (Case 51/88) [1991] Simon's Tax Cases). The reference procedurally was routed under EEC art 177 (see Chapter 10, *Single European market and UK sport* pp 377–379 supra for UK precedents) and the failure to be freed from VAT burdens *at present* has an echo of *Re Nottage* (1895) with the failure of the yacht's prize then to qualify for charitable status.

CONCLUSION

The fluidity at the time of writing which surrounds the fiscal attitudes towards British sport at Government level was emphasised by the support promised for the Manchester Olympic Games bid and the creation of the National Lottery Act which received the Royal Assent on 21 October 1993. By reason of delay due to the Maastricht debates the operations for National Lottery commenced in Autumn 1994. So far as sport is concerned, the CCPR's Annual Report for 1991–92 published in the early summer of 1993 while the Bill was passing through Parliament explained

> 'When first announced there were to be three beneficiaries — sport, the arts and heritage. There are now five — sport, the arts, heritage, charities and the Millennium Fund. The CCPR believes that it is of crucial importance that sport as a beneficiary should be locked into the arrangements through primary legislation'.

Four days after the Bill became law the Secretary of State for the Department of National Heritage appointed a former audit partner with the accountants Price Waterhouse, and subsequently a financial director in the retail and insurance world, Peter Davis, as financial director. He explained during an interview with *Leisure Management* in December 1993 how his first task was to produce a Draft Invitation to Apply (ITA) and a Draft Licence to Run the National Lottery. This would result in contending applications for operating the National Lottery under a two-tiered system which is provided for under sections 5 and 6 of the Act.

With an enthusiastic optimism he explained how

> 'The DNH's research has picked up on the best and worst points of other lotteries [ie from overseas], and with this knowledge we intend to create the best lottery in the world.... The Secretary of State's conservative estimate is £1.5b a year, but there are other prosecutions based on foreign lotteries which suggest a figure nearer the £5b mark'.

Together with the mechanism available for funding for Sport from the Foundation for Sport and the Arts, the Government's Pound for Pound Sponsorship Scheme and the Football Trust, Sir Alan Herbert and his successors might be said to have been partially vindicated.

PART VI

Conclusion

CHAPTER 15

Whither Sport and the Law?

INTRODUCTION

The last two editions in 1988 and 1994 each concluded with the same title ending to this edition. It was inspired, and as stated in the 1988 edition,

> 'unashamedly adapted from Sir Denis Follows' valedictory address before he sadly died - Whither sport - Whither Sport and the Law'.

On each occasion I structured Chapter 15 around a section headed

SPORTS FOUR VICES: and *HOW TO DEAL WITH THEM*
(1) Violence
(2) Drugs
(3) Commercial Exploitation
(4) Political Violation.

Although no authentic statistical yardstick exists for measuring comparable patterns between the position to-day and as it appeared in 1988 and 1994, the proposals which I made in those last two editions for *HOW TO DEAL WITH THEM* for each item were clearly too moderate to appear to have produced any realistic effect. Sadly, each still exists to-day, if apparently not even more emphatically than before, then at least with no diminution for any one category. Furthermore, during the five years since the last edition in 1994, the battlefields of commercial international sport, alongside the always less publicised grass roots activities have produced overwhelming evidence of continuity at every level of everyone of the *Four Vices*.

This in turn has resulted in assessments which echo those cited at the end of the Preface from the *Evening Sports* sports team of *Sporting Spite* in 1991, and earlier this year in David Welch's *Daily Telegraph* editorial and Simon Barnes' *Times'* conclusions of a self-destructive sporting sickness. Yet the questions which they all have posed for analysis were seen fully in 1985, two years after Sir Denis Follows' potentially posthumous lecture, from the late lamented and unforgettable Ron Pickering, Athletics Administrator, Coach and Communicator. In a hard hitting survey to the CCPR Annual Conference at Bournemouth in November 1985 he voiced thoughts under the title of *The Image of British Sport*:

> 'Is this the problem; that the gap cannot be bridged between C.B. Fry and Daley Thompson, or The Corinthian-Casuals and Manchester United, or have the ground rules changed? Have we slipped down the slippery path that far that there is no return? I don't honestly believe so or I wouldn't just be wasting my time or yours saying simply I told you so. But I believe Peter Corrigan was right when he said recently in *The Observer*: "Sport took its soul to the pawnbrokers so long ago that finding the redemption ticket is not going to be easy".
>
> It is not going to be easy, it will need a massive re-think by all that are genuinely concerned with sport. That in turn will need a massive and exciting focal point in my view. The only thing which I can think of is the Birmingham bid for the 1992 Olympic Games. Someone might think up other initiatives'.

Three years later I commented in the First edition

> 'That Birmingham bid, as we knew, was gazumped by Barcelona. Yet there *is* an even more exciting initiative that transcends all others which is at the heart of all lawful sport, i.e. return to the Rule of Law'.

Looking back with hindsight I realise now that I was identifying the Rule of Law in its widest sense, i.e. without the Rule of Law in Sport chaos exists; without the Rule of Sport in Society anarchy prevails. I did not differentiate in those two earlier editions as I do so here, throughout this text, between the *national* Rule of Law and *domestic sports regulated* Laws of Play, both of which are equally essential to be applied for any solution to the Four Vices. Furthermore, I now realise because of my concern with the Rule of Law both generally and within Sport that I did not pay sufficient or any attention to Ron Pickering's earlier requirement to

> 'need a massive re-think by all that are genuinely concerned with sport'.

Yet even if I had, many who 'are genuinely concerned with sport' have had their capacities to *think initially*, even before arriving at the stage to *re-think*, blurred and distorted by such media led disinformation, illiteracies and illegalities such as the 'professional foul'. For if a foul is committed with deliberate designed professional efficiency it is based upon knowledge and intent and clearly a criminally and civilly actionable assault; and in any event it amounts to corruption and prostitution of any self-respecting professionalism in any game.

Therefore, in order to demonstrate how even more emphatically than ever before SPORTS FOUR VICES which I identified in the two earlier editions in 1988 and 1994 have survived until to-day, the comparable tables under the same headings as before, as set out below, are self-explanatory beyond all reasonable doubt, with a further thought which has surfaced since the second edition was concluded in 1994. This is the absence of a coherent penal policy for not only Sport in particular, but also for Society generally.

In October 1994 at the International Bar Association in Melbourne, the Rt. Hon. Lord McClusky a Senator of The College of Justice in Scotland delivered a paper entitled '*Discussing a sentencing policy*'. An edited version was reproduced in the *New Law Journal*, November 4, 1994 under a title 'Middle Class Justice', with a sub-heading

> '*Penal policy in the United Kingdom satisfies no one - neither the 'do gooders' nor the man in the street*'.

Four years forward in the *Criminal Law Review* for October 1998 p 694 the Lord Chief Justice, the Rt. Hon. Lord Bingham of Cornhill, under the head of '*A Criminal Code: Must we Wait for Ever?*' reproduced from part of an earlier speech, developed it to a further dimension with thoughts which are equally applicable to domestic as well as International governing body regulations within the global explosion of International Sports and nearly all of Lord Hailsham's 'heterogenous list of pastimes, with different governing bodies, different ethics and constantly varying needs'.

> 'We are currently witnessing a degree of constitutional, institutional, procedural and professional change of which we have not in combination seen the like for 350 years. One need only mention such expressions as Devolution, House of Lords reform, Human Rights, Freedom of Information, Woolf, Modernisation of Justice for the seismic nature of the current changes to be appreciated. They are, one can have no doubt, changes intended to meet the needs, hopes and expectations of citizens of this modern plural democracy governed as it is by the rule of law. But there is one feature of such a democracy which, I fear, we shall still lack: something enjoyed by our former colonies, and almost all the great countries of the world; something which has the support of the present government, as of its predecessor; something which we have in the past come tantalisingly close to achieving.

I refer to enactment of a clear, authoritative, comprehensive, accessible, modern, written statement of our criminal law. In short, a criminal code.

One hopes that parliamentary time may yet be found to achieve something that has eluded our predecessors but would, I think, come to be recognised as an important milestone in our legal and public life.'

For Sport no legislative Parliamentary or other regulatory sanction-busting body exists, or even a comparable body to the United Nations, or perhaps ever could exist internationally, in the light of the diversity of Lord Hailsham's 'heterogenous list', and as particularised in the Preface at page . Lord Bingham's wider dimension, however, focuses attention on the key issue facing both domestic and International Sport on matters of *organisational* and *penal* policies.

Furthermore in the area of penalties it is worth reflecting that these problems are not new. Sixty years before Lord McClusky's intervention a lecture was delivered on 19 March 1934, at Gray's Inn, London, under the title of '*The Ethics of a Penal Action*' by the then Archbishop of York, the Revd. William Temple, later to become a greatly missed and revered Archbishop of Canterbury after his premature death in 1942. Its thrust was directed to Reformative additional to Retributive and Deterrent elements through the then emerging Probation Service: but its message was in tune with Lord McClusky's and Lord Bingham's concepts about gaps in any comprehensive policies for the problems they exposed for society generally.

How much more difficult it is for Sport to apply their principles is self-evident from the 113 different VAT listed non-profit making disciplines in Sport to which they relate. The most which can be hoped for is adherence to within each particular activity, Archbishop George Carey's reminder on the eve of Euro '96 in the House of Lords debate on '*Society's Moral and Spiritual Well-being*',

'We take it for granted that you cannot play a game of football without rules. Rules do not get in the way of the game: they make it possible',

and *pace* Bill Nicholson, for Rules, read Laws.

Against that background it is now possible to compare, re-consider and update contrasting proposals for

SPORT'S FOUR VICES: and HOW TO DEAL WITH THEM

1988 - 1994 [Summary extracts]

(1) Violence

(i) Within sport itself

(a) Referees and administrators. Consistency is an ideal which can only be aimed for with little hope of perfect attainment. Criticisms of the professional judiciary and the controversial debate about powers for a Court of Appeal on the initiative of the Attorney-General to reconsider allegedly too lenient sentences after mature reflection demonstrate the problems of sporting referees and umpires giving decisions with serious consequences in a blaze of publicity with considerable financial consequences flowing from errors. Every sporting discipline can point to its own examples. No benefit to sport would exist here for raking the embers of burn-out episodes. Six general principles must be identified.

1. The laws and rules of all sports, except for special modifications because of age, size and disability and specially exempted occasions, apply equally at village green and national stadium levels.

2. Referees, umpires, touch judges linesmen as much as the players participate for their love of sport, with no comparable financial reward to those under heir authority at the public level.

3. Administrators and critics should support the referees and umpires except for a flagrant mistake or

1999 Proposals

(1) Violence

(i) Within sport itself

(a) Referees and administrators
On the eve of Sweden's reprieve for England's Euro 2000 qualifying aspirations, Alan Hansen wrote in the *Daily Express* [9 Oct. 1999], under the heading '*F.A. referees and players must act or cheats will ruin football*', *inter alia*

'The real issue here, however, is not so much that referees are making mistakes - they always have and as the games gets quicker they will make even more - but what suits one official does not necessarily suit another ...

The solutions to these problems are not simple. There must be more consistency among our referees, and the players who sometimes deserve Oscars need to realise they are ruining their own game.

But nothing will be resolved unless the Football Association sits down with referees and the players union and tries to sort out the mess before the situation gets out of control.'

1 - 6

For present purposes, sample examples from four different levels prove the perpetuation of this particular vice of *Violence*.
(1) International
(2) Club
(3) School
(4) Administrative

(1) *International*

(a) When Duncan Ferguson then of Rangers was prosecuted, convicted and gaoled for head-butting James McStay of Raith Rovers during a Tennant's Premier Scottish League fixture in 1995 while he was in breach

1988 - 1994 [Summary extracts]

misjudgment amounting to gross error or negligence. Thus, in one publicised soccer precedent the referee admitted that he wrongly penalised a player whose offence was ultimately expunged. On the other hand, the referee who sent off the field for the first time a player in the FA Cup Final of 1985 obtained an agreed amount of ,1,000 damages for libel; and the referee who sent off two internationals at Cardiff in 1977 for fighting was barred from refereeing a subsequent international for England against France because the then French Federation President protested that the referee was too strict!

4. The dynamic growth of sport should inspire administrators to recognise the need for amendments to *penal* playing laws and their administration. Thus professional rugby league introduced the 'sin bin' principle, borrowed from the most violent forms of body contact sports, ice-hockey and water-polo, to douse its more heated confrontations; and amateur rugby union has given authority to touch judges at international levels to act effectively. This is not yet possible at lower grades because of limitations upon numbers of available trained personnel, with a similar verdict awaiting at grass roots level the outcome of FIFA's 1994 World Cup initiatives.

5. Even if referees fail to observe an offence, administrators should act to uphold the Rule of Law when serious breaches occur.

6. Players should be aware not only of the laws of their particular game. They and their officials should also be aware of the manner in which the law of the land transcends and overrides the law of any field of play. Two

1999 Proposals

of Probation Orders, his later club at the date of conviction and sentence, Everton, could not comprehend why he was gaoled for such a clear-cut criminal assault.

(b) Correspondingly, when the Scottish Rugby Union banned Jason Fayers for four years after committing an injurious assault during a game, and he was later prosecuted to conviction, David Sole, Scotland's Grand Slam captain in 1990, wrote a letter to the Court in mitigation, also expressing lack of comprehension for the need to prosecute. He would have sorted it out the scrum.

(2) *Club*

(a) After the jury's conviction of the Gloucester Rugby captain, Simon Devereux and a nine months custodial sentence for smashing a Rosslyn Park opponent's jaw in 1995, the rugby playing fraternity and commentators also expressed a similar incredulity.

(b) Correspondingly in 1999, similar expressions emerged from the Southampton area of Hampshire when a club player was gaoled for injuring by assault during the course of play: and upheld in the Court of Appeal (*R v Moss*, *Daily Echo*, Southampton, 12 June).

(3) *School*

(a) After a schoolboy's sentencing to a Youth Offenders Institution for having broken an opposing school-boy's jaw, the *offender's* father complained: why should my son go to prison? It's only a game (*R v Carlton* (supra)).

(b) In *Casson v MOD* (supra) the defending Army soldiers, held to be in *loco parentis* to youth experience participants, disputed for several days liability for negligent ankle breakage during a game.

1988 - 1994 [Summary extracts]
well-known examples demonstrate
this, in addition to *R v Bishop* (1985)
supra. One concerned the renowned
Liverpool Football Club and the 1978
Football League Cup Final at Old
Trafford, Manchester. The other
concerns the sorry saga of Leeds
United.

(b) Liverpool On 22 March 1978
Nottingham Forest beat Liverpool 1-0
by a disputed penalty goal. The
causation was seen by millions on
television. The controversy
surrounded an allegation that the
tackle which led to the penalty award
took place outside the penalty area,
but the referee behind the actual play
was too far back to adjudicate
correctly. On the following day the
late Denis Lowe was not alone when
in the *Daily Telegraph* (23 March
1978) he reported that the offender,

'Phil Thompson, who foul on John
O'Hare was adjudged by the referee
to have been committed inside the
penalty area, said: "It was never a
penalty. I admit it was a professional
foul, but it was outside the box." '

The extent and nature of that
'professional foul' was corroborated
three years later by Thompson's
colleague, Phil Neal, in a book entitled
Attack from the Back.
    In the chapter, 'Referees',
recorded at page 98; Neal explained

'I have no idea what sort of view
Partridge [the referee] had of the
incident, but it certainly looked bad
from any angle: a wilful tackle, a bloke
hurtling through the air to land with a
fearful smack inside the box, the
screams of thousands of outraged
Forest fans. The result was almost
bound to be a penalty.'

1999 Proposals
(4) *Administrative*

(a) In his book '*Sweet FA*' in 1999
Graham Kelly has sought to justify
his testimony on behalf of Gary
Blissett's defence to his prosecution
for injuring the eye and cheek of John
Uziell of Torquay United during the
trial of 1992.

(b) This hardly helped to diminish
and discourage the circumstances
which created a rash of 27 red cards in
England and Scotland Premier League
games a week after Alan Hansen's
warning and a *Guardian* comment (18
October 1999):

'The FA's spokesman Adrian
Bevington only confirmed that each
side is speaking a different language
when he said: "There is
communication between us, the
Premier League, the Football League,
individual clubs, referees and the
League Management Association. All
the bodies are aware of their
responsibilities." Clearly they are not
if, after the rash of red cards, neither
referees nor the players banished to
the dressing room by them could see
anything wrong with their actions.
The red card will continue to be kept
flying high by referees until players
stop burying their heads in the sand
and pretending that the new laws do
not exist, at least not for them. It
would be a start if they could desist
from burying their heads into the
faces on opponents.'

(c) A month later (23 November
1999) the *Guardian* was further
commenting under the heading, 'Time
to Take on the Cheats':

'Two months ago the chief executive
of the payers' union Gordon Taylor
suggested to the FA that it set up an
independent committee comprising

1988 - 1994 [Summary extracts]

(c) Leeds United. In the case of the Liverpool experiences cited above should be considered exceptional in the world of modern English professional football a more extended impression was given by a contribution to the *Daily Express* on Tuesday 25 August 1987 at pages 30 31. The former Leeds United and Eire international, John Giles, wrote of his club's progress in the 1970s,

'I get a rush of pride when I think of the great years with Leeds United. I also feel shame...now I can see clearly enough that we stretched the rules to breaking point... We went too far, too ruthless. I went too far.... We did and we prospered. We never thought there might be a day when we would wonder if the price was too high.'

The answer to that wonderment is crystallised in the following paragraph in *Soccer Match Control* by Stanley Lover published in 1986, at page 144, the standard work on soccer refereeing.

'Specific acts of gamesmanship, cheating or professional fouls - whatever label one wishes to give them - can be observed in junior football and even in school games within twenty-four hours of being seen on television. Recently an eight-year-old schoolboy returned home after playing for his school team and was heard to boast that he had committed 'a pro foul' on an opponent to stop a goal.'

Mr Lover does not state whether this was inspired from Phil Neal's text cited above. In fact, he continued, 'His justification was that he had seen his idol, a professional of a Football League First Division team, do the

1999 Proposals

representatives of the players, managers, referees and others, including the FA, to view post-match video evidence and charge players practising the black arts of cheating and provocation. The FA, to its credit, is meeting to discuss the issues of TV evidence, its practicalities, implications, reliability, whether it undermines referees or helps them. The League Managers' Association has called some of its members to a meeting to discuss this very subject. Hopefully the game will grasp the nettle and sting the cheats. And what more poetic way than by television, the medium whose very cash has raised the stakes, making it even more important to get every decision exactly right?'

(d) While those hopes continue, consistent with what *Soccer Match Control* published in 1986 at page 144 as recorded in the adjoining column, the *Daily Telegraph* recorded on 13 October 1999,

'DECLINING disciplinary standards are causing almost as much concern in the schools arena as they are in the professional game.

Several incidents were referred to the English Schools' Football Association Council last season and an urgent appeal has been issued for teachers, team managers and head teachers to work together to enhance the image of schools' football.

Malcolm Berry, ESFA chief executive, said: 'Teachers must show the highest level of self-discipline and educate their players on what represents an acceptable level of behaviour. This must not include some of the things young players see when watching the professional game.'

1988 - 1994 [Summary extracts]
same thing a week earlier. Many referees have reported examples of dissent by schoolboy footballers which, a few years ago, were unheard of. One referee was reported to have to dismiss his own son for searing during a friendly match.'

(ii)   Outside sport

If sport cannot control itself adequately to protect itself, and more significantly its victims, from unlawful conduct committed in the name of sport, then the national Law must be wheeled on to the field of play, if only to prevent the corrosive and corrupting effect upon future generations in the manner evidenced here. Road traffic legislation has progressed from the red flag in the Corinthians hey day during the 1890s to compulsory disqualifications for drugged and drunken drivers to penalise such universally acknowledged anti-social behaviour. Why should sporting offenders be excluded from this principle?

When I was preparing initially with Lord Havers and also ultimately Peter Shankland, *The Royal Baccarat Scandal* and its Tranby Croft house party and High Court trial dramas (concerning an alleged cheating at cards on the eve of the Doncaster St Leger horse race classic on 9 September 1890), preparations were also in hand for the first series of *Sunday Telegraph* articles linking Sport and the Law under that title. Both publications appeared in 1977. When the more general survey on *Sport and the Law* was published in booklet form a year later in 1978, the contrast between the punishments for sporting-social misconduct in Victorian England and the permissive society of the 1960s and 1970s was startling. The Plaintiff in the Baccarat

1999 Proposals

(ii)   Outside sport

(a) The necessity to enact the Football Offences and Disorder Act 1999, with its innovation of International Football banning orders, in extension of what I had prepared and proposed in 1978, may be regarded as self-evidence of an almost insoluble problem. The World Cup 1998 in France, with the violence at Marseilles was the catalyst for remedying this 20 years delay in Parliament.

That draft Safety of Sports Persons Act prepared and placed in an Appendix to the 1978 *Sunday Telegraph* production of Sport and the Law in booklet was formulated and tailored with proposals for an 'automatic suspension from further participation in the activity irrespective of any punishment pursuant to the rules or laws of such sporting or recreational activity and of any other statutory or civil cause of action or complaint' an attempt to solve the then domestic problems which Parliament has belatedly accepted in 1999, with the wider dimension for the overseas offender.

(b) Now it is possible to see here the application to the world of sport generally, and not only particularly for association football, of the twin concepts cited at page 507 above of Lord McClusky's belief 'Penal Policy in the United Kingdom satisfies no-one – neither the "do-gooders" nor the man in the street', and Lord

1988 - 1994 [Summary extracts]

Case, Sir William Gordon-Cumming, Bart., a noble Scottish sporting landowner of ancient lineage, lost his High Court slander action in June 1891 to clear his name against the allegation of cheating, wrongly in the opinion of the joint authors and his own counsel at the time, Sir Edward Clarke, the Solicitor-General of the day. Within hours of the jury's verdict he was kicked out of the Scots Guards with whom he had served with bravery and distinction in the Victorian African Wars and ostracised for the remaining forty years of his life by the society in which he had been one of the privileged members of the Marlborough House set centred around the Prince of Wales, later King Edward VII. In our own time, as John Giles explains,

'we stretched the rules to breaking point... and we prospered.'

Against those contrasting backgrounds the draft Safety of Sports Persons Act was prepared and placed in an Appendix to the 1978 *Sunday Telegraph* production in booklet form. Its purpose was to focus attention upon the existing law and to aim for automatic mandatory suspension from play in the manner equivalent to the mandatory disqualification imposed by Parliament reflecting society's will upon drugged and drunken drivers (with certain special exceptions) and Victorian Society's ostracism for foul play at the card table. Its implementation would displace the discretionary power which at present is available to allow courts a free rein to perpetuate a permissive society's penal policy. An immediate sanction would align this social evil with its motoring equivalent under the penal policy contained progressively in

1999 Proposals

Bingham's plea for 'A Criminal Code: Must we wait forever'. The sustained repetitive criminality cited here in each column in the name of a game in flagrant breach of the common law, which has stood the test of time since *R v Bradshaw* (1878) and was re-affirmed in *Venna* (1975) for more than 120 years, clearly proves from the sample illustrations that the message has not yet been received or understood at international, club and school levels: namely, that playing contact sport and games is not a licence to commit crime or civil liability for negligent injury with penal and compensatory damages sanctions for breaches of the laws of play and also of the law of the land.

(c) The former well-known Metropolitan Police Commander and senior rugby referee, George Crawford, who once walked off a rugby field when unable to persuade the players in a senior England rugby club game of the gravity of their criminality committed during the course of play, has explained often orally and in writing that 'a punch-up on a pavement outside a public house is no different from a punch-up during the course of an organised game'. More graphically he has crystallised his attitude with the classic one-liner as a serving police officer concerned as much with the integrity of the game he wishes to serve as with equal dedication for his professional calling: 'I spend Monday to Friday nicking villains. Why should I be obliged to do so when I am intending to enjoy myself on Saturday afternoons?'

(d) Finally, the analogy with road traffic legislation can never be ignored. The introduction of breathalyser legislation in the United Kingdom during October 1967, under Barbara

1988 - 1994 [Summary extracts]
Road Traffic and Transport
enactments.*

Furthermore, the draft Act was
designedly and deliberately aimed also
at a similar withdrawal of discretion
from the courts for sporting violence
off the field. The Public Order Act
1986 absorbs the exclusion order
discretion which Parliament gave to
the courts for offences under its
licensing legislation and to Scotland
during 1980. It falls short of the
mandatory jurisdiction created by
Parliament for all courts when
disposing of driving offences.

The double-barrelled purpose to
hit field and crowd violent offenders
is to target all who are convicted of
sporting violence and (save for
comparable road traffic exceptions)
withdraw any discretion from the
courts for loss of liberty by
attendance or detention centre orders.
The Court of Appeal has exhorted
against leniency by lay justices.
Offenders have ridiculed them and
publicly stated they expected severer
sentences than probation orders or
fines. The draft Act fulfils their
expectations with proposed
compulsory attendance or detention
sentence orders to be implemented at
times of sporting fixtures. In this way
the soul searching for the reasons
which cause sporting violence can be
short-circuited. Mr. Justice
Popplewell stated in his Final Report
that he had read about thirty or forty
sources on the causation of crowd
hooliganism and doubted if he was
any the wiser.

* See page 520 (infra) **Conclusion**,
Violence

1999 Proposals
Castle's imaginative enactment,
produced initially the usual
thoughtless platitudinous protests
about interference with liberties of the
subject. It led dramatically to such a
fall in accident rates, particularly
during the dangerous hours of
darkness, so that by May 1968 866
fewer people had been killed on the
road compared with the same period
in 1966 to 1967; and now 'Don't
Drink and Drive' has become the
norm thirty years later for social and
crime prevention acceptability.

(e) Accordingly, if body contact sport
within its own self-regulation is
incapable of creating sufficient
sanction against criminality to protect
its victims, is there any alternative to
converting the common law criteria
which has stood the test of time for
more than 120 years into a statutory
formula to bring home to the
community reality in lieu of the
continued mythology and
misconceptions about licence to
commit crime from the mere tip of the
iceberg illustrations cited here in each
column?

(2)   Drugs

While this chapter was being
completed the sad story outline in
Chapter 7 *Sports medicine and the*

(2)   Drugs

During an enlightened Sports Medical
Congress in Bruges, Brussels, at the
18th Annual Congress of *Brucosport*,

1988 - 1994 [Summary extracts]

law, has been sustained with a continuing controversy about the extent of the problem: the absence of hard evidence, and the reported death of the first proven fatality in Britain from anabolic steroids. The existing law laid down by Parliament in 1971 under the Misuse of Drugs Act would appear to have been overtaken by chemical and sporting ingenuity. The genetic consequences which the European horse-racing authorities have recognised in contrast to the American states, which permit racing by horses injected with Bute and Lasix to conceal pain, have been ignored for humans. The state of play in this area and the way ahead would appear to point in only one direction. A full in-depth enquiry receiving medical, chemical and legal evidence, to be commissioned by either the Sports Council, the CCPR, severally or jointly, or by Parliament or the Government with power to call witnesses.

Lord Diplock was a member of the Wolfenden Committee on Homosexual Offences and prostitution which reported in 1957 [Cmnd 247]. Inter alia it recommended legislative changes to free this practice between consenting adults from legal and social obloquy. He would tell his Middle Temple Bar students at their Cumberland Lodge wee-end seminars in Windsor Great Park, who enquired how the Committee arrived at its conclusions, that on the medical evidence they had no alternative but to recommend the amending legislation. Only by a comparable in-depth investigation can the extent and remedies for the never-decreasing drug menace to sport and the society it serves be adequately assessed and attempted to be controlled and curtailed.

1999 Proposals

in October 1999, a paper read on behalf of Professor R.E. Leach from the University of Boston, USA, on the subject of

'History of anabolic steroids and other ergogenic aids'

concluded realistically, even if pessimistically

'We will never win the fight against the doping problem.
  All we can do is to reduce it as much as possible.'

By a timely coincidence, on the same morning, Saturday 9 October, the Chief Executive of UK Athletics Dave Moorcroft explained in the *Daily Telegraph*

'We need foolproof doping control, accurate and with controlled scientific processes, and it should be scientist-based, not lawyer-based'

In that context he appears to be acknowledging my earlier proposals in the adjoining column for

'A full in-depth enquiry receiving medial, chemical and legal evidence...',

for which the analogy with the non-sporting Wolfenden Committee would appear to be as appropriate as the other one, established by the CCPR, and advocated in the Preface as pattern for current investigation.

Another contributor at the Brucosport Bruges Congress, Dr. N. Veys, from the Universtair Ziekenuis, Gent, highlighted limitations of any regulatory effect with the warning that there are some competitors' beliefs 'Better be dead than second'. This in turn echoes Michael J. Asken's historical survey noted in the Canadian Government's Dubin Report after the Ben Johnson disclosures entitled: *'Dying to Win'*

1988 - 1994 [Summary extracts]

Within sport, the various International Federations battle against fragmented differences of drug testing arrangements, litigation challenges, debatable administrative practices, and so long as national law enforcement agencies through prosecutions of civil claims for damages are discouraged from intervening, the war between offenders and authority will continue.

(3)   Commercial exploitation [summarised]

Four separate and independent areas here demand attention and action.
(1) Property development
(2) Sponsorship
(3) Television
(4) Government

1999 Proposals

Any legislative attempts at international consistency in sanctions outside the medical profession internationally is difficult to contemplate. Against that, however, a universal condemnation and expulsion from all medical, paramedical and associated activities by peer group administrators, as proposed by the British Association of Sports Medicine to Britain's General Medical Council, could at least limit the area of potential abuse accessories and advisers.

(3)   Commercial exploitation

In the years which have followed my assessment under this head, the acceleration of all four categories
(1) Playing Fields
(2) Marketing
(3) SKY Television
(4) Taxation burdens
have all interacted on each other to leave no doubt about their commercial continuity.

If one example to explain this is required, it is not necessary to do more than cite from 1988 and 1994 a citation still applicable in 1999 from Francis Wheen's *Television A History* (1985). He explained how the American ABC's input of $225 million was the largest single contribution towards the 1984 Los Angeles Olympic Games (the rest of the world's television companies contributed just $125 million); and then he wrote (page 241):

'When ABC is paying the piper so handsomely, it expects to call the tune. At the Winter Olympics in February 1984 (which ABC had acquired for $92 million) there were frequent complaints from performers and journalists about the network's heavy handed behaviour. At one point Princess Anne's private detective

1988 - 1994 [Summary extracts]

1999 Proposals

asked an ABC man to stop poking his camera in her Royal Highness' face [The Princess Royal attended in her dual capacities as the active President of the British Olympic Association and as a former competitor]. 'Listen buddy', came the reply. 'We're ABC television. We bought the Olympics. And we do what the hell we like.' This evidence was not produced to the Monopolies and Mergers Commission on the BSkyB television bid for control of Manchester United Plc. If the man who pays the piper is the one who calls the tune, those who dance with television companies should recognise the limitations of options when seeking to choose a melody. Wheen concluded this section of his History:

More recently in the same spirit, London's *Independent on Sunday* (7 November 1999) observed:

'The elite become even more beholden to their beneficent, but demanding, sponsors. The American basketball star Anfernee Hardaway, when asked whom his first loyalty was to, replied "Nike". Many of Britain's top footballers would be forgiven for answering in the same way.'

(4)   Political violation

The three examples under this head of

(1) Leicester City Council's misguided attempt to operate the so-called Gleneagles Agreement against Leicester Rugby Club, exposed in the House of Lords judgment in *Wheeler v Leicester City Council* (supra)

(2) Learie Constantine's successful challenge to hotel discrimination in *Constantine v Imperial Hotels Limited* (supra)

(4)   Political Violation

The non-sporting Prime Minister Blair's spin doctoring intrusions into the Football Association's Hoddle trouble and Manchester United's withdrawal from defending its F.A. Challenge Cup retention, during 1999, compounded his earlier endorsement at the Labour Party's Brighton conference (29 September 1997) of the photograph of Mrs Blair (nee Booth) holding aloft a replica World Cup for populist political purposes,

1988 - 1994 [Summary extracts]
(3) and Vin Swinson and Andrew
Jennings' assessment of International
sporting power politics in the *Lords
of the Rings*

have all since been and continue to be
overtaken by almost daily events.

1999 Proposals
while later, on Friday 15 October
1999 Cherie Booth, QC, reportedly
said the day before (*The Times*)

'Judges must not stray into politics
when the new Human Rights Act
comes into force'.

Pari Passu, Mrs. Blair without any
known or identifiable sporting
attributions should not stray into
sporting photocalls for her husband's
perceived or perhaps misconceived
political advantage.

4   CONCLUSION

Wither sport and the law: what
direction should sport take today?
Whatever route is taken, the Rule of
Law, on and off the field, alone can
and must guide it within a rapidly
revolving social setting whose pace
can hardly match the kaleidoscopic
changes daily imposed on the public
mind and eye. Ron Pickering's
warning in 1985 that sport need a
massive re-think is evidence by four
separate situations which emerged
nearly 40 years ago in 1957 with no
apparent inter-connection. Yet on
reflection they prove and illuminate
how sport and society and the law
have all changed at the public and
private level and point the clear way
ahead.

(1) The Wolfenden Report on
Homosexual Offences and
Prostitution (Cmnd 247) was
published.

(2) The Wolfenden Report on Sport
and the Community was
commissioned by the CCPR.

(3) The Sportsman's Book Club

4   CONCLUSION

The citation here from the earlier
editions at page 521 below in the
penultimate paragraph in the 1988-
1994 column

'The need for motoring and
techniques to protect the public to
keep pace with each engineering
development is stated here only to
emphasise the contrasts in time. The
radar trap in 1957 and the debates
after it suffice to recall the changes
since the days W G Grace and G O
Smith in 1896'

did not emphasise sufficiently the
essential distinction between Sport
and every other development in
society since its 20th century
explosion. Whether for motor vehicle
or any other industrial progression,
laws have been created to control and
regulate their activity. Sport,
however, is dead without the Rule of
Law, whether in isolation
individually, or competitively against
nature's elements or in contention
with fellow men and women.
     The sanctions for a breach of law
must vary with each different one of

1988 - 1994 Conclusion

edition of *Corinthians and Cricketers* was published.

(4) Radar was used in Britain as a speed check on motorists.

The last of these three *published* items ended with a citation from the reminiscences, *Almost Yesterday*, of the then doyen of modern sporting writers, Trevor Wignall. His columns in the *Daily Express* were woven into Fleet Street's fascinating tapestry alongside his renowned editor, Arthur Christiansen and its legendary proprietor, Lord Beaverbrook.

'Those who assert that the playing of games is not very different from what it was one hundred years ago are not far wrong...the kicking of a goal by Tom Lawton, or the heading of it, is much the same as it was when G O Smith was banging them in, and the scoring of a century by Walter Hammond calls forth the same strokes that were employed by W G Grace. Sport has undoubtedly been developed out of all recognition, but not so much in its expositions as in the finer workmanship that has been acquired, and in the enormous crowds it bails and holds'.

Those crowds are ever greater today - because of television. The kicking of a goal and scoring of a century and the strokes they require are still the same as in the days of G O Smith and W G Grace. Yet the extent to which sport has developed out of all recognition forty odd years later since the citation in 1957 is seen through its administrative structure concurrent with the changes in society generally.

G O Smith and W G Grace were at the peak of their powers in 1896. Dr W G Grace captained England against Australia led by G H S Trott in all three Test Matches played that

1999 Conclusion

Hailsham's hereogenous list. The commercial pressures have distorted attitudes world-wide for preserving that Rule of Law within sport, and attempting to do justice within it.

Looking back on the 1988-1994 and HOW TO DEAL with the Four Vices, an overriding concern for the Rules of Law generally did not target with sufficient precision what the intervening five years since the last edition appear to present arguable potential solutions for each of them.

1.   *Violence*

Parliamentary conversion into statute form what the law has recognised since *R v Bradshaw* in 1878, and the Criminal Injuries Compensation Board has advocated in substance since 1980 as remedial action in the criminal courts for protecting victims of criminal misconduct in the name of a game. Only through legislation via the statute book will the true message be heard and learnt.

2.   *Drugs*

Every professional body associated with drugs should follow on from Canadian Government Dubin Commission's Recommendations and consider expulsion from membership of every practitioner found associated with any sports-related drug offence. In substance this follows the proposals by the British Association of Sports Medicine at its 1998 Annual Congress to the General Medical Council.

3.   *Commercial Exploitation*

Financial progress is inevitable for benefiting sport and recreation at every level. When it appears to conflict with the true meaning of sport at either the public

1988 - 1994 Conclusion

summer. G O Smith as an undergraduate from Oxford University was England's centre-forward alongside a mixture of his fellow Corinthians and the leading professionals of the day in all three home internationals which alone were played at that time. Against the auld enemy Scotland, at Parkhead, Celtic Park, Glasgow, he was one of six Corinthians chosen with five professionals three months before he hit a memorable 132 in Oxford's fourth innings to help win the Varsity match against Cambridge.

1896 was also a landmark year for the area of law which touches the hem of the majority of citizens universally and with uniformity: driving. Two distinguished Professors, D W Elliott and the late Harry Street explained in their survey *Road Accidents*, published in 1968:

'The history of the criminal law about driving shows a gradual development from the range of offences provided by the law as it existed in a pre-motoring age, a range which, as one would expect, was ill adapted to deal with the new phenomenon of highways crowded with powerful and fast motor vehicles.... Until 1896 it was an offence to drive a horseless carriage at more than 4 mph outside town and 2 mph inside them.'

The need for motoring law and techniques to protect the public to keep pace with each engineering development is stated here only to emphasise the contrasts in time. The radar trap in 1957 and the debates after it suffice to recall the degrees of change since the day of W G Grace and G O Smith in 1896.

If society's conscience towards criminally fouling footballers of all codes had kept pace with its readiness

1999 Conclusion

entertainment or grass roots levels, then legitimate vigilance and opposition should be sustained at every point of the legal compass. In this way the Monopolies and Mergers Commission Report concluded in early 1999 after well-publicised hostile evidence

'We were unable to identify any public interest benefits from the proposed merger. We therefore conclude that the proposed merger between BSkyB and Manchester United may be expected to operate against the public interest';

and at the grass roots level in the same geographical area the Oldham Metropolitan Borough Council is still locked in battle with objectors to its proposed sale, even under the Cy Prés system with the Charities legal structure, of the historic Clayton Playing Fields. [*Oldham BC v A-G* (supra) *Oldham Evening Chronicle* 22 November 1999]

4.   *Political Violation*

Correspondingly, a comparable vigilance should be sustained for gratuitous interference contrary to sporting interests of the kind already identified to have been manifested by Prime Minister Blair

(1) in the Hoddle trouble with the Football Association and

(2) his acquiescence in the persuasion evidenced by his junior Minister, Tony Banks' letter to Sir Roland Smith for withdrawal from the challenges to Manchester United's retention of the F.A. Challenge Cup as holders of the trophy in circumstances disputed by FIFA for allegedly benefiting England's 2006 World Cup prospects

1988 - 1994 Conclusion

to pressurise Parliament into action against foul driving and drunk and drugged motorists, then many more international footballers (and perhaps a few coaches and managers and directors as aiders and abettors) would have preceded David Bishop into the dock of different criminal courts throughout the land. By their example Bishop might have been warned to avoid the act which so many have committed before to so many, but for which so few have been punished by the courts, as they could and should have been for violation of sport as well as the law. When a distinguished rugby administrator complained that the decision to prosecute Bishop did more harm to rugby football than the punch which set the law in motion it was necessary to point out through the correspondence columns of the *Daily Telegraph* that if the complainant was not in contempt of court, and it might have been, it certainly was in contempt of sport.

Sport needs all of the associated professions, for whom this book identifies it is intended, as explained in the Introduction if it is to preserve its true integrity and identity in a rapidly dominating commercial market forces world. Lawyers to free it from the feudal grip of administrators in the *Banks*, *Eastham*, *Nagle*, *Packer* and *Welsh FA* line of litigation. Schoolmaster leaders to point the way in the modern traditions created ideally by Rous, Follows, Altham and their successors, to teach those who have to be reminded from time to time or throughout their lives of the basic difference between right and wrong. Doctors to heal the wounded from foul play or natural causes in the tradition of Tucker's insight into Compton's knee-cap problem from

1999   Conclusion

(3) with additional acquiescence in the decision of the Department of Education and Employment to dilute competitive school games in the new national curriculum between the age groups 14-16

(4) and continued appointments of junior ministers in the Department of Culture Media and Arts alongside 14 other different Government departments concerned with sport (see Chapter 2, *Progressive Perspective*)

FINAL WHISTLE

For those who find the intrusion of the Law in Sport itself an evil of necessity, no harm is done to recall how a celebrated Lord Chief Justice between the two World Wars of 1914 and 1939, Lord Hewart, explained in a different context from these pages in his Introduction to Sir Alan Herbert's *Misleading Cases* 'aversion to law and the courts of law is naturally strong in the human mind'. Yet without the Rule of Law to protect victims of its breaches, whether within or without Sport, anarchy and chaos prevail. Correspondingly whenever the less agreeable Americanism than Oliver Wendel Holmes' classic philosophy,

'The Life of the Law is not logic: it is experience',

is recalled,

'Nice guys finish last....'

it is a salutary experience to recall how each of the two previous editions in 1988 and 1994 have ended, as I do on this occasion, with an earlier letter to Corinthians, than my own, which began this text:

'Know ye not that they which run a race all,

1988 - 1994 Conclusion

his rugby days with England; and financiers to benefit sport as well as themselves in the style of Barclays investment in the eccentric finances of professional football to catch up with the legacy left by the member of the family associated with their Gosling's Branch in Fleet Street, perpetuating the memory of another creative schoolmaster amateur international footballer alongside the outstanding professionals of his day, Arthur Dunn. Above all else sport needs a revival of Lord Hailsham's awareness, cited on the opening page, of the absence of a 'coherent body of doctrine, perhaps even a philosophy of government encouragement'.

So, in the end, we return to the beginning. Whither Sport. Whither Sport and the Law? In this Chapter 15 *Whither Sport and the Law?* in the first edition I wrote:

'Has the time come now to move on from the need spelt out by Lord Hailsham of 'a focal point under a Minister' to beyond a Parliamentary Under Secretary with 80 per cent of his time allocated to matters other than sport as evidenced by the former Junior Minister, Mr. Richard Tracey, MP to the House of Commons Committee cited above. Furthermore, has the time come to transfer the 20 per cent of time available for sport away from the Department of the Environment?'

1999 Final Whistle

But one receiveth the prize?
So run, that ye may obtain.
And every man that striveth for the mastery is temperate in all things. Now they do it to obtain a corruptible crown; but we an incorruptible'

[Corinthians: First Letter *from* St. Paul: Chapter 9. Verse 24-25]

Appendices

Contents

How It All Began

Edward Grayson

During early days of practice at the Chancery Bar from Chambers in Lincoln's Inn, before departing to the Temple, I prepared for publication as *Corinthians and Cricketers* what had been my Second World War schoolboy correspondence with England's leading centre-forward at the century's turn, G O Smith, the Gary Lineker of his day. 'G O' like W G Grace, known by his initials and also as 'Jo' Smith, retired after 21 England appearances, many as captain, with only three home international matches played each season from 1894–1901, to become headmaster of the future King William III's preparatory school, Ludgrove in Berkshire, on the death of its founder, Arthur Dunn. C B Fry contributed the Foreword, and research for the two games in the book produced the legal puzzle and paradox that while professional cricketers' benefit matches were tax-free, professional footballers' (and parsons' Easter offerings) were subject to tax.

Encouraged by the then FA Secretary, Sir Stanley Rous, two articles were written for analysing and attempting to solve the puzzle. The first appeared in the *FA Bulletin* for April 1953, while the joint Oxbridge team, Pegasus, were winning the FA Amateur Cup for the second time in three years before 100,000 at Wembley Stadium. The second was published in *Rating and Income Tax* for 8 October 1953 Volume 46, p 652. They are the catalyst for what has followed in a fragmented fashion down the years, to arrive at this third Butterworth edition.

The F.A. Bulletin : April : 1953

The Club and the Player

No 7 TAXATION OF PLAYER'S BENEFITS

By Edward Grayson

The author was an enthusiastic amateur player up to a few years ago when injury at Oxford University put an end to his playing career. He has made a special study of this vexed question of players' benefits, and this article helps to explain the position.

One of the most puzzling problems and anomalies concerning the administration and finance of British sport is the old chestnut—why should a cricketer playing for his county receive a benefit tax free, whereas a footballer's benefit is subject to the full rate of tax? This survey shows why, and considers whether the problem is worth puzzling over again.

It may be said without rancour that before and, indeed, after the First World War, the professional county cricketer, if not drawn from, certainly moved in a different social sphere from that of his association football colleague. The fusion of amateur and professional at soccer had in the main been checked by the 'split' from 1907 until 1914. Only when Herbert Chapman made Highbury an extension of London's fashionable West-End did professional football become *de rigueur*; and C B Fry reflected the change by 1939 when in his autobiography, *Life Worth Living*, he said, 'When the Arsenal players stay at the Grand Hotel at Brighton you would not distinguish between them and the generality of other leisured young men.'*

The Case of James Seymour

During the 1920's, however, the position was little different from before 1914; and when James Seymour, the famous Kent batsman, was assessed

---

*   This was reaffirmed for me recently by the former Arsenal goalkeeper, George Swindin, and later player-manager at Peterborough United at a time when the club captain Norman Rigby's tax appeal to the Special Commissioners of the Inland Revenue succeeded in discharging the local income tax inspector's assessments on his benefit match proceeds (see Chapter 1, *Genesis*). 'The old dears at the Grand Hotel lined up to welcome us back for our cup-tie training visits, and on our departures said how much they had looked forward to our return next year.' The contrast with some, at least, of their more recent successors need hardly be stressed here.

under the Income Tax Act of 1918 in the sum which represented the gate money from his benefit match at Canterbury of nearly £1,000 after Kent played Hampshire in 1920, he appealed to the Commissioners for the General Purposes of the Income Tax Acts. They discharged the assessment at the hearing in 1924. The Inspector of Taxes, through the Crown, appealed to the High Court, and in 1926, Mr Justice Rowlatt, a distinguished income-tax Judge, upheld the Commissioners' decision. Still not satisfied, the Inspector proceeded to the Court of Appeal, two of whose members against one dissentient found in favour of the Crown. Seymour, however, was being guided by a former Harrow batsman against Eton, who is now President of the Surrey County Cricket Club as well as Minister of Labour in the present Government, Sir Walter Monckton, QC; and in 1927, Mr W Monckton and Mr A M Latter, KC, together had little difficulty in persuading the House of Lords by a majority of four to one to reverse the decision of the Court of Appeal and restore the order of Mr Justice Rowlatt. Cricketers no longer were to pay income-tax on their benefit monies, and because their Lordship's conclusions must be the yardstick by which any attempt is made to re-examine the footballers' position, they may be conveniently summarised here.

Personal Gift or Emolument?

The liability to tax in both cases arises under Schedule E to the Income Tax Acts whereby 'Tax ... shall be charged in respect of every public office or employment of profit ...' Rule I applicable to this schedule (which is now found in the Ninth Schedule to the Act of 1952) declares that under it Tax 'shall be annually charged on every person having or exercising an office or employment of profit mentioned in this Schedule ... in respect of all salaries, fees, wages, perquisites or profits whatsoever therefrom for the year of assessment ...' The Lord Chancellor, Viscount Cave, considered these words to 'include all payments made to the holder of an office or employment as such'—that is to say, *by way of remuneration for his services*, though such payments may be voluntary—but they do not include a mere gift or present (such as a testimonial) which is made to him on personal grounds and *not by way of payment for his services*. The question to be answered is, as Mr Justice Rowlatt put it, 'Is it in the end a personal gift or is it remuneration?' If the latter, it is subject to the tax; if the former, it is not.

> 'Applying this test', said The Lord Chancellor, 'I do not doubt that in the present case the net proceeds of the benefit match should be regarded as a personal gift and not as income from the Appellant's (Seymour's) employment. The terms of his employment did not entitle him to a benefit, though they provided that if a benefit were

granted the Committee of the Club should have a voice in the application of the proceeds.'

Lord Carson concluded similarly. Lord Phillimore said, 'I do not feel compelled by any ... authorities to hold that an employer cannot make a voluntary gift to his employee without rendering the gift liable to taxation under Schedule E'; and Viscount Dunedin declared, 'When I think of this little nest egg ... being treated, the whole sum, as income, honestly, had it not been for the fact that honourable Judges, whose opinions I respect, have come to another conclusion, I would have thought that contention preposterous.'

Nearly four years ago, in the House of Commons during its debate upon Footballers' Benefits in the course of the Finance Bill, Mr Justice Donovan, who was then the Member for Leicester East, added to these last words which he cited by saying, 'I also feel that when a footballer, at the end of five years, gets a lump sum as benefit, then it is a little hard to treat it all as the income of one year'. Why is it so treated? Because of a decision of Mr Justice Rowlatt in the High Court a week after the House of Lords judgment in the Seymour Case; and subsequently because of the judgment of Mr Justice Lawrence fourteen years later in 1941.

Question of Agreement with Clubs

The benefit which George Harrison received from Everton in 1924 differed materially in one particular from that existing today. For the Club had expressly agreed in writing that subject to the Football League's consent he should receive a benefit of £650 upon the fulfilment of certain conditions. Today such an express undertaking rarely occurs. When Harrison appealed in 1925 against the tax assessment on this sum, it was contended on his behalf by 'The National Taxpayers' Defence Agency' that the amount in question was not annual profit or recurring income or earnings of office in the sense of the Taxing Acts; rather was it a payment made once only and that its recurrence was impossible; and that further, it was not a payment for services rendered, but compensation for loss of office! Upon this further contention the appeal was allowed.

In the High Court, Harrison did not appear and was not represented. Mr Justice Rowlatt commenced his judgment by saying, 'In this case I am a good deal embarrassed by the fact that I have had nobody to argue against the contention of the Crown'; and he ended by holding, 'The payment is not a compensation for loss of employment; it is not like damages or anything of that sort ... He (Harrison) has earned this just as much as he earned anything else in the service of the club, and I think the appeal must be allowed.'

At some time after this decision, the written promise and guarantee in writing which Harrison had received from Everton was dropped from most contracts. The then Rule 9 of the Football League Regulations had become by the outbreak of the Second World War Regulation 61, and is today numbered 45. Under it 'Clubs may enter into agreements with players after three playing seasons' continuous service providing for a benefit after five playing seasons' continuous service'; and provision is also made for a 'benefit match arranged to augment a benefit for a player and collections'. Further, by the old Regulation 63, now 47, when a player is transferred by a club, the club may pay him a percentage to be worked out in accordance with the regulation of the amount which the club had guaranteed, or would have been likely to guarantee, him for a benefit.

Appeals Against Assessments

Following these provisions, the Football League in 1936 gave their consent to Manchester City paying £200 to F W Corbett as an accrued share of benefit on his transfer to Lincoln City; £650 to William Dale as a benefit after five years' continuous service; and to Notts County for the purpose of arranging a benefit friendly match for Alfred Feebury which brought in £350. Appeals against assessments were lodged and heard in 1939. Dale's and Corbett's were dismissed in Manchester, their benefits being held to be 'wages earned as a professional footballer in the service of the club'. Feebury's in Nottingham was dismissed upon the ground that the monies formed 'part of the Appellant's emoluments of profits of employment'. This time the taxpayers challenged the Commissioners in the High Court. The war was then at its blackest in 1941, but learned Counsel appeared on behalf of all the players. Nevertheless, after a three day hearing, Mr Justice Lawrence dismissed all the appeals with costs. But what were his reasons? He observed,

'As the Cases stated (by the Commissioners), and the Football League regulations indicate, the payments, though *not* obligatory, are expected, are generally asked for, and are usually accorded ... In my opinion, in face of the terms of regulations 61 and 63, and the facts stated in the Cases as to the understanding amongst professional football players, it is impossible to hold that any of the three payments to the Appellants in question was not paid in respect of, and as remuneration for, the Appellant's employment as a football player ... The only difference between the present case and *Davis v Harrison* is that in that case a formal agreement under regulation 61 had been entered into. But that agreement was not acted upon, and the case is really on all fours with Corbett's case'.

But surely that agreement in Harrison's case was acted upon? For he received his monies under the written undertaking.

Summary of Position

Then, is it true these payments have the expectation implied in the judgment? Last year's Report of the Committee of Investigation appointed by the Minister of Labour and National Service to inquire into a difference in the Football Industry expressly showed in Paragraph 46 that no more than 14 per cent, out of 3,200–3,500 registered players for the years 1948–51 received benefits.

Finally, what were the 'facts stated in the Cases as to the understanding amongst professional football players'? There was a reference to the *likelihood* of benefit after five years' service, or an accrued share thereof if transferred before; about *half* the number of players transferred were alleged to receive a benefit or accrued share thereof on transfer; Corbett was given to understand upon joining his Club that 130 first team matches in five years would procure him a benefit, despite no formal agreement; and Feebury's Case mentioned 'large numbers of payments made to footballers playing under the League rules on transfer or otherwise. This fact is well known to all footballers who are not backward in asking for payment'.

Well, there it is. Perhaps it was just as well that Mr Justice Lawrence was never challenged in a higher Court on the Dale and Corbett cases. Yet how a distinction can be made between the facts and circumstances in the Feebury and Seymour benefits is unexplained in his judgment or elsewhere.

'These cases are always difficult to decide,' observed Mr Justice Rowlatt in commencing his judgment in Seymour's Case, 'and not so the less because it is very difficult in my judgment to draw a line between questions of law and questions of fact.' Certainly the law is stated clearly enough in the Schedule to the Acts and in the words of its rule. Of these, Lord Carson said in Seymour's Case, 'They are plain words, of no technical import, and, in my opinion, no previous authorities can assist, as each case must depend upon the particular facts proved'. Whether Mr Justice Lawrence's conclusions coincide today with the particular facts of footballers' benefits only those who are parties to their payments can know. For those facts alone can prove today whether a player's benefit is a personal gift or remuneration; and whether the Commissioners and perhaps the Courts should have to puzzle once more.

1   Six months later the *Rating and Income Tax* article for 8 October 1953, reproduced here verbatim, extended in more formal style what had appeared in the FA Bulletin for April 1953. It is the acorn from which this third edition oak tree of 615 pages has grown. It also explains how Sport and the Law can develop if the appropriate facts are recognised, identified and threaded constructively and progressively to the relevant and applicable law, notwithstanding earlier errors and omissions when earlier assessments have ignored or failed to sport the ball.

TAXATION OF FOOTBALLERS' BENEFITS: 8 OCTOBER 1953

By EDWARD GRAYSON, MA (OXON), Barrister-at-Law

On the 24th July of this year [1953] awards were published by the Industrial Disputes Tribunal, to which the Ministry of Labour and National Service under the Industrial Disputes Order, 1951, had referred a claim by the professional Association Football Players' and Trainers' Union 'for certain specified terms and conditions of employment'. The tribunal, rejecting a claim that the benefit moneys and accrued shares of benefit moneys payable to a player on his transfer from one club to another should be made obligatory, observed: 'it was the union's view that all players should as of right be entitled to benefit payments for meritorious service'. Presumably the submissions of the Football Association and the Football League were accepted, viz., 'that payments of benefits are the reward for meritorious service and that to make them compulsory would be a negation of that principle'.

Sixteen months earlier in March, 1952, the report was published (HMSO 9d.) of a committee of investigation appointed by the Ministry of Labour under the Conciliation Act, 1896, to inquire into a difference in the football industry. Paragraph 46 contained figures showing that no more than 14 per cent out of 3,200 to 3,500 registered professional footballers for the years 1948–51 received payments of benefit moneys. Nevertheless, for over a quarter of a century the courts have held that the obviously non-compulsory and gratuitous payments to professional footballers 'for meritorious service' are taxable, while the corresponding payments made to professional cricketers are not. How this arises typifies the refinements distinguishing similar circumstances under income tax law.

WRITTEN AGREEMENTS

The liability to tax in both cases arises under Schedule E to the Income Tax Acts, Section 156 of the Income Tax Act, 1952, which deals with Schedule E, provides: 'Tax under this schedule shall be charged in respect of every public office or employment of profit.' This was formerly the heading to Schedule E to the Income Tax Act, 1918. Rule 1 of sch 9 to the Income Tax Act, 1952 (formerly r 1 of the rules applicable to Schedule E under the Income Tax Act, 1918) provides: 'Tax under Schedule E shall be annually charged on every person having or exercising an office or employment of profit mentioned in Schedule E ... in respect of all salaries, fees, wages, perquisites or profits whatsoever therefrom for the year of assessment ...' So when George Harrison received £650 from and in pursuance of a written agreement with the Everton Club by way of an accrued share of benefit on his transfer, Rowlatt J, restored an assessment under Schedule E which the General Commissioner had discharged, observing: 'He has earned this just as much as he has earned anything else in the service of the club' (*Davis v Harrison* (1927) 11 TC 707, 723).

Subsequently most contracts dropped that written agreement. Under reg 45 of the Football League, formerly reg 61 and previously reg 9: 'Clubs may enter into agreements with players after three playing seasons' continuous service providing for a benefit after five playing seasons' continuous service'; and provision is also made for a 'benefit match arranged to augment a benefit for a player and collections'. Further, by reg 47, previously reg 63, when a player is transferred by a club, the club *may* pay him a percentage proportionate to the amount which the club had guaranteed him, or would have been likely to guarantee him, for a benefit.

ABSENCE OF WRITTEN AGREEMENTS

Accordingly, the Football League consented in 1936 to Manchester City paying £200 to F W Corbett as an accrued share of benefit on his transfer to Lincoln City, and £650 to William Dale as a benefit after five years' continuous service; and to Notts County's arranging a benefit friendly match for Alfred Feebury, the net proceeds of which were made up to £350 by the club under a voluntary guarantee. In each case the payment was assessed under Schedule E, not in one sum, but as arising evenly over the five-yearly period following reg 63. In the cases of Corbett and Dale the General Commissioners held the amounts received to be taxable as 'wages earned as professional footballers in the service of the club'; and in Feebury's case as moneys forming 'part of the appellant's emoluments or profits of employment'.

In *Corbett v Duff; Dale v Duff; Feebury v Abbott* (1941), 34 R & IT 189, Lawrence J, upheld these findings. He first applied the principles stated by the House of Lords in *Cooper v Blakiston* (1909), 5 TC 347, 355, and *Reed v Seymour* (1927), 11 TC 630, 646: 'namely, that if the payment though voluntary is remuneration for the office or employment, it is taxable; but if it is personal in the sense that it is given to the person not as a holder of

office or employment, but as a personal testimonial, it is not'. Then he held:
'in face of the terms of regs 61 and 63, and the facts stated in the cases as to
the understanding amongst professional football players, it is impossible to
hold that any of the three payments to the appellants in question was not
paid in respect of, and as remuneration for, the appellant's employment as
a football player ... The only difference between the present case and *Davis
v Harrison* is that in that case a formal agreement under reg 61 had been
entered into. But that agreement was not acted upon and the case is really
on all fours with Corbett's case'.

DISTINCTION FROM SEYMOUR'S CASE?

Yet that agreement in *Harrison*'s case, if not directly acted on, certainly
caused the payment of £650, as Rowlatt J, pointed out in his judgment at
p 721. Further, whatever may be 'the facts stated in the cases as to the
understanding amongst professional football players' before 1939, they do
not reflect the position of 86 per cent of the players employed between
1948 and 1951; and how a distinction can be made between the facts and
circumstances in the Feebury and Seymour benefits is unexplained in the
judgment of Lawrence J, or elsewhere.

In *Reed v Seymour* the House of Lords, at p 645 et seq, a week before
the decision in *Davis v Harrison*, reversed the Court of Appeal and restored
Rowlatt J's order. This upheld the General Commissioners' findings that
the Kent batsman, James Seymour, should not pay tax on the sum
representing the gate money from his benefit of nearly £1,000 after Kent
played Hampshire in 1920. Viscount Cave, LC, said (p 646): 'The question
to be answered is, as Rowlatt, J, put it: "Is it in the end a personal gift or is
it remuneration?" If the latter, it is subject to the tax; if the former, it is not.
Applying this test, I do not doubt that in the present case the net proceeds
of the benefit match should be regarded as a personal gift and not as income
from the appellant's employment. The terms of his employment did not
entitle him to a benefit, though they provided that if a benefit were granted
the committee of the club should have a voice in the application of the
proceeds.'

CONCLUSIONS

Undoubtedly, *Harrison*'s terms of employment did entitle him to a benefit,
but it is open to doubt whether those terms before Lawrence, J, likewise
entitled the players concerned to a benefit. Certainly today the position is
completely reversed, with the players attempting to complete their terms
of employment by expressly requesting, in vain, that their benefits should

be made obligatory. In the quarter of a century since *Reed v Seymour* and *Davis v Harrison* the facts surrounding footballers' benefits have completely changed. Even allowing for Lawrence J's conclusions, it would appear from the facts declared by the Ministry of Labour's recent reports that their proper presentation before the Commissioners and, if necessary, the courts, would have a greater opportunity than ever before of destroying the distinction between the two kinds of players' benefits, a distinction which merits Viscount Dunedin's opinion, in *Reed v Seymour* (p 647), of the purported taxation of cricketers' benefits: 'Preposterous'.

2   House of Commons: 26 November 1953
Within two months a House of Commons question to the then Financial Secretary to the Treasury, on 26 November, crystallised the issues with the following succinct exchanges [Hansard: Vol 521 26 November 1953: Cols 504–505/House of Commons Oral Answers]

Cricketers' Benefits (Tax [col 504])

Mr Hamilton: asked the Chancellor of the Exchequer if he is aware that the benefits payable to professional footballers are liable to Income Tax, whilst benefits paid to professional cricketers are not so liable; and what steps he contemplates to remedy this anomaly.

Mr Boyd-Carpenter: The discrimination is not, as the hon. Member suggests, between cricketers and footballers. It is between on the one hand, payments to either cricketers or footballers which accrue by reason of the terms of the employment and are taxable, and, on the other hand, payments which accrue by way of gift of personal testimonial and are not taxable.

Mr Hamilton: Is the Minister aware that if a footballer gets a benefit after five years' service he gets £750 which, after taxation, comes to rather less than £500, and that a professional cricketer, who may get £12,000 or £13,000, receives it free of tax? Does the Minister say that that is not an anomalous situation, however he might defend it? Would he ask his right hon. Friend to have this matter looked into further before next April?

Mr Boyd-Carpenter: [Col 505] It depends in every case, regardless of which sport is concerned, on whether the man gets his benefit as part of the terms of his employment, in which case it is as properly taxable as any other part of his income, or whether he gets it as a gift, in which case it is quite properly, under the present law, not taxable.

Mr K Thompson: Is the Minister prepared to distinguish, for the benefit of the House, between the uncontracted, benefits of the cricketer and the receipts of a vicar at the time of the Easter offerings?

Mr Boyd-Carpenter: There is nothing about vicars in this Question.

3   The Sequel

(1)   Six years later, as explained earlier in the main text, a tax test case experiment to align the two disciplines operated by Peterborough United, then outside the Football League, resulted in the Special Commissioners of Income Tax acceptance of the thrust of the two articles by adapting for professional footballers the cricketing circumstances. This was exclusion *from the terms of employment*, as explained above of any benefit provisions, and more readily capable of facilitation in the then Midland Counties Football League regulations, where Peterborough then played. They also resulted in life-long friendships until death with the late James Guthrie, then Chairman of the then Professional Footballers' and Trainers' Union (now the PFA), and the first shots fired to establish restraint of trade under professional footballers standard form of contract in *Aldershot v Banks* (1955) *Aldershot News* 4th November, a Group Accident Insurance scheme for professional footballers affirmed in *Alder v Moore* (1961) [1961] 2 QB 59, [1961] 1 All ER 1, and also with the Pegasus founder and future FA Council chairman, Sir Harold Thompson. Attempts to establish his romantic Oxbridge creation of the 1950s as a sporting education charity were rejected by the Revenue and unchallenged solely through lack of funds. It was not fought as it could have been, with encouragement from the New South Wales Equity court confirmation as charitable of a bequest to the Sydney University Rugby Club (1957) in *Kearins v Kearins* SR 286 (NSW), until after registration of the FA Youth Trust Deed two decades later in 1971. After an eight year battle against the Revenue through all court levels the House of Lords in *IRC v McMullan* [1981] AC 1, overruled the Revenue, the High Court, a Court of Appeal majority and confirmed the Charity Commissioners Registration of what had been claimed in vain nearly thirty years earlier, for Pegasus.

(2)   Finally, a gap left by the House of Lords in *IRC v McMullan* was filled by a later Lords judicial decision from Scotland in *Guild v Inland Revenue Commissioners* [1992] 2 AC 310 on a successful appeal from the First Division of the Court of Session as the Court of Exchequer in Scotland. It held that a testator's bequest of his estate

'to the town council of North Berwick for the use in connection with the sports centre in North Berwick or some similar purpose in connection with sport' fell validly within the true construction of Section 1(2)(a) of the Recreational Charities Act 1958 and 'the provision of facilities for recreation ... if provided in the interests of social welfare', under section 1(1).

(3)   For tax purposes, the technical English law of charities was to be imported into Scots law for tax purposes; and it is noteworthy that the scourge of *Re Nottage* : *Jones v Palmer* [1895] 2 Ch 649, and its century old diversion from reality with its yacht-racing prize cup, was never cited in argument or speeches when this landmark decision in *Guild* appeared. Its reference in a recent House of Lords debate during the summer of 1999 on sports-related issues demonstrates how far this crucial and developing area of Sport and the Law must travel to be understood by those who purport to practice it.

School Sport
(1) Sport in the Curriculum

Dr Mary Malecka

*PhD education psychology and curriculum; practising
barrister; member Education Law Association schools sub-
committee; author OECD book on integration of
handicapped in schools*

The grass-roots of sport are parched and shrivelled through lack of good
provision from the top. There has been no will at government level in recent
years to save sport in the state system of education. Notwithstanding a
'Minister for Sport', there is no coordination between ministries as to the
whole picture of decline in the availability of physical education to children
and youth.

The Minister for Sport is not in the Cabinet. Autumn of 1999 welcomed
a former physical education teacher as the first woman Sports Minister in
Britain. As an Under Secretary of State within the Department of Culture
Media and Sport, Kate Hoey has no direct input into policy to do with
physical education in schools which is in the hands of the Department for
Education and Employment, whose Secretary of State *is* in the Cabinet.

1 NO REQUIREMENT FOR GAMES FOR CHILDREN 14 AND OVER

The worst aspect and starting point of concern for the fate of opportunities
for young people to participate in sport or make it a career, is the summer
1999 proposal of the Secretary of State for Education and Employment,
based on short sighted advice from the Qualification and Curriculum
Authority (QCA),[1] that games are no longer to be compulsory in schools
for children aged 14 and over:

---

1 A government quango set up in the mid 1990s to replace another quango, the
Schools Curriculum and Assessment Authority. Both organisations directed by
Nicholas Tate.

'At key stage 4 [14-16 year olds] ... that games activities become one option rather than a requirement..., '[2]

thus demoting games in the battle for funds and space in the timetable with the inevitable result that this age group, at least in the state sector, will be able to develop neither interest nor skills in the very games they might otherwise find will enrich their lives as adults, either as amateurs or professionals.

As a result of this change, there are now to be no collective or team sports on the list of compulsory physical education activities for 14 to 16 year olds. All activities are to be individual sports for this age group. It is inconceivable that such a state of affairs is for the educational good of the children, but as there is no reason with evidence in support given by the Secretary of State for this decision to make games a mere option for this age group, one can only wonder.

Sport continues to slip out of the lives of children attending state schools especially. Less so in the private sector where the tradition of a healthy mind in a healthy body continues to be appreciated and enjoyed, and the provision of good varied physical activities including games remains strong.

Prep schools have access to on average more than 18 acres of playing fields per school and their older pupils have on average five-and-a-half hours of sport and PE per week.[3] Leeds Grammar on its new site has a 25-metre indoor pool with seating for 200 spectators, a vast sports hall and extensive playing fields. Charterhouse has recently added an athletics stadium, swimming pool, floodlit all-weather surface, sports centre, and nine-hole golf course to its existing cricket squares and football and rugby pitches.

The present government says it seeks to reduce health irregularities within the population. It has, however, utterly ignored in this context the health implications of the irregularities between private and state schools insofar as time given to and provision for healthy physical exercise at school is concerned. The health implications of such irregularities of provision of physical education in schools is not stated, as it ought to be, as being on the Health Minister's agenda.[4]

---

2   *The review of the national curriculum in England . The Secretary of State's proposals,* page 10. May-July 1999. Published by the Qualifications and Curriculum Authority and the Department for Education and Employment. Copyright by the QCA. All QCA recommendations based on this review were accepted by the Secretary of State in September 1999.

3   *All-Round Excellence ,* Incorporated Association of Preparatory Schools, May 1999.

4   Baroness Hoffman. Hansard 6 July 1999 412 LD 112 page 1, para 2.

2   TWO HOURS PHYSICAL EXERCISE PER WEEK

In the Summer of 1999 the government proposed revisions to physical education in the national curriculum.[5] The proposals state with apparent pride that

'Most schools offer pupils a significant level of physical activity both within and outside the national curriculum. In the *best* schools this amounts to *two hours a week*. Both the Secretaries of State for Education and for Culture, Media and Sport support and encourage this as an *aspiration* for all schools.'[6] (author's emphasis)

That anyone can seriously consider that 2 hours a week at most of physical activity within and outside of the school curriculum should be sufficient to ensure the well being of children aged 5 to 16 is hard to believe (see in contrast the French example below). Even worse, this pathetic 2 hours per week provision is meant to be an *aspiration* for all schools.

It has been the case for some time that physical activity in the school curriculum of the state sector has been declining to as little as 2 hours or even less per week in total; but to be *content* that 2 hours is the best that schools should aspire to is to ignore the sad state of sport in schools today.

It is *both* the Secretary of State for Education and Employment (responsible for the national curriculum) and the Secretary of State for Culture, Media and Sport (in whose department Kate Hoey became an Under-Secretary in the early Autumn of 1999) who support 2 hours physical activity per week for children as an aspiration for all schools. Soon after her appointment the new Sports Minister indicated that 2 hours is a *minimum* in her view, and that school sport is a priority for improvement.

Evidence from OFSTED[7] inspections in schools in 1998 of the number of hours spent teaching PE in primary and secondary schools showed that on average children have between 1 hour 15 minutes and 2 hours teaching of physical education per week:[8]

ages 5-7	1 hour 20 minutes
ages 7-11	1 hour 35 minutes
ages 11-14	2 hours
ages 14-16	1 hour 15 minutes

5   National curriculum introduced in Education Reform Act 1988 and now contained in consolidatory Education Act 1996 ss 353-355. Proposed revisions to the national curriculum were announced by the Secretary of State in September 1999. See also Hyam, *Law of Education* 1998, Sweet and Maxwell, for summary of legislation.

6   QCA review, *op cit supra*, at pages 9-10.

7   Office of Standards in Education; replaced Her Majesty's Schools Inspectorate.

8   Hansard 17 December 1998. Set out in *Report*, journal of the Association of Teachers and Lecturers, March 1999, page 5.

The OFSTED study found that teacher training in how to teach physical education is unsatisfactory in that it often has only a 'tenuous link' with the trainees' later work in schools. Some student teachers in the primary sector have only had seven-and-a-half hours' training in how to teach physical education. A perusal through teacher training manuals in a large specialist bookshop shows a surprising absence of entries in the indexes to PE, sport, games, teamwork and competition. Teacher training for sport and physical education appears to need attention if sport in schools is to improve.

Some state primary schools offer as little as 12 hours physical education *per year* to their pupils according to a consortium of school sports bodies investigating the reduction of hours of physical education in primary schools who seek to follow government curriculum guidelines.[9] This is in stark contrast to the physical education entitlement in the national curriculum in state sector schools in France, which provides young children with at least 4 hours per week of physical education. (See below.)

The Secretary of State's proposals for change in the physical education curriculum in the autumn of 1999 are an expression of Governmental lack of concern for the struggle to provide sport at the grass-roots in state sector schools.

In *Ethics, Injuries and the Law in Sports Medicine* [10] Edward Grayson reviews the case law on sports injury to children, placing it in the context of research classifying kinds of sports injuries to children and reasons for those injuries, set against the World Medical Association's Guideline criteria as to good practice where children participate in sport at competitive level. It is quite incredible that anyone familiar with this data could believe that within a maximum of 2 hours total a week of physical education in school it is to possible for children to learn good 'health and safety' practice when participating in sport.

There is too little entitlement to sport and physical education in the state sector of schools in England to ensure the good health of children and ensure that those who wish to make sport a livelihood or serious amateur pastime will be able to do so.

The relationship to good health and regular physical exercise and sport is only tenuously present in the physical education aspect of the school curriculum. Two hours per week at best are available to children for *all* aspects of physical education both within and outside of the national curriculum and within this time the only teaching they will get in school as to the healthy benefits of physical exercise must be fitted in. The human health aspect of the science curriculum says nothing at all about exercise other than to children aged 4-7.

9   Speednet consortium as reported in the *Evening Standard*, London, 21 August 1999, under the heading "P.E. cut at 1 in 3 primary schools".
10   Butterworth-Heinemann, Oxford, 1999 at pages 65-73.

3   SPORT AND HEALTH IN THE PHYSICAL EDUCATION CURRICULUM

The absence of evidence that there is a real appreciation by the past and present framers of the National Curriculum of the benefit to children of regular physical exercise, let alone sport and games, is frightening.

In the Secretary of State's 1999 proposals for the revised national curriculum based on QCA recommendations, there is a too meagre requirement in the Physical Education programme of study for each Key Stage[11] that children should know the *health* implications of regular exercise. The requirement as stated is that they should be taught

'the importance of being active'

(at ages 4-7 or Key Stage 1)

'why physical activity is good for their health and well-being'

(at ages 7-11 or KS2)

'to understand the benefits of regular exercise...'

(at ages 11-14 or KS3)

'to understand the value of exercise and activity to personal, social and mental health and well-being'

(at ages 14-16 or KS4)

This mention in the physical education curriculum of the relationship between health and physical exercise is meant to be taught within the very little time given to all physical education teaching. Principles of human health are taught in the science curriculum, but there is no proposed cross over between the physical education curriculum and the science curriculum.

To remedy the paucity of provision for sport in schools envisaged as sufficient at the national level, regional initiatives can draw on local enthusiasm. For example, the councils of Rutland, Leicestershire, Leicester and English Sports East Midlands initiative 'Sport through Education 1997-2002' has as one of its principles

---

11   Each Key Stage (KS) corresponds to an age band and indicates the stage of curriculum for most children of that age band: ages 6 to 7 - Key Stage 1; ages 8 to 11 - KS2; ages 12 to 14 - KS3; ages 15 to 16 - KS4.

'to encourage all learners to adopt an active lifestyle and a positive approach to their health and well being'[12]

This is a refreshingly hopeful statement of principle. Unfortunately, even in this document, there is no follow through of this link between physical activity and health from the statement of principle to the three sections in the document setting out the *implementation* of this principle ('Aims, Objectives, and Curriculum Development').

At the time of writing, Dr Nicholas Tate is the Chief Executive of the Qualifications and Curriculum Authority, and was its Director at the time of the 1999 QCA recommendations to the Secretary of State which resulted in the changes to the national curriculum which will make team games no longer compulsory for children aged 14 years and over. In his role prior to the QCA, he had been Director of the now defunct School Curriculum and Assessment Authority (SCAA) during which time he chaired in June 1997 the conference 'Developing the Primary School Curriculum: the Next Steps'. At the back of the published conference papers is a summary of issues raised in conference discussion groups, such as flexibility, information technology and assessment. Not a single issue had to do with the physical education and/or health needs of children. The ubiquitous Dr Tate has held powerful posts influencing sport in state sector schools during its decline in the national curriculum years to date. Ironically, he is moving in September 2000 to the private sector where sport as yet continues to flourish, to become Headmaster of the prestigious Winchester College with its excellent sporting facilities and remarkable sporting history. Perhaps his association with the great sporting tradition of that school may cause him to rethink his lack of attention to sport in state sector schools.

4   PHYSICAL EDUCATION AND HEALTH IN THE ACADEMIC CURRICULUM

In the Secretary of State's 1999 proposals for the revised national curriculum, the science curriculum on human life processes contains almost nothing on the relationship between regular exercise and good health. Principles of human health are taught in the science curriculum and one would expect the effect of exercise on health to be included in this part of the curriculum. The science programme of study starts well enough for the tiny childen, stating that pupils should be taught

'about how taking exercise and eating the right types and amount of food help humans to keep healthy...' (at ages 4-7 or KS1).

12 *The Strategy* , *Sport through Education* published jointly by Rutland County Council, Leicestershire County Council, Leicester City Council and English Sports Council East Midlands.

But thereafter, from the age of seven, children in the state sector will not be taught of the health implications of taking exercise as part of any academic aspect of their national curriculum entitlement.

Obesity in children in the United Kingdom is reported to be a matter of concern along with their general lack of fitness and stamina. Yet in the human health aspect of what pupils should be taught in their science programme of study the Secretary of State's proposal includes *no mention whatsoever* of the relationship between exercise and health for children of 7-16 years (normally KS2, KS3, KS4). When the Health Minister, Baroness Hoffman, was asked recently whether, with sports medicine not contained in her White Paper, there was to be a sports strategy provided, she made no reply as to what if anything the Department of Health is doing relating to action for sports medicine; her reply was to refer only to a 'sports strategy with wider scope for sports participation' which was being prepared by the Department of Culture Media and Sport.

In September 1999, the Secretary of State for Education and Employment asked the QCA to develop curriculum planning guidance for schools so that the scheme of work for children at KS3 (ages 11-14) within the Design and Technology element of the national curriculum would encourage links to be made between food and health in the 'food technology' aspect of teaching.[13] The opportunity has been missed again to include in the academic curriculum entitlement any reference to links between *physical exercise* and health.

That sport in schools and its relevance to the health of children is not taken seriously is evident from the silence on this point in the science curriculum. It is further evident in the context of health education itself in those schools where this is offered. In the Health Education Scheme [14] produced by the University of Nottingham in a document developing an analysis of a health curriculum for schools, there is *no* reference to physical exercise in any form whatsoever in the content of a scheme for health education. Subjects of health education are presented as to do purely with sex, smoking, mental health, alcohol and safety. The only reference to any physical exercise is as one of 14 suggested 'methods' by which to deliver the content of the health curriculum in the scheme: thus, along with 'sorting' and 'site visits' is given 'games and exercise'.

It is simply unacceptable that those formulating the national curriculum should fail to provide that children from the ages of 7 to 16 have any exposure whatsoever within the human health element of the academic curriculum, be it in science, food technology or health per se, to an understanding of the benefit of regular exercise to good health.

13 Letter dated 8 September 1999 from Rt Hon David Blunkett MP to Sir William Stubbs, Chairman of the QCA .
14 *Towards Health. Whole School Approach to Health Promotion*. 1995, University of Nottingham Towards Health Project 1993-96.

5   AN ANALOGY BETWEEN DANCE AND SPORT IN THE CURRICULUM

In the context of school curriculum legislation an analogy can be drawn between the dire position of sport's tenuous foothold in the school curriculum today at the end of the 1990s and the near absence of dance in the school curriculum in England in the 1970s. How it happened that dance came to be included throughout the national curriculum could be a useful lesson for those seeking to pull sport back from the brink of near extinction as part of children's lives in the decade to come.

In dance, following changes to the professional dance scene in the 1970s, which saw the explosion of interest and activity in Martha Graham's contemporary dance and its related techniques, dancers and those who earned their living through dance as an art form became involved in pressure put on the national and local governments of the day to provide dance as part of the curriculum entitlement for children in school. At the time, where there was dance in schools, it was a rarity and probably ballet. In the PE departments a form of non-performance dance akin to gymnastics may have been taught if dance was available at all.

Professional dancers of the day drew on sport themes to entice audiences who might not normally attend dance performances. Ballet for All did a ballet based on athletes; the Janet Smith Company made a very clever dance based on the rules of cricket; Fergus Early choreographed a dance for Northern Ballet based on boxing; London Contemporary Dance Theatre's 'Waterless Method of Swimming Instruction' and 'Troy Games' were popular for years; others made dances based on baseball and tennis.

The introduction, by balletomane Robin Howard, to the United Kingdom of Martha Graham-based professional contemporary training and a performing contemporary company was the spark that set off an explosion of dance in 1970s United Kingdom. The first professional regional contemporary dance company, East Midlands Dance Company (EMMA), an idea suggested by a local person, attracted funding only when the then chairman of the regional arts association, a keen supporter of his preferred football team, understood the analogy between a football team's needs and a dance company's needs. Once he saw the dance company as a quasi football team he was all behind its establishment and fought for funding. This linking of dance and sport has continued to grow, and dance is now part of the Olympic Games and awards Blues between Oxford v Cambridge.

That regional dance company inevitably toured schools and taught workshops, raising the expectations of children and schools as to the availability of dance in the curriculum. Other regional companies started up, feeding off EMMA's success, and bringing dance and professional dancers into schools all over the country. This exposure to dance created an appetite for and expectation of the availability of dance in schools.

At the same time, the concept of a national curriculum for schools began to be developed by the government of the day. An attack was launched from practitioners in dance at the grassroots all over the UK, even by those who had not previously been too much concerned with the relative absence of dance as such in schools, to ensure that dance was available as an entitlement to all children as part of that national curriculum.

Arguments for including dance in the curriculum followed similar lines to those for the inclusion of games and sport in schools.

Issues of gender and health as well as competition are common to both sport and dance in schools. In dance, the argument as to gender had to do in the 1970s with the absence of provision for boys in dance where dance was offered. In sport, the gender issue today has to do with opportunities for girls in amateur and professional sport, eg, World Cup football and women's sport generally.

As to the health issue, in the 1970s in dance the worry was the unhealthy pressure put on children in professional ballet training, anorexia, injuries, stress, exhaustion, not unlike the problems raised in respect of girls training hard in gymnastics at the time. Today a health issue in schools common to all aspects of physical exercise, has to do with the value to the short and long term physical and mental health of children in taking regular exercise as part of their daily school life. (See *Medical Officers Schools Association (MOSA)*'s inspiration leading to *Van Oppen*'s case [1989] All ER 273 at 277 et seq.

The issue as to the benefit or otherwise of competition is controversial as an aspect of physical activity for children. The national curriculum is silent on competition. In eliminating games from required PE activity for 14-16 year olds, the government has left as a requirement only a choice of individual sports for this age group. Working as a team has pedagological benefits such as communication with others in the course of purposeful challenging activity, decision-making, understanding of different rôles played by team members, understanding the benefit of rules and so on (See French Example below). For children of 14-16 years of age, just on the brink of going out into the competitive world of the workplace where experience, skill, and personal excellence in the context of effective team work is highly prized, the national curriculum now is to offer as only *optional*, participation in any team sport.

6   EXPERTISE NEEDED AT POLICY MAKING LEVEL

Since the 1980s at least it has seemed to this writer that the government of the day, or its civil servants, are suspicious of and so ignore experts when consulting prior to formulating policy. The point seems to be that those who work in any particular field of endeavour have a vested interest by definition and so their views cannot be trusted.

As regards the field of education, the lame argument seems to run that businessmen and industrialists — who may know nothing about education — are better placed than teachers and educationalists to advise and participate in formulating policy because they will be the eventual employers; the consumers of the products of the schools, one could say. The composition of the Board of the QCA is an example, where barely half the members have anything to do with education as such. Likewise, neither on the Board of the QCA nor amongst its officers as far as one can see is there anyone who is or has been involved in sport at a high level of expertise. The same absence of expertise appears to exist in the political arena concerned with advising on legislation effecting sport in schools. The appointment of a Minister for Sport who trained as a PE teacher is to be welcomed in this context to some extent.

Those making their living in sport or who are serious amateurs must be tapped for their expertise by the QCA and the Secretary of State and their views made use of and acted upon in advising on the school curriculum. In any event the sources and evidence in support of advice given to the Secretary of State by bodies such as the QCA should be identified and put into the public domain.

7   LOSS OF PLAYING FIELDS

In the first edition of *Sport and Law* Edward Grayson says his target audience is lawyers, administrators, players, referees and umpires. Educationalists can now join this list thanks to legislation setting requirements for a highly prescriptive national curriculum, and also to legislation putting school governors in state schools in charge of balancing mean budgets (unable to take advantage of the economy of scale that had previously been available through Local Education Authorities) selling off land around school previously used for sports.

In the substantial Introductions to the 2nd and 3rd editions of *Sport and the Law* Grayson covers issues arising from the crisis in sport in schools re selling off of playing fields, and this crisis continues to subsist today. State sector school playing fields continue to be under threat. Making team games optional for 14 to 16 year olds essentially removes the requirement that schools provide fields, coaches, facilities and equipment for team games.

Less and less sport is required to be provided by schools, making it inevitable that governors feel they must realize valuable assets such as playing fields. As the 1999 government proposal is that there is to be no requirement to provide any teamwork choice or games at all as part of the physical education curriculum for children 14 and older, do there go the rest of the playing fields off for sale?[15]

Sports and law within the context of education raises important issues; for instance, entitlement to a national curriculum which a) provides adequate academic content as to health and physical exercise, and b) provides sufficient time in school for physical education, sport and games; the effect of selling off of playing fields on sport; the effect on adolescents of the absence of team games; and not least the significant differences between state and private sector school opportunities for sport.

8   THIS IS WHAT MUST BE DONE

- Government expectation of much more time given in state schools to physical education on a daily basis.
- Team games for children at school to remain a required provision up to age 16.
- The health, science and food technology curricula should address the link between physical exercise and human health.
- There should be greater involvement of sportsmen and women, that is practitioners with experience of sport themselves, in forming policy, framing legislation, implementing guidelines for good practice and in practical involvment in schools.

---

15 National Playing Fields Association (NPFA) data show 68 playing fields lost since October 1998, and a further nearly 700 under threat as at end July 1999. See also the letter from NPFA of 28 July 1999 to Edward Grayson reproduced in Chapter 4 on p 181.

School Sport
(2) Draft Act of Parliament for Preservation of Playing Fields

Edward Grayson and Mary Malecka

AUTHORS' NOTE: This proposed Act of Parliament is an attempt to suggest a way to set up mechanisms to preserve from disposal such school and recreational playing fields as are now under threat and others which may be under threat in the decade to come.

Precedents exist in the Transport Act 1962 s 56, and in the Town and Country Planning Act 1971, s 29. In TA1962 s 56, for instance, there was set up a route whereby objections to the closure of railway stations could be lodged and investigated. Section 57 of the Act set up a Transport User's Consultative Committee as part of the investigative process. And in TCA 1971 s 29, an analogous path was laid whereby objections to the change of use of land could be lodged and investigated. In both Acts one objector is sufficient to trigger a halting of a proposal and the setting in motion of an investigation.

The removal of the requirement to provide team games in the school curriculum for 14 to 16 year olds is likely to put further pressure on the tendency to sell off school playing fields which may well be viewed as an extravagance when their use is to be optional.

Already the National Playing Fields Association has found that between October 1998 and July 1999, 68 playing fields were disposed of for other uses, and that a further nearly 700 playing fields are under threat. In this climate of asset stripping, it is imperative that firm steps be taken to protect and preserve playing fields. Once they are built upon, playing fields are lost to future generations when one hopes the school curriculum in sport and games in the state sector may have been pulled back from the brink of extinction, given time and money, and be found to be flourishing again.

A DRAFT ACT TO PROTECT AND PRESERVE PLAYING FIELDS, FOR SCHOOL AND RECREATION PURPOSES, FROM DISPOSAL BY SALE OR OTHER MEANS

1.   A Playing Fields Users Committee (PFUC) shall be established of not more than seven individuals, with the Chair appointed by the Sports Minister. The PFUC shall include inter alia
-   one member appointed by the National Playing Fields
    Association
-   one member appointed by the Central Council of Physical Recreation
-   one sports practitioner
-   one physical education teacher
-   one person with financial expertise
-   one person with legal expertise.

2.   Any proposal that a school or other recreation playing field be sold, changed to another use other than that of a school or other recreation playing field, or otherwise disposed of must be published, not less than 8 weeks before action is taken on the proposal, in 2 successive weeks in 2 local newspapers circulating in the catchment area of the school.

3.   Any proposal that a recreational playing field of any description used by any association, club or organization be sold, disposed of or changed to another use other than that of a recreational playing field, must be published, not less than 8 weeks before action is taken on the proposal, in 2 successive weeks in 2 local newspapers circulating in the area affected by such a proposal.

4.   Where an individual affected by such a proposed disposal objects in writing to the Playing Fields Users Committee, the Committee shall report the objection to the Sports Minister. No disposal may proceed once an objection has been lodged until the conclusion of a full investigation of the objection, either by public enquiry or written or personal consideration with the source or sources of such objection.

5.   A decision of the Playing Fields Committee against disposal of, or change of use of, a school or recreational playing field shall have the effect that disposing of or changing of use of the playing field shall be an offence, for which the penalty to be imposed will be formulated and promulgated by the committee.

School Sport (3)
The French Example
Sport in the Curriculum in France

Sources drawn from *L'Equipe* survey, official curriculum regulations and school documentation in France

Dr Mary Malecka

The Minister for Sport in France is a full Minister of Government, a member of the French Cabinet. This political status at the top for sport is reflected in the provision for sport in schools which is arranged differently in France compared to England. There is no shortage in France of young able team sport players over 16 years of age. Those young players go on to form teams that win: in 1999 at the time of writing France is set to play in the final v Australia for the 1999 World Cup in rugby, having won the 1999 Davis Cup in tennis and the 1998 World Cup in soccer.

According to a survey by the French sports daily, *L'Equipe*, French adolescents accept it as given that French team players are sought after to play in foreign teams.

The grass-roots of sport in France are strong and well cared for in a system of state education that devotes adequate time and money to sport. There is far more physical education and games for all children in state schools under the French national curriculum.

In the basic French national curriculum, schools must provide physical education for children aged

- up to 13 years for 4 hours per week,
- 13 and 14 years for 3 hours per week, and
- 15 and 16 years for 2 hours per week. [1]

All children of school age have team games as part of their physical education entitlement.

---

1   Bulletin Officiel de l'Education Nationale (B.O.E.H.). Programmes des Classes summarised by the Centre d'Information de la Jeunesse, 32.1.99, May 1999.

As well as this basic number of hours in school time, all children have the *additional* opportunity to take part in physical education including team games, other sport and dance on Wednesday afternoons. Wednesday is not a school day for most children and teachers in France, and teachers leading sport, dance, and physical education activities are paid for these Wednesday afternoon sessions. Parents pay a few pounds per year to cover insurance for the Wednesday afternoon sessions only, including related transport and personal injury.

Most children participate in local sports clubs and federations from school. Those who are particularly committed may, from the age of 13 to 15 attend state boarding schools with special sports programs and facilities. A child will apply to the school through his or her local club or federation.

Entry requirements include a good academic record as well as good sporting ability in their chosen sport. Each region has a number of secondary schools with specialist sports programs which might include a *choice* of football, athletics, basketball, hockey, swimming, cycling and a number of others. The pupil of the boarding school will remain a member of their local club during the time he or she is a boarder at the school which might be some distance from home. All transport to matches and to and from home at holidays is paid by the state.

Children receive a full normal school curriculum plus an additional 6 or 7 training sessions per week in their sport. A specialist doctor in sports medicine is on call at no cost to the children. Parents pay fees for room and board of the equivalent of about £600 per year at the time of writing.

The purpose of these schools is not vocational training in sport, but a general education with an opportunity to do more sport than otherwise at club level.

From the age of 15 to 18, children may go on to study sport at vocational level in addition to a normal course of academic study in at least one school per region. There the academic timetable is arranged so as to enable intensive training at regional, national and international level of competition.

The competitive aspect of individual sport and of team games is described in positive educational terms in the national curriculum documentation;[2] for instance, children are to

- gain respect for the rules of the game and an understanding of the purpose of rules
- be encouraged to want to win and to be self-confident
- learn how to keep loss in perspective
- gain an understanding of the contrast in approach between team and non-team sports
- learn tactical play in individual sports

2   B.O.E.N. 15 October 1998, page 151.

- develop coordination, balance, speed
- learn to take responsibility, make decisions, communicate with others at various levels
- gain an understanding of the relationship between team effort and individual effort
- learn effective communication in the course of team play
- learn to appreciate that individual members of a team perform different tasks
- recognize the value of physical activity to good health
- learn the practical importance of warming up before exercise
- work together as a team in offence and defence
- develop an awareness and effective use of open space

A recent survey and report on adolescents and sport in France showed that sport is central to their lives. [3]

Team spirit and self confidence came as top of the list of personal gains the adolescents identified as benefits from participation in sport. Most say that sports lessons are the best moments of their week at school. The vast majority participate in organized sports out of school hours. More than half of adolescents surveyed participate in competitive sport regularly.

The curriculum requirement for physical education in ordinary schools is more generous in France than in England. There are better opportunities for optional sport and physical education out of school hours. From the age of 13 years there is opportunity to spend more time on sport for some children, and from the age of 16 opportunities exist to study sport at national and international level as well as complete academic study and qualifications.

3   *L'Equipe* Magazine Number 906 , 4 September 1999. Report prepared by Pierre Callevaert, pp 46-66.

Sport and the Law and Medicine (1) The Sports Doctors' Role

Donald AD Macleod

MB, ChB, FRCS (Ed), FRCP (Ed), Chairman Honorary Professor of Sports Medicine, Chairman Intercollegiate Academic Board of Sport and Exercise Medicine (UKI), President, British Association of Sport and Medicine, Hon Medical Adviser SRU and Member International Rugby Board Medical Advisory Committee

Modern sport developed in the second half of the nineteenth and twentieth centuries on the basis of healthy exercise with a competitive edge but friendly ethos, stimulating rivalry while strengthening bonds between participants and spectators, between communities and countries. Sport was amateur and fun, developing fit and healthy members of society who played within the rules of the game. Sport bridged underlying social divides — class, colour, creed and nationality. Sport was based on fair play and respect with rules and conventions controlling potentially violent activities. Sport was principally for the benefit of the participants with spectators and society enjoying a secondary role. The oath still taken by all participants in the Special Olympics for Mentally Handicapped Athletes, founded in 1968, epitomises the basis on which sport developed:

'....Let me win but if I cannot, let me be brave in the attempt.'

Sport has changed dramatically over the second half of the twentieth century with paramount importance being given to winning, irrespective of the cost, in conjunction with entertaining the public, usually on the basis of thrills and controversy. Sport is being manipulated by the media, sponsorship and market forces. Success in sport, whether winning medals or securing prestigious events, has become a measure of political success. Public sport is 'showbiz'.

Bill Shankley, manager of the highly successful Liverpool Football Club in the 1970s, was considered slightly eccentric on the basis of his famous quotation.

'Some people think football is a matter of life and death. I don't like that attitude. I can assure you it is much more important than that.'

Shankley recognised the wide ranging forces that were increasingly influencing his game and these forces have now become the norm. Modern sport with its inherent risk, competitive drive and the natural development of athletes carries a significant price tag in medical terms. Exercise for health should be risk free and beneficial to the participant but sport implies competition and therefore risk. This immediately exposes the participant to the possibilities of illness, injury and the early onset of degenerative joint disease. In addition to the physical consequences, there is also increasing evidence of psychological effects of both winning and losing in sporting competitions.

Edward Grayson, in the third edition of his authoritative text on *Sport and the Law* has identified many of the increasing pressures placed upon participants in the highest levels of sport which 'enjoy' public interest. The pressures applied to participants, coaches and administrators must be balanced against the potential medical consequences that the participant may have to face.

Medical practitioners involved with sport must increasingly recognise their dual responsibilities when working with sports participants or individual governing bodies of sport. Doctors must ensure that they achieve the highest professional standards of clinical practice when dealing with the individual patient. Sport and Exercise Medicine can no longer be looked upon as a hobby. In addition, doctors must recognise their duty to identify the risk and injury patterns in a sport so that they can make a positive contribution to injury and illness prevention without in any way significantly changing the nature of the sport in question. Members of the medical profession must also be prepared to make an active contribution to minimise cheating in sport whether this is on the basis of abuse of drugs, use of inappropriate artificial aids and equipment or violence. Edward Grayson's text has highlighted several legal precedents where the medical profession has failed to meet its responsibilities and identified circumstances in which the medical profession has made a positive contribution to the development of sport.

I can recommend the third edition of Sport and the Law to all interested doctors who are striving to achieve the highest standards of clinical practice in Sport and Exercise Medicine as educational, stimulating and at times cautionary reading.

Sport and the Law and Medicine (2) Violence, Drugs and Trial by Television

Professor John Elfed Davies

MRCP, Eng, LRCP, Lond D Phys Med Eng Hon Medical
Officer Welsh Rugby Union, International Rugby Board and
Chairman Medical Commission on Accident Prevention
Sport's Committee

As we approach the end of the century, we enter a new millennium hopefully having learnt a great deal from the achievements and mistakes that have been made in the past. Sport is no exception to the labyrinth of cultural and sociological changes that have taken place, and in many ways reflects these changes in so many different ways. The advent of the telecommunication industry, as one example, into sports is having far-reaching effects if only for the following reasons.

Many amateur sports are achieving exposure on a global scale, and one has only to look at rugby union, where the present Five Nations Championship commands a viewing audience of 200 million each match. Instant replays and highlights of the best moments to be savoured are alas tarnished by occasional needless acts of violence or professional foul and trial by television has now arrived, with video recordings used as evidence in disciplinary hearings. To the role of the administrators in sport has been added a new dimension of judgmental ability and possibly involving legal procedures of civil and criminal liability.

A further area of grave concern to many sports is the introduction of drug testing to participants, many of whom partake in sports and in certain parts of the world where the drug testing procedures are unfamiliar and no government agencies exist. The injection of substances, potions or elixirs to try and enhance performance has existed for centuries. However, the advent of modern powerful drugs such as anabolic steroids and stimulants with potentially life-threatening side-effects has created the era of the chemical athlete and a molecular war with the laboratories and drug detection authorities. During the last few years there have been instances of wide discrepancies by tribunals of governing bodies of sport with regard to penalties and sanctions imposed in the event of positive dope tests and the legality of resolutions imposed by governing bodies has also been challenged. In professional sports such as athletics, this has led to multi-million dollar law suits, and even in the amateur game of rugby union, an amateur game, players have been represented by leading not inexpensive legal counsel.

The two areas outlined above, in trial by television involving possible civil and criminal liability, and the issue of drugs in sport, both raise more questions than answers. It is into these areas that both the medical and legal professions have combined in an advisory capacity to sport in general.

The recognition of sports medicine as an integral part of preventive medicine worldwide, and its acceptance as a speciality with the creation of postgraduate degrees and diplomas, follows the traditional pathway of medicine. This is with regard to responding to healthcare demands in society, and in this instance, the sporting population.

The famous quote 'the Law follows medicine, albeit slowly, but limping a bit, and in the rear' is very apt, with interest now shown by the legal profession in the sporting scene. The recent formation of the British Association for Sport and Law augurs well for the future and follows the pathway pioneered by the medical profession in eventually having sports medicine recognised as a speciality.

It has been my great pleasure to have collaborated with Edward Grayson over the years as co-authors of *Medicine, Sport and the Law* and *Medico-Legal Hazards of Rugby Football Union*, and this third edition of *Sport and the Law* reflects not only his unbounded enthusiasm, but his chosen profession's demand for knowledge on this subject.

Many sports are entering dangerous waters and with the threat of increased exposure as outlined above, medico-legal expertise and support, together with administrators of great character and strength are all necessary for healthy survival.

Soccer Behaviour

Jack Rollin

Editor of Rothmans Football Yearbook

During the inter-war years, two-fifths of the 88 Football League clubs attracted their highest attendance figures. None of these events were accompanied by serious crowd disturbances. However, during the same period there were minor incidents at other venues, involving a handful of spectators which resulted in the closure of grounds for short periods.

In an era of strict discipline and general respect for authority, the Football Association's response was in keeping with the nature of the offences. Usually a two-match ban on home games was sufficient punishment. In some instances, clubs were even able to rearrange fixtures, while others had to play on a neutral ground.

Millwall, who had experienced one closure in 1920, found themselves fined £50 in 1934 in addition to another ban and erected a tunnel for match officials to enter the pitch. The referee had been the target of misbehaviour.

The other clubs affected were: Wolverhampton Wanderers 1919, Crystal Palace 1920, Stockport County 1921, Queen's Park Rangers 1930 and Hull City 1934. Rowdiness and pitch incursions were the primary cause.

The dismissal of players was rare, punishment severe. Jack Barrick, who towards the end of his refereeing career controlled the 1948 FA Cup Final, had sent off only six players in over 23 years. It was not unusual for suspensions to last for several months.

Frank Barson was probably the most suspended player during the period with twelve dismissals. Unfortunately, he used a strong shoulder charge which was sometimes interpreted as foul play. Playing for Watford against Crystal Palace in the opening game of the 1928–29 season, he was cautioned early on by the referee. Shortly afterwards Joe Davison, who bore some resemblance to Barson, tackled a Palace player apparently legitimately, only to find himself sent off. According to the official history of Watford Football Club, the referee was alleged to have said: 'Off you go, Barson!' Such was his reputation.

Davison received a 14-day suspension and a few weeks later on 29 September 1928, Watford were beaten 6–2 at home by Fulham. Barson was sent off after a collision in which his legs became entangled with those of a Fulham player. Both sets of players pleaded on Barson's behalf and the referee needed police protection at the end of the match. Subsequently a petition with 5,000 signatures was sent to the Football Association claiming that Barson had been the victim of his own reputation. But the FA upheld the referee's decision. The player received seven months' suspension.

Watford had had only one other dismissal since 1912 and that had been in 1923. The same month as the Barson incident, Cecil Poynton was sent off playing for Tottenham Hotspur against Stoke City. It was to be nearly 35 years before another Spurs player was dismissed, the longest such period enjoyed by a Football League club.

In the inter-war years, clubs were often ruthless in dealing with indisciplined players. Tommy Black's tackle on Walsall winger Gilbert Alsop which resulted in a penalty kick during Walsall's famous 2–0 FA Cup win over Arsenal on 14 January 1933, resulted in manager Herbert Chapman banning him from Highbury. Black was transferred to Plymouth Argyle within a week.

The quickest sending-off remains at 20 seconds from the kick-off. Ambrose Brown of Wrexham was dismissed by referee Bert Mee of Mansfield at Hull on Christmas Day 1936 in a Division Three (North) match.

Much of the good conduct of spectators emanated from an orderly society, the majority of whose members obeyed the Rule of Law and fully expected harsh treatment if they erred. The father-son predominance among football crowds helped sustain this atmosphere, though barracking and good-natured banter were traditional features.

In contrast, the last 30 years have seen a radical change in the composition of crowds, the largest percentage of those watching have been teenagers and young people without their parents. The lowering of standards of behaviour at home, school and in workplaces has created a climate where indiscipline has flourished.

The media, particular television, have been responsible for promoting tribal-like allegiances to clubs, often at the expense of the uncommitted football follower who has become an endangered species.

In the 1992–93 season, the number of arrests at first-class League and Cup matches totalled 6,329, compared with 6,378 the previous season. But there were a series of incidents in city centres involving football followers, sometimes prior to and often hours after matches had finished, which were not reported as being related to the game.

Moreover, the increasing use of stewards by clubs to offset the escalating cost of policing matches, has obscured the problem, because they were only able to eject unruly spectators, not charge them.

Hooliganism is at best being contained and the National Criminal Intelligence Service has its own football unit, which is kept busy during every season. During the 1993–94 season undercover police officers seized pocket rocket launchers, CS gas sprays, hammers, knives and martial arts equipment among other weapons. Hypodermic needles were even used at a pre-season friendly.

The vast majority of matches at still trouble-free, but Superintendent Brian Appleby, head of the football unit was quoted in the *London Evening Standard* of 27 August 1993 as follows: 'There are small groups, totalling abut 500 people who are capable of orchestrating violence, whether against each other, decent fans or other members of the public miles away from the grounds.'

In the last five years the hardcore hooligan element has become more organised along military lines, using the Internet to arrange for violent confrontations to, from and at selected matches. The use of mobile phones has finely tuned their operations.

The Republic of Ireland v England match in Dublin on 15 February 1995 had to be abandoned after only 27 minutes play, due to crowd disturbances, the first time such a fixture involving the England team had had to be called off for such a reason.

Discipline on the field has also been in question with an escalation of yellow and red cards. Widespread coverage of the game on television with such an effect on the next generation of idolized players misbehaving must be of the utmost concern. On the weekend of 16/17 October 1999, no fewer than 27 red cards were issued in England and Scotland, a record of shame.

Officials controlling matches are finding it increasingly difficult to handle situations and calls for two referees per game and professional referees to be appointed are becoming more vociferous, but in a climate where society is tending to disregard standards previously acknowledged, there appears to be no easy solution to the problem.

The post-war years have seen an increase in the number of players sent off in Football League matches. Pressures caused by the fear of defeat and with a much faster game being developed have been contributory causes. The maximum wage was lifted in 1961.

The number of players dismissed in Football League matches are as follows:

1946–47	12	1952–53	15
1947–48	5	1953–54	14
1948–49	10	1954–55	13
1949–50	14	1955–56	20
1950–51	7	1956–57	15
1951–52	14	1957–58	27

1958–59	20	1968–69	51
1959–60	19	1969–70	37
1960–61	18	1970–71	28
1961–62	25	1971–72	36
1962–63	35	1972–73	83
1963–64	45	1973–74	76
1964–65	46	1974–75	97
1965–66	46	1975–76	89
1966–67	50	1976–77	100
1967–68	48		

Figures doubled in the 1980s and trebled in the late 1990s.

1981–82	132	1990–91	202
1982–83	211	1991–92	244
1983–84	150	1992–93	226*
1984–85	163	1993–94	233*
1985–86	185	1994–95	304*
1986–87	193	1995–96	278*
1987–88	195	1996–97	295*
1988–89	172	1997–98	305*
1989–90	161		

* includes FA Premier League

Hooligan-free Football Grounds: Record Attendances in England and Wales (1919–39)

Harry Grayson

Solicitor

Note: This Appendix was prepared for my first Butterworth edition at my specific request for the period 1919–39 during national unemployment of an estimated 3 million; but no recorded violence or crime appears at any of the crowd attendance records in the schedule listed below. It is retained here to illustrate the point made in Chapter 15, *Whither Sport and the Law?*, which refers to Mr Justice Popplewell's experience (shared by the author) of having read 30 to 40 sources on the causation of crowd hooliganism, and doubted if he was any the wiser.

The hard facts contained in this Appendix have been included with the (at present unfulfilled) hope that they may perhaps stimulate research among the many survivors from these record attendances (including the author!) for comparison with the current crowd consequences of the self-styled permissive society. It is an area for research so far untapped by purported seekers of the truth behind one of sport's many ailments.

LIST IN ORDER OF CROWD SIZE

	Club	Crowd	Date	Occasion
1	Manchester City	84,569	3 Mar 1934	FA Cup 6
	(British record for any game outside London or Glasgow)			
2	Chelsea	82,905	12 October 1935	FA Cup 5
3	Manchester United	76,926	25 March 1939	FA Cup
	(Wolves v Grimsby Town)			Semi-Final
4	Sunderland	75,118	8 Mar 1933	FA Cup 6
5	Tottenham Hotspur	75,038	5 Mar 1938	FA Cup 6
6	Charlton Athletic	75,031	12 Feb 1938	FA Cup 5
7	Arsenal	73,295	9 Mar 1935	Div 1

	Club	Crowd	Date	Occasion
8	Sheffield Wednesday	72,841	17 Feb 1934	FA Cup 5
9	Bolton Wanderers	69,912	18 Feb 1933	FA Cup
10	Birmingham City	68,844	11 Feb 1939	FA Cup 5
11	Newcastle United	68,386	3 Sep 1930	Div 1
12	Sheffield United	68,287	15 Feb 1936	FA Cup 5
13	Huddersfield Town	67,037	27 Feb 1932	FA Cup 6
14	West Brom Albion	64,815	6 Mar 1937	FA Cup 6
15	Blackburn Rovers	61,783	2 Mar 1929	FA Cup 6
16	Wolverhampton W	61,315	11 Feb 1939	FA Cup 5
17	Burnley	54,775	25 Feb 1924	FA Cup 3
18	Stoke City	51,380	29 Mar 1937	Div 1
19	Fulham	49,335	8 Oct 1938	Div 2
20	Milwall	48,672	20 Feb 1937	FA Cup 5
21	Oldham Athletic	47,671	25 Jan 1930	FA Cup 4
22	Leicester City	47,298	18 Feb 1928	FA Cup 5
23	Plymouth Argyle	43,596	10 Oct 1936	Div 2
24	Bristol City	43,335	16 Feb 1935	FA Cup 5
25	Preston NE	42,684	23 Apr 1938	Div 1
26	Barnsley	40.255	15 Feb 1936	FA Cup 5
27	Brentford	39,626	5 Mar 1938	FA Cup 5
28	Reading	33,042	19 Feb 1927	FA Cup 5
29	Grimsby Town	31,657	20 Feb 1937	FA Cup
30	Chesterfield	30.968	7 Apr 1939	Div 2
31	York City	28,123	5 Mar 1938	FA Cup 5
32	Newport County	24,268	16 Oct 1937	Div 3 (S)
33	Exeter City	20,984	4 Mar 1931	FA Cup 6
34	Wimbledon	18,000	1932/33	FA Amateur Cup

AUTHOR'S COMMENT

Since these statistics were prepared for the first Butterworths edition in 1988 and retained for the second edition in 1994, the comment I made as cited

> 'no recorded violence or crime appears at any of the crowd attendance records in the schedule listed below'

can be placed alongside and read together with the table of 'Disasters and incidents involving United Kingdom stadia or supporters' reproduced from Frosdick, S and Walley L (1997) Sport and Safety Management in Chapter 1 at pp 83-85, above, and also *'Ethics, Injuries and the law in Sports*

Medicine'. The comparison shows that the following ground record attendances coincided with injuries caused by crowd crush circumstances:

1924	Burnley	1 dead	54,775	25 Feb 1924	FA Cup 3
1932	Huddersfield	100 injured	67,037	27 Feb 1932	FA Cup 6
1938	Fulham	unknown injuries	49,335	8 Oct 1938	Div 2

This limited numbers of casualties reaffirms the title to this particular Appendix.

Draft Safety of Sports Persons Act

Edward Grayson

Author's Note: For the 1st edition, published in 1988, I wrote: 'It is at least arguable in 1987 that no responsible citizen would object to compulsory disqualification for drunk and drugged drivers as an automatic penalty upon proof of a road traffic offence (except in special circumstances such as malicious or irresponsible 'lacing' of drinks). In 1987 it was also arguable that fewer citizens would protest against breathalyser tests than those who complained against their purported interference with personal freedoms and liberties upon their introduction twenty years earlier by the Transport Minister, Mrs Barbara Castle, under the Road Safety Act, 1967.

Accordingly, the question arose in 1987 whether any responsible citizen would object to my proposal initiated in 1977 and converted into concrete form as an Appendix to the slender *Sunday Telegraph* version of *Sport and the Law* in 1978 in the circumstances explained in Chapter 15 '*Whither Sport and the Law*'. As appears there, the idea was inspired by the contrast between the wide ranging discretionary penalties imposed by sporting sentencing tribunals for what may be described as 'field' offences, and the equally discretionary penalties imposed by magistrates and crown courts for 'crowd' offences, on the one hand; and the fate of the unsuccessful plaintiff who failed to clear his name of the allegedly unjust charge of cheating at cards in the Tranby Croft Baccarat Case [*Gordon-Cumming v Green and others* (1891) 7 TLR 408], and the *Royal Baccarat Scandal* (at pp 439 and 513 above).

The initial publication of the book in 1977 coincided with the initial series of *Sunday Telegraph* articles under the *Sport and the Law* title; and the contrast between that Plaintiff's peremptory military and social dismissal within hours of the jury's adverse verdict after a six-day trial in 1891, and the mid-1970s soft options which operated at all levels of sentencing against violent 'field' and 'crowd' offenders was too much for me to stomach without an attempt to propose a practical alternative. Its advocacy regularly in the same [*Sunday Telegraph*] source where it began, and elsewhere, during the intervening ten [now twenty] years has not been answered by the Exclusion Order principle in recent licensing and pubic order legislation. An overriding *discretion* whether or not to operate that sentencing disposal still remains. If the public's attitude and will towards these offenders is, as is argued, consistent with its attitude to drunken and drugged motorists, then Parliament should reflect it by legislative withdrawal of that discretion and its replacement with *mandatory* sanctions.'

That *mandatory* (as distinct from discretionary) power still remains for implementation, notwithstanding recent legislation. More significant, however, is the absence generally throughout the whole administrative sports world of an effective *penal* policy with a coherent code of sanctions. This is consistent with the citations in Chapter 15 '*Whither Sport and the Law*' from Lord McCluskey's paper 1994 paper '*Discussing a sentencing policy*' and Lord Bingham of Cornhill's *Criminal Law Review* contribution '*A Criminal Code: Must we Wait for Ever?*'

AN ACT TO PROTECT ALL PERSONS ENGAGED IN AND CONCERNED WITH SPORTING AND RECREATONAL ACTIVITIES FROM INJURY CAUSED TO THEM BY OTHER PERSONS CONCERNED WITH SPORTING OCCASIONS

1. Any person deliberately or recklessly causing any harm or injury in any manner whatsoever to any person concerned with, before, during or after any sporting or other recreational activity shall be guilty of an offence.
2. The said offence shall be committed by any participant during the course of any authorised sporting or recreational activity when it occurs in breach of the rules or laws of such sporting or other recreational activity.
3. The penalty for such offence committed by any participant during the course of such authorised lawful sporting or recreational activity shall be automatic suspension from further participation in the activity irrespective of any punishment pursuant to the rules or laws of such sporting or recreational activity and of any other statutory or civil cause of action or complaint.
4. The penalty for conviction of any offence committed by any non-participant before, during or after the course of any such authorised lawful sporting or other recreational activity shall include disqualification from or further attendance at any such sporting activity from the date of such conviction and also compulsory attendance at an appropriate attendance or detention centre to be designated by the Secretary of State on every Saturday afternoon between the hours of 2.00 p.m. (14.00 hours) and 5.00 p.m. (17.00 hrs.), and every evening between the hours of 7.00 p.m. (19.00 hrs.) and 10.00 p.m. (22.00 hrs.) for a period of 12 months from the date of such conviction; and in default of the availability of such attendance or detention centres, a community service order for the same time within the same period shall be directed.

Amateur Football

WP Goss

Honorary Secretary Amateur Football Alliance

It is probably not surprising that in the era of the multi-thousand pounds per week professional footballer there are many who presume the entire game has taken an upward lift into a new prosperity. It has not, and there can be no doubt that it has been the politicians, and particularly the previous administration, who have been - both directly and indirectly - responsible for outright neglect.

Having earlier tried an ethical approach, in which only Commissioners for Oaths benefited and some clubs hastily fled the sham-amateur ranks, in the mid-70s the Football Association had little option but to grasp the nettle again and face up to the fact of continued illegal payments to so-called amateurs. Instead of 'professional' and 'amateur', 'Contract' and 'non-Contract' categories resulted as alternative status descriptions. In fact, these determine player-club administrative arrangements significantly more than the implied financial rewards, and the true amateur player has by media neglect been consigned to near public oblivion. That being so it is relatively easy for the politicians to minimise this aspect of their undoubted responsibility for the state of the nation's sport, since every International stems originally from the bottom layer.

A decade ago adherents of the current government were not only loud in their desire to remove competition from school sport but were often simultaneously protesting about under use and therefore accessibility of private grounds, where often the grass certainly looked greener. In due time many of these sites accepted pitch hiring, often on generous terms. However, subsequently many such facilities have been sold or even just closed to lie fallow rather than continue to encourage or to subsidise sport, even for employees of the owners. This has been true of central London corporate facilities and also Universities. Hiring facilities frequently terminate after a sale or, in the case of Universities, squeezing of government funding has contributed to the extreme arguments perhaps not for sale, but groundstaff redundancies and draconian lifts in hire charges to highest bidders. And not only for playing facilities but also food and drink charges, where West End prices are now the norm in some London suburban playing fields. In many cases these arrangements have coldly ignored the historical contribution made by users of the facilities over many decades. Furthermore, such moves will have adverse effects on participation, which is a serious issue in the case of Universities given that the age band 16–18 is said to be where the greatest losses are said to result in many sports, due to lack of facilities.

Those who operate in the *grass-roots* sectors of Association football are responsible for development and regulation of the game, for both genders, including players, referees, coaches, premises in the community, and *more than* 40,000 Clubs and 25,000 Referees are involved. These are probably conservative figures but greater accuracy will never prevail until modern information technology is used to create a national database of participants in the game. In evidence submitted by The Football Association in November 1972 to a Select Committee of the House of Lords on 'Sport and Leisure' it was argued that if estimating the number of adult players is demonstrably very difficult 'doing the same for schoolboys is virtually impossible'.

Meanwhile, at these lowermost and principally *recreational* levels there have been increasingly higher costs for diminishing facilities, and increasing needs for protection in an increasingly litigious society. It is not a pleasant scenario to learn of groundsmen who have had to sell their homes to settle court awards or, after redundancy, their intended retirement homes, unable to continue to pay mortgages without security of tenure.

Given the *lack of playing fields* and the basic charges levied to use them, the associated VAT regulations are patently draconian and an example of governments, both national and local, which not only allow facilities, such as pitches, to be lost to developers, but then compile nonsensical regulations to tax use of the diminished remainder. One such regulation concedes alleged exemption from VAT on a block booking for regular use of — for example, football pitches — but then disallows the exemption if the interval between any two dates in the block is in excess of 14 days. Given that all such facilities are bound to close for one and possibly two week-ends over the Christmas holiday it is virtually impossible to secure the benefit of the exemption. Another, equally ridiculous regulation is the concept that premises with, say, a basketball net attached to walls counts as a 'sports facility' and therefore taxed, but not so if there are merely floor markings for games! One has to wonder about the imaginings and competence, even the motives, of those who draw up these regulations.

Given that facility hirings, including VAT, are these days high enough, the *truly amateur* player has then to pay his/her own travelling expenses to games, and additionally a club subscription for all the other running costs, such as playing clothing and equipment, hospitality for visiting teams, and personal insurance - often also a share of the premium for public liability cover.

Clearly, current costs promote thoughts of seeking assistance from the private sector by way of sponsorship, where there is a clear imbalance between the huge sums offered at national levels and the surprising relatively small interest and magnitude of largesse spread across the majority of sports. Five years ago there was a temporary lifting of spirits in the sporting world with the inception of the National Lottery, which has since aggregated a public income of £8 billion, only half of which has so far been paid out to good causes. This includes a substantial amount of interest, since revenues are banked bi-weekly whilst assessments of applications and eventual grants take much longer. This is hardly surprising considering the *complex nature of a lottery application pack* which leaves one feeling not that a punter's joy of giving is to be matched by sport's joy of receiving, but that the latter is *hedged with many reasons why an application will not succeed*. Principal among these are that the requirement of minimally 35% of project costs must be borne by the applicant, and that funding can be applied only to capital costs. Given that even the smallest of constructions is likely to require at least £1,000 from the applicant's own funds, it is not surprising to find that politicians deviously enhance their political reputations by using surplus lottery monies for funding which should be derived, both morally and fiscally, from national taxation. As long ago as May 1995 Sports Council and Lottery representatives declared — in response to a dearth of inner-city applications and speculation that the 35% element may be a prohibitive cause — 'We will look at the situation carefully. We have always said that our policies would be flexible and we are prepared to make changes if necessary'. Four years on, nothing has changed.

Sportsmanship and Respect for Authority

Doug Insole CBE

Former Essex and England cricketer and amateur footballer,
Corinthian-Casuals Football Club, vice-President, Football
Association

During the period of about 50 years which covers my involvement in the playing and administration of football and cricket at senior level there have been fundamental and wide-ranging changes in the attitudes of players in both games, even though the laws encompassing fair and unfair play have in each case remained unaltered throughout.

Many powerful influences, all of them reflected in society generally, can be cited as contributing towards what undoubtedly amounts to a significant deterioration in what might be described loosely as 'sportsmanship' coupled with, and probably consequent upon, a steadily decreasing respect for the laws of the game and for those appointed to ensure that those laws are applied. The law and its custodians, on and off the field, are being tried to the limit and not infrequently to the point at which umpires and referees, but especially the latter, are being abused to such an extent that they decide to sever their connections with a 'sport' which has such unpleasant associations.

I have little doubt that the so-called glory of winning and the alleged ignominy attached to losing are the most important factors in the current approach to sporting contests. Big money is, of course, a crucial factor where it exists, but lack of respect for authority in almost all sports is as pronounced at the bottom of the scale as it is at the top. It can justifiably be said that performers in the lower echelons are simply imitating those who play at the highest level, but money and national prestige are a relevance only where star professionals are involved.

My own clear recollection of early experiences in top level sport — amateur and professional — is that dissent and the disputing of decision were almost non-existent and that a substantial majority of players were prepared to assist the officials in charge of a match in taking decisions. An obvious example of this tendency is that batsmen frequently — in fact, usually — 'walked' when they snicked the ball to the wicket-keeper. It was customary if a catch was made close to the ground, or if it was unseen by the batsman, for the fielder to be asked if the catch had been cleanly taken and for the batsman to depart, if the answer was in the affirmative, without reference to the umpire. Fielders, similarly, would make it known immediately if what appeared to have been a catch was in fact a 'bump' ball. The claiming of a catch when the ball had not carried was almost unheard of, but not quite. There were one or two performers in the English first-class game who were regarded with some suspicion, and Frank Chester, widely regarded as the best umpire ever, told me that in a Test Match in 1948 he was asked by his colleague at the bowler's end whether a possible catch at the wicket had actually 'carried' to the keeper. Chester had seen clearly that the ball had bounced a couple of feet in front of the wicket-keeper and as a result his pronouncement of 'not out' was loud and disapproving. At the end of the over he was informed very firmly by the Australians that the umpire's job was simply to announce a decision, and not to make moral judgments.

Cricket, of course, is the only major sport in which the appeal is part of the formal structure of the game, and this in itself is a cause of controversy and of potential animosity. The very act of appealing means that the fielding side — often, in these days, in concert and unanimously — claims that the batsman is out and, much more often than not, the umpire is obliged to disagree with them. Concerted appealing, combined with premature celebration and much congratulatory embracing, is a fairly recent and entirely unacceptable means of putting pressure on the umpire and so influencing him to make wrong decisions. It is intimidation aimed at bringing about a miscarriage of justice and it is the aspect of 'gamesmanship' that umpires regard as the most objectionable of all.

In soccer, too, there was in the early days of my participation a ready acceptance of the referee's decision and even a general inclination to take the most obvious decisions for him. There was nothing quite as obvious as the occasion on which the Corinthian goalkeeper moved out of his goal to allow his opponents to score from the penalty spot and do something to expunge the disgrace of having committed a foul in the penalty area — that goes back a bit further still. But players would acknowledge a corner, or a goal-kick, or a throw-in by presenting the ball to the opposition to enable them to get on with the game. With very few exceptions a player who had injured an opponent would, at the very least, inquire after his health. That this kind of friendly gesture so rarely happens in these days is perhaps not surprising in that the assailant has probably committed an intentional, 'professional' foul and that the victim may be feigning fatal injury in order to influence the referee to dismiss the offender from the field of play. No wonder that the game is littered with disciplinary hearings and appeals procedures at which legal representation on both sides is now commonplace.

The shadow of the law influences the judgment of sporting administrators the world over. Recourse to the legal process in the settlement of which might previously have been regarded as 'internal' matters is almost the norm. Most governing bodies have recently tried to enshrine within their Rules the principle that clubs will not sue if decisions within the game go against them, but feelings sometimes run so high that the law of the land is called into play to settle 'sporting' disputes.

The modern administrator is constantly seeking the advice of lawyers about the 'reasonableness' of rules and regulations applying to his particular sport in order to avoid possible legal implications arising as a result of sporting legislation.

It would be comforting to think that what may broadly be described as 'the Corinthian spirit' may one day be revived, but for a number of reasons such a development seems a very remote possibility.

'Player power', which has played such an important part in the deterioration of behaviour in sport, could in theory be kept in check by administrators and governing bodies, but firm action is unlikely when spectators at sporting events often approve, support and give every indication of admiring those performers who challenge authority in the most ostentatious manner. To take effective punitive action against the stars of a sport which is anxious to attract and to retain public interest in a highly competitive world is a step that most administrators would take only with the greatest reluctance, and under extreme pressure. Their situation is made no easier by the fact that the media is inclined to recruit these 'characters' and to invite them to project their image of the sporting ethic to the world at large.

The situation may well be irretrievable unless respect for the law returns to society as a whole but happily there are still clubs, organisations and individuals prepared to perform within the spirit and according to the laws of their chosen sports. While they and the concept of sportsmanship still exist, they must be given all possible help and encouragement.

What is crystal clear is that modern attitudes, the worst aspects of which include such legally unacceptable practices as the professional foul and the use of drugs to enhance performance, must be altered if the word 'sport' is to retain anything of its original and time-honoured meaning.

The Corinthian Ideal

Hubert Doggart, OBE

'Corinthian and Cricketer', past President of MCC and ex-Headmaster of King's School, Bruton

For a sportsman to be called a Corinthian is perhaps the highest accolade he can receive. We recall from the last quarter of the Victorian age, for instance, the sporting prowess of C B Fry, a Corinthian to his finger-tips, and G O Smith, the finest amateur centre-forward of his day, to whom Edward Grayson once paid a seminal visit on leave-out from school. Both could be said to have upheld the Corinthian ideal.

Today the word 'Corinthian' has ringingly favourable overtones, but it was not ever thus. In the Greek language, 'to be a Corinthian' was to suggest a lowly man or woman, or both together, whose idea of sporting activities was decidedly below the belt. In his letters to the Christians in Corinth St Paul stresses that they must be on their guard — against their own divisions as well as against the seedy diversions available at the drop of a hat.

Words, as Philip Howard tells us in his books and articles, often undergo a rich sea-change. At the inaugural meeting of the Corinthian Football Club, called by N L Jackson, the honorary assistant secretary of the Football Association, in Paternoster Row, London, in 1882, the name 'The Wednesday' was discarded and, by a happy chance, 'The Corinthian Football Club' decided. To the proposer, Mr H A Swepstone, the name may well have seemed a halfway house between Spartan and Athenian, with a healthy dose not only of sporting prowess but also of the 'Muscular Christianity' of the day.

The word 'Corinthian' can cross frontiers. When Mr Peter Bills wishes to pay Jean-Pierre Rives, the great French Rugby player and sportsman, a special compliment, he sub-titles his book, 'A Modern Corinthian', implying those standards of 'sport for sport's sake' achieved by the Corinthian teams, of the 1880s and the 1920s especially.

Bills expresses it word-perfectly at the end of the book:

'All his career Rives has fought to enshrine a special spirit, a joyous approach. He will be remembered as a man who cherished such spirit, in himself and in others. His lasting testimony to the game is not of tries scored or matches played or jerseys swapped: such are peripheral matters. It was always 'spirit' which motivated Rives, that is love for the game, played in the finest traditions with love for those involved, even one's fiercest opponents.'

The same kind of tribute could surely also be paid to the 'legendary' Bobby Jones, that outstanding Amateur golfer for the United States, whose sense of fair play, exceptional character and four Grand Slams (as they are now called) in tournament victories in 1930 are writ large in the annals of sport. Thus, we have an American Corinthian and a French Corinthian as well as those English Corinthians who have given their name to the ideal which is the subject of this appendix.

I was fortunate to be reared in a Corinthian environment, having Graham Doggart as my father, Gilbert Ashton as my prep-school headmaster, Colin Hunter as my housemaster at Winchester, and Hubert Ashton as my godfather — all four of them fine 'Corinthians and Cricketers', as Edward Grayson called his excellent book in 1955. It is true that they lived in a more innocent age in terms of sport and life, when the Corinthian ideal came to them more naturally, but that, for us, is the nub of the matter.

In his chapter in the first edition of *Sport and Law* entitled '*Genesis*' (and in the Introduction to his second edition), Edward Grayson has a delightful list of those 'concerned with, affected by or interested in whatever is believed or understood to be sport'. Alliteratively and engagingly it includes 'the tea ladies and the team agents', and he concludes: 'in fact, participants at every level from aspiring and fading stars with feet of clay to all who know that, in the beginning and at the end, sport exists for fun and the never changing ideal embodied in "mens sana in corpore sano"'.

Those in the list (the tea-ladies almost certainly excluded, since they know it already!) need to be constantly reminded of the Corinthian ideal. For without it — in this more complex, more commercial, more cynical, and more street-wise age — sport can so easily cease to be true to the practical hopes and personal dreams of its founders. Cricket — though, of course, sponsors are a blessing rather than a blight — can all too easily become market-led rather than cricket-led. And, mutatis mutandis, all other sports can also. We need a crusade to stop this happening.

From that list, those involved in the administration of sport have a self-evident duty to see the wood from the trees and to stop sporting 'Dutch Elm Disease' — with no aspersion being cast on the Dutch — from spreading. But I choose to select three specific groups whose efforts could be harnessed to stop the rot and ensure the survival, relatively intact, of the Corinthian ideal.

First, the doctors, whose Hippocratic oath can be construed as an upholding of the Corinthian ideal in medicine. Second, the lawyers, who once played without a thought that their services qua lawyers would be needed, but cannot now be sure. And, third, schoolteachers, whose *raison d'être* could be called 'the upholding of the Corinthian ideal in body, mind and soul'. To the barricades, then, in the cause of the Corinthian ideal!

Football Litigation and Insurance - Full-Time for Corinthian Values?

Andrew Deans

*Head of sport and leisure liability team, Solicitor, of
Hextall Erskine, solicitors to the insurance industry*

Justin Clayden,

Solicitor, of Hextall Erskine

The recent record award of damages of £959,000 in early 1999 to Gordon Watson of Bradford City following the tackle by Kevin Gray of Huddersfield Town in February 1997 has thrown the spotlight once again onto the tortious duties of players to one another in relation to incidents occurring during the heat of a fast moving game. It also brings into sharp focus the potential difficulties of assessing damages not only at the higher levels of the game, but also at amateur and junior levels.

The developments in football over the past few years have been extraordinary. The explosion in media coverage, especially satellite television, together with the effect of the *Bosman* decision (which gives more freedom of movement between clubs at the end of their contracts and greater negotiation strength) has promoted the value and earning potential of players out of all proportion to the levels of pay enjoyed less than a decade ago. Michael Owen is reputedly insured for some £20 million which compares interestingly to insurance on Betty Gable's legs for $1m forty years ago!

Although careers are relatively short in comparison to other areas of employment, the lucrative levels of pay and bonuses available to top players mean that the premature curtailment of a player's career by perhaps some four or five years can generate a significant claim for future loss of earnings. The assessment of future loss of earnings or notional career path is also far from an exact science relying not only on past goal scoring records and opinions on past performance but at the end of the day on the opinion of the player's worth and marketability.

The legal development of players or sporting participants' duties to either participants or spectators has been comparatively recent. The starting point is perhaps the case of *Woolridge v Sumner* 1963 (2 QB p 43). Mr Woolridge, a photographer, was injured at White City stadium when he fell or stumbled under the path of a heavy hunter horse which in the law reports was stated to have 'excelled' at galloping. The horse appears to have taken a turning either too wide or too fast with the result that it was outside the main eventing arena and alarmed the claimant who was trying to remove himself from the area. The horse went on to win the event.

Mr Woolridge's claim was unsuccessful. The Court of Appeal found that the extensive speed of the horse did not constitute negligence, but was rather an error of judgment and had ceased by the time of the accident. Neither did the rider's attempts to bring the horse into the arena at speed constitute negligence. The court expressed considerable sympathy for the rider (or indeed any participant) having to make a difficult decision in the heat of the moment. The main judgment was given by Lord Justice Diplock who set out the spectator's legal position as taking:

'...the risk of any damage caused to him by any act of a participant done in the course of and for the purposes of the game or competition notwithstanding that such act may involve an error of judgment or a lapse of skill unless the participant's conduct is such as to evince a reckless disregard of the spectator's safety'.

A similar formulation was also made by Lord Justice Sellers who stated:

'...If the conduct is deliberately intended to injure someone whose presence is known, or is reckless and in disregard of all safety of others so that it is a departure from the standards which might reasonably be expected in anyone pursuing the competition or game, then the performer will be held liable for any injury his act caused'.

The question of consent was also discussed. The court found clearly that the maxim would only have any merit in a case where, having established the existence of a duty of care, the claimant could be shown to have consented to the defendant's lack of reasonable care and the defendant could in turn demonstrate the claimant's full knowledge of the nature and extent of the risk.

In *Harrison v Vincent and Others* 1982 RTR 8, a case following an accident involving a motorcycle and sidecar combination, the Court of Appeal was of the opinion that the same duty would apply as between competitors provided the acts occurred during the course of or for the purposes of the game or competition. On the facts, the cause of the accident was found to be due to negligent mechanics prior to the competition and, therefore, the 'normal' test of negligence was applied.

Condon v Basi 1985, 1 WLR 866 concerned a football case involving players of two clubs in the Leamington League. The decision of the County Court was upheld in the Court of Appeal with supporting references to the

Australian case of *Rootes v Shelton* 1968 ALR 33 which discussed the relative standards to be expected of players at different levels. The trial judge's summary that the defendant '...*was clearly guilty, as I find the facts, of serious and dangerous foul play which showed a reckless disregard of the claimant's safety and which fell far below the standards which might reasonably be expected in anyone pursuing the game*' was given approval in the judgment of Sir John Donaldson, MR. The decision therefore echoes the test applied on a participant to a spectator in *Woolridge*.

The Master of the Rolls went on to suggest that the main issue was whether the defendant failed to exercise the degree of care which was appropriate in all the circumstances or acted in a way to which the claimant cannot be expected to have consented.

Two more recent football cases also deserve some mention before turning to the case of *Watson v Gray: Elliot v Saunders*, (June 1994), and *McCord v Swansea City Football Club*, (December 1996). Both concerned career terminating tackles on professional footballers in the Premier and the Third Division respectively. In the former, and after considering the application of the principle in *Condon*, Mr Justice Drake found that the claimant had failed to demonstrate that the defendant committed dangerous or reckless play or was in breach of any duty. The tackle was no more than an error of judgment and not one giving rise to a finding of negligence. With regard to the duty the judge appeared to doubt whether, as suggested in *Condon*, the level of the match amounted to any more than one of the circumstances to be considered, as compared to a specific finding on the level of the duty of care itself.

In *McCord*, Mr Justice Kennedy had to consider whether the player's tackle was late and found that he '*was guilty of a serious mistake when he made his challenge or tackle...*'. The judge declined to label his actions however as reckless or rash. He also went on to rule interestingly that, irrespective of his decision in that case it did not follow that players do not consent to the '*...great majority of errors of judgment, mistakes or even fouls.*'

Coming at last to the record damages case of *Watson*, Mr Justice Hooper at the trial on liability in the autumn of 1998 considered that the claimant would have to show that, on a balance of probabilities, a professional player would have known that there was a significant risk that the defendant's actions would result in a serious injury to the claimant. On the facts the judge found that a forceful high challenge was one that a reasonable professional football player would have known carried with it a significant risk of serious injury. It is unlikely that the factual findings in the judgment in *Watson* will open the floodgates to other claims of negligence.

The judge in *Watson* appears to have used at least a semantically different test (*significant risk of personal injury*) from that applied both in

Condon and earlier in *Woolridge* (*reckless disregard for the claimant's safety*). The former suggests a primarily objective test, the latter an element of personal appreciation of the risks. It may be that ultimately the description of the test to be applied is not so important provided there is some consistency in determining the appropriate degree of care in all the circumstances. Nevertheless in an action determined since *Watson* at Bradford County Court (*Maxwell Casson v MOD*) during early 1999 and which involved a teenager sustaining injuries whilst participating in a football match, the judge was prepared to make a finding of negligence based on the concept of 'reckless disregard', thus adopting the terms in the *Woolridge* and *Condon* list of cases.

One of the interesting features which has emerged from the three professional football cases mentioned above is the value of the evidence which the judge has had to consider. In all the cases there has been extensive witness evidence — as would be expected from a match watched enthusiastically by thousands — which has often been quite contradictory and in some cases wrong after analysis of the video evidence available to the court. Some witnesses have had to amend their views after reviewing the available video evidence, and in both *Elliott* and *Watson* the judges were able to make findings of fact with very considerable assistance from the taped replays of the incidents rather than witness evidence. Perhaps this is scarcely surprising given the speed of the game and the split second nature of the incidents which have given rise to the claims in all three cases.

Another unusual feature of the recent judgment which has been touched on at the outset of this article is the basis of the assessment of damages in the professional football field. Where it is claimed the incident had terminated or seriously highlighted the player's career, a court will need to assess not only the likely career pattern of the player, but also the relevant level of remuneration which would have been enjoyed by him. In short, in a field which is so open to passionate debate at all levels as to a player's worth or rating, wildly varying opinions are bound to be advanced.

Any such evidence on this issue must inevitably involve a degree of speculative estimation in particular the subjective assessment of 'loss of chance'. Furthermore expert evidence by managers and agents commenting on the large diversity of players' pay may result in assessments which might vary by many hundreds of thousands of pounds. It is likely that neither party would wish to see this aspect of claims in the future being handled by a sole expert as envisaged by the new CPR. No doubt similar principles and calculations will also apply to other professional contact sports.

It is not crying wolf to predict that, in a professional game where an estimated 50% of leavers do so as a result of some injury involved on the pitch, there may well be more cases like *Watson* in the future. The financial rewards in pursuing cases, linked to the possibility of conditional fee agreements, would also suggest the likelihood of an increase in litigated cases unless some form of 'no fault' compensation scheme is set up, into which players and clubs contribute. While this would not banish the threat of litigation it would hopefully remove much of the emotional element from such situations, thus reducing the temptation to go to law. For the time being however, there does not seem to be any prospect of this, and the insurance market will no doubt be revisiting the levels of cover and premiums paid by all clubs and associations for the insurance of liability risks on the playing field, as well as other areas of sporting pursuits, at both the amateur and professional levels.

Insurance Needs of Sport

Tony O'Brien

*Perkins Slade Ltd, Insurance broker to the Central Council of
Physical Recreation and other similar national organisations*

The preferred path in insurance is to seek to bring about a resolution long
before a matter goes to trial. Any matters which have been before the Court
are best left for comment in the hands of Lawyers rather than an insurance
broker.

Insurance needs at most levels in sport are little different from the needs
of the rest of the community — individuals, commerce, industry or other
organisations. Property, premises, equipment and the like can sustain
damage by fire or other perils or loss by theft and the insurance market can
quite readily provide such cover, extended if required to embrace
consequential losses. Motor insurance needs are also much the same
although, at a top professional level the rather exotic machinery paraded
in what are usually far from peaceful pastoral surroundings hardly appeals
to the little red telephone type of Insurer.

Money insurance can be a problem where Sports Clubs with a
dependence on enthusiastic, or as is more often the case, reluctant
treasurers are perhaps susceptible to occasional malpractice and Fidelity
Guarantee insurance is inappropriately expensive or cumbersome. Despite
Insurers reluctance to respond individually to athletes, Sports Clubs or
other small groupings, schemes are available either through or with the
approval of Sports Governing Bodies to provide the insurance protection
sought at economic prices.

Having disposed of their *'ordinary, every day insurance problems'* there
is a need to recognise the most vital protection needed which is without
doubt Liability closely followed by automatic compensation for death or
serious disabling injury.

LIABILITY INSURANCE

Where individuals are employed as athletes, coaches, administrators and general staff there is the legislative need for the Employers be they club, activity business or any other organisation to carry *Employers Liability* insurance cover. Such insurance originally known and generally understood as Workmen's Compensation provides cover for bodily injury, death or disease arising out of employment with a minimum indemnity level of £5M for any one incident.

Recognised however as the absolute essential insurance protection is *Public Liability*. This should cover anyone participating in sport against any action for damages by another party and meet any associated legal expenses — but the insurance industry just doesn't seem to have come to terms with this! Policy wordings, the bible of any insurance company, carry within such wording limitations that cause one to question their real intentions and suitability for use in the total area of sport. Liability for accidental bodily injury or damage to property, the standard cover offered and therefore considered all that is available by the general insurance intermediaries/advisers may well provide for most of what happens in the *'arena'*, be it grass, water, board or cement, but it is totally inadequate beyond. Sport doesn't begin and end at touch lines or perimeters but relies on layer upon layer of administrators, coaches, managers, advisers etc. making up the structures enabling it's very existence and certainly continuity.

Their role is such that it calls for insurance protection in respect of errors or omissions, libel/slander and other eventualities, not just *'accidental'* bodily injury or damage to property — a *Professional Indemnity* cover akin to that provided to Doctors, Lawyers, Architects, Accountants etc. Quite apart from the traditionally recognised administration, budgeting, planning, and maintaining the rules and regulations the enforcement of discipline and rule interpretation makes them very vulnerable to those affected by any disagreeable decisions seeking damages, exemplified by the distressed coaches/instructors suspended under the Child Protection measures now considered essential!

Additional to *'Professional Indemnity'* full cover there is need for insurance whilst they operate as *Directors* and *Officers* of their organisations and their operational activity within the sport.

There are very few insurers who provide such three different classes of insurance, *Liability*, *Professional Indemnity* and *Directors & Officers* and even those that do would utilise three different insurance policies — hardly seam free! An all-embracing Civil Liability Policy providing, under one document for all these needs and underwritten by a single large UK Insurer, can provide the answer to the problem. In practice the only exclusions are:

(a)   The criminal act of the individual perpetrator.
(b)   Road vehicle risks.
(c)   Loss or damage to property in the Insured's custody or control.

The former is not insurable in the general market with *Criminal Injuries* Act handling compensation, and the other two latter aspects are the subject of separate insurance considerations.

This *Civil Liability* insurance can be best arranged by the Governing Body of individual sports who, by providing as part of membership and funded out of fees, can make dramatic savings in the administrative expenses. It is not unusual to find an annual fee of under £1 per capita providing all the members, officials, executive, clubs and the Governing Body itself with Civil Liability insurance in a £5 indemnity limit.

AUTOMATIC [NO-FAULT] COMPENSATION

The insurance market response to this need takes the form of *Personal Accident* insurance and this cover is readily available in a selection of forms. Traditionally, and particularly in those sports with a significant artisan participation, the priority was deemed to be the payment of lost wages following sports injuries. Particularly has soccer [Association Football] clung to this fixation not recognising that a large majority of participants nowadays are unlikely to suffer a wage loss — salaried workers, students, unemployed etc; and even where income would cease if there was an inability to attend work, particularly self-employed etc. there is much more time spent apart from sport when accidents can happen! It must be recognised that any income replacement benefit needs to embrace an individual's total life style, not just that small percentage when playing sport. Such full time *Personal Accident* cover is readily available to embrace all business, social and recreational time not excluding sport.

Death benefits also vary in their needs but are best accommodated within *Life Assurance* where apart from high hazards there would be no sporting exclusions. There is also a limitation by law in respect of death benefits for people under age 18 and thus it is far more sensible to provide £5,000 for death compensation [funeral expenses] but recognise the need to rebuild a shattered life following permanent and total disablement and provide a benefit of £100,000. This should be in respect of any activity associated with their sport and when Governing Body-arranged to all members the premium could be as little as £1 per member or even less as part of their membership fees.

PROFESSIONAL SPORT

Whilst facing similar insurance problems the substantial variation in benefits mean that the simple overall scheme philosophy cannot apply. It is necessary to cater for the wide variation in earnings and asset valuation of individual athletes up to £ multi-million, also recognising where, following injury, a player's ability to perform at the level expected cannot continue. This calls for a distinct specialisation involving a very wide underwriting market to readily identify and arrange such a programme. There is a need to take into account varying financial interests focussed primarily on the Clubs, the employers of what has now become incredibly expensive assets with high individual values over an agreed contract period along with remarkable operating costs [wages].

Premier League Football Clubs are most publicly prominent important users [employers] of professional athletes, and other senior leagues are not far behind, followed by both Rugby codes. With star players valued in excess of £20M exposed to ferocious conflict in a crowded seasonal agenda it is fair to assume that the local insurance shop cannot help! Nor for that matter are major insurance companies really interested in such high exposure but a sophisticated underwriting market, capable of providing for these needs, exists in London. Involving a major spread of carriers at Lloyds it provides a primary level of benefit per player or team of £7M and a second layer of £6M over this subscribed to by most of the London market with a selective few prepared to provide £8M over the £13M for top quality players — a limit of indemnity comparable to a fair sized industrial/commercial premises but brickwork is more readily repaired than an athlete's carefully honed body [and mind].

Within professional sport there are possibly four interested parties who would seek insurance protection:-

(1)   International Teams

If one looks at the present needs of the English FA in controlling an England XI they need to have insurance cover in place to indemnify clubs for loss of a player following each international appearance in amounts possibly around:

Up to £21 Million per player Capital value
Up to 100 weeks wages to the Club when unable to play at the appropriate level
£250 Million for a travel catastrophe - Aircraft
6 months wages to the player for disablement either permanent or temporary — a contractual feature for the Home International controllers.

(2)   Football Clubs

A most sophisticated assessment of insurance needs is called for where even individual players have massive wage differences. Young players would normally carry a full value identified against their planned career time, present costs and possible future transfer potential to be reviewed annually. Advancing years will reduce these levels as will the remaining contract time — three years to expiry could call for a purchase cost of £3M reduced annually for insurance purposes by £½M for year 1 and year 2 down to zero by year 3 termination. A free transfer in would usually carry as a sum insured the replacement cost.

Clubs seldom insure against their loss of wages recognising that reserve players can maintain the gate. Thus the experience of a major specialist insurance broker can help identify acceptable controls which when in place can dramatically reduce the cost of the required insurance package — exclusion of pre-existing conditions and specific clauses relative to previous injuries along with risk assessment [MRI scan and comparable services] can all help in saving premiums or funding higher benefits.

(3)   Professional Players

It is readily understandable that given the present high earnings Clubs/ Employers are not inclined to provide paid athletes with anything other than what will enable them to return to action, namely medical treatment and continued salary payment. They are however usually quite willing to include players in the overall accident insurance plan through their own insurance advisers. Foremost is a cover for up to five times annual wages for young players prevented from pursuing their role at elite money-earning level following injury, paid for by the player along with possibly a capital sum in tune with transfer value. There is however a limited take-up of this insurance by footballers and other professional athletes have also not taken this thinking on board.

The PFA have recently arranged a *'fund'* which looks like providing a fixed annual lump sum of £15,000 a year for their members unable to pursue careers in sport following injury.

(4)   Sponsors

Where considerable expense has been undertaken by a sponsor with an individual athlete or a team it is desirable they take out *'death or disgrace'* cover to protect their investment. The insurance market is readily able to provide for such losses at a fairly modest premium where enterprises have been unable to use their prepared publicity following death of a chosen celebrity or, more commonly the case now, a scandal bringing the celebrity into disrepute.

Thus, in conclusion, the preferred path in insurance to bring abut a resolution, long before a matter goes to trial, travels alongside the unfolding development of Sport and the Law.

'Physical Education is Education like Latin and Greek'
(Re Mariette [1915] 2 Ch 284 at 288–289)

(1) MR JUSTICE EVE

Eve J. The admonition with which Mr Clayton[1] commenced his argument is by no means to be disregarded. One must be careful not to allow one's natural inclination to give effect to a gift of this sort to lead one to disregard well-established principles. The gift[2] in question is a gift by a gentleman who had served this school for twenty-four years as an assistant master[3] and who had obviously come to entertain for it in a marked degree that affection which most men feel for the old school, and which would certainly tend to increase in the case of a man who had given the best part of his life to its services. The amount is to be laid out in the erection of additional fives courts at the school, and the question is whether it is a gift which in law can be supported or whether it is void as not being charitable and tending to a perpetuity. It is a gift to an institution which admittedly is a charity within the Statute of Elizabeth, but I accede to the argument of the residuary legatees that it is quite possible that a gift is charity may be of such a character as not to be in itself a charitable gift. On the other hand I think in considering whether a gift is charitable or not one must not confine oneself to the character of the gift itself, but must pay regard also to the character and objects of the charity who are the intended recipients of the gift.

---

1   Counsel for objectors to the bequest as a charity.
2   '£1,000 to the Governing body of Aldenham School for the purpose of building Eton fives courts or squash rackets courts, or for some similar purpose that shall be decided by a majority of the housemasters at the time of my death.'
3   Edgar Henry Mariette.

The object of this charity is the education, in the widest sense, of boys and young men between the ages of ten and nineteen. No one of sense could be found to suggest that between those ages any boy can be properly educated unless at least as much attention is given to the development of his body as is given to the development of his mind. It is necessary, therefore, in any satisfactory system of education to provide for both mental and bodily occupation, mental occupation by means of the classics and those other less inviting studies to which a portion of the day is devoted, and bodily occupation by means of regular and organised games. To leave 200 boys at large and to their own devices during their leisure hours would be to court catastrophe; it would not be educating them, but would probably result in their quickly relapsing into something approaching barbarism. For these reasons I think it is essential that in a school of learning of this description, a school receiving and retaining as boarders boys of these ages, there should be organised games as part of the daily routine, and I do not see how the other part of the education can be successfully carried on without them. It is not disputed that if this sum — I am dealing now with the 1000*l*. — had been left to the charity, for the general purposes of the charity, it might have been applied to any of the purposes to which moneys coming to the hands of the governing body are in fact applied; it might have been expended in the repair or in additions to the class-rooms, laboratory, and other buildings of that sort; or it might equally, as it seems to me, have been applied to the repair or enlargement of the swimming bath, the gymnasium, the fives courts, or other buildings employed in those branches of education which have exclusively to do with the bodily welfare of the students. I cannot, in these circumstances, bring myself to think, because the testator has indicated his intention that in the hands of the charity this money shall be used for the particular purposes stated in his will, that the gift is thereby vitiated. On the contrary I think the gift is a good charitable gift. It is a gift to a charity for purposes which seem to me to be included in the objects of the charity.

The same reasoning applies to the 100*l*.[4] It is given not to the charity but to the headmaster, but it is given for a purpose which, though not quite so specific as the purpose for which the 1000*l*. is given, is in my opinion within the objects of the charity, that is to say, the advancement of bodily and physical development of the students. I think both legacies are valid charitable legacies, and I so hold.

I have said nothing about the 100*l*. for the classical prize; that is clearly good, and the contrary has not really been argued.

---

4   '£100 to the headmaster for the time being of Aldenham School upon trust to use the interest to provide a prize for some event in the school athletic sports every year agreed upon by the committee of the athletics sports.'

(2) THE ERRATIC CHART

Date	Charitable	Non Charitable	Source
(1895)		Yacht-racing Prize (Cup)	*Re Nottage: Jones v Palmer* [1895] 2 Ch 649
(1915)	School Fives Court (Aldenham School)		*Re Marriette: Mariette v Aldenham School Body* [1915] 2 Ch 284
(1925)	Army Regimental Fund for promotion of sport		*Re Gray: Todd v Taylor* [1925] Ch 362
(1929)		County Cricket Nursery Fund	*Re Patten: Westminster Bank v Carlyon* [1929] Ch 276
(1945)	Chess tournament for under 21-year-olds		*Re Dupree's Deed Trusts* [1945] Ch 16
(1953)		Police Recreation	*IRC v City of Glasgow Police Association* [1953] AC 380
(1957)	University Rugby		*Kearins v Kearins* (1957) SR (NSW Australia) 286
(1978 1979)		FA Soccer Youth Trust	*IRC v McMullen* [1979] 1 WLR 130, CA
(1980)	FA Soccer Youth Trust		*IRC v McMullen* [1981] AC 1, HL
(1992)	Sports Centre Recreational Charities Act 1958		*Guild v IRC* [1992] 2 AC 310, HL

House of Lords Summary — decisions overturned

Edward Grayson

Clarke v Dunraven : The 'Satanita' [1897] AC 59

Contract competition rules exclude limitation of Merchant Shipping (Amendment) Act 1862

[Court of Appeal reversal of lower court]

Seymour v Reed [1927] AC 554 Professional cricketer's tax free benefit.

Reversal of lower court

Rowlatt J Upheld by House of Lords.

Tolley v Fry [1931] AC 330 Defamation decision of trial judge reinstated; retrial ordered.

Reversal of lower court

Acton J Defamation direction upheld by House of Lords.

Bolton v Stone [1951] AC 850 Cricket ball hit out of ground not establishing negligence or nuisance.

Reversal of lower court

Oliver J Negligence and nuisance rejected and upheld by House of Lords.

Inland Revenue Commissioners v City of Glasgow Police Athletic Federation [1953] AC 380 Police force athletic, sports and general pastimes association rejected as charitable. Reversal of first decision of the Court of Session affirmation of Special Commissioners.

Brutus v Cozens [1973] AC 854 Anti-apartheid demonstrators disrupted Wimbledon's men's doubles tennis match

Reversal of divisional court

Magistrate's dismissal of insulting behaviour charge affirmed.

Arsenal Football Club v Smith (Valuation Officer) [1978] AC 1 Ratepayers can have interest in rates paid by others

[House of Lords affirmation of the Court of Appeal's reversal of the lower tribunal]

Inland Revenue Commissioners v McMullen [1980] AC 1 Sporting educational trust funded by football for general sporting sources

Reversal of Court of Appeal confirmation of lower court

Walton J Rejection of Charity Commissioners registration of charity and overruled by House of Lords.

Wheeler v Leicester City Council [1985] AC 1054 Reversal of local authority's decision penalising amateur rugby club's players' decision to play for England in South Africa funded from private sources.

Reversal of Court of Appeal confirmation of lower court

Forbes J Affirmation of City Council overruled by House of Lords.

Shilton v Wilmhurst [1991] All ER 148 1991/STC 88 Professional International goalkeeper's golden 'hello' taxable as emolument from employment.

Reversal of Court of Appeal confirmation of lower court

Millet J Reversal of Tax Commissioners in turn reversed by House of Lords.

Guild v Inland Revenue Commissioners [1992] 2 All ER p 10 Social Welfare extended beyond Sports Centre under Recreational Charities Act 1958.

Reversal of Court of Session of Inner House

Tax Commissioners confirmed by Court of Appeal but reversed by House of Lords.

NB *Customs & Excise Commissioners v Professional Footballers' Association (Enterprise) Ltd* [1993] STC 86 For the first time House of Lords upholds lower court, Nolan J and also Court of Appeal majority, all confirming VAT Tribunal decision that an awards dinner ticket price payment including trophy presentations was for a consideration rather than a supply of goods for no consideration (for the provision or supply of the trophies on the cost of which no VAT was payable separately).

Judicial Review of the Decisions of Sporting Bodies

Catherine Bond

Former Solicitor

The question of whether sporting bodies' decisions in England [as distinct from Scotland where it is acceptable] are susceptible to judicial review is one which the courts have dealt with on many occasions in recent years. However, time and time again the courts have refused to allow judicial review to extend its parameters this far. This Appendix is designed to give an overview of this topic by providing a summary of the legal arguments which have taken place in court in the last ten years. One of the main attractions and advantages which judicial review offers above the writ is that of a swift remedy. This is probably the reason why so many have challenged the precedent that sports governing bodies' decisions cannot be challenged by way of judicial review.

GENERAL BACKGROUND TO JUDICIAL REVIEW

Judicial review is the process by which the High Court exercises a supervisory jurisdiction over:

(i) proceedings and jurisdiction of inferior courts;
(ii) tribunals;
(iii) bodies or persons carrying out quasi judicial functions; and
(iv) bodies or persons who perform public acts and duties.

The last three groups can all be applicable to sporting bodies, so why not allow judicial review of their decisions?

Many forward the argument that sporting bodies should be able to sort their problems out within their own ranks and if the courts were to interfere in any way, it should be through the route of private law in contract. Judicial review certainly should not be perceived as a great evil which would take away the power of the individual sporting bodies and leave them to the mercy of the courts. In *R v Secretary of State for Education and Science ex parte Avon County Council*, Glidewell LJ commented on the role of judicial review:

'It is not intended to take away from those authorities the powers and discretions properly vested in them by law and to substitute the courts as the bodies making the decisions. It is intended to see that the relevant authorities use their power in a proper manner.'

Is there any reason why in addition to the route of private law in contract and negligence, 'public' sporting bodies should not be subject to the same supervision? The questions which the courts have to consider in the judicial review function are questions of legality and not of fact. The courts are concerned with the decision-making process and not concerned with the decision itself. These fundamental concepts of judicial review do not offend good sporting practice.

The traditional test for establishing whether a body is subject to judicial review is the source of its power. The power must derive from either statute or prerogative. In *R v Panel on Take-Overs and Mergers, ex parte Datafin plc* ([1981] 1 All ER 564) Lloyd LJ discussed the scope of judicial review. He stated that on one hand, there were bodies whose source of power was statute or subordinate legislation, who would of course be subject to judicial review, and on the other hand there were other bodies whose source of power is purely contractual and therefore would not be subject to judicial review. Lloyd LJ went on to say that within these two extremes there may be bodies who exercise public law functions or their functions will have public law consequences and that may be sufficient to bring the body into the scope of judicial review. This case dramatically changed the jurisdictional question for judicial review and brought the question of whether a sporting body could ever be subject to judicial review to the fore.

One of the most forceful arguments for allowing sporting bodies to be subject to judicial review is that it is in the public interest to do so because the enormous power which is now vested in some sporting bodies should be subject to scrutiny by the courts. However, in *R v East Berkshire Health Authority ex parte Walsh* ([1985] QB 152 at 164; [1984] 3 All ER 425 at 430), Sir John Donaldson said that there was no warrant for equating public law with the interest of the public: 'If the public through Parliament gives effect to that interest by means of statutory provisions, that is quite different, but the interests of the public per se is not sufficient. The crucial consideration will be whether the decision made by the body is made under a statutory power'. Thus, the source of power is still considered to be an important criterion when considering the applicability of judicial review even after the *Datafin* case.

The arguments for and against the use of judicial review in a sporting context can be illustrated by following the most recent cases on the subject and following the progression of argument. The cases start with *Law v National Greyhound Racing Club Ltd* in 1983 and finish with the most recently reported case on this subject, *R v Disciplinary Committee of the Jockey Club; ex parte Aga Khan* decided in December 1992.

1   *Law v National Greyhound Racing Club Ltd* [1983] 3 All ER 300

The defendants, the National Greyhound Racing Club Ltd, were a limited company acting as the judicial body for greyhound racing in Great Britain. The plaintiff was a trainer whose licence had been suspended by the defendant as prohibited substances had been found in a greyhound which had been in the charge of the plaintiff. The plaintiff issued an originating summons seeking, inter alia, declarations that the stewards' decision was void and ultra vires.

The National Greyhound Racing Club applied to strike out the claim for want of jurisdiction on the ground that judicial review under s 31 of the SCA 1981 should have been sought. This contention was rejected at first instance and then by the Court of Appeal. Lawton LJ held that the stewards' powers were derived from contract which is a private law and a stewards' enquiry concerned only those who voluntarily submit themselves to the stewards' jurisdiction. Lawton LJ stated that there was no public element in this jurisdiction, even though the consequences of the powers did have benefits which affected the public.

Slade LJ re-emphasised Lawton LJ's argument by saying that the NGRC's authority to perform judicial or quasi-judicial functions in respect of persons holding licences from it is not derived from statute, statutory instrument or the Crown and as such, the case is a claim against a body of persons whose status is essentially that of a domestic as opposed to a public tribunal.

2   *R v Jockey Club ex parte Massingberg-Mundy* [1990] COB 260

The applicant sought judicial review of a decision that his name be removed from the list of those qualified to act as chairman of a panel of local stewards on the grounds of lack of natural justice. Notably, the divisional court held that if the matter were free from binding authority, the court might (per Neill LJ) or would (per Roch J) have concluded that at least some of the decisions of the Jockey Club were susceptible to judicial review. This was because the Jockey Club held a position of major national importance and it held near monopolistic powers in an area in which the public had a general interest and in which many persons carried their livelihoods. The court stated that whilst some decisions of the Jockey Club were capable of being susceptible to judicial review, the question being considered in this instance did not have any public element in it at all and as such did not have any bearing on judicial review.

3   *R v Jockey Club, ex parte RAM Racecourses Ltd* [1991] COD 346

The applicants were a racecourse management company who sought judicial review of the decisions of the Jockey Club not to allocate at least 15 racing fixtures to it at Telford Racecourse. On the jurisdictional question, Stuart-Smith LJ felt bound to follow the *Massingberg-Mundy* decision and added that but for that authority he would have held that the Jockey Club was amenable to judicial review. Simon Brown J felt similarly so inclined criticising the grounds of the decision in *Massingberg-Mundy* and stating that the court could have distinguished *Law* in the light of *Datafin*. He said that he was much attracted to the idea that the

> 'Jockey Club in discharging its functions of regulating racecourses and allocating fixtures is strikingly akin to the exercise of a statutory licensing power. I have no difficulty in regarding this function as one of a public law body, giving rise to public law consequences. On any view it seems to have strikingly close affinities with those sorts of decision-making that commonly are accepted as reviewable by the courts.'
>
> Plainly the Jockey Club for the most part takes decisions which affect only — or at least essentially — those who voluntarily and willingly subscribe to their rules and procedures. The wider public have no interest in all this, certainly not sufficient to make such decisions reviewable. But just occasionally, as when exercising the quasi-licensing power here under challenge, I for my part would regard the Jockey Club as subject to review.'

However, the Divisional Court still felt bound to follow its previous decision.

4   *R v Football Association of Wales ex parte Flint Town United Football Club* [1991] COD 44

The applicant was a football club which was a member of the Football Association of Wales playing in the Welsh Amateur League. The applicant sought to change football leagues. The respondent league argued that the applicant required their permission which incidentally had also been given to other clubs. Permission was not granted by a committee as a result of a proposed reorganisation of the football league in Wales. The applicant appealed to a commission of the respondent association who upheld the decision. The applicant sought judicial review of the decision of the committee and the commission. Again the court reiterated the *Law v National Greyhound Racing Club* decision and stated that even though the law had developed since this case, the courts were still bound by precedent. Indeed, a contractual relationship had been established between the applicant and the respondent and so it was not possible to distinguish *Law* in the way Simon Brown J had suggested in *R v Jockey Club, ex parte RAM Racecourses Ltd.*

5   *R v Football Association Limited ex parte Football League Limited* [1992] COD 52

The FA wished to create a new Premier League for the 1992–93 football season. The Football League Ltd is the most important football league sanctioned by the FA and it sought judicial review of the FA's decision. Rose J held dismissing the application:

> 'Despite its virtually monopolistic powers and the importance of its decisions to many members of the public who are not contractually bound to it, it is, in my judgment, a domestic body, whose powers arise from and duties exist in private law only.'

Rose J referred to other major popular sports:

> 'But they are all essentially forms of popular recreation and entertainment and they are all susceptible to control by the courts in a variety of ways. This does not, of itself, exempt their governing bodies from control by judicial review. Each case will turn on the particular circumstances.'

6   *R v Disciplinary Committee of the Jockey Club, ex parte His Highness the Aga Khan* [1993]

The Aga Khan's filly, Aliysa, won the Oaks at Epsom in 1989. In tests after the race, a metabolite of camphor was found in the filly's urine and the Aga Khan sought leave to move for judicial review of the respondent's decision to disqualify the filly and fine the trainer. The Court of Appeal in December 1992 upheld the Divisional Court in dismissing the application.

The Master of the Rolls held that notwithstanding the fact that the Jockey Club was created by Royal Prerogative and it exercised broad and monopolistic powers over a significant national activity, it is still not in its origin, history, constitution and not least of all its membership, a public body.

Yet again, the court refused to state categorically whether sporting bodies would ever be susceptible to judicial review. The Master of the Rolls stated:

> 'It is unnecessary for purposes of this appeal to decide whether decisions of the Jockey Club may ever in any circumstances be challenged by judicial review and I do not do so.'

However, Farquharson LJ did give more reasoning on this point by suggesting that the question of whether the Jockey Club was susceptible to judicial review did not have to be answered on an all-or-nothing basis:

> 'While I do not say that particular circumstances would give a right to judicial review, I do not discount the possibility that in some special circumstances the remedy might be. If for example the Jockey Club failed to fulfil its obligations under the charter by making discriminatory rules, it may be that those affected would have a remedy in public law.'

7   *Finnigan v New Zealand Rugby Football Union* [1985] NZLR 159

As a final case in this list and in contrast to the conclusions which the English courts have reached so far in *Finnigan*, the New Zealand courts found that the New Zealand Rugby Football Union was subject to judicial review. This was on the grounds that the Union was in a position of major national importance, even though it was a private and voluntary sporting association. The plaintiffs who were members of local rugby football clubs and linked to the Union by contract were held to have standing to challenge the decision of the Rugby Union to send a team to tour South Africa. Since there was also a contractual relationship present, it would seem that the English courts would currently never follow this New Zealand line of reasoning.

SHOULD JUDICIAL REVIEW BE APPLICABLE TO SPORT?

The arguments which pervade either side apparently seem to be evenly balanced. On the one hand it is argued that sporting bodies' decisions are subject to attack using the private law route and on the other hand it is argued that the courts should be able to intervene on powers which are often monopolistic and have an undeniable effect on the public.

Rose J in *R v Football Association Limited ex parte The Football League Ltd* stated a compelling practical argument:

'But, for my part, to apply to the governing body of football on the basis that it is a public body, principles honed for the control of the abuse of power by government and its creatures would involve what, in today's justifiable parlance, would be called a quantum leap. It would also, in my view, for what it is worth, be a misapplication of increasingly scarce judicial resource. It will become impossible to provide a swift remedy, which is one of the conspicuous hallmarks of judicial review, if the courts become even more swamped with such applications than they are already. This is not, of course, a jurisprudential reason for refusing judicial review, but it will be cold comfort to the seven or eight other substantive applicants and the many more ex parte applicants who have had to be displaced from the court's lists in order to accommodate the present litigation to learn that, thought they have a remedy for their complaints about the arbitrary abuse of executive power, it cannot be granted to them yet.'

This is indeed a powerful argument, yet it does not tackle the real jurisdictional question. The law should not be prevented from developing and allowing people to use judicial review purely for the reason that it might inhibit the progress of applicants who are currently allowed to resort to its use.

Many sporting bodies such as the Football Association and the Jockey Club have extraordinarily wide powers which affect hundreds of thousands of people within this country on a regular basis. A powerful and cogent argument was put forward in this case that those who contract with the Jockey Club have no alternative but to accept the obligations imposed since the Jockey Club's powers are monopolistic. This would therefore undermine the reality of consent in a contractual situation. Farquharson LJ argued that nearly all sports are subject to a body of rules to which an entrant must subscribe and dismissed this argument. This is true, however, and the reality of the situation with the Jockey Club is that an individual simply does not have an alternative set of rules to abide by if he wants to be involved in the horse-racing industry in this country. As such, monopolistic powers exist which may be open to abuse by the sporting body and the use of judicial review would appear to be appropriate in such circumstances.

If a contractual relationship does exist then there is a form of redress. However, this leaves open the situation where a private law remedy does not exist. It seems just that the judicial review remedy should be available when a private law remedy is not. This view that judicial review should be used where a contractual situation does not exist has not been specifically dismissed by the higher courts and is one which may well be tested in the future.

In such a non-contractual situation, the Divisional Court in *RAM Racecourses* reluctantly felt bound by its own decision in *Massingberg-Mundy* even thought he *Massingberg-Mundy* decision was criticised.

If a contractual relationship does exist, it would be necessary for an applicant to argue his case to the House of Lords in order to overturn the *Law* and *Aga Khan* decisions if the facts could not be distinguished. So far applicants* have not appeared willing to face up to the reality that they have to reach the higher courts in order to have a chance of overturning the binding precedent which steadfastly exists in this area.

The jurisdictional boundaries of judicial review should not be extended to include sporting bodies just because it is convenient for people to have further redresses to the courts when wrongs are done unto them. However, there may be circumstances where a person is affected by a decision of a sporting body which does have a significant public role and therefore its actions and business has a significant effect on the public at large and there is no remedy in private law available with which to gain redress. For example, a situation could arise in which a football supporter would wish to question a decision of the Football Association. As no contract would arise between the parties and since the FA is not a body susceptible to judicial review, the supporter would have no remedy. In such circumstances, it would be impossible to predict which way the courts would turn — judicial review or no recourse in all at all? Even after *Datafin* which widened the judicial review boundaries the courts still feel bound by *Law* which was decided before *Datafin*. The courts have subsequently balanced these two authorities providing dicta that judicial review may be relevant to sporting bodies in limited circumstances.

[* This, of course, is essentially a crucial question of funding, resources and costs. His Highness the Aga Khan possessed the capacity for this route; but for reasons which have yet to be disclosed publicly, he and/or his advisers, side-stepped the opportunity to test the arguments which failed on his behalf in the lower courts, by reason of the existing binding precedents. Instead, he withdrew his support of the British racing industry for a damaging period to it, as I have explained in my text, in favour of France and Ireland. **Edward Grayson**.]

Sanctions for Fair Play in Sport

Edward Grayson

1. The concept of fair play in sport is the ideal result of operating the Rule of Law within any sport on and off the field of play. To that end the Central Council of Physical Recreation created a Charter of Conduct and the Council of Europe created a Code of Sport's Ethics.

2. The Charter referred in paragraph 1 to

'rules...properly enforced'

and the Code referred to

'sanctions applied'.

3. Neither completed the logical corollary to each ideal, namely, what are the consequences of proper enforcement and applying sanctions?

4. The gap was filled with admirable timing for the 1994 World Soccer Cup Competition in the USA by the little known International Football Association Board, which monitors the Laws of the Game, as distinct from FIFA which hitherto has been remiss in enforcing them. This the whole world witnessed in 1966 when the jewel in Brazil's crown, Pele, was hacked and assaulted off the England field by brutality which today would end in either a criminal prosecution or civil claim for damages.

5. At its annual meeting in FIFA House, Zürich, Switzerland, on 5th March 1994, the International Football Association Board made a number of amendments to the Laws of the Game and International Board decisions.

The Board also issued two important instructions. All amendments, decisions and instructions **must be enforced from 1st July 1994**. Instructions for referees

1.   Reckless Challenges

The Board showed much concern about the increasing tendency among players to move their arms and elbows, without due care, too near to opponents whilst competing for the ball. Referees should, therefore, take stringent measures against the offenders by applying the sanctions available to them under Law XII.

2.   Kicking an opponent

The Board discussed the increasing number of incidents where violent challenges were made **from behind** with little or no attempt to play the ball. It emphasised the fact that the current Laws of the Game forbid such actions and condemn it as Serious Foul Play.

Such violent and unacceptable challenges can result in serious injury. Referees must apply the sanctions laid down in Law XII and **send off** any player guilty of this offence.

The International FA Board gave FIFA permission to implement the aforementioned amendments as from the first match of the 1994 World Cup Finals on 17th June 1994.

6.   As these pages have argued from the commencement in the Introduction, the Rule of Law on the field of play is essential for the Rule of Law in society generally. It is also arguable that if the 1994 IFAB sanctions had been in force during 1966, Brazil with Pélé could even have won the world Cup on that occasion as they have in 1994. Certainly these sanctions prove how fair play can flourish if, and only if, effective sanctions exist to punish offenders who break the law during play.

(A)   THE CENTRAL COUNCIL OF PHYSICAL RECREATION

A CHARTER OF CONDUCT FOR ALL THOSE INVOLVED IN SPORT AND PHYSICAL RECREATION

TERMS OF THE CHARTER

General

Members of governing bodies, officials, competitors and spectators are perceived by the general public as representatives of their sports and must always attempt to set a good example, particularly to the younger generation, by the way in which they carry out their duties and responsibilities both on and off the field. The media plays a particularly vital role in this respect. It is urged, in keeping with the spirit of the Code of Practice agreed by Editors of national newspapers, to maintain the highest standards of responsible journalism in its reporting of sport and in its comments on sporting personalities.

Coaches

1. Must insist that competitors understand and abide by the principles of good sportsmanship.
2. Must not countenance the use of drugs by competitors.
3. Must never employ methods or practices that might involve risks to the long-term health or physical development of their charges.
4. Must not attempt to manipulate the rules to the advantage of their charges.

Competitors

1. Must abide by both the laws and the spirit of their sport.
2. Must accept the decisions of umpires and referees without question or protestation.
3. Must not cheat and in particular must not attempt to improve their performance by the use of drugs.
4. Must exercise self-control at all times.
5. Must accept success and failure, victory and defeat with good grace and without excessive display of emotion.
6. Must treat their opponents and fellow participants with due respect at all times.

Sponsors and Promoters

1. Must not seek improperly to influence the outcome of non-professional competitions by financial inducements.
2. Must understand and agree that the administration, operation and arrangements for the conduct of competitions and events are the exclusive responsibility of the governing bodies.

Conclusion

In order to bring about the raising of standards of behaviour across the wide spectrum of sport in Britain, the CCPR expects all governing bodies of sport and recreation, clubs, teachers, coaching organisations and spectators to give study to the Chapter and take the necessary action to incorporate its relevant principles into their own rules and codes of practice and appeals to the Press Council to do the same.

(B)   COUNCIL OF EUROPE

CODE OF SPORTS ETHICS

In setting a proper context for fair play

Sports and sports-related organisations have the following responsibilities:

- to publish clear guidelines on what is considered to be ethical or unethical behaviour and ensure that, at all levels of participation and involvement, consistent and appropriate incentives and/or sanctions are applied.
- to ensure that all decisions are made in accordance with a code of ethics for their sport which reflects the European Code.
- to raise the awareness of fair play within their sphere of influence through the use of campaigns, awards, educational material and training opportunities. They must also monitor and evaluate the impact of such initiatives.
- to establish systems which reward fair play and personal levels of achievement in addition to competitive success.
- to provide help and support to the media to promote good behaviour.

Sport is governed by a set of rules and, often unwritten, principles of behaviour which usually come under the banner of Fair Play. Sadly, it is often these principles which are not strictly adhered to in a range of sports. The Council of Europe's Code of Sports Ethics is a valuable reminder of the need to demonstrate and practice ethical behaviour in Europe.
The Sports Council has been delighted to play a significant part in drawing up the Code and fully endorses its content.

(C)   GUIDELINES FOR CONDUCT IN SCHOOL SPORT

From the HMC Sports Sub-Committee (Headmasters' Conference)

These guidelines should be seen in the context of a long tradition of sportsmanship in our schools. They simply restate basic principles in a rapidly changing world of sport. It is assumed that all the off-the-field courtesies which are an essential part of inter-school fixtures are taken as 'read'.

1. Basic Premise: That it is the responsibility of Heads to ensure that high standards of conduct obtain in school sport. To this end, the rapport between Heads and the Director of Sport (or 'individual staff in charge of games') is crucial.
2. There should be no foul or abusive language in any area of school sport.
3. Teams should never seek to claim unfair advantage. By verbal abuse or any other means.
4. Open criticism of, or, dissent from, umpiring or refereeing decisions by those playing or watching, is always unacceptable.
5. The committee would recommend that any pupil who is in the breach of the above guidelines, should be formally warned — with further sanctions to include suspension from matches.
6. All the above is relevant to sport within schools as well as between schools.
7. The school has a responsibility for the conduct of every aspect of its sport — including the behaviour of supporters (pupils/parents/other adults alike).
8. Staff i/c individual teams should assume responsibility for the conduct of their teams and supporters and should be conscious of their role as examples to both.

C H Hirst, Sedbergh School, Cumbria, November 1997.

Index